WASHINGTON JOURNAL

WASHINGTON JOURNAL

Reporting Watergate and Richard Nixon's Downfall

ELIZABETH DREW

OVERLOOK DUCKWORTH
NEW YORK • LONDON

To those who rose to the occasion

This edition first published in the United States and the United Kingdom in 2014 by
Overlook Duckworth, Peter Mayer Publishers, Inc.

NEW YORK
141 Wooster Street
New York, NY 10012
www.overlookpress.com
For bulk and special orders, please contact sales@overlookny.com,
or write us at the above address.

LONDON
30 Calvin Street
London E1 6NW
info@duckworth-publishers.co.uk
www.ducknet.co.uk
For bulk and special orders, please contact sales@duckworth-publishers.co.uk,
or write us at the above address.

Most of the material in this book appeared originally
in *The New Yorker*, in slightly different form.

Library of Congress Cataloging in Publication Data
Drew, Elizabeth.
Washington journal.
"Most of the material ... appeared originally in
the New Yorker."
1. Watergate Affair, 1972-   2. Nixon, Richard
Milhous, 1913-   —Impeachment. 3. Nixon, Richard
Milhous, 1913-   —Resignation. I. Title.
E860.D73   973.924   75-9803

2 4 6 8 10 9 7 5 3 1
ISBN US: 978-1-4683-0918-8 (HC)
ISBN US: 978-1-4683-0999-7 (PB)
ISBN UK: 978-0-7156-4916-9

Manufactured in the United States of America

CONTENTS

INTRODUCTION

On the day after Labor Day in 1973, I was in the office of William Shawn, the justly legendary editor of the *New Yorker*, for which I had begun to write a few months earlier. In his whisper of a voice he asked me what I was thinking about writing. (He never imposed a subject.) I told him that I had an intuition that within a year this country would change vice president and president. At the time, this was a seemingly outlandish thought, but I go a lot on instinct, and I just sensed it. I began with the vice president because the nearly—or not so nearly—forgotten Spiro Agnew, formerly governor of Maryland, was under criminal investigation on suspicion that he'd been accepting post-facto bribes right in his vice-presidential office.

The Watergate scandal hadn't yet caught up with Nixon, but there was already plenty of evidence that serious wrongdoing had taken place in the White House and that Nixon had surrounded himself with rudderless aides willing to carry out most anything against the President's various real and imagined "enemies."

We knew that there had been an "enemies list," which we joked about but wasn't really funny: the President was willing to use the levers of government at his command, or retain outside goons to spy on, "get the goods on," and "destroy"—Nixon's terms—those who he saw as "out to get him." Nixon confused political opponents with enemies, but his suspicions swept a much wider field. And so tailing, break-ins, wiretaps, and IRS audits, among other things, proceeded against political opponents, journalists, university presidents—all manner of people.

Shawn, whose interest level was perpetually high, was fascinated and, as usual, he landed on a point I hadn't thought of: even if the trouble stopped with Agnew, this country had no idea how to remove and install a new vice president. We could start with that and see what followed. The word impeachment was totally foreign to us then—we were vaguely aware of some sort of unsuccessful and ill-regarded act after the Civil War. It was an alarming word that awed us. (The term hadn't yet been cheapened by the partisan and fundamentally unserious impeachment of Bill Clinton.) Shawn and I came to the conclusion—symbiotically, as I cannot honestly say if it was his idea or mine—that I should write a journal of the period we were entering into that Fall. Not a diary, but a journal of reporting and insight into the events of that time. We couldn't be sure what would unfold when; we would just start and then see. Back in Washington, when I told my mentor John Gardner about this assignment, he said to me, "no one will be able to go back and recapture this. Write it so that forty years from now people can say, 'So that's what it was like.'" (He actually said forty.) Thus I was writing for both a current and a future audience. As time went on, and Nixon's problems deepened, Shawn called me one Saturday and said, "Don't you think you'd better keep going?" "Yes," I replied, "I'd better keep going." We still could have no idea how it would end, but we knew that great drama was afoot. And so I kept going—until Nixon climbed aboard the helicopter to take him to the plane that would carry him to San Clemente and retirement.

The reader may be struck early with a sense that these events took place in a somewhat archaic atmosphere. In fact, the rhythms of our daily working lives were quite different then: no cable television, no Internet, no Twitter. We lived in information vacuums between the morning papers and the evening news broadcast and the evening papers that existed then, and the occasional radio bulletin. News and rumor in equal measure buzzed around Washington through telephone calls and chance enounters. "*Did you hear . . .?*" In retrospect, this was somewhat liberating: we went about our business while we awaited the next bombshell or confirmation of the latest wild rumors—which all too often turned out to be true. As I recount in the first chapter, "it's harder than ever to know where reality stops and fantasy begins." Facts outran our imagination.

The journal ran in the *New Yorker* as sets of three parts each. Later, Joe Fox, an editor at Random House, came to see me in Washington and said that he wanted to publish the series as a book. I turned the series into a book, adding some material at the beginning, to give a backdrop as to how we had reached the situation we—and Nixon—were in by that Labor Day, and the book was first published in 1975. But it fell out of print and hardback copies became almost nonexistent. It was distressful that as we were heading into what happened to be the fortieth anniversary of Nixon's resignation this book was essentially unobtainable. It seemed worth keeping alive, not simply as a commemoration of Nixon's resignation but as a way of looking at this extraordinary period, at what led to its dramatic climax, to remind those who lived through it and to inform those who were too young at the time what it was really like. What may appear inevitable in hindsight seemed at the time anything but. We laughed at some of the ridiculous characters and at the absurdities—but by and large we were alarmed. It was a frightening time, and the stakes were enormous. Thus, the purpose of this book is to show what it was really like during the turbulent months that led to Nixon's resignation.

To my delight, Peter Mayer of Overlook Press, with whom I had worked happily before, strongly agreed that *Washington Journal* should be kept alive and be offered to those who were there—but couldn't see it for all the debris, or for whom memories have faded—and those who weren't. Even when I reread it I'm astonished at what went on then. It looks quite different now than it did when we were in the middle of it, but no less dramatic, alarming, and even amusing in parts. And as it happens, Nixon has never really left us. He would be most surprised that he's become a cult figure, the subject of endless fascination.

I have added an Afterword about what happened to Nixon after he left office—a period that very few know much if anything about. I think it's about as fascinating as any other time in his life. The man didn't change. I won't spoil it here, but just say that this was the Nixon who never gave up. He just couldn't. The Afterword also provides new insights I've had into what Watergate was actually about, some of which came as a bit of a surprise and can still shock me. This new section also provides a more comprehensive view of Nixon: what shaped him and (without delving into psychobabble) might explain his behavior that got him in such terrible trouble—making him the first president forced to leave office. I have included some important and sometimes bizarre, sometimes alarming, things we learned about Nixon in the Watergate period and after he resigned, and also—and this was new to me when I later learned it—how Nixon very methodically climbed his way back into respectability sufficient enough that he was given a hero's burial. The story of how he did this also shed new light about this most extraordinary figure.

I hope that those who go through this for the first time and those who re-live it will realize what an amazing period this was, and how we almost lost our democratic system.

—E. D.

FIGURES IN THE EVENTS OF 1973–1974

Robert Abplanalp: New York businessman and friend of President Nixon.

Spiro T. Agnew: Vice-President of the United States

Howard Baker (Republican of Tennessee): vice-chairman of the Senate Select Committee on Presidential Campaign Activities

Bernard L. Barker: participant in the break-ins at the Watergate and the office of Daniel Ellsberg's psychiatrist

Richard Ben-Veniste: Assistant Special Prosecutor

Robert H. Bork: U.S. Solicitor General, and later Acting Attorney General of the United States

Jack Brooks (Democrat of Texas): member of the House Judiciary Committee

Patrick J. Buchanan: special assistant to the President (speechwriter)

Stephen B. Bull: White House staff assistant

Dean Burch: counsellor to the President

Warren E. Burger: Chief Justice of the United States

M. Caldwell Butler (Republican of Virginia): member of the House Judiciary Committee

Alexander P. Butterfield: deputy assistant to the President, and later administrator, Federal Aviation Administration

J. Fred Buzhardt, Jr.: special counsel to the President

John J. Caulfield: private investigator retained by the White House

Dwight L. Chapin: deputy assistant to the President

Ken W. Clawson: deputy director, and later director of White House Office of Communications

William S. Cohen (Republican of Maine): member of the House Judiciary Committee

Charles W. Colson: special counsel to the President

John B. Connally: former Democratic governor of Texas, chairman of Democrats for Nixon, Secretary of the Treasury and then special adviser to the President

John Conyers, Jr. (Democrat of Michigan): member of the House Judiciary Committee

Archibald Cox: Special Prosecutor

George E. Danielson (Democrat of California): member of the House Judiciary Committee

John W. Dean, III: counsel to the President

David W. Dennis (Republican of Indiana): member of the House Judiciary Committee

Felipe de Diego: participant in the break-in of Daniel Ellsberg's psychiatrist's office

John M. Doar: special counsel, House Judiciary Committee impeachment inquiry

Harold D. Donohue (Democrat of Massachusetts): member of the House Judiciary Committee

Robert F. Drinan (Democrat of Massachusetts): member of the House Judiciary Committee

Don Edwards (Democrat of California): member of the House Judiciary Committee

John D. Ehrlichman: assistant to the President for domestic affairs

Joshua Eilberg (Democrat of Pennsylvania): member of the House Judiciary Committee

Sam J. Ervin, Jr. (Democrat of North Carolina): chairman, Senate Select Committee on Presidential Campaign Activities

Hamilton Fish, Jr. (Republican of New York): member of the House Judiciary Committee

Walter Flowers (Democrat of Alabama): member of the House Judiciary Committee

Gerald R. Ford (Republican of Michigan): House Minority Leader, and later Vice-President of the Unites States

Harold V. Froehlich (Republican of Wisconsin): member of the House Judiciary Committee

Leonard Garment: special consultant to the President, and later assistant to the President

Gerhard A. Gesell: judge, U.S. District Court for the District of Columbia

L. Patrick Gray, III: acting F.B.I. director

General Alexander M. Haig, Jr.: White House chief of staff

H. R. (Bob) Haldeman: White House chief of staff

Bryce N. Harlow: counsellor to the President

Richard Helms: C.I.A. director, and later ambassador to Iran

Lawrence J. Hogan (Republican of Maryland): member of the House Judiciary Committee

Elizabeth Holtzman (Democrat of New York): member of the House Judiciary Committee

William L. Hungate (Democrat of Missouri): member of the House Judiciary Committee

E. Howard Hunt, Jr.: consultant to the White House, and participant in the break-ins at the Watergate and the office of Daniel Ellsberg's psychiatrist

Tom Charles Huston: associate counsel to the President

Edward Hutchinson (Republican of Michigan): member of the House Judiciary Committee

Leon Jaworski: Special Prosecutor

Albert E. Jenner, Jr.: minority counsel, House Judiciary Committee impeachment inquiry

Barbara C. Jordan (Democrat of Texas): member of the House Judiciary Committee

Herbert W. Kalmbach: the President's personal attorney and associate chairman of the Finance Committee to Re-Elect the President

Robert W. Kastenmeier (Democrat of Wisconsin): member of the House Judiciary Committee

Henry A. Kissinger: Secretary of State and National Security Adviser to the President

Richard G. Kleindienst: Attorney General of the United States

Rabbi Baruch Korff: chairman, National Citizens Committee for Fairness to the Presidency

Egil Krogh, Jr.: deputy assistant to the President for domestic affairs, and co-director of the Social Investigations Unit (the "Plumbers")

Philip Lacovara: counsel to the Special Prosecutor

Melvin R. Laird: Secretary of Defense, and later counsellor to the President for domestic affairs

Frederick C. LaRue: special counsel to the President, and later special assistant to the Committee for the Re-Election of the President

Delbert L. Latta (Republican of Ohio): member of the House Judiciary Committee

G. Gordon Liddy: White House staff assistant and later counsel to the Finance Committee for the Re-Election of the President, and participant in the break-ins at the Watergate and the office of Daniel Ellsberg's psychiatrist.

Trent Lott (Republican of Mississippi): member of the House Judiciary Committee

Jeb Stuart Magruder: deputy director, Committee for the Re-Election of the President

James R. Mann (Democrat of South Carolina): member of the House Judiciary Committee

Joseph J. Maraziti (Republican of New Jersey): member of the House Judiciary Committee

Robert C. Mardian: Assistant Attorney General in charge of the Internal Security Division of the Justice Department, and later political coordinator for the Committee for the Re-Election of the President

Eugenio R. Martinez: participant in the break-ins at the Watergate and the office of Daniel Ellsberg's psychiatrist

Wiley Mayne (Republican of Iowa): member of the House Judiciary Committee

Robert McClory (Republican of Illinois): member of the House Judiciary Committee

James W. McCord, Jr.: security coördinator for the Committee for the Re-Election of the President, and participant in the break-ins at the Watergate and the office of Daniel Ellsberg's psychiatrist

George Meany: President, A.F.L.-C.I.O.

William H. Merrill: Associate Special Prosecutor

Edward Mezvinsky (Democrat of Iowa): member of the House Judiciary Committee

John N. Mitchell: Attorney General of the United States, and later chairman of the Committee for the Re-Election of the President

Rev. Sun Myung Moon: Korean evangelist and supporter of President Nixon

Carlos J. Moorhead (Republican of California): member of the House Judiciary Committee

Richard M. Nixon: President of the United States

Wayne Owens (Democrat of Utah): member of the House Judiciary Committee

Kenneth W. Parkinson: attorney for the Committee for the Re-Election of the President

Henry E. Petersen: Assistant Attorney General in charge of the Criminal Division of the Justice Department

Herbert L. Porter: White House staff assistant, and later scheduling director, Committee for the Re-Election of the President

Tom Railsback (Republican of Illinois): member of the House Judiciary Committee

Charles B. Rangel (Democrat of New York): member of the House Judiciary Committee

Charles G. (Bebe) Rebozo: Miami banker and friend of President Nixon

Elliot L. Richardson: Attorney General of the United States

Peter W. Rodino, Jr. (Democrat of New Jersey): chairman of the House Judiciary Committee

William D. Ruckelshaus: Deputy Attorney General

James D. St. Clair: special counsel to the President

Charles W. Sandman, Jr. (Republican of New Jersey): member of the House Judiciary Committee

Paul S. Sarbanes (Democrat of Maryland): member of the House Judiciary Committee

William B. Saxbe: Attorney General of the United States

James R. Schlesinger: Secretary of Defense

Donald H. Segretti: attorney employed by the President's aides to engage in political tricks

John F. Seiberling (Democrat of Ohio): member of the House Judiciary Committee

John J. Sirica: judge, U.S. District Court for the District of Columbia

Henry P. Smith, III (Republican of New York): member of the House Judiciary Committee

Maurice H. Stans: Secretary of Commerce, and later chairman of the Finance Committee for the Re-Election of the President

Gordon C. Strachan: White House staff assistant (aide to H. R. Haldeman)

Ray Thornton (Democrat of Arkansas): member of the House Judiciary Committee

Anthony Ulasewicz: private investigator retained by the White House

Robert L. Vesco: financier

Jill Wine Volner: Assistant Special Prosecutor

Jerome R. Waldie (Democrat of California): member of the House Judiciary Committee

Lieutenant-General Vernon A. Walters: C.I.A. deputy director

Gerald L. Warren: deputy press secretary to the President

Charles E. Wiggins (Republican of California): member of the House Judiciary Committee

Rose Mary Woods: the President's personal secretary

Charles Alan Wright: professor, University of Texas Law School, and special consultant to the counsel to the President

David R. Young, Jr.: aide to Henry Kissinger on the National Security Council, and later co-director of the Special Investigations Unit (the "Plumbers")

Ronald L. Ziegler: press secretary to the President

AUTUMN

1

T HE DAY AFTER Labor Day. Tomorrow, the Congress will reconvene,
the President will hold a press conference, and the clashing between
President and Congress—or at least the noise—will resume. The President will undoubtedly use his press conference to urge the Congress,
via the people, at whom the press conference is really aimed, to put
"Watergate" behind it and get on with "the nation's business." All year,
the Congress has bobbed and weaved, and has taken only an occasional
jab at the President. The Ervin committee has shown signs of losing its
nerve, and direction. The Congress has as yet done nothing concrete
to change the conditions that made possible that spreading cluster of
events which have been coming to light, or to prevent these things from
happening again.

It is unusually hot here today. It gets so hot here in the summer that
the British foreign service used to consider this a hardship post. In
recent years, the Congress has adjourned during August. The month is
set aside for the congressmen to be with their families, take vacations
and junkets, so that, at least theoretically, they can be here for the rest
of the year. As a consequence, Washington, like Paris, empties out in
August. August is a good time to stay in Washington. The restaurants are
less crowded, the tennis courts are more available, friends are less busy.
Fewer press releases and newsletters and statements by the politicians
come across one's desk, and it takes less time to read the newspapers.
But it is crucial to get out of Washington from time to time—to change
the scenery and the perspective, to clear the mind, to be with people who
think about things other than those that people here spend most of their
time thinking about. So I took the Labor Day weekend off, and flew
back this afternoon. It is good to have had a breather. This is going to be
no ordinary autumn.

Historic events are coming at us now with a swiftness and in a profu-
sion never before experienced in our national life. The close view we
get of these events—in our newspapers, on our television screens, in our
gossip—may seem to reduce their magnitude, but they remain the stuff

of history. Our Constitutional system is being tested. Decisions are being made that may determine the future of our two-hundred-year democratic experiment. We keep learning new things about our government, and the uses of power. In following events here in Washington, one tries to see them on various levels, tries to understand the implications and hidden meanings of what people say and do. People here deal in power, and implications. They proceed out of a combination of ambition, concern, rivalry, patriotism, fear, and responsibility which is often hard to parse. Now the stakes are high. We watch as fallible human beings struggle over the office that has the ultimate power in this country, and over the ultimate compact in our political life—over the Presidency and the Constitution. This is a deadly struggle. Speeches, stories in the press, tactics, the musings of men as they decide how to proceed must be seen accordingly.

SEPTEMBER 5

President Nixon returned from a vacation in San Clemente a few days ago. It can't have been much of a vacation. On August 22nd, the President held an outdoor press conference at the "Western White House"—the first press conference since the Watergate story broke wide open last spring. The week before that, he gave a televised address on the subject. At the press conference, as he stood on the lawn, in the bright California sunshine, he answered questions on break-ins, on wiretaps, on investigations of his Administration. He appeared to be under great strain, and gave a number of answers that left him open to further questions, but his aides thought he had done so well that he should have another press conference soon.

Today the East Room of the White House was jammed for the President's press conference. It was at once a social and a political event. Many of the reporters had not seen each other in some time. Today, Nixon was on the attack. (He explained in *Six Crises,* his political autobiography, that when he was under attack, his reflex was to counterattack.) And he was trying, as he has tried since last spring, to change the subject. His subject today was the failure of the Congress to enact his legislative program. He began with substantive issues: inflation, defense, energy, domestic programs, taxes. Many of the questions followed the agenda that the President had set, but the uninvited guests, the other questions, were also there. Last week, Judge John J. Sirica ruled that the President must turn over to him nine tapes subpoenaed by Special Prosecutor Archibald Cox. The Judge said that he would review the tapes to determine whether they were protected by executive privilege or should be given to the Special Prosecutor. The President is planning to appeal the ruling to the Court of Appeals and then, presumably, to the Supreme Court. The President's strategy, *Newsweek* reports

this week, is to postpone a Supreme Court ruling until he h[
popular support. *Newsweek* also says that if the President de[
the courts, he might "purge both Attorney General Elliot Ric[
Special Prosecutor Archibald Cox" if they oppose him. Th[
has said only that he would obey a "definitive" decision of th[
Court. Today, as before, he refused to define "definitive."

Dan Rather, of CBS, asked Mr. Nixon why he felt that he was different from Abraham Lincoln, who had said, "No man is above the law."
President Nixon responded that during the Civil War President Lincoln
had suspended the writ of habeas corpus.

Asked about the fact that he had said last month that he had ordered a
new investigation after March 21st—first by John Dean, his thirty-four-
year-old former White House counsel, and then, when Dean was unable
to write the report, by John Ehrlichman, formerly one of the President's
two top assistants—whereas others had testified that they did not know
of any such investigation, the President replied that this was because
he "had ordered the investigation from within the White House itself."
(In his August 15th statement, the President changed his story and
said some surprising things, and, in a pattern that is becoming familiar, some things that raised new questions. He said that on March 21st
he was told "for the first time that the planning of the Watergate break-in
went beyond those who had been tried and convicted," that he had
"learned of some of the activities upon which charges of cover-up are
now based," and was told that "funds had been raised for payments to
the defendants, with the knowledge and approval of persons both on the
White House staff and at the Re-Election Committee," but that he was
"only told that the money had been used for attorneys' fees and family support, not that it had been paid to procure silence." He also said:
"I was told that a member of my staff had talked to one of the defendants about clemency, but not that offers of clemency had been made."
He said he learned then that one of the defendants was "attempting
to blackmail the White House by demanding $120,000 as the price of
not talking about other activities, unrelated to Watergate, in which he
had engaged." The President said that "these allegations were made in
general terms" and "were largely unsupported by details or evidence."
He also said that he "turned over all the information I had" to Henry
Petersen, the Assistant Attorney General in charge of the Criminal
Division of the Justice Department, and "I ordered all members of the
Administration to testify fully before the grand jury." At his press conference the following week, on August 22nd, the President said that
H. R. (Bob) Haldeman, his other former top assistant, had made an
"accurate" statement to the Ervin committee about the President's conversation with Dean on March 21st in regard to paying the defendants
to keep silent. Nixon said that "the problem was, how do you get the
money to them, and also, how do you get around the problem of clem-

ency, because they are not going to stay in jail simply because their families are being taken care of. And so, that was why I concluded, as Mr. Haldeman recalls . . . and did testify very effectively . . . I said 'John, it is wrong, it won't work. We can't give clemency and we have got to get this story out.' ")

The President refused today, as he had at San Clemente, to comment on the Justice Department's investigation of charges that Vice-President Agnew accepted bribes and kickbacks from building contractors while he was serving as county executive of Baltimore County, Maryland, and as governor of the state. (There have also been reports that the payments continued after Agnew took office as Vice-President.) When, early last month, the papers reported that Spiro Agnew, Vice-President of the United States, was under federal investigation in Baltimore for criminal wrongdoing, it felt like an earthquake. The Vice-President held a press conference, calling the charges "damned lies." The Agnew story collided with the Watergate story, and spun it around. Until then, Agnew had been the respectable alternative to Nixon, untouched by the unfolding scandals, very likely the Republican candidate in 1976, and even possibly, if the President's troubles continued to mount, the successor to the Presidency before then. It is not yet clear whether formal charges will be made against the Vice-President. Today the President expressed his "confidence in the Vice-President's integrity during the period that he has served as Vice-President."

The question of the financing of and improvements on the President's houses at Key Biscayne, Florida, and San Clemente, California—one more issue that exploded in our midst in the past few months—came up today at the press conference. The story was a nuisance. Until it broke, it had been a truism of Watergate that such a banal matter as personal gain was not involved. The issue of the houses was also a diversion from the main question. Today the President was asked if he paid a capital-gains tax on that part of the San Clemente property he had sold to his friends, Charles G. (Bebe) Rebozo and Robert Abplanalp. (The White House has said that Rebozo and Abplanalp helped him finance the purchase of the California property.) Both are obscure figures—Rebozo a Miami banker, and Abplanalp, a Bronxville, New York, businessman and perfector of the aerosol-spray valve. We know little about them except that they are the President's most frequent companions in his frequent seclusion. Rebozo has a house in the Key Biscayne compound where the President has two houses. The President uses one of these houses as a home, the other as an office. Abplanalp has a retreat on Grand Cay Island, where the President seeks isolation. When the President goes to Florida, the three men often go out on Bebe Rebozo's boat, the *Coco Lobo*.

Today, the President replied that the I.R.S. said that he did not have to pay a capital-gains tax on the sale of the land in California—even though an accounting firm retained by Mr. Nixon had found that he made a profit on the sale. The President said that this was "a matter of difference between accountants." The President said that he resented "the implications" that "my private property was enriched because of what the government did." He said that, actually, "what the government did at San Clemente reduced the value of the property," that the gazebos and fences ordered by the Secret Service blocked the view. Presumably, they could never be removed. He said that he was a man of little wealth—"the first President in this office since Harry Truman" who did not own stocks or bonds.

Asked how he would restore confidence in his leadership, he said that it has been difficult "for four months to have the President of the United States by innuendo, by leak, by, frankly, leers and sneers of commentators, which is their perfect right, attacked in every way." That, he said, caused the confidence to be "worn away." He said that it was restored "by the President not allowing his own confidence to be destroyed." The President continued, "And second, it is restored by doing something. We have tried to do things. The country hasn't paid a great deal of attention to it, and I may say the media hasn't paid a great deal of attention to it because your attention, quite understandably, is in the more fascinating area of Watergate. Perhaps that will now change." The President's demeanor changed when he dealt with the questions about Watergate and about his property. He became tense, and he breathed hard. If one stood far enough to his right, one could see that, behind the lectern, his hips swivelled in a circular motion, as if within an invisible Hula Hoop.

SEPTEMBER 6

Each time the Congress reconvenes after a long recess, there's a ritual whereby the press asks the returning politicians about the mood of what is known in Washington as "the country." According to today's papers, most of the returning politicians are saying that in the minds of their constituents the economy is the most important issue. They are saying that "the country" is tired of Watergate. But according to a study conducted within the television industry—and to the surprise of the industry itself—daytime television viewing increased, by seven percent, during the period between May and August in which the hearings of the Senate Select Committee on Presidential Campaign Activities, headed by Sam Ervin, Democrat of North Carolina, were televised. This is contrary to the history of the televising of such events. It may be that it is the politicians who are tiring of Watergate, and want to get it behind them.

Some of the politicians feel that the President's position may grow stronger, and they do not want to be caught on the wrong side of the issue. The politicians also sense that Watergate is lowering still further the public's esteem for politics. There has been uneasiness on Capitol

8

Hill as the Ervin committee has moved toward the conclusion of its hearings on the actual break-in at the Watergate, and toward the beginning of hearings on campaign practices and money. Other politicians did not break into their opposition's campaign headquarters, but many politicians did flout the spirit, and some even the letter, of the laws covering the raising and spending of campaign funds. Today's Washington *Post* reports that the Ervin committee will resume hearings in about two weeks and hopes to conclude them by November 1st. Howard Baker, Republican of Tennessee, the vice-chairman of the committee, says that the committee will be "less meticulous" on the next subjects, because they are "less spectacular."

Yesterday afternoon, in considering a bill appropriating money for the White House, the Senate rejected two amendments to bring expenditures for the White House under stricter congressional control. The amendments, offered by Senator Walter Mondale, Democrat of Minnesota, would have reduced the size of the staff of the Domestic Council and deleted an appropriation of one million dollars to the White House for what is called the "special-projects fund." (The Domestic Council, set up to "coördinate" the work of Cabinet Departments, had been headed by John Ehrlichman, and at one point had a staff of about seventy.) The issue, said Mondale, was "the relationship between the executive and legislative branches of the government, and more fundamentally it is a question of whether we have learned from Watergate the essentiality of forcing executive decisions out into the open again."

The issue was also whether the Congress wished to assume responsibility for knowing what the White House was doing. If the Congress had insisted on knowing how public moneys were being spent by the White House, or who was doing what there, perhaps we would have known that there were, or perhaps there would not have been, the private investigators Anthony Ulasewicz and John Caulfield, hired in 1969, and the Special Investigations Unit, or "plumbers," set up in June, 1971. Congressional "oversight" of the executive is one of the few checks there are on that branch. One of the best ways for the Congress to exercise such oversight is to question how appropriated funds are spent. Mondale pointed out that two of the plumbers—Egil Krogh and G. Gordon Liddy—had been on the payroll of the Domestic Council. The White House had refused to account for how the "special-projects fund" was spent.

The debate was symptomatic of the Congress's aversion to confrontation, and of its disinclination to exercise oversight of the executive branch. Its habit of deferring to the White House—out of fear, and out of its own view of patriotism—bespeaks institutional confusion, a mixup over the roles of the two branches of government. It is difficult under any circumstances to mobilize the Congress for significant action. The Congress is composed of five hundred and thirty-five egos—not a situation conducive to collective work. The Congress is essentially a reactive branch. Fewer and fewer enterprises are initiated by the Congress. The Constitution says that the Congress should make the laws and that the President should "take care that the laws be faithfully executed." It stipulates that, in the oath of office, the President swear "to faithfully execute the office of President of the United States," and "preserve, protect, and defend the Constitution." But increasingly the laws are written in the executive branch, then passed—perhaps in revised form—by the Congress. The Congress often pays little attention to how the laws are carried out by the executive, how the office of the President is executed, or whether the Constitution is being preserved. The Congress has a limited attention span. It wearies of issues. Its primary instinct is to play it safe, and its primary motivation is to get reëlected. All this is not, of course, true of every senator or representative in the Congress, but it is true of the collective body.

President Nixon has understood these things about the Congress, and he has exploited its unheroic streak, its cumbersome ways, and its institutional confusion. There is much in the process of governing, as there is in human relations, that cannot be defined or codified; it depends on shared understandings of undefined limits. The Nixon Administration, in its dealings with the Congress, as in other behavior, did not recognize limits. It placed unprecedented power in the hands of White House assistants who were not accountable to the Congress. They were not confirmed by the Congress, and were protected by the doctrinal shield of "executive privilege" from testifying before the Congress. Earlier this year, Richard Kleindienst, then Attorney General, told the Congress that the President could extend the doctrine of executive privilege to all two and a half million members of the executive branch. The Nixon Administration's claim was unprecedented. There is no mention of executive privilege in the Constitution, and Presidents Truman and Eisenhower were the first to make any extensive use of it—against the onslaughts of the late Senator Joseph McCarthy. Earlier Presidents had impounded funds appropriated by the legislature, but President Nixon carried this practice, too, to new lengths. Other Presidents had gone to war without the approval of the Congress, but, at least in the view of some legislators, President Nixon continued to wage war in Southeast Asia after the Congress had specifically withdrawn its approval. These legislators believed that the Administration's continued bombing of Cambodia until this past summer was illegal, and so was its secret bombing of Cambodia in 1969 and 1970. The Congress's reaction to the policies of the President on impoundment, executive privilege, and the war was to try to write legislation to codify the limits. It became fashionable to say that Congress was reasserting its powers, but these and other actions were less exercises in courage than instinctive reactions to the President's weakened position. The Congress has a kind of animal instinct about changes in the flow of power. Moreover, the bills on war powers, impoundment and executive privilege can be seen as conferring more power on the President to impound money and wage war and invoke executive privilege, since they specify conditions, subject to varying interpretations, under which he may do so. Senator Mondale's amendment to limit the number of members of the Domestic Council was not necessarily the best approach to the problem. Presidents need some flexibility. Such are the problems that spring from not respecting the guidelines and the ambiguities that the framers of the Constitution settled on. They knew that not everything could be codified.

James Madison wrote in Federalist Paper No. 48 of his uneasiness over whether the separation of powers was a sufficient hedge against tyranny. "It will not be denied that power is of an encroaching nature, and that it ought to be effectually restrained from passing the limits assigned to it," he said. He continued, "A mere demarcation on parchment of the constitutional limits of the several departments is not a sufficient guard against those encroachments which lead to a tyrannical concentration of all the powers of government in the same hands."

The Washington *Post* reporters Bob Woodward and Carl Bernstein, who did more than any other journalists to break the Watergate story, write in this morning's *Post* that the Secret Service, on the President's instructions, wiretapped F. Donald Nixon, the President's brother. Donald Nixon is a problem. In 1960, the revelation that Howard Hughes had loaned two hundred and five thousand dollars to Donald Nixon in 1956 to rescue his restaurant chain, Nixon, Inc., which specialized in "Nixonburgers," was an embarrassment to Richard Nixon, then running for President. Woodward and Bernstein say, "In the last five years, there have been periodic news reports referring to attempts to keep Donald Nixon out of trouble," and they note that John Ehrlichman and Bebe Rebozo were reported to have made such attempts. Woodward and Bernstein also cite a White House memorandum obtained by the *Post* which was written by Caulfield, the secret White House investigator, to John Dean. It said that Donald Nixon had visited the Dominican Republic in 1969 with "wheeler-dealers" who were believed to be connected with enterprises owned by Hughes. The wiretap on the President's brother may have been illegal. Today, the White House said that if the President's brother had been wiretapped, it would have been in order to protect him. Just how is unclear.

Today, the President appealed Judge Sirica's ruling on the tapes to the Court of Appeals.

It is harder than ever to know where reality stops and fantasy begins. When, time after time, the incredible proves to be fact, it's quite an achievement for something to remain incredible. The borders of fantasy keep receding as fantasy is overtaken by reality. Today, there was a story in the Washington *Post* about the transcript of a taped telephone conversation between Charles Colson (former special counsel to the President) and E. Howard Hunt (formerly an agent for the Central Intelligence Agency and later a consultant to the White House). The conversation was included in a memorandum from Colson to Haldeman. Colson wrote to Haldeman on July 2, 1971, "The more I think about Howard Hunt's background, politics, disposition, and experience, the more I think it would be worth your time to meet him. . . . If you want to get a feel of his attitude, I transcribed a conversation with him yesterday on it. Needless to say, I did not even approach what we had been talking about, but merely sounded out his own ideas."

Colson did talk to Hunt, about Daniel Ellsberg, who had in June, 1971, a few days before this conversation, been charged by the government with unauthorized possession of the "Pentagon Papers," the newspaper publication of which the Administration had tried to stop. "It could be another Alger Hiss case," Colson said. Colson and Hunt continued:

COLSON: Let me ask you this, Howard, this question. Do you think with the right resources employed that this thing could be turned into a major public case against Ellsberg and co-conspirators?

HUNT: Yes, I do, but you've established a qualification here that I don't know whether it can be met.

COLSON: What's that?

HUNT: Well, with the proper resources.

COLSON: Well, I think the resources are there.

HUNT: Well, I would say so absolutely.

COLSON: Then your answer would be we should go down the line to nail the guy cold?

HUNT: Go down the line to nail the guy cold, yes.

At another point in the conversation, Colson asked Hunt, "Weren't you the guy who told me . . . that if the truth ever came out about Kennedy and the Bay of Pigs, that it would just destroy them?"

"Yes," Hunt replied. "I've written my memoirs of that, but, of course, I never published them. . . ."

"Might want to talk to you about that, Howard," said Colson. "I'll be back to you."

In the current *Newsweek,* Stewart Alsop reminds us of some things about G. Gordon Liddy. Liddy, formerly a special assistant in the Treasury Department, worked at the White House on the staff of the Domestic Council, then was counsel to the Finance Committee to Re-Elect the President. It was Liddy, we had been told, who presented plans to a supposedly dismayed John Mitchell for kidnapping members of radical groups at the Republican National Convention, providing prostitutes for Democrats at the Democratic National Convention, and bugging the offices of the Democratic National Committee and of key figures at the Democratic Convention. Mitchell, the former Attorney General and later chairman of the Committee for the Re-Election of the President (CREEP), told the Ervin committee that he rejected this and a scaled-down plan, and denied that the Democratic National Committee was discussed as a "target" for surveillance. Jeb Stuart Magruder, Mitchell's former deputy at the Re-Election Committee, had testified that it was. Magruder also told the Ervin committee that Colson "called me one evening and asked me, in a sense, would we get off the stick and get the budget approved for Mr. Liddy's plans, that we needed information, particularly on Mr. O'Brien." (Lawrence O'Brien, chairman of the Democratic National Committee.)

On June 20th, three days after the break-in, Colson wrote a memorandum for the file in which he said, "While Liddy and Hunt were in my office, I called Jeb Magruder and urged them to resolve whatever it was that Hunt and Liddy wanted to do and to be sure he had an opportunity to listen to their plans. At one point, Hunt said he wanted to fill me in and I said it wasn't necessary because it was of no concern to me, but that I would be glad to urge that their proposals, whatever they were, be considered. There was no discussion that I can recall of what it was that they were planning to do other than the fact that I have the distinct impression that it involved security at the convention and/or gathering intelligence during the Democratic National Convention."

Alsop reminds us of some other testimony last summer by Magruder when he was questioned by Samuel Dash, Democratic counsel to the Ervin committee:

> MAGRUDER: I simply put my hand on Mr. Liddy's shoulder and he asked me to remove it and indicated that if I did not, serious consequences would occur.
> DASH: Was he more specific than serious consequences?
> MAGRUDER: Well, he indicated he would kill me.

In his testimony, Magruder later said, "I do not now regard that as a specific threat. It was simply Mr. Liddy's mannerism."

People "in the Nixon entourage," Alsop says, "were uneasily aware that Liddy often carried a gun and was quite capable of using it." One evening, Liddy, spying on the McGovern headquarters, shot out a light.

"On another occasion," writes Alsop, "Magruder was complaining in Liddy's presence about some 'enemy' and muttered something about 'getting rid' of him. A few minutes later, a Magruder subordinate met a grim-faced Liddy, who mentioned the well-known name of the 'enemy' and remarked that 'I have been ordered to kill him.' A horrified Magruder finally persuaded Liddy that murder was not quite what he had in mind." These people make it very hard to be imaginative anymore.

The Nixon Administration boasted at the outset about its methodical and businesslike ways. Now it is having trouble because so many were so eager to record, and to protect, themselves on paper and on tape.

SEPTEMBER 9

Sunday. There is much speculation about where the President stands—about whether he can, as the current phrase goes, "tough it out." There are, as usual, two schools of thought. A more important question is what sort of precedent will have been set. Last spring, when the story was breaking, one friend of mine here said that the conclusion that those who come to power in the future might draw from what we have been learning is not that these things should not be done but that they should be done more skillfully.

The New York *Times* says today that Stephen Bull, a White House aide has reportedly told Senate investigators that President Nixon on several occasions asked White House aides to play tapes, including two of his conversations with White House counsel John Dean, and to brief him on their content. This was said to have happened both before and during the time Dean testified before the Ervin committee. Dean, in five days of testimony in June, had said that last September the President had praised him for his work on the case—which Dean took to mean that the President was pleased that no one higher than Liddy had been prosecuted. Dean told the committee that on March 13th he told the President that the Watergate defendants were asking for more money. He said that the President had asked him how much they were demanding and, when Dean said that it might be a million dollars or more, the President said that that would be "no problem." The President then said, according to Dean, that he had discussed the "fact that Hunt had been promised executive clemency" with Ehrlichman and Colson. (Haldeman and others subsequently told the committee that this conversation took place on March 21st.) Dean said that at a meeting on March 21st, he told Mr. Nixon that "there was a cancer growing on the Presidency," and he said that when he and the President met on the evening of April 15th, after Dean had begun to coöperate with the prosecutors, the President said that he had only been "joking" about raising the money for the defendants. And then, said Dean, the President went to a corner of the room and whispered that he had probably been "foolish to discuss Hunt's clemency with Colson." Dean said that he had the impression that the conversation was being taped. (All this was before Alexander Butterfield, a former White House aide and later Federal Aviation Administrator, revealed to the Ervin committee, on July 16th, the existence of the tapes. It was hard to believe that they existed, much less to think that the President had not taken care that there was nothing incriminating on them.)

Haldeman later told the Ervin committee that the President's questioning of Dean on the payments to the defendants was just the President's way of drawing people out. Haldeman also told the committee that, at the President's request, he had listened to two of the tapes. After the Ervin committee requested the tapes, the President on July 23rd declined to turn them over, and on the same day the committee subpoenaed them. The President wrote to the committee that he had listened to a number of them and that they were "entirely consistent with what I know to be the truth and what I have stated to be the truth. However, as in any verbatim recording of informal conversations, they contain comments that persons with different perspectives and motivations would inevitably interpret in different ways."

There is much about the recent period that we still do not know. We do not know all the ways that the power of government was used to further the Administration's ends, or even what its ends were. We have to learn everything we can, because we have to know what we are capable of. The framers of the Constitution understood a lot about human nature, and recognized its darker side. It is not ordained—except, perhaps, in our hopes—that America is immune to the effects of mankind's darker impulses. But while the investigations into what happened continue, it is also important to consider what we already know: the President and his top assistants believed they could suspend the First and Fourth Amendments in the Bill of Rights when they perceived a threat to the national security. The White House attempted to use the instruments of government against political opponents and other citizens exercising their right of free speech. One of the most disturbing parts of John Dean's testimony before the Ervin committee was the memoranda he submitted about the White House "enemies." One memorandum, written in August, 1971, by Dean to members of the White House staff put it clearly enough. Dean wrote: "This memorandum addresses the matter of how we can maximize the fact of our incumbency in dealing with persons known to be active in their opposition to our Administration. Stated a bit more bluntly—how can we use the available federal machinery to screw our political enemies?" The "enemies"—about two hundred of them—were contributors to the opposition party, political activists, journalists. (A number of people spoke as if they thought the "enemies list" was amusing. But beneath much of the amusement there seemed to be an undertone of anxiety.) One memorandum singled out twenty people for "Opponent Priority Activity." It was not clear to what extent these lists were acted upon, but there was little doubt that they were at least an accurate reflection of White House attitudes. We know that agents of the incumbent in the White House, in order to secure his reëlection, went to unprecedented lengths to affect the internal processes of the other party. We know that people acting on behalf of the incumbent President went to unprecedented lengths to solicit funds to finance his reëlection from those who did business with the government. And we know that the White House is continuing to use its power to keep us from learning what happened. If it succeeds, what constraints will there be on future executives?

It has been difficult to absorb all that we have been learning, because of the very speed with which it came at us, and because of what it was. In fact, the word "Watergate" may have undergone one of the swiftest and greatest enlargements of meaning in the history of the English language. A place became a metaphor. Like "Waterloo." It is hard to remember now that until a little over a year ago "Watergate" was simply the name of an expensive complex of buildings—containing a hotel, apartments, offices, shops, restaurants—that was constructed on Virginia Avenue, near the Potomac River and the Lincoln Memorial, in the nineteen-sixties. After Nixon was elected President in 1968, several leading figures of his Administration moved into the Watergate. It was said to be the Nixon Administration's answer to Georgetown. When the Democratic National Committee moved its offices to the Watergate in 1967, many thought their selection was in poor taste. The buildings were plush and expensive, and party headquarters—especially Democratic Party headquarters—are supposed to have the look of earnest poverty. It even seems long ago now that "Watergate" came to mean also the break-in on June 17, 1972, of the Democratic headquarters by four Cuban Americans and James McCord, security coördinator for the Committee for the Re-Election of the President, acting under the direction of Hunt and Liddy. When we heard about that break-in on a weekend in June, it seemed odd—we didn't know what to make of it—and it was hard to decide what to think when the President's press secretary, Ron Ziegler, dismissed the break-in as a "third-rate burglary attempt," and John Mitchell informed us that McCord had a number of clients and that "this man and the other people involved were not operating either in our behalf or with our consent." We wondered when Mitchell suddenly resigned on July 1st as director of the President's reëlection campaign in order, he wrote to the President, to "meet the one obligation which must come first: the happiness and welfare of my wife and daughter," an action which followed by six days an announcement by his wife, Martha, that she was leaving her husband because of "all those dirty things that go on" in the campaign. The word from the Nixon entourage was that the outspoken Mrs. Mitchell was—well, a bit unstable. There were widespread suspicions when five of the seven break-in defendants pleaded guilty in January of 1973, but we were nevertheless stunned when Judge Sirica later made public a letter from McCord, who said that "there was political pressure applied to the defendants to plead guilty and remain silent" and that perjury had been committed during the trial. Sirica's conduct of the trial—his expressions of concern that the full story was not coming out—made him something of a hero, but there was reason to be uneasy about that conduct, too. And while it became widely believed later that Sirica had "cracked" the case, McCord's letter was written before Sirica—albeit known as a harsh sentencer—imposed provisional maximum sentences on the defendants and urged them to coöperate with the grand jury and the Ervin committee. The letter was made public and the sentences were delivered on March 23rd. Three days later, the grand jury was reconvened.

It was hard to think about what all of this might mean—and to connect it with other things we knew about the Administration. The mind resisted making the connections. Then the investigatory processes multiplied. In the fall of 1972, Common Cause, the citizens' lobby headed by John Gardner, brought a suit to force the disclosure of secret contributions. And early in 1973, the Senate decided to set up a special committee to investigate 1972 campaign activities.

It was hard to adjust to how increasingly skeptical we had to become about statements issued by the White House. When the President said in August of 1972 that an investigation by John Dean had shown that "no one in the White House staff, no one in the Administration presently employed, was involved in this very bizarre incident," some time elapsed before questions were raised about the qualifying phrase "presently employed." When, on last April 17th, the President announced that there had been some "major developments"—this was the same day that Ron Ziegler termed all previous White House statements on the case "inoperative"—we could almost feel the ground shaking beneath us. (It was also on that same day that Dean issued a statement that he would not be a "scapegoat." We learned later that by then Dean and Magruder had begun to coöperate with the prosecutors.) There was the sense that we were in for things we had never experienced before.

But even then we had no idea. It is hard to believe now that the President's speech on April 30th—the one in which he announced the dismissal of Haldeman and Ehrlichman and Dean and Kleindienst—was to have been the climactic one, the one that cleared things up. In May, the President issued his astonishing four-thousand-word statement confirming that there had been a program of wiretapping, a domestic intelligence-gathering plan ("the Huston plan"), and the "plumbers" operation "to stop security leaks and to investigate other sensitive security matters." (The President also said then that "I took no part in, nor was I aware of, any subsequent efforts that may have been made to cover up Watergate," and he also said that "the name of Mr. Hunt had surfaced" and in order to ensure that the investigation of the break-in "not expose either an unrelated covert operation of the C.I.A. or the activities of the White House investigations unit," which he said was involved in "national security matters," he instructed that the F.B.I. investigation of the break-in be "coördinated with the C.I.A.") We had suspected wiretapping, had even joked—nervously—about it, and the thought that one might be wiretapped was an indicator of self-esteem. But it was easier to live with abstract invasions of privacy than with real ones.

And as the story unfolded before the Ervin committee, it began to take on the characteristics of a Russian novel. Someone we had never heard of suddenly emerged as an agent in activities that were almost inconceivable. McCord led us to people named Ulasewicz and Caulfield, and we had to try to absorb the idea that the White House had maintained its own private investigatory force. It became a major effort just to keep the names straight, not to mention comprehend what these people were doing. (The Ervin committee put its information in a computer.)

The Ervin hearings, which began in May, were flawed and fumbling and marked by some showboating by and tensions among its members; but they did show an attentive public a picture of those who had been in power. And the comprehension became more difficult, as we learned—through the Ervin hearings, through the government's trial of Daniel Ellsberg, through newspaper reports—of illegal wiretaps, of another break-in (this one at the office of Ellsberg's psychiatrist), of documents shredded after the Watergate break-in was discovered, of money for the Watergate defendants being handled with gloves and left in telephone booths and airport lockers. We learned that there had indeed been a plan for espionage and sabotage of the opposition party—a plan with the name of "Gemstone."

Also in May, the demands for an independent investigation outside the Justice Department grew, and on May 18th, the office of the Special Prosecutor was established, with Archibald Cox heading it. From then on, four sets of investigations proceeded: in the Congress, in the courts, in the press, and in the office of the Special Prosecutor. By this August, two grand juries in Washington were investigating various charges.

And so we know now that in 1970 the President approved a "domestic intelligence-gathering" plan that proposed to use the combined resources of several investigative agencies for a program that included breaking and entering, electronic surveillance, and mail covers. The plan's author —Tom Charles Huston, then a White House aide—had said in a memorandum that the President's name should not be on the plan, because parts of it were "clearly illegal." J. Edgar Hoover objected to the plan, and the President has said that after five days it was "rescinded." Last summer, Huston told a House subcommittee that the plan was never formally cancelled. Parts of the plan were incorporated into the plumbers operation, established in the White House in 1971.

The President has said that the limits on "the inherent power in the Presidency to protect the national security" were "the limitation of public opinion and of course Congressional and other pressures that may arise." This assertion presupposes that the Congress and the public know what the executive is doing. The White House investigators, the wiretapping, the Huston plan, and the plumbers were established in secrecy. Last summer, before the Ervin committee, John Ehrlichman defended the President's right to suspend the Fourth Amendment guarantee against "unreasonable searches and seizures" in the interests of "national security." Senator Herman Talmadge, Democrat of Georgia, and a member of the committee, asked him about the principle, derived from English law, that not even a king can enter a man's cottage without his consent. Ehrlichman replied, "I am afraid that has been considerably eroded over the years." Ehrlichman approved a memorandum in which the plumbers proposed "a covert operation . . . to examine all the medical files still held by Ellsberg's psychoanalyst," and after initialling the memo he added the notation "if done under your assurance that it is not traceable." He told the Ervin committee, "Now, if you are asking me whether this means that I had in my contemplation that there was going to be a breaking and entering, I certainly did not." Ehrlichman argued before the Ervin committee that the break-in was "well within the President's inherent Constitutional powers." In May, the President took responsibility for the plumbers, but he said that he had not authorized, and had no knowledge of, any illegal actions they may have taken. Later, he said that he had not been aware of the Ellsberg break-in until March 17th, 1973, and still later he said that it was "illegal." The government has admitted that it wiretapped its own employees—and that some of these taps continued after the employees left the government—and that it wiretapped newsmen. The government has admitted to seventeen taps without court orders, four on newsmen and thirteen on government employees. The wiretapping program was begun after the New York *Times* in May, 1969, revealed that the United States was conducting bombing raids in Cambodia. Presumably the Cambodians were already aware of the bombing, and the news had already appeared in a British newspaper. Subsequent taps were justified on the basis of other leaks of foreign policy information. Three taps were on White House aides who did not deal with national security matters. The taps on two aides to National Security Council Director Henry Kissinger were maintained after they left the government and served as advisers to Democratic

Presidential candidate Edmund S. Muskie. The taps continued into 1971, and the Administration went to some efforts to keep their existence a secret. Records of them were removed from the files of the F.B.I.— apparently out of concern that J. Edgar Hoover, who knew something about blackmail, might reveal them—at the suggestion of William Sullivan, then Hoover's deputy and opponent, and Robert Mardian, then Assistant Attorney General in charge of the Internal Security Division of the Justice Department and later deputy manager of the Committee for the Re-Election of the President. The Administration at first denied the existence of the taps, but later the records of them were discovered in John Ehrlichman's safe.

The President has said that the warrantless taps instituted between 1969 and 1971 were "legal at the time." The President defends his "inherent power" to take special actions "to protect the national security" by suggesting that in an opinion on wiretapping in 1972 the Supreme Court said some things that it did not say. In June, 1972, the Supreme Court, by a vote of eight to nothing, rejected the Administration's claim that the government had the right to wiretap, without obtaining a court order, those who constituted a domestic threat to the national security. A government practice, which has never been tested in the Supreme Court, permits such taps in cases of foreign threats to the national security. Attorney General John Mitchell had argued, in effect, that there was no longer any distinction between foreign and domestic threats. The Court said, "Fourth Amendment freedoms cannot properly be guaranteed if domestic surveillances may be conducted solely within the discretion of the executive branch." In San Clemente, in an answer to a question on the Ellsberg break-in, the President referred to "a recent decision of the Supreme Court or at least an opinion . . . which indicates inherent power in the Presidency to protect the national security in cases like this." The Supreme Court explicitly stated that it was not deciding the legality of warrantless wiretaps in cases involving "foreign powers or their agents," and gave no indication that it was considering break-ins. The President introduces the nonexistent Supreme Court approval of his actions when questions about the wiretapping or the break-ins start to close in on him. At the time the Fourth Amendment was adopted, the government of England was conducting searches against traitors to the Crown. If a President can suspend a guarantee in the Bill of Rights, is it still a guarantee?

In dealing with these issues, the President often cites precedents. He says that previous Presidents wiretapped, and that there have been break-ins before; he says that Abraham Lincoln suspended habeas corpus. The citations of precedents confuse the questions and do not answer them. The fact that these things, to some extent or other, may have gone on before is not particularly comforting. And at what point do differences of degree become substantive differences? The question of the accountability of a President for the acts of his aides may be an instance in which differences of degree at some point become substantive. It stands to reason that a President should not be held accountable for each act of each assistant secretary throughout the government, or for every act of every member of his own staff. But can it be argued that a President is never responsible for his subordinates' acts?

Recent events have forced us to reconsider old assumptions about what can and cannot happen here. We did not want to face the implications of the fact that the union leader whose workers beat up peace demonstrators on Wall Street in 1970 was thereupon invited to the White House to meet the President and present him with a hard hat, and is now the Secretary of Labor. Charles Colson was the White House aide who maintained liaison with that union leader. According to John Dean, Colson suggested to Caulfield in 1971 that to facilitate the retrieval of some documents belonging to a friend of Ellsberg's who worked in the Brookings Institution, a Washington research organization, the Institution's building be firebombed. Woodward and Bernstein have reported that Caulfield himself has told this to federal investigators. Colson denied making the suggestion. An "associate" of Colson's told reporters that if Colson did say such a thing, it might have been as a "joke."

It was also difficult to face the implications of the fact that there were attempts by the Administration to checkmate every institution that could check the executive—the Congress, the Supreme Court, the press, the bureaucracy, even the opposition party. We saw more clearly in some instances than in others that it was happening, and were uneasy, but it was difficult to face what it could mean. Many people take comfort from the thought that our institutions have responded to the challenges. Perhaps they almost didn't. It is not clear that they have. We have learned something about how those in power can use power to retain power. We do not know what, ultimately, would have happened but for the fateful bungling. There may have been less purpose or pattern than hindsight sometimes suggests. The Nixon Administration may not have thought in terms of checkmating institutions. It may not have thought in terms of institutions at all.

Something about the Nixon staff. Every President must have aides whom he can totally trust. Every President must have at least some aides who are willing to carry out, and accept the blame for, some unpleasant tasks. But the price of having loyal people around one is not demanding things that are beyond ethical limits, and one must have a taste for people who recognize limits. Nixon seems to have had a taste for associates who did not recognize limits. Many of the Nixon White House men seemed to have no gyroscopes.

In Federalist Paper No. 51, James Madison wrote:

> But what is government itself but the greatest of all reflections on human nature? If men were angels, no government would be necessary. If angels were to govern men, neither external nor internal controls on government would be necessary. In framing a government which is to be administered by men over men, the great difficulty lies in this: you must first enable the government to control the governed; and in the next place, oblige it to control itself.

SEPTEMBER 16

Last week, the President's lawyers and Archibald Cox submitted briefs to the Court of Appeals on the issue of the tapes. Charles Alan Wright, who has come to the White House from the University of Texas Law School to advise on the tapes issue, said that there were no circumstances under which the President could be forced to give up the tapes. He disputed Judge Sirica's view that if the interest served by executive privilege was abused, the privilege did not obtain. "The privilege is the President's," said Wright.

John Connally, the former Democratic governor of Texas and former Nixon Administration Secretary of the Treasury, who has been a Republican since early this year, defended the President's position on the tapes. (Until just recently, it had been widely believed that Connally and Agnew were the chief rivals for the Republican nomination in 1976. Connally served as a White House adviser for a little more than two months earlier this year. The press reports when he left were that he could not get through to the President after he first advised him that Watergate was a disaster and recommended a housecleaning of the White House staff. Now Connally is tacking back toward those who support the President.) Connally told the press, "We're leading ourselves into believing the Supreme Court is the ultimate arbiter of all disputes, and I don't believe it. I think there are times when the President of the United States would be right in not obeying a decision of the Supreme Court."

A couple of days later, Senator Edward Kennedy, who is widely believed to be the front-runner, if he runs, for the Democratic nomination in 1976, made a speech on the Senate floor about the tapes. Kennedy said, "If President Nixon defied a Supreme Court order to turn over the tapes, a responsible Congress would be left with no recourse but to exercise its power of impeachment. . . . The President has no argument from history for such defiance. The only argument he has is the law of the jungle, the law of raw and naked power."

2

YESTERDAY, the Washington *Post* ran a banner story saying that Vice-President Agnew has been discussing the possibility of resigning. The way the Agnew story swept through Washington—the speculation about its truth, its sources, and their motives—is characteristic of the way things work here, especially in recent times. There is the quality of a nervous system about Washington, or, at least, about that part of Washington which professionally concerns itself with official events. Obviously, there are people here who sell shoes and insurance and fix teeth and automobiles and live as people do anywhere else. But there is a constantly growing, bipartisan collection of people here—journalists, politicians, politicians' aides, lawyers, lobbyists, government workers, hangers-on, and the geological strata of several Administrations' worth of former officials—who make up what is usually referred to as "Washington," as in "What does Washington think?" or "What is the mood in Washington?" These people concern themselves with what is going on, whether or not what is going on concerns them. They talk about it over their meals and on their telephones. "Washington" not only does a great deal of talking about what's happening but also does a great deal of speculating about what might happen. It speculates on the question, say, "Is Teddy going to run?" even though no one—perhaps not even Senator Kennedy himself—really knows the answer as of now.

The news here is more than just news—it is an event, which often affects the subsequent news. The flow of news is to "Washington" what the stock-market ticker tape is to "Wall Street." People here develop expertise in reading the news, in recognizing signals and spotting shifts in power, and in determining who is leaking what and who is doing what to whom. This, like the speculation, is not just a matter of curiosity. The careers and fortunes of many here rest on their capacity for knowing—or for convincing others that they know—what is what and who is up and who is down and who is on the rise. There are many here who are investors in power—people who aid or befriend a politician, or an important aide or friend of a politician, whose success could enhance their own. Some investors in power propel a Presidential candidate

along, fuelling his ambitions and dreams, in the hope of thereby realizing something on their investment. Washingtonians read several
newspapers. Washingtonians do not live like other people. On Sundays,
when other people are hiking or sailing or doing nothing, many
Washingtonians are earnestly going through the thick Sunday papers
and watching *Meet the Press* and *Face the Nation.* Washingtonians do
this even when there is little going on. Someone once said, in a quieter
era, "We are in the thick of thin things." Now we are in the thick of thick
things, and at times we are very nearly overwhelmed.

Watergate has been hard on the Washington nervous system. The nervous system responds with some intensity to great, unexpected public
events. They alter patterns and assumptions, and that can be disturbing.
It is harder to escape the events in Washington, to turn the conversation
and the mind to other matters. Most of the people here are here because
they want to be; they came from other places and decided to stay. They
have an odd combination of idealism and cynicism about the government they watch closely. They impute a certain majesty to the White
House and the Capitol, and yet they know that inside those buildings
fallible human beings are fumbling their way through the complexities
of running the country. They know how fallible those human beings can
be, but they still address senators as "Senator" and Cabinet officers as
"Mr. Secretary" and think it matters who is Attorney General, and stand
up when they hear "Hail to the Chief." The creation of illusions is part
of the process of clothing our government in some dignity. The predis-
position to trust our leaders, despite some of the things we know about
them, bespeaks an understanding that every free society has to proceed
on trust. There is something healthy about our reluctance to shed that
trust. We may derive some pleasure from shedding illusions imposed
on us by others; there is little pleasure in shedding the illusions we have
imposed on ourselves.

Today's papers report that the White House has invoked executive
privilege on a tape of a meeting between President Nixon and milk
producers in 1971. It was two days after this meeting that Agriculture
Secretary Clifford Hardin, reversing a decision announced thirteen
days earlier, ordered an increase in the price support of milk. Following
this decision, dairy groups contributed more than four hundred thousand dollars to Republican political committees. Much of the money
was given through dummy committees with names like Committee
for a Better Nation and Association for More Effective Federal Action
Committee. Ralph Nader's Public Citizen, Inc., sued charging that the
increase in price supports was in exchange for early contributions to
the President's reëlection. The White House is also claiming executive
privilege on a memorandum suggesting a "photo opportunity" between
dairy-industry leaders and the President. A "photo opportunity" is when

press photographers are permitted a few minutes of picture-taking during a Presidential meeting.

Some of the milk funds were collected by Murray Chotiner, a long-time associate of Richard Nixon's and now a Washington lawyer. Reading about the milk case last spring, I discovered that one of the dummy committees had been headed by E. Howard Hunt. It was one of those unexpected connections that keep turning up.

The inflation—and who knows what else?—is doing strange things to this country. We have shortages. America is not supposed to have shortages. Shortages are among the things to which we were supposedly invulnerable. There haven't been this many shortages since the Second World War. Now there appears to be a gasoline shortage—no one seems to know the facts—and the oil companies are advertising on television that we should not buy their products. As of now, there appear to be shortages of lumber, energy, audio- and video-tape, copper, blue-jean dye, meat, paper, bloodworms, gasoline, and tennis balls.

At lunch today, an assistant to the President told me that the worst was over for the President. The situation had, he said, "bottomed out." The problem for the President now was to reestablish his popularity. The aide said that perhaps the President needed a foreign-policy crisis to divert attention from Watergate and reassert his capacity for leadership in the foreign-policy field.

SEPTEMBER 30

Sunday. Things came unglued last week. On Tuesday, Vice-President Agnew asked the House of Representatives to conduct an inquiry into the charges against him. That same afternoon, Attorney General Richardson released a statement to the effect that he and other officials had been meeting with Agnew's lawyers "to discuss procedural aspects of the case and options available to the Vice-President," that the negotiations had broken down, and that the evidence against the Vice-President would be presented to the grand jury. In his letter to the House, the Vice-President said that an investigation by the House provided the best means of "preserving the Constitutional stature of my office and accomplishing my personal vindication." He suggested that an impeachment inquiry was in order, because "the Constitution bars a criminal proceeding of any kind . . . against a President or Vice-President while he holds office."

The Vice-President cited the precedent of a House impeachment inquiry into charges of war profiteering by Vice-President John C. Calhoun. A House committee found Calhoun blameless, and no further action was taken. In the case of Calhoun, however, there were no grand jury or other legal proceedings on the charges taking place. Others

felt that another precedent went against the Vice-President's conten-
tion that he could not be prosecuted before he was impeached. In 1872,
Vice-President Schuyler Colfax came under investigation for bribery
that had taken place earlier in his career. A congressional committee
decided that Colfax could not be impeached for crimes that occurred
before his election as Vice-President.

On Wednesday, House Democratic leaders rejected Agnew's request,
because, said House Speaker Carl Albert, it "relates to matters before
the courts." Behind the high Constitutional principles evoked by both
sides, there were other considerations: Agnew's hope that the Congress
would extricate him from his legal troubles, and the Democrats' lack of
interest in doing so.

On Friday, Agnew's lawyers moved in court to block the grand-jury
proceedings, on the ground that a Vice-President cannot be investigated
or indicted by a grand jury unless he is first impeached and removed
from office by the Congress. The precedents cited on this question
are confusing, and may not even be precedents. Agnew's lawyers also
said that leaks to the press about the investigation had made it impossible for the Vice-President to receive a fair trial. They said that Justice
Department officials were responsible for the leaks and were trying "to
drive the Vice-President from the office." The Justice Department issued
a statement calling the charges against Department officials "patently
ridiculous."

The case is a skein of conflicting ambitions and exigencies.
Richardson, who may have further political ambitions, must maintain a
certain distance from both the White House and Agnew. The President
is believed by some to want the Vice-President out, because his presence, and a long legal battle, would further scar an already damaged
Presidency. But another way to look at it is that as long as there is a
Vice-President under a cloud and in the office, the President's tenure
is more secure. Agnew is fighting to save his skin, and he has a very
powerful weapon—a following. Agnew has taken to the road to evoke
that following. Yesterday, he told the National Federation of Republican
Women in Los Angeles that he is "innocent of the charges against me.
. . . I have not used my office," said the Vice-President, "nor abused
my public trust as County Executive, as Governor, or as Vice-President
to enrich myself at the expense of my fellow-Americans." The Vice-
President accused Justice Department officials of trying to "destroy
me politically through the abuse of the criminal-justice system of the
United States." He said they were doing so in order to compensate for
"their ineptness in the prosecution of the Watergate case." Pointing to
Henry Petersen, the Vice-President made an unusual—for the Vice-
President—remark about the Watergate case. "A recent examination of
his record," Agnew said, "will show . . . that he failed to get any of
the information out about the true dimensions of the Watergate matter."

The Vice-President said, "I'm a big trophy." He told the cheering women, "I will not resign if indicted. . . . I intend to stay and fight."

In the course of the week, one wise Washington lawyer whom I consulted on the Constitutional question of the impeachment of a Vice-President, professed himself "unwildered" by the rush of events. The Vice-President racing to Capitol Hill, and then his lawyers racing back to the courts. Perhaps the President was "unwildered," too. Suddenly we were soberly examining "the Calhoun precedent" and "the Colfax precedent"—things most of us had never heard of a week ago.

The Ervin committee resumed its hearings last week. Hunt, released from prison in order to testify, and under pressure from Judge Sirica to coöperate with investigators, was pale and subdued, the disillusioned soldier-at-arms betrayed by friends and by his country. Hunt said, "I am crushed by the failure of my government to protect me and my family, as in the past it has always done for its clandestine agents." He told the Ervin committee that payments for legal defense and family subsistence for himself and for his fellow Watergate defendants had stopped before all of the bills had been paid. It was Hunt's name in the address books of two of the men caught in the Watergate that first linked the break-in to the White House. Hunt, a former employee of the C.I.A., a participant in the Bay of Pigs invasion, seems like a character out of his own forty-odd adventure novels. He was dashing and adventurous, and it was hard to take him seriously, to know what to think about him. It was reported that Hunt, wearing a red wig, had gone out to Denver to see Dita Beard, formerly the I.T.T. Washington lobbyist. What was one to think about that? (Later we learned that the C.I.A. had supplied the wig, and its officials said it was brunette, and objected to reports that it was "ill-fitting.") Charles Colson testified before a House committee that he had sent Hunt to see Mrs. Beard. Last spring, it was reported that Hunt told the grand jury that, acting on instructions from Colson, and drawing on his own C.I.A. experience, he fabricated cables in an attempt to link the Kennedy Administration with the assassination of South Vietnam's President Diem in 1963, and tried to leak the cables to the press. What was one to make of that? Hunt also told the grand jury—referring with perhaps unconscious irony to one of Richard Nixon's triumphs—that there were "technical problems" in preparing the cables "because after the Alger Hiss case everyone was typewriter-conscious."

The break-in was actually the second one that took place at the Democratic headquarters. The first, on May 27, 1972, was undiscovered and apparently also fruitless. Hunt told the Ervin committee that Liddy "indicated to me in the strongest terms that it was Mr. Mitchell who was insisting" on the second break-in. He said that after taking orders from the C.I.A. for twenty-one years without question, "it never occurred to me to question . . . the legality, the propriety of anything that might be ordered by the Attorney General of the United States." The committee released a memorandum from Hunt to Colson, written in July, 1971, on how "to destroy [Ellsberg's] public image and credibility." One of the suggestions: "Obtain Ellsberg's files from his psychiatric analyst." In a memorandum written in August, 1971, to Colson, Ehrlichman wrote, "On the assumption that the proposed undertaking by Hunt and Liddy would be carried out, and would be successful, I would appreciate receiving from you by next Wednesday a game plan as to how and when you believe the materials should be used." When Hunt tried to tell Colson about the raid afterward, Colson said, according to Hunt, " 'I don't want to hear anything about it.' " (Colson has refused to testify before the Ervin committee.) The raid had failed to produce the psychiatric files. In his San Clemente press conference, the President referred to it as a "dry hole."

Hunt said that the "parameters of the Gemstone operation" were in two notebooks that he had left in his safe in the White House. Some of the items in Hunt's safe had been turned over to the former acting F.B.I. director, L. Patrick Gray, who destroyed them. The disclosure in late April of this year that Gray had destroyed the evidence led to Gray's resignation as acting director of the F.B.I. on the following day. Ehrlichman and Dean gave him the material, Dean saying it "should never see the light of day." Gray burned the material. The material from Hunt's safe— including a revolver, microphones in simulated ChapStick containers, bugging equipment, fake cables about Vietnam, a psychological profile of Ellsberg prepared by the C.I.A., and information gathered on Edward Kennedy and Chappaquiddick—left its legacy of damage, and also some of the most striking language of this series of events. Dean has said that Ehrlichman suggested that he shred the sensitive documents, and "deep six" the other material in the Potomac one evening on his way home to Virginia. Ehrlichman denied later that he had made either suggestion. He said that he had never in his life proposed to anyone that they shred papers. He said his practice was to burn them.

Gray had the misfortune of being the acting director of the F.B.I. for a protracted period—he was named in May, 1972, but his nomination was not submitted for confirmation until the following year because, the White House said, the President did not want this sensitive position subjected to election-year politics. And so he was serving as the acting director in the days after the break-in, and also in the following year when the cover-up was coming unravelled. His nomination to be permanent director of the F.B.I. was withdrawn from the Senate in early April. It was disclosed during his confirmation hearings that Dean had sat in on F.B.I. interviews with White House personnel about Watergate, and that Gray had forwarded F.B.I. files on the Watergate investigation to Dean. Gray's revelations to the Senate Judiciary Committee were also disturbing to the White House, and the subject, Dean has testified, of several meetings with the President. It was during Gray's extended agony before the Judiciary Committee that Ehrlichman got off another of the memorable lines of this period: "Well, I think we ought to let him hang there. Let him twist, slowly, slowly in the wind."

Hunt told the Ervin committee of another break-in—one that he and Liddy had planned in 1972—that had not been carried out. The plan was to raid the office safe of Herman M. (Hank) Greenspun, the editor and publisher of the Las Vegas *Sun*. The plan was drawn up with the coöperation of a security aide to Howard Hughes, with whom, Hunt said, there was a "commonality of interest." The Washington *Post's,* story about Hunt's testimony says that among the items that Jack Anderson wrote in 1971 and 1972 was one saying that the White House was unhappy about Donald Nixon's association with an associate of Hughes, and that Bebe Rebozo had once intervened to keep them apart; and that a payment of a hundred thousand dollars had passed from Richard Danner, a Hughes aide, to Bebe Rebozo.

Something else that Hunt said to the Ervin committee stays in one's mind. He said that he could not "say that the C.I.A. has ever stayed out of domestic activity." The revelations about the C.I.A., the F.B.I., and the White House investigators raise a number of questions concerning the uses of covert agencies in a democratic society. Congressional "oversight" of the covert agencies has been something of a joke. Can we train people in the black arts and then control their practice of their craft?

Last summer, Woodward and Bernstein reported that Hunt had told Ervin-committee investigators that he had been ordered by Colson, within hours after Arthur Bremer shot George Wallace, on May 15, 1972, to break into Bremer's apartment in Milwaukee. Colson, Hunt said, wanted him to reach the apartment before the F.B.I. did. He said that Colson wanted him to look for evidence that Bremer was connected with left-wing political causes. Hunt, according to the reports, said that the risk of getting caught was too great, and he did not go. Colson denied the reports, calling them "utterly preposterous." Colson said that he had dined with the President that evening and could not have spoken with Hunt until later. Woodward and Bernstein wrote, "One White House source said that when President Nixon was informed of the shooting, he became deeply upset and voiced concern that the attempt on Governor Wallace's life might have been made by someone with ties to the Republican Party or the Nixon campaign. If such a tie existed, the source said, the President indicated it could cost him the election."

A memorandum of a telephone conversation in November, 1972, between Colson and Hunt, taped by Colson, was released by the committee today. It shows Hunt saying to Colson, "There's a great deal of unease and concern on the part of the seven defendants. . . . there's a great deal of financial expense that has not been covered and what we've been getting has been coming in very minor [dribs] and drabs. . . . I thought that you would want to know that this thing must not break apart for foolish reasons. . . . This is a two-way street and as I said before, we think that now is the time when a move should be made and surely the cheapest commodity available is money." It shows Colson telling Hunt, "I'm reading you. You don't need to be more specific. . . . The less specifics I know, the better off I am, we are, you are."

Patrick Buchanan, a Presidential speechwriter and the first Ervin-committee witness on the subject of "dirty tricks," was self-assured and combative. He testified on Wednesday. Buchanan's memoranda about campaign strategy contained lines such as "We ought to go down to the kennels and turn all the dogs loose on ecology Ed," and "Who should we get to poke the sharp stick into his cave to bring Muskie howling forth?" Said Buchanan to the committee, "The exaggerated metaphor is really the staple of American political language."

The Washington *Post* reported this morning that Tom Charles Huston, author of the President's 1970 plan for admittedly illegal intelligence-gathering, who is now a lawyer in Indianapolis, has been serving for the past year on a Census Bureau advisory committee on privacy and confidentiality.

OCTOBER 1

Monday. On page 28 of this morning's New York *Times,* there is a story about testimony and other evidence gathered for the trial in Los Angeles of a suit against Howard Hughes by a former employee, Robert Maheu. Maheu has given more details of Richard Danner's delivery of a hundred thousand dollars in cash from Howard Hughes to Bebe Rebozo in 1969 and 1970. He said that the money was delivered in two installments of fifty thousand dollars each. Danner is a former F.B.I. agent, an associate of former Florida Senator George Smathers, and a friend of Rebozo. It was Smathers who introduced Rebozo to Nixon. The *Times* story also says that in January, 1970, Danner was sent by Hughes to Washington to see Attorney General John Mitchell. In 1968, the Justice Department blocked further acquisitions of casinos in Las Vegas by Hughes. (Negotiations by Hughes interests to buy another casino later went forward, but then fell through.)

Over the weekend, there have been stories about campaign contributions to Mr. Nixon that were revealed as a result of the suit brought by Common Cause to force the disclosure of secret contributions for the President's reëlection. A story in Saturday's Washington *Post* said that

Calvin Kovens, a Miami Beach contractor who was convicted, with former Teamsters president James Hoffa, of mail fraud, contributed thirty thousand dollars in cash. It said that Kovens was pardoned eight days after former Senator Smathers called Charles Colson and argued for Kovens' release. In March, Colson left the White House and joined a law firm in Washington. A few months before he joined the firm, the Teamsters had transferred their business to it from one headed by Edward Bennett Williams and Joseph Califano, which had been counsel to the Democratic National Committee. In 1971, James Hoffa's sentence was commuted by the President, and Hoffa was released from prison after serving about one-third of his term. Jack Anderson reported in May of this year that the Teamsters raised large amounts of money, most of it in cash, for the President's 1968 and 1972 campaigns. Much of it, said Anderson, came via Las Vegas casinos financed by Teamsters pension funds. Hoffa was released on terms that prohibited him from participating in Teamsters politics until 1980. In July of this year, Hoffa was reported in the Washington *Post* to have said he believed that Colson received sizable contributions for the President's campaign in exchange for keeping him out of Teamsters politics. Colson responded, "No money, not on any occasion, was ever paid to me regarding Mr. Hoffa. The charge would be funny if it was not so serious."

The information on campaign contributions released last Friday in response to a federal-court order showed that the President's reëlection committees raised eleven million four hundred thousand dollars in the one-month period before April 7, 1972, when the new campaign finance disclosure law went into effect. The Common Cause suit maintained that the law in effect before April 7th also required disclosure. We had read that lists of those who contributed before that date had been destroyed at the offices of the Finance Committee to Re-Elect the President. Common Cause, in the course of its suit, discovered, almost by chance, that one list survived—in the desk drawer of the President's secretary, Rose Mary Woods. There is no way of knowing whether the information that has now been supplied as a result of the suit is complete.

The newly released figures show that sixty million two hundred thousand dollars was raised to reëlect the President. This is almost twice as much as was reported to have been raised for his nomination and election in 1968, and the total of sixty million two hundred thousand dollars does not include funds raised by "Democrats for Nixon," headed by John Connally, and from certain Republican groups.

Common Cause released a preliminary breakdown of contributions made to Nixon between January 1, 1971, and April 6, 1972. The amounts were: the auto and tire industry, $307,000; chemicals, $950,000; construction, engineering, and architects, $370,000; dairy, $232,000;

entertainment, $580,000; financial (banking, securities, and insurance), $4,470,000; food and food processing, $295,000; mining, $125,000; oil and gas, $1,410,000; pharmaceutical and health, $1,120,000; real estate, $1,005,000; textiles, $312,000; transportation (airlines, railroads, and shipping), $425,000; government officials (including ambassadors), $1,011,000; defense and aerospace contractors, $501,000.

The Ervin-committee hearings showed how rivers of cash flowed from contributors to Maurice Stans, former Secretary of Commerce and chairman of the Finance Committee to Re-Elect the President, and to Herbert Kalmbach, associate chairman of the Finance Committee to Re-Elect the President and the President's personal attorney; and to safes and secret funds; and to the "Gemstone" plan for espionage and sabotage of the Democrats; and to the "legal-defense fund" for the Watergate Seven. Stans and former Attorney General Mitchell were indicted, along with the financier Robert Vesco, last May, for conspiracy to defraud the United States and to obstruct an investigation by the Securities and Exchange Commission into Vesco's financial affairs, and Mitchell and Stans have also been indicted for perjury, in connection with a contribution by Vesco of two hundred thousand dollars. (This case was brought by the United States Attorney's office in New York and was not part of the Special Prosecutor's efforts.)

The material released last Friday shows that the President's reëlection committees spent almost five million dollars in the two days before the new law took effect. According to Common Cause, most of it went in prepayments for services that the committees would apparently rather have had remain undisclosed. Among the recipients of funds listed on Friday with the Clerk of the House were G. Gordon Liddy, Anthony Ulasewicz, Donald Segretti (retained to carry out "dirty tricks" against the Democrats), John Caulfield, Seymour Freidin (one of two journalists retained by Murray Chotiner to spy on the McGovern campaign), and Chotiner.

OCTOBER 2

At the White House, John Love, former governor of Colorado and now in charge of the Administration's energy program, and Rogers Morton, the Secretary of the Interior, explain to the press a new program of mandatory allocation of propane gas and a plan for federal supply-management of heating oil. This is the first energy allocation since the Second World War. The energy officials say that it will be "temporary."

The President and Mrs. Nixon dined last night at Trader Vic's restaurant. Yesterday, the President went for an automobile drive with General Alexander Haig, now his chief of staff. Several of the reporters are edgy, and wonder what's going on. They also become edgy, and wonder what's going on, when the President stays secluded.

Last weekend, a special Senate committee issued a report that says there are now over four hundred and seventy statutes in which the Congress has given the President special powers that he may use in a period of national emergency. The report also points out that we have been in a state of national emergency since 1933. Among the things that these statutes say the President may do in a period of national emergency are declare martial law, send troops anywhere in the world, call up the Reserves, seize and control all means of transportation, regulate all private enterprise, restrict travel, and seize property. Some of the emergency powers have been around for some time, and have been put to imaginative use. The Feed and Forage Act of 1861 was passed in order to permit the President to provide food and clothing to Civil War troops and forage for their horses without the specific approval of the Congress. In that period, the Congress met in short sessions; the law was passed, amid a general tightening of restrictions on the President's powers, to assure that the troops would be fed and clothed while the Congress was not in session. The Feed and Forage Act of 1861 has been used in recent years to circumvent congressional restrictions on paying for the war in Southeast Asia. It has been estimated that more than ten billion dollars was spent for the war by this circumvention alone.

The committee, headed by Senators Frank Church, Democrat of Idaho, and Charles Mathias, Republican of Maryland, is considering legislation to repeal the state of national emergency.

There was a time last spring when it seemed that the most dramatic question was whether John Dean would "finger" other members of the White House staff. Now we hear people considering the possibility that both the Presidency and Vice-Presidency will be vacated before their four-year term has been served. Ever adaptive, people here are beginning to consider this heretofore inconceivable possibility. One can hear conversations about what should happen next. There are discussions as to whether Carl Albert, the Speaker of the House and second in line for the Presidency, should step down in favor of someone else who might then be made President. It has been noted that one does not have to be a member of the House of Representatives to be Speaker of the House. Neither Democrats nor many Republicans are interested in having Agnew replaced by someone who would run for President in 1976, and might profit from incumbency. One hears all manner of schemes for filling the highest and second-highest offices in the land.

OCTOBER 3

The President came into the pressroom today. This usually means that he wants to be seen, and heard, and make some point, without submitting to a regular press conference. Because most of the reporters

must stand, the President was almost impossible to see—a disembod-
ied voice. A brief glimpse of him showed that he was wearing a blue
suit and makeup. The television lights were on, and it was hot in the
crowded room. This part of the White House used to hold a swimming
pool. Early in the Nixon Administration, it was transformed into comfortable quarters for the press. The press used to lounge around in the
West Wing lobby, where there was some opportunity to observe some
of the comings and goings there. These new quarters have put the press
at a further remove.

Today, the President confirmed an announcement just made by the
White House press office that Secretary of State Henry Kissinger is going
to Peking. But it was clear that the President was prepared for questions
about Agnew. That may be why he was there. He praised Agnew's "distinguished service as Vice-President" and said that he regarded Agnew's
decision to remain in office as "an altogether proper one." He said that
the charges against the Vice-President "do not relate in any way to his
activities as Vice-President of the United States." Nixon said, however,
that the allegations against the Vice-President were "serious and not friv-
olous." Afterward, the President's statements were closely scrutinized
for their meaning. The President appears to be trapped by, and somewhat
frightened of, the Vice-President. Reporters' conversations with White
House staff members confirm this. The President is said to be worried
that the Vice-President will turn his constituency against the President.
The President is trapped, politically and Constitutionally.

The Presidential candidate bestows the opportunity to run for Vice-
President on some grateful politician, but there is no way for a President
to oust a Vice-President. The assumption has always been that the Vice-
President is in the President's thrall. It could also be the other way
around. Richard Nixon selected Spiro Agnew as his running mate in
1968 in order to build a certain constituency, and kept him on the ticket
in 1972 because Agnew had succeeded in doing so. Now that Nixon is
in trouble, he needs Agnew's constituency. It is the conservative constituency of the Republican Party. It was also what George Will, of the
National Review, has called the "constituency of the discontented."
Agnew, like Nixon, appealed to the anger and discontent in America.
He articulated grievances. His speeches against the media were powerful because they reached that part of people that distrusted the power of
the media, and its control in "Eastern" hands. These were old themes,
to which Agnew gave fresh currency. His vocabulary articulated the historic streak of anti-intellectualism, anti-liberalism, in America. It was
the dark side of populism. It caught the illiberalism of liberalism, liberalism's own distrust of the people. It was never clear whether Agnew
believed these things or not.

Maryland is just down the road from Washington, yet we in Washington were only vaguely aware of Agnew as he rose in Maryland politics. Many of our friends live in Maryland, yet for many of us Maryland is as remote as, say, Illinois or Louisiana and its politics as impenetrable. I first recall hearing about Agnew on my radio, when he was running for governor, and he had a campaign song, to the tune "My Kind of Town." The first line of his song went, "My kind of man, Ted Agnew is," and I wondered who Ted Agnewis was. He defeated a many-times candidate who ran on the slogan "Your home is your castle," which, in that context, was anti-integration, not pro-Fourth Amendment. So we had the impression that Agnew was a moderate. Agnew, the Vice-President, gradually came to be looked upon—as people who might actually attain the office are—as a possible President. His style encouraged that process. There was a certain dignity about Agnew, a peculiar sort of elegance. Erect, with those narrow eyes and silky voice, he was always very neat, well-groomed. In style, he was manicured and mean. It was never clear whether the Presidency was Agnew's ambition or that of those around him, the investors in power. From time to time, he gave interviews suggesting that he really did not care to be President, and his statements did not sound like the standard demurrers. Agnew said he might prefer to make some money. But he adapted to the trappings of the Vice-Presidency—his own plane, the Palm Springs spa of his new friend, Frank Sinatra.

Agnew was, at first, given an office in the White House. Then he was shunted across the way, to the Executive Office Building. It was said at the outset that he would have an important hand in domestic policy. He ended up dealing with Indians and taking trips and making speeches. When he went out to make speeches, it was said that the President had "unleashed Agnew." In 1972, there was a slight flurry over whether Agnew would be kept on the ticket or might be "dumped" in favor of John Connally. But Agnew had built his constituency. At the conventions in 1968 and 1972 "Dick" and "Ted" stood arm in arm, beaming and waving to the cheering conventioneers. Now they are locked in a death grip.

OCTOBER 6

A Justice Department memorandum printed in today's papers argues, by somewhat tortured reasoning, that the Vice-President can be indicted before he is impeached but the President cannot. The memorandum concedes that the Constitution makes no such distinction. The distinction is made, rather, it says, because of "the singular importance of the Presidency." It says that should a Vice-President who is under indictment succeed to the Presidency, the criminal proceedings could stop and impeachment could begin.

This week, the Providence *Journal* reported that the President and Mrs. Nixon paid $792.81 in income taxes for 1970, and $878.03 for 1971. Other papers picked up the story. Gerald Warren, who now conducts the White House press briefings, said, responding to queries, "We consider that the President's tax returns are private, just like any other citizen's, and we're not going to comment further."

The *Green Book,* Washington's social register, was published this week. The Haldemans, the Ehrlichmans, the Deans, the Magruders, and the Stanses have been dropped. A press release accompanying publication of the book said that the changes were the result of "an upheaval in Washington officialdom unprecedented without a change in Administration." In an interview, Mrs. Carolyn Hagner Shaw, who says that she compiles the book with an anonymous five-member board, observed that compiling it this year was "some job."

This morning, war broke out in the Middle East.

OCTOBER 10

The phone call that comes in the early afternoon saying that the Vice-President has resigned is astonishing. I had thought about the event, even anticipated it. Now reality, as it has done in other instances, other contexts, has betrayed anticipation. We had been getting ready for this, and we hadn't.

Agnew is on television, coming out of the courthouse in Baltimore. His face is expressionless. He has pleaded nolo contendere to a single charge of federal-income-tax evasion. Moments earlier, he resigned as Vice-President. The judge called the no-contest plea "the full equivalent of a plea of guilty." Agnew has been sentenced to three years of unsupervised probation and a fine of ten thousand dollars. In exchange, the government has agreed not to press the other charges, of alleged acts of extortion and bribery, the details of which shall be made public. Agnew has told the court that he chose to resign, and not to fight the charges against him, because to do otherwise "would seriously prejudice the national interest." On television, Agnew is still defiant. He points out, "The principal witnesses of the government are not being fully prosecuted," and goes on to say, "I will make an address to the nation within a few days."

On a CBS Special this evening, we see the congressional leaders leaving the White House. Carl Albert, as Speaker of the House, is now first in line of succession for the Presidency. After Albert, the next in line is Senator James Eastland, Democrat of Mississippi. Eastland is now second in line for the Presidency by virtue of having served in the Senate longer than any other member of the majority party. He thereby holds the ceremonial post of president pro tempore of the Senate, who under normal circumstances is third in line of succession.

Walter Cronkite says that "the big question tonight" is who will succeed Agnew. Cronkite lists some names that are being mentioned: Governor Nelson Rockefeller, of New York; Governor Ronald Reagan, of California; John Connally; Representative Gerald Ford, Republican of Michigan, the Minority Leader of the House; Senator Hugh Scott, Republican of Pennsylvania, the Minority Leader of the Senate; William P. Rogers, the former Secretary of State; Elliot Richardson; Melvin Laird, former Secretary of Defense and now a White House adviser; George Bush, chairman of the Republican National Committee; William Scranton; Howard Baker.

Now the procedure for selecting a new Vice-President will have to be invented. There is no precedent for this situation. The Twenty-fifth Amendment to the Constitution, which provides for filling the office of the Vice-President if it should become vacant, says simply, "Whenever there is a vacancy in the office of the Vice-President, the President shall nominate a Vice-President who shall take office upon confirmation by a majority vote of both Houses of Congress." The Amendment was approved by the Congress in 1965 and was ratified by the required three-fourths of the states by 1967. Now no one is sure how it should work.

When the Congress enacted the Twenty-fifth Amendment, it had other concerns besides filling a Vice-Presidential vacancy. The section dealing with this was in fact added almost as an afterthought. The main concern, which the Amendment also deals with, was the question of what to do in the case of disability of the President. Some think that this section is unclear, too. The Twenty-fifth Amendment was enacted in part because the men who were next in line when Lyndon Johnson assumed the Presidency, after Kennedy's assassination, in 1963, were very old. Johnson had suffered a heart attack some years earlier. The Speaker of the House, John McCormack, was in his seventies; the president pro tempore of the Senate, Carl Hayden, was in his eighties. We watched them uneasily as they sat, slack-jawed, behind the President when he addressed the Congress.

The Washington *Star-News* reports that, through a set of transactions arranged by Charles Colson, five thousand dollars in money contributed by the milk producers in 1971 was used to finance the break-in at Ellsberg's psychiatrist's office.

OCTOBER 11

Today will be a day of speculation and rumors and attempts to grasp the situation. We've never been here before.

Yesterday's "Dear Mr. President" and "Dear Ted" letters between the President and the former Vice-President are in this morning's papers. They are at once cordial and guarded, each man protecting his position.

DEAR MR. PRESIDENT:

As you are aware, the accusations against me cannot be resolved without a long, divisive and debilitating struggle in the Congress and in the Courts. I have concluded that, painful as it is to me and to my family, it is in the best interests of the Nation that I relinquish the Vice-Presidency.

Accordingly, I have today resigned the Office of Vice-President of the United States. A copy of the instrument of resignation is enclosed.

It has been a privilege to serve with you. May I express to the American people, through you, my deep gratitude for their confidence in twice electing me to be Vice-President.

Sincerely,
SPIRO T. AGNEW

DEAR TED:

The most difficult decisions are often those that are the most personal, and I know your decision to resign as Vice President has been as difficult as any facing a man in public life could be. Your departure from the Administration leaves me with a great sense of personal loss. You have been a valued associate throughout these nearly five years that we have served together. However, I respect your decision, and I also respect the concern for the national interest that led you to conclude that a resolution of the matter in this way, rather than through an extended battle in the Courts and the Congress, was advisable in order to prevent a protracted period of national division and uncertainty.

As Vice President, you have addressed the great issues of our times with courage and candor. Your strong patriotism, and your profound dedication to the welfare of the Nation, have been an inspiration to all who have served with you as well as to millions of others throughout the country.

I have been deeply saddened by this whole course of events, and I hope that you and your family will be sustained in the days ahead by a well-justified pride in all that you have contributed to the Nation by your years of service as Vice President.

Sincerely,
RICHARD NIXON

The Agnew story dominates this morning's papers, but there are other items of interest. The war in the Middle East is growing worse. The United States government says it believes that the Soviet Union is airlifting supplies to Egyptian and Syrian forces. The State Department says that this would "put a new face on" the Middle East conflict. There are reports that the United States may increase its military supplies to

Israel. The 1967 war lasted six days. It is now the sixth day since this war broke out, and there is no prospect of an end.

It is a gray, chilly day. In Washington, the autumns are usually warm and lovely. It is often warm enough here to play tennis, and sail on Chesapeake Bay, through November. Along Pennsylvania Avenue today, there are flags with orange, green, and white stripes, marking the official visit to the United States of the President of the Ivory Coast, Félix Houphouet-Boigny. Some things don't change. For as long as I can remember, Félix Houphouet-Boigny has been President of the Ivory Coast and has been visiting Washington. As I approach the White House, cannons fire, and a helicopter rises from the South Lawn. The President has seen his official visitor off.

On television, Elliot Richardson is holding a press conference at the Justice Department on the way in which the Agnew case was settled. The Department has released a document titled "Exposition of the Evidence Against Spiro T. Agnew Accumulated by the Investigation in the Office of the United States Attorney for the District of Maryland as of October 10, 1973," which covers forty pages. It tells of the transactions by which Agnew allegedly arranged for cash payments from engineering firms and others with state business in exchange for state-awarded work. According to the charges, some of the payments were made while Agnew was Vice-President. Agnew has claimed that the evidence is false.

Victor Gold, to my surprise, keeps a lunch date we made last week for today. Gold was Agnew's press secretary for a time, and has just begun to work as a newspaper columnist. His career has been closely tied to that of Agnew. During Agnew's recent troubles, Gold was an outspoken defender of the Vice-President, and suggested that the Vice-President was the victim of a White House plot—perhaps to replace Agnew with Connally, or, at least, to divert attention from the President's troubles. Gold has a rather famous temper, but he is popular with the press, because he understands its job and he has a sense of humor. Today, Gold, usually a voluble man, is subdued. He seems to be in shock. We eat at the Sans Souci. The Sans Souci, around the corner from the White House, is Washington's "see-and-be-seen" restaurant. Today, William Safire, former Nixon speechwriter and now a columnist for the New York *Times,* is lunching with Patrick Buchanan; Ken W. Clawson, deputy director of the White House Office of Communications, is here; and so is Charles Colson. One day last summer, I saw James McCord lunching at the Sans Souci.

"I should have been more cynical," says Vic Gold, shaking his head sorrowfully. "I grew up in Louisiana, and when I was twelve years old

I saw my governor go to jail." A bit later, he says, "It's like Watergate. You don't know what you're in." Gold says that conservatives are telephoning him, very upset. When the former Vice-President said emphatically that he would not resign, they had believed him. Gold says that conservatives are also upset about what is going on at the White House. And some still suspect the President "dumped" Agnew. Gold himself is in a difficult position. After lunch, I walk back with him to his office, at 1701 Pennsylvania Avenue. There is a thick stack of slips noting phone calls that came in while he was at lunch. He is being besieged by requests for interviews, television appearances. "Frankly," he says, pacing the floor of his office, "I don't know what to do." On the walls of his office are large photographs of Agnew and Gold conferring, and of Agnew, waving and smiling, emerging from a plane that bears the seal of the Vice-President.

The flags of the Ivory Coast have been removed from Pennsylvania Avenue. Supporters of Israel are demonstrating in front of the White House. Supporters of the Arabs are demonstrating across Pennsylvania Avenue, in Lafayette Park. Six years ago, it was the other way around: Arabs in front of the White House, Israelis in Lafayette Park.

The town is dense with rumors and speculation. A reporter encountered after lunch on Connecticut Avenue says, "It'll be Warren Burger on Tuesday." John Connally is believed to be out of the running for the Vice-Presidency, because he would meet strong opposition from the Congress. His change of parties doesn't make him particularly popular with either one. And there is something about Connally that stirs dislike in politicians. He is big, noisy, and unpredictable. He not only opposes—he rubs it in.

A new word has been given currency—"caretaker." Words become fashionable quickly here, even when, as in this case, they do not quite fit. In the present context, a "caretaker" would be a Vice-President without further ambitions. If he became President, he would not run again. Some politicians want a "caretaker" for what they see as statesman-like reasons—to provide stability. Others, of course, have less detached reasons, but few will talk about them out loud. Everyone wants to appear statesmanlike now. The removal of a Vice-President on a relatively "minor" charge is seen by some as making it more possible that a President might be removed on less than grand grounds. If the President selects someone who attracts wide support, a figure of "national unity," he might have more trouble remaining President. These thoughts must have occurred to Mr. Nixon.

Just before six this evening, the President took off in his helicopter for Camp David, his Maryland retreat. A few minutes later, House

Minority Leader Gerald Ford and Senate Minority Leader Hugh Scott drove up to the White House. Ford told reporters he had come to deliver the House members' proposals for the Vice-Presidency—a hundred and sixty-three of them.

OCTOBER 12

On the evening news, it is announced that the President made his decision about the next Vice-President at dawn today at Camp David. It is reported that he has chosen from among five men who were under final consideration. He will disclose his decision at the White House this evening. This is earlier than had been expected. Presumably, the information that the choice was made at dawn is included to add drama, but dawn has bad connotations. The President chose Agnew at dawn. At dawn, in 1970, the President went to the Lincoln Memorial to talk about football with the peace demonstrators.

It is also announced on tonight's news that the Court of Appeals has ruled that the President must turn the tapes over to the court. The court said that for the President to be able to decide what information he must surrender would be "an invitation to refashion the Constitution." The court said that it had hoped the President and the Special Prosecutor could work out a compromise on the tapes.

Yesterday, Egil Krogh, thirty-four, was indicted for lying to the grand jury about the work of the plumbers. This was the first in what is expected to be a series of indictments obtained by the Special Prosecutor, Archibald Cox.

It is hard to know what to call the television spectacle that is broadcast from the East Room of the White House tonight. The Cabinet is present. Many members of Congress are also there, including some Democrats—by and large, Southern senators and senior members of the House. The President has played on their institutional confusion. The Supreme Court declined to come. Members of the Joint Chiefs of Staff are there. The President says, as he has said before, that it is "vital that we turn away from the obsessions of the past." He says, "This is a time for a new beginning." He succeeds, maddeningly, in drawing us into his guessing game about his choice. It will be someone who agrees with him on foreign policy and defense matters, he says. It will be someone with executive ability. Someone who can work with the Congress. (Maybe Senator Henry Jackson, Democrat of Washington? That would be a stroke, neutralizing the Democrats.) He says that his choice has served in the Congress for twenty-five years. That still leaves a number of possibilities. But the congressional leaders, and then the others in the room, are standing and clapping and cheering. I am embarrassed for Gerald Ford when he does not stand up. There must be some mistake.

Can it be Ford? Ford has the reputation of being a somewhat limited spear-carrier for the Republicans. Ford is a clubman, steady, courteous, and well liked on Capitol Hill. There are no sharp edges on him—of brilliance or of meanness. His name was not taken very seriously when it came up in the speculation. But now it is clear that Nixon's choice is Ford.

The President congratulates his nominee, and the crowd in the East Room is jubilant. "They like you," the President says to Ford. They do; Ford is one of them. The President and the Vice-President-designate, arm in arm, smile at the crowd in the East Room.

OCTOBER 15

Monday. Behind the statements of several members of Congress today about how deliberate the consideration of Ford must be, there is some embarrassment over the scene in the East Room on Friday night, and there is also the idea that Ford's confirmation should be delayed until the President's situation becomes clearer. There is the issue of the tapes. The Ervin-committee staff is reported to have been told four conflicting stories about the circumstances of the payment of a hundred thousand dollars by Howard Hughes to Bebe Rebozo. Some people are questioning why a President in so much trouble should be able to choose his successor. But who else could do it? The Twenty-fifth Amendment did not foresee this situation. Who could?

Today, I asked a Democratic Senate aide who is in the traffic patterns on Capitol Hill why the issue of whether the President obeys a court decision on the tapes was the focus of the impeachment talk. This man knows a lot about not only just what is going on, but what it might mean. "Because it provides a high-minded reason for impeachment," he replied. "If the President defies the Supreme Court, that would overturn the concept of how America works which has held since Marbury v. Madison." In Marbury v. Madison, in 1803, the Supreme Court ruled that the Supreme Court did not have to enforce an act of the Congress which it found un-Constitutional. The aide also said that defiance of the Supreme Court was "something clear-cut that the members of Congress could seize on, as opposed to corruption, break-ins, or the Fourth Amendment."

At lunch, a Republican member of the House said that Ford had been more a "White House man" than a leader of the House Republicans. He also said, "Jerry is popular because he is not a leader. If he were a leader, he would not be popular."

A Democratic senator said today that he did not think Ford was Presidential material, and that a lot of his colleagues shared his view. I asked him why others did not say so publicly. "Because if they say something nice about him, he'll be nice to them," the senator said. "A lot of those people spend their time currying favor. He might be President, you know."

Agnew, in his television address tonight, suddenly looks like an old man. He seems shrunken, his face more creased. Perhaps it is the gray suit that makes his face appear ashen despite the makeup. The former Vice-President is sitting in a mock office in a television studio. It is painful to watch the former Vice-President speak tonight, but this seems to be something he needs to do. Mr. Agnew says that his plea last week was "not an admission of guilt but a plea of no contest, done to still the raging storm." He has some bitter words for the Maryland contractors who allegedly participated with him in the kickback scheme, and then did him in. "They know where the questionable propositions originate," he says. "They know how many shoddy schemes a political man must reject in the course of carrying out his office." Then the Vice-President gives, in effect, a little chalk talk about the process of corruption of politicians. He explains the "pressures for favoritism" under systems of noncompetitive contract bidding—pressures that exist "at every level of government in this country." He also explains that public officials "face the unpleasant but unavoidable necessity of raising substantial sums of money to pay their campaign and election expenses." Then he explains, "In the forefront of those eager to contribute always have been the contractors seeking non-bid state awards." He says that the series of charges against him "boils down to the accusation that I permitted my fund-raising activities and my contract-dispensing activities to overlap in an unethical and unlawful manner." Then the former Vice-President says, in a bitter tone, "Perhaps, judged by the new, post-Watergate political morality, I did." And he calls for "public financing for every political candidate." This is a more radical reform than almost anyone else has suggested.

After the former Vice-President finishes speaking, Victor Gold, appearing on CBS, is asked what the point was of Agnew's speaking at this stage. Gold replies, slowly, "I have no idea."

OCTOBER 16

Just before lunchtime, the news came over the tickers that Marines were boarding an aircraft carrier headed for the Mediterranean. Nobody knows what it means.

At a restaurant, some aides of former Vice-President Agnew are being taken to lunch by reporters. It may be the last time.

The city seems to be reeling around amidst the events and the breaking stories. In the restaurants, the noise level is higher. At the end of the day, someone says, "It's like being drunk."

This morning's papers report that Melvin Laird told reporters yesterday that he had warned the President to expect an impeachment move
by the Congress if he rejected an order by the Supreme Court to surrender the tapes. The President, of course, could have known this if
he read the newspapers, but it has never been clear to what extent the
President reads the newspapers, or to what extent the news summaries prepared under the supervision of Patrick Buchanan give him the
bad news. Laird, a former House Republican leader and then Defense
Secretary who went to the White House to serve as counsellor in June,
is proficient at playing the press, and he is shrewd, and he is enmeshed
in Republican politics, and from long habit we read stories about Laird
to try to figure out why he is saying what he is saying. We even read
stories that do not mention Laird—such as columns by the team of
Rowland Evans and Robert Novak, who are close to Laird—to try to
figure out why Laird is saying what he is saying. Laird usually has a
reason. It is fair to guess that two purposes of yesterday's comment by
Laird were (1) to send a message to the President, to whom Laird is
said not to have much access, and (2) to keep Laird's public record on
the issue of the tapes clear. Laird also said that "several weeks ago" he
discussed with Gerald Ford the possibility of Agnew's resignation and
of Ford's replacing Agnew.

A House subcommittee has just completed hearings on federal spending on the President's private homes. Among the disclosures during
the hearings were that two thousand dollars in government funds was
spent for a black-and-white terrazzo shuffleboard court and that eleven
thousand five hundred dollars was spent for a redwood, rather than a
wire-mesh, fence. The hearings showed that on a number of occasions
the improvements were ordered by Herbert Kalmbach or by others handling the President's private affairs, who later billed the government. We
have also read that the government supplied the President's home at San
Clemente with Mexican lanterns designed by the President's architect.

In the October issue of *Fortune,* Dan Cordtz writes of the "monar-
chical life style to which U.S. Presidents have grown accustomed." He
says that "only the budget of the Central Intelligence Agency is harder
to calculate than that of the Presidency." He says that the thirteen-
million-dollar White House budget "ludicrously understates" the cost
of maintaining the Presidency, and says that the cost may be as high as
a hundred million dollars a year. He says that the air fleet now at the
disposal of the President, his family, and his staff includes five specially
fitted Boeing 707 jetliners (President Johnson had three), sixteen specially soundproofed helicopters, and Lockheed Jetstars that often serve
as courier planes to carry mail and staff assistants when the President is

away from Washington. The Presidential air-conditioning bill, he says, is increased by Mr. Nixon's habit, copied by some of his aides, of keeping a fire burning in his fireplace even in summer. Cordtz reports that an official car has been used to provide private transportation to Camp David for the President's Irish setter, King Timahoe. He also reports that a group of Californians have given the President a golf course at San Clemente.

Early in the Nixon Administration, the Nixons began the custom of having, at social occasions, smartly uniformed trumpeters, their medieval horns draped with heraldic banners, trumpet the imminent approach of the President of the United States.

At dinner, a House Democrat of some influence says that he would like Vice-Presidential nominee Gerald Ford to become President soon. He says he would not mind if Ford were to be the Republican candidate for President in 1976. "It'll be easy to knock him off," he says.

OCTOBER 18

Yesterday, officers of three corporations—American Airlines, the Goodyear Tire & Rubber Company, and the Minnesota Mining & Manufacturing Company—pleaded guilty to making illegal corporate contributions to the President's reëlection campaign. Archibald Cox said that some other corporate indictments could be expected.

On the evening news, Senator Kennedy says that Congress should reject Ford's nomination "if Mr. Ford refuses to acknowledge the obligation of the President to obey the Supreme Court" in the matter of the tapes.

3

TODAY IS THE LAST DAY on which the President can appeal the Court of Appeals ruling that he must comply with Judge Sirica's order to give the subpoenaed tapes to the court. The assumption is that he will appeal. The President might gamble that the Supreme Court would not hand down a "definitive" judgment. Moreover, there are a number of ways in which the issue of the tapes could sputter along for a considerable time, with compromises, challenges over the meaning of "national security," and so on. The matter could end ambiguously. This morning's Washington *Post* reports that Attorney General Richardson and Special Prosecutor Cox have been meeting during the week in an effort to avoid a Supreme Court showdown over the tapes.

Most of today's stories are about the Middle East. Israeli tanks are on the west bank of the Suez. Saudi Arabia has announced that it has cut its oil production by ten percent, and has threatened to cut off all supplies of oil to the United States unless the United States ceases its military aid to Israel.

There are further stories about the President's problems. In Washington, Egil Krogh has pleaded not guilty to charges that he lied to the grand jury about the plumbers' raid of Ellsberg's psychiatrist's file. Krogh contends that in ordering the break-in he was acting as "an officer of the United States" in defense of national security.

In his opening speech at the biennial A.F.L.-C.I.O. convention today, George Meany said, "Never in history has a great nation been governed so corruptly."

Gerald Warren told White House reporters yesterday that the hundred thousand dollars given by Howard Hughes to Bebe Rebozo was a "potential campaign contribution." Warren would not specify which campaign.

On the evening news, it is reported that John Dean pleaded guilty today to conspiracy to obstruct justice and defraud the United States. In return for being permitted to plead guilty to this single charge, carrying a maximum sentence of five years in prison and a ten-thousand-dollar fine, Dean has promised "complete coöperation" with the Watergate prosecutors. He must have more to tell, and Cox must feel that what Dean has to tell is of sufficient value to warrant this arrangement.

Richardson is reported to be still trying to work out a compromise on the tapes. Reporters spent the day at the Supreme Court awaiting the President's appeal, but nothing happened, and now the Court is closed. It is possible that the appeal might still be sent this evening (the Court would probably not turn it away)—too late for the event to be seen on tonight's news. Another "normal" day, as days, these days, go.

The tailspin begins with the late-evening television news programs. It is announced that the President will not give up the tapes and will not appeal to the Supreme Court on the tapes. Instead, he will make summaries of the tapes available to the courts and the Ervin committee. Senator John Stennis, Democrat of Mississippi, will verify the authenticity of the summaries. Senators Ervin and Baker have met with the President and agreed to the arrangement. The President has also ordered Archibald Cox to cease his efforts to obtain, through the courts, other evidence from the White House. Cox has replied that to obey the order would be a violation of his duties, and that he will not obey. Fred Graham, of CBS, announces the story dressed in black tie. He has rushed from a dinner at the National Press Club, where the first annual Fourth Estate Award was presented to Walter Cronkite.

The news is stunning and makes little sense. On what authority could Ervin and Baker agree to such an arrangement? What on earth is Stennis doing in the picture? Stennis, seventy-two, is chairman of the Senate Armed Services Committee—one of the most powerful men in the Senate. Stennis had kept the secret of the secret bombing. Stennis had presided over a subcommittee to oversee the C.I.A., but it had rarely met. Stennis is one of the Senate's barons. When he returned to the Senate recently, after recovering from being shot by a holdup man outside his Washington home early this year, he received a hero's welcome. Stennis is unlikely to be challenged by his fellow-senators. And Ervin and Baker are now getting at least some access to the tapes, which they have been denied by Judge Sirica. Apparently, the President has played to both senators' institutional pride, and to their confusion. He has brought them into an agreement that deals out the courts and Cox. Now the issue is drawn over the role of the courts and the Special Prosecutor. Tomorrow, Cox will hold a press conference.

The radio is kept on, as if war had broken out. At twelve-forty-five A.M., CBS radio announces a "net alert," meaning an alert to the network stations. It sounds very ominous when a network announcer says

"net alert"—as if, perhaps, war had in fact broken out. The announcement that follows is that Henry Kissinger has left, in secrecy, for
Moscow.

OCTOBER 20

It is a spectacularly beautiful day, warm and springlike. It's unfair to
have to give it up for a Constitutional crisis. Besides, it is Saturday, and
Washington is supposed to stop on Saturdays. The term "Constitutional
crisis" has been overused in the course of the year. It has been applied
to situations better described as Constitutional challenges or congressional failures or institutional confusions. But now this may be the real
thing. The President has sought to define and limit the investigation of
the executive branch. The President's offer of summaries of the tapes
does not seem to comply with the court order that he turn over the tapes
themselves. So there is no choice today but to submit to the events, to
watch and listen as men struggle over the meaning of the Constitution.
This crisis is ahead of schedule.

The Washington *Post* has a story by David Broder entitled "Stennis
Is Logical Choice." The story reminds us that last April, as the Watergate
dam was cracking, "Stennis left his hospital bed to fly with Mr. Nixon
to the dedication of the Stennis Center at a naval air station outside
Meridian, Miss.," and that "in a clear reference to the scandal then
emerging in the President's official family, Stennis said: 'Mr. President,
we admire you for the worker you are. You worked your way up against
adversity and you do not panic when things go the wrong way or when
the going gets rough.'" Stennis is what a friend of mine who works in the
Senate calls a "King's-party" man. The concept goes back to the debates
of the Constitutional Convention over the proper powers of the executive—over whether, in the President, the framers of the Constitution
were establishing a King by another name. They solved this, or thought
they did, by stipulating that the power of the executive derives from
the people. The "King's party," according to my friend's definition,
is represented by those in the Congress who impute to the President
extraordinary powers and duties, which only he is capable of dis-
charging. "King's-party" men pay particular obeisance to the concept
of the President as Commander-in-Chief. "King's-party" men add to
legislative directives the qualifying phrase "as the President may determine." "King's-party" men accord a majestic aura to the Presidency,
and equate it with whoever is President. They are men close to power,
accustomed to power, who in a crisis feel a special bond with the
President as the ultimate symbol of power. To John Stennis, the higher
duty was to keep the Administration's secret bombing, and secret C.I.A.
operations in Laos, from becoming known to his fellow-senators or to

the people. In Washington, this way of proceeding is regarded as a mark of "integrity." Stennis has played a major role on those rare occasions when the Senate has sat in judgment on one of its own: Joseph McCarthy, Thomas Dodd. In the wake of the Bobby Baker scandal, Stennis headed a Senate ethics committee, which faded from view after making a few recommendations. These exercises relieved the Senate of major embarrassment without disturbing basic arrangements. And they contributed to John Stennis's reputation for "integrity." Stennis has said that he is "honored" by this new assignment.

There is a great deal of confusion this morning. It is not at all clear where we are. Will the President fire Cox? What, then, will Richardson do? Richardson keeps ending up in the middle of it. Beneath the suspense is the disturbing sense that people are not proceeding according to the processes. The President is circumventing the courts, and the senators are a party to his action. If the President succeeds in ridding himself of the Special Prosecutor, how can he, or any President, be held accountable? This is a time for the "definers"—those who by speaking out shape the debate on public questions. Who the definers are can change from issue to issue. Sometimes there are no definers. The reaction of other members of Congress will be very important. Senator Lowell Weicker, Republican of Connecticut and member of the Ervin committee, has already called the arrangement a "hollow deal." Mike Mansfield, the Majority Leader of the Senate, has said that he thought Cox had independent authority. This is important; Mansfield does not often speak out. Carl Albert has said that the arrangement is "interesting."

The idea of a Special Prosecutor presents a Constitutional dilemma. The problem is how to empower someone to investigate the executive branch who is not also beholden to it. There are but three branches of the government, and the Prosecutor has to be accountable to one of them. If he should be accountable to the Congress, he would not, without further legislation, have sufficient prosecutorial powers. There is no precedent for establishing a Special Prosecutor under the authority of the courts. Last May, the idea just seemed to catch on that the investigation of Watergate could no longer be entrusted to the Justice Department, which was subject to White House authority. But there remained problems of executing the idea. Liberal Democrats on the Senate Judiciary Committee were holding up Richardson's nomination to be Attorney General (the President had announced on April 30th that he would name him to replace Kleindienst) until institutional safeguards for an independent Special Prosecutor could be arranged. Richardson at one point tried to make it an issue of his own personal honor, but the senators insisted that the issue was an institutional one. When Richardson reached for Archibald Cox, it seemed a neat stroke. Cox, a Harvard Law School professor, had been Solicitor General in the Justice Department under Robert Kennedy in the Administration of John F. Kennedy. Edward Kennedy and his allies applauded the appointment and eased up on their demands for institutional arrangements. Archibald Cox was one of theirs. Richardson and the committee worked out a set of guidelines covering the office of the Special Prosecutor. They included the following: "The Attorney General will not countermand or interfere with the Special Prosecutor's decisions or actions," and "The Special Prosecutor will not be removed from his duties except for extraordinary improprieties." The President said last night that he was issuing his orders to Cox "as an employee of the executive branch."

Word comes that Ervin and Baker are saying they did not know that Cox was to be forbidden to proceed. Ervin is said to have thought that he would receive the full transcript of the tapes. One keeps wondering what they thought they were doing yesterday. Why did they even go to the White House without consulting their colleagues? Even now, perhaps an invitation to the White House has a majesty that is irresistible. They may have been acting out of a sense of patriotism. Ervin and Baker are among those who are reluctant to tear at things too much.

The President's statement, printed in today's papers, suggests the strategy he used with the two senators—and will be using with the public in the next days—and something of what is on his mind. He speaks of "the strain imposed on the American people by the aftermath of Watergate." "What matters most, in this critical hour," he says, "is our ability to act—and to act in a way that enables us to control events, not to be paralyzed and overwhelmed by them." (This sentence is reminiscent of *Six Crises*.) The President says, "There are those in the international community who may be tempted by our Watergate-related difficulties at home to misread America's unity and resolve in meeting the challenges we confront abroad." Patriotism, then, is to be equated with putting aside the issue of the tapes. The war in the Middle East is dangerous. Kissinger has gone to Moscow.

It is odd how natural it seems that the networks are televising a press conference by the Special Prosecutor. This folksy, tentative, Jimmy Stewart-like character I see on my television screen is not the cool, starchy Professor Cox I remember from attending his classes in labor law with frightened Harvard Law students. The lanky build is familiar, and so is the crew cut. But his casual manner now is disarming—and devastating. Fiddling with his jacket pocket, he says, "I'm certainly not out to get the President of the United States." He says he worries that "I'm getting too big for my britches." And then Cox gets to the point, speaking of "what seems to me to be non-compliance with the court's order." He slices up the President's arrangement with the senators, stating that it is "not a question of Senator Stennis's integrity." It is important, he says, "to adhere to the established institutions." The President's instruction not to pursue the evidence is unacceptable not "because it interferes with Archie Cox" but because it represents "a basic change in the institutional arrangement that was established." It is, he says, "inconsistent with pledges that were made to the United States Senate and through the Senate to the American people."

Cox refers to the "slippery term . . . national security"—a term the President uses to defend, and to keep secret, many of the things that were done. Cox makes it clear that the issue was not just the tapes but the "repeated frustration" of his attempts to obtain several papers, some of which were "put into a special category called 'Presidential files.' " He emphasizes his "respect and affection" for Attorney General Richardson. Of his conversations with Charles Alan Wright on Thursday evening, he says, "It was my impression that I was being presented with things that were drawn in such a way that I could not accept them." He has slipped a hook into Richardson and the Senate. If he goes, he intends to take their honor with him. He says he does not believe that the President can fire him; only the Attorney General can. Otherwise, he will go to court and challenge the President.

Elliot Richardson is caught in the ultimate conflict in the role of Attorney General—of being both the President's lawyer and the people's lawyer. That's what the establishment of a Special Prosecutor was supposed to resolve. It seems that we have been thinking about Richardson's conscience, and crises thereof, for years now. His complaisance, when he was Under-Secretary of State, in the Administration's policy of continuing the war in Vietnam and extending it into Cambodia. His support, when he was Secretary of Health, Education, and Welfare, of the Administration's position against busing. His defense, when he was Secretary of Defense, of the bombing of Cambodia. How many crises of conscience can Richardson stand? How many can we?

The afternoon is one of rumors and speculation. No one knows what the President will do. Since Cox's press conference, reporters have speculated—and speculation has developed into assumption—that the President would not, as they put it, "let this go" for twenty-four hours. If he did, the theory runs, there would be too much time for support for Cox to develop. So if the President is to rid himself of his Special Prosecutor he should do it soon, and fast. The speculation has been fed by the fact that the President's helicopter, to take Mr. Nixon to Camp David, has been delayed on the South Lawn of the White House. There are rumors that a statement will be forthcoming from the White House by nightfall. Reporters are deployed at the White House, at the Justice Department, and at Cox's office, waiting.

Senators Kennedy, Birch Bayh, Philip Hart, and John Tunney, all Democrats, have issued a joint statement saying that the compromise may be acceptable to the Ervin committee but that it may "cripple the role" of the Special Prosecutor, and that the President's instructions to Cox are an "unjustified challenge" to his authority. The ostensible purpose of the statement is to bring pressure on the President to proceed with caution in the matter of firing Cox—to warn him that such an action would bring trouble. But the senators seem to have something other than the President's interests in mind. Their preferred ground for a showdown with the President would be over a Supreme Court ruling on the tapes.

As the evening news programs go on the air at six-thirty, there is still only rumor and speculation. Nothing has actually happened since Cox's press conference. At a news bureau in Washington shortly after six-thirty, bulletins begin to cascade from the wire-service machines:

6:48. BULLETIN. WASHINGTON (UPI)—KNOWLEDGEABLE SOURCES CLOSE TO THE WHITE HOUSE SAID SATURDAY NIGHT THAT PRESIDENT NIXON WOULD FIRE SPECIAL PROSECUTOR ARCHIBALD COX FOR "BLATANT AND OPEN DEFIANCE" OF THE PRESIDENT.

6:53. BULLETIN. WASHINGTON (UPI)—PRESIDENT NIXON'S COMPROMISE OVER RELEASE OF THE WATERGATE TAPES BLEW UP SATURDAY NIGHT WITH REPORTS THAT ATTORNEY GENERAL ELLIOT L. RICHARDSON MIGHT BE RESIGNING.

6:56. BULLETIN. (AP) (WASHINGTON)—ATTORNEY GENERAL ELLIOT RICHARDSON APPEARS READY TO RESIGN. THIS IS IN THE WAKE OF PRESIDENT NIXON'S ORDER BARRING FURTHER COURT ACTION TO GET THE WATERGATE TAPES. DEPUTY ATTORNEY GENERAL WILLIAM RUCKELSHAUS GAVE THE IMPRESSION AS HE TALKED WITH NEWSMEN AFTER A DAY OF MEETINGS WITH RICHARDSON AND OTHERS. . . . RUCKELSHAUS . . . REFERRED REPORTERS TO A WHITE HOUSE STATEMENT TO BE MADE LATER TONIGHT.

Cox's office is at work. At 7:03 P.M., the Associated Press reports, "Phone calls and telegrams poured Saturday afternoon into the office of Watergate Special Prosecutor Archibald Cox supporting his opposition to President Nixon's proposed compromise in the Watergate tapes case. 'Only two out of a hundred calls that we've gotten have been against Mr. Cox,' a spokesman said."

At 7:31 P.M., the Associated Press reports: "Newsmen at the White House were expecting an announcement there relating to the controversy, but the White House would not comment. After returning to the Justice Department from a brief trip to the White House, Richardson remained unavailable for comment."

7:32. (UPI) ADVISORY. EDITORS: THE WHITE HOUSE HAS NOT PROMISED AN ANNOUNCEMENT TONIGHT, ALTHOUGH THERE ARE MANY INDICATIONS THAT A STATEMENT WILL BE ISSUED BEFORE THE NIGHT IS OUT.

8:31. WASHINGTON (UPI)—PRESIDENT NIXON THREW OPEN THE DOORS OF HIS OVAL OFFICE AND THE CABINET ROOM SATURDAY TO THOUSANDS OF VISITORS ON THE FALL GARDEN TOUR OF THE WHITE HOUSE GROUNDS. THE TOUR FOLLOWED A BEAUTIFICATION AWARD CEREMONY IN WHICH PAT NIXON AND DISTRICT OF COLUMBIA MAYOR WALTER E. WASHINGTON PRESENTED AWARDS FOR CONTRIBUTIONS TO ENHANCE THE BEAUTY OF THE NATION'S CAPITAL.

8:31. BULLETIN. WASHINGTON (UPI)—PRESIDENT NIXON ACCEPTED ATTORNEY GENERAL ELLIOT L. RICHARDSON'S RESIGNATION SATURDAY NIGHT AND FIRED SPECIAL WATERGATE PROSECUTOR ARCHIBALD COX.

At 8:31 P.M., on CBS, Nelson Benton is on the White House lawn, breathless and seemingly shaken. He delivers his report in much the same manner that war correspondents did from battlefronts in Vietnam. The President has ordered that Cox be fired. Richardson refused to fire Cox, and has resigned. William Ruckelshaus, Richardson's deputy, refused to fire Cox, and was fired. Robert Bork, formerly Solicitor General, has fired Cox and is now the Acting Attorney General. The office of Special Prosecutor has been abolished.

At this time, in this verbose city, no one seems to know what to say.

The journalists, at least, have something to do. Tomorrow's papers must be published. There will be television specials later this evening. There is research to be done on Robert Bork. Nobody knows very much about the Acting Attorney General. All the telephone lines at the White House are busy. Word comes that the F.B.I. has sealed off the offices of Cox, Richardson, and Ruckelshaus. Thoughts turn to the President's emergency powers. We had given little thought to Clarence Kelley, the new director of the F.B.I.—to what manner of man he is.

The news is coming too fast. Faster and harder than anyone expected. It is almost impossible to absorb. Summary firings are not our style. Something about Saturday night—a private time, the dark. Too much disarrangement at once. The speed of the events has become part of their substance. One journalist says that it's like being in a banana republic. Another, ordinarily an outspoken defender of the Administration, says it's like downtown Santiago. Their statements bespeak anxieties that are beyond matters of atmospherics. An enigmatic President has summarily fired three men—men who had built some public trust. What seemed logical, and even inexorable, this afternoon has taken on unpredictable and disturbing proportions. There is no way of telling what the President was thinking. Did he consider the impact that these events would have? Could he know? Did he care? There is another question people are asking. It's whether the President has acted in an irrational burst of temper. It is clear that the President will go to some lengths to assert his independence of the courts and of prosecution. Will he succeed in this? Is there to be any check on him—or any President—ever again? Do we have a system of laws?

Where are we? The United States had three Attorneys General today. Carl Albert is still first in line of succession for the Presidency. Then James Eastland. We have had our first public resignations over policy. The Special Prosecutor's office has been abolished, and the investigation of Watergate returned to the Justice Department, by Presidential fiat.

The reactions of the politicians begin to come over the wires. What the definers will say is important.

10:03. (AP). URGENT. WASHINGTON. SEN. EDWARD M. KENNEDY, D-MASS., CALLED COX'S FIRING "A RECKLESS ACT OF DESPERATION BY A PRESIDENT WHO IS AFRAID OF THE SUPREME COURT, WHO HAS NO RESPECT FOR LAW AND NO REGARD FOR A MAN OF CONSCIENCE. . . . THE BURDEN IS NOW ON CONGRESS AND THE COURTS TO NULLIFY THIS HISTORIC INSULT TO THE RULE OF LAW AND TO THE NATION'S SYSTEM OF JUSTICE."

Gerald Ford: "The President had no other choice" than to fire Cox.

Senator Edmund Muskie (Democrat of Maine): The President's action "threatens to destroy our system of laws. It smacks of dictatorship." Muskie suggests holding hearings on impeachment.

Senator Edward Brooke (Republican of Massachusetts): "This act on the part of the President, under the circumstances, is sufficient evidence which the House of Representatives should consider to begin impeachment proceedings." The subject of impeachment is now in the open. It is here.

Senator Charles Percy (Republican of Illinois): "We have a tremendous quandary . . . tragic war in the Middle East. . . . Thank heavens we have Dr. Kissinger in Moscow."

Archibald Cox: "Whether ours shall continue to be a government of laws and not of men is now for Congress and ultimately the American people."

Late in the evening, I caught up with more of the details of Ron Ziegler's announcement at the White House a few hours ago. He said that the President's compromise was accepted by responsible leaders of Congress and the country. Ron Ziegler said that the Watergate prosecution will continue "with thoroughness and vigor."

It is announced on the radio that Saudi Arabia has cut off its oil supplies to the United States. Can't think about that now.

4

SUNDAY. The newspaper stories reconstructing the events of the last week have begun. There will be many of them before we are through, told from the perspective, and to the advantage, of various figures in the drama. We are in for another *Rashomon,* and we shall read the many versions and may never know the truth. An important part of the truth lies in what was going through the mind of the President.

The Washington *Post* has a story that seems to reflect the view of Richardson, Ruckelshaus, and their aides. Busy as they must have been last night, these people understood the importance of getting their versions to reporters in time for the morning papers. From the *Post* we learn that Richardson was directed last Monday "by a high-ranking Presidential aide to dismiss Cox." The *Post* says that "Richardson agreed to try the negotiating route, according to Justice Department associates, in an effort to forestall the outright firing of Cox—a course that he knew would require his own resignation." The *Post* adds, "At no point, these sources insisted, did Richardson give his final blessing to the various compromise proposals." Ruckelshaus says that he was not fired but had resigned. When Ruckelshaus declined to fire Cox, the story says, General Haig told him, "Your Commander-in-Chief has given you an order."

There are confusing reports as to whether Senator Ervin still agrees to the compromise plan. Melvin Laird is on *Meet the Press.* He had arranged more than a week ago to make the appearance. Laird had, through well-planted leaks, kept his distance from the President on the matter of the tapes. Now, amidst the wreckage, Laird, on national television, must defend the President's actions.

Laird talks calmly about the President's compromise plan on the tapes. It is as if we should wonder what all the excitement was about. "It's just a question of trusting Senator Stennis," he says. In a novel turn, he refers to him at times as Judge Stennis. (Stennis was a circuit judge in Mississippi before he was first elected to the Senate, in 1947.) Laird says, "It's a question of whether you would rather have Senator Stennis make this review and produce this product, or whether you would rather have a federal judge." At one point last summer—when the Ervin committee appeared to be the greater threat—the President argued that "the time has come to turn Watergate over to the courts, where the questions of guilt or innocence belong."

The Washington *Post* has a story that, according to a memorandum written to Haldeman by Gordon Strachan (staff assistant to Haldeman), the White House expected to receive two million dollars from dairy groups.

Dairy groups. Dean's guilty plea. The increasing questions about Bebe Rebozo and Howard Hughes. The Krogh case. Cox getting into the milk case. Cox's revelations about the scope of the issue between himself and the White House—over whether the President must surrender other documents besides the tapes. The indications, for weeks, that the White House wished to rid itself of Cox. It appears that the issue of the tapes was one of many, and provided a means for a showdown with Cox in which important senators appeared to be on the side of the White House. Perhaps the White House hoped that Cox would quit. But Cox was uncoöperative to the end. And perhaps the White House underestimated the reaction.

The radio says that four more Arab countries have cut off supplies of oil to the United States.

Some people are trying to proceed as if this were an ordinary Sunday, but many cannot. Some have even given up the opportunity to attend the football game. There are few ways in which Washington behaves like a city, few connecting threads that give it community, few features of civic pride. It may have been this vacuum, this need, that led to Washington's fanaticism about its football team. The Redskins provide the one bond among Washingtonians, government and nongovernment, Democratic and Republican—Richard Nixon and Earl Warren and Edward Bennett Williams. Today, someone tried to reach Earl Warren to talk with him about what was to be done. Earl Warren was at the football game. Many people are receiving calls from friends around the country expressing a sense of helplessness. The worry that there does not seem to be any means, any machinery, by which to do anything. It is not yet clear what sort of national reaction, if any, there will be. Despite some strong statements last night, it is not yet clear what the politicians will do, or whether they will do anything. A number of meetings are being held today: at the White House, on Capitol Hill, in some downtown offices. Nerves are frayed, and tension is deep. Imaginations have been set loose by events. A friend of mine went out to her front lawn to collect the newspaper this morning and, not seeing it, said to herself, "They've stopped the presses."

James Doyle, press assistant to the Watergate Special Prosecution Force, formerly headed by Archibald Cox, has called a press conference for four o'clock this afternoon at the Prosecution Force's offices, at 1425 K Street. Doyle, of medium height and in his late thirties, is an experienced former reporter for the Washington *Star-News* and the Boston *Globe*. He has a large number of friends in the press corps, and knows what, to them, is good copy. The Special Prosecutor's office was a scene of some drama last evening. To the press, Doyle said, "I think I'll go and read about the Reichstag fire." A member of the Cox staff has told me that when the F.B.I. arrived last night, a young member of the staff was surprised to see a young F.B.I. agent who had been working with the staff in its investigations. "What are you doing here?" the young lawyer asked. Both the young F.B.I. agent and the young lawyer burst into tears.

Today's papers carried stories of how staff members, learning by radio and by word of mouth last evening that they had been fired, had gone to their office, as much to draw together as to take any action. They did vow to continue their work, if possible. They were forbidden by the F.B.I. to remove either papers or personal effects. Some staff members, sensing the storm coming, had already taken some papers home. And what they know can't be shredded.

This afternoon, reporters and television cameras are jammed into the small, hot law-library room of the Special Prosecution Force offices. It is someplace to go, something to cover. A press aide hands out some releases. "Each one has been checked by a federal marshal," he says dryly. A few hours ago, the F.B.I. was replaced by federal marshals. Doyle says that "the mood of the staff is that we're going to continue." He is asked about the fact that the White House has announced that the Special Prosecutor's office was abolished. "The White House announced we were abolished," he replies, "but, you know, if they announce the sky is green and you look up and see the sky is blue . . ."

OCTOBER 22

Monday. Veterans Day. It is a government holiday, and it should be a day of quiet, but that is not possible. The Congress is in recess, and many offices are closed. But around the city, people are examining the situation, holding meetings, getting their bearings.

According to the papers, there were discussions yesterday within the White House on when the President should make a televised statement about the Stennis compromise. "Conservative White House advisers, who applauded the showdown move," says a Washington *Post* story, "predicted yesterday that [the President] will achieve a political vindication comparable to the one that Harry S Truman eventually won for his firing of Gen. Douglas MacArthur." It quotes Patrick Buchanan as saying, "And you don't go after a President for making an unpopular decision, especially in a period of international crisis like this." Senators Ervin and Baker say that their committee may now broaden its inquiry.

I went to see Ken Clawson, the White House deputy director of communications, to get his version of the events—to find out the way he was thinking, or wanted me to think he was thinking. We sat in Clawson's office—a blue-and-white office in the northeast corner of the Executive Office Building. Clawson is one of the voices that speak for the White House, and he deals with writers, editors, and television executives. Thirty-seven, round-faced, and slightly beefy, he is a former reporter for the Washington *Post,* who joined the White House staff in 1972.

"Think back to February or March," Clawson said. "Ninety-nine percent of the people here did not know things that we now know from the hearings, and from all that's transpired. When two things became apparent—that there was more than we thought, and that the Democrats were going to take our, you should pardon the expression, blank off—some of us said, 'There's going to be one hell of a fight and we should gear up.' There were others who were not looking so much at the fact that the Democrats would capitalize on this as that there were these truths that would come out. They were saying, 'Let them come out and let the Democrats capitalize on them and then it will pass.' They were saying, 'Since these things were true, take the damage.' They asked, 'How can you justify battling it?' My argument was that the President is the only lion in the forest, and when there has been a cut in him the ants will grow in number, and by the time he gets back on his feet, only his carcass will be there. As I saw it, and some others saw it, we should have waged a political battle. Had our argument won, we might not be where we are today. The appointment of the Special Prosecutor was the result of a negative decision that was permitted to go forward because of inaction, not because of action. The deal over which Richardson resigned was between Richardson and the committee. No one here said 'Make it,' but no one said 'Don't do it.' Richardson reported to the White House that a Special Prosecutor should be picked. The pistol was pointed at the old man's [the President's] head, and there wasn't much else we could do. So we're coming out of six or seven months where we kind of rolled over and let anyone have at us who wanted to. How many times have you seen the White House strike back? It just hasn't occurred. But now we've put it on the line, for the first time since this thing began. The thing that is different now is that it has now shifted to our initiative. What makes me very happy now is that we know how to fight this kind of battle. We know how to cope with it. What we didn't know how to cope with was the *mea-culpa* attitude that we have had for the last several months. That is foreign to us and our nature."

Clawson then spoke of the events of the weekend. "Let's take this weekend," he said. "Every action that the President took was completely within his legal right and prerogative, and yet what's the talk? The talk is of impeachment. What crime or misdemeanor did he commit this weekend? And as for bringing Baker and Ervin along—you watch it. That agreement won't fall apart. The Kennedys and the Tunneys are simply carrying on a P.R. fight. There are no grounds for impeachment on the basis of what the President did this weekend. Now we have the mechanism for hitting back at Ted Kennedy when he hits us. We haven't done it yet, but we might, and we can. When a nothing, jerk Democratic politician issues a press release saying that the President should be impeached, it ends up on page 1. We've found out that if we roll out George Shultz to say the jerk has his face on backward, that ends up on page 36, unless we get it in the same news cycle. The liberal wing of the Democratic Party appears to be coalescing around this issue. So what are our choices? To turn to the Republican senators and congressmen who are with us, the Republican National Committee, the President's Cabinet, the White House staff."

The first problem, Clawson indicated, was to get the White House point of view across in the press. "Have you read anywhere," he asked. "that what the President did this weekend is legal and lawful?" And then he made an argument that Nixon White House staff members had been making for some time. "Decisions and public opinion are molded outside of New York and Washington and Boston," he said. "We know that and we've always known that. We have a proper duty to articulate the President's positions, to engage in political debate with our opponents. We have talked to about a hundred editors and about fifty publishers. We have three lawyers who can speak for us—Charles Wright, Fred Buzhardt, Leonard Garment. We can maximize the President's own participation in this—a very potent weapon. We'll take what you'd have to call 'the spiritual lead.' When those groups that are our natural allies see us not doing anything, as they saw us over the last few months, they do nothing. If it gets as tough as I think it's going to get, we'll call them up and say, 'God damn it, make our case.'"

White House aides had prepared a chronology of the past week's events, to give to inquiring reporters. According to the White House chronology, the President made up his mind the Saturday before last (the day after he selected Ford) that he wanted to reach an accommodation on the tapes. Otherwise, the issue would go to the Supreme Court and would be a major issue for months. The President thought that the issue was causing an erosion of America's position in the world. The Middle East was explosive. The choice of Mr. Stennis was the President's; the lawyers had discussed, in general terms, letting someone of impeccable integrity listen to the tapes. Contact was made with Stennis on Monday, and he asked that, because of his age, the White House prepare a draft of what the tapes said. The arrangement was that the

Senator would work with the draft, would listen to all the tapes, and could expand or alter the draft in any way he wished.

There was, as one "White House source" put it, "the language factor." (For months, word had circulated in Washington that the President was disposed to use some rather strong, off-color language. This was said to be one reason it would be embarrassing to make tapes public.) The "source" said that while any President would be sensitive to being discovered to use off-color language, Richard Nixon was especially so. When Lyndon Johnson reached the White House, said the "source," everyone knew how he talked. But Nixon, he went on, "makes Lyndon Johnson look like a piker." However, the "source" said, Richard Nixon reached the White House without this being known.

According to the White House version, everybody, including Richardson, was "on board" until Friday. Then Richardson began to hedge, citing his pledges to the Senate. The White House did not know whether Richardson would resign if Cox was fired. What Ruckelshaus would do had apparently not been considered.

One of my colleagues was told, in a briefing by another White House assistant, that the final problems with Cox were that Cox objected to having only one person hear the tapes, that he wanted access to other materials, and that he wanted to be able to determine whether the tapes had been altered. The White House objected not to the final request, my colleague was told, but to the fact that Cox made it in "an insulting and offending way."

It is another beautiful day, and a colleague and I eat a sandwich lunch in Lafayette Park. Lafayette Park is the closest thing we Americans have to Hyde Park. But—perhaps because we are more scattered and diverse than the English, perhaps because we do not put the same value on language and debate, perhaps because our differences are deeper and angrier—we do not really have a Hyde Park. Lafayette Park has drawn an occasional demonstration, or someone who was fasting for peace. For some time, it was boarded off, ostensibly for a beautification project begun in the Johnson Administration. A friend who worked in the White House at the time has told me that while the boards were up, some highly sophisticated electronic equipment was laid underneath the park. Someone who served in the Nixon White House in the early years has told me that the boards were kept up around Lafayette Park to prevent demonstrations there. There comes to mind John Dean's testimony before the Ervin committee about how the President was distressed by a solitary demonstrator outside the White House and wanted him removed from the scene. The park covers one square block. In it there are nine statues—of, among others, Lafayette, Kosciusko, the Comte d'Estaing, and Chevalier Duportail—and four fountains. Pigeons circle the statues, and the benches, where there might be food. Across the way is the front lawn of the White House. A large fountain plays there, surrounded now by bright-yellow chrysanthemums. It is a lovely picture—reminiscent of the ones on the jigsaw puzzles of our nation's capital that, as a child, I used to try to piece together.

Today, there are some demonstrators in Lafayette Park. Several carry signs saying "Honk for Impeachment," and the horns of some cars on Pennsylvania Avenue are honking. A sound truck advertising a lecture by the Reverend Sun Myung Moon, of Seoul, Korea, on "Christianity in Crisis" circles the park. Over its loudspeaker comes a voice saying, "President Nixon, we offer our support to you." A couple passes the bench where we are sitting. The man is, with one hand, pushing a stroller holding a baby and, with the other hand, carrying a sign that says "Impeach Now." A derelict sitting on the next bench says to the couple, "I don't agree with you, but I admire your spirit."

The early edition of the Washington *Star-News* has Judge Sirica pondering his next move, Democrats pondering their next moves, Kissinger flying to Tel Aviv, and the White House spreading the word that people should remember all the heat that Truman took for firing MacArthur. There are, around town, discussions of various strategies. Some people want to push for impeachment. Some fear that this is exactly what the President wants—an impeachment move that ends in failure. He could interpret it as a vindication. The fact that there is no Vice-President complicates the decisions. There is some talk about repealing the Twenty-fifth Amendment and calling a special election, but this is no time for special elections. There appears to be substantial sentiment among congressmen and their staffs—those who have been in touch with each other—for pushing for legislation to establish a new Special Prosecutor. Some think that there is enough support for the idea to override a Presidential veto of such a bill. Pushing for Special Prosecutor legislation will give the politicians something to do—a vehicle for an indirect confrontation—without their having to face the difficult issue of impeachment. Everyone is in new territory.

For all its talk about public opinion's being formed "out there," the Nixon White House obviously believes that public opinion is manufactured here—either by the "Eastern press" and the networks or by the White House. In part it is right, and in part it is quite wrong. There are other ways, some of them almost mysterious, in which public opinion is formed. There have been many times when "the public" (sometimes called "the country") perceived things before "Washington" did. "Washington" can become accustomed to the way things are, its thinking imprisoned by insiders' knowledge. It can find a certain amusement in the Congress's more outrageous characters and quaint rituals. "Washington" knew that the campaign-contribution laws had been flouted since, it seemed, the beginning. "Washington" knew that the regulatory agencies tended to serve the industries they were to regulate. It knew that public officials lied. It knew these things. It just didn't talk about them much. That was the way things worked. "Washington" is often surprised when questions are first raised about these matters. The deep uneasiness about Lyndon Johnson took form in "the country" before it was felt in Washington, where we were used to him, and where many of us were on friendly terms with his assistants.

"The public" has a more complex set of views and reactions than many politicians think—or, at least, appear to think. "Realistic" politicians learn the lore of their trade: that "the public" dislikes taxes and welfare; that it can be angry and it can be militaristic. This is probably all true, but so are other things about "the public"—feelings about human justice and fair play and peace. That accounts for some of the wild swings in the polls. "Realistic" politicians can mistake a public impulse to rally around the President in a time of crisis for a lasting belief that what the President is doing is right. "Realistic" politicians operate under certain delusions. But so do many of those who oppose them. The "realists" are not the only ones who oversimplify human nature. "Realistic" politicians set themselves apart from "elitists." It is true that liberal intellectuals often proceed on the assumption that they know what is best for America. But Lyndon Johnson and Richard Daley and Richard Nixon also proceeded on the assumption that they knew what was best for the people. What is more "elitist" than saying, as Richard Nixon did after his 1972 reëlection, "The average American is just like the child in the family"? "Realistic" politicians see the public as manipulable. They act on their belief that they can reach it by speaking to its lower motives, its baser instincts, and often they are right. But at the same time another part of human nature is there and alive. That other part can gather force silently, and then suddenly lash out and bowl the "realists" over. The important thing is not the number of people who think what at any given moment, but the relative power, and momentum, of ideas. As the peace marchers went by the White House, President Johnson asked how many troops they had.

The White House is offering spokesmen to appear on the *Today* show and the CBS *Morning News*.

At the bookstores, there has been a run on Raoul Berger's *Impeachment: The Constitutional Problems*.

The evening news programs give the first real picture of the intensity, and the dimensions, of the coming struggle. It is announced that Carl Albert and other House Democratic leaders will ask the House Judiciary Committee to take up the question of impeachment. George Meany, speaking for the A.F.L.-C.I.O. at its biennial meeting, calls on the

President to resign, "in the interest of national security." If he does not, Meany says, the labor federation will call for his impeachment. NBC says that an Oliver Quayle poll shows that seventy-five percent of the people interviewed disapprove of the firing of Cox and fifteen percent approve. It reports forty-four percent in favor of impeachment, forty-two percent opposed. More than seventy thousand telegrams have been sent to Washington in the thirty-six hours since Cox was fired. Western Union is swamped. Bork says the Watergate prosecution will be continued and Henry Petersen, the Assistant Attorney General in charge of the Criminal Division who directed the first Watergate investigation, will be in charge. This would seem to bring us back to where we began. The President has left for Camp David.

5

CHARLES ALAN WRIGHT, on the *Today* show, defends the President's actions.

Senator Edward Gurney, Republican of Florida, says, on the radio, that the President was "forced" by Democrats to hire Cox. He says the President "had a gun to his head."

Carl Albert is reported to want the House to hurry its approval of Gerald Ford as Vice-President.

Morris Udall, an independent-minded liberal Democrat in the House, suggests, in a news story, that Congress hasten confirmation of Ford as part of an agreement that Nixon resign in Ford's favor. The idea had been bruited about in the past few days, but this is the first time I have seen it in print. There have been proposals that various people—Rockefeller, Richardson—be made Speaker of the House, and then President. It is perhaps a reflection of the times that in the minds of intelligent men Constitutional procedures should give way to improvisational fantasies.

Two Cabinet officers—James Lynn, the Secretary of Housing and Urban Development, and Caspar Weinberger, the Secretary of Health, Education, and Welfare—have made speeches defending the President's action.

The name the Great Hall of the Justice Department has always had an Arthurian ring. Other Cabinet departments make do with an "auditorium." The Great Hall is two stories high. On its platform are two giant aluminum statues, of a semi-nude man and woman. A Justice Department spokesman says that the man represents the majesty of justice and the woman the spirit of justice. Behind the section reserved for reporters, and in the balcony that rings the second story of the Great Hall, hundreds of Justice Department employees are gathered for Elliot Richardson's televised press conference. One wonders about their state of mind. The Justice Department lawyers had traditionally been considered a select group. Justice was seen as a good place for law-school graduates to spend a few years, before moving on; its career lawyers were highly respected. But recent times have been hard on them. Their morale has been sapped, and many of them feel that their reputations are in question.

Before the press conference begins, the correspondence between the President and Richardson on the Friday and Saturday of last weekend is released. There, in the form of polite letters, are two powerful men cold-bloodedly staking out positions that were to lead to a confrontation with profound consequences both for them and for the nation. A Constitutional crisis, the issue of Presidential accountability, drawn in an exchange of letters. Letters such as these are for the record, intended for public release if necessary. They state positions as the writers want them to be read; otherwise they would not have been written. These people know how to deliver messages by telephone.

In his "Dear Elliot" letter of Friday, Nixon says he has "reluctantly agreed to a limited breach of Presidential confidentiality" to spare the country further "agony." He says the "very limited" intrusion on the "independence that I promised you" would not have been necessary "if the Special Prosecutor had agreed to the very reasonable proposal you made to him this week." Richardson, in his "Dear Mr. President" letter, says he found the Stennis proposal "reasonable and constructive" but did not agree that the "price" to the Special Prosecutor should be "renunciation" of further judicial proceedings. Richardson also points out that the compromise he submitted to Cox "did not purport to deal with other tapes, notes, or memoranda." He suggests in his letter that the Stennis solution be a precedent for other tapes and documents.

A television technician calls out "Thirty seconds!" This is a television show as well as a press conference. As Richardson and his wife, together with Ruckelshaus, step through the blue velvet curtain, the Justice Department workers burst into prolonged applause. It is the sort of emotional applause that, once started, feeds on itself—the applauders' way of making a statement. The ovation also expresses the Justice Department workers' desire for a hero—a moral standard to which they can repair.

Richardson looks different today. He is tired; his eyes are bleary. His voice is tremulous. His delivery lacks the customary crispness. He is apparently struggling for control of his emotions; it seems to be the fatigue—a reaction to the ovation the Justice Department workers have given him and to what he has been through. It is all the more noticeable in Richardson, who always seemed to be in such control. It had come to be the cliché about Richardson that he resembled the stiff, square-cut comic-strip character Clark Kent. But, as usual, behind the cliché there was some truth. And the extent of the control, the fact that it came across as control, suggested that there was something else there. And the now former Attorney General has a certain fame in Washington as an uninhibited dancer. It is hard to imagine George Shultz, the Secretary of the Treasury, or Earl Butz, the Secretary of Agriculture, as an uninhibited dancer. Before the press conference, a friend of Richardson's described him as "sad, tired," and without any "sense of exultation." "That's good," said the friend, "but it makes him vulnerable to entreaties from all sides—and he's getting them."

In his prepared statement, Richardson says, "At stake, in the final analysis, is the very integrity of the governmental processes I came to the Department of Justice to help restore." But his statement leaves an impression of ambiguity. He professes his loyalty to "the general purposes and priorities" of the Nixon Administration. He says he does not believe "that Mr. Cox was guilty of anything approaching an 'extraordinary impropriety.' " He says he does not share the feeling among some congressional Republicans and in the White House that the Cox staff might "be tipped by partisanship," or believe that Mr. Cox was out "to get Mr. Richard Nixon." He says, "I believe that he was exercising a very difficult responsibility with conscientiousness, with a real effort to be fair."

Asked if the President had reason to expect him to resign, Richardson says, "The question of what I would do, I think, was unclear from his perspective up to the point on Saturday afternoon when I came to see him. There had been issues drawn earlier in the week in which I had made clear that if certain action were taken I would be forced to resign."

On the question of impeachment—one for which he is clearly prepared—Richardson answers carefully, saying that it is "a question for the American people." But he avoids saying whether there can be an independent investigation run by the Justice Department. He suggests that there will be no real problem over obtaining other documents for the investigation. It is hard to see how he can say this now.

After lunch, it was a pleasure to walk for a while in the sunshine, along Connecticut Avenue, accompanying a friend as he did the mundane errands I take some pains to avoid—getting shoes fixed, cashing a check at the bank.

The news came over the radio in the early afternoon that the President, after all, has agreed to turn the tapes over to the court. Another startling turn. From the news reports, it seems that there will still be issues over which material is to be withheld on the ground of "national security." And this move does not resolve other key issues. The move indicates that the President did believe himself to be in some trouble. Politicians and their aides are probably scrambling again. Statements made this morning, positions taken, may now be outdated. On the radio, it is announced that the House inquiry into impeachment will go on. By 4 P.M., Richardson, who was to have been today's big story, seems a footnote.

In the late afternoon, Haig, Wright, and Ziegler brief the press on the President's decision. It is crowded and hot in the White House press-room. The reporters are tired and snappish. They are wearying of the twists and turns, of being told things today that render what they were told yesterday "inoperative." Haig says that the President is making this "single exception" to his stand on the importance of the confidentiality of the President's documents. He refers to "the firestorm of this week-end." He says that the White House position was "subject to a great deal of misunderstanding, a great deal of misinformation over the past weekend." He says that there were problems of "semantics" over the weekend. As for the compromise, he says that Senator Baker "was a catalyst in the thing, and a very important one." In response to a question, Haig says that now the Senate committee will not get the tapes or summaries of them. For one thing, the committee is continuing its suit for the tapes, and, for another, he says, the White House is concerned for Senator Stennis's health. "As you know," says Haig, "Senator Stennis has experienced a very grievous wound recently." The President, he says, did not want to "presume to impose on Senator Stennis."

Haig reënacts his conversation with Ruckelshaus, in which his "Commander-in-Chief" comment now sounds very casual; and he makes a little joke about himself. "Anybody who knows me knows what a militarist I am," he says.

Alexander Haig, now forty-eight, was an affable, able major in the Pentagon when he was discovered, during the Johnson Administration, by Joseph Califano, then special assistant to Defense Secretary Robert McNamara. Haig had proved a competent aide to McNamara and then to Kissinger—the organizer, the expediter, the one who saw that orders were carried out. Now he is in charge of the White House staff, is the President's top adviser. One wonders how much he understands about the country.

Haig, standing before the microphone in his gray suit, speaking with his slight Southern accent, says that he is not blaming the press, but there was "the impression at large that this compromise . . . was a contrived subterfuge to (a) not turn over the information, or (b) design some devious scheme by which to relieve ourselves of the burden of Professor Cox and his investigating team." He says, "I think that is a terrible disservice to the President of the United States."

"Firestorm." I had always thought of the word in connection with the firestorm of Dresden, in the Second World War—a word of terrifying connotations, like "holocaust." A word one would use with care. Reporters believe that the word was first used in connection with last weekend by Ron Ziegler.

It is dark now. On the White House lawn, equipment is set up so that television newsmen can report the late developments. The television spotlights cast a ghostly glow on the White House lawn. Along Pennsylvania Avenue, an unusual number of car horns are honking.

Some thoughts, and questions, at the end of the day. Has Nixon succeeded in putting all the focus on the tapes? If there is no independent Special Prosecutor, who will be in a position to challenge him on other issues? Haig referred to future questions about White House documents as a "minefield." (More wartime terminology.) Is he right? Was getting rid of Cox, and perhaps gaining control of what was referred to in some Republican circles as "the breakaway Justice Department," worth all this to the President? Did Nixon figure that Richardson would be sufficiently malleable not to give him trouble? Richardson's resignation is widely viewed as the first Administration resignation "on principle"—an act of courage. But did Richardson really have any choice? He had made a contractual arrangement with the Senate committee as the price of his confirmation. Moreover, if he had agreed to fire Cox, Richardson would have been finished politically. He was already in some trouble with his moderate Republican constituency. Is he destroyed anyway? Has he been torn up by his conflicting constituencies within the Republican Party, and by a demanding press corps and involved outsiders?

Do we in fact destroy those who try to bridge some of the divisions in American politics? A Muskie is devoured. In turn, a Goldwater or a McGovern is set upon by his own constituency if he tries to broaden his base. But the thought that "politics is the art of compromise" is not without meaning. When public men show some principle, are we then insatiable in our demands on them?

Tomorrow evening, the President is to address the nation on television. Another speech to be analyzed and debated about. We could all use a rest. Tonight, Mr. Nixon has gone to Camp David. He went there last night also. It is said that the President is taking his leave of the White House nightly now to escape the sound of the car horns honking.

At dinner, someone remarks that there is a new bumper sticker in California. It says "Don't Blame Me. I Voted for Voorhis."

OCTOBER 24

This morning, on the radio, Leonard Garment says that the President did the right thing by bowing to public opinion on the tapes.

There is a new cease-fire in the Middle East.

The Associated Press has a copy of a letter sent to the President by Patrick J. Hillings, lawyer for the Associated Milk Producers, Inc., pledging two million dollars in reëlection contributions. The letter is dated two weeks before the President, in 1970, imposed import quotas on ice cream and other dairy products. That was the year before he raised the price supports for milk, reversing his Secretary of Agriculture, after he met with milk producers. Hillings is a former representative of the same congressional district Nixon once represented, and an old friend of Nixon's, and for a time he was a law partner of Murray Chotiner.

Murray Chotiner had been with Nixon from the beginning, when Nixon defeated Jerry Voorhis for Congress. He was in the Nixon campaign against Helen Gahagan Douglas, and, in 1952, when Nixon was under attack for "the Nixon Fund," Chotiner urged Nixon to counterattack with the "Checkers" speech. Chotiner worked in the White House for a while after Nixon was elected President. He was particularly involved, along with Charles Colson, in the 1970 mid-term elections. That was when the Nixon White House tried very hard—and failed—to get an "ideological majority" in the Senate. Some Republican politicians were persuaded to give up secure positions in order to make the race. Some moderate Republicans were given the back of the hand. Conservative Southern Democrats, such as John Stennis, were treated benignly. Edmund Muskie and Edward Kennedy, both running for reëlection to the Senate that year, were targets, not because the White House thought they could be defeated but because it thought they could perhaps be made less formidable for the Presidential race in 1972. The theme of the campaign, set by the President, was "law and order." Stones were thrown at the President in San Jose. He thereupon stood atop his limousine waving his arms in a victory sign and saying, "This is what they hate to see." In *Six Crises,* Nixon tells of how he stood up on the rear seat of his limousine in Lima when a mob was attacking him. "I could not resist the temptation to get in one other good lick," he wrote. (There were always some questions about who threw those stones in San Jose.) Attorney General John Mitchell let it be known later that he thought the 1970 campaign a disaster. He said it would be different in 1972.

It was said that Haldeman and Ehrlichman got Chotiner out of the White House in 1971 because they thought he would embarrass the President. After that, he turned up in the news from time to time. The milk fund. Chotiner had been involved in obtaining Hoffa's release from prison. I once asked him why. He said because Hoffa's son had asked him to help in getting his father out of prison, because Hoffa was a "political victim," and because he thought "the rank and file of the Teamsters would be most appreciative."

There are also stories, and speculation, that the President is acting to protect not just himself but also his former aides, who might be in a position to do him damage. One gets a picture of the President and several of his formerly most trusted aides circling each other, each of them in a position to put the knife to the others. It is the court of the Borgias. It is the government of the United States.

A House Democrat, one in touch with many members, says that impeachment is now being moved along by an irresistible force. "The genie is out of the bottle," he says. "The unspeakable is being spoken." He says that the House leadership wants to get on with the confirmation of Ford's nomination, lest it appear to be trying to replace the President with a Democrat. "The shock of the past weekend changed everything," he says. "There had been the ordinary forbearance toward the President here, a great reluctance to move. I think the people were out ahead of us. They saw a frightening threat to the democratic process. What the President did over the weekend may not have been a high crime or misdemeanor, but it opened things up."

The President's speech scheduled for tonight has been postponed until tomorrow, and there will be a press conference instead. Tom Brokaw says on tonight's NBC news that the White House has asked several groups to issue statements of support of the President after his press conference: the National Association of Manufacturers, the United States Chamber of Commerce, the American Legion, the Veterans of Foreign Wars, the Disabled American Veterans, the AMVETS. The President has vetoed the war-powers bill, saying that it "would seriously undermine this nation's ability to act" in a crisis. George Meany has referred to "the dangerous emotional instability" of the President. The White House has called this "one of the most incredible, inexcusable, irresponsible statements ever made by someone who is in a position to have his remarks and comments carried in the national news media."

There are unspoken things, things that are in the air, in private conversations, but do not enter the public dialogue—the news stories, the editorials, the speeches. There are forms of responsibility and civility with which we surround our public discourse. This is good, in that it helps to keep things from flying apart, but it also extends the charade, perpetuates illusions. These unspoken things are not facts, but they are factors. They have to do with things people are uneasy about. Lately, they have had to do with concern about what the President would do, how far he would go, to get himself out of trouble. They have had to do with theories about what else might have been done by members of the Nixon Administration, with concern about shocks still to come. These things, because they are not facts, and because we proceed, in our public discourse, according to certain unwritten rules, ordinarily do not appear in newspapers, ordinarily are not spoken about by public figures. But the silence can be deceptive. It can conceal part of what is motivating people of power. When George Meany spoke aloud of the President's "emotional instability," he was saying something that others felt they could not say. And he was someone whom it was legitimate for the press to quote. The White House understood that.

Senate Republican leaders today urged the President to name a new Special Prosecutor.

Kennedy and Nixon. There is something ineluctable about their struggle. The bad blood between Nixon and the Kennedys—it has been something far deeper than the usual political rivalries—goes way back. The clashes of their ambitions started in the Eisenhower years. John and Robert Kennedy and their congressional investigations of the Teamsters and "labor racketeering." Among those they damaged were Murray Chotiner, and the Teamsters. Robert Kennedy, counsel to a Senate investigations subcommittee, probed Chotiner's dealings before the government in the nineteen-fifties on behalf of newfound clients, including a racketeer. Robert Kennedy brought about Murray Chotiner's disgrace. John Kennedy versus Richard Nixon in 1960, with Nixon losing the Presidential race to Kennedy by a narrow margin. Nixon was gracious about the defeat, but was said to remain bitter, to resent the Kennedys' money, glamour, acceptance. Robert Kennedy, Attorney General, sent James Hoffa to jail.

Robert Kennedy and then Edward Kennedy became major threats to Richard Nixon's enduring ambitions. When Chotiner worked in the White House in 1970, he had on his desk a report on Chappaquiddick. He instructed political strategists on how not to appear to be raising the subject of Chappaquiddick while doing so. Neither Nixon nor any of the Kennedys was the forgiving type. Some of Edward Kennedy's friends say, and have told him, that he should not be so out front now, so public in his attempts to bring down Richard Nixon. They say it will not do him good if he intends to run for President in 1976. But Kennedy does not seem to be able to help himself.

There is something striking about the way great pending Constitutional issues are discussed these days. The Constitution itself is rarely mentioned. There are discussions of whether various people "want" to have Nixon, or Ford, or Albert, as President. Issues are put in terms of political preferences, and tactics, rather than processes. That is not the way the Constitution is supposed to work. That's the point of having a Constitution.

OCTOBER 25

We awakened to the news that the President has declared a worldwide military alert.

United States air, ground, and sea forces around the world have been put in a state of readiness. The radio reports say that the alert may be a reaction to Soviet moves to enforce the ceasefire in the Middle East. There were meetings of government officials throughout the night. The National Security Council is said to have convened. Congressional leaders are meeting at the White House. "We still have very sketchy details," the radio announcer says. Kissinger will hold a press conference at noon.

The news is chilling—and bewildering. It is not clear what it would mean if the Russians were moving to enforce the ceasefire in the Middle East, or why that would call for worldwide military alert. What is our government planning to do? And there is the cynicism. The cynicism is very unpleasant, but it is there: the question—spoken and implied in conversations throughout the tense morning—whether the crisis is real.

Marvin Kalb, of CBS, puts the question to Kissinger at his press conference. Marvin Kalb is a thoughtful man, and he puts the question carefully. He says, "Mr. Secretary, could you tell us whether the United States received a specific warning from the Soviet Union that it would send its forces unilaterally into the Middle East? Do you have intelligence that the Russians are preparing for such an action? The reason I raise these questions—as you know, there has been some line of speculation this morning that the American alert might have been promoted as much perhaps by American domestic requirements as by the real requirements of diplomacy in the Middle East. And I wonder if you could provide some additional information on that."

Kissinger answers slowly, in a tone that is more in sorrow. Kissinger, of course, knows Marvin Kalb. Marvin Kalb and his brother Bernard are writing a book about Kissinger. Kissinger says, "Marvin, we are attempting to conduct the foreign policy of the United States with regard for what we owe not just to the electorate but to future generations. And it is a symptom of what is happening to our country that it could even be suggested that the United States would alert its forces for domestic reasons. We do not think it is wise at this moment to go into the details of the diplomatic exchanges that prompted this decision. Upon the conclusion of the present diplomatic efforts, one way or the other, we will make the record available, and we will be able to go into greater detail. And I am absolutely confident that it will be seen that the President had no other choice as a responsible national leader."

The question comes up at other points, in other forms, in the course of the press conference. To one question, Kissinger replies that "one cannot have crises of authority in a society for a period of months without paying a price somewhere along the line."

The price, simply put, is that in what may be an international crisis there is widespread disbelief in our leaders. Either way, it is not good. If the crisis is, as some think, manufactured, that is not good. If it is real, and the public confidence in our leaders is at such a low ebb that they are widely disbelieved, that is not good, either. Democracy, if it is to work, requires more public trust than this.

The government lied about more than three thousand bombing raids conducted in secret in Cambodia. The Secretary of State and National Security Adviser to the President is asking the press, with a combination of pleading, accusation, and agony in his voice, to believe him now. "It is up to you, ladies and gentlemen, to determine whether this is the moment to try to create a crisis of confidence in the field of foreign policy as well," Kissinger says to the press. "We have tried to give you as much information as we decently and safely and properly can under these conditions. As soon as there is a clear outcome, we will give you the full information. And after that you will be able to judge whether the decisions were taken hastily or improperly. . . . We will be prepared, however—and I'm certain within a week—to put the facts before you. But there has to be a minimum of confidence that the senior officials of the American government are not playing with the lives of the American people."

Extraordinary questions, in an extraordinary situation, and then there is another—one that, if memory serves, has never been asked before. The Secretary of State is asked if the President's order for a worldwide military alert is "a totally rational decision." Kissinger replies that he usually does not "provide a checklist of what advice I give to the President," and goes on, "But, due to the particular implications of your remark, I may say that all of the President's senior advisers, all the members of the National Security Council, were unanimous in their recommendation, as the result of a deliberation in which the President did not himself participate, and which he joined only after they had formed their judgment, that the measures taken, that he, in fact, ordered, were in the essential national interest."

Over the years of the Nixon Administration, the President's assistants, explaining the President's requests for large military budgets, have said, with striking regularity, that the President was concerned that the United States be sufficiently strong to face down the Soviet Union as John F. Kennedy did in the Cuban missile crisis of 1962.

The President's press conference has been postponed until tomorrow evening. It is still unclear why the alert was ordered.

All week, it has been said within the Administration that Leonid Brezhnev, the Soviet leader, was exploiting the vulnerability of the President caused by Archibald Cox.

A Democratic senator says that he does not know what sort of statement to make about the worldwide military alert. "I'd like to know what's going on, first," he says. "I can't get any information about it. How can the country listen to us if we don't know what the hell's going on?"

Imaginations have been set loose again. Ordinarily sensible people are thinking the ordinarily unthinkable. A Washington lawyer says that he is studying the question of how to declare a Presidential disability.

Someone tells me that he has been called by a politician from out of town who wants to know if there are national leaders who can prevent a coup.

By midafternoon, the Middle East crisis is over. The United Nations Security Council has voted to send a peacekeeping force to the Middle East. But the alert is still in effect.

Tonight, we watch, on our television screens, American troops and tanks mobilizing for we don't know what. We are reminded this evening that American planes loaded with nuclear bombs are in the air. Does the President believe that these scenes convey the impression of a strong Commander-in-Chief, with powerful weapons at his command, in charge? Perhaps to many it does. The President makes a point of being photographed as he sees Kissinger off after a White House meeting. Then he is photographed springing up the steps of the Executive Office Building. The scenes emphasize the point that it was considered necessary that we see our President.

Robert Schieffer, the CBS Pentagon correspondent, says that certain Soviet actions led United States military planners to "suspect" that Soviet troops were on their way to the Middle East. The Pentagon is chronically suspicious. Its job is to be suspicious and to plan reprisals. It is for others to decide whether the suspicions are well founded and the reprisals are in order. Dan Rather says that White House aides are "furious" that anyone would suggest that there were not good reasons for the President's action. Rather says, "Anyone who suggests otherwise, they say, will be humiliated by history."

Today, someone says, was "a Strangelove day." In thirty-two minutes, United States intercontinental ballistic missiles can destroy the Soviet Union. Some say that these missiles can destroy the Soviet Union twenty times over; some say only ten times. In any event, in thirty-two minutes the United States can destroy the Soviet Union as a civilization. And vice versa.

There is the inescapable feeling that things have changed—that the atmosphere shifted again today. The talk of impeachment has been more serious. More people have seemed to be suggesting plans for replacing the President. It is a result not just of the suspicion that the crisis was unreal but of the fear of real crises, with the President not being believed. There is deep concern that our domestic troubles might in fact, just as the President says, make us vulnerable. Atmosphere is substance, too.

Is there a national trip wire? When the country seems to be in danger and the regular processes seem to offer little hope, are there other ways out? One hears suggestions that a group of our more estimable citizens step forward and take charge. One hears all manner of suggestions now for unusual procedures (or is there a savior somewhere?) for resolving our difficulties. In times of trouble, it is all the more important to move according to legitimate procedures.

The events of the day almost obliterated the other news of this morning, but some items in the papers still caught one's attention. The White House has claimed executive privilege to prevent former Agriculture Secretary Clifford Hardin from testifying about a meeting in 1971 with President Nixon and top White House aides on the question of increasing the price supports for milk.

The President has gone to Camp David again tonight.

OCTOBER 26

The President's press conference tonight is another television show. It has been three weeks since the reporters have had an opportunity to ask him questions. This has been one of the most exhausting weeks in the reporters' professional lives. There are too many questions to ask. Under the best of circumstances, the press conferences have serious limitations for questioning the Chief Executive. The more time that has elapsed between press conferences, the greater the limitations. There are few questions for which the President, any President, has not prepared. Only if there is a series of follow-up questions—questions that take off from a previous answer—is there a chance of eliciting more information than the President is prepared to give. A series of questions can, at the least, show the viewer the gaps in the information. But the reporters have diverse things on their minds—questions that they have come prepared to ask—so follow-up questions are rare. A few years ago, some White House reporters met to discuss this problem, to prepare for follow-up questioning. In a subsequent press conference there was a series of follow-up questions concerning whether the Administration had exceeded Constitutional limits in its arrests of "May Day" anti-war demonstrators in 1971. The White House attacked the press corps for organizing its questions, and the press dropped the tactic. Tonight, the fatigue, tension, and frustration of the reporters play into the President's hands. He seems to allow more time than usual for them to jump up and shout at him (*"Mr. President!"*) for recognition.

The President begins as the Commander-in-Chief, speaking of his achievement in the Middle East. "The ceasefire is holding. . . . The outlook for a permanent peace is the best that it has been in twenty years." He says that this week's military crisis "was a real crisis," and adds, "It was the most difficult crisis we have had since the Cuban confrontation of 1962." Then he says, "Turning now to the subject of our

attempts to get a ceasefire on the home front, that is a bit more difficult."
He laughs—the slightly delayed, tense, brief Nixon laugh—and says
that a new Special Prosecutor will be appointed. He is attempting to
head off moves in the Congress to establish an independent prosecutor
by legislation. But can the Congress accede to him on this issue now?

The President says that the new Special Prosecutor should bring the
thing to an "expeditious conclusion," because "under our Constitution
it has always been held that justice delayed is justice denied." He gives
the now familiar explanation of the "Stennis compromise"—he refers to
"Judge Stennis"—and says that "Mr. Cox was the only one that rejected
it," and therefore "I had no choice but to dismiss him." He gives a curious answer to a question about the one hundred thousand dollars that
Bebe Rebozo received from Howard Hughes. It is a question for which
he clearly is prepared. He says that Rebozo kept the money and returned
it when "the Hughes Company . . . had an internal fight of massive
proportions."

We learned about the one hundred thousand dollars from Hughes to
Rebozo through a lawsuit by a disenchanted former Hughes employee.
The money, then, appears to have been returned, finally, not because
anyone thought it was wrong, but from what the President has just said,
because information about it might become public. "And I would say,"
says the President, referring to Rebozo, "that any individual, and particularly a banker who would have a contribution of a hundred thousand
dollars and not touch it—because it was turned back in exactly the form
it was received—I think that is a pretty good indication that he is a
totally honest man, which he is."

Suddenly, as if from nowhere, the President lashes out at the press.
Referring to the electronic media, he says, "I have never heard or seen
such outrageous, vicious, distorted reporting in my twenty-seven years
of public life." He refers to "frantic, hysterical reporting." Sometimes,
we had seen the tension in the President in his public performances,
and sometimes the scarcely disguised contempt for the press, and
sometimes the seemingly calculated attack on the political opposition.
But this appears to be the most open display of emotion on the part
of Richard Nixon since the "last press conference," after he lost the
California gubernatorial race in 1962. Perspiring, he says, "The tougher
it gets, the cooler I get." This, too, is reminiscent of the self-absorbed
passages in *Six Crises*. As is the self-pity: "It has been my lot throughout my political life [to be attacked by the press] and I suppose because
I have been through so much . . . [that] I have what it takes." He says
that people printed and broadcast things they knew to be wrong, and that
during the recent military alert the commentators had used the "same
words" on the networks as they had after the December 18th bombing
by B-52s of North Vietnam—"tyrant, dictator, he has lost his senses, he

should resign, he should be impeached." The reporters ask him how he is "bearing up emotionally" under the stress of recent events and goad him, through questions, into further attacks on the press. The civility has broken down. The scene is painful to behold.

OCTOBER 27

Robert Bork, the Acting Attorney General, is quoted in the papers as saying that the new Special Prosecutor should have a mandate "no less free" than that of Archibald Cox. It is not clear whether he is speaking of the mandate as interpreted by the President or by Cox, but Bork does say, "If his independence were interfered with, I would feel that my position was untenable." Last night, the President said that he "will not provide Presidential documents to a Special Prosecutor," and that he thought that issues of documents "can be worked out" without "having a suit filed by a Special Prosecutor within the executive branch against the President of the United States."

James Schlesinger, the Secretary of Defense, is quoted as having said yesterday that one reason for the military alert this week was that "I think that it was important, in view of the circumstances that have raised a question or may have raised a question about the ability of the United States to react appropriately, firmly, and quickly." Schlesinger, however, said, "I think we were very far away from a confrontation. . . . I think that the probability of Soviet forces being en route was considered by some to be quite low, but that the probability might rise was a matter of concern universally."

Last night the President likened the situation to the Cuban missile crisis. On Thursday, Kissinger said, "We are not talking of threats that have been made against one another. We are not talking of a missile crisis-type situation."

6

IT's A QUIET SUNDAY. We need some quiet days now. Spiro Agnew resigned only two and a half weeks ago, and so much has happened since that it's hard to remember him. Within the past eight days alone, the President fired Special Prosecutor Archibald Cox, reversed himself and said he would turn the subpoenaed tapes over to the court, ordered a worldwide military alert, and, in his press conference on Friday night, striking out at the press, put on his greatest public display of anger since taking office.

Democratic congressional leaders have rejected the President's proposal that he appoint a new Special Prosecutor rather than have the Congress establish one by legislation. "No soap," says Senate Majority Leader Mansfield.

The papers point out that tomorrow William O. Douglas, seventy-five, becomes the Justice who has served longer than any other in the history of the Supreme Court. Douglas was named to the Supreme Court by President Franklin D. Roosevelt in 1939. Three years ago, Gerald Ford led a drive to impeach Douglas. In 1969, Abe Fortas was forced to resign from the Court after it was disclosed that he had accepted a fee as consultant to a foundation headed by the industrialist Louis E. Wolfson at a time when Wolfson was under investigation by the Securities and Exchange Commission. The move to drive Fortas from the Court was, writes Robert Shogan in his book *A Question of Judgment,* directed by Attorney General John Mitchell, with the knowledge and approval of President Nixon. The Fortas vacancy led to Nixon's confrontations with the Senate over his attempts to appoint first Clement F. Haynsworth and then G. Harrold Carswell to fill it. If Nixon has the opportunity to make one more appointment to the Supreme Court, he will have appointed a majority. His appointments have already had a substantial impact on the direction of the Court; and, of course, the Nixon Presidency will be outlived by the Nixon Court.

Today, James Reston, in whom powerful people confide, writes in his New York *Times* column that "Mr. Nixon is encouraging even his best friends to question his judgment and think about his resignation or impeachment."

The Constitution does not give much guidance on the subject of impeachment. Section 4 of Article II states, "The President, Vice-President and all civil officers of the United States, shall be removed from office on impeachment for, and conviction of, treason, bribery, or other high crimes and misdemeanors." Four other sections of the Constitution specify that the House of Representatives has "the sole power of impeachment"; that the Senate, by a vote of two-thirds, has "the sole power to try all impeachments" and that punishment shall be removal from office, but that someone so punished can still be liable to "indictment, trial, judgment and punishment, according to law"; that the power of Presidential pardon does not extend to impeachment; and that the right to trial by jury does not include cases of impeachment. The framers of the Constitution debated for some time the methods by which the President and other high officials could ultimately be held accountable. In the end, the phrase "treason, bribery, or other high crimes and misdemeanors" was, as Raoul Berger, the author of *Impeachment: The Constitutional Problems,* points out, "lifted bodily from English law." Even the division of functions between the House and the Senate parallels the respective responsibilities for impeachment and conviction of the House of Commons and the House of Lords. Impeachment was the English Parliament's method of stripping the king's ministers—and thus the kings—of absolute power, and holding them accountable. The impeachment procedure had fallen into disuse in England until Parliament, in the seventeenth century, used it against usurpations of power under the Stuarts. More than fifty impeachments came to trial in England between 1621 and 1787—the year the Federal Convention was meeting in Philadelphia. While we were drafting a Constitution for the United States of America, the English Parliament was considering the impeachment of Warren Hastings, the former governor of British India. The group meeting in Philadelphia followed the debate in England. Edmund Burke, opening the trial of Hastings in the House of Lords, said:

It is by this tribunal that statesmen who abuse their power are accused by statesmen, and tried by statesmen, not upon the niceties of a narrow jurisprudence, but upon the enlarged and solid principles of state morality. It is here that those who by abuse of power have violated the spirit of law can never hope for protection from any of its forms . . . it is here that those who have refused to conform themselves to its perfections can never hope to escape through any of its defects.

There are a few indications of what, exactly, the framers of the Constitution intended by the words "high crimes and misdemeanors." At the Federal Convention, George Mason said that "corruption" would be impeachable. Berger points out that James Madison, at the Virginia Ratification Convention, stated that the President might be impeached if he "be connected in any suspicious manner with any person, and there be grounds to believe that he will shelter him." Alexander Hamilton, in Federalist Paper No. 65, said that impeachment was intended to reach "the misconduct of public men" and "abuse or violation of some public trust." Hamilton said that impeachable offenses were political, "as they relate chiefly to injuries done immediately to the society itself." During the first Congress, James Madison said that since only the President could remove his own subordinates, the President had to be accountable, and was therefore subject to impeachment, for their actions:

> I think it absolutely necessary that the President should have the power of removing [subordinates] from office; it will make him, in a peculiar manner, responsible for their conduct, and subject him to impeachment himself, if he suffers them to perpetrate with impunity high crimes or misdemeanors against the United States, or neglects to superintend their conduct, so as to check their excesses. On the Constitutionality of the declaration I have no manner of doubt.

Berger concludes that " 'high crimes and misdemeanors' appear to be words of art confined to impeachments, without roots in the ordinary criminal law and which, so far as I could discover, had no relation to whether an indictment would lie in the particular circumstances." In other words, according to what the drafters of the Constitution said, an impeachable offense need not be one that is, strictly speaking, a crime. And, whatever Constitutional and legal niceties are advanced as the basis of impeachment, the process is inescapably conducted in a political atmosphere.

The talk of impeaching Richard Nixon began shortly after his April 30th speech, in which he dismissed his top aides, took responsibility for Watergate, and said that the investigation of it would be continued. The idea of impeachment required getting used to; it seemed unreal. On July 31st, House Resolution 513 was introduced in the House of Representatives. It said simply, *"Resolved,* that Richard M. Nixon, President of the United States, is impeached of high crimes and misdemeanors." This first resolution for impeaching the President was introduced by Father Robert F. Drinan, a Jesuit priest and Democratic representative from Massachusetts. Father Drinan is one of the most liberal of the liberal Democrats in the Congress, so his move was not taken very seriously. There was some thought that it was a setback to the idea of impeachment. Serious moves, it was believed, do not begin with the likes of Father Drinan. It was the same political wisdom that dismissed the early opposition of Senators Wayne Morse and Ernest Gruening to the war in Vietnam. It is the political wisdom that overlooks the fact that someone has to go first, and that those who go first are likely to be those who are not governed by the prevailing political wisdom. In time, other impeachment resolutions were introduced in the House—several of them after the weekend before last, when Archibald Cox was fired. Having no useful precedent to guide them, the members improvised: some stated specific reasons for impeaching the President; others drafted their resolutions in general language, calling on the House Judiciary Committee to, for instance, "inquire into and investigate the official conduct of Richard M. Nixon to determine whether in the opinion of said committee he has been guilty of any high crime or misdemeanor which in the contemplation of the Constitution requires the interposition of the powers of the House of Representatives under the Constitution."

OCTOBER 29

John Connally is putting some distance between himself and the President now. Connally is quoted in the Washington *Post* as saying that the President "owed the country a better explanation for his actions than we got" on the matter of the tapes and on the matter of the firing of Special Prosecutor Archibald Cox.

The New York *Times* says that this week's *Time* will say that Cox was dismissed after the White House challenged his determinations to pursue four areas of inquiry: the "national-security" wiretaps of government officials and newsmen; the plumbers; the handling of anti-Nixon demonstrators in the 1972 campaign; and the raising of four million dollars in campaign funds for congressional and gubernatorial candidates in 1970. There have been other reports that Cox was fired because he was looking into the financial affairs of Bebe Rebozo and the hundred-thousand-dollar payment from Hughes. All or none of these reports may be true. The President may have fired Cox because he wanted to fire Cox and perhaps shut down the Special Prosecutor's office.

At lunch, a Democratic member of the House says that now Gerald Ford's nomination will move through the House Judiciary Committee with some speed, because "we would get more votes for impeachment if there was a Republican Vice-President." He says that before the weekend of the firing of the Special Prosecutor he and many of his colleagues "would have liked to hold up Ford until the tapes issue, or even Watergate, was resolved—on the ground that a President who might be impeached or suspected of criminal conduct ought not to name his successor." I ask what happened to change this principle. He replies, "It has changed because impeachment is a real possibility now."

The President's decision to turn over the nine subpoenaed tapes after all, says the congressman, "had zero effect on Capitol Hill and in our constituencies." He says, "It almost made him look worse. Tricky Dick. He tried his trick and got caught. And there was his misjudgment about the importance of the issue. We have got no mail saying, 'Now that he has complied with the court order, back off.' "

This afternoon, I talked with a Republican member of the House. He is one of the more junior members, and has already become a leader among what are called the "moderate" Republicans (not too conservative, not too liberal). This group would like to think that it can make the House of Representatives, and the Republican Party, reflect what it regards as its more contemporary attitudes. "A lot of my kind of Republicans are very confused," he said. "We don't feel we can tell the Democrats we will go along with them on the Special Prosecutor bill. I don't know how you get one appointed and keep him accountable to someone. We have the feeling that Cox was going too far. I guess most guys of my type in the Congress find it hard to see ground for impeachment. Of course, everyone has his own definition of 'high crimes and misdemeanors.' It looks as if the Judiciary Committee is really going to conduct an inquiry into impeachment. I kind of take the pessimistic view that we're going to be locked into this thing for quite a while. It seems unlikely that the President will resign. That would be out of character. We can't make impeachment stick as of now, so we might limp along. A resignation might set a worse precedent for the long run than impeachment, or than his staying in office. That would mean that every President hereafter would be subjected to questions of judgment, and an important group, particularly an economic one, could call for his resignation. So I'm reluctant to talk about resignation. The public outpouring against the Cox dismissal—at least as far as my district goes—was from basic middle-of-the-road types who had voted for the President. It must have scared the President to death. So maybe that isolation booth he lives in has some holes in it."

I asked the congressman what course, given the alternatives, he would prefer.

He replied, "We want him out."

He then said, "I sense a lot of feeling among my colleagues, especially the older ones, that they didn't come here to face crises every day. The load's getting kind of heavy. And some of the old-timers are feeling that the investigatory air is getting heavy. They think that they will be second-class citizens, that politics will be more trouble than it's worth.

The newer guys here are more used to election laws that require disclosure. But the President's problems are going to ruin a lot of Republican congressmen—some good ones, even some who have put some distance between themselves and the White House. Everyone around here is terribly depressed—kind of worn down by the sequence of events. It's taken over everything. People have their heads down. They don't talk up anymore. They don't know what to say. It's a pretty unpleasant business. Last spring, when this thing started to break, we watched agape. Then curiously. Now we're depressed—thinking about resignation, impeachment, crisis. I can't write a script that brings us out whole. Resignation is a bummer. Impeachment is long and messy. And lurching along like this for three more years is almost the worst of the three alternatives. If that becomes the possibility, then, horrible as the precedent is, maybe someone has to go to him and say he'd better resign."

This afternoon I also talked with another Democratic member of the House. He is of medium seniority, and is one of the most effective members of the liberal wing of the party. I asked him why the Democratic House leaders had set impeachment in motion. "The leadership is responding to public sentiment, not leading," he replied. "The leaders really didn't have much choice. And on the face of it an investigation is not that threatening. But now the investigation has its own momentum. I think the investigation should go on, to see what more there is. I would vote for impeachment now, on the basis of what I know, but it isn't enough for a lot of others, so the investigation has to go forward."

I asked him why he was ready to vote for impeachment.

He replied, "The President has said that he learned within a few days after the Watergate break-in that an investigation might lead to an uncovering of activities by the C.I.A. That he remained ignorant of what happened for almost a year is unbelievable. That a burglary could have to do with overseas intelligence is also incredible. Either for gross negligence or for culpability, he ought to be out of there. There is the additional problem that the country has lost faith in him, but this is not an indictable offense."

The Democratic congressman said he thought that the President should resign. "I think it could be a good precedent," he said. "The President has accepted responsibility for these things. If he resigned on that ground, that would be all to the good. We can pay more respect to executive privilege if the President takes responsibility for what happened."

Still later today, I talked with a Republican senator of medium seniority and moderate persuasion. He had at times, early in the Nixon Administration, taken stands against the President, and had thereby come under some attack by the White House and by Republican Party workers in his state. Last week, his office received six thousand letters about the President's firing of the Special Prosecutor; they ran seventeen to one against the President. "We're in very bad shape," the senator said. "The Veterans Day weekend"—the weekend Cox was fired—"set us on some irreversible courses, in which I see one of two things happening: one, something blows up and it is 'strike three' and the President has to either resign or be impeached; or, two, we have a Presidency with no leadership base. If I had to guess, I would guess it's the first. Time's running out. The surprising thing about that weekend was the feeling among conservative Republicans that the time had come to do something. The 'Saturday-night massacre' wiped out the protective line of the conservatives who used to defend him. The collision may come soon. One of the big questions is who goes in as President. I can't bring myself to say what kind of President Jerry Ford is going to make. Three years is a long time. Right now, there isn't a very viable alternative, and that's the problem. Ford going in as Vice-President is one thing; his going in as President is quite another. It's very sobering." He shook his head and fell silent.

The current issue of *Human Events,* the conservative weekly, says that Democrats are trying for a "legal *Putsch*" to put Speaker of the House Carl Albert in the White House. It writes of "the operation to countermand the 1972 election results and install a Democrat in the White House." It also reports that mail to several conservative senators and representatives has been running against the President.

OCTOBER 30

Cox has given the Senate Judiciary Committee more details about the information he was trying to obtain from the White House. Each time he does this, of course, it sets loose some speculation about what he was looking for. Much of the material he was trying to obtain had to do with the plumbers—one of the more mysterious aspects of the whole business. We still know very little about what they did. The President has said that what they did was in the interests of national security, and we must not be told about it, because that might jeopardize the national security.

Among the things that Cox says he was seeking were records removed from Egil Krogh's files in the Department of Transportation and placed in the President's files, and documents regarding matters that Ehrlichman, David Young, and Charles Colson were handling, which have been placed in Presidential files. (Krogh and Young were in charge of the plumbers, and, as part of the Haldeman-Ehrlichman plan to place people loyal to them throughout the bureaucracy, Krogh served as Under-Secretary of Transportation after he left the White House.) Cox says that "Presidential files have a way of expanding." Cox also says that he was seeking records about the plumbers and two of their efforts—labelled "Special Project M-1" and "Project Odessa."

The New York *Times* reports that Cox was told by former Attorney General Richard Kleindienst that President Nixon had personally ordered him not to press anti-trust action against I.T.T. The White House has called this revelation "an inexcusable breach of confidence on the part of the staff of the former Special Prosecutor." The White House also says, "The President's direction to Mr. Kleindienst was based on his belief that the . . . case represented a policy of the Justice Department with which he strongly disagreed, namely, that bigness per se was unlawful. When the specific facts of the appeal were subsequently explained in greater detail, the President withdrew his objection and the appeal was prosecuted in exactly the form originally proposed." The *Times* points out that in the hearing in 1972 on his confirmation as Attorney General, Kleindienst told the Senate Judiciary Committee that the White House had not interfered. (The hearings had been reopened, at Kleindienst's request, to look into the question of whether I.T.T. had received favorable anti-trust treatment—eventually, the case in question was settled out of court—in exchange for a commitment by I.T.T. to contribute four hundred thousand dollars to the 1972 Republican convention which was originally scheduled to be held at San Diego.) If this story was in fact leaked by Cox, it could be helpful to the White House in its continuing battle against him. But some people notice that today's story was written by Nicholas Gage, who is known to have contacts in the Justice Department. There is also a theory that the story was leaked by Kleindienst. That is how we read newspapers these days.

Carl Albert and Mike Mansfield have issued a statement calling for the Ford nomination to "proceed with all due deliberateness in both houses."

The *Wall Street Journal* reports that the Ervin committee has subpoenaed access to three accounts in the bank owned by the President's friend Bebe Rebozo. The *Journal* says that, according to Rebozo's lawyers, Rebozo is refusing access not because he is trying to conceal anything but because the accounts are covered by executive privilege.

In both the House and the Senate, the Special Prosecutor issue is becoming a partisan one, with Democrats supporting a court-appointed prosecutor, Republicans a Presidentially appointed one.

There is a kind of lull now—a calming down from the tumultuous events of last week, and bracing for events to come. The politicians are confused. Even those who want to challenge the White House seem to be without a strategy. They stagger from crisis to crisis, regroup, and then change plans as events unfold. Or they get bored. The politicians' limited attention span is affecting the Constitutional issues. Now some politicians are tiring of the Special Prosecutor issue. In getting rid of

Cox, the President has bought time. He may, if the Congress permits, establish his own authority over the investigation and prosecution of his own Administration.

OCTOBER 31

The Senate Democratic Caucus met yesterday. Mansfield said that legislation for an independent Special Prosecutor should be enacted, and, as a threat to the White House and to some senators who for various reasons wanted an end to the Ervin-committee hearings, suggested that the life of the Ervin committee should be extended if an independent Special Prosecutor is not established by law. The senators gave Mansfield a standing ovation. But Senator Ervin is reported to be reluctant to extend the life of the committee. At the time that the Congress reconvened, Mansfield was reported to be pressing Ervin to conclude the hearings.

Senator Ervin has said that he and Senator Baker had agreed to the White House tapes compromise—the so-called Stennis compromise—without being aware that a similar offer had been made to Cox and that he had refused it. Ervin and Baker have also told reporters that they did not agree to anything with the White House on behalf of the committee on the matter of the tapes. Ervin said, "It was a proposal—not a compromise or an agreement."

The House Armed Services Committee's Subcommittee on Intelligence has issued a report saying that the C.I.A.'s involvement in some of the things we have been learning about "had no support in reason or law." This is the first congressional report to result from an inquiry into this set of events. It is more sympathetic toward the C.I.A. than toward the White House. It says that the C.I.A. did not know it was being used for improper purposes. But that leaves the question of why C.I.A. officials did not know this. The subcommittee says that the C.I.A. and its highest officials were "the unwitting dupes for purely domestic White House staff endeavors that were beyond the realm of the C.I.A." It says that the C.I.A. operated outside the law that prohibits its participation in domestic activities by providing two wigs, speech-altering devices, a tape recorder, a clandestine camera, one-way tinted spectacles, film-developing facilities, and other equipment to E. Howard Hunt; and that it was an "abuse of C.I.A. facilities" for it to prepare a psychological profile of Daniel Ellsberg for the White House. It says that requests from White House aides were taken by C.I.A. officials to have the authority of the President, and that the aides made the requests not of C.I.A. chief Richard Helms but of his deputies, who owed their jobs to Mr. Nixon. (After the 1972 election, Helms was removed as C.I.A. director and made ambassador to Iran. Vernon Walters, the deputy director beginning in May, 1972, had accompanied then Vice-President Nixon on his tour of Latin America, and was in the car with him when he was mobbed in Caracas.) The subcommittee says that it will prepare legislation to prohibit the C.I.A. from participating in domestic activities without the authorization of the President. This does not seem to solve the problem.

The Internal Revenue Service has rejected a request—made by a public-interest tax-law firm, Tax Analysts and Advocates—that it name an independent auditor to examine the President's tax returns and assess the validity of his five-hundred-and-seventy-thousand-dollar deduction in 1969 for the gift to the government of his Vice-Presidential papers. The question has been raised whether the gift was made before the tax laws were changed, in 1969, to eliminate deductions for gifts of papers. (Why Mr. Nixon or Presidents before him, or other politicians, were able to consider official papers, written on government time, on government salaries, and usually by government-paid assistants, "theirs" is a mystery.) The question of how the government handles top officials' tax returns is a dilemma not unlike the Special Prosecutor dilemma.

The Ervin committee resumes its hearings today in the caucus room on the third floor of the Old Senate Office Building. On the ground floor, the yellow ropes to contain waiting spectators are still there, but the spectators are not. The television cameras have been dismantled, and fewer reporters are present. Berl Bernhard, a Washington lawyer, who was the manager of Edmund Muskie's Presidential campaign, is testifying on the subject of unethical campaign practices. Bernhard is talking of a question we have almost forgotten in the current confusion—the question of whether we really had an election in 1972.

Bernhard does not suggest that but for the interference in Muskie's campaign Muskie would have won. He is candid about Muskie's political failings and about the difficulties of Muskie's position as a "centrist" trying to bridge the gap between wings of the Party. Bernhard also gives a clear picture of the time and energy that a candidate for the Presidency must expend in the effort to raise money for his campaign. "If I had to choose the one reform which is most urgently needed, it would be the public financing of campaigns, not because Ed Muskie ran out of money but because he, and Senator Humphrey, and Senator Jackson, and Senator McGovern, and all the rest of them had to spend so much time just passing the hat," says Bernhard. "America deserves candidates who have enough time to consider the issues, enough funds to present their views to the voters, and to compete equally on the merits—not men who make the best fund-raisers, because they appeal to particular interest groups or because they are in a position to put pressure on people with money."

And Bernhard documents extensively the degree to which the party in power used its power—as it interfered in the processes whereby the other political party selected its candidate for President—to maintain itself in power. A memorandum written in March, 1971, by the White House aide Patrick Buchanan to the President of the United States said:

> And if Mr. Muskie is not cut and bleeding before he goes into New Hampshire, he will very likely do massively well there, building up irresistible momentum for the nomination. This scenario is not in our interest—as Muskie today is a figure ideally situated to unite the warring factions of his party, and if they are united, that is bad news for us.

According to Bernhard, Muskie campaign-planning documents disappeared. The contents of some turned up in newspaper columns. Spies were planted in the campaign organization. Bernhard's law office was broken into and his files were ransacked. Confidential documents relating to the Muskie campaign were later discovered on the Xerox machine in the campaign offices. (Bernhard does not assert that this was the work of the opposition; his point is that it was like things the opposition was known to have done and therefore was disturbing.) Days were lost in trying to track down spies within the organization. The campaign was constantly disrupted. Muskie fund-raisers were put on the White House "enemies" list. Campaign advisers—those who had worked for Henry Kissinger—were wiretapped. "We were never able to understand how it was that there was so much conjecture in the press which seemed to relate to staff discussions on the issue of Vietnam," says Bernhard. It is now reported, as a result of the civil suit brought by Morton Halperin, one of the advisers who were wiretapped, that summaries of the taps were given by the F.B.I. to Haldeman. Telephones in Muskie offices did strange things. A Muskie fund-raising dinner was nearly ruined by the chaotic arrival of food that had not been ordered and guests who had not been invited. There were more than the usual number of pickets at Muskie appearances; the pickets held up signs saying "Muskie is a racist pig," "Muskie supports draft dodgers," and the like. At some appearances, almost all the questions were about gay liberation and abortion and whether Muskie would accept a black running mate.

Bernhard acknowledges that "it is not always a simple matter . . . to make precise philosophic distinctions between rough but fair politics and rough unfair politics." And he says something to the committee which is arresting:

> I would point out that there is nothing in the resolution establishing your committee that says this conduct is reprehensible only if it has decisive significance. It speaks rather of whether the object was "to disrupt, hinder, impede or sabotage" the campaign. Does anyone here doubt that

this was the objective of the dirty tricks? If they were not successful, that's a comment on the ineptitude of the perpetrators, not their moral fiber. I am troubled by the moral viewpoint implicit in offering that line of reasoning as a defense. The doctrine that the end justifies the means is pernicious enough. The doctrine that the failure to attain the end justifies—or at least excuses—the means is terrifying.

On April 12, 1972, Patrick Buchanan and Ken Khachigian, a White House staff assistant, wrote a memorandum to John Mitchell and Haldeman. "If so much had not been done to sustain it," says Bernhard, "I would have written [it] off as no more than an act of self-satisfied puffing." The memorandum said:

> Our primary objective, to prevent Senator Muskie from sweeping the early primaries, locking up the convention in April and uniting the Democratic party behind him for the fall, has been achieved. The likelihood—great three months ago—that the Democratic Convention could become a dignified coronation ceremony for a centrist candidate who could lead a united party into the election is now remote.

This afternoon, I dropped in to see the Democratic Senate aide who is in the traffic patterns of Capitol Hill. "The eggs have been scrambled," he said. "Impeachment is being spoken of openly. There is a lot of feeling that Nixon's term can be measured in months. The presumption among senators is that when they are talking about confirming Nixon's nomination of Gerald Ford for the Vice-Presidency they are talking about choosing a President. The Republicans are floundering, and very worried. Ford is going to go zipping through. The issue of his competence is now a back-burner crisis." He said that "once impeachment became an acceptable term, it remained an acceptable term." He said he believes that Nixon's "days are numbered" because of issues that "won't stay hidden"—I.T.T., Rebozo, the milk fund, the break-in at Daniel Ellsberg's psychiatrist's office, the amounts the government has spent on the President's houses. Now that the issue of the tapes is gone, he said, these issues will combine to bring down the President. The issues are diffused, he said, but one issue or another makes everyone angry. He argued that the issue of the invasion of privacy, involving a government break-in at someone's psychiatrist's office, goes very deep with the public—deeper than the politicians had at first suspected. The aide said he could not predict exactly how the events would evolve. "The Congress is like a school of fish," he said. "They dart one way, and then another. You don't know which fish will dart out and make the next move that they will all follow. There aren't built-in leaders and followers."

As we were talking, two reporters burst into the office, and one asked, "Did you hear the news?"

There is the expression "The heart stopped." That's the way it felt. Each jolt seems more severe. Literally gripping our chairs, the Senate aide and I asked the reporters what had happened.

One of them said, "Two of the tapes are missing."

After a pause, the aide said quietly, "He's playing for days now."

The stunning news of the missing tapes dominates tonight's news programs. The two conversations that the White House now says were not taped could be of some importance. One was the President's telephone conversation with John Mitchell on June 20, 1972, three days after the break-in at the Watergate. The other was a conversation between the President and John Dean on April 15, 1972. NBC, ABC, and CBS show Dean testifying about that conversation. It was the one in the course of which, Dean told the committee, the President "got up out of his chair, went behind his chair to a corner of the Executive Office Building office, and, in a barely audible tone, said to me he was probably foolish to have discussed Hunt's clemency with Colson." Of the many surreal images of this past year, this is one of the lasting ones—the President cowering in a corner of his own office to whisper to an aide. Dean had told the committee that "leading questions" which the President asked at that same meeting "made me think that the conversation was being taped." J. Fred Buzhardt, one of the White House attorneys, told Judge John Sirica's court today that the conversation with Dean, which took place on a Sunday evening, was not recorded because the recording device had "a malfunction." NBC replays the testimony of Alexander Butterfield to the Ervin committee about the existence of White House tapes. It shows Butterfield saying that the tape system was "checked at least daily." It is recalled that Haldeman had taken some tapes home, and that the President had listened to some tapes, and that the President had asked Buzhardt to listen to a tape. The White House says that it discovered just this past weekend that the two tapes were missing, and therefore had not mentioned the matter until now.

Buzhardt is interviewed as he comes out of the courthouse. He is asked, "Do you think the public will believe this?"

He replies, "I don't know."

Senator Ervin says, "Everything about this has been curious from the first day."

The matter of the missing tapes almost drowns out other news of today. Kleindienst has said that he threatened to resign after the President ordered him not to proceed with the I.T.T. anti-trust case and that then the White House changed its position. We see on our television screens William Saxbe standing on the White House lawn and saying he is "relatively sure" that the President will name him Attorney General. Saxbe, the maverick Ohio Republican senator, recently announced that he would not run for reëlection. Saxbe is the senator who last December, during the carpet bombing of North Vietnam, said, "The President appears to have left his senses." Like George Meany more recently, Saxbe was widely quoted at the time. It is hard to believe that the President would now make him Attorney General. In his press conference Friday, the President complained that during the recent military alert network commentators had used the "same words" they had used after the December bombing of North Vietnam—that he had "lost his senses." But the only person who appears to have said anything like this, for quotation on television, is Saxbe. Now, in casually announcing his own appointment, he is being characteristically brash. Saxbe's irreverence is the source of his popularity here. He is something of an unguided missile; it is hard to locate him. He has a kind of talent for gut statements that strike people as honest and candid, but essentially he has been loyal to the Administration. In selecting a man who said that the President must have "left his senses," the President appears to be selecting an independent man. But it may be just that—a matter of appearances. Saxbe says that he thinks the President will be coöperative on issues of White House documents. He also says that on these matters the President "has gone further than I would have recommended."

The worldwide military alert, which the President put us on six days ago, has been called off.

Spiro Agnew paid his ten-thousand-dollar fine today.

This evening, a friend who covers the White House says that this afternoon Ron Ziegler said to some skeptical reporters that he could not understand why people did not believe the White House about the missing tapes. My friend says that White House aides admonished reporters that in reporting the story they should be clear that it was not that the *tapes* were missing—it was that the *conversations* were missing.

There is a plausibility to the White House explanations of the missing conversations. From long habit, we still make the effort to see the story from the White House point of view, to entertain the idea that the President of the United States is telling the truth. The tape machine might have run out on the President and Dean. The President might have taken the precaution of speaking to Mitchell from an untaped phone. Untaped. Untapped. The President of the United States taking care not to be overheard by his own listening system. The atmosphere of absurdity has been building up. One friend called me tonight and asked, "Do you suppose they confused the things they were supposed to put in the burn bag with the things they were supposed to deep six with the things they were supposed to put in the shredder?" Another friend, a serious man, called and, before either of us had gone beyond saying hello, broke into uncontrollable laughter.

NOVEMBER I

It has been announced by the White House that Saxbe will be named Attorney General, and that Leon Jaworski, a Texas lawyer who was a friend of Lyndon Johnson's and is a former president of the American Bar Association, will be named Special Prosecutor. The A.B.A. had been calling for legislation for a court-appointed Special Prosecutor. Check. Ford checks the House. Saxbe checks the Senate. The chess game goes on.

It is already clear that those missing conversations will be costly to the President. On page 2 of the Washington *Post* are stories headed "CONGRESSMEN SHOCKED BY TAPE DEVELOPMENT" and "GLOOM GRIPS REPUBLICAN SENATORS." The second story, written by Spencer Rich, the *Post's* Senate correspondent, leads off with the statement that "President Nixon faces a massive hemorrhaging of support from G.O.P. senators unless he acts immediately to dispel all suspicions of a Watergate cover-up, key Senate Republicans warned gloomily yesterday." Rich quotes some of the senators. Senator James B. Pearson, of Kansas, says, "I'm shocked: I'm surprised—I thought all the surprises were out of me." Senator James L. Buckley, of New York, says that the disclosure of the missing tapes "has dramatically shifted the burden of proof," and continues, "As of this moment, President Nixon has the clear burden of satisfying the American people that he has been speaking the truth. If he fails in this, then we are faced with a political crisis of the most profoundly disturbing proportions."

Mrs. Leon Jaworski, speaking yesterday of her husband's expected appointment as Special Prosecutor, says, "It's a terrible job. I just feel sorry for him."

Egil Krogh's attorneys have asked that his indictment on October 11th in Washington for giving false statements to the grand jury be dismissed. They argued that Krogh testified falsely—in saying he was not aware that E. Howard Hunt and G. Gordon Liddy had travelled to Los Angeles for the purpose of the break-in into Ellsberg's psychiatrist's office—because to have told the truth would have disclosed information "that had been officially classified by the highest security office in the government of the United States, the President himself." Krogh's lawyers also asked that there be a change of venue, that the trial be moved to Peoria. "How will it play in Peoria?" Ehrlichman, Krogh's old boss, used to ask about policy decisions.

The hearings on the nomination of Gerald Ford to be Vice-President begin today in the Senate Committee on Rules and Administration. Room 1202 of the New Senate Office Building, where the hearings are to be held, is not quite full. One long press table is almost vacant, and several of the seats for the public are empty. The drama now is elsewhere. The hearings on the confirmation of the next Vice-President of the United States—perhaps its President—seem almost routine. In their opening statements, the senators do their best to convey a sense of occasion. They speak of their "solemn responsibility" and of the "utmost gravity" of the proceeding. Ford begins with the observation that "this is a new experience for me," and goes on, "I realize it is also a new experience for you, and for the American people. I feel that I am among friends. . . . I am deeply conscious that today the Congress and the citizens we represent are embarking upon an historic voyage into uncharted waters." Ford, speaking in his flat, Midwestern voice, his large frame hulking over the microphone as he faces the committee, says, "These are not ordinary times." He says that he supports the President's programs, as Vice-Presidents are supposed to do. He poses the question "What makes you, Jerry Ford, qualified to be Vice-President of the United States?" And then answers it: "My answer is that I believe I can be a ready conciliator and calm communicator between the White House and Capitol Hill, between the reëlection mandate of the Republican President and the equally emphatic mandate of the Democratic 93rd Congress."

The problem for the committee is what to ask him. There is some debate and confusion within the Congress now as to whether in confirming a Vice-President members of Congress should act as "surrogates for the people" and examine his qualifications more closely than they do— at least sometimes—those of other Presidential appointees or whether they should be predisposed to give the President "his own man."

Afterward, in the hallway, I encounter a Democratic senator. "It just gets worse and worse, doesn't it?" he says. "They're picking a President in there. We're so traditional and conventional. Should we act this way in picking a President? That's what they're doing in there. Nixon can't last. Jerry Ford President? There are other Republicans we could agree to—Nelson Rockefeller, even Barry Goldwater. We know who they are. Who is Jerry Ford? If we had a parliamentary system, he wouldn't be President."

I ask the senator if he would prefer a parliamentary system.

"Yes," he replies.

Senator Birch Bayh, Democrat of Indiana, also encountered in the hallway, says that Saxbe and Jaworski are "O.K."—probably as good nominees as there could be—but that Richardson and Ruckelshaus and Cox were good, too, and "they were canned." Therefore, he will continue to press for legislation establishing a court-appointed Special Prosecutor. Then he steps in front of the cameras across the hall from the Senate Judiciary Committee room, where hearings on legislation to establish a new Special Prosecutor are being held, and repeats what he has just said.

Inside the Judiciary Committee room, Senator Adlai Stevenson, Democrat of Illinois, is testifying on legislation to establish an independent Special Prosecutor rather than leave this power in the President's hands. He was instrumental in establishing the guidelines for the role of the Special Prosecutor last spring. Stevenson says that "this Administration cannot be trusted to investigate itself," and that if the President has nothing to hide he has nothing to fear from an independent Special Prosecutor. Stevenson says that the President's choice of a new Special Prosecutor reminds him of something Zsa Zsa Gabor said after one of her numerous marriages: "This time, darling, it's for real."

At noon, the military honor guard is on the South Lawn of the White House. Golda Meir will meet with the President today. Tourists are peering through the fence.

At my office, I watch the Ford hearings on television. The camera zooms in on Ford. His large, plain face—straight-back hair, smallish eyes, high forehead, slightly bulbous nose—fills the screen. This is probably as close an examination as we have ever had of a prospective Vice-President. But the camera, which often reveals things that the politician is trying to hide behind his words, reveals little. Ford deals in football imagery: "After a play is called, you shouldn't tackle your own quarterback." And in the irrelevant absolute: asked about impoundment, he says, "That would scare both of us, actually, because if we forced every President to spend every dime Congress, for one reason or another, gave them—you would have a tax increase of astronomical proportions." Senator Mark Hatfield, Republican of Oregon, talks of impeachment—"a problem that is, I think, paramount in everybody's mind," he says. The pretense that this is the confirmation of simply a Vice-President begins to slip away.

The military alert of a week ago has left its residue of tension. There are more conversations about who will go to whom to get the President out. A Washington lawyer says that several of his business clients are concluding that the present situation is unacceptable, and are asking him what they should do. He is advising them to see Melvin Laird and Bryce Harlow, both Presidential advisers. Laird, in the view of some, is an *éminence grise*. Ford is perceived as Laird's instrument. Ford was Laird's choice for Vice-President. When Ford is in office, it might be easier to oust Nixon. The idea is widely entertained now that at some point Republicans will go to the President and tell him they cannot support or protect him any longer. No one can know whether this is really what is in the minds of the people to whom such thoughts are imputed. But the thoughts are factors in other people's calculations. They are part of the atmosphere. The conversations about who will go to the President began last spring. They sounded fanciful then.

NOVEMBER 2

Friday. Republican politicians are suggesting that the President appear before the Ervin committee to clear things up once and for all. The idea that such an appearance would clear things up once and for all is exactly what is wrong with the suggestion. The committee is not capable of questioning the President closely. It does not have all the legal powers that a prosecutor has for gathering evidence. It has not done the necessary research into all the aspects of all the issues. Senator Goldwater, urging that the President appear before the Ervin committee, says that Mr. Nixon's credibility "has reached an all-time low, from which he may never be able to recover." This is considered significant. Goldwater is considered a moral arbiter and also a signal tower for the right wing of the Republican Party. Goldwater's moral authority seems to stem from the widespread perception of him as a politician who says what he means. In 1964, it was his undoing. Now it is making him a hero—especially among those who want to bring down the President. Goldwater's political authority stems from the perception of him as a leader of the conservative Republicans, whose disaffection might doom the President. The President used the conservative wing of the Party to gain the nomination in 1968, and the conservative wing of the Party used Nixon to gain power. The conservatives had learned in 1964, when Goldwater was the Presidential candidate, that they could not win with one of their own. Winning with someone who needed them, and would accommodate some of their wishes, was the next-best thing. Now Nixon is undoing their work.

Today, Joseph Alsop, the columnist, calls for Nixon's resignation. This is an event, not necessarily because Alsop is influential but because of the thinking he represents. His columns often reflect the point of view of the military and its supporters, and he had been a supporter of the President. Alsop says that he has reached his conclusion "with extreme reluctance." He is worried that the Soviet Union will try to exploit our weaknesses, as he believes it did last week. He argues that the United States has permitted the Soviet Union to pull ahead in weaponry, and that now the President is too weakened politically to redress the balance.

Today, James Reston also calls for Nixon's resignation. Earlier this week, Howard K. Smith, of ABC, said that the President should resign or be impeached. ABC has been the White House's favorite network.

Bebe Rebozo has given an interview to the Miami *Herald*. His version of how the hundred thousand dollars from Hughes reached him is said by the Washington *Post* to conflict with two sworn accounts. (Rebozo said that he told the President's secretary, Rose Mary Woods, about the money from Hughes.) Rebozo said, as the President did in his press conference last week, that he kept the money for three years—according to Rebozo, in a vault. And, also as the President said last week, Rebozo said he returned the money after an internal dispute broke out in the Hughes organization. He said, as the President's comment suggested, that there was concern that the fact that Hughes had sent the money would become known. The spectre of Hughes' loan, in 1956, of two hundred and five thousand dollars to Donald Nixon persists. Speaking of the recent problem in the Hughes organization, Rebozo said, "They had all that flap out there, and I began to get memories of that two-hundred-and-five-thousand-dollar situation. . . . It just got worse and worse, and I gave it back."

The Washington *Post* reports that eleven days after the Watergate break-in Richard Helms, then C.I.A. director, wrote a memorandum to his deputy, General Vernon A. Walters, noting that the F.B.I. should be requested to restrict its investigation "to personalities already arrested or under suspicion." The memo asked that the F.B.I. be urged to "desist from expanding this investigation into other areas which may, eventually, run afoul of our operations." The *Post* reporter, Laurence Stern, says that the memorandum "appears to be in sharp conflict with testimony by the former C.I.A. director to five Congressional committees and federal prosecutors" investigating the Watergate break-in. He says that "the thrust of testimony by Helms and Walters, as well as other principals in the case, has been that despite heavy White House pressure the C.I.A. steadfastly denied that F.B.I. inquiries into Watergate matters would expose C.I.A. activities." The debris—the damaged people and institutions—keeps growing.

White House witnesses were in court yesterday explaining the missing conversations. Characteristically, their explanations raised more questions. They said that the tape ran out before the President's conversation with Dean on April 15th. Yet today testimony was elicited that a box of tapes of conversations that preceded the meeting was marked "Part I." The White House lawyers could not explain why. There was, they said, no "Part II." It was also revealed that the tapes had done a good bit of travelling in and out of a storage room in the Executive Office

Building. The logs of their travels were incomplete and casual; some of them were kept on pieces of brown-paper bags. There is a photograph in today's papers of a log of the tapes of the President's conversations on these scraps of paper.

I do not think of myself as a terribly orderly person. The idea that I am more orderly than the people running my country is disconcerting.

Carl Albert has been asked his reaction to the missing conversations. He replies, "I have passed the point of reacting."

Chesterfield H. Smith, the president of the American Bar Association, told the House Judiciary Subcommittee on Criminal Justice yesterday that, despite his friendship with Jaworski, he supported a court-appointed Special Prosecutor. He said that "the appearance of justice" is important.

Robert Bork, the Acting Attorney General, said yesterday that the President had given his personal assurances that he would not fire the next Special Prosecutor without obtaining the agreement of a "substantial majority" of the Democratic and Republican Senate and House leaders, and the chairmen and ranking members of the Judiciary Committees of the Senate and the House. As it happens, the majority of these men are likely to support the President in most actions he takes. The swing vote would be cast by James Eastland, who is even more conservative, and even more likely to support the White House, than his colleague from Mississippi, John Stennis. In any event, it is a strange arrangement. It confuses institutional roles. It makes the tenure of the investigator of the executive branch subject to agreements between the President and the congressional leaders—not to processes. It rests, in the end, on assurances given by the person being investigated.

Jaworski goes to work as the Presidentially appointed Special Prosecutor on Monday. At the Special Prosecutor's office, he is awaited with interest. Members of the Special Prosecutor's staff have contacts throughout Washington, in the press and on Capitol Hill, and they can make things very difficult for Jaworski if he does not proceed with actions that they have initiated or that they recommend. In the end, a great deal may rest on what manner of man Jaworski is; on the President's assurances that he will not—or his fear that he cannot—fire the new Special Prosecutor; and on the strength of the spine of congressional leaders. Jaworski, in mixed advance notices, has been described by people who know him as "the servant of princes" and as "a cobra." The Congress is losing interest in the legislation to establish a Special Prosecutor. And many politicians, as they often do, are equating a drop in the level of mail on an issue with a loss of public interest in it. The impact of mail on Capitol Hill is felt when it arrives. This overlooks public sentiment of the sort that welled up, and burst out, when the

President fired Archibald Cox. It is likely that that kind of sentiment is still there. Politicians, to their sorrow, often overlook public opinion that is welling up, and forget that it can be cumulative. They read today's polls. Today's polls can be very misleading. Before long, they are yesterday's polls.

The stock market is dropping sharply this afternoon. The decline stopped for a while when a rumor swept the floor of the New York Stock Exchange that the President was resigning. When the rumor was found to be untrue, the decline resumed.

A businessman in New York calls. He is by temperament an optimist. He says that his business friends in New York want the President out of office but they do not know what to do. He says that the businessmen are afraid to take the President on. He says that they are particularly fearful of the President now, when he is in trouble. He says that some of the businessmen he knows are calling politicians in Washington.

Someone speculates about whether Kissinger might be an instrument in the President's downfall. Kissinger has great power, through his contacts, his cachet with the press, his reputation as the reassuring presence in the Administration. He is, perhaps, unrivalled in the art of cultivating the press. Kissinger is thought to see complexities that others would not take into consideration. He is widely viewed as having exercised a restraining and responsible influence. All this may be true; there is no way of knowing what would have happened if he had not been there. But there are also the things that did happen when he was there: the continuation of the war in Southeast Asia for four more years, the secret bombing, the military alert. Kissinger has a penchant for secrecy and surprise. He permitted the wiretapping of his own staff, and turned over a list of names of staff members who had access to information that had been leaked. Our "allies" were expected to accept diplomacy-by-surprise. The way our foreign policy has been conducted under Nixon and Kissinger is also part of its substance. It has avoided public debate over choices. It has shown distrust of the political process, and of the people.

On the evening news, it is reported that Stephen Bull, a White House aide, told Judge Sirica's court that on June 4th the President spent ten or twelve hours listening to tapes, and that there might be a tape of him listening to his tapes. The prosecutors asked for *that* tape—the tape of the tapes. The President's lawyers objected. The day before the day in June that the President spent listening to tapes, the Washington *Post* had published a story by Bob Woodward and Carl Bernstein describing some of Dean's expected testimony before the Ervin committee.

We have become so accustomed to talking about the tapes that we've almost forgotten how strange it is that these tapes exist at all.

Gerald Warren, who now handles the White House press briefings, said today that the President would not resign.

At dinner, a friend said that for him Washington has lost much of its beauty. He also said, "I want a President I am not afraid of."

NOVEMBER 3

In the past twenty-four hours, the thought seems to have spread that the President must leave office. It is one of those sharp changes in atmosphere which have characterized this year. It does not appear to be linked to any particular event. It may be the result of anxieties that have been accumulating since the firing of the Special Prosecutor and the ordering of the military alert. On Thursday, the President left Washington suddenly for Key Biscayne, taking no members of the press along. There's the drop in the stock market. And there are the phone calls. The phone calls that tense people are making to each other must be having an impact. There is a word-of-mouth communications system—operating totally apart from the communications media—by which ideas travel around the country. And there are the tapes. That issue has taken too many bizarre turns. And there is fear. The fear of a President in trouble. In the House, there is a sudden urge to hurry the approval of Ford, so as to have someone in place if, or when, the President leaves office. Edward Kennedy has issued a statement calling for the prompt confirmation of Ford. The White House is not likely to announce that the President will resign until, and if, he does. Agnew said that he would not resign.

On tonight's news, it is announced that tomorrow's Gallup poll will show the President's popularity at twenty-seven percent. The Detroit *News* and the Denver *Post,* former supporters of the President, have called for his resignation.

7

SUNDAY. Betty Beale, the Washington *Star-News* social columnist, writes, "During this shattering period in the Presidency, the White
House seems to be a veritable tomb, socially."

The New York *Times* reports Representative Robert Michel,
Republican of Illinois, as saying that there was "a lot of discussion"
of the President's resignation in the cloakrooms of the Congress.
Newsmen reported seeing Barry Goldwater and William Buckley at the
airport in Wichita, Kansas, in "deep discussion." Later, Buckley, in a
speech at Kansas State University, said that he thought the President
would resign. Goldwater told the reporters that he was in Wichita "on
vacation."

Julie Nixon Eisenhower, in an interview with the Associated Press,
said that she wrote "Fight. Fight. Fight" on her calendar on October
25th. That was the day on which the President ordered the military alert.

The New York *Times* says, in an editorial, that the President should
resign.

On *Issues and Answers,* Senator Edward Brooke, of Massachusetts,
becomes the first Republican senator to call on the President to resign.
Two Democratic senators, Daniel Inouye, of Hawaii, and John Tunney,
of California, have already done so. Brooke says that he does not think
the country "can stand the trauma that it has been going through for the
past months."

In the afternoon, word comes that tomorrow *Time* will call for the
President's resignation. It is as if a fever were sweeping the nation.

President Nixon, at Key Biscayne, issues a statement, through his
press spokesman, that he has "absolutely no intention of resigning."

On a CBS Special Report on "The Embattled President" this evening,
Joseph Alsop is interviewed. He says that he thinks the President should
resign, not for moral reasons but "because he can't work." Ron Ziegler

talks about the tapes. He says, "We have a good story to tell there." Ziegler concedes that it is difficult to "project" that story. He says that the talk of impeachment comes from "the President's traditional adversaries . . . his strong political adversaries from the past twenty-seven years." He then asks, "Where is the impeachable offense?"

The Constitution does not say that a President should leave office if his standing in the polls is low, or if he "can't work." The framers of the Constitution were trying to protect us from both kingly authority and popular passions of the moment. They knew what they were doing.

NOVEMBER 5

I made some calls to Capitol Hill to ask about the mood and events of the weekend. A Democratic senator says that he thinks the talk of resignation is "politically premature." He says that Congress should proceed to establish the Special Prosecutor by legislation. "The system is being tested now, and we ought to see it through," he says. "If the President were to resign tomorrow, there would be a sigh of relief from one end of the country to the other, but we would not have seen it through. We should get more of the facts. The country is way ahead of the Congress on wanting him out of office. If we are going to impeach him, we need more facts. That is why we must proceed with the Special Prosecutor." Another Democratic senator says, "I'm confused. I don't know what to think. I think he's going to leave." The Senate Democratic aide who is in the traffic patterns of Capitol Hill tells me, "Congress is on dead center. There is no movement. These guys have no capacity for movement. Nothing that has happened is the result of action by the Congress—only of ineptitude in the cover-up by the executive branch. Everyone who is looking at the Congress for leadership is misdirecting his attention. Being statesmanlike is synonymous with being inactive."

Senator Peter Dominick, a conservative Republican from Colorado, said in a speech today in Denver that there is "a crisis of confidence in our leadership." Dominick, who will be up for reëlection in 1974, urged Republicans "to follow a more independent course" from here on. He headed the Republican Senatorial Campaign Committee in 1972 and is said to be bitter, as are other Republicans, over the President's lack of support of Republicans seeking reëlection then. Gordon Allott, who had been Dominick's Republican colleague from Colorado, was defeated for reëlection last year.

I phoned a Texas businessman, a supporter of the President. He said, "No corporate executive would survive this—surrounding himself with that many bad people. It's hard to believe that no one went to him and said, 'We've got a problem.' Things that would have been little things are now big things. Why does this guy go off every weekend during crises? A businessman would stay there if he discovered he had a massive problem. This guy goes off alone. These things are what have the businessmen disturbed. Bebe Rebozo and Robert Abplanalp aren't their people. He's got to get rid of the trappings of royalty. He's got to get around the country and listen."

Woodward and Bernstein report in the Washington *Post* that the prosecuting attorneys are planning to subpoena the tape of June 4th, the day on which the President listened to some tapes, but that the White House says there could not be a tape of the tapes, because the President listened to them through earphones.

The Washington *Star-News* reports that John Dean shredded Howard Hunt's notebooks last January. It says that Dean found them while he was going through a file folder containing material on the President's estate plan.

Last night, on the CBS Special, William Saxbe said, "If somebody upstairs wants me to be the Attorney General at this time in our history, it'll work out."

"When you say someone 'upstairs,'" Daniel Schorr asked him, "you don't mean upstairs in the White House?"

"No," replied Saxbe. "I mean God."

NOVEMBER 6

Tuesday. Courtroom 2, on the second floor of the United States Court House, on Constitution Avenue, a short distance from Capitol Hill. Judge John J. Sirica's courtroom. About forty reporters and two courtroom artists are here. The press fills the jury box, a table on the other side of the room, and the first several rows of seats in the section reserved for the public. The courtroom is full, but there are no lines of people waiting to get in. The room is plain, with a panel of marble in the center of the front wall. The seal of the United States is on the wall above where the Judge sits.

At one table is Douglas Parker, a lawyer for the White House, pale and slightly stout; he wears horn-rimmed glasses. Parker is on loan to the White House from the Department of Housing and Urban Development. There is a heavy demand for lawyers at the White House these days. At the Special Prosecutor's table is a group of lawyers, their average age clearly under thirty-five. There are three pairs of steel-rimmed glasses, one beard, one mustache, and one woman, blond and in a miniskirt. She is Jill Wine Volner, an Assistant Special Prosecutor. One can understand the resentment that must be felt at the White House against the prosecution lawyers, whose questions its witnesses must answer and whose salaries the government pays. In one corner of the courtroom,

John J. Wilson, lawyer for H. R. Haldeman and John Ehrlichman, sits unobtrusively, flag in lapel, taking notes.

Because neither of the chief White House lawyers, J. Fred Buzhardt and Leonard Garment, is here, the reporters who regularly cover the proceedings think something may be afoot. The White House has been putting it about—and it has been reported in the press—that the President would like to make the tapes public, if Judge Sirica would permit. On Friday, Stephen Bull testified in this courtroom that the President had told him five weeks ago that the two nonexistent tapes did not exist. This raised the question of why the court was informed of the "missing conversations" just last week. Over the weekend, White House aides explained to reporters in Key Biscayne, in "guidance"—a term meaning that the White House aides were not to be quoted—that the "ascertainment" that the tapes did not exist had been made just the previous weekend. They explained Bull's revelation by saying that there had been an "awareness" on the part of the President earlier that the conversations had not been taped but that there had been no urgency about "ascertaining" this, because at that point the President had no intention of giving up the tapes. After the President changed his mind, his aides explained to the reporters at Key Biscayne, the search for the nonexistent tapes began to "intensify." As a result of this "intensive" and "extensive" search, they explained, it was "ascertained" that the conversations were not recorded. Stephen Bull was at Key Biscayne over the weekend. Today, he is back in the courtroom for more questioning.

Bull is tanned from his weekend in Key Biscayne, and young, his clean-cut looks not unlike those of Ron Ziegler and Jeb Stuart Magruder. He is wearing a gray suit, with a flag in its lapel. A reporter says that Bull had intended to clear matters up quickly on Friday and then go to Key Biscayne for some sun and tennis. Now he is being questioned again, by Richard Ben-Veniste, another Assistant Special Prosecutor. Ben-Veniste, short, with curly hair and steel-rimmed glasses, lobs questions slowly and quietly, and they land in the witness box like grenades. Ben-Veniste's aim is so accurate that it is hard to believe he does not already know the answers to the questions. But he does not, and as new information comes forth from the witness, Ben-Veniste does not quite suppress a satisfied smile. As Ben-Veniste, considering the next question, walks back and forth behind his lectern, the slight smile remains. "Sir," says Bull at one point in the questioning, "if I could distinguish between a missing tape and a conversation that apparently was not recorded . . ." At another point, he refers to "conversations that may have not been recorded." He slows up when he comes to this, as if to be careful to get it exactly right. I notice that he does not say "were not recorded." Sirica, with the familiar wavy hair and bushy eyebrows, watches, expressionless. He says little. Sirica is now one of the lions of Washington. He is a major attraction at parties.

Bull explains that Buzhardt understood two weeks ago "that I was unable to find those two conversations." But, he says, no one was sure at the time "that these conversations were unequivocally unavailable." At one point, Ben-Veniste elicits testimony that in late September Bull took a number of tapes to Camp David. Bull also says that he did not return all the tapes.

Now Judge Sirica starts to question Bull. He asks him how many tapes he received. Bull tells him that he received "approximately one dozen tapes."

"How many did you return?"

"Approximately four or five, sir."

"To whom did those four or five go?"

"Returned them to John Bennett, Your Honor." (General Bennett, who is an assistant to General Alexander Haig, now the President's top adviser, is the latest custodian of the tapes.)

"What happened to the rest of them?"

"The remainder were retained by the President's personal secretary, who is working with the President."

"What is her name?"

"Rose Mary Woods, sir."

"How long did she keep them?"

"At least a week, but I do not know beyond that period, sir."

"Is that the last time you saw those seven or eight, or whatever the number was, when you turned them over to the personal secretary?"

"Perhaps a period of two weeks afterwards—I can't recall the precise date I saw it, sir."

"They were in her possession away from you for about two weeks?"

"Yes, sir."

"Where, in the White House or Camp David?"

"The White House."

"What part?"

"Miss Woods' office."

"She kept them in her office for a period of two weeks?"

"Presumably."

"She returned them to you?"

"No, sir."

"Do you know what happened to the seven or eight tapes?"

"No, sir."

"You don't know to this date what happened?"

"No, sir."

"All right."

Judge Sirica suggests that "someone get word to Miss Woods that she will be called as a witness in this case."

Ben-Veniste then draws some tales from Stephen Bull about the adventures of the White House tapes. On the last weekend in September, Rose Mary Woods was working with them in a cabin at Camp David. The President of the United States went to the cabin where his secretary was at work. Then someone from the "camp-support element" came to the cabin, and, says Bull, "I think we took precautions to obscure from his view the tapes and tape-playing device." In his appearance in court on Friday, Bull testified that on two occasions in April and May he had given Haldeman twenty-two tapes. Today, Bull testifies that in July, with the President's approval, he had sent "about a half-dozen" tapes to Haldeman. The President, says Bull, told him to tell Haldeman that when he testified before the Senate committee he should base his testimony on his personal recollections rather than on information from tape recordings.

Just after he has finished his questioning of Bull, Ben-Veniste has a new thought, and returns to his lectern. He asks if any tapes were carried anywhere else.

"Yes."

"And where was that?"

"They were carried to Key Biscayne."

"And when was that?"

"That was, approximately, October 4th. I think that is—Let me look at a calendar here. That is the week after the September 29th Camp David—Make that October 4th or 5th, please."

The President and Miss Woods, says Bull, were continuing to review the tapes. Bull says that in the meantime the tapes were locked in Miss Woods' safe.

Bull says, "Miss Woods was reviewing the tapes at Key Biscayne."

"Do you mean she was typing transcripts from the tapes?" Ben-Veniste asks.

"No, sir, I did not say that she was typing a transcript."

"Did you make some conscious effort to avoid looking at what she was typing?"

"I certainly did."

Judge Sirica establishes that the tapes at Key Biscayne were those covered by the grand-jury subpoena.

"Do you know when those tapes were returned?" Judge Sirica asks.

"No, sir," replies Bull.

"Were you aware of any statement by the White House press personnel that the tapes were being secured in the White House itself under the President's personal control?" asks Judge Sirica.

Bull replies, "I read that recently in the newspaper."

As Bull leaves the courthouse, the cameras and television reporters close in on him. This scene will be on tonight's news. Cameramen have been waiting outside in the cold. The reporters ask, for the cameras, "Exactly when did the President know the tapes were not there?" Bull says that he wants to emphasize "very strongly" the distinction between missing tapes and nonrecorded conversations.

The tapes were not "missing." They were "unequivocally unavailable."

At noon, there are rumors that the President will go on television soon, for the purpose of everything from "clearing things up" to resigning.

This morning, in the New York *Times,* John Herbers writes, "The narrowness of Mr. Nixon's day-to-day contacts has become a matter of growing concern to a number of Republican leaders in Congress and to some White House aides." There have been several stories in the papers about how the President's circle has contracted to General Haig and Ron Ziegler, neither of whom is likely to question the President's judgment or bring him perspective from "the outside world." But the President's circle was never very wide, nor did it ever contain many people likely to question his judgment or bring him perspective from "the outside world."

The familiar cycle has started up again. The President suffers some misadventure, and his standing goes down. Some of the politicians call for drastic action. The President recovers, but not quite to the point where he was before. The politicians, fingers ever to the wind, temporarily back off. On Capitol Hill, it has been noticed that no Republican senators joined Brooke in his call for the President's resignation. He was left alone out on that limb. Many Democrats say that they cannot call for the President's resignation, because that would appear partisan. "We are in a holding pattern," said someone on Capitol Hill today. But the events are not in the control of either the President or those on Capitol Hill.

The Washington *Star-News* reports, "The trucking industry poured more than $600,000 into the Nixon campaign last year while it was fighting a government proposal that would have caused more competition in highway shipping." This was, says the *Star-News,* more than was contributed by the milk industry.

NOVEMBER 7

A year ago today, Richard Nixon was elected to his second term as President of the United States, with the support of just over sixty percent of those voting. The conclusion had been foregone. The only question was the size of the victory. John Chancellor, on NBC, announced the President's reëlection a very few minutes after 7 P.M., when the election-night coverage began. It was generally accepted that the President had won in a "landslide." His opponent, George McGovern, carried only Massachusetts and the District of Columbia. Mr. Nixon's loss in 1960 had been narrow, and his victory in 1968 had been narrow. In 1972, he had scored a triumph.

But something odd happened. Just before the election, the President gave an interview to Garnett Horner, of the Washington *Evening Star and Daily News* (now the *Star-News*), and the bitterness poured out. The interview, released just after the election, caused a sensation at the time, and is even more interesting in retrospect. The President attacked federal programs and the "bloated" bureaucracy. He said that in order to set an example the White House staff would be reduced—in which he may have been unconsciously, or perhaps even consciously, prophetic. The President said that he expected all his appointees to submit their resignations so that he could, if he chose, dismiss them. He said that the country had passed through a "spiritual crisis" in the nineteen-sixties, which should be attributed not simply to the war but also to the "break-down" in the "leadership class" and to "permissiveness." The President said, "The average American is just like the child in the family. You give him some responsibility and he is going to amount to something. He is going to do something. If, on the other hand, you make him completely dependent and pamper him and cater to him too much, you are going to make him soft, spoiled and eventually a very weak individual. . . . Now I realize what I have just said, in many quarters of Washington in which we live, in the Georgetown cocktail set, that will be tut-tutted by those who are living in another era." The President said he was going to "encourage [people] to do more for themselves, not only to encourage them, but to give them incentive to do more for themselves on their own without government assistance."

There followed a rather grim period in which word came from the White House about impending "shakeups." It is routine for Presidential appointees to submit their resignations after an election, in order to give the President the option to select his new "team." But the post-election tone set by the Nixon Administration was different. The President had been vindicated in the election, and now there would be vengeance against those who had been giving him trouble, thwarting him in his efforts to achieve his goals: the Congress, the press, liberals, even people within his Administration who disagreed with him on some issues. At the time, an Administration official told me that because of the narrow victory in 1968, and because the Nixon Administration was new to Washington, it had been somewhat intimidated in the first term by the power of the Congress and the press and the bureaucracy to determine the mood in Washington and to define issues. But this time, said the Administration man, "We beat the bastards." There followed the carpet bombing of North Vietnam, the impoundments, the Presi-

dent's display of contempt for the Congress by not delivering the State
of the Union address in person, and the unprecedented claims of executive privilege. There followed the shakeups, and the dispatch to the
departments and agencies of men whose credentials were their loyalty
to Haldeman and Ehrlichman, in an attempt to take total control of the
government. Through Haldeman and Ehrlichman, Nixon tried to create
a government within a government. John Ehrlichman once said, "The
President *is* the government."

Tonight, the President will go on television to give an address on the
energy crisis. All day, he has been holding meetings on energy with
labor leaders, industry leaders, governors, mayors, and congressional
leaders. If he comes across as the leader dealing with a difficult problem
that affects us all, this can help him. We need someone to handle this
problem. The Congress can't do it. The energy crisis is the President's
opportunity.

There is, of course, a large element of theatre in the Presidency, and
even though we know it, like any theatre, it often draws us in. Whoever
is President can pull back the curtain at will and use all manner of
props. As Commander-in-Chief, the President can review troops, view
awesome weapons, decorate heroes. If the President goes to church, it
is noted in the papers. The President can command television coverage.
Tonight, the President will be on television as our leader in the energy
crisis.

It is not exactly clear when the energy problem became a "crisis."
There had been predictions for years that an energy shortage was coming. A Senate subcommittee headed by Senator Philip Hart, Democrat
of Michigan, predicted it four and a half years ago. Consumption of
energy grew at exponential rates. The timetable for the crisis was
speeded up by the still unexplained sudden shortage of fuel last summer and by the cutoff of supplies by the Arab countries this fall. But all
that does not entirely account for the crisis. Government has difficulty
in dealing with a crisis before it is perceived as a crisis. Government is
not anticipatory. Our prophets are without honor. Then, when a problem
is ordained a crisis, it becomes all the rage. Congressmen hold hearings,
and Presidents announce programs. There are conferences and commis-
sions and television specials. We write books about it, spend money on
it, and set it to music. And then we become bored with it. The transportation crisis. The urban crisis. The race crisis. The environmental crisis.
Now the energy crisis. How long will the crisis of the Constitution hold
our attention?

In tonight's speech, the President announces a number of energy-
saving measures. He asks for authority to relax environmental standards,
so that more coal and high-sulphur oil can be used; to limit the number

of hours that stores and other commercial establishments may stay open, and to curtail outdoor lighting; to control highway speed limits. He asks us to drive at fifty miles an hour or less, and to lower our thermostats to sixty-eight degrees. The President of the United States setting our speedometers and our thermostats. Even though the compliance is to be voluntary, this is an unprecedented reach of federal authority. But it's probably necessary, and probably just the beginning. The President calls on Americans to "unite in the service of their country"; he calls for "a time of renewed commitment."

In a postscript, he says he will not resign. "I have no intention of walking away from the job I was elected to do," says the President. "As long as I am physically able, I am going to continue to work sixteen to eighteen hours a day for the cause of a real peace abroad and for the cause of prosperity without inflation and without war at home." At one point, he says "enemy" when he means "energy."

Today, Congress overrode the President's veto of the war-powers bill. Several people had misgivings about the bill—were concerned that in fact it gave the President more powers. But by now it had become symbolic—a contest, no matter what the bill actually said, between the President and the Congress. It is believed that one reason several Republicans voted for the first time to override a veto by President Nixon is that Republicans suffered some defeats in elections yesterday. The national significance of such off-year elections is never clear, but politicians think that they are significant, and therefore they are. Earlier this week, one Republican member of Congress said that it was important to override the veto in order to give the Congress more confidence. Therapy.

George Aiken, of Vermont, the senior Republican in the Senate, said today that Congress should impeach the President or "get off his back." People are trying to figure out what he meant. He may have meant exactly what he said.

At dinner, a Democratic senator says something startling. He says, "I hate Richard Nixon with a deep, personal hatred." Politicians don't usually say things like that. He says, "I hate Richard Nixon with a deep, personal hatred not just because of what he has done to the country but because of what he has done to politics."

NOVEMBER 8

In a White House briefing yesterday, Ron Ziegler said that the President will give detailed answers to Watergate issues and questions. It is not yet clear how this will be done. Said Ziegler, "We are compiling information on all of these problems that have come in such a rush, and we are going to communicate to the Congress, the press, and the American people the President's position more effectively than we have done in the past." Ziegler was asked some unprecedented questions. Has the President been seeing a psychiatrist? "Absolutely not" was the answer. "After the briefing," reports the Washington *Post,* "Ziegler told another reporter that Mr. Nixon also was not taking tranquillizing medicines or any other drugs."

In Egil Krogh's trial in California for the break-in of Dr. Fielding's office, the attorney for the defense has demanded that the President turn over information dealing with the creation of the plumbers. Krogh's attorney said that the documents would show that "any action which may have been taken by Krogh was pursuant to a directive of President Nixon." Krogh has asked the court to subpoena Mr. Nixon to testify. Krogh seemed somewhat different from the others. While he was in the White House, he used to engage in earnest and troubled, though not disloyal, conversations with friends. He had practiced law with Ehrlichman in Seattle. He talked about his respect for the President and Ehrlichman, but he also talked about his concern over what he said he saw to be the President's divisive stands on crime and the war. After Krogh, in trouble, resigned from the Administration in May, he said that he wanted to be part of "the healing process." The others did not say that. Krogh is said to be weighing the possibility of coöperating with the Special Prosecutor.

The A.F.L.-C.I.O. today announced a drive for the President's impeachment. The White House calls this "unseemly."

Today, in court, Rose Mary Woods said that the quality of some of the tapes was "very bad."

Elliot Richardson says that two days before Cox was fired the White House complained about his investigation of Rebozo.

William Ruckelshaus, the former Deputy Attorney General, says that the White House complained about an investigation by the Cox staff of allegations of violations of the civil rights of some peace demonstrators who sought to attend a rally held by the Reverend Dr. Billy Graham.

Representative Wilbur Mills, Democrat of Arkansas, chairman of the House Ways and Means Committee, and a powerful man, says that pressure from the news media, the Congress, and the public will force the President to resign "within a short period of time."

NOVEMBER 9

The Washington *Post* has a story saying that the President's energy proposals are too late to help in this coming winter. I am keeping my thermostat at sixty-eight degrees, and I feel very patriotic, and I'm cold.

The Dow Jones stock-market average dropped twenty-four points today—its biggest drop in eleven years.

It is considered a major event that today the President met with Republican leaders at the White House and was reported to have listened to them.

Today, Judge Sirica reduced the sentences for all those—except G. Gordon Liddy, who has refused to coöperate with any investigators—convicted in connection with the break-in at the Watergate.

NOVEMBER 12

On *Meet the Press,* Senator Charles Percy, Republican of Illinois, announces that in the coming week the President will meet with all members of Congress, in six sessions, to be "interrogated" by them. Percy says that he thinks "this is the beginning of full and total disclosure." A crescendo of Republican calls for "full and total disclosure" has been building. It is not clear what the Republicans mean by the term. The White House has been at pains to make as little "disclosure" as possible. Outsiders have no way of judging what there is to disclose. Therefore, we would have to take the President's, or the politicians', word that there has been "full and total disclosure." Are the politicians, in their eagerness to get this thing behind them, going to coöperate in the President's new maneuver? Institutional confusion is growing.

Today, there is a news story headed "GOP HILL SUPPORT AT 38-YEAR LOW." A Gallup poll shows that if national congressional elections were being held now, the Republican loss of seats in the House of Representatives would be far greater than that normally suffered by an Administration in off-year elections.

NOVEMBER 12

An important House Democrat reached into his wallet and pulled out a bill of particulars for the impeachment of the President. "I keep it there because one time I dropped it in the hallway," he explained.

I asked him why he wanted Mr. Nixon out of office.

"Because I haven't wanted that guy to have power ever since he was a member of the House and was a sore loser over a twenty-five-dollar pot in a poker game," he replied, and he continued, "The best thing for the Democrats, as many people have said, would be to keep Nixon in. If he were still in next fall, we'd sweep the congressional elections. If he were still in in 1976, we'd be sure to win. If Jerry Ford should become President before that, he could run and win. Truman did. Coolidge won, after the Harding scandals, on the argument that he had restored integrity in government. Jerry Ford could run on the ground of having improved the situation, which it would be very hard not to do."

I asked the Democrat again why, then, he wanted to get Mr. Nixon out of office.

"You have to think of the nation," said the House Democrat. He appeared to mean it. I had heard this kind of answer before when I asked why the Democrats would want to get Mr. Nixon out of office. I had been told that I had to consider the possibility that they were putting patriotism ahead of Party interests.

The Democrat said that the pressure on the President to resign would become very strong after Ford was confirmed as Vice-President. He said that the Republicans were very much concerned, and were in touch with each other now, and with members of the financial and diplomatic communities. "They are very much concerned, especially, about the military alert last month," he said. "The alert did it. For us, too."

A number of people say that there has to be "one more thing," one more big revelation, one more earthquake, before the President can be removed from office. Some people have almost become addicted to these earthquakes, and take some satisfaction in their horror. I asked the Democrat if he subscribed to the "one more thing" theory. He said that the movement for impeachment would proceed in any event. "The House Judiciary Committee will build the case before the vote," he said. "It won't turn back."

The tapes have struck again. Today, the White House announced that the President could not find the dictation belt that recorded his recollections of his April 15th meeting with Dean, of which it is also said that there is no tape. Twelve days ago, Buzhardt had promised that the dictation belt would be produced, and in June, in a letter to Cox, he referred to such a dictation belt. This latest loss came to light in the course of a White House effort—which included a statement issued by the President—"to help dispel those doubts" about the two nonexistent conversations. The President offered to make available to the court a dictation-belt recording of his recollections of his March 21st conversations with John Dean, as well as a dictation-belt recording of his recollection of the telephone conversation on June 20th, 1972—three days after the break-in at the Democratic National Committee headquarters—with Mitchell, of which the White House says there is no tape. In his statement, the President expressed concern over "misconceptions about this matter" which have arisen "simply because certain basic facts are not being presented to the American people."

Ziegler gave a briefing to the press and also made himself available to network correspondents for interviews. In the briefing, Ziegler said, "Now I know that the dramatic news lead would be—and I say that respectfully—that something else is missing." Ziegler said that the "objective" of the briefing was to convince the American people that the President was being forthcoming with the information. The President ended his statement as follows: "It is my hope that these steps will clear up this aspect of the Watergate matter once and for all."

The stock market dropped eleven more points today.

NOVEMBER 13

In today's Washington *Post,* there is a photograph of Donald Segretti ("dirty tricks"), thirty-two, going to jail.

Leon Jaworski, the new Special Prosecutor, filed a brief in court yesterday arguing that "not even the highest office in the land" has the authority to break the law in the name of national security. Jaworski said, "In the recent past, national security has become a kind of talisman, invoked by officials at widely disparate levels of government service to justify a wide range of apparently illegal activities."

Cox said in a speech yesterday—he is still at it—that he had been told that the President had said that Cox should "keep the hell out of" the matter of the raid on Ellsberg's psychiatrist's office. Cox also said today that the White House had refused to give him access to the files on the milk industry's campaign contributions.

A Gallup poll says that the public is against removing the President from office by a percentage of fifty-four to thirty-seven.

NOVEMBER 14

The rift between the President and the Republicans is even wider than I had thought. Today, I went to see a Republican senator who had been very loyal to the President. I asked him if it was, as some said, just a matter of time before the Republicans broke with the President. He replied, "Yes. I considered myself a Nixon supporter. I faulted those around Nixon—felt that they used us and then cast us aside. When we got into Watergate, my gut reaction was to stand up and flail at the critics. But, as you may have noticed, not many of us did that. We didn't know. There was a suspicion on the part of the senators. We figured, why should we stick our necks out? We don't know what to think. There is one disclosure after another. Some of us would be willing to lose our Senate seats if we felt that the President was not involved. But I won't stand on this desk and take an oath that the President has convinced me that the President is totally innocent. It's going to take more than a statement by the President. I'll need an independent source now—maybe Judge Sirica, maybe the House of Representatives. I'll go out and charge into the critics if I feel that I'm armed with the facts, but I can't feel that now. I call it a no-win situation for the Republicans now. If you go to speak to a Republican group, they are probably for the President, and they'll say afterward, 'Senator X didn't stand up for the President,' but there's probably a reporter there, who will write about it if you do. It's bad. I think many Republicans are waiting now. They've been used. I don't see what the President can do himself to restore the lost confidence. Hedging is legal, and a lot of it is done in politics, but it's difficult for us now. So we have to ask ourselves, 'If there's no way out for the President, how many others should suffer?' Senators and House members will lose seats. And there are all the people outside the political arena who are losing faith. If he's clean and he can find a springboard, and it doesn't break with him jumping up and down on it, we might survive next year."

The senator said there were three groups of Republican senators: those who had not supported the President at any point, and who, the other Republicans noticed, were now the strongest politically; those who remained loyal to the President; and those he described as "back and forth." "There aren't many gung-ho Nixon types in the cloakroom these days," he said. "We wonder how he can stay. We wonder how much he can be enjoying this. The main thing is that there is now a disbelief. How can we believe? What can we tell the people? I have decided that I don't know of any recourse but an impeachment inquiry. That or Judge Sirica. It's too late for him to get up and say, 'I didn't tell the American people about this or that, and I regret that.' It's too late. But he won't give up. He just doesn't give up. There's nothing you can really point to about which you can say that that is what is causing time to run out, but a lot of us feel that it is running out. People here seem to feel Jerry Ford has gone over well with the American people. They find him acceptable—more acceptable than Nixon." The senator said that if, as many thought, Ford had been chosen to provide insurance against the President's impeachment, because of his apparently lacklustre credentials for becoming President, it was turning out to be "just the reverse." The senator continued, "At first, when they said to us, 'Come to the White House,' we thought that was quite something. But that doesn't work anymore. We're not awestruck anymore. They kept telling us that this story would go away. It's still here."

Said another Republican senator, "We keep weighing having him out of office versus limping along for three years. We are losing confidence in his ability to turn it around." The senator said he was getting letters from third-grade children who were troubled about the President. He said, "This is deeper on the college campuses than Cambodia was." Finally, he said, "When it's a question of me and thee in politics, it's usually thee who has to go."

A federal judge ruled today that the firing of Archibald Cox was illegal. He said that the action by Acting Attorney General Robert Bork violated a federal regulation that had the force of law. The ruling did not have the effect of reinstating Cox.

I shared a taxi from Capitol Hill this afternoon with two men who were getting off at the Justice Department. "You work at the Justice Department?" the taxi-driver said to one of them. "I guess you stand a pretty good chance of being Attorney General."

NOVEMBER 15

The Washington *Post* reports that Representative John Anderson, Republican of Illinois, who is an important member of the House, has said that he has decided not to run for the Senate next year. Anderson cited "the spectre of Watergate" as the reason for his decision. He said a private poll taken for him in Illinois showed that forty-six percent of the voters there thought Watergate was the most important issue.

The Administration is reported to be divided over whether to impose gasoline rationing.

A Washington *Post* feature on Peter Rodino, the sixty-five-year-old Democrat of New Jersey, and chairman of the House Judiciary Committee, brings to the surface a question that there has been in conversation about Rodino, whose committee is to conduct the impeachment inquiry. Rodino was close to, and at one time shared a Washington apartment with, former Representative Hugh Addonizio, who, like Rodino, represented Newark. Addonizio later became mayor of Newark and recently went to jail on charges of corruption. The *Post* points out that Rodino represents "a region where organized crime has been entrenched and political corruption common." It quotes the United States Attorney who prosecuted Addonizio as saying, "There's never been an inquiry about Rodino, never the slightest anything. In my opinion, Pete Rodino is an honest man and a fine public servant." The *Post* quotes Rodino as saying that he would not know a mobster "if I fell over him." Rodino told the *Post* that there was nothing in his background that the Administration could use to induce him to go easy on impeachment.

It has come to that. We wonder, because we have to, who has what on whom. We assume that the question of potential blackmail extends to many levels—staff members, lawyers, anyone in Washington peripherally involved in the question of the President's fate. It is an unpleasant way to have to think about the Constitution, but there is no escaping it.

In Senate hearings yesterday, Ford's record on civil rights was attacked by leaders of the civil-rights movement. But now even less attention is being paid to the hearings on Ford.

Yesterday, Judge Sirica issued a statement saying, "If the President thinks it advisable to waive any privilege and make tapes or other material public, he of course is free to do so at any time."

Leon Jaworski has told the court that he has been assured of access to White House tapes and documents regarding the work of the plumbers. Earlier this month, in the court in Washington, Krogh's attorney indicated that the defense will seek to show that Krogh lied about the work of the plumbers because he had been under orders from the President to maintain secrecy about the plumbers' activities. Two days ago, the judge in the case, Gerhard Gesell, termed Krogh's argument that he lied under orders "a Nuremberg defense." (In the Nuremberg war-crimes trials, some former Nazi high officials defended themselves on the ground that they had been following orders. This line of defense was not accepted by the tribunal.) Judge Gesell said, "I don't think that's an argument I can entertain. We would have no society." Today, Judge Gesell dismissed the motion by Krogh's lawyers to dismiss the indictment on the ground that Krogh had been ordered to lie.

Tonight, on the television news, the President is standing in front of a giant replica, with colored lights, of the American flag. It may be the largest replica of the flag that I have ever seen. The President is beaming and waving his arms over his head. The scene is from his appearance this morning before the National Association of Realtors, meeting at the Sheraton-Park Hotel here. He says, "As far as the President of the United States is concerned, he has not violated his trust and he isn't going to violate his trust now."

As a powerful man starts to fall, or as his power begins to decline, one can almost sense people pulling in their lines of credit. It is a cruel but sure judgment that people who know about power make. Unseen, an enormous alteration in his situation takes place. The alteration affects the kinds of people he is able to hire, the willingness of people to go to great lengths, take risks, for him. One senses that this has happened to Richard Nixon. But there is also a deep fear of moving against him. The fear is felt even by some of those who believe that he should be removed from power. He is still the President, and the levers of power are still within his reach. In part, the paralysis stems from fear of making a move that will not succeed. This is not the sort of struggle one can afford to lose. Many businessmen want the President to go, but they are afraid to speak out—which is characteristic. Businessmen who were disturbed about the continuing war in Southeast Asia were reluctant to speak out on that. I have asked a number of businessmen, and their Washington lawyers, about this reluctance. Most of them offer the same explanation: that business has too much business with the government to speak out against it. There are the merger applications, the contract bids, the airline-route requests, the license renewals. The President's power to reward or punish continues, even if the President is in trouble. Businessmen believe that the enemies list was real. When others were laughing at the enemies list, one businessman, whose politics are very liberal, was admonished by his board of directors not to take any action or any position that might land him on an enemies list.

Many politicians are also frightened. They do not want to be on the losing side of this issue. Many politicians are less frightened of Richard Nixon than they used to be, but the fright is still there. Some citizens are frightened. Perhaps the sense that this was a tough and punitive Administration, one that would give trouble to those who gave it trouble, was deeper—and has had more lasting effect—than we may have thought. Perhaps, in fact, it was a very effective posture for an Administration to take. Perhaps, in fact, it has set another precedent. Memoranda written by Nixon Administration members on how to frighten the media—through license challenges, anti-trust suits—have recently been made public. We also know that many of their recommendations were carried out. There was a time, not long ago, when many people stopped to consider whether to speak out on an issue, sign a petition, file a lawsuit—for fear of retribution. Some still do.

John Connally is interviewed by Daniel Schorr on the CBS news tonight, and appears to be very upset. He has been subpoenaed by the Ervin committee. There are allegations that Connally helped collect funds from the milk producers, and helped persuade the President to override other officials and raise the price supports for milk. On television tonight, Connally complains about "the atmosphere and the times in which we live, the inferences, the innuendos, the rumors." Connally says, "And I must say, Dan, that if this environment prevails that exists today in the United States and in Washington, I tell you very frankly, I'll have no plans for '76."

NOVEMBER 16

The President is going South, where the climate and his political reception promise to be warmer than in Washington or other parts of the country. He will make some public appearances. It is becoming more complicated for the President to travel. Now he is under criticism for the amount of fuel that such trips consume. Yesterday, Gerald Warren told reporters that the cruising speed of the President's jet, the "Spirit of '76," will be reduced from five hundred and twenty-five miles an hour to four hundred and seventy-five, and that the spare plane usually sent on such trips will be grounded for this one. The Presidential helicopters will, however, fly to Key Biscayne for the President's use, and his special limousine will be flown South in a separate plane.

This week, the Ervin committee—for three days—was instructive on the subject of money. Executives of various kinds of corporations, including shipbuilding, oil, and airlines, told how they raised and turned over illegal campaign contributions. Some of the executives and the corporations themselves have been charged by the Special Prosecutor with making illegal corporate contributions. The testimony illustrates how the illegal funds were gathered—through entering fake bonuses and false expense reports, through disguising the funds as investments in land, or through transferring the funds from foreign subsidiaries. Last spring, when the revelations of large cash contributions had begun, a Washington lawyer was asked at a party how it was that corporations could come up with such large sums in cash. We had read that oil-company executives had stuffed seven hundred thousand dollars in cash and checks into a suitcase, which was then flown to Washington, in a jet owned by Pennzoil. A successful businessman, puzzled, said to the lawyer that he did not understand how a business could secure substantial amounts of cash. The lawyer, who knows a lot, said, "Oil companies can."

The businessmen who testified before the Ervin committee spoke of the "pressure" on them to contribute to the President's reëlection. One said that both John Mitchell and Maurice Stans had asked him for funds on various occasions. He said, "That is just a little bit different than somebody collecting for the Boy Scouts." An oil-company executive said he feared that if his company did not contribute, it would be on an Administration "blacklist" or at the "bottom of the totem pole." He said he was aware that other oil companies were contributing.

There is in this subject of money a problem of definition. The law makes a distinction between "extortion" and "bribery." The distinction may be much clearer in the words of the law than in reality. The way the act of making a contribution is interpreted may depend upon what a prosecutor is looking for. The more the businessmen portray themselves as having been, in effect, victims of "extortion," the less they are subject to prosecution for "bribery." This is what made Agnew so angry. Moreover, many contributors can say, in all honesty, that they gave because they believed in the politician. And many politicians can say, in all honesty, that they took an action that happened to be in the contributor's interest because they believed the action was right. It is usually fruitless to search for the specific *quid pro quo* between a campaign gift and a political decision by the recipient. The parties to these acts usually do not talk to each other about them. It is rare that the *quid* and the *quo* are discussed. Dita Beard's memorandum (which she later described as a "forgery" and a "hoax") received so much notoriety precisely because it broke this well-established rule of procedure. It contained the suggestion, at least, of a *quid pro quo* concerning "our noble commitment"—for I.T.T. to contribute four hundred thousand dollars to the Republican convention that was not held in San Diego in exchange for a favorable anti-trust decision. Many politicians make a point of not knowing what their fund-raisers do. In his October 26th press conference, President Nixon said that he has made it a practice to refuse "to have any discussion of contributions."

The Ervin committee's attention to the subject of money was limited. We still do not know to what extent the government was sold in the last election. Many businessmen give to the Republican Party because they believe that its policies are better for America. Some believe that this is the only way to balance the influence of unions on the Democrats. Nixon officials often point to the "checkoffs" of union dues which go for political activities, and ask how these are different from the corporate contributions to the Nixon elections. They point out that corporate executives have often contributed to Democrats, too.

As with other areas in which Nixon officials cite precedents, they have a point, and at the same time they miss the larger point. For years, it has been widely known that labor, through its contributions of money and manpower, has had a strong influence on the Democratic Party. It has been widely known that there have been underground rivers of money flowing into campaigns, and that some government decisions have been guided by the access of money to power. In recent years, two things made this a problem of a different order, and of a different nature. The first was the sudden, rapid growth in the costs of campaigns in the nineteen-sixties, largely because of television advertising. The second was that in raising money, as in other things, the Nixon Administration overreached. Like others around Nixon, Nixon's fund-raisers did not recognize limits. Maurice Stans and Herbert Kalmbach carried to unprecedented lengths the practice of raising money from those who did business with the government. In the process, they broke the game wide open. The Common Cause suit helped us to see what they had done. And Watergate changed the atmosphere. Some candidates for Congress are now said to be having difficulty finding treasurers for their campaigns. It is said that businessmen do not want to get trapped again, and will be reluctant to be so generous in the future. The politicians are beginning to wonder what they will do for money.

Inevitably, stories are leaking out about this week's meetings between the President and members of Congress. Members of Congress are notorious sieves. Senator Percy was not exactly correct in saying that the President would meet with every member of Congress. The President met with Republicans and selected Southern Democrats. The President has done his arithmetic: this is the group that could save him in a vote on impeachment in the House or conviction in the Senate. At some of the meetings, the President spoke at length on the energy crisis and foreign policy as well as Watergate, leaving little time for questions. Someone has told me that at one meeting Senator Eastland, in a burst of enthusiasm, said, "We believe in you, Mr. President," and that Senator Stennis then said to Senator Eastland, "Quiet! Let the boy speak." At another meeting, Senator Roman Hruska, Republican of Nebraska, said, "The State of Nebraska is behind you, Mr. President." Some senators are reported in the papers to have told the President that he must be more "frank and open." The President is said to have suggested that Elliot Richardson had not told the truth when he said he would not be a party to prohibiting Cox from trying to secure more documents. The President is said to have suggested that Richardson took the position he did at the end because he wants to be governor of Massachusetts. Addressing Senator Charles Mathias, Republican of Maryland, during a discussion of the Administration's problems, the President mentioned that contributors to former Vice-President Agnew had also contributed to Senator Mathias. (There has been no suggestion that Mathias has been connected in any way with illegal contributions.) The senators interpreted the President's remark to Mathias as an indication of the kind of research that the White House had done on those who might oppose him. Mathias later said to the President that it was no longer adequate for the President to assert executive privilege or national security as a reason for doing certain things. He asked for a detailed explanation of his approval of the plumbers and of the Huston plan for admittedly illegal intelligence-gathering on American citizens. The President said that he would send a report to the Congress on the plumbers and the Huston plan.

This week, Senator Howard Cannon, Democrat of Nevada and chairman of the committee examining the nomination of Ford, said, "There's always the chance that we may be confirming a President, not just a Vice-President."

The President said some optimistic things about the energy crisis today as he signed a bill permitting the construction of an oil pipeline in Alaska, and the stock market went up. The energy crisis has caused the environmentalists several reverses. Like civil rights and poverty activists, the environmentalists were indulged until their objectives were seen as inconveniencing the majority.

On the news tonight, Julie Nixon Eisenhower and Anne Armstrong, a Presidential counsellor, pose with a suitcase containing messages of support for the President. The suitcase was not the happiest choice of container.

At 7 P.M., there is no choice but to watch the President being questioned by newspaper editors meeting at Walt Disney World, in Orlando, Florida. The buildup to this appearance has been akin to that which precedes the Super Bowl. One television announcer says that this is part of the President's "new campaign to increase his credibility." The President will submit to questions about Watergate. He has, of course, submitted to questions about Watergate before, but this, the week of what has come to be called Operation Candor, is the week to "turn it around." The President is forceful, strong-voiced, landing on certain words for emphasis. He says he spoke on the telephone with John Mitchell "at the *end* of the day in the *family* quarters." He talks of things he will "disclose to this audience." Politicians and officials usually prepare some "disclosures" for press conferences and interviews. The point is to try to set the agenda and assure the headline—on the right subject.

Tonight, the President discloses that he telephoned John Mitchell on June 20, 1972, in order to cheer him up after the men were caught in the Watergate. He goes into detail about why a tape ran out, and we are farther and farther from the point. He explains that his taping system was "a Sony, a little Sony that they had," and that "what they had are these little lapel mikes in my desk." As he says that, he rubs the flag in his lapel. He says, with a smile, that the equipment President Johnson had "was, incidentally, much better equipment." (There have been reports that Presidents Kennedy and Johnson had some telephone conversations and meetings recorded, but even these reports do not indicate that either had a taping system on anything like the scale of Nixon's.) He adds that he is not criticizing Sonys. An editor asks him his reaction to the discovery that tapes of the conversations with Dean and Mitchell did not exist, and the President replies that it was one of "great disappointment, because I wanted the evidence out." He says that the plumbers were established to stop leaks of information that were endangering the national security, including one "so serious that even Senator Ervin and Senator Baker agreed it should not be disclosed." Asked how Watergate could happen, the President replies, "Seventy-two was a very busy year for me." Arguing that measures have been taken to hold down the consumption of fuel during his trip to the South, Nixon points out that the back-up plane had not been brought on this trip. He adds that if his own plane goes down, "it goes down, and then they don't have to impeach." He talks about his Vice-Presidential papers and gives some details of his finances, and then he says, "Let me just say this: I want to say this to the television audience—I made my mistakes, but in all of my years of public life, I have never profited, never profited from public service. I have earned every cent. And in all of my years of public life, I have never obstructed justice." He says that he welcomes "this kind of examination, because people have got to know whether or not their President is a crook," and then he says, "Well, I am not a crook."

Societies need unifying symbols, and the Presidency has been ours. We cling to the idea that the Presidency is worthy of our respect, because we want it to be. In linking his fate with the fate of the Presidency itself, Nixon is making his ordeal ours. In trying, through his office, to protect himself against the damage from all that has happened, he has attached the damage to the office. That is part of what makes this such a painful time. It is humiliating to see a President subjected to humiliation, whatever its origin. It's hard to watch him struggle to answer questions that should never have to be asked. It is difficult to watch a President running and maneuvering like a hunted man. There are stories in the papers these days about the Afo-A-Kom, the sacred statue of the kingdom of Kom, in Cameroon. The statue, a symbol of the political and religious heritage of the people of Kom, had long been missing, and was recently found in the United States. It is being returned to Kom. The well-being of the tribe depends upon its presence. When the totem is gone, the tribe is in trouble. We seem to have an almost totemistic view of the Presidency. Our well-being is involved with it. In Nixon's frequent reminders that he is the President, he speaks to something in us.

8

MONDAY. At a press briefing in Macon, Georgia, where the President spoke yesterday, Ron Ziegler said that the response to the President's performance Saturday evening was highly favorable, and "quantitatively larger" than the adverse reaction to the firing of Archibald Cox. Ziegler also said that "a lot" of the reaction to the firing of Cox was "manufactured and coördinated" by "traditional adversaries of the President." When the President's plane landed at Robins Air Force Base, outside Macon, a crowd estimated at about twenty thousand met him. The crowd cheered. It carried signs saying "We Love and Support President Nixon" and "Keep Up the Good Work."

On the Op-Ed page of the New York *Times* is an article by Charles Colson calling for public financing of political campaigns; for the barring of elected officials from any source of personal gain beyond their salaries while they are in office; for complete financial disclosure, including disclosure of tax returns, by public officials; and for a law requiring publication of all contacts by members of Congress with the executive branch. This is almost as thoroughgoing a reform agenda as any that has been suggested. Colson, forty-two, delighted in being known as the "tough guy" in the White House—even cultivated the image. His memorandum saying that he would "walk over my grandmother if necessary" to get Richard Nixon reëlected was famous—if, in the light of what we now know, perhaps understated. Colson seems to have been thrashing about for a way to confront Watergate. He left the White House in March of this year, and began to practice law in Washington, where he might have hoped to benefit from his well-placed contacts. After Watergate broke, he kept his distance, at least publicly, from the White House for a while. Then for a while he was all over the media, defending the President. Then he disappeared again. Now, like Agnew, he is calling for political reform. The Bible tells us to welcome penitents.

The stock market dropped twenty-eight points today.

The current *Newsweek* reports that Charles Colson and the President met with representatives of the milk industry in 1970, a year before the better-known meeting between the President and the milk producers which preceded the raising of price supports for milk. It has also been revealed recently, as a result of the suit brought by Ralph Nader against the price-support increase, that in 1969 the milk producers made a retroactive payment of a hundred thousand dollars to the President's 1968 campaign in order to win a more sympathetic hearing from the new Administration. The payment was made by Milton Semer, a Washington lawyer and former assistant to President Johnson. Semer, according to a deposition presented to a federal court last week, delivered the hundred thousand dollars in cash in a briefcase to Herbert Kalmbach in California. Semer said that Kalmbach told him the money would be used for White House favorites in the 1970 campaign. It has subsequently been learned, according to Saturday's Washington *Post,* that Kalmbach accumulated a "trust fund" of one million seven hundred thousand dollars in money ostensibly left over from the 1968 campaign. Among the expenditures from it, according to the *Post,* was one of about a hundred and forty thousand dollars to pay Anthony Ulasewicz, the private investigator hired by the White House in 1969, and Donald Segretti. The *Post* story goes on to say that four hundred thousand dollars was to have been expended in an effort to defeat George Wallace in his 1970 campaign for governor of Alabama. Kalmbach has testified before the Ervin committee that he was instructed to disburse four hundred thousand dollars to people whom he did not know, and that half of this was disbursed by Haldeman's brother-in-law. Kalmbach said he subsequently heard that "part or all" of this money went into the Alabama campaign, but he said he had never been told by anyone in authority that its purpose was to defeat Wallace. Haldeman testified before the Ervin committee that he authorized the transfer of campaign money left over from 1968 to support Wallace's 1970 opponent. Kalmbach has testified that most of the remainder of the money purportedly left over from 1968 was spent on the President's reëlection.

In 1970, I asked Murray Chotiner, sitting in a White House office, his desk littered with computer print-outs and a catalogue of federal grant programs, what he was doing. He replied, "To infer that the White House is engaged in any political endeavors isn't correct. The White House isn't the place for it, and the public would resent it."

NOVEMBER 20

The White House has been granted a six-day delay in turning over the seven tapes to the court. It told the court that it needed more time to prepare an analysis and an index of the materials, because one of the lawyers was ill.

George Gallup told the Republican governors, who have been meeting in Memphis, that it was "wishful thinking" to believe that the Republican Party would not be damaged badly by Watergate.

A Harris poll published in today's paper shows that only twenty-five percent of those surveyed consider themselves Republicans. This is an all-time low. It represents a drop of two percentage points since August. But the Democratic allegiance has also dropped—by one percentage point, from forty-eight to forty-seven. The most interesting figure is the one for those who call themselves independents, which has risen from twenty-five percent to twenty-eight percent. There are now, according to this survey, more people who call themselves independents than people who call themselves Republicans. The study shows that the professed allegiance to both parties has been dropping constantly since 1968, when this particular survey began, while the percentage of those who identify with neither party has steadily grown.

NOVEMBER 21

Yesterday, the Senate Committee on Rules and Administration unanimously approved the nomination of Gerald Ford to be Vice-President of the United States. The approval came one month and eight days after Ford's nomination. Senator Cannon said that the committee had conducted "the most exhaustive investigation of a nominee ever undertaken by a Senate committee." The House Judiciary Committee plans to complete its hearings on Ford's nomination today.

In today's New York *Times,* David Binder reports that the Soviet note that led to the worldwide military alert "carried an implied threat rather than an actual threat of the dispatch of Soviet troops to the Suez war zone." Binder reports that the Soviet note said: "We strongly urge that we both send forces to enforce the cease-fire and, if you do not, we may be obliged to consider acting alone." Binder also reports that during the period that decisions were made on how to respond to the note, and the alert was ordered, the President remained in his living quarters in the White House. He reports that the note was the second one delivered to the State Department on the evening of October 24th by Soviet Ambassador Anatoly Dobrynin: the first had urged the United States to participate in a joint peacekeeping force, and we declined. After the second note was received, Binder reports, Kissinger telephoned the President and suggested that the response "should be military as well as political," and the President agreed. Binder reports that the President is said by his aides to have "remained in charge throughout" but that he remained in his White House residence, receiving messages from Kissinger and Schlesinger, empowering them to manage the crisis, to decide the form and method of the United States' response. What had been described as a meeting of the National Security Council was essentially a meeting of Kissinger and Schlesinger, with the Chairman of the Joint Chiefs of Staff, Admiral Thomas Moorer, attending, and the Director of the C.I.A., William Colby, called in belatedly. The Soviet Union was not notified directly of the alert. The "hot line" was not used. The Soviet Union was expected to learn of the alert through its own electronic intelligence. It is not clear why it was assumed, or whether it was assumed, that the Soviet Union would react to the discovery calmly. The Israeli and British ambassadors were informed of the alert, and the other NATO allies were notified through the North Atlantic Council in Brussels, which was slow, because of mechanical failures, to get the news to other allied capitals. Binder says that in retrospect associates of Kissinger acknowledged that the process of informing our allies was "botched up."

Yesterday, the President met with the Republican governors, who were meeting in Memphis. Governor Winfield Dunn of Tennessee reported afterward that when the President was asked if there were "any more bombs" about to explode in regard to Watergate, the President replied, "If there are any more bombs, I'm not aware of them."

This morning, I called on an official of the A.F.L.-C.I.O. The labor federation's offices are in a mammoth building on Sixteenth Street. The building has a marble façade and is on the north side of Lafayette Park, across the park from the White House. There had seemed to be, for a time, a cordiality between the A.F.L.-C.I.O.—or, at least, its president, George Meany—and President Nixon. In 1970, Meany was the honored guest at a White House Labor Day dinner. Meany appeared to support the President's reëlection. The White House had designed several of its policy positions to please the labor leader, because it needed the political support of his troops. The Administration had talked of fashioning "the New Majority," wherein the interests of both business and labor would be accommodated. Charles Colson, the man in charge of White House liaison with interest groups, was matchmaker for Mr. Nixon's courtship of labor. George Meany grumbled over the President's trips to China and Russia, and growled over his economic controls, but when it mattered—in the 1972 election—he remained neutral. His distaste for George McGovern was undisguised.

The A.F.L.-C.I.O. is now leading a drive to impeach President Nixon. It is the largest and most important organization to be doing so. The A.F.L.-C.I.O. represents a hundred and eleven unions, with a total membership of nearly fourteen million workers. I wanted to find out why it was seeking the President's impeachment. I asked the labor official—who requested that he not be named—what had caused the final falling out. "There was never any falling together," he replied. "Labor's feelings about Nixon go back to the Jerry Voorhis campaign. We opposed him in every election except the last one. We never had any regard for him as a politician or as a person. There was a considerable amount of misconstruction of the nature of any relationship we had with the Nixon Administration after the 1968 election. The Nixon Administration went through the period of its so-called 'New Majoritarian' enterprise. There was some romancing. The highlight was that Labor Day dinner at the White House, which we were not enthusiastic about to begin with—but the President of the United States is hard to refuse. As soon as that thing was held, all the labor reporters wrote about the 'love affair' between us and Nixon. But what would they have written if the President had extended the invitation and we had said no? They'd have written 'Labor Boycotts White House,' 'Labor Insults Nixon.' We knew we were being sort of used at the Labor Day dinner, but there wasn't a hell of a lot we could do about it. We have a long string of issues in the executive and on Capitol Hill." He named Social Security, the budgets for the Department of Labor and the Department of Health, Education, and Welfare, appointments to the National Labor Relations Board, the money spent for medical research, and the appointment of labor attaches in American embassies. The list of issues, he said, "could be as long as your arm." He continued, "We can't say publicly that the wrong guy got elected. We'll talk to whoever we can. When the White House was working on 'the New Majority,' it worked around the A.F.L.-C.I.O. leadership. Colson built up telephone contacts with their own labor buddies they thought they could build up around us. They used to have little meetings in Blair House with industrialists and a few labor people. We'd usually hear about it." Blair House is the government's guest house for state visits.

I asked him about the relationship between the A.F.L.-C.I.O. and Peter Brennan, who was formerly the head of the New York Building and Construction Trades Councils and is now the Secretary of Labor.

"We hardly ever used to see Pete," he said.

The A.F.L.-C.I.O. did not anticipate McGovern's nomination, felt that it would be a disaster for the Democratic Party, and tried to stop it at the Convention. The A.F.L.-C.I.O. also worried that McGovern's nomination might cost the Democrats control of the Congress. The A.F.L.-C.I.O. cares very much about maintaining Democratic control of the Congress; therefore, it declined to endorse McGovern.

Between the 1972 election and the drive to impeach the President, there occurred the following events, as the A.F.L.-C.I.O. official recounted them: the President's veto of a bill raising the minimum wage; the impoundment of funds; the development of "government by veto." "Comes Watergate," said the labor official, "and we became convinced that not only was this man going to use his last four years to dismantle a great many programs that we thought were vital. We had thought maybe this man would want to use his last four years to make a record for history. We found out he was a man who wanted to use his last four years to get even, in a vindictive sense. There was no reservoir of good will toward Richard Nixon in this organization. We had gone through the fights over Haynsworth and Carswell against him."

For the A.F.L.-C.I.O., as for others, the impetus to try to remove the President from office developed from a combination of motives. The labor official cited "the spectacle of the apparatus he had set up to pervert the Justice Department, the F.B.I., the I.R.S.," and said, "It wasn't a confrontation between the Presidency and the Congress or the courts. It was a confrontation between the Presidency and the American people. That's what was at stake." He continued, "The Brennan thing was an exacerbating factor. Peter Brennan was not our nominee; he was Chuck Colson's. We never felt it was a good idea to put a trade unionist in as Secretary of Labor. We'd rather have a civilized employer or a professional middleman. A trade unionist is always going to be put in an anomalous position. We accepted the Brennan appointment and supported him, and then became rapidly disillusioned with the guy." The official said that "Brennan double-crossed us" on the minimum-wage issue by supporting the A.F.L.-C.I.O.'s position in his confirmation hearings and then opposing it in testimony after he became Secretary of Labor. He said that Brennan's predecessor, James Hodgson, "used to come over and tell us what positions he was going to take, and we could argue with him." Brennan, he said, "never darkened our door."

At its meeting in May of this year, when Watergate was breaking, the A.F.L.-C.I.O. Executive Council called on the President to ensure a full and independent investigation into Watergate. "It was quite obvious," said the official, "that we could not go into a fall convention and duck that question." The official did not mention it, but one A.F.L.-C.I.O. official was on the enemies list. At the biennial convention in Miami Beach in October, the A.F.L.-C.I.O. Executive Council held a breakfast meeting and decided to call for the President's resignation or impeachment. "Logic leads you that way," said the official, "unless you decide that nothing is going to be done about it." He then said, "We believe that there are grounds. The A.F.L.-C.I.O. has published its bill of particulars, and is devoting a section of each weekly newsletter to an item in the list. Beyond that, it is for the good of the country. As long as this guy is in power, it means that every damn issue that's up is going to be filtered through Watergate. Remember, he put the country on a military alert. It's a terribly dangerous way to live for three years. We don't have any illusions that by impeaching Nixon we'll find a shortcut to progressive government. That's not in the cards."

I asked the labor official what he thought would happen on the question of impeaching the President.

"It is always true that in a closely contested issue there are a lot of people who want to wait and see," he said. "It's a mass of fuzz at the moment. It depends on developments. Remember, we're dealing with a guy who has been laid out for dead many times."

I asked the official how he felt that his own constituents—workers— viewed Nixon. His answer said some interesting things about how judgments are formed by "the public."

"Our people never cared for Nixon," he said. "The suspicion was always very deep. He played on an element that working people have, that most people have—they don't think it's wrong to be patriotic. He understood that. It's simply astute politics to know your clients. The tragedy of the Democrats is that they didn't know their clients. Nixon used to be a very effective television performer, but more and more, people have gotten inoculated against his devices. And now Nixon stands exposed as a hypocrite. Of *course* most people believe in law and order. But they believe it should apply to everyone."

It is the afternoon before Thanksgiving, and the city is quiet. A number of people have already left town. Others are leaving their offices early. This year, people seem to be particularly eager to close up shop and stop thinking about what we have been thinking about.

On the news tonight, another "bomb" explodes. It is announced that one of the seven tapes is "inaudible" for eighteen minutes. The tape is of the meeting on June 20th, three days after the Watergate break-in, between the President and Haldeman. The White House has said that during the portion that has been obliterated by a "tone" the President and Haldeman were discussing "scheduling."

On tonight's news, government officials say that the energy shortage will be greater than has been predicted.

NOVEMBER 22

Thanksgiving, and the tenth anniversary of the assassination of John Kennedy. It is a beautiful day—warm enough to play tennis outdoors.

It is reported in the papers that yesterday Gerald Ford, in his confirmation hearings, said he favored Constitutional amendments to permit school prayers, to forbid school busing for racial integration, and to let states decide whether abortions should be permitted.

At a press conference yesterday, Kissinger, reminded of his pledge to give out the information justifying the military alert, said, "It's a mistake to assume that everything that is said in a press conference is fully considered."

Yesterday, a federal judge ruled that the Administration's impoundment of money for education was un-Constitutional. There have been several court tests of the Administration's impoundments. In almost every decision thus far, the Administration's action has been held illegal.

Evans and Novak report in their column that after Jaworski filed his brief in court on November 12th contending that the President could not break the law in the name of national security, he was summoned to the White House and told of a national-security matter that the White House said was so sensitive it should not be divulged. They write that Jaworski decided to proceed with his inquiry into the activities of the plumbers.

In court yesterday, Buzhardt said that "all of the other tapes subpoenaed have been audible throughout." Richard Ben-Veniste said that the tape recording of the conversation between the President and Haldeman had been "partially obliterated." A panel of six scientists has been chosen jointly by the White House and the Watergate prosecutors "to study the authenticity and integrity" of the tapes. Someone has told me a number of interesting things about the scientists. One of the six is the director of the Haskins Laboratories. There is a certain symmetry to this. A few years ago, the Haskins Laboratories invented a machine that can create a human-sounding voice. Another member of the panel was involved in restoring Enrico Caruso records by removing scratches and other obstructive noises. There is some thought that he might be able to restore the voice of Haldeman. Some of this expertise grew out of an interest on the part of the Pentagon in finding ways to stop the Russians from jamming *Voice of America* broadcasts. Now it will be applied to Richard Nixon's tapes.

CBS has released a poll showing that more people believe the news media than believe the President.

A Harris poll says forty-three percent of those polled think that the President should resign. Previous percentages registered in favor of this proposition were thirty-six in October, thirty-one in September, twenty-eight in August, and fourteen last May.

The President has gone to Camp David, where, according to his aides, he will work on the energy crisis.

The Washington *Post* has a summary of "more than three dozen types of crimes that were either committed or proposed in connection with the Watergate scandal." The categories of crimes are: conspiracy; breaking and entering; bribery; perjury and suborning perjury; lying to the F.B.I.; illegal wiretapping; bribing a witness; contempt of court; contempt of Congress; destruction of evidence; campaign-finance violations; blackmail; showing classified documents to an unauthorized person; falsifying government documents; income-tax violations; defrauding the United States; embezzlement; extortion; distributing false or unsigned campaign literature; slander; libel; malicious mischief; intercepting mail; flight to avoid prosecution or to avoid testifying in a criminal investigation; theft.

Time for Thanksgiving dinner.

This is a semi-holiday. Many offices are closed, and the city is once more moving at half speed, as it did on the Monday following the firing of Cox. The telephone is quieter than usual. One colleague took his wife for a bicycle ride through Rock Creek Park. Another called, sounding depressed. For some, the quiet, too, is hard to take. The sudden availability of time, the sudden drop in the flow of adrenaline can be difficult.

According to the news, the President's secretary, Rose Mary Woods, will go to court to explain the eighteen-minute gap in the tape. Evans and Novak report that before Special Prosecutor Jaworski informed the court about the gap, White House lawyers "pleaded" with him to delay making the information public. According to Evans and Novak, Fred Buzhardt and Leonard Garment went to Jaworski's office to ask for more time to get their "ducks in a row before shocking the nation once again."

A Harris poll in today's Washington *Post* says that forty-four percent of the people believe that the President has violated the law. A month ago, a survey showed that thirty-nine percent believed this.

There are stories in the Washington *Post* today about Robert Vesco, another of the shadowy and elusive figures in this whole affair. Vesco is in the Bahamas, and is fighting extradition to the United States, where he faces charges on a number of matters. Four federal warrants have been issued for Vesco's arrest. He has sought and been granted permanent residence, and immunity from extradition, in Argentina. He has also established a base in Costa Rica, where he is reported by the *Post* to have invested more than sixty million dollars belonging to mutual funds, some of the money going into a company founded by the President of Costa Rica, Jose Figueres. Costa Rica has refused a United States request to extradite Vesco. It has also been reported that Donald Nixon, Jr., the President's nephew, who is an aide to Vesco, has spent time in Argentina on Vesco's behalf. According to a recent story in the New York *Times,* Donald Nixon, the President's brother, of whom we have heard in other connections, has said that a lawyer who had done work for Vesco helped his son obtain employment with the financier. The lawyer, Howard Cerny, has said, according to the *Times,* that he also represented both Donald and the President's youngest brother, Edward. The papers point out that Edward Nixon helped to arrange Vesco's secret contribution of two hundred thousand dollars in cash to the President's reëlection campaign. It is in connection with that contribution that John Mitchell, Maurice Stans, and Vesco have been indicted for trying to obstruct an investigation into Vesco's affairs by the Securities and Exchange Commission. (Mitchell and Stans are the first Cabinet officials to be indicted since the Harding Administration.) The S.E.C. has brought a two-hundred-and-twenty-four-million-dollar civil-fraud suit against Vesco and forty-one other individuals and corporations. In 1971, Vesco took over control of Investors Overseas Services, a Swiss-based mutual-fund operation, from Bernard Cornfeld, who is in jail. The S.E.C. fraud suit against Vesco is in connection with his handling of the funds of Investors Overseas Services. Vesco and his associates have indicated in interviews that they have information of pertinence to the investigations into Watergate. In an interview with a Costa Rican newspaper last August, Vesco said, "My presence in the United States would aggravate the Watergate case." A close associate of Vesco has said that he and Vesco had a "missing link" to Watergate. The associate has also termed the two-hundred-thousand-dollar contribution an "extortion." The cash contributed by Vesco went into the secret fund in Maurice Stans' safe. The fund financed the espionage-and-sabotage activities against the Democrats. There is a photograph of Robert Vesco in this morning's *Post*. He has a full head of dark hair and a mustache. He is thirty-seven years old.

Two days ago, the Washington *Post* reported that John Caulfield, one of the private investigators hired by the White House in 1969, told the Ervin-committee staff that the President's brother Donald not only was wiretapped but was apparently under physical surveillance by the Secret Service. At Disney World, the President said that his brother Donald was wiretapped because, among other reasons, someone might have been trying to "get him" in order to "use improper influence," and that whoever that was might have been in a "foreign country."

The stock market dropped twenty-nine points today—the fifth-largest drop in its history.

The President today addressed the Seafarers International Union, which has supported the President. Paul Hall, the union's president, voted against the A.F.L.-C.I.O.'s action calling for the impeachment of Mr. Nixon. Tonight, we see the President on television, addressing the union. Rocking back and forth on the podium, he says, "I don't get seasick, however rough the seas are. . . . You don't need to worry about my getting seasick or jumping ship. I am going to stay at that helm until we bring it into port." This week's *Time* reports that the office of the Special Prosecutor is investigating the arrangements by which the Seafarers Union made a contribution of a hundred thousand dollars to the President's reëlection.

Today, the President turned the seven tapes over to the court.

Rose Mary Woods explained in court today that the gap was caused by the fact that in the course of transcribing the tape, on October 1st, she received a telephone call, touched the "Recording" button instead of the "Stop" button of the tape recorder by mistake, and kept her foot on its pedal, thus causing the tape to be erased while she talked. She said, however, that she thought she had been on the telephone for only about five minutes, whereas the gap in the tape lasts for what is now said to be eighteen and a quarter minutes. Miss Woods said that she had not mentioned this during her appearance in court two and a half weeks ago, because she had been "petrified," and because she did not think the tape had been subpoenaed. "All I can say," Miss Woods said to the court, "is that I am most dreadfully sorry." In her testimony yesterday, Miss Woods said that the President had listened to the tape on a Sony machine she used at Camp David. She said, "The President listened to different parts of the tape, pushing the buttons back and forth."

NOVEMBER 27

Notes written by Haldeman after his June 20th conversation with Nixon (the one with the gap) and introduced in evidence yesterday say, "What is our counterattack? PR offensive to top this. Hit the opposition w/ their activities. Point out libertarians have created public callousness. Do they justify this less than stealing Pentagon Papers, Anderson file, etc? We should be on the attack for diversion." Jill Wine Volner, one of the Assistant Special Prosecutors, charged that the notes showed that "the portion obliterated related to Watergate." Leonard Garment objected. Judge Sirica commented that "the exhibit will speak for itself."

In court yesterday, Miss Woods said that when she realized she had erased part of the tape she went in to tell the President "just as soon as I saw his office was empty." Miss Woods said that she told the President she was "terribly embarrassed," and that the President said, "It's too bad, but don't worry about it. That is not one of the subpoenaed tapes." Buzhardt told the court that "it was not until the evening of Wednesday, November 14th" that the President's lawyers realized that the tape of the conversation between Nixon and Haldeman was covered by the subpoena. The White House analysis submitted to the court yesterday said that what is now referred to as "the hum" on the tape "was caused by the depression of a record button during the process of reviewing the tape, possibly while the recorder was in the proximity of an electric typewriter and a high-intensity lamp." In claiming executive privilege on

the tape, the White House said that the conversation between the President
and Haldeman "relates primarily to scheduling and travel." The claim of
executive privilege was based on the need to "protect the confidentiality
of advice given to the President."

The President told a group of senators yesterday that he would release
his income-tax returns by the end of this week.

This afternoon—Tuesday—the Senate is debating an amendment to
provide for public financing of elections for the Presidency, the Senate,
and the House. The amendment is being offered to a bill to raise and
extend the expiration date of the ceiling on the national debt. The current legal debt ceiling expires at midnight on Friday. The Congress
regularly extends the debt ceiling for only a few months at a time, and
uses the legislation, which is essential for running the government, as a
vehicle for attaching amendments on other subjects. The idea is that the
debt-ceiling bill is not likely to be vetoed, so the amendments are likely
to become law. The amendment for public financing of campaigns is
sponsored by a group of senators, including Hugh Scott, the Senate
Minority Leader; Edward Kennedy; Walter Mondale; Charles Mathias;
and Richard Schweiker, Republican of Pennsylvania. For some time,
while the senators were busy competing over whose bill to establish
public financing of campaigns would be pushed, the reform languished.
Finally, a bill combining provisions of the various bills was worked out,
and the names of the senators were attached to it in alphabetical order.

The idea of public financing of campaigns seemed radical not long
ago. The fact that it is now before the Senate, and seems likely to pass,
shows how quickly things have changed. Maneuvers by conservative
Republicans and Democrats to kill the amendment are failing. In the
debate, Mondale says, "The shakedown tactics of the Nixon fund-raisers
have shown many businessmen what can happen when the present
system is pushed to its outer limits. It becomes simple extortion, the
collection of protection money."

In the "President's Room," a small, dark, musty room off the Senate
floor where senators come from the floor to meet reporters, I ask a
Republican senator, a moderate, how things stand with the Republican
senators and the President.

"Everyone is sort of at the head-shaking stage," he says. This morning,
an emissary of the President had breakfast with the Republican senator, and asked him what message he would like to send the President.
"I said, 'Hell, none,' " says the senator. " 'I don't have anything to tell
him, and he wouldn't listen.' " He continues, "I think that's how a lot
of people feel. It's got to the ridicule stage. In politics, criticism is a
healthy stage. Ridicule and sarcasm are the unhealthy stage. That's
where it is now, even among serious people. The two missing tapes

probably took it to that stage. The White House meetings didn't do him any good." The senator says that his colleagues have been talking with each other about this week's Harris poll showing that forty-four per-cent of the people think that the President violated the law. "You hear senators all giving their opinions about what he has to do to get out of trouble," he says. "They aren't talking about what *we've* got to do to get him out of trouble. They look at it like spectators. Most people don't think he'll get out of it—some because they think he's guilty, and some because they think he's not adroit enough. You know, one of the things in human nature is that there is an almost inevitable wave of sympathy that builds up. Anyone who has as much power as he has with the press and television, with as much power to manipulate the press, has every chance to build the sympathy backlash. The President hasn't been able to do it. Then we voted that piece of legislation on energy the other day which gave him almost total power."

I asked him why the Senate had done this.

"We didn't want to deal with it—couldn't. Also, it's a nice hot potato to pass to him. He won't be able to manage it."

At three-forty-eight, the Senate begins its consideration of the nomi-nation of Gerald Ford to be Vice-President of the United States. It has reserved one hour for the occasion. The voting on the public-financing amendment is temporarily suspended. Most of the senators depart. There is some question about what the Senate is to do with this hour, since the confirmation is a foregone conclusion. There is nothing to "debate."

Edward Brooke says, "This is an historic occasion." I had expected more of this kind of talk. But the senators do not seem to have it in them to try to infuse history or majesty into the occasion. They seem tired and distracted. They are treating this as a routine necessity. It is difficult to infuse drama into an occasion if there is no drama available to infuse. But behind that quiet scene down there on the Senate floor an invisible, and very great, drama may be taking place. There are some references—oblique, fleeting—to the fact that the senators may be con-firming someone who will succeed the President before the President's term has expired. They seem to be aware that in confirming Ford they may be taking a step toward driving the President from office. They cannot say this, of course, but in some of their comments the senators indicate what may really be going on.

Brooke praises Ford highly. Brooke has called for the President's res-ignation. He says that Ford "is well qualified for the Vice-Presidency and, if necessary, the Presidency." He goes on to say, "Jerry Ford is a man who gives me hope." Some of the speeches sound like nominating speeches at a political convention. But the senators' confusion is under-standable. They have never been here before. The country hasn't.

Charles Percy, who is interested in running for President in 1976, says, "Many of us are under no illusion that we are advising and consenting to . . . a name that will go down in the annals of history like such great former Vice-Presidents as John Adams, Thomas Jefferson, John C. Calhoun, and Theodore Roosevelt. . . . I believe that Jerry Ford would be the first to say that though he probably would not yet be classified as one of the potential great Vice-Presidents, he nonetheless will strive to achieve this stature."

"There is a certain exhilaration," says Carl Curtis, Republican of Nebraska. There isn't, but Curtis is trying. "Is Congressman Gerald Ford of Presidential calibre," asks Curtis. He replies, "I can answer, with unequivocal and positive enthusiasm, yes."

At four-thirty, there seem to be no more speakers available. It is time for the roll to be called, and the senators return to cast their votes. The only senators who vote against the nomination are three Democrats: Thomas Eagleton, of Missouri; William Hathaway, of Maine; and Gaylord Nelson, of Wisconsin. (Hathaway has argued that under the current circumstances, the President should not be permitted to select his Vice-President. He has proposed a statute to provide that in the event of a vacancy in both the Presidency and the Vice-Presidency, there be a special election. A statute to this effect was enacted in 1792 and remained the law for ninety-four years. Eagleton and Nelson opposed Ford on the basis of his record.) The vote is ninety-two to three for Gerald Ford to be Vice-President of the United States.

NOVEMBER 28

The new required subject, in this year in which there has been much to learn, is the operation of tape recorders. Last night, television newsmen went through some contortions to demonstrate what Miss Woods said had happened while she was playing the tape and answering the phone. We were shown how to keep a foot on a pedal, take off earphones, push a "Recording" button, and answer a phone, all at about the same time. Electronics experts were interviewed on television. When Miss Woods demonstrated in court yesterday what is now becoming known as "the Rose Mary stretch," she took her foot off the pedal.

Great scandals are often remembered for their symbols. Deep freezes, vicuña coats. By now, one legacy of Watergate is an abundance of symbols. The symbols gave the issues force. It was not that Howard Hunt went to see Dita Beard. It was that Howard Hunt, wearing a red wig, went to see Dita Beard. And even the symbols changed on us sometimes. The red wig turned out to be brunette. Suitcases stuffed with money. The money symbol used to be hundred-dollar bills, but then, like Watergate itself, the money symbol swelled: a hundred thousand dollars. Mexican lanterns and Mexican laundries. And now we have come to tapes and recorders and tape gaps. Great Constitutional issues reduced to a hum. And even the hum got longer.

Last night, the Senate, by a vote of fifty-seven to thirty-four, approved the amendment to provide public financing of federal campaigns. This morning, I asked a senator why it had passed so easily. "No one wanted to vote for 'corruption,' " he said.

In another act of *Rashomon,* Richardson has released to the press two documents to support his version of the story of the firing of Special Prosecutor Archibald Cox.

The Ervin committee announced the suspension of its hearings, and Senator Baker said that they may never be resumed.

Leon Jaworski will pursue the I.T.T. question.

On the evening news, Buzhardt, coming out of court, says, as he has just told the court, that there are more gaps in the tapes. He tells reporters, "It's nothing to get excited about."

NOVEMBER 29

In court today, Buzhardt said that there was "no innocent explanation" for the eighteen-and-a-quarter-minute erasure.

There are press reports that the President will get a new team of lawyers.

Dwight Chapin, thirty-two, former appointments secretary to the President, was indicted today for lying to the Watergate grand jury about his association with Donald Segretti.

Today, Ron Ziegler attacked the Special Prosecutor's staff as having "an ingrained suspicion and visceral dislike for this President and this Administration." Ziegler said that Jaworski was exempted from his remarks. Ziegler also said today that the President's current lawyers had made "some mistakes" and might be replaced. Buzhardt, asked about this by reporters at the courthouse, said, "I've never pretended I was perfect."

NOVEMBER 30

Today's Washington *Post* reports that Laird met with reporters at the White House yesterday and said that he does not believe that as of now there is a "great desire" in the House to impeach the President. This cannot be very reassuring to the President. And Laird knows that these things are matters of momentum. What members of the House say now about how they would vote on impeachment is not very significant.

What is significant is the chain of events that will precede their having to cast the vote. Moreover, the House Judiciary Committee will have made its study and recommendations. If it recommends impeachment, House members will have to cast a vote for or against impeachment on specified grounds. Then the question will not be as theoretical as it now seems. Representative John Rhodes, Republican of Arizona, who will replace Ford as House Minority Leader, said earlier this week that it was "quite possible" that the House committee would approve a resolution calling for impeachment. Laird has confirmed earlier reports that he will leave the White House shortly. He says that he will depart after Ford becomes Vice-President, because then Ford can assume Laird's responsibilities. If the Vice-President became an adviser to the President, it would be a new turn. Bryce Harlow, a Presidential counsellor, is also said to be planning to leave the White House soon.

Yesterday, Hugh Scott, the Senate Minority Leader, said in an interview, "I've had a terribly difficult job trying to strike a balance as a Party leader and at the same time trying to hold the confidence of people that I'm telling the truth. . . . I've never been more uncomfortable." Scott said that the President must make "a complete, all-out disclosure," and continued, "I think that promise of candor is fine, but actual, complete candor is essential."

Ron Ziegler said yesterday that next week the White House would make public "a full report" on the President's finances. The statements, said Ziegler, would clear up "all questions" about the President's personal finances.

9

EGIL KROGH pleaded guilty yesterday to conspiracy to violate the civil rights of Ellsberg's psychiatrist, and promised to make a "full and truthful disclosure" of what he knows about the incident. Krogh said, "I simply feel that what was done in the Ellsberg operation was in violation of what I perceive to be a fundamental idea in the character of this country—the paramount rights of the individual." The plan is that Krogh will be sentenced in January and then will coöperate with the prosecutors. He said he had sought this arrangement in order to "avoid any possible suggestion that I am seeking leniency through testifying."

Under ordinary circumstances, all grand juries expire within eighteen months. At the request of the Justice Department, the Congress, in what may be an unprecedented action, passed a bill extending the life of the Watergate grand jury for another year. Yesterday, the President signed the bill.

The President is at the White House this weekend. Gerald Warren said, "The President will do everything he can to conserve energy and set an example for the nation." Last week, the Washington *Star-News* reported that the President had spent only four of the forty-four weekends of his second term at the White House.

The Senate is meeting today—Saturday—because Senator James Allen, Democrat of Alabama, is filibustering the debt-ceiling bill. He objects to the amendment authorizing public financing of Presidential campaigns. The sections providing for public financing of Senate and House elections have already been stripped from the bill, because the House members objected. House members gave high-minded reasons for their objections, but the reason they give among themselves is that public financing of campaigns would guarantee financing of challengers. The advantages of those candidates in office over those not in office are impressive. There is the franking privilege, giving members of Congress an average of seventy thousand dollars in free mailings each year. Last

week, Common Cause released a study showing that incumbents in the
House and the Senate were able with striking regularity to raise about
twice as much campaign money as could their challengers. This was true
of Democrats and Republicans, liberals and conservatives. The figures
released by Common Cause also showed that special economic groups—
banking, business, labor, farm interests, physicians, and so on—contributed
almost three times as much to incumbents as they did to challengers.

The White House, too, opposes the public-financing provisions. One
would think that it had enough on its mind, but it is still fighting its
fights in the Congress.

In any event, the manner in which the public-financing amendment
was added to a bill on another matter may not be the best way to proceed to make such a fundamental change.

On tonight's news, it is reported that the President is planning to
announce that he and Mrs. Nixon will give their San Clemente estate to
the American people when they die.

DECEMBER 2

Last week, Ron Ziegler said to a White House reporter, "Don't they
realize what they're doing to our institutions?"

"Who's 'they,' Ron?" the reporter asked.

"Those people on Capitol Hill," said Ziegler. "How will they feel
in 1978, when the Republicans and Southern Democrats impeach a
Democratic President?"

There is to be another shakeup of the group that advises the President
on energy policy. It is the fourth such reorganization this year. Now
former Governor John Love, of Colorado, is out, and will be replaced
by William Simon, who is Deputy Secretary of the Treasury. Simon is
said to be opposed to rationing, and in favor of dealing with the shortage by letting the prices of oil and gas rise. He is said to believe that if
the price of gasoline rises sufficiently consumption will drop. The move
is interpreted as a victory for Secretary of the Treasury George Shultz,
who is philosophically opposed to controls.

Jack Anderson reports that the figures on campaign contributions
show that oil and gas interests contributed at least five million dollars
to the reëlection of the President. Anderson reports that "major stock-
holders, directors, and officers" of Exxon contributed four hundred and
forty-two thousand dollars. Anderson also reports that Exxon's profits
for the first three quarters of 1973 were one billion six hundred million
dollars—an increase of fifty-nine percent over 1972. Anderson may be
reaching to make connections between some of the contributors and the
oil companies, but his basic point seems documented well enough. He

notes that executives of Gulf, Ashland, and Phillips have admitted to making illegal contributions of a hundred thousand dollars to the Nixon reëlection campaign. He reports that Gulf "laundered" its money through a Bahamas subsidiary, and that Ashland routed its payment, in hundred-dollar bills, through Africa.

DECEMBER 3

The Senate, meeting in Sunday session yesterday, failed to cut off the filibuster against public financing of Presidential campaigns. Senator Allen was assisted in the filibuster by Robert Griffin, of Michigan, the Republican Whip. Two Republican senators were flown back on a government plane from Oklahoma, where they were on a quail hunt, so that they could vote against ending the filibuster. The White House hinted strongly that the bill would be vetoed. Senator Wallace Bennett, Republican of Utah, opened yesterday's session with a prayer asking forgiveness for meeting on the Sabbath.

A congressionally commissioned study by Louis Harris shows that Americans place more confidence in garbage collectors than in—in declining order—the police, the press, church, business, Congress, or the White House.

On the evening news, it is reported that General Motors will lay off a hundred and thirty-seven thousand workers before Christmas, because of the energy shortage.

DECEMBER 4

On the television news tonight, the President introduced William Simon, his new energy "czar." The President's delivery was wooden, and fatigue showed in his face. Simon told reporters today that he and the President did not believe that the profits of oil companies were too high. He said he and the President believed that high profits, "properly reinvested," were the best way to solve the problems. Truck drivers, protesting the lower speed limits and higher fuel costs, are blocking interstate highways.

In court, it was learned today that Haldeman still gives instructions to the White House staff. An aide, Lawrence Higby, told of being asked in November by Haldeman to obtain Haldeman's notes of the June 20th meeting—the one recorded on the tape in which there is that gap—and to read them to him before giving them to anyone else at the White House. Higby said that after he read the notes of the meeting to Haldeman, Haldeman said, "That's not a problem."

In the Washington *Post* this morning, it is reported that "President Nixon and his lawyers have given skeptical Republican congressmen an account of his personal finances that substantially contradicts previous Presidential statements." The President is reported to have stayed at the meeting for only ten minutes and then left his tax attorneys to answer questions, in what one congressman called "a frank and free session that included more than a little profanity." The President's net worth is reported to have more than tripled since he became President, rising from about three hundred thousand dollars to about nine hundred and eighty-eight thousand dollars. It turns out, according to the report in the *Post,* that the President has two hundred and fifty thousand dollars in certificates of deposit at Rebozo's bank. An officer of Rebozo's bank has said that the President purchased a hundred-thousand-dollar certificate of deposit soon after he sold his New York apartment, in 1968, and has had it ever since. In his statement at Disney World, the President, in addition to saying that he "put everything into real estate," said he had a hundred thousand dollars "coming to me from the law firm."

Yesterday, a lawyer for Howard Hughes opened a briefcase and dumped a hundred thousand dollars in hundred-dollar bills before startled members of the Ervin committee, meeting in executive session. Said the lawyer, Chester Davis, "Here's the goddam money." Davis said it was the same money that had been sent from Hughes to Rebozo and had been said by Rebozo and Mr. Nixon to have been kept by Rebozo and then returned to Hughes. Senator Ervin said there is "very little doubt" that Mr. Rebozo will be called to testify.

Ron Ziegler said yesterday that more information would be released and would "clear up" any questions about the President's finances, and he said that the White House objected to the "piecemeal disclosure" on the subject. The White House has been making most of the disclosures.

The President has proposed that the Joint Committee on Internal Revenue Taxation decide whether the President acted properly in taking an income-tax deduction of five hundred and seventy thousand dollars for donating his Vice-Presidential papers to the government. The committee is reported to have agreed. There is some question as to the authority of this or any congressional committee to make such a finding.

Senator Stennis has told Woodward and Bernstein that he had "no idea" that the White House wanted him to authenticate a transcript of the tapes to be given to the court. He has said that he thought he was authenticating the transcript simply for the Ervin committee. Woodward and Bernstein write that Stennis also understood that he was to authenticate a verbatim transcript of the tapes—not, as the White House announced, a summary.

After lunch, I encountered a reporter talking with a former official of the Nixon Administration. "We were just discussing who Jerry Ford will pick as his Vice-President," the reporter said.

Today, Senator Jacob Javits, Republican of New York, said that, now that Gerald Ford's swearing-in as Vice-President is imminent—it is to take place tomorrow—the possibility of the President's resignation will "properly come to the front, and I and others will have to give every thoughtful consideration to that possibility."

The truckers are still blocking the highways. In some states, National Guardsmen and state police have been called out.

DECEMBER 6

Shortly after five-thirty, the swearing-in, in the House chamber, of Gerald Ford as Vice-President of the United States is on national television. Earlier this afternoon, his nomination was confirmed by the House by a vote of three hundred and eighty-seven to thirty-five. The swearing-in is a strange occasion—improvised. Once more, there is no precedent. It is not taking place outdoors, where Inaugurations are held, or in the East Room, where the President announced Ford's nomination. Albert and Eastland, who until now have been first and second in line for the Presidency, sit on the rostrum. An American flag is draped above their heads, and on the wall above that there is carved, in marble, the words "In God We Trust." Mrs. Nixon and Rose Mary Woods are in the gallery, both wearing red suits. General Haig is next to Mrs. Nixon. As Mr. Nixon and Mr. Ford enter, it is not clear whom the congressmen are applauding for. The applause seems full but not exuberant. The members of Congress seem to be relieved that they have got through this passage without disaster. The President is beaming.

As Ford takes the oath of office, Mr. Nixon hovers close, within camera range, as if now drawing on Ford's reflected glory. Nixon is remarkable. He presents a seamless professional exterior. There he is, with all that he has endured, all the damage that he has suffered, looking well and carrying out with total aplomb this ceremony that may be his undoing. As Chief Justice Burger administers the oath to Ford, Ford's wife, in a red dress, looks moved, and then Ford gives a little speech. It is a sort of combination Convention acceptance speech and Inaugural Address. He thanks the Chief Justice for swearing him in and the Supreme Court for attending. "You have my support and loyalty," he tells the President. Ford praises the separation of powers and the two-party system and the members of Congress, who he says are "Americans who love their country, Americans who work and sacrifice for their country and their children," and he promises to uphold the Constitution and to "do the very best I can for America." He asks for our prayers. And then it is over. Albert and Ford wave to the room. Albert looks overjoyed. Like other ceremonies, happy or sad, the purpose of this ceremony was to depersonalize. It was an occasion of state, meant to sweep away personalities, misgivings, politics. There is a special lift to ceremonies that mark beginnings. The thing whose beginning is being celebrated may, miraculously, escape the common fate. These people on the screen are involved in the roughest and most desperate maneuvers, and what we see is a smooth ceremonial occasion. It is not a human transaction. Sometimes we need ceremonies, but they should not be confused with reality.

On tonight's news there are pictures of Ford receiving a briefing at the State Department. According to the reporters, Kissinger said to Ford, "I want to pose with you. After tonight, you'll outrank me." Representative Clarence Long, Democrat of Maryland, says that Ford votes "wrong most of the time, but he's decently wrong."

The stock market has gone up twenty-six points.

The court hearings on the tapes and their gaps and their nonexistences are over. Today, General Haig said in court that perhaps "some sinister force" erased Haldeman's conversation with the President. That makes as much sense as anything else.

Spiro Agnew was out of town today.

DECEMBER 7

It's starting again. The radio announces that the Chicago *Daily News* and the Chicago *Sun-Times* have called for the House Judiciary Committee to proceed with the impeachment investigation.

Tonight's news programs focus on the Vice-President's first day on the job. It is reported that he was up late last night "celebrating" with a thousand friends. Bronze, silver, and gold-on-silver medals were made to commemorate his swearing-in. There are pictures of the President and the Vice-President sitting at the White House, smiling, conferring. In a press conference, Ford says that "the President has no intention whatsoever of resigning . . . and I don't think he should resign."

DECEMBER 9

What comes through the myriad details of the President's tax returns —published in today's papers—is a cumulative impression: the imaginative and controversial deductions, including the one for the Vice-Presidential papers; the minimal tax payments ($792.81 in 1970, $873.03 in 1971, $4,298.17 in 1972); the charitable contributions up to, but no more than, the deductible amount. In a statement, the President said that his gift of San Clemente to the nation would help the American people "maintain a truly national perspective for the Presidency." A White House spokesman, briefing reporters, said, "The people who dealt with the President's tax returns dealt with them without talking to the President."

Seymour Hersh reports in the New York *Times* that the plumbers' code names Special Project M-1 and Project Odessa are both believed by federal investigators to stand for the Ellsberg break-in. He also reports that Ehrlichman, on Nixon's instructions, urged the plumbers to read the chapter in *Six Crises* about Alger Hiss. In that chapter, Nixon wrote that "the Hiss case aroused the nation for the first time to the existence and character of the Communist conspiracy within the United States." Nixon's use of the Hiss case got him national attention and started him on his way to the top; his attempt to repeat the episode might now contribute to his downfall. Nixon built much of his career on his tough stands against the world Communist threat; now his troubles are being perceived by people of various political views as making us more vulnerable to the Russians.

DECEMBER 10

Yesterday, on *Issues and Answers,* Vice-President Ford, asked if he thought President Nixon had acted with propriety in paying so little in taxes, said that the President's promise to give his San Clemente home to the American people should "wipe out any alleged—and I say alleged—impropriety."

A Harris poll shows that Gerald Ford "has become the preferred candidate for President on the Republican ticket in 1976." Ford now leads Reagan, Percy, Baker, Connally, and Rockefeller, in that order.

DECEMBER 11

The Congress is in that peculiar state it reaches toward the end of each session. Appropriations bills and other legislation are rushed through. The lobbyists are out in force. Amendments, some of them mischievous, many of them not understood by anyone but the sponsor, are added. The voting is speeded up, and the representatives and senators are even more in the dark than usual about what it is they are voting on. The main thing that members of Congress want to do now is to get out of town.

Events are often "one-day" stories. This is a comfort to politicians. But the stories about the President's tax returns—on which tax lawyers and accountants are advising the press—continue.

On the evening news, Herbert Stein, chairman of the Council of Economic Advisers, is quoted as saying that the energy crisis may not be as bad as has been predicted.

Republican campaign officials met with the President today, at his invitation, to talk about next year's elections. Reporters ask if Watergate was discussed. "The word was never mentioned," says Republican National Chairman George Bush.

Congress gave up today on its efforts to establish a Special Prosecutor by legislation. The legislators could not reach agreement on an approach to pass a bill with sufficient support to survive a Presidential veto. The idea of a court-appointed Special Prosecutor, sponsored by fifty-five senators, mostly Democrats, suffered a blow when Judges Gesell and Sirica issued statements opposing it. Some Republicans, led by Percy, had offered another approach, and the White House suggested still a third one. Moreover, many of the senators were impressed by Acting Attorney General Bork's pledges that this time the Special Prosecutor would not be interfered with, and by Jaworski's performance thus far. Since he assumed the job, Jaworski has been cultivating the image of a relentless prosecutor. He has no choice; if he falters, his staff and the press, working together, could give him trouble. Like many people here these days, Jaworski is trapped. Some concern was also expressed that if the Congress did pass legislation to establish a Special Prosecutor, the President might use it as an opportunity to fire Jaworski. The President may be too trapped himself to do that, but the concern that he might do so, nurtured by Jaworski and his staff, was there—a factor. Congressional leaders saw themselves to be over a barrel on the question of the Special Prosecutor, and gave up.

The move to set the bill aside was made by Senate Majority Leader Mansfield after a meeting today of the Democratic Policy Committee. Senators Kennedy and Bayh objected strongly to the move. One theory advanced by the congressional leaders is that the President would perhaps fear that if he interfered with the Special Prosecutor, Congress would retaliate with legislation to establish one. It's not clear, as of now, that he need be so fearful of this. The question of how to establish an independent prosecution of a President has not been resolved. Thus far, it has twice been settled, ad hoc, on the basis of personalities and the perceived relative strength of the President and his opponents.

DECEMBER 12

Today, Vice-President Ford joined other Republicans in urging the House Judiciary Committee to hurry its impeachment inquiry. Ford said that if the committee did not resolve the question by April, "then you can say it's partisan." A line commonly used by Republicans, beginning, it seems, with Aiken, is that the Congress "should impeach the President or get off his back." The Republicans are disturbed by the possibility that the question of impeachment might drag on well into the election year; some believe that the sooner the vote is taken on impeachment, the more likely it is that the move will fail. But the Republicans' call for the hurrying of impeachment may be deepening the President's problem. Each Republican voice that is raised in favor of impeaching the President or getting off his back lends more legitimacy to the concept of impeachment. The fact that Republicans feel that they have to say this at all shows how the respectability of the idea has grown. There is a cumulative effect. The idea is there; the Republicans, in their agony, say "Get it over with," and in doing so they give strength to the idea. Almost without anyone's noticing, a bipartisan consensus has grown that the Congress must proceed on the question of impeaching the President.

The House Judiciary Committee has begun to make preliminary arrangements. On television last night, Rodino said he did not think that "these matters should be formalized" until the committee had chosen a special counsel.

DECEMBER 13

There is a U.P.I. report in today's Washington *Post* that President Nixon claimed a twenty-five-dollar deduction for a dogwood tree he donated in 1972 to the State of Connecticut.

According to Harris and Gallup polls published today, approval of the President has risen by four (Gallup) or five (Harris) points. The polls mark the first time since February that the President's standing has not dropped. The Gallup poll shows thirty-one percent of the people approving of the way the President has handled his job, and fifty-nine percent disapproving. The Harris poll shows thirty-seven percent of the people rating Mr. Nixon's performance as "good" or "excellent," and sixty-one percent describing it as "fair" or "poor." To judge from conversations in Washington today, the politicians are finding the President's rise in the polls significant, and it is giving pause to some who were set to oppose him.

Yesterday, Senator Saxbe, in a hearing on his nomination as Attorney General, told the Senate Judiciary Committee that Bork had fired Archibald Cox for "an extraordinary impropriety." This was the only reason for firing the Special Prosecutor permitted by the guidelines establishing the office. However, Saxbe also assured the senators that he would refuse to carry out an order to fire Jaworski.

In the New York *Times,* there is one of those stories within a story that, it seems, we may hear more about. The story, with a San Francisco dateline, says that the Ervin committee has subpoenaed the records from the San Clemente Inn concerning visits there by people involved with Howard Hughes, the plumbers, and some friends of President Nixon. What catches the attention is a mention, well down in the story, of one name on the subpoenaed list—that of William Griffin, the attorney for the Precision Valve Company, owned by Robert Abplanalp. The story says that, according to transcripts of testimony given to the Ervin committee in executive session, and on file in court in Washington, Griffin was the man who returned the one hundred thousand dollars in cash from Bebe Rebozo to a representative of Howard Hughes in New York in June. A few days ago, we read that last December Griffin bought two Key Biscayne lots from Nixon, at about three times their original cost.

Evans and Novak report today that Gerald Ford has "dismayed supporters by rejecting important advice from long-time political intimates." These unnamed intimates think that the Vice-President should not go skiing, as he has planned, over the Christmas holidays but should stay in Washington and build his "take-charge" image. They also think that Ford should hire a "sophisticated politician of wide experience as his chief aide." Ford's "political friends," write Evans and Novak, are also disturbed at the extent to which the Vice-President is defending the President. This is worrisome to those who see Ford as "the party's only salvation," the columnists write. Evans and Novak report that Ford has shown some resistance to the President. The President, the columnists reveal, wanted Ford's swearing-in as Vice-President to take place in the White House. They say that the President was dissuaded only by Ford himself, who told Mr. Nixon, "with candor," that to walk down the aisle of the House of Representatives with Ford might help Mr. Nixon. That's candor.

In New York, a wise man who used to be in Washington says that if this all ends ambiguously the lessons will still be clear. "Don't think of it in terms of punishment for crime which prevents people from doing it again. The history of law enforcement shows that it doesn't work that way. The erosion of the President's support is the lesson. He's helpless now. He can't push buttons or do something mad. That would be the 'tilt,' and the end of him. Politicians will learn that lesson."

DECEMBER 14

The panel of technical experts studying the tapes reported yesterday to Judge Sirica that they did not think the eighteen-and-a-quarter-minute gap on the tape could have been caused in the manner suggested by the White House. They said that neither the lamp nor the electric typewriter used by Rose Mary Woods was "a likely cause" of the noise, as the

White House had said. Judge Sirica said there were "some indications" that the Uher recorder used by Miss Woods could have produced the buzz.

Yesterday, Britain announced a three-day work week because of the energy crisis.

Various individuals and organizations are trying their hand at drawing up a bill of particulars for impeachment. Some of the bills of particulars contain as many as twenty items. Some of them go beyond matters related to Watergate, and include such matters as bombing and impoundment. Some of the lists give an appearance of equal importance to large and small matters. Some of them include charges that have been proved and charges supported only by hearsay. Some members of the House Judiciary Committee see the possible grounds for impeachment as falling into three categories: acts that are statutory crimes; matters that are generally perceived to be wrongdoing, such as tolerating malfeasance and corruption by one's appointees and assistants; and acts that may not be legal wrongs but are essentially political, such as the cover-up of activities in Southeast Asia. It will be the job of the Judiciary Committee and its staff to sort these things out. It is possible that events and public opinion will impose themselves on the House of Representatives.

Inevitably, the judgment about the President will be both legal and political. It will be political in the small sense—in the sense that the politicians will be weighing the decision in terms of how it will affect their own hides. The Democrats may perceive the issue in terms of the greatest damage to the Republicans. Similarly, many Republicans are talking of impeaching the President not out of concern that he did anything wrong but because they are worried about what is happening to the Republican Party. The judgment will also be political in the larger sense—in the sense that a judgment will be made about the damage that has been done to our political system.

It was said not long ago that the issues of Watergate, and particularly the Constitutional questions, were too abstract for "the public." This recent period has shown us something about the growth of public awareness and the movement of opinion. The periods of quiet are deceptive. "The public" might not keep a copy of the Constitution under its pillow, or fret aloud to pollsters and politicians about the Fourth Amendment, but a large segment of "the public" appears to have a deep instinct that one's home is indeed one's castle. "The public" seemed to understand early this year, when the President defied congressional authority time and again, that checks and balances were not working. The reaction to the firing of Archibald Cox was a deep, instinctive reaction—apparently not manufactured, as Ron Ziegler says it was—to what appeared to be a President holding himself above the law. Someone here says it was similar to the reaction in 1937, when President Franklin Roosevelt tried to "pack" the Supreme Court—an attempt he followed with an effort, also unsuccessful, to "purge" the Congress of those who opposed him. The reaction to Cox may not have represented the opinion of the majority, but it was the sort of reaction that shapes events. It appears that "the public" has some fairly deep feelings about the ideas and principles that the Constitution represents. Our roots in the past may be deeper than we knew.

Yesterday, the Senate Judiciary Committee approved the nomination of William Saxbe as Attorney General. The committee acted after receiving more assurances from Saxbe that he would not interfere with Jaworski. Senators Hart and Kennedy wanted written assurances to this effect from the President. Saxbe said that such assurances were not necessary. Senator Scott said he would "seek further clarification" from the President, and the committee voted to approve Saxbe.

Today, I talked again with the exasperated Republican senator whom I spoke with at length a month ago. He said, "There hasn't been much cloakroom talk lately. We're caught up in the energy crisis. But we Republicans are not in much of a position to help the President now. We could form a choir and go to the White House and sing over him and it wouldn't make any difference."

The papers report that Kissinger and Le Due Tho are to meet again in Paris next week, presumably to discuss the increased fighting in Vietnam. Two months ago, Kissinger and Le Due Tho were awarded the Nobel Peace Prize; Le Due Tho turned it down. At the moment, Kissinger is in the Middle East, trying to arrange truce talks.

Late this afternoon, President Nixon presided over the lighting of the national Christmas tree. At his side were a Camp Fire Girl and a Boy Scout. Robert Pierpoint, of CBS, reported that, under the direction of the Interior Department, a large number of Nixon supporters, holding posters and little American flags, were in the front rows. Many of them were followers of the Korean Reverend Sun Myung Moon, whose sound truck had circled Lafayette Park, offering prayers for the President, on the Monday after he fired Archibald Cox. The audience cheered the President. On one giant banner—of the type held up for the television cameras at baseball games—there appeared, in block letters, the message "GOD LOVES NIXON." The ceremony of the President lighting the Christmas tree was carried live on the television networks.

DECEMBER 15

The Joint Committee on Internal Revenue Taxation has decided to make a full investigation of the President's tax returns and has asked the

Internal Revenue Service to re-audit the returns of several of President Nixon's friends. The committee has also received a preliminary report from its staff which says that the I.R.S. resisted pressures by the White House for audits of its enemies. The report says that if enemies were audited it was because they had been selected by computer "at random." The staff of the committee has close ties with the staff of the I.R.S.

DECEMBER 17

Nine inches of snow has fallen on Washington in the past two days, and the city is nearly paralyzed. For reasons that have never been quite clear, the city reaches near-paralysis whenever it snows, and even when it rains.

The Reverend Dr. Billy Graham, the evangelist and friend of Presidents, conducted the worship service at the White House yesterday. The Washington *Post* says the Reverend Dr. Graham interrupted a crusade in Europe, at the President's special request, to appear at the White House yesterday. Introducing Dr. Graham, the President said, "He always leaves us with a message." "Ladies and gentlemen," said Dr. Graham, "I believe America stands on the threshold of divine judgment. . . . Who should repent? Everybody." Following the service, Edward Nixon, the President's youngest brother, said to reporters that Watergate was "a tempest in a teapot."

The Washington *Post* carries a front-page story headed "Colson, 'Mr. Tough Guy,' Finds Christ." Colson says, "I have found in my own life the relationship with Christ. I think I realize now that your abilities as an individual are much more limited than I believed them to be before." Colson says that he expects people to be cynical about his spiritual awakening.

Tonight, we await the President's decision on whether to sign or veto a bill that gives the U.S. District Court here authority to enforce subpoenas issued by the Ervin committee—an authority that Judge Sirica had said he did not have. Republican leaders are reported to have told the President that they could not support him in a vote to override a veto. Late this evening, the news comes that the President has allowed the bill to become law without his signature. He calls it "bad" legislation, but says that nevertheless he has decided not to veto it, "under the circumstances."

Over the weekend, a White House aide said to one of my colleagues, "Just because a couple of those Republican congressmen might go down the chute doesn't mean he's going to quit."

DECEMBER 18

Yesterday, as part of a campaign for "high visibility," the President and Mrs. Nixon went out to the South Lawn of the White House to view a snowman, and today there are pictures of the event in the papers. The President doesn't seem to know quite what to do in relationship to the snowman. In the picture in this morning's Washington *Post,* he gestures at it vaguely, and Mrs. Nixon smiles. In the Washington *Star-News;* the President is alone with the snowman and is touching its hat. The snowman is smiling. The President is not.

On WTOP, a Washington television station, Gordon Peterson reads the Christmas card that Bebe Rebozo has sent to the customers of his Key Biscayne bank. Bebe Rebozo's Christmas card says "Neither material wealth, fame, power, nor admiration necessarily brings happiness."

DECEMBER 19

Around Washington, lawyers are doing research on the possibility of plea-bargaining by a President. Some lawyers say that a bargain could be struck between a President and the Attorney General. They base this theory on the fact that the Supreme Court has held that when a duly qualified representative of the law strikes a bargain with a defendant, the bargain sticks.

An interview with Barry Goldwater has appeared in the *Christian Science Monitor.* Senator Goldwater says, "I've never known a man to be so much a loner in any field. . . . The President, I think, thinks of himself as the supreme politician in this country. And being a loner, I think he sits by himself and tells himself what he's going to do. Now we went through this gesture period of having congressmen and senators down to see him—but it seems to have ended. . . . And as a result he's not getting advice. That's his problem, he's not getting it. And when he gets it, he doesn't listen to it. . . . My God, we've never had so many serious problems in the history of this nation."

Melvin Laird announces that he will leave the White House on February 1st—a month later than he had planned. Laird says that the House should vote "on the question of indictment" by March 15th. When he uses the word "indictment" rather than "impeachment," he makes the action the House must contemplate sound even more severe. Peter Rodino says that the House Judiciary Committee will finish its inquiry into impeachment by April 1st. Laird and Rodino are not so far apart.

Sam Dash, the Watergate committee's majority counsel, says that the White House has "graciously" agreed to accept the committee's subpoena for over two hundred documents and tapes.

The first segment of an interview with Bebe Rebozo by Walter Cronkite is shown on CBS tonight. Rebozo speaks softly, and fingers a piece of paper as he talks. Cronkite asks Rebozo why he was the conduit for the hundred thousand dollars from Hughes. Rebozo explains that in political campaigns people "are not sure" that the money gets to the proper place. He says that "many people made contributions through me or would send me a check and would say, 'Put this in to help our friend' and so on."

DECEMBER 20

John Doar was named counsel to the Judiciary Committee's impeachment inquiry today. Doar, fifty-two, had been an attorney in the Justice Department's civil-rights division during the Eisenhower Administration and had remained on under the Democrats, eventually becoming head of the division, and establishing a reputation for calm and integrity.

DECEMBER 21

Another heavy snowfall today. Again the city is entangled in itself. So is the Congress. The emergency energy bill is being filibustered in the Senate by senators from oil-producing states. The House and the Senate seem to be unable to agree on the final terms of the bill and may adjourn without passing the emergency legislation. This episode adds to the feeling that one conclusion to be drawn from recent events is less that the Presidency as an institution will have to be, as many people say, weakened than that it will have to be surrounded by methods of holding it accountable for its acts.

John Rhodes, the new House Minority Leader, who is a conservative, said to reporters yesterday that if the House votes to impeach the President, the President should consider resigning. Rhodes said he had "no feeling" on what action the House might take, but he said he thought the chances that the Judiciary Committee would recommend impeachment were "pretty good." Rhodes, unlike other Republicans, said he did not think that the committee was "stalling."

The Joint Committee on Internal Revenue Taxation has disclosed that in September, 1972, John Dean turned over to the I.R.S. a second list of names—five hundred and seventy-five of them, including those of McGovern supporters and members of his staff—with a request that the I.R.S. "see what type of information could be developed" on those named. This was in addition to the some two-hundred-name "enemies list" which Dean told the Ervin committee about last summer. The Joint Committee said that there was no evidence that those on the new list were singled out for harassment by the I.R.S.

Joseph Alsop reports that Wilbur Mills is giving consideration to backing a joint resolution that would free the President of the threat of any prosecution or other court proceedings if he should resign.

Quietly, an ad-hoc group of senators and their staffs have been making plans to begin work next year to reaffirm some of the guarantees in the Bill of Rights. Two subcommittees of the Senate Judiciary Committee and a special subcommittee of the Foreign Relations Committee will look into encroachments on the First and Fourth Amendments.

On the evening news, it is announced that government figures released today show that consumer prices are now eight and four-tenths percent higher than they were a year ago. This increase is the highest in peacetime, and higher than any annual increase during the Vietnam war.

The Congress, ending its first session, will adjourn tomorrow and go home.

Today is the first day of winter.

WINTER

10

IN COLD PRINT, and in stark language, the fifty-page indictment handed up by the Watergate grand jury today charges that seven former associates of the President "and other persons to the Grand Jury known and unknown, unlawfully, willfully, and knowingly did combine, conspire, confederate, and agree together and with each other to commit offenses against the United States." The first count charges that the conspiracy began on or about June 17, 1972, the date of the break-in at the Watergate, and continued "up to and including the date of the filing of this indictment."

The past two months have been relatively quiet. To the extent that there were significant events during this period, I'll touch on them later. Now with the indictment, and concurrent preparations by the House Judiciary Committee's impeachment inquiry staff, this struggle has entered a new and still more dramatic phase.

The major attention today is not so much on the details of the indictment as on a sealed report handed to Judge John Sirica by the grand jury foreman, Vladimir Pregelj, and on a locked briefcase handed to Sirica by Richard Ben-Veniste, Assistant Special Prosecutor. Immediately, the speculation was that it contained information about President Nixon and was intended for the House Judiciary Committee. We know already, as a result of a disclosure by the President at his press conference last week, that the grand jury sought to question him and he declined.

Among those named in the indictment today were John Ehrlichman, H. R. Haldeman, John Mitchell, and Charles Colson. Also indicted were Gordon Strachan, former aide to Haldeman; Robert Mardian, former Assistant Attorney General in charge of the Internal Security Division of the Department of Justice; and Kenneth W. Parkinson, an attorney for the Committee for the Re-Election of the President.

Even though the indictment was expected, it came as a hammer blow. That keeps happening: the impact of the actual event is sharper and more disturbing than was anticipated. We can anticipate the facts but not their impact, their emotional reverberations. So we are unnerved when seven former Administration and reëlection-committee officials—

including the President's closest associates, men who held great power—are indicted. The indictment is for conspiracy to cover up the Watergate break-in. The purpose of the cover-up was to keep the public from finding out the extent of official involvement in the break-in and the surrounding activities and so prevent damage to the President's chances of reëlection. (John Mitchell told the Ervin committee last summer, speaking of the period following the discovery of the break-in, "I still believe that the most important thing to this country was the reëlection of Richard Nixon.") In that sense, the cover-up worked.

There are those who believe that the cover-up has proved far more damaging to the President than the discovery of what was being covered up would have. Many discussions have taken place here as to whether the President could have spared himself this agony, and, if so, when. But the problem for the White House, as we keep learning, was that there was so much to cover up. The break-in at the Watergate combined the elements of covert operations, espionage, secret funds, hidden contributions, and aggression against political opponents (real and perceived) which also characterized other activities carried out under the Administration. Perhaps the President was trapped all along. The indictment charges that the seven men and others "known and unknown" conspired "to obstruct justice . . . to make false statements to a government agency . . . to make false declarations . . . and to defraud the United States and Agencies and Departments thereof, to wit, the Central Intelligence Agency (C.I.A.), the Federal Bureau of Investigation (F.B.I.), and the Department of Justice, of the Government's right to have the officials of these Departments and Agencies transact their official business honestly and impartially, free from corruption, fraud, improper and undue influence, dishonesty, unlawful impairment and obstruction." The defendants, it says, did "knowingly make and cause to be made false statements" to the F.B.I. and the grand jury; they did, "by deceit, craft, trickery and dishonest means, defraud the United States by interfering with and obstructing the lawful governmental functions of the C.I.A." It accuses them of seeking the release of one or more of the men imprisoned for the Watergate break-in; of destroying records; of "covertly" raising cash and paying it to the Watergate defendants; of making and causing to be made "offers of leniency, executive clemency and other benefits" to Hunt, Liddy, McCord, and Magruder; and of attempting to obtain financial assistance from the C.I.A. for the Watergate defendants. The indictment includes thirteen counts against the various defendants and lists forty-five "overt acts" to describe the conspiracy. Several of the charges are based on the word of John Dean.

When, last June, Dean described the cover-up to the Ervin committee, there was reason to suspend belief, reserve judgment. Dean himself had been deeply involved in several of the less attractive activities in the White House; he had been a true believer, and now this cold, seemingly almost bloodless young man with the pale, pinched face and tortoise-shell glasses, was saving his own skin. Much of what he said seemed suggestive but not conclusive. There were many layers of authority and circles of power at the White House; it was not a place where people dealt openly with one another. Also, many pieces of the story were missing. And, anyway, despite all we were learning, it was hard to accept the notion of an elaborate conspiracy on the part of the President's top aides, and perhaps even the President, to cover up a crime.

One of the overt acts charged against Colson is the conversation he had in November, 1972, with Hunt, who was asking for additional payments for the Watergate defendants. It was in that conversation that Colson said to Hunt, according to a transcript released by the Ervin committee last fall, "The less specifics I know, the better off I am . . . we are, you are." John Mitchell is charged with "knowingly" making "false material declarations" to the grand jury on September 14, 1972, when, upon being asked whether he knew of any plans to spy on the Democrats, he said, "Certainly not, because, if there had been, I would have shut it off as being entirely nonproductive at that particular time of the campaign." Nonproductive at that particular time. Haldeman is charged with lying to the Ervin committee when he said that in a meeting on March 21, 1973, at which the raising of money to buy the silence of the Watergate defendants was discussed, the President said, "It would be wrong."

The White House has issued a statement, approved by the President, that the President hopes the country "will join him in recognizing that those indicted are presumed innocent unless proof of guilt is established in the courts."

The Democratic National Committee yesterday agreed to settle for seven hundred and seventy-five thousand dollars its civil damage suit against the Committee for the Re-Election of the President for the break-in at the Party's offices at the Watergate. Somehow, it seems a bit unseemly for the Democrats to collect the money. Last summer, Dean told the Ervin committee that the reëlection committee's lawyers "were very hopeful of slowing down" the Democrats' suit, "because they had been making *ex-parte* contacts with the judge handling the case [Judge Charles R. Richey] and the judge was very understanding and trying to accommodate their problems." Dean said, "The President was pleased to hear this and responded to the effect that 'Well, that's helpful.' "

A poll commissioned by Republicans which was conducted last month showed that seventy-three percent of the voters in Vice-President Ford's former congressional district thought Watergate the most important issue in the recent election there. On February 18th, Ford's seat, which he had held for twenty-five years, and which Republicans had held for sixty-four, was won by a Democrat. Though much was made of the fact that the victor, Richard F. Vander Veen, had called for the President's resignation, it is also true that he had pointed out that the resignation would make Gerald Ford President. The Michigan election was the second of two special elections held so far this year. On February 5th, in Pennsylvania, a Democrat narrowly defeated a Republican in an election to fill a seat that had been held by a Republican who died.

MARCH 2

Richard Cohen writes in the Washington *Post* that as of now charges have been brought against twenty-eight persons formerly associated with the White House or the President's reëlection campaign. "In addition," he writes, "ten corporations or their officers, or both, have been accused of making illegal contributions," eight of them to the Nixon campaign. And six people are now in jail for Watergate-related crimes: three of the seven original co-conspirators for the break-in; two who were sentenced for "dirty tricks" in the campaign; and Egil Krogh. In January, Krogh, the former White House aide and director of the plumbers, having pleaded guilty to violating the civil rights of Dr. Lewis J. Fielding, Daniel Ellsberg's psychiatrist, was sentenced to serve six months in prison.

When he was sentenced Krogh said, as part of a somewhat vague statement, "I received no specific instruction or authority whatsoever regarding the break-in from the President, directly or indirectly." Specific. Krogh said that when he saw the photographs of Dr. Fielding's office after the break-in, "the visibility of physical damage was somehow disturbing beyond the theoretical impression of covert activity." He said that he then recommended to Ehrlichman that "no further actions of that sort be undertaken," and that Ehrlichman "concurred and stated that he considered the operation to have been in excess of his authorization." Krogh's subsequent conversations with the prosecutors yielded little: he could not, he kept saying, remember a number of things.

In February, Herbert Kalmbach, the President's personal attorney, pleaded guilty to charges of secret and illegal fund-raising, and is now coöperating with investigators. The charges to which Kalmbach pleaded guilty had to do with the 1970 congressional elections, in which the White House was trying to secure an "ideological majority" for the President in the Senate. Kalmbach also pleaded guilty to promising a prospective contributor an ambassadorship in exchange for a donation of a hundred thousand dollars, to be divided between the 1970 and 1972 campaigns. (The appointment never materialized.) The charges did not have to do with Kalmbach's other strenuous efforts to raise money for the President's reëlection in 1972, or with his role in raising and seeing to the delivery of money for those convicted for the Watergate break-in. Kalmbach, sad-faced and appearing shaken, told the Ervin committee last summer that Ehrlichman assured him that what he was doing was proper. Now Kalmbach is said to be disillusioned, and is talking.

There is little to guide those who must design and direct the impeachment process. They virtually have to invent it. England, from which the framers of the Constitution borrowed the idea, hasn't used the impeachment procedure since 1805. Warren Hastings, whose trial on impeachment charges was taking place in London while the framers met in Philadelphia, in 1787, was an ex-Governor General of India—a situation not exactly analogous to that of a sitting President of the United States.

In all of American history, the House has impeached thirteen officials: one Cabinet officer, one senator, ten federal judges, and one President. Of a total of eleven impeachments tried by the Senate, four resulted in conviction, six in acquittal, and one in dismissal. All four of the convicted officials were federal judges, and only two of the convictions—of Associate Judge Robert W. Archbald, of the U.S. Commerce Court, in 1913, and Judge Halsted L. Ritter, of the southern district of Florida, in 1936—took place in the twentieth century. Ritter was acquitted of six charges of substantive misconduct but convicted for behavior that "has brought his court into scandal and disrepute." The impeachment of Andrew Johnson, ostensibly for his removal of the Secretary of War, Edwin Stanton, in violation of an act of Congress—the Tenure of Office Act, which was itself later held un-Constitutional—was surrounded by post-Civil War bitterness and partisanship. It is not the sort of precedent that contemporary legislators wish to rely on.

It is the current impeachment proceeding that may be setting the precedents for future generations.

This week, the White House issued a paper setting forth what it views as constituting an impeachable offense. The White House analysis concludes that the Constitutional definition of impeachment—"for treason, bribery, or other high crimes and misdemeanors"—inherently requires not only a criminal offense but one "of a very serious nature committed in one's governmental capacity." It argues that "the use of a predetermined criminal standard for the impeachment of a President is also supported by history, logic, legal precedent, and a sound and sensible public policy which demands stability in our form of government." To hold otherwise, it says, would be to expose the executive branch to "political impeachments."

The paper further argues that English precedents were inconclusive and should be rejected, because even though impeachment had been used in England to deal with what were, in effect, high crimes against the state committed by officeholders, impeachment had also been used there to establish "Parliamentary supremacy," whereas the framers of the Constitution were establishing a system of separation of powers. And even in England, the White House paper points out, many of the impeachments—including that of Warren Hastings—charged breaches of criminal law. The White House paper argues that the word "high" in the Constitutional definition of impeachment—for "treason, bribery, or other high crimes and misdemeanors"—applies to "misdemeanors" as well as "crimes," because otherwise it would have read high crimes *or* misdemeanors, and that they must be as serious as "treason" and "bribery." It points out that the Constitutional Convention rejected noncriminal definitions, such as "maladministration," "malpractice," and "misconduct." It points out that the Constitution says that "Judges . . . shall hold their Offices during good Behavior" but that no such language is applied to the President. It also argues that a different standard should be applied for the impeachment of judges from that applied for the impeachment of Presidents, because judges cannot otherwise be removed from office, while Presidents can be defeated at the next election, are prohibited from running for reëlection after serving two terms, or can be declared incapacitated under the Twenty-fifth Amendment. And in the impeachment of Andrew Johnson, the paper points out, most of the articles had to do with what the House of Representatives viewed to be a violation of the Tenure of Office Act, which specified that a violation of the Act would be a "high misdemeanor."

The report of the staff of the House Judiciary Committee's impeachment inquiry, issued in late February, rejects the argument that an impeachable offense must be a crime. "Impeachment is a Constitutional remedy addressed to serious offenses against the system of government," the report says. The report notes "three major Presidential duties of broad scope that are explicitly recited in the Constitution: to 'take care that the laws be faithfully executed,' to 'faithfully execute the Office of President of the United States,' and to 'preserve, protect, and defend the Constitution of the United States.' " All three of these are in the Constitution, the second and third as parts of the oath of office which the Constitution prescribes. The report argues that "the duty to 'take care' is affirmative," and "so is the duty faithfully to 'execute the office.' " It says, "The duty of a President to 'preserve, protect, and defend the Constitution' to the best of his ability includes the duty not to abuse his powers or transgress their limits—not to violate the rights of citizens, such as those guaranteed by the Bill of Rights, and not to act in derogation of powers vested elsewhere by the Constitution." It argues that these duties cannot be precisely spelled out, nor can the limits on the President's exercise of power. "Some of the most grievous offenses against our Constitutional form of government may not entail violations of the criminal law," it says. The report also says, "Not all Presidential misconduct is sufficient to constitute grounds for impeachment," adding that there is the further requirement of "substantiality." "In deciding whether this further requirement has been met," it says, "the facts must be considered as a whole in the context of the office, not in terms of separate or isolated events."

The Judiciary Committee's report also points out that the term "high misdemeanors" was defined in Blackstone's *Commentaries on the Laws of England*—to which the delegates to the Constitutional Convention had reference—as "maladministration of such high officers, as are in public trust and employment . . . usually punished by the method of parliamentary impeachment." The term "high crimes and misdemeanors" was adopted by the Convention, the report says, after "treason or bribery" alone was considered too narrow and the addition of "maladministration" was opposed by James Madison as too broad. The Constitution did not substitute impeachment for criminal prosecution, the report says, since it specifically did not immunize an impeached and convicted official from criminal liability. The report also points out that in English history the power of impeachment was designed to curb abuses of power by the King's Ministers, and that the phrase "high crimes and misdemeanors" was confined to impeachments, and "had no roots in the ordinary criminal law." The framers of the Constitution, it says, adopted impeachment as one way of seeking to "build in safeguards against executive abuse and usurpation of power." One reason that the Articles of Confederation had been rejected "was that they provided for a purely legislative form of government," but in adding an executive the framers explicitly rejected a plural executive, the report argues, "because a single person would give the most responsibility to the office."

In Federalist Paper No. 70, the report continues, Alexander Hamilton wrote that a plural executive would deprive the people of "the two greatest securities they can have for the faithful exercise of any delegated power . . . responsibility . . . to censure and to punishment." It was, Hamilton wrote, "far more safe [that] there should be a single object for the jealousy and watchfulness of the people." The report points out that William Davie, a delegate to the Constitutional Convention, told the North Carolina ratifying convention that the "predominant principle," on which the Convention had provided for a single executive was "the more obvious responsibility of one person," so that "the public were never at a loss" to fix the blame. But several safeguards were added to insure that the single chief executive did not arrogate powers like those from which the inhabitants of the new nation had fought a revolution to free themselves: the safeguards of checks and balances, a limited term of office, and impeachment.

The report also makes the point that the framers of the Constitution debated the question of whether the requirement of standing for reëlection, if the incumbent should choose to run again, would serve as a sufficient check on the executive. One of the framers argued against impeachment on the ground that the executive "would periodically be tried for his behavior by his electors," and Gouvernuer Morris suggested that an executive could "do no criminal act without coadjutors who may be punished." George Mason replied that no man should be "above justice," and that the principal as well as the coadjutors must be punished when great crimes are committed. James Madison, arguing in favor of an impeachment provision, said that it was "indispensable" in order to defend the people against "the incapacity, negligence, or perfidy of the chief magistrate." Madison argued that with a single executive, as opposed to a legislature, "loss of capacity or corruption was more within the compass of probable events, and either of them might be fatal to the Republic." The President "is not the King but the prime minister," said Gouverneur Morris at the Constitutional Convention. "The people are the King."

In Federalist Paper No. 65, Alexander Hamilton wrote:

A well-constituted court for the trial of impeachments is an object not more to be desired than difficult to be obtained in a government wholly elective. The subjects of its jurisdiction are those offenses which proceed from the misconduct of public men, or, in other words, from the abuse or violation of some public trust. They are of a nature which may with peculiar propriety be denominated POLITICAL, as they relate chiefly to injuries done immediately to the society itself. The prosecution of them, for this reason, will seldom fail to agitate the passions of the whole community, and to divide it into parties more or less friendly or inimical to the accused. In many cases it will connect itself with the pre-existing factions, and will enlist all their animosities, partialities, influence, and interest on one side or on the other; and in such cases there will always be the greatest danger that the decision will be regulated more by the comparative strength of parties than by the real demonstrations of innocence or guilt.

There is, inevitably, a certain selectivity with which arguments are marshalled for and against the various interpretations of the purpose and use of the impeachment process. For example, people who favor the broad interpretation of impeachment often quote the first part of Alexander Hamilton's statement about the political nature of impeachment but leave out the second part. In the end, therefore, the arguments have to come down to some root meanings of what this country is about and how democracy is supposed to work, and to common sense. And in the end, political beings have to make "POLITICAL" judgments. As of now, and more than ever, the Congress seems to dread that prospect.

The White House paper is widely dismissed as taking a predictably narrow view of impeachment, but it does suggest some questions worth considering. If the grounds for impeachment need not be criminal, how is it to be decided whether noncriminal grounds that are chosen have been chosen "responsibly"? If the grounds for impeachment must be criminal, what is to be done about abuse of the public trust or failure to carry out Constitutional duties? What if by the next election it might be too late? It stands to reason that grounds for impeachment cannot be confined to the items in the criminal statutes. There is no chapter in the criminal code covering the activities of Presidents. This is another example—there have been so many examples recently—of how not everything can be codified. In the end, the Constitutional system will always rest on the reasonableness and the sense of responsibility of those to whom it was entrusted. Depending on one's view of human nature—of the ultimate wisdom of man—one can decide how firm or how precarious a base that is.

After the staff report was released, Peter Rodino, Democrat of New Jersey and chairman of the House Judiciary Committee, said, "It has been my view all along that grounds for impeachment need not arise out of criminal conduct." Edward Hutchinson, Republican of Michigan and the committee's ranking minority member, said, "There should be criminality involved," and added that he did not endorse the staff report.

For a time, the Judiciary Committee considered holding meetings to discuss what constituted an impeachable offense, but, for reasons of both philosophy and politics, the idea was shelved. There was no way that the committee could consider this subject without becoming entrapped early in the process in a partisan dispute. Moreover, such a discussion would have involved reducing the intentionally abstract to the concrete. This was a situation in which the maxim "The law arises from the facts" applied. That might seem subjective, but then the concept of impeachment called for subjective judgments. By and large, the members agreed that what behavior constituted an impeachable offense was something on which they would have to decide individually.

At a press conference last week, his first in four months, the President said, "You don't have to be a Constitutional lawyer to know that the Constitution is very precise in defining what is an impeachable offense. And in this respect it is the opinion of White House counsel and a number of other Constitutional lawyers, who are perhaps more up to date on this than I am at this time, that a criminal offense on the part of the President is the requirement for impeachment." At the press conference, too, for the first time in our lives, we watched and heard a President say, "I do not expect to be impeached."

One senses today, instead of excitement, a subdued atmosphere. Perhaps it is an atmosphere of foreboding. Things are quieter, and grimmer. Large and difficult events lie ahead. People seem to be digging in, getting ready—or trying to. But the rumors and the speculation still sweep through this city. They move along the familiar paths among the press corps, the members of Congress and their aides, interested onlookers (of whom there seem to be an unprecedented number), and even the Administration and former members thereof. They travel by word of mouth in the Congressional cloakrooms and gyms, by telephone throughout the city, and from table to table in the Senate and House dining rooms, the Federal City Club (patronized largely by journalists and Democratic lawyers), and the Sans Souci restaurant. A colleague calls and says that the information in the briefcase given to Judge Sirica is "very damaging" to the President. "It could be over in two weeks," the caller says. A Judiciary Committee member says that "what with the indictments and the mysterious documents, it could be over before April."

Widely accepted "truths" about the President's situation keep shifting. The Congress returned to Washington in January, having found its constituents in an angry mood. The mixed distress over gasoline shortages, inflation, and the questions raised about the Nixon Administration was difficult to sort out, but the politicians sensed the over-all mood and were uneasy. Around the same time, the President emerged from a period of seclusion and vowed to "fight like hell" to stay in office. (One member of Congress quoted him as saying, "There is a time to be timid. There is a time to be conciliatory. There is a time to fly and there is a time to fight. And I'm going to fight like hell.") The period of Presidential seclusion had seemed both to reflect and to feed a sense of the deep trouble he was in. In the course of that period, the White House had issued two "white papers"—on the I.T.T. and milk controversies—which raised still more questions; a White House plan to make public some transcripts of tapes of Presidential conversations was cancelled; and Operation Candor was declared ended. (A White House spokesman said that release of summaries of the tapes "could lead to confusion in the minds of the American public and further distortion of the matter.")

The report in mid-January by the experts appointed by Judge Sirica and agreed upon by the Special Prosecutor's office and the White House about the eighteen-and-a-half-minute gap in the tape of the conversation between the President and Haldeman held three days after the break-in at the Watergate sent shock waves through Washington. The experts said that the erasure was the result of five—and perhaps as many as nine—separate manual erasures. There were reports that the President faced more trouble on his taxes. The Special Prosecutor's staff was said

to have made new discoveries. There was a sense that the net was closing, and there were rumors that the President might resign.

Then the President's confident delivery of his State of the Union message—conciliatory about domestic programs, noncommittal about the
degree to which he would coöperate with investigations into his own
conduct, adamant, once more, about getting the issue behind us ("One
year of Watergate is enough")—gave pause to many politicians. They
began to think that perhaps he should be taken at his word when he said
in his State of the Union speech that "I have no intention whatever of
ever walking away from the job that the people elected me to do for the
people of the United States." Shortly thereafter, Capitol Hill was filled
with rumors that the President was prepared for a strong "counterattack." Very thinly veiled warnings went from the White House to some
of the media that there might be trouble if what were viewed by the
White House as "attacks" on the President continued. The idea spread
that perhaps the President would in fact survive, and certainly it was
clear that he would "fight like hell"—and this was not the sort of battle
in which many people wanted to be on the losing side.

But other processes were also in motion. The staff of the Ervin committee was still at work. The House Judiciary Committee's inquiry into
the President's impeachment was getting organized. And by now three
grand juries in Washington were examining evidence presented by the
staff of the Special Prosecutor.

There are press reports today that the grand jury considered indicting
the President but did not do so after Special Prosecutor Leon Jaworski
advised that the Constitution precluded the indictment of a President
while he was in office.

A Gallup poll shows twenty-seven-percent approval of the way the
President is handling his job. This figure has remained about the same
since the beginning of the year. In January, a Harris poll found that
only twenty-one percent looked favorably on the way the Congress was
doing its job.

As of early March, twenty-six members of the House—an unusually
high number—have decided not to run for reëlection. Politics is getting
harder on its practitioners.

Yesterday, the President signed into law a bill that requires Senate
confirmation of appointments to the posts of director and deputy director of the Office of Management and Budget. Passage of the law was one
small move by Congress to regain some of its power from the executive.
Last year, the President vetoed a similar bill, and his veto was sustained.
In 1970, when the White House was beginning to try to consolidate

control over the bureaucracy, a White House aide explained to me at lunch one day, "It works in the Vatican. It works in the Mafia. It ought to work here."

MARCH 5

This morning, Mike Mansfield, the Senate Majority Leader, told reporters that he was not giving any thought to a trial of the President in the Senate. This may have been Mansfield's idea of the proper thing to say at this moment, but thought about such a trial, accompanied by research, has been going on in the Senate since the beginning of this year. There were, in fact, several senators who believed as early as January that the case against the President was strong enough so that if it reached the Senate—and they believed it would—on the basis of the evidence, and the momentum of the issue, the Senate would convict. But out of a sense of propriety and a desire to appear decorous, they of course would not speak this way for the record. They tried to convey the impression that they were preoccupied with other matters.

MARCH 6

The Democrat, Thomas Luken, defeated the Republican, Willis Gradison, in a congressional election in Cincinnati yesterday. The district had gone Democratic only three times in this century. In California, a traditionally Republican seat was won by the Republican candidate, Robert Lagomarsino. On tonight's television news, Lagomarsino says that he won "in spite, perhaps, of what has happened in Washington." At a conference of governors here, Governor Francis Sargent, of Massachusetts, a Republican, said that the country would be better off if the President were out of office and were replaced by Ford.

Two days ago, Harold Wilson, the Labour Party leader, was asked to form a government in England after Edward Heath, the Conservative leader, failed to do so. Neither party won a majority in the recent election. The French government resigned last week and has been reorganized. Golda Meir announced today that she had managed to form a Cabinet in Israel, ending a stalemate of nine weeks. Italy has no government.

In court today, James St. Clair, the President's new attorney, announced that the President had decided to turn over to the House Judiciary Committee the nineteen tapes and seven hundred documents he had given to the Special Prosecutor. He said that the President would answer written questions from the committee and was willing to be interviewed by a few members of the committee. This offer of material is true to another pattern: when the President appears to be in serious trouble, when the net appears to be closing, he tosses out more tapes, documents, statements. But what he tosses out has never been enough. Moreover, the President has given the Special Prosecutor some items he did not want, and has not given him some items he did want—including some promised material about the plumbers.

St. Clair's announcement was made in the course of a hearing by Judge Sirica on what to do with the grand jury's sealed report and what has now come to be called "the bulging briefcase." In court, St. Clair took no position on the question of referring the grand-jury report. Arguments against a referral to the committee were made by John J. Wilson, the lawyer for Haldeman and Ehrlichman, and by other defense counsel, on the ground that their clients might be harmed by pre-trial publicity. (In the age of television, the concept that trials might be harmed by pre-trial publicity seems antique, but it is still with us.) It is widely assumed that Wilson was carrying the argument for the White House, though he denied this.

On tonight's news, it is reported that although the White House said that the President spoke with Haldeman over the weekend to congratulate him on his wedding anniversary, the anniversary was actually some ten days earlier. Gerald Warren, the White House Deputy Press Secretary, speculated that perhaps the President had just been reminded of it. A prevalent theory is that the President may be acting to protect his former aides, who, in turn, are protecting him. There is even a theory that the aides are working collectively to keep him in office so that in the end, if it comes to that, he can give them Presidential pardons.

At his press conference tonight, attempting to confront the problem of Haldeman's indictment for perjury for telling the Ervin committee that the President had said "it would be wrong" to buy the silence of the Watergate defendants, Mr. Nixon got himself in deeper trouble. He said that John Dean told him "for the first time on March 21st" that payments were being made to the Watergate defendants "for the purpose of keeping them quiet, not simply for their defense." And, said the President, "if it was for the purpose of keeping them quiet . . . hush money, that of course would have been an obstruction of justice." In August, 1973, the President said he had been told only that the payments were for the defendants' lawyers and families, and said that Haldeman's testimony was "accurate." Tonight, describing the March 21st meeting with Haldeman and Dean, Mr. Nixon said, "We examined all of the options at great length during our discussion. . . . Then we came to what I considered to be the bottom line. I pointed out that raising the money, paying the money, was something that could be done. But I pointed out that that was linked to clemency; that no individual is simply going to stay in jail because people are taking care of his family or his counsel, as the case might be; and that unless a promise of clemency was made that the objective of so-called hush money would not be achieved. . . . I then said that to pay clemency was wrong. . . . I said, 'It is wrong; that is for sure.' . . . Now, when individuals read the entire transcript of the twenty-first meeting or hear the entire tape where we discussed all these options, they may reach different interpretations. But I know what I meant and I know also what I did. I meant that the whole transaction was wrong."

MARCH 7

John Ehrlichman and Charles Colson were indicted today for conspiring to violate the civil rights of Dr. Fielding, Daniel Ellsberg's psychiatrist, by arranging for the break-in at his office. The indictment says that the conspirators did "without legal process . . . covertly and unlawfully enter" Dr. Fielding's offices, "thereby injuring, oppressing, threatening, and intimidating Dr. Lewis J. Fielding in the free exercise and enjoyment of the right and privilege secured to him by the Fourth Amendment to the Constitution of the United States to be secure in his person, house, papers, and effects against unreasonable searches and seizures," and that they did "thereafter conceal such activities, so as to prevent Dr. Lewis J. Fielding from securing redress for the violation of such right and privileges."

Also indicted for participation in the conspiracy to deprive Dr. Fielding of his rights were G. Gordon Liddy, Bernard Barker, and Eugenio Martinez, who were also convicted for the break-in at the Watergate, and Felipe de Diego, a Cuban refugee recruited, as was Martinez, by Barker. Barker and Martinez participated in the Bay of Pigs invasion. Barker, Martinez and De Diego had been in the real estate business in Miami. Liddy has been cited, in addition, for contempt of Congress for refusing to testify before a House subcommittee investigating the involvement of the C.I.A. in various events related to Watergate. Liddy has refused to testify anywhere, has been convicted of contempt of court for refusing to testify before the grand jury, and is now in prison. He has also been sentenced for his role in the Watergate break-in.

Also named today as unindicted co-conspirators were Krogh, Howard Hunt, and David Young, an assistant to Henry Kissinger until Young was assigned, with Krogh, to establish the plumbers unit. Hunt and Young had been granted immunity in return for testimony. Ehrlichman was charged, further, with lying to the grand jury and the F.B.I. during their investigations of the Fielding break-in. Among the overt acts listed in the indictment are several memoranda the White House aides wrote, which came to light during the Ervin committee hearings. One of the overt acts was the memorandum written by Krogh and Young to Ehrlichman proposing a "covert operation . . . to examine all the medical files still held by Ellsberg's psychoanalyst." This was the memorandum to which Ehrlichman had, after initialling it, added the notation, "If done under your assurance that it is not traceable." Another was the memorandum written by Ehrlichman to Colson entitled "Hunt/Liddy Special Project No. One," and asking Colson to prepare a "game plan" for using the materials derived from "the 'proposed undertaking by Hunt and Liddy.'" (We now know that "Special Project M-1" was really "Special Project No. One.") Ehrlichman, the indictment further charges, had a telephone conversation with Krogh and Young "in which Krogh and Young assured Ehrlichman that the planned entry into the office of Dr. Lewis J. Fielding would not be traceable." Also among the overt acts documenting the conspiracy was the arrangement by Colson to use five thousand dollars from one of the milk funds to finance the break-in. The nineteenth, and last, overt act was that "On or about March 27, 1973, John D. Ehrlichman caused the removal of certain memoranda related to the entry into the offices of Dr. Lewis J. Fielding from files maintained at the White House in which such memoranda would be kept in the ordinary course of business."

When we heard the news, one Friday in April of last year, in the course of the Ellsberg trial that Hunt and Liddy had been involved in a break-in at Ellsberg's psychiatrist's office, it made little sense; we were not yet able to fit it in with other events. The Ellsberg trial seemed unrelated to Watergate then. There were so many other events at the time—the Watergate case was still breaking—that we were hardly able to absorb it. When Daniel Ellsberg portrayed himself as a major target of the Nixon Administration, many dismissed this as Ellsberg's delusion. The connection between the Fielding break-in and other events did not begin to become clear until the President, late in May, 1973, issued his statement that told something about the plumbers and "the Huston plan." In May, the President said that "because of the extreme gravity of the situation [the leak of the Pentagon papers] and not then knowing what additional national secrets Mr. Ellsberg might disclose, I did impress upon Mr. Krogh the vital importance to the national security of his assignment." (We have read of how the President instructed those setting up the plumbers operation to read the chapter in *Six Crises* in which he tells how he, as a congressman, carried out the investigation of Alger Hiss. Mr. Nixon wrote there, among other things, that the Justice Department could not be trusted to do it.) But, said the President in May, "I did not authorize and had no knowledge of any illegal means to be used to achieve this goal." Perhaps the meaning of the Fielding break-in did not become entirely clear until Ehrlichman gave it definition during the Ervin hearings last summer. It was then that Ehrlichman suggested that the concept that lay behind the Fourth Amendment had "eroded." And now it is becoming apparent that what have been seen as efforts to cover up the Watergate break-in were efforts to cover up the Fielding break-in as well.

The President has said that he first learned of the Fielding break-in on March 17, 1973. Henry Petersen, the Assistant Attorney General who was then in charge of the Watergate investigation, testified before the Ervin committee that when, in mid-April, he told the President that the prosecutors had just learned of such a break-in, the President said, "I know about that. That is a national-security matter. You stay out of that."

Following the return of the indictment today, a White House spokesman reread the statement that had been issued with the President's approval after the indictment of last Friday.

MARCH 8

The President's latest challenge to the House Judiciary Committee is his most audacious yet. In a letter—released by the committee yesterday—from St. Clair to John Doar, special counsel to the committee's impeachment inquiry, St. Clair implied that the committee should limit its inquiry to the Watergate break-in and cover-up. "In the President's opinion," St. Clair wrote, "the Watergate matter and widespread allegations of obstruction of justice in connection therewith are at the heart of this matter." In addition, his letter strongly implied that the President would not provide the tapes and documents that the committee requested on February 25th. These items included six conversations involving the cover-up that were not turned over to the Special Prosecutor. St. Clair's letter also stated that the committee should define an impeachable offense before proceeding with the inquiry. "Furthermore," he wrote, "before such an inquiry is undertaken, it would seem clear that fundamental fairness would require that the 'allegations involving the President' under investigation be identified." Of the committee's request for other materials, St. Clair said, "You appear to have requested, in effect, access for your staff to other Presidential papers, conversations and memoranda without apparent limitation." At a committee meeting yesterday, Rodino called this "a distortion."

In February, the House passed a resolution affirming the committee's authority to conduct the impeachment inquiry and to issue subpoenas—by a vote of 410-4. At the meeting yesterday, the committee decided, at the suggestion of Doar and Albert Jenner, the minority counsel, to postpone until later this month any move to subpoena the material. A subpoena would be a major move, perhaps provoking a confrontation. Rodino wants to appear patient, move cautiously, to exhaust—and to appear to have exhausted—other remedies, so as to have the broadest possible committee support behind any moves he makes. It has been an article of faith among Democrats that impeachment must have strong bipartisan support, just as it has been an article of faith among them—

sometimes broken—that if the President resigns, it must be at the Republicans' behest. This puts the Republicans in the vortex.

The Watergate break-in and cover-up constitute one of six broad areas under investigation by the committee staff. Earlier this week, the committee issued a report, ostensibly from Rodino to the members, about the status of the impeachment inquiry. The report is also a reminder of the breadth of the potential case against the President. The list included in the new report is divided into the same six areas as an earlier report: domestic surveillance, including the plumbers, the Huston plan, and wiretapping; intelligence activities and "dirty tricks" conducted for the purpose of the President's reëlection; the Watergate break-in and cover-up; alleged improprieties in connection with the President's finances; the use of government agencies for political purposes; and other misconduct, including the secret and perhaps illegal bombing of Cambodia, impoundment of funds, and dismantling of the Office of Economic Opportunity. The staff does not give all of the areas equal weight. The list is based on allegations submitted by members of Congress or on material gathered by the staff. There is no serious intention to consider impeaching the President for dismantling the O.E.O., and there is little interest in taking him on over the bombing of Cambodia. Some members say that this is a "political" issue—one of policy differences. Some say that the bombing is something that the Congress should have known, or done, something about. Moreover, some feel that the vote of the Congress to end the bombing as of August 15, 1973, in effect sanctioned the bombing until then. And there is something else, perhaps, at the heart of it: members of Congress do not want to fight the impeachment issue over the bitter question of the war.

The committee on which the responsibility for conducting the inquiry into the impeachment of the President landed last autumn was then largely an unknown quantity. With a few exceptions, little attention is paid in Washington to House members, much less to the particular characteristics of each House committee. But each committee does have its own characteristics, and in 1973 the Judiciary Committee's were in the midst of change. The committee had long been dominated by Emanuel Celler, a Democrat from Brooklyn, who had been its chairman (except for two years when the Republicans controlled the House) since 1948. But in 1972, at the age of eighty-four, Celler was defeated in a Democratic primary by Elizabeth Holtzman, who herself joined the Judiciary Committee. In 1973, Celler was replaced as chairman by the Democratic member next in seniority—an unknown figure named Peter Rodino, a Democrat from Newark, New Jersey. Celler had developed the practice of running the committee in tandem with the ranking minority member, William McCulloch, of Ohio, and, as it happened, McCulloch retired in 1972. He was replaced as ranking minority member by Edward Hutchinson, of Michigan, who was even less well known than Rodino. Furthermore, the committee started out in this Congress with an unusual number of new members—eleven.

The Republican side of the committee has a disproportionate number of conservatives, just as the Democratic side has a disproportionate number of liberals. Even the Southern Democrats on the committee— James Mann, of South Carolina; Walter Flowers, of Alabama; and Ray Thornton, of Arkansas—while they are no liberals, are less attached to the old order than their Southern predecessors on the committee were, or than many of their Southern colleagues in the House still are. The preponderance of liberals on the majority side stems partly from the fact that members interested in civil rights and civil liberties have gravitated toward the House Judiciary Committee. This follows a congressional pattern: members interested in promoting legislation that concerns them—members interested in protecting agriculture, say, or members from areas dependent on defense contracts—gravitate toward the committees with jurisdiction over their interests. The result is imbalances in the committee system: the Agriculture Committee is more interested than the House as a whole in protecting agricultural programs, and the Education and Labor Committee is more interested than the House as a whole in protecting education programs and the concerns of labor. The theory has been that the House as a whole acts as an arbiter of these interests, usually by a process of mutual accommodation. The committees, therefore, are highly influential, often decisive, in the final actions of the House. But there is a question as to whether House traditions will apply when it comes to the issue of impeaching the President.

It was, then, on an unformed and disparate group that there suddenly fell such issues as the confirmation of a Vice-President-designate, legislation to establish a Special Prosecutor, and the conduct of an inquiry into impeachment of the President. When the first biographical sketches of Peter Rodino appeared, the other committee members were surprised to learn that he was an amateur poet. Rodino had been "one of the boys"; he had been considered a man of unimpressive talents, and had been better liked than Celler, in part because he was less feared. As a member of the House, he had shown little creativity (he had interested himself mainly in immigration legislation) and almost no leadership (he was responsible for making Columbus Day a national holiday). So when responsibility for the impeachment inquiry fell upon Rodino, the widespread assumption was that he wasn't up to it. But gradually he began to find his style—low-key, easygoing, but firm—and as time went on he became increasingly adroit in working with other Democratic committee members. Even the committee Republicans began to sense that they would be ill-advised to criticize him. The evolving impression of Rodino became self-confirming, as such things do in Washington: as he was perceived to be more of a leader, he was able to be more of a leader.

Sometime last summer, the House leaders and Rodino saw that impeachment was not the remote possibility it had once seemed. And since there were no recent precedents to go by, Rodino directed his staff to begin to collect information on impeachment. When, last fall, the question became a live one, the Judiciary Committee had published one of the few useful volumes on the subject. Spiro Agnew's request, late in September, that the House conduct an impeachment inquiry because, he claimed, he was immune from criminal proceedings as long as he remained Vice-President—even though quickly rejected—heightened the committee's sense that it had better brush up on the subject of impeachment. When resolutions to impeach the President were referred to the committee after the weekend when Archibald Cox was fired, the committee still had to hold confirmation hearings on the first Vice-President selected under the Twenty-fifth Amendment. (House leaders referred the impeachment resolutions to the Judiciary Committee, rather than appoint a special committee, as some House members sought, both because there were precedents for giving the issue to the Judiciary Committee and because the selection of a special committee would have involved a great deal of House politics and, therefore, trouble.) Further, the search for a counsel—a critical matter—took some time, and John Doar was not named until December 20th.

When Rodino named Doar as special counsel, the Republicans wanted someone of note as minority counsel. At the importuning of Tom Railsback, an Illinois Republican on the committee, and with the approval of Robert McClory, the other committee Republican from Illinois, Albert Jenner, the prominent Chicago attorney, agreed, in January, to take the job of minority counsel. Jenner was a flourishing trial lawyer who had been active in the American Bar Association, was senior counsel to the Warren Commission on the assassination of President Kennedy, and was a member of the National Commission on the Causes and Prevention of Violence—a lawyer well known in the legal circles in which well-knownness counts. He also had been one of the many lawyers considered by Rodino for the job of counsel.

Doar, for at least the first month, had to spend much of his time selecting a staff and working out methods of procedure. By early March, the staff numbered a hundred and one, of whom forty-three were lawyers. The staff went to work on the second floor of the old Congressional Hotel—an office annex across the street from the House office buildings—under arrangements of maximum security. Doar rented an apartment a few blocks away, made it a point not to talk with the press, and fastidiously absented himself from Washington social life.

The committee, sensing that there was no way a coherent investiga-

tion could be managed by thirty-eight members of the House, took unusual vows of noninvolvement in the early processes of the inquiry. Only
Rodino, Hutchinson, Doar, and Jenner were to have access to the information that was being assembled. In the first weeks of the inquiry, most
committee members had only vague knowledge of what the staff was
doing. It is, of course, standard practice for congressional committees
to rely heavily on their staffs, but these procedures went well beyond
that. Thus, the counsel played an unusually strong role—defining the
nature and the strategy of the inquiry—and once they were selected the
process was under way.

Most of the talk one hears now and much of the press attention
focus on what the President said at his latest press conference about
the meeting of March 21st. There is speculation about whether the
President may be guilty of misprision of a felony for not reporting to
the appropriate authorities what Dean had told him about the payments
to buy silence. While it is inevitably tempting to some to try to find
a specific instance of wrongdoing on the part of the President—the
"cookie-jar syndrome"—such an approach gets in the way of understanding the breadth and the depth of the issues and of dealing with
them. Maybe it is easier to zero in (as we did just a few weeks ago)
on a particular question like "Who erased the tape?" Our minds are
getting tired. The focus shrinks into ever-smaller circles, until it lands
on a tiny dot.

There is, moreover, a certain absurdity to the discourse about the
March 21st meeting. (I held out for as long as possible against thinking of this mosaic of issues in terms of dates of meetings, but the
dates have a way of forcing themselves into our minds and our discourse.) In order to talk of the meeting in terms of what the President
says about it, one has to begin with a number of assumptions: that
it *was* the first time he learned that money was being used to buy
silence; that for almost a year after the break-in the President was
either extraordinarily uninterested in what was going on or unable
to inform himself about it; that Dean, an underling, could, unbeknownst to Haldeman and Ehrlichman, have made the arrangements
to buy silence; that Ehrlichman and Haldeman really believed that
the money was going for a "legal-defense fund" for the Watergate
defendants; and that, in some sudden access of compassion, those
determined opponents of federal assistance to so many would have
approved the payment of money for the families and the legal fees of
the men indicted for the Watergate break-in. (Ehrlichman, in his testimony before the Ervin committee, likened this fund, with apparent
retrospective approval, to defense funds that had been established for
Daniel Ellsberg, Angela Davis, and the Berrigan brothers. According
to testimony, over four hundred thousand dollars was paid to the Water-

gate defendants.) And there is a certain absurdity in assuming that the major question is whether, in the midst of all these misdeeds and frantic meetings, the President ever said, "It is wrong."

Dinner-party conversations these days, when they are not about the President's fate, are about the movie *The Exorcist* and about the gasoline shortage. In Washington, as in some states, one has the opportunity to wait in line for gas only on alternative days—odd-numbered days if the last number on one's license plate is odd, even-numbered if it is even. A woman came up to me at dinner recently and asked, "Are you an odd or an even?" An ad-hoc, berserk system of in-effect rationing, but the President is adamant against rationing. People now tell stories of their adventures in obtaining gasoline with all the detail that might go into an account of an airline trip. And they are just as interesting.

Dean Burch, forty-six, a former aide and close associate of Barry Goldwater, and, until recently, chairman of the Federal Communications Commission, has just joined the White House staff as counsellor to the President. Laird left on February 1st, and Harlow is leaving soon. The question is why, if the President is in such deep trouble, Burch would want to join the staff, and why, if the President is not in deep trouble, Laird and Harlow are leaving.

The President has lately been at some pains not to give further displeasure to conservatives—or, at least, that is how several of his actions have been perceived. The cross-pressures on Nixon are fiercer than ever. In a vote in the House to impeach or in the Senate to convict, it is the conservatives who could save him or do him in. Even some Administration officials concede that certain of his recent energy policies, including the veto of the energy bill, were designed not so much to please the oil companies as to please conservative senators from oil-producing states. Similarly, the White House recently dropped its support of a relatively mild bill to encourage the states to devise land-use policies when the bill was strongly opposed by politicians from Western states interested in development. Conservatives are taking aim at a possible new arms-limitation agreement, in the hope of shooting it down. Also, after the President's State of the Union message, which proposed a number of new domestic programs, *Human Events,* a conservative weekly, ran a headline asking "WHY WERE ALL THOSE REPUBLICANS CHEERING?" It took exception to the President's willingness to "embark upon sweeping new and untried spending programs, thus escalating the budget ever upwards." An earlier edition of the weekly, noting that a new family-assistance plan was in the works, was headlined "HOW MUCH CAN CONSERVATIVES TAKE?" The President has not yet proposed his new welfare-reform bill.

The government announced yesterday that wholesale prices rose again in February. The rise put the index 20.3 percent higher than it was a year earlier, and the consumer price index was rising in February, 1974, at an annual rate of 14 percent.

Two indictments, involving eleven people, and a troublesome Presidential press conference in one week. The feeling is in the air that the President is in terrible trouble. But he is still in power, and we are all, in a sense, riding his back. Tomorrow, the seven men indicted last week for the Watergate cover-up will be arraigned. I have decided to take the weekend off and get out of town. It is becoming more important than ever to break free of this nervous system that is "Washington" once in a while—to escape the talk and the rumors and the speculation. The nervous system is getting overloaded these days, and as it becomes more important to get away, there is so much going on that it becomes more difficult to do so. Many here are taking a certain pleasure in the fact that tomorrow men who recently held great power will be brought before the court to be arraigned. It reminds me a bit of the song from *Candide:* "What a day, what a day, for an auto-da-fé." People ask me if I can bear to be out of town for "the arraignment." I can.

11

Monday. The seven men indicted for the cover-up of the Watergate break-in pleaded not guilty Saturday. Their trial has been tentatively set for September 9th.

The question persists: What manner of men were these who once ran the Nixon Administration and the country? Of course, we do not yet know whether they are guilty as charged, but we already know much of what happened. If they are found not guilty in strictly legal terms, they nevertheless chose strangely conspiratorial subordinates and created an atmosphere of punitiveness wherein they tolerated or encouraged an array of misdeeds which is still hard to comprehend. They also seemed to take some pains to establish "deniability"—to not know the details of deeds that were done. We shall never know now where, if anywhere, it all might have led. What does all this mean for our country and our Constitution? Given that we entrust power to fallible human beings, how can we prevent things like this from happening again?

We are not giving much thought to these questions now. Too much is going on. We are absorbing, one after another, events that outrun our imaginations, and trying to prepare ourselves for the months of bitter struggle to come. Someone close to the Administration has said to me that the story of the Nixon Administration is one of people who were in over their heads. There may be something to that. But that does not explain it. There was a fanatic quality to some of the Nixon men, a weaving together of their public piety and their venom which may have deceived even them. And one cannot escape the thought that the President set the tone. Lonely and suspicious, a man with a striking lack of deep human connections, he seems to have gone through life as if in constant combat. He confused legitimate opposition with vendetta, and so did his staff. Most of us have what a friend of mine calls our "inner jury"—people whose judgment we trust and whose esteem matters to us and whom we count on to level with us. Nixon does not seem to have an inner jury.

We used to be told that the man Nixon respected, the one who could get to him, was John Mitchell. Mitchell had some of the surface attributes that sometimes pass for wisdom: he puffed on a pipe and said little.

But now we know that behind that smoke there was no judgment. The White House circle began as a relatively broad one, containing people with varying points of view. Then the circle grew narrower and nar- rower. The once highly touted policy debates vanished, and so did most of the people who engaged in them. When Secretary of the Interior Walter Hickel was fired, in 1970, after complaining, in a letter to the President which was leaked to the press, that he could not get access to the President, it seemed that perhaps he was being theatrical. But he was being prophetic. Someone who went through those White House years has pointed out to me that when the President began to run into trou- ble—after the Senate defeated his nominations of Clement Haynsworth and G. Harrold Carswell to the Supreme Court; after the war was extended into Cambodia and there were protests on the campuses— he drew closer to him those who spoke to his own suspicious nature: Haldeman and Mitchell. It was in 1970, after the student protests, that the Huston plan was drawn up, and one year later that the plumbers unit was established. Haldeman, now forty-seven, had worked for Nixon on and off since 1956, and it is said that these two men were most alike in outlook. Haldeman, crew-cut and quiet, ran the White House by a system of fear. It was a place of suspicions and rivalries and of making points by acting and talking tough. Haldeman recruited his old college friend Ehrlichman to work as an advance man for Nixon's 1960 Presidential campaign, and later Ehrlichman worked on Nixon's 1962 race for the governorship of California, and on the 1968 Presidential race. In between, Haldeman worked for the J. Walter Thompson adver- tising agency in Los Angeles (from which he recruited Ron Ziegler and Dwight Chapin), and Ehrlichman was a Seattle zoning lawyer.

The unusual tough-guy talk of the President's aides was the very atmosphere of this White House. We have now seen it in their memos. We have seen it carried out in their deeds. And those who have heard the Presidential tapes have come away shaken. (One man who worked at the White House told me—perhaps without realizing what he was saying—that in an attempt to persuade the President to give him more responsibilities he had said, "I can do bad things, too.") These people seem to have understood little of what politics and government are sup- posed to be about. But they had power. And, as they compromised the public morality, they were not alone. There were those who aided and abetted: the businessmen who bought in, went along, and would not speak out; those politicians and members of the press who were truly frightened. Nixon and his aides were subjected to that process by which we impute authority to those in authority, give them power because they have power, accord them respectability because they are in positions to which we, for a variety of reasons, accord respect. This imputation process begins before these people attain power, because they might

attain it. The "new Nixon," before he was elected in 1968. Before Spiro
Agnew resigned in disgrace he was assumed by many politicians and
political observers to be the next Republican candidate for President.
One of the wisest people I know says that we must take care not to over-
correct for what has happened. He argues that the Nixon group was an
accidental one, not likely to be replicated for perhaps a century. Perhaps
this group was accidental, but we cannot count on that.

In the future, beyond all this, we cannot look to some leader to save
us; that would be one of the wrong lessons to draw from this period.
Nor can we put our faith in the Congress; the Congress almost failed
us, or perhaps it did fail us. We cannot put our faith in new legislation;
laws are not self-enforcing. We cannot put our faith in the private sector, because so much of the private sector bought in. We cannot put our
faith in the press; the press almost failed us. Another wrong lesson to
draw would be that the Presidency must be greatly weakened. That idea
is enjoying some fashion now, but the Congress, by the nature of the
institution, cannot manage foreign policy or economic policy or energy
policy. The Presidency must be strong, but it must be accountable. That,
after all, was the original idea. It is true that not everything can be codified. Democracy, like any noncoercive relationship, rests on a shared
understanding of limits. Our recent experience has been with people in
power who did not recognize limits.

The solution, it seems, is to build a web of accountability around the
Presidency, around the Congress. The problem is not power; it is unaccountable power. To begin with, we cannot hold institutions accountable
if we do not know what is going on. We did not know that secret investigative and intelligence units had been established in the White House.
We did not know that decisions had been taken which had the effect
of suspending some of the guarantees in the Bill of Rights. We did
not—and still do not—know the degree to which government was sold
and to which there were attempts to use the instruments of government against citizens expressing legitimate opposition. Any President
would want a responsive bureaucracy and a coöperative Cabinet, but
we have now seen the dangers of an executive branch that is unac-
countably responsive to an unaccountable White House. The only thing
between us and that is us—and the Congress. The Congress may not be
able, institutionally, to "manage" the complexities of society, but it can
help to shape policies and it can exercise "oversight." And the oversight
functions can be rearranged so as to break up the sweetheart contracts
between the Congress and the agencies it is supposed to oversee. The
Congress can write curbs on lawless government and see to it that they
are enforced. It can help to protect independence and integrity in the
bureaucracy. It can open its own methods to scrutiny, so that we know
more about what it is doing and to whom it is responding. Congress is

the accessible branch. The executive branch can become remote and inaccessible and arrogant. The Supreme Court is remote and inaccessible, guided by canonical doctrine. The Congress responds to great outside pressures. So, in the end, it comes down to us.

MARCH 12

The crocuses are up, and the forsythia is in bloom. There is still a chill to the breeze. We often get one more snowstorm or cold spell here after the crocuses appear, as if winter won't give up and let us have our spring. Spring in Washington is unlike anything I have seen anywhere else. When the azaleas finally reach full bloom, toward the end of April, the city has an astonishing, almost exotic look and feel.

At Key Biscayne this past weekend, a spokesman for the President said that the White House was aware of the "semantical differences" between the accounts of the March 21st meeting which the President gave last week and last August.

A Harris poll published yesterday showed that fifty-four percent of those interviewed believed that "if President Nixon fails to turn over the information the House Judiciary Committee wants, that committee should vote to bring up impeachment charges against the President." By sixty-four percent to seventeen percent, the respondents said they did not believe that the President would turn over all the evidence to the committee. And by seventy-one percent to eighteen percent the respondents said they believed that the President had withheld important information. A Minnesota poll published two days ago showed that fifty-eight percent believed that President Nixon had "broken his oath of office."

Gerald Ford is quoted in today's New York *Times* as having said yesterday that he is still convinced that President Nixon was not involved in Watergate or the cover-up. "But time will tell," he added. In January, Hugh Scott, the Senate Minority Leader, said he had seen some "information" not made public by the White House which would "exculpate the President" on some specific items in the Watergate affair. A couple of days later, Ford said he had been offered an opportunity to examine this evidence but had chosen not to. A week before the Vice-President said this, he had made a speech in Atlantic City in which he said that "a few extreme partisans" were trying to drive the President from office. The speech caused an uproar, and Ford's allies let it be known that White House aides had written the speech.

In an interview with Lesley Oelsner which appeared in today's New York *Times,* St. Clair said that the President did not fail to tell law-enforcement authorities about the payment of money to buy silence, because "the President is the chief law-enforcement officer of the country."

The White House has leaked to the press a letter from John Doar to St. Clair requesting more information, the object of the leak being to show that the committee had asked for tapes of forty-two—some press reports say forty-three—conversations, rather than, as earlier reports had suggested, six. "Committee sources" explained to the press that they had been seeking conversations surrounding "six events." Committee members, meeting this morning, were furious that the White House had leaked Doar's letter. By the end of the day, anyone who was interested knew it was Ken Clawson, now communications director for the President, who had leaked the letter, and that he was the "official" who had said that Doar's letter showed that the committee wanted "carte blanche to rummage through every nook and cranny in the White House on a fishing expedition." He was referring to a request by Doar that arrangements be made for committee staff members to examine the files of Haldeman, Ehrlichman, Colson, and Dean "for the purpose of selecting materials which, in our opinion, are necessary for the investigation."

It is interesting to consider what this story would be like tapeless. (I have been told by someone whose word is to be trusted on this that destruction of the tapes was considered at the White House shortly after their existence was revealed.) A tapeless story would have left us with just the events that took place under the Administration, and a judgment would have had to be made on them. The talk of impeachment and resignation—a sense of the seriousness of what had happened—began several months before we heard about the tapes. There would still have been the question of one person's word against another's, and struggles over documents. These people wrote a lot down, too. And, despite the compulsive recording, not everything that the Nixon Administration said or did was committed to tape. Logically, the story should not be much different tapeless. But then this story is not burdened by a surfeit of logic. So we can never know what it would have been like without the tapes, which have produced, or have seemed to produce (even this is not entirely clear), some of the more spectacular events. We are as deeply entangled in the tapes now as is the President.

This afternoon, I went to see the Democratic Senate aide who is in Capitol Hill's traffic patterns. We sat in the senators' dining room drinking tea. On the Senate floor, the senators were debating a bill to restore the death penalty. "It's all finally going to turn on him," said the Senate aide. "It's going to become clear that it's he who is bringing down the office of the Presidency—that if he left the office it would be restored. This wrapping of the Presidency around himself is going to militate against him. It's going to be seen that *he's* the problem—we still revere the office. An impeachment vote will be one to clear the air and bring the case to trial. I don't think he's going to stay. I think he's definitely going to get convicted. Who knows what would happen in a Senate trial? The senators are keeping quiet now and letting the House do its will. They're not going to stick their necks out until they have to. This is one time when cowardice is an act of statesmanship. All the stories that have been published showing that there are only about two dozen senators who would vote today to convict are meaningless. It's the classic case of how all these guys don't take a position on anything they don't have to take a position on: it might go away, he might resign, the House might not vote impeachment. But if it comes to a vote in the Senate it's an entirely different picture."

The aide said that we might be in for some very rough times before the process was over. "I'm not worried about the Russians," he said. "I'm worried about Nixon—the possibility of diversion. Remember the Middle East alert. It's very important to get him the hell out of there, yet the control of the speed is in his hands."

I asked him why he wanted Nixon out. One had to keep considering that way in there, unspoken, was the thought among Democrats that it might be politically advantageous for them to keep Nixon in office. What this man said would reflect the view of many Senate Democrats.

"The President sets the moral tone," he said. "His being there is eating away the whole notion of government. However atrocious the idea of six years of Gerald Ford is, it's better than this. It's not going to be easy. You just have to say that ten years from now you might look back and see that it was worth it all."

On tonight's news, Ron Ziegler says that what the Judiciary Committee is doing is like "backing a truck up to the White House." Ziegler says it would be "Constitutionally irresponsible" for the President to comply with the committee's request. He says the committee should study the material it has already received before asking for more.

MARCH 13

Last night, the President spoke to the Veterans of Foreign Wars at the Sheraton-Park Hotel here. John Stennis, of whom we heard much last fall, and George Mahon, chairman of the House Appropriations Committee—two of the most powerful men in the Congress—were at the head table. The President said, "In the remaining three years I have in this office, one goal will be mine above everything else—to build a peaceful world." Some White House reporters have concluded, on the basis of background briefings they have been given, that the White House strategy is to push the House into a vote on impeachment as soon as possible, on the theory that it is now in position to win such a vote. The purpose of leaking Doar's letter, it is said, was to try to divide the committee and its staff, or to force committee votes on all staff actions and inquiries. The matter of appearing seemly is of more interest to the committee than it is to the White House. One gathers that the White House has rather counted upon the committee's comporting itself in an unseemly fashion, and the committee is disappointing it. Rodino is gaining command, and moving cautiously. Last week, Robert Drinan, the Massachusetts Democrat, and Jerome Waldie, the California Democrat—both sponsors of impeachment resolutions—were ready to move to subpoena the President, but even some of the other most liberal Democrats, taking their cue from Rodino, refused to go along.

Perhaps the White House is trying to goad the committee into acting quickly, but one can argue just as convincingly that the White House strategy is one of delay, on the theory that the longer the time that goes by, the more likely it is that the opposition to the President will become confused or uninterested. The President knows about the limited attention span on Capitol Hill. He is encouraging public weariness with the whole business. Something might turn up. Play for time. Besides, if the tapes do have incriminating evidence, the better gamble might be that the House would not impeach without convincing evidence, that the President's failure to supply the tapes would not be enough, or, if it was enough for the House to warrant impeachment, it would not be enough for the Senate to warrant convicting the President and thus remove him from office. The mistake may be to assume that there is such a thing as a White House strategy. In the matter of impeachment, there is no White House—there is only the President. Others may act in his behalf or speak for him, but it is not clear that anyone knows his mind. And, like any human being caught in a complex difficulty, in which forces and people beyond his control are at work, the President may not have a strategy other than taking it day by day, getting through each dangerous passage as best he can, and hoping for the best. No one really knows. The center of this drama is still the hidden, enigmatic President.

This is a deadly struggle, yet only part of what the White House is doing, other than trying to define the issues, is visible. The advertisements to support the President lead back to his friends. We can see the political appeasement of powers on Capitol Hill. (Recently, Goldwater objected to the appointment of Paul Nitze to a potentially important Pentagon job, and it appears that the appointment will not go forward. Nitze had served in the Pentagon under Robert McNamara, and had also been a member of the President's negotiating team for SALT; he has the reputation of being a "hard-liner" on defense issues. Goldwater's opposition was puzzling, but it was sufficient to block the appointment.)

Not long ago, Bryce Harlow suggested to a White House reporter that Republicans in Congress were going to have to think twice before voting against the President, because they would have to go back to their "money." It is clear that the White House is using what political leverage it has within the Party. But how much leverage does it have? And is the leverage likely to grow or diminish as time goes by?

Today, Attorney General William Saxbe said that the President was not different from "any other citizen" in his duty to report information about the commission of crimes.

A sense of excitement is building over a possible "confrontation" between the House Judiciary Committee and the White House. (The New York *Times:* "HOUSE AND NIXON SEEM NEAR CLASH ON WITHHELD DATA." The Washington *Post:* "PROBERS, NIXON CLASH.") Confrontations are comprehensible and exciting, and it has been a while since we have had one. It seems as if we have almost come to miss them. During the day, word comes that the committee Democrats met and have decided to back off "temporarily." Doar and Jenner are "negotiating" with St. Clair. The White House has let out the word, through Senator Norris Cotton, of New Hampshire, that perhaps some third person who is "entirely trustworthy" could decide which information is relevant to the inquiry and should be released to the committee. In the light of the disastrous result of the "Stennis proposal" last fall, it is hard to believe that the White House would suggest such a thing again. It is impossible to believe that the Judiciary Committee would accept the suggestion. No one knows whether the White House is putting forth the idea seriously. Harlow, Buzhardt, Clawson, and Ziegler have been holding meetings with the press to present the White House arguments. St. Clair is making television appearances. (In this morning's New York *Times,* St. Clair is quoted as saying that he is representing "the office of the Presidency," not the occupant of the office "individually.") Harlow told reporters, "The House Committee is somewhat in the position of a lot of children. . . . When you are at meals and you want seconds, you have to clean up your plate first." He also argued that if the precedent were set that the Congress could obtain any documents it sought, some future member of Congress—someone like the late Joseph McCarthy—could obtain whatever he wanted, because "all he would have to do would be to introduce an impeachment resolution."

The big Constitutional confrontation between the Congress and the President may be building—one for which we have no precedent. However this one is settled, crucial history will have been made. Mere mortals are feeling their way along, making history as they go, shaping our Constitutional future. This is now happening so frequently that one finds it difficult to realize that it is happening. Despite the fact that we have come to expect earthquakes, it seems unlikely that there will be anything like the events of last fall, when the President fired Special Prosecutor Archibald Cox. That was unique, defined to some degree by the setting (the dark Saturday night) and the number of events—the immediate departure of two successive Attorneys General. Among the things that made that such a frightening time was that there appeared to be no processes. But the President's attempt to rid himself of one Special Prosecutor landed him with another one. The public outcry forced him to obey the courts. And now the real drama is taking place quietly, behind the scenes, in the work of the staffs of the House Judiciary Committee and the Special Prosecutor, and in the accumulation of events and facts that will eventually be put before the House of Representatives and the public for a judgment.

Tomorrow, the President begins another swing around the country—the first since last November, during Operation Candor. He is to leave for Chicago tomorrow, will be back in Washington Friday evening, will go to Nashville for the day on Saturday, and then, on Tuesday, to Houston. The President is in terrible trouble, and is trying to save himself. This is a desperate trip. I'm going along.

12

ANDREWS AIR FORCE BASE. Andrews, eleven miles southeast of Washington, toward the Eastern Shore of Maryland, is the point of departure for Presidential trips. In the flat, red brick air terminal this afternoon, military personnel lounge in the waiting room, hoping to "catch a hop" on one of the planes flying to another base. To judge from the map of those bases, one could make a grand tour of the United States on military planes. On the large airfield are about a dozen planes— what an Air Force officer explains to me are VC-137s, VC-135s, and VC-140s—all saying on them "United States of America," and all having the American flag painted on the tail. This is part of the fleet of twenty-seven planes at the command of the President. The President's plane, named the "Spirit of '76" by Mr. Nixon (whatever Air Force plane the President rides in is referred to officially as Air Force One), is taxiing onto the field. It is a 707, white across the top and dark blue across the bottom. Its number, painted below the flag on the tail, is 27000. The interior of the "Spirit of '76" was redone a few months ago. The original interior arrangement, worked out by H. R. Haldeman when the new plane was put into service in early 1973, had not pleased Mrs. Nixon—her quarters constituted a passageway, and were separated by staff quarters from those of the President—and so, after several months, and Haldeman's departure, it was overhauled.

At noon tomorrow, the President is to appear for a question-and-answer session before the Executives' Club of Chicago. Bryce Harlow has said that on this trip the President can be seen by the people without "the filter" of the Washington press corps. The President has been telling Republican congressmen that the real issues in the November election will be peace and prosperity, and he is trying to make them the issues in another election—the one that is to take place in the House of Representatives.

When the President travels, the press, ostensibly along to cover him, inescapably becomes part of his entourage, and so enhances the aura that surrounds him—and vice versa. The aura of the Presidency extends to the White House press corps. The reporters fly on a privately chartered plane, and their employers are billed for the trip. Ray Zook, a slight, bald, bespectacled man who appears to be constantly speaking into a walkie-talkie, sees to it that the proper arrangements are made for the press. At Andrews, one is given a hexagonal badge, of a specified color (Chicago: blue), which one strings around one's neck, along with the White House press pass. These badges serve as a signal to the Secret Service and the local police, and part the seas of crowds on Presidential trips. The airlines, aware that they are carrying national communicators, people close to power, lay on fine food, and as soon as one boards the plane the stewardesses proffer Bloody Marys, beer, champagne. Tonight, there will be shrimp cocktail and steak for dinner. The pilot welcomes us over the public-address system and says that the plane's crew will be with us for three days "on this junket."

There are sixty-five representatives of radio, television, and the press aboard this flight. Also aboard are representatives of the Army Signal Corps, who will record the President's words; a representative of the telephone company, to see that the phone connections at the airport and other spots are in order; and members of the White House press office, who must answer questions (or appear to), shepherd us around, and provide transcripts of the President's remarks as quickly as possible. The President's limousine and the Secret Service follow-up car, together with several Secret Service agents, have already been flown to Chicago. On Air Force One, five reporters serve as pool reporters for the rest of the press. In previous Administrations, pool reporting was a sought-after assignment; it could lead to conversations with the President, or, at least, with his closest aides. Now reporters are reluctant to do pool duty; the most that can be hoped for is a few crumbs from Ron Ziegler. Some of my colleagues say that the press plane for this Nixon trip has an unusually keyed-up atmosphere—somewhat like one of a political campaign. More and more, this trip is talked about as Nixon's "campaign for survival."

We land at a part of O'Hare Airport that is reserved for the military. When we get off the plane, several of the reporters go to the phones that have been set up on the field, and call their desks; there is nothing to report, of course, but they say that their desks get very edgy, want to make sure they have arrived. One reporter tells me that we will not be able to hear what the President says when he arrives. A solution to this, the reporter says, is to befriend a network soundman, who will tell you what he is hearing through his earphones. No crowd has been mustered to greet the President, but off to one side Mayor Richard Daley waits in the back seat of his Cadillac limousine. In the dark, one can barely make out the familiar features beneath the gray fedora. After a while, he gets out of his limousine and walks toward the roped-off section where we are standing. It is mercifully unfrigid in Chicago tonight; I had expected the worst. The Mayor is wearing a navy-blue suit and a bright-blue shirt. We wonder what he is doing here. One reporter said there was some pressure on Daley to "lay on" an event for the President; he wouldn't, or couldn't, but he is meeting him at the airport. The only other politician in sight is Roman Pucinski, a former Democratic member of Congress who lost a Senate race against Charles Percy in 1972. No Republican politicians are here. A crowd of reporters gathers around Daley. What does the Mayor think of Senator Jackson? "Great man." What does the Mayor think about Watergate? "The real issue is not Watergate. The real issue is the cost of living." "You have just witnessed a non-event," a colleague says to me.

Air Force One arrives. Nixon comes down the ramp, wearing a gray overcoat. He is followed by Alexander Haig, Ron Ziegler, Patrick Buchanan, and Rose Mary Woods. They are smiling. The President waves vaguely to the reporters and a few military men standing at the edge of the apron. One military man shouts "There he is!" and starts to applaud, and then, noticing that no one is joining him, shrinks. The President says something to Daley we cannot hear and gets in his limousine—an American flag on one front fender and a Presidential flag on the other—which has been driven up to the plane. Haig, wearing a camel's-hair coat, jogs around to the other side of the limousine and gets in. We are handed the pool report for the President's flight out. It says, "Trip uneventful all the way . . . slightly bumpy, but nothing special. Started rolling at Andrews at 7:36 31,000 feet, average speed 520 mph. Col. Ralph Albertazzie, pilot. President and 13 others . . . Haig, Ziegler, Miss Woods, Pat Buchanan, Steve Bull, Wm. Henkel jr, adv [advance] man, John Guthrie, speech writer, Dr. Wm Lukash, Lt Comdr Steve [cq] Todd, mil aide, Maj Geo A Joulwan, aide to Haig, Mrs. Nellie Yates, Miss Sarah Currence, Miss Judith Gagliardi, secretaries."

Many of us had not seen the Conrad Hilton Hotel, corner of Michigan and Balbo, since the Democratic National Convention of 1968, when we watched the military jeeps with the large metal screens attached to the front, and we choked from the stink bombs and the tear gas, and heard the crowd in Grant Park, across the street, shout "Dump the Hump!" Someone points out the hotel bar whose plate-glass window was smashed then. Tonight, the Chicago police are in their winter uniforms: dark-blue leather Eisenhower jackets, dark-blue trousers, dark-blue caps with a dark-blue-and-white checked band above the visor. Outside the hotel, there is a small crowd. Some carry signs saying "IMPEACH DICK" or "DOWN WITH NIXON." In the lobby, there is a small, friendly crowd to receive the President, and a bagpipe band called the Shannon Rovers is playing. (The Shannon Rovers are from the eleventh ward—Mayor Daley's—and seem to be to him what the Marine Corps Band is to the President.) People are cheering, and some carry signs that say "DON'T GIVE UP" and "AMERICA NEEDS NIXON." The President is nowhere to be seen. The police are shouting, very excited, to clear an aisle—perhaps for the Mayor. We don't know what is going on, and head for the pressroom, where our room keys are ready.

Those summer events in Chicago helped elect Nixon in 1968. But Chicago was also once the scene of his undoing—the site of his first "debate" with John Kennedy in 1960. Nixon wrote later, in *Six Crises,* that he had not appeared sufficiently well and rested for that encounter: "I had concentrated too much on substance and not enough on appearance." Perhaps that is the answer to the puzzle of why the President came to Chicago tonight, so long in advance of his question-and-answer session tomorrow.

MARCH 15

The Chicago *Daily News* reports this morning that the reception for the President in the lobby last night was arranged by Rabbi Baruch Korff, head of the National Citizens Committee for Fairness to the Presidency, and that Nixon introduced him to Daley as "my rabbi." Rabbi Korff, of Taunton, Massachusetts, appeared out of nowhere, began taking newspaper advertisements (paid for in part by Teamsters money) supporting the President last fall. The paper also carries a U.P.I. story about a story in the Washington *Post* (the President cannot escape the *Post* even here) saying that "informed sources" who have heard the tape of the March 21st meeting agree that the President used the word "wrong" but assert that the context in which he used it suggests that he meant only that the payments for silence would not work. The Washington *Post* story says, too, that the members of the Special Prosecutor's staff believe they have proof that the last payment of money to E. Howard Hunt was made about twelve hours after the meeting. There are several other stories in the Chicago papers about the President's problems. So much for the supposed lack of attention to the President's problems "out there."

Shortly after twelve-thirty, we are led, via a maze of back passageways, to the Hilton's International Ballroom, a vast gold room whose front wall is of wood panelling on which gilt curlicues have been painted. We stand crowded together on one side of the room, cordoned off by a red ribbon. In front of us, at one of a hundred and ninety tables for ten, some men are eating crepes stuffed with chicken or turkey (they aren't sure which), boiled peas and carrots, and cherry pie. "It's not very good," one of the men says of the lunch. On the dais, the long head table is draped with a gold tablecloth, and there is a gold curtain behind it. Mayor Daley is at the head table, and so is W. Clement Stone, wearing a peach-colored shirt and a black bow tie. Stone, an insurance magnate and author of a book espousing a "positive mental attitude," who gave the President two million dollars for his reëlection, is one of the more important members of the Executives' Club. He has a thick, dark mustache, matching his hair, which is combed straight back. At the microphone, a man is saying to the audience, "The indications are that you are being a little bit reticent about asking questions. Come on, now, don't be bashful." Stone is introduced, and he stands up and waves both hands in the air, Nixonlike. At one end of the dais is the regional commissioner of the I.R.S., which seems a bit surprising. When he is introduced, there are some laughs and boos. A man at the table in front of me says, "This is a conservative bunch." The average age of the crowd appears to be about fifty. There are few blacks and few women. One man has wandered over to a group of reporters for a quick briefing on the complexities of March 21st, and wandered away, confused.

Nixon, reaching the dais, looks tanned and healthy. He is wearing a navy-blue suit. As he shakes hands with Daley, the applause increases. It is not clear for whom. The President takes a seat at the center of the head table. When the president of the club introduces Nixon, Clement Stone is the first to his feet to applaud. Nixon thanks the group for having invited him to appear when he was senator and when he was Vice-President and when he was out of office—"and that I appreciate *very* much." He says that he will come back after he has completed his term, "which I expect to do three years from now." He breaks into his sudden laugh. The President is asked whether he would encourage young people to go into politics (he would), and he is asked about energy and the economy. He talks about America's having "won a peace," and the country's efforts to "keep the peace for a generation and longer abroad." The economy: "That future is good. It is going to be strong." Energy: The worst is over; he has been able to move allocations from heating fuels to gasoline. "As I told Mayor Daley driving in, in the car, Mr. Simon is watching the situation in Chicago very closely, in the Chicago area as well as other areas of the country. If shortages occur, we believe we will be able to handle them so that there will not be an undue problem for your constituents." Gasoline is the new public-works project.

The President points out that he has made "an unprecedented turnover of confidential materials"—the tapes, the documents, and also "caseloads of documents" from the executive branch. He says that Jaworski "said that he had what he considered to be the full story of Watergate, and we want the full story out." And then he says, "There are those who I think very logically would raise the question: Well, why not just give the members of the Judiciary Committee the right to come in and have all of the tapes of every Presidential conversation, a fishing license or complete right to go in and go through all of the Presidential files in order to find out whether or not there is a possibility that some action had been taken which might be and might result in an impeachable offense? The reason why we cannot go that far . . . it isn't a question that the President has something to hide." It is that he does not want to further weaken the Presidency. Every President, he says, "has recognized the necessity of protecting the confidentiality of Presidential conversations," and he says that otherwise a President "will be surrounded by eunuchs." He adds that he will continue to fight for the confidentiality "that [Thomas] Jefferson fought for."

The President's last answer is worth some attention, for what it tells us about Nixon and how he is carrying on his struggle. The distortions are transparent. Jaworski had said he *would* need more material. The New York *Times* reported on February 27th that Jaworski had said that he thought his office now knew the "full story of the Watergate affair," and that there was enough evidence to bring some indictments but that he would still need, and seek, more evidence for the cases. Moreover, the impeachment inquiry is not limited to the Watergate break-in. And other Presidents were not facing an impeachment inquiry. Jefferson did not "fight for" confidentiality; this is a new twist on an old distortion. (The case of the Jefferson letter is confusing enough, subject to various theories and a bit of obscure history. There were, in fact, two letters— written to Jefferson—which were requested by the defense in two trials of Aaron Burr. In each instance, it appears that the letter, or a copy of it, was made available to the Court, as ordered by Chief Justice John Marshall, sitting as a circuit court judge. It also appears that Jefferson or his attorney did make excisions in one of the letters of material claimed to be irrelevant but also left the final judgment on this to the Court. In both instances, it appears that Marshall held that the production of evidence was for the Court to decide.)

Standing here, away from Washington, I try to listen to what the President is saying as if I were hearing it for the first time, and had no opportunity to compare notes with my colleagues or to check with others involved in the issue. I hear an answer that has a certain plausibility. The Special Prosecutor had enough material to bring indictments, and the committee has the same material. The committee won't say what particular offenses it is looking into but seems to simply want to go through everything to see what it can find. Wrapped in the context he has given it, the argument appears to make sense. Perhaps the President can put it across. If he does, he will have established the precedent that Presidents can set the terms of impeachment inquiries.

The President looks good today—as good as I have seen him look since this whole issue broke. He seems calmer and more in command than he has in almost a year. He hunches over the lectern, his shoulders forming a curve up over his neck, but there are fewer nervous gestures. From time to time, his knees do pump into the rostrum. When he says, "One year of Watergate is enough," he gets applause, and when he says, "I will do nothing to weaken the office of the Presidency," he gets applause again. Whatever impression this is giving the television audience, it must be reinforcing to him—telling him that the approach is effective.

The President, not being asked about the March 21st meeting, works it into an answer to a question about whether it might not be better if he resigned. (Some of the audience hiss at the question, but the President assures them it is "a perfectly proper question.") Nixon refers to some "charges" that he says the audience has probably read "either in your news magazine, possibly in a newspaper, certainly heard on television and radio." He then lists such things as Dean's having said that the President was informed on March 13th, rather than on March 21st that payments were being made to the defendants, and that a blackmail attempt was being made on the White House (the White House has made much of this as an example of Dean's faulty memory); "that the President helped to plan the Watergate thing"; "that the President had ordered the burglarizing" of Dr. Fielding's office. These charges, the President says, "are all totally false, and the investigations will prove it." Then, sliding into the meeting of March 21st, he says, "Correcting what may have been a misapprehension when I spoke to the press on March 6th in Washington, it was alleged that the payments that had been made to defendants were made for the purpose of keeping them still. However, Mr. Ehrlichman, Mr. Haldeman, Mr. Mitchell have all denied that that was the case, and they certainly should be allowed the right in court to establish their innocence or guilt without our concluding that that was the case." Thus his "explanation" of the March 6th statement. The President went through the "charges" and this "explanation" so quickly that one had to put the mind in overdrive to keep up with him. There was a "misapprehension" connected with what he said—whose misapprehension he does not specify. Now "it was alleged" that the payments were made for silence.

The question of resignation is a good one from his point of view. "If the President resigned when he was not guilty of charges," he replies, "then every President in the future could be forced out of office by simply levelling some charges and getting the media to carry them and getting a few congressmen and senators who were on the other side to exploit them." That is not an exact description of what has been happening, but the President is circling an important issue. "Why doesn't the President resign because his popularity is low?" he asks, and he answers, "From a personal standpoint, resignation is an easy cop-out. But on the other hand, apart from the personal standpoint, resignation of this President on charges of which he is not guilty, resignation simply because he happened to be low in the polls, would forever change our form of government."

As the President is given a round of applause, he goes back to the dais to talk with and smile at Daley. Daley applauds but does not smile.

Clement Stone is beaming and applauding. Nixon steers Daley to the
rostrum. Daley does not appear pleased but goes along, his solid body
propelled by Presidential command. The President says that though
"at times" he may appear partisan, he does not intend to be. While
the President greets some others on the dais, the president of the club
thanks him for the "wonderfully interesting and informative and candid
performance." Nixon goes back to the rostrum again. He seems not to
want to leave the applause and the approval, and return to his limousine,
his plane, and his troubles. "While I leave the podium," he says, "I don't
expect to leave the Presidency until January the twentieth, 1971." And
then he says, "I mean 1977."

Outside the hotel, it is chilly and raining. Near the door on Michigan
Avenue are picketers with signs saying "IMPEACH NIXON," "NIXON PAY
YOUR TAXES," "NIXON IS A CROOK." Someone in this group is playing a
tuba. Across the street in Grant Park, demonstrators are carrying neatly
lettered signs that say "GOD BLESS AMERICA" and "GOD LOVES NIXON."
Many of them are also waving red-white-and-blue paper pennants that
say "SUPPORT OUR PRESIDENT," "GOD LOVES AMERICA," and "GOD LOVES
NIXON." A man, using a bullhorn, is leading them in a singsong chant:
"God Loves America." They are followers of the Reverend Sun Myung
Moon, the evangelist from Seoul, Korea, whose trucks circled Lafayette
Park blaring prayers for the President after he fired Archibald Cox, and
whose followers have been turning up for the President—at a Christmas-
tree lighting, at a prayer breakfast, at crucial moments—ever since. One
of them, a young man in his twenties, tells me that the Reverend Moon
has about three hundred and fifty followers in Chicago. He says that the
man with the bullhorn came to Chicago from Washington to organize
this demonstration. The man with the bullhorn, who appears to be in his
mid-thirties, is staring intently at the Hilton and seems lost in his chant.
He changes the chant to "Support the President."

Where are the definers? The politicians are reluctant to speak out—
partly because of fear, and partly because they will have to vote on
impeachment and possibly in a Senate trial and do not want to appear
to be prejudging the case. There is an awareness now that the Andrew
Johnson impeachment was an unattractive episode, and the politicians
are becoming conscious that their behavior during these days and weeks
will be the stuff of history. They have not been confronted with this kind
of situation before. It is not an easy time for people to find their roles.
Some are reluctant to speak out for fear of being painted as part of a
"lynch mob," or as "out to get" the President. This is how the White
House tries to paint those who call for his impeachment. By the White
House definition, it is acceptable to speak out against the President's
impeachment but not for it. As they define it, it is not proper to have
come to a conclusion—an unfavorable one, at least—about the things

that have happened and have been known for some time. Perhaps the members of the House Judiciary Committee will eventually be definers. But a battle for public opinion is going on now.

When the framers of the Constitution were searching for methods of constraining power, of holding the trustees of power accountable, it was a much simpler time. Now the arsenal of power is far, far greater: television networks, regulatory agencies, federal laws and federal grants to be selectively applied, large staffs, responsibility for economic management, a private fleet of planes, international diplomacy, and nuclear weapons. Somehow, Nixon seems to turn the fundamental idea of democracy on its head—saying, in effect, that the more powerful the President is, the less accountable he should be. It is a long way from Warren Hastings to this.

MARCH 16

The Nashville Airport. A crowd has been gathered in an Air National Guard hangar. The advance men have done their work. Airplane hangars are very good for amplifying the cheers of a crowd. Little Girl Scouts, in their green uniforms, are shivering in the cold. People in the crowd are holding signs saying "AMERICA LOVES NIXON" and "WELCOME TO NASH-VILLE." Across the back of the hangar is a large sign that says, in block letters, "WELCOME HOME PAT." Many in the crowd are carrying miniature American flags. The flags are plastic. The Bellevue High School Band, dressed in red and black, rehearses "Ruffles and Flourishes" and "This Is My Country" and "Tennessee Waltz," the last of which it is having some inexplicable difficulty with. Another band, wearing tall black Beefeater hats, plays country music. Some reporters who got here earlier say that the crowd has been practicing cheers. A man named Fred Boyd has written, to the tune of "Okie from Muskogee," a song called "Stand Up and Cheer for Richard Nixon": "Now, I'm not from Muskogee, Oklahoma,/ But I believe in right and being free./And I'm sick of what I'm reading in the papers, I'm tired of all that trash that's on TV. . . ./Stand up and cheer for Richard Nixon,/ For he's the President of our great land./With a little help and a lot less criticism,/He well could be the best we ever had." What seems to be becoming a nationwide sign contest is taking place here, too. Outside and to the left of the hangar there is another crowd. Among its signs are two that say, "RICHARD THE RAT" and "HE AIN'T COUNTRY, HE'S CROOKED." A truck has on it, in large white letters, "THROW THE BUM OUT."

Winfield Dunn, the Republican governor of Tennessee, and the Tennessee senators, Howard Baker and William Brock, both Republicans, approach the hangar. Dunn, who was a dentist until he was elected

governor, in 1970, is handsome, with a thick shock of dark hair. He
asks the crowd inside to be polite to "the beautiful and charming First
Lady." It is not clear what he is worried about. Today is Mrs. Nixon's
birthday. Dunn has been a strong supporter of the President. (He is the
one who relayed to the public the President's word last November that
he was not aware of any more "bombs" just before the news broke of
the eighteen-and-a-half minute gap—it's grown to that—in one of the
tapes.) Senators Baker and Brock could obviously play an important
role in deciding the President's fate. The politicians are here for the
dedication of a new building for the Grand Ole Opry, and the President
has landed in their midst. So they have come to the airport to greet him.

Eventually, the President's limousine pulls up outside the hangar,
the President emerges, and the crowd cheers. The Bellevue High
School Band plays "Hail to the Chief." I am standing on some
bleachers, and can only occasionally glimpse—over the signs—the
President, who is talking with the senators. The cheering crowd cannot possibly see him. But it cheers anyway. Then a plane numbered
26000—the First Lady's plane—and also blue and white, matching
the President's, taxis dramatically right up to the hangar. Good theatre, and a remarkable piece of timing: she has flown in from Brasilia
after a six-day tour of Latin America. The President, wearing a gray
overcoat, springs up the ramp to her plane, and shortly emerges,
holding Mrs. Nixon's arm and waving to the crowd. Mrs. Nixon
is wearing a white raincoat and a bright-green scarf. The Bellevue
High School Band plays "Happy Birthday." In the hangar, some
hitherto hidden signs go up. One says, "IF IT WAS WRONG, WHY DID
YOU DO IT?" Another lists the former Presidential aides who have
been indicted. "This is truly a wonderful homecoming," says the
First Lady. While she speaks, her plane is in the background, the
dashing pilot watching from the controls. The President smiles and
applauds. Dunn introduces "our beloved President." There are a few
boos, but the cheers drown them out. There is an indistinguishable
chant from the crowd outside the hangar. It holds up a huge white
banner with, written on it in red, "IMPEACH."

The President talks to the crowd of his wife's trips and his trips all
over the world. "And when I come here to the heartland of America, just
let me say two things," he says to the shivering Girl Scouts and others.
"From a military standpoint, I know that in this great State of Tennessee,
as indicated by the votes of your senators and your congressmen, the
people of Tennessee support strongly my position that the United States
must never become the second strongest nation in the world."

We run for the bus, and the motorcade begins. On the way into the
city, we pass one group along the road holding a three-part sign that
says "RES IPSA LOQUITUR."

The auditorium of the new Grand Ole Opry building, a fifteen-million-dollar edifice, in a park called Opryland, U.S.A. The interior of the auditorium is a cross between an opera house and a tabernacle; the pews are upholstered in burnt-orange carpeting. The performers mill around the stage, just as they used to do at the Ryman Auditorium, a converted tabernacle and something of a national shrine, from which the Opry has moved. On a backdrop at the rear of the stage is painted a big red barn. When we arrive, the Grand Ole Opry radio program is on, and the announcer, in a yellow suit, announces a break for a commercial. Then he proclaims "the Grand Ole Opry's finest hour in its forty-eight-year history," and Governor Dunn and Senators Baker and Brock come into the balcony just above the right-hand side of the stage. Spotlights are turned on them, and, after the applause, the politicians look at the people on the stage and the people on the stage look up at the politicians and there is dead silence—except for the sound of a popcorn machine on the other side of the auditorium where some of us are standing. I think it is the loudest popcorn machine I have ever heard. No one had arranged this moment, and no one seems to know what to do about it. Then, mercifully, someone announces the President and Mrs. Nixon, and they file into the balcony. The President waves. The applause is polite but not exuberant. The audience consists mainly not of regular Opry-goers but of music industry executives and Nashville business leaders. Also in the audience is James Neal, a former member of the Special Prosecutor's staff who will return to Washington to try the case of the seven indicted for the Watergate cover-up. (As a member of the Justice Department under Robert Kennedy, Neal conducted the prosecution that convicted Hoffa.) The announcer says that the show will continue, and the President of the United States, who is facing impeachment, sits, like a Roman emperor, in the balcony and watches while Roy Drusky sings "Satisfied Mind."

After the show has continued for a while, the President has faded into the audience, and so has George Wallace, who is also here. Nixon is turned in his seat and is talking at length with Howard Baker, seated behind him. Roy Acuff, the country singing star, in a dark-blue jacket, blue-and-white checked trousers, a red tie, and white shoes, and wearing glasses, is at the microphone. Roy Acuff, after saying he has "only been with the Opry since nineteen hundred and thirty-seven," says that tonight we have "the very first President to be here." He asks President and Mrs. Nixon "if they would mind honoring us" by coming onto the stage. The President would not mind in the least. As he comes onto the stage, "Hail to the Chief" is played country-music style. The audience applauds politely. The President and Mrs. Nixon are seated on the stage—he sitting stiffly, his hands folded on his right knee. Dorothy Ritter, Tex Ritter's widow, presents Mrs. Nixon with a dulcimer. Mrs. Nixon is in a bright-green dress with bone-colored pumps. Roy Acuff suggests that we sing "Happy Birthday" to Mrs. Nixon, and asks if he would "be imposing should I ask, Mr. President, will you please play the piano for us." There is applause, and Nixon stands and briefly grasps the dulcimer, waves it in the air, and then suddenly pulls a yo-yo out of his pocket. He does it so quickly, saying "I haven't even learned to play with this thing," that the incident—like his explanation of the March 21st meeting—is over almost before one realizes what has happened. The yo-yo is Roy Acuff's trademark, and the President has appropriated it. He grasps what he can—Mayor Daley, a dulcimer, senators, a yo-yo. The yo-yo hangs there loosely, and one watches, transfixed, sensing that one is seeing a moment that will be remembered. We are there, and at the same time we are visualizing pictures of this scene in *Time* and *Newsweek*.

The President goes to the piano, announces, "In the key of G," and firmly bonks out "Happy Birthday." Back at the microphone, the President talks about his wife's birthday and suggests that the audience join him as he plays another song. Then, with exaggerated motions, hands pawing the air in front of him, the President creeps toward the piano as if to attack it. The clowning is strange; I have not seen it before. The emperor appears to be courting the favor of the audience. After playing "My Wild Irish Rose," the President makes some remarks to the audience. He points out that his wife has flown in from Brasilia for the occasion, and he makes a little joke about country music and country moonshine. He tells the audience that "country music is America" and that he has brought country music to the White House "on many occasions." He tells of the night in May, 1973, when they had a White House dinner for the returned prisoners of war, "the largest dinner ever held at the White House," and "we had some fine Hollywood stars, you know, singing some of the more modern music that is—well, it is a little hard to understand." He emphasizes the words "modern" and "understand," and manages to look baffled as he says them. And then he says that the biggest hit of that evening was Roy Acuff. (As he talked, my mind went back to that dinner. It was then that Watergate was breaking, and the President launched a brief overt attack on Daniel Ellsberg, saying that it was time to "quit making national heroes of those who steal secrets and publish them in the newspapers.")

The President tells the audience that country music talks about family life and religion and patriotism—"those combinations which are so essential to America's character at a time that America needs character," because the peace of the world "for generations, maybe centuries, to come will depend not just on America's military might, which is the greatest in the world, or our wealth, which is the greatest in the world," but on our character and our willingness to wear the flag and stand up for the flag—and, coming miraculously full circle, he says, "And country music does that." Then Roy Acuff gives him a little lesson in how to use a yo-yo, and Nixon says, "I will stay here and try to learn how to use the yo-yo, and you go up and be President." Good line. Then Roy Acuff asks the audience to sing "Stay a Little Longer," and it does, and he asks the President to play the piano again, and the President plays "God Bless America," and the audience, standing, sings along.

MARCH 18

Yesterday, Sunday, Dr. Norman Vincent Peale delivered the sermon at the White House prayer services, and Wilbur Mills went on *Face the Nation* and predicted that the President would be out of office by November.

That's what it's like here now. A babel of voices and rumors and prophecies, a battle for public opinion, antagonists sending messages while they issue their prophecies. Mills' prediction, which he based on a combination of Republican disaffection from the President and public dismay over the President's tax returns, was aimed, through us, at the President. The President's attacks on the Judiciary Committee are aimed, through us, at the Congress. It is obviously an important part of the White House strategy to discredit in advance the committee that might recommend the impeachment of the President.

John Anderson, Republican of Illinois, who is chairman of the House Republican Conference (a body made up of all House Republicans), and an important moderate member of the House, said on *Meet the Press* yesterday that if the President's strategy is "to go to the country, in effect to go over the heads of Congress and to go over the heads of the members of the Judiciary Committee, I think this is a mistake"; and that "I don't think that the committee should be reviled or should be demeaned in any way." Yesterday, it was reported that the President's tax lawyer had said that the original deed turning the Vice-Presidential papers over to the National Archives had been destroyed. (In January, two lawyers for the President said that the deed—not signed by the President—had been backdated.) Last week, Leon Jaworski sent John Doar a list of all the evidence that the Special Prosecutor has asked for and been denied. This will help the impeachment inquiry staff. Treasury Secretary George Shultz is leaving the government, and though he denies that Watergate has anything to do with his decision, it is widely believed that it does. A Gallup poll shows that sixty percent of the respondents favor impeachment if the word "impeachment" is not used in the question—if the question asked is whether a congressman should vote for the Senate to hold a trial to determine whether the President should be removed from office. A few days ago, Representative Lawrence Hogan, Republican of Maryland, who had previously been one of the most vigorous defenders of the President on the Judiciary Committee, said, "It is not the White House's job to tell the committee how to discharge its Constitutional function. The President's lawyer is off base when he stated the committee should first define an impeachable offense. There is not a set definition. Each member will have to subjectively determine this in his own mind." The subject of the inquiry is broader than Watergate, said Hogan, and he went on, "If the President continues to follow the lines being drawn by his counsel and press secretary, he will lose even those on the committee who are trying to keep an open mind on the impeachment issue. . . . And if the President ignores a subpoena from the committee, this could be considered an impeachable offense."

Today, I decided to spend some time talking with members of the House—preferably, members of the Judiciary Committee. William Cohen is a very youthful-looking man with dark-blond hair, blue eyes, and even, white teeth. He is thirty-three, a Republican from Maine, in his first term in the House. His district, reaching from the top of Maine down to a point south of Lewiston, is the largest in area east of the Mississippi. It is a "swing" district; Cohen won the seat, which was formerly held by a Democrat, by fifty-four percent.

Cohen is soft-spoken; his manner is earnest. He is aware that, as a member of the committee conducting an inquiry into the impeachment of the President, he is on display. Under ordinary circumstances, he might not have been heard of for years. Cohen and I had lunch at the far end of the House members' dining room, which has been newly refurbished in pale blue and white. There is a huge blue-and-gold chandelier in the center. On each table is a bud vase containing a fresh red carnation. The blue-and-white paper placemats depict George Washington at Yorktown. The dining room is noisy and crowded—there is never enough room for all the members of Congress who want to eat there— and the cuisine is, at its zenith, mediocre. But the congressmen have seen to it that it is inexpensive. And it is convenient: close enough to the House floor, one story above, for members to dash off to answer quorum calls or to vote.

"I've approached the entire impeachment question in terms of what the facts are and what the law is—the law being the Constitution," Cohen said. "I am determined to follow that course, regardless of political influence." This is rather what one would expect to hear, but I asked him to go on. I wanted to see what I could learn about how some members of the committee are thinking about the issue before them—or thinking that they should be talking about how they are thinking about it. "I solicit the opinions of my constituents," Cohen continued. "It's an ugly mood that's building out there—an anger coming from both sides. But it's really not a matter of nose counting. Ultimately, I'll have to cast a vote depending on what the evidence is. Even if sixty percent of the people of this country were opposed, if the facts supported the allegations I would vote for it, and the converse is true. I, like most members, am going to get burned no matter what happens. These are forces beyond my control. All I can do is make a very careful, scrupulous examination of all the facts and then try to do the right thing, and then go back and try to explain to my state what I've done and why. If I can't, I don't belong down here."

I asked Cohen what kind of conduct he thought was impeachable.

"Do I think I have to find a specific link between the President and these acts? No. Do I think most of the committee members think so? Yes. I have a special problem with the issue of accountability for the acts of subordinates. The issue is so controversial that the staff report made only a quick reference to it. I happen to feel that if someone sets in motion an essentially illegal operation, without guidelines, restrictions, inhibition, and it results in the commission of a number of offenses, then the person who set the thing up might very well be held accountable. I don't believe that one should be able to set up situations or procedures in a way that gives one deniability. You may take a searchlight and look for the footprints and come to a dead end. Then you have to ask another question: Must it be a specific offense or do you come to a conclusion that—*in toto*—the rule of law and the Constitution have been subverted?"

Cohen went on, "I can see what's taking place in terms of strategies, but it's not going to affect my decision. From the President's point of view, his going public and St. Clair's strategy are very good moves. The President doesn't have many options. He's doing what he can to remain strong and viable in the eyes of the public. I think the short-term reaction will be to galvanize the support. But in terms of the committee it will be counterproductive. The committee will continue to search for the documents. We may go the subpoena route, but it is sort of an empty gesture. We're not about to send a sergeant-at-arms to arrest the President, and rent a room in the Rayburn Building to contain him. There are legal questions that can be raised about his refusal to supply documents. The President will be active, will shower the public with legislation—veterans, education, health insurance—to show that he is an active President and to seek the support of groups backing such things. I would anticipate a trip to the Soviet Union a week or ten days before we vote"—Cohen stops and smiles—"juxtaposed against the image of thirty-eight members of a committee dealing in 'small-minded unsubstantiated allegations.' Which will generate a great deal of pressure on the committee. We'd be living in a fool's paradise not to appreciate that. As for now, there is an attempt to blur the line between appearance and reality. The President took to television last week to tell the public he was coöperating with us, saying he's giving us the material he gave to Jaworski. Well, obviously you can't give material for an indictment but not for an impeachment. As for the offer to answer written questions, any trial lawyer worth his salt knows that written interrogatories aren't worth anything as far as discovery is concerned."

I asked him what would happen if the President should continue to withhold material.

"It's very difficult to compete with the President," he said. "We don't have the access to the media. We can't call a press conference any time we want. A member can get maybe forty seconds on television to say that what the President is saying is wrong. We can't counter the power of the Presidency. And people are becoming immune to shock. I don't think the next revelation will make that much difference. I don't see an issue so stirring up the public that it piles up on the Congress again. When the tax report comes out, Kissinger might be in the Middle East, and we might see Henry and Sadat and Golda toasting. So it's hard to predict what the evolution of this thing is going to be."

I asked Cohen if he had been under any pressure from the Party.

"Not much," he replied. "Three or four months ago, some members of the White House staff were asked to get together our statements. I had a visit from the Party state chairman and the state chairman of the Committee for the Re-Election of the President. They came down here to find out what my thinking was. I made it clear that I was basing my decision on the facts."

I asked Cohen to describe the political problems of this issue for Republicans.

He replied, "There is that hard reality that twenty-five to thirty percent of the Republicans don't want him removed or out, and see it as a Democratic-inspired move, aided and abetted by 'the Eastern-media conspiracy.' So there is a gnawing feeling among Republicans that they are going to lose that vote, and there would be very little reason for Democrats to cross over and vote for them. They—meaning we, I—are caught between the Scylla and Charybdis of American politics right now. I've been taking some steps to deal with this—to make the point that this has to be in perspective, that the country is going to survive with Nixon in office in 1976 or without him, that, in any event, in 1977 there is going to be another President, that we can't link one man with our destiny."

Shortly after noon, word comes that Judge Sirica has ruled that the Judiciary Committee can have the material given him by the grand jury. (The Special Prosecutor's office had expected him to make this ruling, but, apparently, to make it more automatically than he did.) Sirica has given Haldeman's and Ehrlichman's attorney, John Wilson, two days to appeal the ruling.

I next went to see the moderate Republican member of the House— who is not on the Judiciary Committee—with whom I had spoken on a number of occasions since last fall. When I saw him after the firing of Archibald Cox and asked him what, generally, he thought Republicans wanted the President's fate to be, he had replied, "We want him out." After the President's State of the Union message, he was talking as though he would oppose impeachment. This afternoon, he said, "I still find myself in a no-win situation at home. There's a certain number of people who, no matter how bad the President is, won't forgive a vote against him. Most Republicans are like me. They face the erosion of the Republican base or of the independents they need. So we stand between Scylla and Charybdis. [This was the second Republican to use that expression today—a sign that it is making the rounds of the cloakroom.] And, no matter how fast we vote, we'll still be looking down the throat of Watergate in November. It's clear even to those most favorable to the President that the White House is holding up evidence. Some of us are pretty discouraged. A lot of Republicans think they are going to get reëlected, but nobody comes to Congress to be a member of the minority, and it seems to a lot of us that we're never going to get out of that status."

I asked the Republican member of the House if he and other Republicans still wanted the President out of office.

"Even more so," he replied. "Republicans think the farther the Party gets from Nixon the better off it will be. But what's beginning to sink in is that we'll never get away from this. We'll be running against Nixon for a generation. When I first ran for office in my state, in the early nineteen-sixties, I had to run against Herbert Hoover. Now Democrats should say, 'Here's the Party of Nixon, someone who supported Nixon,' or, best, 'a Nixon rubber stamp.' Any Democrat who didn't campaign that way would be a dunce."

He continued, "I'd want to know beyond a reasonable doubt that he was directly involved in the commission of a serious crime. That's what I've been telling my people. Maybe they can make a case of enough association that is convincing, or of crimes committed after the President was aware of what was going on."

I asked him if Republicans still talked among themselves about the possibility of asking the President to resign.

"There were a couple of abortive attempts at that before Christmas, but no one could put the act together," he replied. "He has stomped on it so hard that I think the feeling of most Republicans is that that is a lost cause at the moment. And also, from the standpoint of a citizen, and not a Republican, I wouldn't like it. If he should be impeached, he should be impeached. The only way he would resign is if there were enough votes to impeach him, and if there were he should be impeached, and the word should be got out about a trial—for the good of the Republic."

Late in the afternoon, I went to see Tom Railsback, who is one of the Judiciary Committee members on whom attention is being focussed. Railsback, forty-two, has developed a reputation in the House as one of the next generation of leaders, and he is already instrumental in the reform movement. He is one of those representatives on whom the word "promising" has been conferred. The process by which someone becomes promising in Washington is somewhat mysterious—arising out of the mists of press attention and word of mouth. It is a fickle process, inflating reputations and then deflating them. And there are several members of Congress who have never been anything more than promising. Now Railsback is in a spot. It is believed that his position on impeachment will be persuasive to other House Republicans—particularly the moderates. A vote by Railsback for impeachment would make such a vote by them more respectable, and safer. Railsback is a member of the Chowder and Marching Society—one of the House Republicans' informal clubs, an old-line and generally conservative one. (Richard Nixon and Gerald Ford were members when they were in the House, and remain lifetime members, as all members of the club do.) Railsback spends time in the House gym, where the traffic is thick, and where party and club affiliations give way to the commonality of human flesh and conversation is candid. He is friendly, is believed to have strong political instincts, and touches a lot of bases in the House. Tom—or Rails, as he is alternatively referred to—is one of the crowd and is watched carefully now. At this point, he is considered unpredictable on the question of whether to vote for impeachment. The Nineteenth Congressional District of Illinois, which he represents, is made up of the area around Rock Island and Moline. In 1972, he ran unopposed. This year, he has a Democratic opponent.

When I saw Railsback, he had just come from one of the occasional meetings between the Judiciary Committee Republicans and the House Republican leaders. The meetings are presided over by John Rhodes, the House Minority Leader. Railsback has blue eyes and thinning blond hair and a distinct Midwestern manner. He was wearing a brown-and-white plaid wool sports jacket and brown trousers. We sat in large black leather chairs in his office.

I began by asking him his opinion of the President's attack on the committee.

"We don't think we're on a fishing expedition," he replied. "They're orchestrating a public-relations campaign. It has driven some of his supporters into wanting to respond."

I asked Railsback how effective he thought the President's campaign against the committee might be.

"I doubt whether the public is going to buy this," he said. "I don't think the President will establish his criterion for impeachable offenses, because almost every allegation that can be seen as an impeachable offense is a criminal offense. I don't think criminality is essential, but, in effect, Congress will impeach him on a criminal offense. I don't think we'll do as they did with the Judge Ritter case, where the House couldn't impeach him on one charge and therefore lumped them." He went on, "I don't think you substitute your judgment for that of the sixty percent of the American people who voted for the President in 1972 unless you have specific evidence of criminal involvement, and I don't think you impute criminal responsibility for the acts of others. I don't like it, but then he's going to be out of office anyway after 1976. It's not like a judge."

Railsback said he thought that the strongest potential cases were in the Watergate cover-up and in the alleged manipulation of the F.B.I. and the C.I.A., and, he said, "there might be indictable offenses." If the charge of raising milk-price supports and imposing import quotas on dairy products in exchange for campaign contributions from the dairy industry was proved, he said, that would be bribery, and an impeachable offense.

I asked Railsback about the plumbers.

"What clouds the plumbers issue is the national-security thing," he replied. "Not that I approve." He added that he did not think it an impeachable offense "where you have a series of happenings and call it an abuse of power."

Railsback asked whether I minded if he shaved while he continued talking. It was after six o'clock, and he had a birthday party to get to. From time to time, he popped his head through the doorway of his bathroom to emphasize a point. I worried that he might cut himself.

"Our requests are very reasonable," he said. "And if we don't get the material in one fashion or another I think he's in trouble. I think it would offend many members of Congress. I think it would offend the American people."

Unlike many of his colleagues, Railsback would refer the issue of Presidential noncompliance with a committee subpoena to the courts. "We can't go down and arrest him like a common criminal," he said, and then, throwing his arms in the air, he said, "We've got to *do* something." Waving his razor, he added, "I'll be glad when this thing is over. It's a real headache."

MARCH 19

The Arab nations, except Libya and Syria, agreed yesterday to lift the embargo on oil shipments to the United States. The effect on supplies for the United States is uncertain. Besides, there were fuel shortages here before the embargo was imposed. That's why it seemed to make such a difference.

Judge Sirica's opinion justifying his ruling yesterday that the committee could have the tapes and documents that the grand jury asked to have sent to it is printed in this morning's papers. In it he said that "there can be no question regarding their materiality to the House Judiciary Committee's investigation." Concerning the President, he wrote, "The report's subject is referred to in his public capacity, and, on balance with the public interest, any prejudice to his legal rights caused by disclosure to the Committee would be minimal."

On the press plane to Houston. The President is to speak there to the National Association of Broadcasters tonight. Several reporters have copies of this morning's statement by Senator James Buckley, conservative Republican of New York, calling on the President to resign. "Watergate has expanded on a scale that has plunged our country into what historians call a 'crisis of the regime' . . . a disorder, a trauma, involving every tissue of the nation, conspicuously including its moral and spiritual dimensions," says Buckley. "I speak of the spreading cynicism about those in public life and about the political process itself. I speak of the pervasive and undeniable sense of frustration and impotence that has become the dominant political mood in the nation. I speak of a perception of corruption that has effectively destroyed the President's ability to speak from a position of moral leadership. . . . The character of a regime always reflects and expresses the character of its leader. It is he who appoints his executive staff. If he does not explicitly command what his aides and agents do, they in any event do what they sense and believe he wants them to do." Few politicians have said this.

Buckley also fears the "melodrama" of a Senate trial, in which "the Chamber would become a twentieth-century Roman Colosseum as the performers are thrown to the electronic lions," and the "sordid dregs dug up by the Watergate miners would inflame the passions of the domestic audience." And there is the political consideration. He fears "the risk of a runaway Congress that could commit us to new and dangerous programs"; that is, although he does not say so explicitly, if the President is not removed from office, Republicans will suffer substantial losses in November. The "trauma" that Buckley foresees is one that a good many politicians, for all their professed concern about not wanting to put "the country" through it, do not want to go through themselves. They fear "the passions of the domestic audience," and do not want to be subjected to them and, in their midst, have to cast a vote. The President would make it easier if he would kindly leave office.

Jesse Jones Hall, in Houston. The National Association of Broadcasters is holding its annual convention here. It is just a few blocks from the hotel where the President is staying, but the President travelled that distance in his limousine, and we followed in our bus in a motorcade.

On the block between Capital and Texas Avenues was a group carrying signs that said "THE EMPEROR HAS NO CLOTHES," "IMPEACH NIXON," "NO MORE YEARS," "HOW ABOUT DOING MY INCOME TAX?," and "NIXON IS A YO-YO." Police, with German shepherds, held the sign-carriers back.

The hall is a large, modern, red-carpeted building, and we are seated in the balcony. It is like having a bad ticket to a concert. The stage is set like an amphitheatre for gladiators, or a bear pit, where the President and his questioners will confront each other. There are four wooden platforms, draped in blue, for the questioners, and one, also draped in blue, for the President. The President can do much to control the event—answer questions, not answer them, give answers that are unrelated to the questions. The President may be wise to make these public appearances. It was easier for his opponents to deal with him, talk about his fate, when he stayed hidden. Now he is out there, public, a force. A force not to be treated lightly. A person and a personification. The President. In staying hidden, he had failed to use one of his most effective props: the Presidency.

Now the President deals again, at some length, with the question of why he should not resign. It is a good question for his purposes and there is a good answer to the question—that ours is not a parliamentary system, that Presidents should not resign because they are unpopular, that there is a Constitutional procedure for removing Presidents from office. But he does not seem to be able to present this argument without overstating it. And so he talks about charges levelled against him which he knows are false, and about making the difficult decision to carpet-bomb North Vietnam last December, with the result that the prisoners of war were brought home "on their feet rather than on their knees," and he says that we should not have "a President who every time the polls go down says, 'Well, maybe I better resign.' " The right of a President to make unpopular decisions is not the issue, of course, but it is an interesting and perhaps a useful argument for the President to advance. His answers are long—little speeches. The Middle East. The economy. From here we can see only his head and shoulders and something in his lapel that is shiny and must be the American flag. The realization sets in how strange this is—sitting in this balcony watching the President on that stage with his questioners. There is no news here—not even any information. It is the President doing his road show.

Asked whether he would honor a subpoena from the House Judiciary Committee, Nixon says he wants to put the issue "in perspective." He talks about all the material the committee already has, and says that nonetheless it wants "access to every document and/or tape, in effect, which is in the White House," and he says, "The reason that we do not say, 'Come in and bring your U-Haul trailer and haul it out,' very simply is this: It is not because of a lack of desire to coöperate." The committee, he says, "has enough information to conduct its investigation," and "insofar as additional documents are concerned, in other words, virtually a hunting license or fishing license or whatever you may want to call it, I am following the precedent that every President, Democratic and Republican, since the time of Washington has followed, and that is of defending the confidentiality of Presidential conversations and communications." The President has not answered the question of whether he will respond to a subpoena by the House committee. His precedents are not precedents. (Tom Brokaw, of NBC, points out in his question that Andrew Johnson turned over all the material sought in his impeachment investigation.) Nixon says, "Dragging out Watergate drags down America, and I want to bring it to a conclusion as quickly as we can."

MARCH 20

The Lyndon B. Johnson Space Center, outside Houston. We hear "Ruffles and Flourishes" and "Hail to the Chief," and the President and some NASA officials are standing on a platform on the lawn. Citations of awards for the Skylab 3 astronauts are read by an official, and during the reading the President stands sidewise, his arms folded. His graying hair blows in the breeze. His face is ruddy—almost unnaturally ruddy. When his face is in repose, he looks very tired, older. His eyes are barely visible. But then he poses with each astronaut, and reworks the tired face into a broad smile. And when he begins to speak he can pump the emphasis into his voice and gestures. He can make the effort. He is a pro, remarkably resilient. The President speaks without notes. He refers to the astronauts' medals, "which I hope they will never have to hock." He says that he has invited the astronauts and their wives to Camp David, and then goes into an almost mystical description of the place; the President rarely speaks of nature, beauty, physical things. "The clouds are right around you; when it is like that, you may think you were in space." He says he would like to volunteer for a space voyage. He tells the audience what his blood pressure is. He thanks the people who work on the space program and goes into a discussion of the importance of American-Soviet coöperation. He says he is aware of the differences between the two systems of government. "But I do know that the Russian people are a great people, the American people are a great people, and we can be so much together, and when we work together, let's work together. That is what this program is about. . . . A great people must always explore the unknown. Once a great people gives up or bugs out, drops out of competition of exploring the unknown, that people ceases to be great." He talks about the Spanish and French and British explorers and about the American pioneers and again about the space project and then about coöperation in medicine between the United States and the Soviet Union. I have seldom heard him so discursive.

An advance man rushes over to Dan Rather and says he has arranged for cameramen to get a "back shot" of the President speaking to the crowd. Against a backdrop of a concrete arch, gum trees, and scrub oaks, the President is now talking about his crash program to cure cancer and about speaking on the phone to a little boy who was dying of leukemia and how the little boy guessed a football score. "Today, that boy is dead. And thousands of others here, in the Soviet Union, in Europe, Africa, Asia, Latin America will die of cancer and other diseases because we haven't found those answers." And then he is talking about Boy Scouts ("I was not a Boy Scout, and I see one here") and about rubbing sticks together to create a spark. "And so it might be that Soviet doctors working together with American doctors, rubbing together, may find that spark." Then he talks about the nation's being at peace "for the first time in twelve years," and about the fact that "all of our prisoners of war are at home," and about his negotiations with Russia and China. He looks at his watch, says it is time for the coffee break, and keeps talking. Praising the astronauts of the aborted Apollo 13 mission, he says, "They didn't fail. The men and women on the ground didn't fail, because you are only a failure when you give up, and they didn't give up."

The reporters, thinking the President has concluded, race toward the bus and board it, and then they realize that he is still talking. A band strikes up "Hail to the Chief." The President again seems reluctant to leave the platform; he waves to the crowd, and then he waves at the band as if trying to stop it from playing his exit music. The band stops, and the President asks for a hand for the Clear Lake High School Band for learning to play "Hail to the Chief." The crowd applauds, and then the band resumes "Hail to the Chief." We are getting on and off and back on the bus like so many characters in a Marx Brothers movie. The President moves through the crowd, shaking hands as he makes his way to his limousine. As Nixon finally departs, the Clear Lake High School Band plays "The Washington Post" march.

SPRING

13

Today is the anniversary of that now famous meeting between the President and Dean and Haldeman, and we are still waiting to learn whether or when the President ever said, "It is wrong."

Today is the first day of spring.

Small events—measured by contemporary standards—have been happening quickly in the past week, and give a sense of the pattern of the times. Leon Jaworski disclosed that he has subpoenaed more documents; their subjects are unknown. Jaworski told reporters, "It'll ripen in a few days." The more Jaworski shows that he needs additional material, the more reasonable the Judiciary Committee appears. The White House has suggested that St. Clair screen the tapes sought by the House Judiciary Committee and give it edited transcripts. Reports out of the White House are that some White House aides concede the possibility of impeachment but are confident that the President will not be convicted by the Senate. The United States Court of Appeals has refused to overturn Judge Sirica's order that the grand-jury material be sent to the Judiciary Committee. The cost of living has risen again. (It is the first time since 1948 that the cost of living has gone up ten percent or more twelve months in a row.) The Senate has passed a bill revising the procedures that the Congress uses when it is dealing with the federal budget. (The House has passed a similar bill.) The bill also attempts to limit the President's power to impound funds appropriated by the Congress. Before the Senate bill passed, senators made speeches saying that the bill would restore the Congress to the status of a co-equal branch of the government. The new procedures are cumbersome, and it is not clear how well they will work. "They will work as well as the senators want them to work," one Senate aide told me.

According to the Los Angeles *Times,* "government sources" say that the tape of the March 21st meeting is "explosive" and "unambiguous." Rumors to this effect had been floating around Washington. Gerald Warren says, "We are not going to comment further on this totally expected story planted by someone with apparent political motives, however false it is." Hugh Scott has let it be known that he told St. Clair that the President "would be impeached" if there should be a confrontation with the House over the tapes, and that such a confrontation would "imperil" the President's position in the Senate.

The Marriott Corporation has announced that F. Donald Nixon, the President's brother, who has been the company's vice-president for community and industrial relations since 1970, will retire early. The company cited as the reasons Mr. Nixon's "ill health in recent months," and an austerity program brought about by the energy crisis. The White House announced that the President will nominate Leonard K. Firestone as ambassador to Belgium. Firestone contributed a hundred thousand dollars to the President's 1972 campaign, and Firestone's two brothers contributed $48,712 and $63,441. Henry Kissinger, in Moscow, arranging for the President's summit visit, has said he expects to make "concrete progress on a number of outstanding issues." A confidential report approved by the House Government Operations Committee says that seventeen million dollars in federal funds has been spent on the President's homes. The government had been saying that only ten million dollars was spent. Jack Brooks, chairman of the subcommittee that held hearings on the expenditures, announced the higher figure. Ken Clawson said, "Either deliberately or unwittingly, Brooks has become a member of an unprincipled gang of Democratic congressmen bent on destroying the President without regard to the national interest." The subcommittee's ranking Republican member, John Buchanan, of Alabama, said that the report was "absolutely untrue." On Saturday, the President made a radio address endorsing an aid-to-education bill pending in the House this week, and also a pending anti-busing amendment. The amendment would permit the reopening of previous court rulings ordering desegregation. Even before the President endorsed the amendment, it was expected to pass the House.

At the White House yesterday, Ron Ziegler, referring to the pace at which the House Judiciary Committee was moving, said that the committee staff "should perhaps work late into the evening." In a speech in Millburn, New Jersey, Gerald Ford said that the Republican Party might suffer "disastrous" defeats in November. Yesterday, the President met with Republican political leaders and said that he would support Republican candidates in the fall. In an interview in California yesterday, Robert Finch, former Secretary of Health, Education, and Welfare and former Presidential counsellor, a longtime associate of President Nixon's, and a man who was once considered a possible candidate for governor of California, said that he "couldn't run for dogcatcher without it turning into a referendum on Watergate."

At lunch today, a friend of mine who works in the Senate—a Senate aide who is unusually wise and thoughtful—says he thinks that the President may be succeeding in defining the terms of the impeachment. This man has the view, which I share, that the committee appears most anxious to find a specific criminal act by the President—the "cookie-jar syndrome." Catching him at something would be easier than impeaching him for violations of the Fourth Amendment or for the Huston plan or on general grounds of abuse of power or failure to protect the Constitution or to take care that the laws are "faithfully executed." This aide and others on Capitol Hill believe that the politicians are most reluctant—even afraid—to impeach the President on such grounds.

So, for now, Nixon and the committee are going down the same definitional track. The legal and the political questions are merging. The committee seems to be focussing on who-said-what-to-whoms. The Howard Baker approach, reiterated during the Ervin committee's hearings: What did the President know and when did he know it? The problem with the "cookie-jar syndrome" is that it is unrealistic. It is unlikely that the President sat there instructing his aides to carry out misdeeds. Most executives know how to get things done without asking that they be done. Many know how to establish deniability. The search for the specific link between the event and the order may be quite instructive to future leaders, who could perhaps conclude from all this not that these things should not be done but that they should be done more skillfully. The more disturbing things that went on—the adoption of the Huston plan, the work of the plumbers—the President has admitted, wrapping them in national security. It is not inconceivable that, left to itself, the Congress would accept the national-security rationale. Officials of the F.B.I. refer to certain things it has done—some of them (infiltration of groups, mail covers, breaking and entering) proposed by the White House in the Huston plan—as "illegals." An amazing term for government activities. And we know that Tom Charles Huston himself wrote in a memo that the President's signature should not be on his plan, because parts of it were "clearly illegal." The trouble is that if illegal things can be done in the name of national security, there is no law. The statutes themselves are already riddled with exceptions made in the name of national security.

The Senate man thinks that if it were simply up to the Congress, the President would not be impeached. "So much of what Nixon did they either did themselves in some degree or blinked at," he says. "The difference is that Nixon did it more, that he got caught, and that the country has changed."

But it is not up to Nixon and the Congress; there is also the Special Prosecutor and his staff, who have been gathering evidence. And in time the House Judiciary Committee could become heavily influenced by the way the issues are formulated by its own staff. Still, there is a lack of definers now. Except for the President.

The President's citation of precedents for some of the illegal actions carried out under his Administration—wiretapping, break-ins—cannot be entirely dismissed. It is true that he is talking about matters in which the differences of degree may be so great as to be substantive. And the fact that the Nixon Administration proposed to carry out these activities through secret White House units, drafting secret and unauthorized plans and employing free-lance agents, was also a substantive difference of some magnitude. But still some precedents were there. To what degree we don't know. John Ehrlichman was not entirely wrong when he told the Ervin committee that the concept of the Fourth Amendment had been "eroded." Perhaps, in fact, we owe him a great deal for saying it—for being, if unintentionally, a latter-day Paul Revere. The erosion goes back to methods that the government, starting in the nineteen-thirties, adopted to "protect" us from successive real and suspected external and internal threats. And to the extent that in recent years protesters against government action broke the law, those in charge of law enforcement apparently felt justified in doing the same. There thus emerged "precedents" to be summoned, and statutes riddled with exceptions, all in the name of national security. Perhaps it was inevitable that sooner or later a group would come to power which lacked a sense of limits and would encourage the process of erosion. And the issue is not yet settled.

When Judge Gerhard Gesell sentenced Egil Krogh to prison in January for violating the rights of Dr. Lewis Fielding, he quoted the late Justice Louis Brandeis: "If the government becomes a lawbreaker, it breeds contempt for law; it invites every man to become a law unto himself; it invites anarchy."

MARCH 27

The shad roe is in the restaurants. Another sign of spring. It is a comparatively quiet spell. There is time to clear out the debris of the cluttered winter, put the new license plates on the car (they commemorate the bicentennial in 1976), and anticipate the opening of the tennis courts this weekend. Time to try to live somewhat normally. It won't last.

At a restaurant, at lunchtime, Marsh Thomson, who used to be Spiro Agnew's press secretary, walks up to a table of reporters and hands out his card. Reporters used to vie for Marsh Thomson's favor and implore him for tidbits, or for an audience with the Vice-President. His card says that he is now executive vice-president of the National Oil Jobbers Council.

The generic term "Watergate" is rarely heard anymore. Gradually—
almost imperceptibly—the word for what we are going through has
become "impeachment."

Last night, the Republicans held their thousand-dollar-a-plate dinner here to raise funds for congressional campaigns. The turnout was
considerably lower than in previous years. But so was it at a five-hun-
dred-dollar-a-plate dinner held here by the Democrats last week. Last
night, President Nixon told the Republican diners that Republicans
would surprise the experts and win in November on a platform of
"peace abroad and prosperity at home."

The President's strategy may be aimed at the Senate, but then so is
that of the House Judiciary Committee impeachment inquiry staff. If
the President should be impeached, members of the House committee
would try the case against the President in the Senate, if there is such
a trial. The staff of the House Judiciary Committee is proceeding with
this in mind. Doar has tried some cases, and Jenner is primarily a trial
lawyer. The work of the impeachment inquiry staff can be thought of as
taking place in three stages: the gathering of evidence (which is going
on now); the presentment of the evidence to the House committee; and
the trial in the Senate. The efforts of the staff work back from that third
stage: it must gather enough incontrovertible evidence that if impeachment is voted, conviction will follow. Although the House committee is
not bound by the strict rules of evidence, the Senate trial must be kept
in mind. The Constitutional word "trial" for the Senate proceeding is
taken more literally, perhaps, than the framers intended. And prosecutors in any lawsuit proceed on the theory that they must obtain as much
evidence as they can as early as possible; later, the defense counsel and
the judge can have a voice in responding to requests for more evidence.

Therefore, the staff will seek material beyond the forty-two tapes
over which it is now disputing with the White House. The White House
may know this, and may be carrying on this fight against surrendering
these tapes in the hope of making the Judiciary Committee seem even
more unreasonable when it asks for still further evidence. But there are
signs on Capitol Hill that the President's strategy may be backfiring.
His struggle over procedures increases suspicions that he fears a battle
over substance. Yesterday, Senator Robert C. Byrd, Democrat of West
Virginia and the majority whip, said in a speech—widely noted here,
since few have said it, and Byrd is usually neither very outspoken nor
very liberal—that the President's strategy is to "mislead the American
people" and "is calculated to sabotage the legitimate and Constitutional
impeachment inquiry."

It is a lovely afternoon. There are more birds, squirrels, and tourists than usual on the lawns of the Capitol. For all the talk about the cynicism and apathy of the public, the tourists are here again in great numbers. Their presence suggests that they still take their government seriously, still care about it.

I called on a Republican senator I have spoken with from time to time. He is the one who, when I talked with him in December, told me that the President's situation had become subject to ridicule, and that he therefore didn't see how the President could recover. "The last time we talked was a time when most of us were on a teeter-totter of opinion," he said this afternoon. "One week, we felt the House was going to send a bill of impeachment over; the next week, we didn't. Now there's no doubt in my mind, or anyone else's, that an impeachment's going to come over. When the indictments happened, I was amazed by the reaction here. I had thought they had been discounted. We knew they were coming and who was involved. Yet they created a great stir. The tax thing is coming. It's a cumulative effect—it just keeps piling on: the Saturday-night massacre, the two missing tapes, the eighteen and a half minutes. You can't get anybody to take seriously that the failure to turn over the tapes on the ground of executive privilege is a real protection of the institution of the Presidency. That argument just won't wash. You can't go out on the street and find anyone who believes that. A senator said to me today that he had given up any hope that there was anything that would bail the President out, and that he hoped that when it came over, it would be cut and dried."

The Republican senator went on, "The talk now in the cloakroom is about the procedures for a trial. They say, 'Say, did you know that? Did you know that senators take a separate oath for the trial?' The little stories go around. The question is raised about whether we will have it on TV. That's a very different dialogue from what you were hearing three or four months ago. Senators who are up for reëlection see themselves sitting here day after day while their opponents are running against them."

I asked the senator what had happened to change the attitude among the senators.

"A number of people are beginning to think in terms of history," he replied. "At least, I am. Senators rarely think in terms of history. And I think part of the reason the senators have changed from doubts to a sense of certainty is that the attitude of the people at home is changing. Something happens to a country when support of the President goes down to twenty-five percent, and something else happens to a country when it stays at twenty-five percent."

At the beginning of the annual Radio and Television Correspondents Association dinner, there is the usual proposal of a toast to the President. This year, it is got through quickly. (I had never noticed before: the President is toasted but not the Congress or the Supreme Court.) Watergate and impeachment have been ruled out as subjects of what are supposed to be humorous speeches tonight, so a debate is staged about the energy crisis. It is hard to be funny about the energy crisis. The new lions are here: Leon Jaworski, Peter Rodino—and Sam Ervin and Judge Sirica, who are sort of lions emeriti. Leon Jaworski and Ken Clawson are at the same table, and Albert Jenner and Pat Buchanan are at the same table. That wouldn't happen in Chile.

MARCH 31

Sunday. It rained so hard yesterday that part of the Cherry Blossom Festival had to be called off. The President and Mrs. Nixon, escaping the rainy weekend, have gone to Key Biscayne. The President avoided a showdown with the Special Prosecutor on Friday by agreeing to turn over the subpoenaed materials that were due then. The materials are believed to cover alleged promises of ambassadorships in exchange for contributions.

In a speech yesterday, Gerald Ford called the President's 1972 reelection committee "an arrogant elite guard of political adolescents." As this came over the radio, the thought occurred that Ford had retained one of Spiro Agnew's former speechwriters. The statement was typically cryptic: it could be taken as critical of the President or as an attempt to separate the President from those who committed misdeeds. Within a few hours, it was announced on the radio that Ford said he had not meant by his comments to criticize President Nixon.

APRIL 1

Sitting in his office this morning, John Anderson, the Republican representative from Illinois and chairman of the House Republican Conference, said, "Out in Rockford, Illinois, they are more interested in busing than they are in impeachment. It seems that the impeachment sentiment is almost a function of age: younger people see impeachment as a method of rejuvenation; older people think of it and tremble." Anderson is a moderate, a thoughtful man, highly respected. He is fifty-two, white-haired, with a youthful face and large brown eyes. He speaks quietly. "I think the vote is going to be to impeach," he said. "I feel the pall of inevitability. I feel on this first day of April, 1974, that unless there is a dramatic change he has sealed his doom—primarily because of his uncoöperative attitude with regard to the Judiciary Committee. I don't foreclose the possibility that it could change, given the bizarre events."

I asked him at what point he felt that the President's fate had been decided.

"I doubt if there is any single point in the whole thing," he replied. "This is a cumulative series of events that drained away any support he might have had—ounce by ounce, it has gone out of the vial. His lack of coöperation, the results of the off-year elections, a growing feeling that this whole affair is an incubus hovering over the scene and poisoning the whole atmosphere. It's very difficult for members day after day, month after month, to live under this strain: the realization that you're going to have to vote on this issue; the realization that as this goes on longer and longer the lines are being etched deeper and deeper, and hardening. The twenty-five percent hard-core Nixon supporters are vitriolic in their defense. I think that even if a vote is necessary we're never going to satisfy that group that we didn't succumb to the blandishments of 'the Eastern-establishment press.' That twenty-five percent may not seem very big nationally, but when a member of Congress realizes he will alienate one out of every four voters . . . The young, who are most articulate about impeachment, are often not very enthusiastic about going to the polls. Members weigh these political consequences. After his State of the Union address, I really thought he'd brought himself back. But since then this obdurate, foot-dragging attitude has increasingly turned off a lot of Republicans. He's in a bind on foreign policy. Increasingly, the bloom is off the détente rose, and the conservatives are gunning for him if he makes an arms agreement."

At lunch, I talked with Richard Schweiker, Republican senator from Pennsylvania and a moderate—one who had opposed some Nixon Administration policies in earlier years, when it was politically risky to do so, and is now up for reëlection.

"I think things have changed dramatically in the last four weeks," he says. "It went from an unlikely House vote for impeachment to a most likely House vote for impeachment and a Senate trial."

I asked him why.

"A convergence of things," he replied. "First, the Administration is almost thumbing its nose at the Judiciary Committee—delaying, and saying 'One year is enough.' Second, the broad-scale indictments of his aides. I don't know if I agree with the Madison opinion that a President is impeachable for the acts of subordinates, but there is the fact that the opinion is there, and I do think the definition of an impeachable offense is broader than a criminal offense. Third, his contradictory statements about the hush money. Fourth, withholding of vital evidence would itself be grounds for impeachment. Until three or four weeks ago, I was fairly sure that the votes in the House were not there. Now, from talking to House members, I think the votes are there."

I asked him if he was having trouble raising money for his campaign.

"I can still raise decent money from moderate and independent bases," he replied. "It shows that in the year of Watergate they want to give to independent candidates. The White House is living under a delusion if it thinks that money is going to affect our stands on this. All of a sudden, my liabilities—having been independent of the White House—have become my greatest assets."

John Rhodes is still settling into Gerald Ford's old premises—Room H-232, the office of the House Minority Leader, down a labyrinth of corridors winding around the Capitol's rotunda. The walls of Room H-232 are still bare. Rhodes is deeply involved in the Republican Party; he is one of the people who try to shape it. A conservative, he was active in the Goldwater campaign in 1964 and was chairman of the platform committee at the 1972 Convention. He is considered part of the network (it also includes Gerald Ford and Melvin Laird) whose interest is in the strength of the Party. So Rhodes sits at the point at which several Republican groups converge. He, like Laird, is a longtime ally of Ford's. Along with Goldwater, in the Senate, and Dean Burch, in the White House, he is part of what is referred to here as "the Arizona Mafia." Moreover, Rhodes presumably would like to maintain his position as House Republican leader, and so he is watched carefully in this power struggle. Rhodes is informal and friendly—Capitol Hill friendly. He is accustomed to reporters, relaxed in their presence.

"Right now, April 1st, the House is beginning to jell," he said. "Up until this time, the atmosphere has been amorphous. People weren't talking very much—they were waiting to see what Judiciary would do. Now people are clearer on what the Judiciary Committee's procedure will be, and I think most people approve. I think it is jelling here because of the time that elapsed and the water that has gone over the dam. People have begun to get a feel for the situation, and to react. The far right is concerned with Nixon over the détente with Russia."

Rhodes said he had told the White House that he had not made a count of how House Republicans would vote on impeachment, and would not do so until the evidence was in. "But I have said that my visceral reaction was that the votes were not there for impeachment. But as of today the margin may be narrowing."

I asked Rhodes if he thought the need to raise reëlection money would be a factor in members' minds.

"Depending on the district, it would be quite a factor," he replied. "The President is much more popular in certain areas than he is in others. I'm not saying that members will cast a vote according to the constituents, but it would be naïve not to think they might." Rhodes went on to list the factors that House members would be influenced by as they considered how to vote on impeachment. "Their own reëlection, of course. A genuine concern for the future welfare of the two-party system. But I hope and believe the overriding factor will be whether there has been a high crime and misdemeanor. Is he so powerless that he can't govern? He's not in that position yet, but it is deteriorating."

The fear of the twenty-five percent presumed to be deeply opposed to the President's removal seems to stem not just from the fact that it might withhold its votes in November but from the fact that it represents, for the most part, those who work hardest within the Party—the activists. I asked Rhodes whether any Republican seeking the Presidency had a particular problem in this situation, since this group is also heavily represented at Republican Conventions.

"Yes," he replied. "Anybody in the Party who aspires to national office and high state office could earn the undying enmity of the hard core and might never succeed. The only thing to do is wait, look at the evidence, get down on your knees, and hope that your conscience will give you the right direction."

Senator Robert Dole, of Kansas, former chairman of the Republican National Committee, former outspoken defender of the President, is running for reëlection this year. When he is asked how he is or what he thinks, he jokes nervously. More than once, he has said, "I'm reading Edmund Ross biographies." Ross, a Republican senator from Kansas, voted, in the face of great pressure, against the conviction of Andrew Johnson. Later, Ross wrote that as he announced his vote "I almost literally looked down into my open grave." The act ended Ross's political career (but earned him a chapter in John F. Kennedy's *Profiles in Courage*). Dole talked with me this afternoon in the President's Room, the small, dimly lit room, off the Senate floor, where senators meet reporters. The room has an ornate chandelier, a tile floor, large brown leather chairs and couches, a grandfather clock, and frescoes of George Washington and his Cabinet.

"I don't think there's been any change for the better," Dole said. "If there's been any change, it's been downhill. It's been so long since there's been any good thing happening. The President is combatting bad news every day—it's either inflation or energy or Watergate. He hasn't anything good to announce. Among Republicans, there's a widespread feeling that unless there's a turnaround it's going to be bad in November. I ask everybody in the cloakroom every day, 'Has anyone heard any good news?' And I can't get an answer in the affirmative. There used to be the hope that he was innocent and would skyrocket in the polls. The latter just hasn't happened. I don't know what the President can do. You look down the road. You've got the tax report coming, possibly some more missing tapes, impeachment more of a reality. Those of us who are running this year don't know what to do. We think that the bread-and-butter issues—inflation, unemployment, energy—are the key ones, but who knows, if this impeachment heats up? How do you gear up your campaign for this impeachment thing? It really is a puzzler. Normally, you would be out running with the Administration. I don't think the alternative is running against the Administration. You just hope that enough voters feel you weren't involved in some way. I talked with Al Haig at the Radio and Television Correspondents' dinner the other night, and he said it's going to get better. He's probably programmed that way—to say it's going to get better. It'll be a lot clearer when Judiciary makes its report. Then you've got the question right on the table. A lot of the rest of us are getting flak because the thing is still going on. A lot of people who have been fed up with Nixon may get fed up with all of us. I guess the irony of it all is that, unfortunately, those who surrounded the President had no use for the Republican Party, and if the President survives it will be because of the Party. You can stand up and talk for an hour about things you think Nixon has done that are constructive, but that doesn't deal with the problem."

APRIL 2

In Acapulco, H. R. Haldeman is to speak before a group of young executives on White House management techniques. His subject is "Crisis Management."

George Meany, the president of the A.F.L.-C.I.O., was cheered enthusiastically yesterday by officers of the building and construction unions—the hardhats—when he told them that "the American people have completely lost confidence" in President Nixon. At one time, the construction unions had good relations with the Nixon Administration, having been cultivated by Charles Colson. Meany said in his speech, "I pray every night that Henry Kissinger won't give the Russians the Washington Monument—he's given them every goddam thing else."

Some Republican congressional leaders have urged the White House to restrain the comments of some of its spokesmen—particularly Ken Clawson and Ron Ziegler. The leaders have tried to explain that the comments give offense to the House. The White House has been warned not to, as the phrase goes, "Zieglerize" the Judiciary Committee.

Today, I met with Clawson and asked him, "Where are things?"

"Where are things?" Clawson said. "The opposition has got things around to where it wanted them, because we didn't do anything. It wasn't them opposing us and them winning—it was us not doing anything at all."

"Who's 'them'?" I asked.

"The opposition."

"Who's that?"

"The Democrats."

Clawson continued, "Since the first of the year, we've been in a position of playing catch-up ball, because we let all that time go by. But it's clear that the more forceful we are, the more effective we are. We shoot back when we are shot at. The opposition, sensing that the body was inert, started getting careless. I was the author of the 'cheap-shot' comment about Wilbur Mills [after Mills, the chairman of the House Ways and Means Committee, said that the President might have to resign over his taxes], and I was right, because on the following Sunday he said that all he knew was what he read in the papers. Did you see the story where I took on Jack Anderson? I let Anderson have it very forcefully—I said one of his stories was an example of the Watergate syndrome gripping the Washington press corps."

I asked Clawson if he felt that the White House offensive against the House Judiciary Committee had been effective.

"Yes it has been," he replied. "I released John Doar's letter to St. Clair. I did it because no one on the committee knew what was in the letter—that he was asking for forty-two conversations instead of six, that he wanted to look through the files. All weekend, the Democrats and the Republicans were talking about how reasonable the request was. The thing that really ticked me on this was when they had McClory and [Don] Edwards on the CBS *Morning News* or the *Today Show* saying that they were very surprised that he wouldn't give up the six tapes. I called St. Clair, and he said, 'Obviously, you haven't read the letter.' So I read the letter, and I said, 'My God! Nobody even mentioned this on the television or in the newspapers.' I said, 'It seems to me we're pretty dumb sitting here taking all this flak from the bastards,' and St. Clair said, 'That's your department,' and I released the letter."

Speaking of impeachment, Clawson said, "We think we can stop it in the House. What they think is a mountain is going to come out a molehill. We don't think they can come out with a meaningful bill of impeachment. It will come out with a bill of ballyhoo. Tip O'Neill is now running this. [House Majority Leader Thomas P. O'Neill is not really managing the impeachment process, but he likes to give the impression that he is.] Rodino is a guy out of Essex County, New Jersey. What else do you need to know? Albert is Albert. If the bill of impeachment is thin, it's going to hurt the impeachment drive. Many of the congressmen are lawyers and have a sense of history. And you have in this mix that the President has been and will continue to be seen publicly and talk about this publicly. There is no question that every time the President goes out and talks about this thing his stock goes up. Americans like to see their President. Secondly, the more he talks about Watergate, that boredom, irritation point gets closer and closer, and, in fact, the President's own appearances hasten it. What's taking place here is that people who were completely rejected at the polls in 1972 are trying to bring down the Presidency."

Clawson went on, "I don't think congressmen are going to want to buck their constituents, who will say, 'Get off this Watergate crap and get the price of hamburgers down.' And this country doesn't take as lightly as I think the national press takes to the idea of kicking a President out of office. It's one thing to talk to a pollster about high prices, but it's another to throw an elected President out of office. Historically, that works in our favor, not just in the initial stages but when it comes to a vote. We know how to fight this kind of fight. We're really quite good at it."

14

ROOM 2141 of the Rayburn House Office Building. The House Judiciary Committee's room. The room is on the first or second floor, depending on which street you enter from. (Including a garage, there are entrances to this building on three levels.) Police are stationed outside the door. Television cameras are being set up in the hallway. Also in the hallway are yellow ropes to hold back waiting spectators. One could almost follow the story of Watergate and the impeachment by tracing the route of the yellow ropes. Nearly a year ago, they were outside the meetings of the Ervin committee. Then they were outside the hearings of the Senate Judiciary Committee, which was inquiring into the firing of Special Prosecutor Archibald Cox. And they were outside the hearings of the Senate Rules and Administration Committee, briefly, in November, at the time of the confirmation of Vice-President-designate Ford. Now they are here, for the inquiry into the President's impeachment.

The walls and the carpeting of the Judiciary Committee's room are pale green. On the walls are paintings of Peter Rodino's predecessors as committee chairman: Hatton W. Sumners, of Texas; George S. Graham, of Pennsylvania; Emanuel Celler, of New York. The committee is to meet at ten o'clock, but at ten the thirty-eight members are just beginning to file in. Today, there is to be another "briefing," at which members merely talk, as opposed to a "meeting," at which they vote or make decisions. Rodino has been calling the briefings as a kind of cathartic exercise while postponing potentially divisive questions until he can find a consensus, and while giving the staff time to gather the evidence and prepare papers on procedural questions as they arise. Reporters are still taking their readings of the committee members, getting to know them, cultivating them. The committee members do not seem to mind having these newfound friends or to shrink from their sudden celebrity. Estimates are made of which members are "hard-line" for the President, which ones are "pro-impeachment," and which ones are the "undecideds." It is generally assumed that a majority of the Republicans are hard-line, but it is difficult to be sure even of that. It may be that some statements are being made now for public consumption; the evidence may crack the hard-line. It is also generally assumed that most of the Democrats feel that the President's actions warrant impeachment. Whether committee members who are put in the undecided column really belong there only they know.

As the members file in, the reporters surround them, asking questions, and the photographers take pictures—especially of Rodino. He is wearing a dark-blue pin-striped suit, a blue-and-white striped shirt. A rosette of the Knights of Malta is in his lapel, and a blue silk handkerchief is in his pocket. He looks almost dapper. Rodino is of medium build. His complexion is ruddy—setting off his full head of wavy hair, which is partly gray and partly white—and he smiles a lot. The members take their seats on two tiers—the Democrats to Rodino's right, with the exception of the thirty-two-year-old Elizabeth Holtzman, of New York, and the thirty-six-year-old Wayne Owens, of Utah, junior Democrats, who spill over onto the Republican side. Doar and Jenner, with two assistants, sit facing the committee, at what would ordinarily be the witness table. Word spreads that two White House aides are here. They are spotted quickly: two young men who look much alike, pale, sitting stiffly.

At ten-twenty-five, Rodino gavels for order and says, "The chair will first read a statement." He reads, "It has been two months since the House of Representatives, by an overwhelming and historic vote, authorized and directed this committee to investigate whether grounds exist to impeach Richard M. Nixon, President of the United States." In his slightly high-pitched voice, laced with a New Jersey accent, Rodino continues reading: "As regards the President himself, we have been respectfully patient. The courts were patient. The House has been patient. The people have been patient for a long, long time. The patience of this committee is now wearing thin." This is no ordinary opening statement. It is a major maneuver in a major struggle, and Rodino is listened to attentively by members of the committee. "On February 25th," he reads, "the committee made a specific request to the counsel of the President for specific evidence of specific facts of specific relevance to our inquiry. That request [for tapes and documents] so far has not been honored. . . . We can subpoena them if we must."

Edward Hutchinson, Republican of Michigan and the senior minority member, sitting just to Rodino's left, says, "Mr. Chairman, this committee has displayed an extreme amount of patience . . . and I cannot understand why there should at this late date still be any doubt in anybody's mind as to what it is we are after."

Robert McClory, Republican of Illinois, and the second-ranking minority member, has been trying to speak, but Rodino says that he will first call on John Doar. (Hutchinson is passive, and McClory is angling for the leadership of the minority side.) This has been carefully choreographed. Doar and Rodino meet almost every evening—sometimes for hours. (Someone says that Doar was up until 3 A.M. last night. Another staff member is in the hospital with an ulcer.) Doar reads a letter to St. Clair which Rodino says he has instructed Doar to send. The committee also listens attentively to Doar as he reads, in his throaty, boyish voice, the letter spelling out once more what the committee is seeking. He is letting the committee, and the public, know how important that material might be. The letter has to do with "action or nonaction" by the President or any of his senior aides and "the President's knowledge or lack of knowledge of, or participation in, or lack of participation in" acts to obstruct justice. It restates the committee's belief in its Constitutional authority to obtain these tapes and documents, and refers to the resolution passed by the House on February 6th which authorized the committee to conduct the inquiry and subpoena material. Rodino and Doar sought the authorization—it was approved by a vote of 410-4—in order to have an underpinning for subsequent committee action. "We therefore request a reply by Tuesday, April 9th, at the latest, with respect to whether or not the conversations referred to in our letter of February 25, will be delivered to the committee," Doar concludes. "Sincerely, John Doar, Special Counsel." There it is, a line drawn in the dust.

APRIL 5

As Americans struggle with their income-tax returns, we read the continuing stories about the President's taxes. White House aides say that the President's decision to pay the $432,787.13, plus interest, that the Internal Revenue Service said he owes has "almost virtually wiped out" his personal savings. The President cannot sell his home in San Clemente, because he promised last December, when his tax returns were made public, to give it to the nation. Although he said last fall that he would "be glad to have the papers back" if the Internal Revenue Service disallowed the deduction, as it now has done, the National Archives has maintained that his pre-Presidential papers are now the property of the government. The White House has put out a statement saying, "Any errors which have been made in the preparation of the President's returns were made by those to whom he delegated the responsibility for preparing his returns and were made without his knowledge and without his approval."

The *Wall Street Journal* reports today that the Maurice H. Stans Award for Distinguished Federal Financial Management has been abandoned.

Edwin Reinecke, lieutenant governor of California, was indicted in Washington this week by one of the Watergate grand juries on three counts of lying to the Senate Judiciary Committee during its investigation of the I.T.T. case.

On the CBS news tonight, Frank DeMarco, one of the President's tax lawyers, says that he went over the President's tax returns with him "page by page."

APRIL 6

Today's Washington *Post* reports that the President still has pre-Presidential papers valued at one and a half million dollars. (He also, of course, has his Presidential papers.) The staff of the Congressional Joint Committee on Internal Revenue Taxation, which reported last week that the President owed $476,411 in back taxes, has found that many valuable pre-Presidential papers were not included among those donated to the Archives. It has said that included among those donated were three boxes—apparently valued by Ralph G. Newman, Nixon's appraiser, at fifteen thousand dollars—dealing with Nikita Khrushchev's visits to the United States as Premier and consisting only of newspaper clippings.

At dinner, a Democratic senator says, "We're all very weary."
I ask him why.
"I don't know what we're doing, but we're worn out from it," he replies. "This thing is a strain on all of us. We're all on trial. We all want it over with. We Democrats are counting on the Republicans' great desire to get Ford in by November."

APRIL 8

Monday. The Howard Hughes hundred thousand dollars is with us again. As in a Bach fugue, the themes recur and overlap and become more complex. (Last December, when Chester Davis, a Hughes attorney, flung the money down before the Ervin committee—"Here's the goddam money"—there was one hundred thousand one hundred dollars. Nothing stays in place. Like that gap in the tape which grew by quarter minutes from eighteen minutes to eighteen and a half.) It has been leaked to the papers that Herbert W. Kalmbach, the President's former personal attorney, who had served as a campaign fund-raiser, gave new testimony on the subject of the Hughes money to the Ervin committee in executive session a few weeks ago. (There are now frequent leaks out of the Ervin-committee staff's investigation. In January, the committee postponed further hearings, and the leaks—in a pattern of congressional-committee behavior which has appeared before, in unpleasant form—are keeping the issue of the Hughes money alive.) According to the leak, Kalmbach said that the President's friend Bebe Rebozo had told him that part of the money was given or lent to Donald and Edward Nixon and to Rose Mary Woods. Rebozo, in testimony, and the President, in his press conference last fall, had said that the money had been kept by Rebozo—according to Rebozo, in a safe-deposit box. According to today's stories, Kalmbach also said that Rebozo, at the President's request, met with Kalmbach at the White House on April 30th of last year to ask him what to do about the potentially embarrassing money from Hughes. It was on April 30th that the President dismissed his highest aides and went on television to say that the Watergate matter would now be cleared up. It must have been quite a day at the White House. Last December, we read in the New York *Times* that the money was returned to Hughes' lawyer, Chester Davis, in June in New York by an associate of Robert Abplanalp.

Pieces of the puzzle are beginning to fit together—or are they? For example, the hundred-thousand-dollar payment was first disclosed by Jack Anderson in August, 1971. The information was believed to have come from his friend Hank Greenspun, publisher of the Las Vegas *Sun*. It has now been reported that Ehrlichman sent Kalmbach to see Greenspun, to learn if he had other memos about Hughes, including any information about Lawrence O'Brien, who once did public-relations work for Hughes. (Greenspun's safe was broken into—it has never been clear by whom. Hunt told the Ervin committee that he and Liddy had planned such a break-in, but that it was not carried out.) Magruder testified before the Ervin committee last June that among the targets for the first surveillance efforts discussed in a meeting in Mitchell's office on February 4th, 1972, were Greenspun and O'Brien. This has led to one theory that the Ervin-committee staff members have been putting forward—that one purpose of the Watergate break-in, at least, was to obtain information about O'Brien's connections with Hughes, or to see if O'Brien had information about Hughes' connections with the Nixons. But this theory about the case-within-the-case also seems to be misleading. It is at odds with the fact that the "Gemstone" plan was one for widespread political intelligence; O'Brien's and McGovern's headquarters at the Democratic Convention in Miami were discussed for possible bugging, too, and there was a tap on the phone of another member of the Democratic National Committee staff. And we now know that wiretapping and surveillance by the Administration was not limited to the opposition party.

Over the weekend, the President flew to Paris to attend memorial services for the late French President Georges Pompidou, and extended his visit to meet with a number of world leaders. Alexander Haig, the White House chief of staff, told reporters, "It was very evident that European leaders and world leaders with whom the President met continue to look to the United States and President Nixon as an essential factor in the realization of the continuing efforts to develop a structure for stable international environment." Haig said that the world leaders in Paris could not conceive of Mr. Nixon's being impeached and convicted.

A Harris poll published today said that the President's popularity rose five points after his trips to Chicago and Nashville and Houston in March and before the report on his taxes was made public.

In the Judiciary Committee briefing this morning, Republicans—particularly McClory—complained about the lack of business meetings at which votes could be taken, and about the failure to settle the issue of James St. Clair's role. St. Clair has asked to participate in the impeachment proceedings. Rodino—in accordance with a style that he seems to be developing—has not yet called a meeting on the issue, which might divide the committee. He is slowly establishing a reputation for fairness—even among the grumbling Republicans—and, to the astonishment of many, has managed to cool the more hotheaded committee members. But Rodino and Doar are opposed to St. Clair's participation. The argument they give is that this proceeding is analogous to that of a grand jury, but there is also a fear that St. Clair's presence would be intrusive. Nonetheless, precedents exist, in the cases of judges, for the subject of an impeachment inquiry to have counsel present.

"Let me explain to you what I think is happening," Tom Railsback, the Illinois Republican, who is considered an "undecided" member of the House Judiciary Committee, said at lunch. "There are many members of the minority who don't like the idea of Doar and Jenner working together. You have to differentiate between trying to get at the truth and these procedural things. But the procedural things are very important to us. It is going to be easier for members of the minority to vote for impeachment if they feel that the President has got a fair deal. I want to be able to go back to my Republicans in my district and say, 'Look, we fought to get him every break, but the evidence was thus and so.' Also, cross-examination is one of the best ways to get at the truth." (Railsback did not say so, but I have been told that another reason the Republicans are anxious to win participation for St. Clair is that it would relieve them of the burden of defending the President.)

Railsback talked of his own current thinking about whether the President should be impeached. "I just don't know," he said. "I want to hear the March 21st tape. I want to see what was in the bulging briefcase" (the briefcase that was forwarded to the committee by the Watergate grand jury). Railsback said he felt that in the matter of the cover-up or of manipulation of sensitive agencies, such as the C.I.A. or F.B.I., which would be serious offenses, there had to be "direct evidence" of Presidential involvement.

What if a leader took care not to give orders that could be traced, I asked.

"I think you have to prove his involvement," Railsback replied. "I don't mean that if Nixon was in the room when these things were discussed and then didn't do anything about it, that would be all right. We would want to investigate those circumstances closely. That might make him a conspirator. I think he's got to have knowledge. It's a tough question."

I asked Railsback if it worried him that there could be a President under whom all kinds of acts were carried out but who, because he was not found to be personally involved, was not held responsible.

"Yes, yes," he replied. "The saddest indictment of this Administration is the pervasive attitude of top-level aides that they could do anything they pleased and get away with it. I don't think that's O.K. It has brought an impeachment proceeding that has been a disgrace to the President. His aides have been fired and indicted. I just don't think that if a President has been elected by more than sixty percent of the people you reverse that decision unless you find serious offenses."

I asked if he felt, then, that a President should not be held responsible for the acts of subordinates.

"Under our general criminal law, in order to convict a superior you have to have conspiracy or complicity," he said. "I don't buy the Madison concept that a President can be impeached for the acts of his subordinates. I don't think there are any precedents for that. If it was implied that subordinates could commit criminal acts, that would be a problem. Say the plumbers' operation envisioned criminal acts. You have to bear in mind that national security will be raised as a defense. But if the President said, 'Go out and get the evidence and I don't care how you do it,' that could be grounds. This could be one of the most critical issues in defining an impeachable offense—the extent of his participation or knowledge. Most people have not gone into it much yet. Don't forget one thing. Some people are under indictment. Some people have lost their means of livelihood. There's some reason for some of them not to take the rap for the President if he was involved. I don't think he'd pardon them. That would be too unseemly."

APRIL 10

Last night, the White House responded to the Judiciary Committee's request for a reply by tomorrow to the committee's request for materials by releasing a letter from St. Clair casually saying that "a review of the material in question is under way," and might be completed after the Easter recess, twelve days from now.

Rodino and some of his colleagues, for all of their surface assurance, are aware that in fact the White House may be controlling the timing, and even the substance, of the committee's deliberations. The committee has held back from asking for still further material it believes it needs, not wanting to blur the question of the first request, or to be vulnerable to charges of making excessive demands, as the Ervin committee was when it subpoenaed five hundred documents last December. Still, the White House delay on this material will further delay subsequent requests, at the same time that the pressure on the committee will grow to "get it over with." (Rodino has a way of quietly slipping the date on his own deadlines. In December, he was saying that the inquiry would be completed by April. When the House voted to give the committee the subpoena power, he was saying "by the end of April." Now Rodino has said that the presentation of evidence will begin on May 7th and that the committee staff is talking of finishing in six weeks.) Yesterday, the committee Democrats caucused and agreed to let St. Clair participate in the impeachment proceedings—details still to be determined. Rodino was opposed to letting St. Clair participate—and Doar was deeply opposed—but since some Democrats felt he should be allowed to, Rodino knew he did not have the votes to prevent it.

There are valid reasons for the committee's deadline postponements thus far: the mass of material, the procedural questions, the delays by the White House in producing information. The Special Prosecutor's office has still not completed its work. An argument can be made that, if anything, the impeachment process may be too hasty. But the political realities are intervening. The members of the House have to run for reëlection, and they are getting edgy. The President's gambit of encouraging and playing on public fatigue over the issue—while dragging it out—seems to be effective. At some point, the committee staff will have to go ahead with presenting the evidence without having much of the evidence it requested. The thought is that when the committee sees the pertinence of the gaps in information, it will become more assertive in its demands and have more public support. Rodino and Doar and most of the Democrats have settled on the strategy of not moving to hold the President in contempt if he does not supply subpoenaed material but, rather, to add up the noncompliance and put it in the list of charges against the President. Despite statements that have been made by some House members, it is not at all clear that when it comes down to it the House will consider failure to provide the material a sufficiently serious offense to impeach the President. The White House may have succeeded in establishing the criterion for an impeachable offense (a serious criminal act), the timing of the inquiry, and even the substance.

This afternoon, I went to see Representative Walter Flowers, a Democrat from Tuscaloosa, Alabama, who is a member of the Judiciary Committee. When Flowers first ran for Congress, in 1968, he campaigned as a supporter of George Wallace, and that year, too, he worked to get Wallace on the national ballot. Flowers' vote is considered one of the crucial votes on the committee—one that could not only affect the outcome in the committee but influence the votes of other Southerners if he supports articles of impeachment that go to the House floor. On the walls of his office, in the Cannon House Office Building, there were pictures of Flowers with George Wallace and of Flowers with James Allen, the very conservative Democratic senator from Alabama. There was also a framed poster of the Capitol, with a quotation from Alexander Hamilton: "HERE, SIR, THE PEOPLE GOVERN." Before being elected to Congress, Flowers was an attorney. Now, as he entered his office from having voted on the House floor, he removed a beige suède jacket. He was wearing tinted glasses, a flowered shirt, and brown-and-beige plaid trousers. He has dark-brown hair, which is curly and slightly graying. He is forty-one, relaxed, and friendly. He speaks softly, with a gentle Southern accent.

"I have an open mind," Flowers said. "But I'm miffed, just as a lot of people are, at the fancy footwork on the part of the President's lawyer. I don't look at this as a partisan thing at all. Hell, I come from a no-party state. I'd say that seventy-five to eighty percent of the people who voted for me voted for Richard Nixon in the last election. I feel as independent on this as anyone could. I feel I could vote either way and survive. I don't intend to run a poll and go by it. I think of this as a once-in-a-lifetime proposition. I don't mean to be melodramatic. I feel I just happened to be in the breach when the gun got loaded with this particular shell. I'm hearing less political talk out of the Congress on this than on anything else. They talk about doing what's right for the country, and most of the members want that, but they don't know what that is yet. I'm probably a good case study as a Southern Democrat."

Behind Flowers, as he sat at his desk, were the American flag, the Confederate flag, and the flag of Alabama. "As a Southern Democrat, I'd say my thinking probably represents that of most Southern Democrats whose districts are pro-Nixon. People in our state have an innate loyalty to the institutions of their government and the occupant of the office. That helps me, and the governor. They equate supporting the President with supporting the country. I sincerely feel that there is a difference of attitude between the New York-Washington corridor and the rest of the country. These grand jurors here in Washington are no more representative of the average grand jury than the man in the moon. This thing has a national character. It's unusual to take a grand jury from the nation's most unusual city—seventy-five percent black. The grand jury was mostly black, and a couple of the members were unemployed, and the foreman was a naturalized American. Now, there's nothing wrong with that, but it isn't typical. I go from here to Alabama every weekend. It's like going from the Sahara to Antarctica. I just don't think grass-roots America is getting heard. As far as the national press is concerned, you take the newsmen, the television producers. I think it's clear a majority don't like Nixon and would like him to be removed from office. They've set the scene that makes it easier for it to happen. I hear all these predictions that the House is going to impeach the President. Ain't no way anyone can know. *We* don't know. Rodino doesn't know. I hear Democrats say in the cloakroom that the Republicans will have to vote for impeachment. Well, I just don't know. I hear that the Republicans want Ford in. Well, a guy's natural reaction is going to be to defend his own man. I'd speculate right now that a large majority of the Republicans are going to vote against impeachment, and I'm *afraid* that it's going to get down to what the Southern Democrats do. I'd like it to be as bipartisan as possible."

I asked Flowers to tell me more about the point of view that equates the man with the office.

"It's a patriotic support of the institution that works in Nixon's favor," he said. "Also, this country went so overwhelmingly for Nixon two years ago, and against the Democratic candidate. In my section of the country, Nixon still enjoys large support, because in some areas being against Nixon is equated with being pro-McGovern. My district is forty percent black, and the blacks largely went for McGovern. Nixon got eighty-five to ninety percent of the white vote."

I asked Flowers what would persuade him to vote for impeachment.

"I have purposely left that open," he said. "I haven't stretched my imagination to say, 'If Nixon and John Dean were talking and Nixon said this, I'd vote for, or if they said another, I'd vote against.' I substantially support the broad view of what constitutes an impeachable offense, but that seems moot, because most of the things that have been talked about are criminal offenses."

What if you have a pattern of offenses by the President's aides, I asked.

"Then you have a pattern of offenses by his aides, and you have to see what they are," he replied. "One of my professors in law school told me that out of the facts the law rises, and I'll never forget it. That's why I think the broad view is the right view, and Jerry Ford wasn't all wrong when he said that an impeachable offense is whatever the House thinks it is." (In 1970, when Ford, then House Minority Leader, led a drive to impeach Supreme Court Justice William O. Douglas—reviving the antique notion of impeachment—he said, "An impeachable offense is whatever a majority of the House of Representatives considers it to be at a given moment in history." Ford did go on to say that the removal from office of a President, who, unlike judges, could be voted out of office after four years, would "require crimes of the magnitude of treason and bribery," but what entered our political lore was the first part of his statement.)

Flowers showed me a petition from some law students at the University of Alabama. "We urge you to vote for and push for the impeachment of Mr. Nixon," it read. "Only a trial in the Senate can clear the air of the many doubts and frustrations engendered by Mr. Nixon's so-called 'law and order' Administration and restore public confidence in our government and its leaders." Flowers said, "The news media have been largely responsible for this—the idea that we should send it to the Senate. I have come to the firm opinion that at least this member is going to cast his vote on the same basis as he would if he were a senator. The emotion in the House is a little lopsided for impeachment now, because the members get a lopsided view of it, but the degree of proof needed is the same. I think most of the members feel that way. I think most of the members will not cop out and pass the buck to the Senate. I think that would be morally irresponsible."

I asked Flowers if he felt that failure of the White House to coöperate with the inquiry would be a factor in the outcome.

"It would certainly be a factor," he replied. "I'm more than disappointed in their response so far. If they flagrantly disregard a subpoena, I think it will be very bad. If requests have been flagrantly disregarded, I think that the assumption will be that it goes against the President. There is a principle of evidentiary law that comes down from merry old England—and most of us are lawyers—that says that if one party to a controversy has under his dominion or control evidence or a body of fact and he fails to present it to the jury or the court, you may presume that that evidence goes against him."

Did Flowers, I asked, give any credence to the idea that the President was protecting the principle of confidentiality?

"Bull," he replied. "Bull."

The House and the Senate are working late tonight, trying to clear away some legislation before the Easter recess begins, on Friday. In an elevator in the Cannon House Office Building, a member of Congress was in a great hurry to get to the House to vote, and the elevator operator took him directly to the subway, not stopping at other floors. To make conversation, I said to the congressman, "You're working pretty hard these days, aren't you?"

"Sure am," he replied.

"Well, you've got a week off coming," I said.

"I've got to leave here and go home and face the music," he said. "That's not time off. Anytime I'm *here* or *there,* it's *not time off.*" He grasped my arm and, looking quite perturbed, said, "Listen, in the year of Watergate and you're a Republican in a Democratic district . . ." Then he threw his arms in the air and left the elevator. The elevator operator smiled.

By 9:30 A.M., an hour before the Judiciary Committee is to meet, the line of spectators stretches from the committee room to the sidewalk outside the South Capitol Street entrance to the Rayburn House Office Building. Numb as people are, they still recognize when a major event is to happen, and head for it. This is a new one: the first subpoena of a President by a committee of the House of Representatives; the first subpoena in an impeachment inquiry. The committee room is not very large, and the press takes up more than half the seats. The scramble for seats will get worse before this is over. More representatives of the foreign press are arriving in Washington. Some people are already trying to arrange for seats for a Senate trial.

And after some confusion caused by a last-minute offer from St. Clair of part of the material, and after some procedural maneuvers, and roll-call votes on ancillary questions, when the roll is finally called on whether to issue this first subpoena in the impeachment of a President the vote is thirty-three to three. Hutchinson votes against it, and casts a proxy vote for Charles Wiggins, California Republican, who is absent. (Hutchinson has said that he does not believe that the President has committed an impeachable offense, and that he does not believe in subpoenaing the President.) The third vote against the subpoena is cast by Trent Lott, a thirty-two-year-old Mississippi Republican. (Lott's district gave Nixon the highest percentage in 1972—eighty-seven percent.) The atmosphere in the room is subdued.

Directed to Benjamin Marshall, chief of security for the impeachment inquiry, the subpoena, to be returned by April 25th, says, in printed form, "You are hereby commanded to summon," and then, filled in by typewriter, "Richard M. Nixon, President of the United States of America."

Later in the afternoon, I went to see James Mann, a conservative Democrat from Greenville, South Carolina, whose vote on the Judiciary Committee, like Flowers', is considered crucial for the outcome both in the committee and on the floor of the House of Representatives. Mann, who is fifty-four, had practiced law in Greenville before he was elected to Congress, in 1968. He had also served in the South Carolina state legislature, had been a prosecuting attorney in the state's courts, and had been widely involved in civic, fraternal, bar, and church activities. On most issues, he has supported the President. His congressional district is still heavily in favor of Nixon. (In 1972, Nixon won it with seventy-eight percent of the vote.)

"I'm having no difficulty whatsoever in putting myself in the posture of a judge or a juror who is listening to evidence with an open mind and for the first time," Mann said. "I have not paid attention to the press analyses or the Watergate hearings. I'll see what the facts are and make a decision. It's a common legal maxim that the facts make the law. Depending on what the facts are, the definition of what is an impeachable offense becomes moot." Flowers had said a strikingly similar thing. Mann went on, "In the end, there can be only one definition, and that is: conduct that is so damaging to the national interest that it requires impeachment. That may seem simplistic, but in the end it's what the members will have to go by. The technical definition of crime or no crime is unrealistic. There can be a hundred crimes that don't affect the national interest or morality. I also reject the Ford definition that it is a political decision. There will be some degree of politics—so there is in all life's decisions. One just has to isolate oneself from it to the greatest degree possible. I have no difficulty in assuming a position of impartiality—which increases my distress at some of the members' politicizing a very serious issue."

Mann, who is tall and slim, has thinning gray hair and was wearing a gray suit. His voice is flat, and his pale face is aging. He is soft-spoken and speaks slowly. Many members of the committee, when they are interviewed, are anxious to convey an impression of concern about the magnitude of the issue they are facing. Mann really seemed to feel it. "I find it very distressing," he continued. "I think there's a great vacuum in the media in stressing the procedures. They fail to stress that the staff is proceeding objectively under the explicit instructions of the committee. Mr. Jenner, because of his objectivity, finds himself in difficulty, and even in jeopardy. The real evidences of partisanship are not analyzed well, and so we come up with a continuing battle by the minority to use partisanship as a defensive weapon. There are those on the minority who would inject partisanship into the process solely for the purpose of damaging the process and solely for the purpose of preventing getting the truth determined. I charge that."

I asked him how he assessed the problem of the committee's needing even more material than it has subpoenaed.

"It appears that dilatory tactics fit the strategy of Mr. St. Clair and the President," he said. "Their idea seems to be that when the White House coughs up material after all the agonizing and quibbling, the American people, wearying of the whole thing, are fruitful soil for the President's saying, 'We gave you all this and now you want more.' It's *frightening* how the electronic throne can be used for this kind of story. It's important that the public understand that impeachment is part of the process, and not the final action, and there's no one to educate them on this. We're handicapped, because our position is too delicate. An explanation of the process in a thoughtful, rational manner becomes an advocacy position."

I asked him if he did not think that the meaning of impeachment would become clear as the proceedings went on.

"Very gradually," he replied. "But as it becomes clear, the weariness of the American people will counterbalance that, and the other side continues to make its argument, so that those of us who are going to do what is objective and fair and right are going to pay a price. A lack of understanding should not cause that to be so. I'm willing to pay, but it's unfortunate that one has to pay for doing one's duty."

I asked Mann about what had been perceived as the need of some committee members to find the commission of a crime by the President, and about the fact that the White House could withhold any such evidence that exists.

"Obviously, that's going to make it very difficult," he said. He shifted his big blue leather chair and removed his jacket. "There will be a tough problem because of tones of voice, and expressions of outrage that weren't made, thrustings of people from his bosom who weren't thrust—on which inferences will be drawn," he said. "As a prosecuting attorney, I feel capable of drawing those inferences, but I'm reluctant to present to the House and the American people a case based on a sophisticated analysis of those items. Yet we're simply not going to be given incriminating evidence. It's said that a very large segment of the American public goes along with that reluctance to give us that evidence, on the basis of a lack of understanding of the process and almost a not wanting to understand the process, because of a fixation on the Presidency versus a willingness to govern themselves and this country through elected representatives. It is characteristic of human nature to want to transfer the responsibility for self-government to a strong central figure. And that characteristic of human nature is played upon by the electronic throne. The media do the President more favors than anyone will ever say. The President can sign a goody and get it announced. Bad announcements are made by others. A President can get on TV, and who responds for the people? Nobody. When the networks say the Congress can respond, we have what is seen as some little politician yapping back in a partisan manner, and it's counterproductive, because of the tendency of the American people to view the Congress as a monolithic body conspiring against the President."

I asked Mann if there was some process he would prefer to that of impeachment.

"The big shortcoming is the failure of the House of Representatives to maintain an ongoing mechanism for these purposes," he replied. "The failure over the years to exercise oversight on behalf of the people contributed to the point zero from which we had to start. Congress should have had a mechanism for overseeing the conduct of the elected officials and the civil officers of this country. Last year, I proposed that the Judiciary Committee have a subcommittee conduct oversight. Because of my concern about the deterioration of the system, I think that the Watergate affair can be nothing but a tremendous stride toward a return to a more viable self-government."

But, I asked him, what if the precedent set is that these things can be done and, as long as the President does not provide the information and is not held accountable for the acts of his aides, can be done with impunity?

"The fact that the Watergate affair came to light will at least make some people aware of what they are surrendering when they surrender self-government," he replied. "But I'm optimistic enough to believe that even if the public does not want to go through with the trauma of the process, it will give notice as to what it is willing and not willing to tolerate. What there was before this convulsion was a lot more dangerous and powerful than the situation you describe."

APRIL 12

Friday. A perfect spring day. There is something healing, reassuring about it. We have been through so much, and so much is still uncertain, but in Farragut Square, a few blocks from the White House, where I had a picnic lunch with a friend, the red-and-white tulips were out. The white and magenta azaleas that surround the statue of Admiral Farragut are beginning to blossom.

There are all kinds of rumors going around. Rumors about some of the language that the President used while being taped. Rumors that St. Clair is not really being kept informed by his client. (It was apparent that St. Clair's predecessors weren't.) In the Judiciary Committee meeting yesterday, Doar said it was his impression that St. Clair had not heard the tapes. There is talk about the interview that Gerald Ford gave to John Osborne, of *The New Republic,* in which he outlined the membership of a possible Ford Cabinet. Osborne also reported that Ford said that the President's tendency to ramble at their meetings drove him "close to distraction." While great Constitutional issues are being raised and a President is struggling to maintain power, "Washington" discusses the Ford Cabinet. It is all the more remarkable in that—Kissinger excepted—little thought is given to the Nixon Cabinet.

The unease, even the fright, of the politicians is quite noticeable. I have never seen them like this before. The impeachment vote is becoming a reality for them. They can often practice the art of not having to cast critical votes. They fudge, and obscure issues, and wrap them in motions to table motions and in technical amendments. We saw some of that yesterday, as they bobbed and weaved around the subpoena. But— unless they are more imaginative than now seems possible—they won't be able to do that when the time comes to vote on whether or not to impeach the President.

After a debate that lasted almost two weeks, the Senate mustered the necessary two-thirds vote to close off a filibuster and yesterday passed a bill providing for public financing of all federal campaigns. A couple of

weeks ago, Common Cause, the citizens' lobby, released figures showing that as of that time special-interest groups had raised eleven million
six hundred thousand dollars in cash to contribute to candidates in the
1974 congressional elections—already more than such groups donated
in 1972. It has also been reported that dairy groups now have a contributions fund of two million dollars. In a message to Congress last month,
Nixon said that he would oppose public financing, because it would
have the effect of "undermining the very foundation of our democratic
process."

Earlier this week, Senator Lowell Weicker, Connecticut Republican,
released a set of documents showing that a special I.R.S. group, dis-
banded last year, had been set up in 1969 to collect information on
"individuals promoting extremists' views or philosophies." The documents included a summary of fifty-four undercover investigations made
by the White House detective Anthony Ulasewicz, including investigations into whether there were "any scandals or skeletons" in the
backgrounds of Senators Edmund Muskie and Hubert Humphrey. The
I.R.S. memorandum establishing the special I.R.S. group said that it
would examine the tax records of "ideological, militant, subversive,
radical or other" organizations. It also said, "We do not want the news
media to be alerted to what we are attempting to do or how we are operating, because the disclosure of such information might embarrass the
Administration."

Herbert Porter, the former scheduling director of the Committee for
the Re-Election of the President, was sentenced this week to fifteen
months in prison—all but thirty days suspended—for lying to the F.B.I.
in its investigation of Watergate.

Senator James Buckley said this week that the President should not
go to Moscow while impeachment proceedings were pending. Another
problem with which we have no experience: a President conducting
international negotiations while facing impeachment.

Recently, Senator Jacob Javits, Republican of New York, held a press
conference and said that he had noted "some disquieting tendencies,"
and warned the President not to play "impeachment politics" with
domestic legislation and foreign policy. Nixon is caught in the crossfire
of his own "centrist" politics. A Republican senator once described him
as "the man with the portable center." Javits suggests that if the President
feels he cannot govern effectively he should step aside, under the section
of the Twenty-fifth Amendment that provides for the Vice-President to
serve as President in cases of Presidential disability. This idea had been
bruited about, but I think Javits is the first politician to mention it publicly.
It is seen by some as a way of having Nixon resign without resigning, of providing him a harbor in which he would still have immunity.

But it is unclear how this would resolve uncertainty at the head of the government. And the Twenty-fifth Amendment's provisions for transfer of power in the event of Presidential disability have never been tested.

Some people, concerned at the length of time the impeachment process is taking, and at the difficulties of having such a process take place in the case of a sitting President at all, are proposing alternatives that would be more along the lines of the British system of resignation and new elections after a finding of a loss of confidence. But apart from the practical difficulties—the British opposition party has its leader in place, but it is hard to imagine, for example, the Democrats coming up with a candidate in short order—a Constitutional crisis seems to be precisely the wrong time to think about changing the Constitution. Changing it at all should be approached with caution. That is a game anyone can play.

Golda Meir resigned this week as Prime Minister of Israel.

Almost imperceptibly, the gasoline lines have disappeared. In the course of the week, I made some inquiries about what had happened to them. The recent end of the Arab boycott was not sufficient to eliminate the lines. One reason the gasoline shortage diminished was that the winter was so mild that in the course of it the government was able to tell producers to shift production of fuel oil back to gasoline. But the main reduction was in the lines, not in the shortage. Reacting to public anger and political pressure, the President ordered reallocations of gasoline supplies in February and March. But, rather than take supplies away from the states that had more gasoline per capita, which happened to be the oil-producing Southern and Western states—the states whose politicians might decide the President's fate—the government drew on gasoline inventories it normally keeps in reserve. So it is gambling. It is also gambling that the Arab boycott will not be renewed. The gasoline lines are gone, but the problems that caused them are not. More shortages are predicted, not only in energy but also in raw materials and food. Politicians don't like to talk about these things, or get us ready for them. Does our cohesiveness as a society depend upon a situation in which the pie keeps getting larger?

On tonight's news: For the first time, a plurality of those queried in a Harris poll favor the impeachment of the President.

15

A SECOND SUBPOENA to produce materials was served on the President this week, this one requested by Special Prosecutor Leon Jaworski and signed by Judge John Sirica. The subpoena was for tapes, memoranda, and Dictabelts covering sixty-four conversations between the President and his aides which occurred between June 20, 1972, three days after the break-in at the Watergate, and June 4, 1973, the day on which the President is said to have spent from ten to twelve hours listening to tapes. The materials have been requested in connection with the forthcoming trial, scheduled for September, of Haldeman, Ehrlichman, Mitchell, Colson, and the rest of the seven defendants in the cover-up of the Watergate break-in. Twenty-four of the conversations are among those subpoenaed by the House Judiciary Committee last week.

The Republican loss of the election in Michigan's Eighth Congressional District on Tuesday—a seat that Republicans had held for forty-two years—inevitably led to political and press speculation that the President was in worse trouble than ever. The politicians and the press have become accustomed to making the link between election outcomes and the President's fate. If the President is to be impeached, it should be on solid grounds, which will be understood by contemporary Americans and by history. Some Republicans are saying he should be removed from office not because he did anything wrong but because his presence hurts the Party. But the Constitution was not designed to protect political parties.

In the Vesco trial in New York this week, the defense rested its case after both John Mitchell, the former Attorney General, and Maurice Stans, the former Secretary of Commerce, took the stand in their own defense. They are being tried for perjury and conspiracy to obstruct an investigation by the Securities and Exchange Commission into the activities of the financier Robert Vesco in exchange for a contribution of two hundred thousand dollars from Vesco for the President's reëlection. Stans said that Vesco had made the contribution in secret because "privacy was his Constitutional right under the law." Mitchell said that he had called the S.E.C. because he had received reports that the agency was harassing Vesco and he did not want it to take precipitate action. "I wouldn't flatter myself that the call would be a help," the former Attorney General said.

During the week, I talked with one of the President's aides. Here are some of the things he said: The mood at the White House is sad, melancholy. "It's kind of like a hospital." There is no way things can come out well, and there is a feeling of inevitability about what still has to be gone through. The President is finished anyway, and will be unable to govern. The number of people leaving adds to the pall. (A week ago, Bryce Harlow, one of the President's chief advisers, quietly took his leave of the White House. Other departures are rumored.) Whenever tapes or other materials are requested, the President's attitude is "Don't give them anything. No. Never." Advice is received from the Republican leaders on the Hill, from Haig, from Ron Ziegler, from St. Clair, and all this is put together, and what comes out is homogenized decisions. Haig can and does tell the President that he should yield tapes and materials requested by investigators. None of the lawyers have been levelled with and know all. The Nixon Administration was the last outpost in defense of a discredited policy; Vietnam is part of the story. The Nixon Administration was up against the fact that so many people disagreed with its belief that what was "right" for America was necessarily moral. Up against that—up against a bureaucracy that it did not trust and that it perceived as opposing many of its policies—it inevitably formed its own groups to deal with problems, and became a garrison. The House has not been given up on. It is true that no one can talk very knowledgeably about this, knows the President's mind. But a fight will be made in the House. The House is "the crucible." The President's resignation should not be ruled out. If the House comes up with a strong bill of impeachment, which will be tough to beat in the Senate—a bill with a heavy vote behind it—that might be the end.

The Nixon White House group, the aide said, had been a collection of little groups—sometimes of factions of one. In one place there were Haldeman and Ehrlichman; somewhere else there was Colson; somewhere else there was Dean; somewhere else, Mitchell; somewhere else, Leonard Garment, the President's former law partner who had become an adviser on cultural affairs, minorities, and occasional legal matters; somewhere else, Patrick Buchanan and Raymond Price, the speechwriters; somewhere else, Robert Abplanalp and Bebe Rebozo, the friends. So when this thing came undone there were no half-dozen people who could get together and talk with the President and plan.

The White House man said that he thought all the subpoenas would be complied with but that it took time for Buzhardt to listen to the tapes. I asked him why, if the subpoenas were going to be complied with, Buzhardt had to listen to the tapes. He looked at me in astonishment.

The White House man also said that we are in a period of McCarthyism, of a "witch-hunt." He said that many people who think of themselves as caring about balance and fairness and civil liberties are going to look back at this period with regret. It was time, I realized, to think very carefully about what he said. He said that the testimony of one person, for example, is now reported as fact. That is not quite the case, but it is true that the testimony of one person and allegations as well, even rumors, are now printed as news stories and given more prominence and authority than they would be in another time, another context. There is no question that great effort is expended to find misdeeds on the part of the Administration, but it is also apparent that there have been many misdeeds to find. The secrecy in which so much was done and the pains that have been taken to keep us from discovering the facts have heightened the zeal to get at them. And we are living in a supercharged atmosphere, in which the competition within the press is strong. It is easy to see how the White House might view this as a witch-hunt, but that does not make it one.

It was announced this week that in the first three months of this year the gross national product dropped by the greatest amount since 1958, and that the rate of inflation for the same period was fourteen and a half percent.

APRIL 27

Another week of maneuvers and suspense. The showdown, or whatever it will be, between the President and the House Judiciary Committee has been postponed. The White House requested, and was granted, five more days to respond to the committee's subpoena. Rodino was anxious to appear "reasonable." Ron Ziegler says the White House is not delaying: "Our objective is to move as quickly as possible." There have been rumors, based on leaks from the White House, that the President will submit edited transcripts of what he considers "relevant" material, and also rumors that, in the face of prior notice by several committee members that this would not suffice, he is reconsidering. The President is reported to be "deeply involved" in forming the response to the committee, and to be listening to tapes. Rodino said this week that transcripts would be an "emphatically" unsatisfactory response. John Rhodes has proposed that Rodino, Hutchinson, Doar, and Jenner listen to the tapes and decide what is relevant, or that perhaps this could be done by Gerald Ford. I had thought that Rhodes was Ford's friend.

Ford said this week that he "hopes and trusts" that the White House will hand over all "relevant" material. The Vice-President did not offer his own definition of the term, or say who is to determine what is "relevant." (The New York *Times* had a story this week, based on "sources," and on "close friends" in whom Ford confided—meaning that the story probably came from Ford himself, or had his sanction—to the effect that Ford is "perplexed by what he senses to be the feeling of some White House aides that he is attempting to undercut President Nixon." The story continued, "The Vice-President has concluded, according to those sources, that certain members of Mr. Nixon's staff don't understand the close relationship, dating back more than a quarter of a century, that Mr. Ford has had and continues to have with the President.")

Henry Petersen, the Assistant Attorney General in charge of the Justice Department's Criminal Division, yesterday opposed proposals to broaden restrictions on wiretapping and electronic surveillance. (Hearings are planned in the Senate on proposals to ban any wiretaps without a court order and to require that notice of all approvals of taps be referred to the Congress.) Petersen told a House subcommittee, "I can be very brief. We oppose the bills. That's it."

APRIL 28

Sunday. Telephone calls today begin, "Did you hear about the acquittal?" Mitchell and Stans have been acquitted, and at once the talk and the reflections turn to the implications. The White House will be able to say that this shows that John Dean, who testified for the prosecution, is not a credible witness.

APRIL 29

An affidavit that Charles Colson has filed with Judge Gerhard Gesell, who will preside over the trial for the break-in at the office of Dr. Lewis J. Fielding, Daniel Ellsberg's psychiatrist, says that the President said, "I don't give a damn how it is done, do whatever has to be done to stop these leaks and prevent further unauthorized disclosures; I don't want to be told why it can't be done."

The President, on television again, one American flag behind him and one in his lapel, says that he has been examining "the very difficult choices that were presented to me." His actions will show, he says, that all the statements he has made about "the Watergate break-in and cover-up" were correct, "just as I have described them to you from the very beginning." He talks about some transcripts he is releasing—more than twelve hundred pages—and the camera pans to two high stacks of notebooks imprinted with the Presidential seal. "Portions not relevant" are not included, he says. The President looks grave—somewhat haggard but very much in command. He tells us how hard he has worked on this, and how much of "my own time" was spent listening to the tapes. He says that Rodino and Hutchinson may come to the White House to listen to the tapes on which the transcripts are based. Will they go? Dare they? Dare they not? Baker and Ervin went last fall. The President refers to the Judiciary Committee counsel, who are not invited to listen to the tapes, as "staff employees." Now, he says, he will make "a major exception" to the doctrine of executive privilege. He refers to "the current impeachment climate," and how he wants to spare the nation "a wrenching ordeal." Is he resigning? It seems not. He smiles as he refers to "the morning newspapers" and "the evening newscasts" and how they aired charges that became part of the atmosphere, and then he says, "The distinction between fact and speculation grew blurred. . . . The basic question at issue today is whether the President personally acted improperly in the Watergate matter. Month after month of rumor, insinuation, and charges by just one Watergate witness—John Dean—suggested that the President did act improperly." The transcripts, he says, will lead to some "sensational" stories; there are parts that "will be in conflict with some of the testimony given in the Senate Watergate committee hearings." He continues, "I have been reluctant to release these tapes not just because they will embarrass me and those with whom I have talked—which they will—and not just because they will become the subject of speculation and even ridicule—which they will—and not just because certain parts of them will be seized upon by political and journalistic opponents—which they will." Of what the transcripts will reveal, he says, "I wanted to do what was right, but I wanted to do it in a way that would cause the least unnecessary damage in a highly charged political atmosphere to the Administration. . . . I was striving to sort out a complex tangle." He is telling us how to read the transcripts, and characterizing other interpretations as the work of his "opponents." A very effective performance.

Almost as an aside, the President says the transcripts "should place in somewhat better perspective the controversy over the eighteen-and-a-half-minute gap in the tape of a conversation I had with Mr. Haldeman back in June of 1972." He says, "Now, how it was caused is still a mystery to me, and I think to many of the experts, as well." Disputing Dean's testimony, he says that the Hunt "blackmail" concerned "a potential national-security problem." He says that he even considered letting a payment to Hunt go forward, "at least temporarily." This is new; is it to deal with the fact that the grand jury says that a payment did go forward? There are holes in what he is saying, many of them, but even if one has studied the issue, it is hard to keep up with him. He is smart; *he* is releasing a transcript of the March 21st tape, which the Judiciary Committee already has, and giving it his own interpretation. It's a daring gamble. Why are there all those notebooks? "I intend to go forward," he says, and he again attaches himself to Abraham Lincoln, quoting Lincoln at a time when "he was being subjected to unmerciful attack." He smiles, and it is over.

APRIL 30

In a CBS interview this morning, Buzhardt says that nine of the conversations subpoenaed by the House committee were "non-recorded."

The telephone-book-size document in pale-blue covers—my copy of the transcripts, which arrives this evening—is a surprise. The image of all those notebooks had stayed in my mind. The document, titled "Submission of Recorded Presidential Conversations to the Committee on the Judiciary of the House of Representatives by Richard Nixon," has been published by the United States Government Printing Office. There is a little Presidential seal on the cover. The pages are in typescript, double-spaced. But still this is a formidable document, covering forty-six conversations (including eight already in the possession of the committee, and omitting some that the committee already has)—one thousand three hundred and eight pages, beginning like a script for a play. Dean enters the Oval Office:

P Hi, how are you? You had quite a day today didn't you. You got Watergate on the way didn't you?
D We tried.

The script ends, incredibly, with the President's speech of last April 30th, exactly a year ago—the speech in which he announced the resignations of Haldeman, Ehrlichman, Dean and Kleindienst, and called Haldeman and Ehrlichman "two of the finest public servants it has been my privilege to know." He told us then that he had not become aware until March of a possible involvement of White House staff members in a cover-up of the Watergate break-in, and that he had "personally assumed the responsibility for coördinating intensive new inquiries into the matter"; that he had directed his aides to appear before the Ervin committee, and to coöperate with the prosecutors and the grand jury; that he had been so busy pursuing peace in 1972 that he delegated the management of his campaign and sought to remove campaign decision-making from the White House, but that "in any organization, the man at the top must bear the responsibility." He said that when the Watergate break-in occurred, "I was in Florida trying to get a few days' rest after my visit to Moscow," that "I immediately ordered an investigation by appropriate government authorities," that he had "discounted the stories in the press that appeared to implicate members of my Administration or other offi-

cials of the campaign committee." He said he would then turn to "the
larger duties of this office," including another visit to Moscow. "We
must maintain the integrity of the White House. . . . There can be no
white-wash at the White House," he said.

And then we go back and read in these transcripts how the President,
on the day that the original Watergate defendants were indicted, congratulates John Dean for being "very skillful putting your fingers in
the leaks that have sprung here and sprung there." (The White House
summary in the front of the book says that this comment was made
"in the context of the politics of the matter such as civil suits, counter-
suits, Democratic efforts to exploit Watergate as a political issue and
the like.") We read, in the March 21st conversation, of Dean telling
the President that Haldeman was reading information gathered from
the bugging of the Democratic headquarters, and that Haldeman did
not "necessarily" know where it was coming from but that Haldeman's
aide, Gordon Strachan, did. It is never quite clear whether the President
is saying things for the benefit of Dean or the tape or as a simple statement or a question. He says, "I don't know about anything else," when
Dean explains that Hunt is threatening to expose some of the "seamy"
things he did. At one point, when the President starts to make a suggestion, Haldeman, who knows the room is taped, says (because of Dean?
the tape?), "Be careful."

Even things said casually are astonishing: Dean telling the President
that he had told John Caulfield, the White House investigator, to "come
up with a plan that, you know—a normal infiltration, buying information from secretaries and all that sort of thing." But Ehrlichman and
Mitchell felt that Caulfield was not the man to do this and asked Dean
to look around for someone who could run the campaign intelligence-
gathering program. Dean then selected Liddy, he says, because "they
needed a lawyer." Of Liddy, Dean says, "I was aware that he had done
some extremely sensitive things for the White House while he had been
at the White House and he had apparently done them well. Going out
into Ellsberg's doctor's office—" To which the President says, "Oh,
yeah." (The President has said that he learned about the Ellsberg break-
in on March 17th.) The incident was not reported to the Judge in the
Ellsberg trial until late April—the report apparently made at the insistence of Petersen and Kleindienst. In the March 17th conversation, when
Dean tells the President that Hunt and Liddy—"geared up with all this
C.I.A. equipment, cameras and the like"—had directed the break-in of
Ellsberg's psychiatrist's office and that Ehrlichman had some connection with the operation, the President says, "What in the world—what
in the name of God was Ehrlichman having something (unintelligible) in the Ellsberg (unintelligible)? . . . This is the first I ever heard
of this. I, I (unintelligible) care about Ellsberg was not our problem."
The problem, says Dean, is that a camera was returned to the C.I.A.

with film still in it, that the C.I.A. developed the pictures, "and they've got Gordon Liddy standing proud as punch outside this doctor's office with his name on it."

In the March 21st conversation, discussing the question of the payment to Hunt: Dean telling the President, "This is the sort of thing Mafia people can do: washing money, getting clean money, and things like that." And then, when Dean tells the President that it would cost a million dollars to continue to buy the silence of the defendants, the President's response: "We could get that. On the money, if you need the money you could get that. You could get a million dollars. You could get it in cash. I know where it could be gotten. It is not easy, but it could be done. But the question is who the hell would handle it? Any ideas on that?" When Dean tells the President that Fred LaRue, former assistant to John Mitchell at the Committee for the Re-Election of the President, has gone out "trying to solicit money from all kinds of people," the President's response is "No!" When Dean says that LaRue "has apparently talked to Tom Pappas"—a Boston businessman—the President's response is "I know." The President asks Dean whether he would put the money "through the Cuban committee," and "Is the Cuban committee an obstruction of justice, if they want to help?" Dean informs the President, "Well, they have priests in it." And the President responds, "Would that give a little bit of a cover?" Dean says, "You have to wash the money. You can get $100,000 out of a bank, and it all comes in serialized bills." And the President says, "I understand." The counsel to the President tells the President, "And that means you have to go to Vegas with it or a bookmaker in New York City."

One comes to that line "No—it is wrong that's for sure." One reads backward and forward from it. The President says it just after he has said that "politically" he cannot give clemency to Hunt until after the 1974 elections and asks Dean if "Your point is that even then you couldn't do it," and Dean replies, "That's right. It may further involve you in a way you should not be involved in this." Before that, the President has asked Dean whether "the million bucks" could "hold that side," and when Dean says "Uh-huh," the President replies, "It would seem to me that would be worthwhile." Dean tells the President that Hunt has a commitment from Colson to receive clemency by Christmas of 1973. Remarks Haldeman: "That is your fatal flaw in Chuck. He is an operator in expediency, and he will pay at the time and where he is to accomplish whatever he is there to do. . . . I would believe that he has made that commitment if Hunt says he has."

Observes the President of Hunt: "The only thing we could do with him would be to parole him like the (unintelligible) situation. But you couldn't buy clemency." The President also says, referring to Hunt's wife, who was killed in an airplane crash in late 1972 (ten thousand dollars in hundred-dollar bills were found in her purse): "Great sadness. As a matter of fact, there was a discussion with somebody about Hunt's problem on account of his wife and I said, of course commutation could be considered on the basis of his wife's death, and that is the only conversation I ever had in that light." Later the President agrees with Dean that it is worth while "buying time" with Hunt. Says Nixon: "I think Hunt knows a hell of a lot more." Later, he says, "Time is of the essence." And, several pages later:

> P That's why for your immediate things you have no choice but to come up with the $120,000, or whatever it is. Right?
> D That's right.
> P Would you agree that that's the prime thing that you damn well better get that done?
> D Obviously he ought to be given some signal anyway.
> P (Expletive deleted), get it. In a way that—who is going to talk to him? Colson? He is the one who is supposed to know him?

There are other lines by the President, such as "Complete disclosure isn't that the best way to do it? . . . That would be my view," to which his defenders will be able to point.

Going to the grand jury is viewed as a means—a more manageable one—of avoiding testimony before the Ervin committee. Dean says to the President, "You are chancing a very high risk for perjury situation." The President replies, "But you can say I don't remember. You can say I can't recall. I can't give any answer to that that I can recall."

The President is told by Dean in this March 21st meeting that Magruder has perjured himself before the grand jury. (Magruder, formerly deputy director of the reëlection committee, was at that point an official at the Commerce Department. He resigned in late April, after he began to coöperate with the prosecutors.) The national-security rationale for the Ellsberg break-in is suggested by Dean.

> P National Security. We had to get information for national security grounds.
> D Then the question is, why didn't the C.I.A. do it or why didn't the F.B.I. do it?
> P Because we had to do it on a confidential basis.
> H Because we were checking them.
> P Neither could be trusted.

Says the President, on March 13th, referring to William Sullivan, a former F.B.I. official with whom Dean was in contact, and from whom they were hoping to obtain information, on the theory that he might coöperate—because, Dean says, Sullivan "wants to get back in the bureau very badly"— "If he would get Kennedy into it, too, I would be a little bit more pleased." (It was Sullivan who removed the wiretap records from the F.B.I.'s files.)

And then Dean tells the President that an investigation of Kalmbach's bank records would show that Anthony Ulasewicz, the private detective hired by the White House, had been paid to investigate Chappaquiddick. (Caulfield, one of the private investigators, was on the White House payroll; Ulasewicz was paid out of funds said to be left over from the 1968 Nixon campaign—funds we now know to have been replenished by the milk interests in 1969.) Says Dean, "Right after Chappaquiddick somebody was put up there to start observing and within six hours he was there for every second of Chappaquiddick for a year." Later, the President asks, "Does he have any records? Are they any good?"

We are shown the President's view of the public: referring to an item in Patrick Buchanan's news summary about a crisis in confidence in the Presidency, the President says, "How much of a crisis? It will be—I am thinking in terms of—the point is, everything is a crisis. (expletive deleted) it is a terrible lousy thing—it will remain a crisis among the upper intellectual types, the soft heads, our own, too—Republicans— and the Democrats and the rest. Average people won't think it is much of a crisis unless it affects them."

The document is far more dramatic than had been anticipated. Unbelievably dramatic. This is not just the usual difference between anticipation and reality. We are actually *reading their conversations*—living through these conversations, sensing their overtones and undertones. It is intimate theatre indeed.

First impressions, as one leafs through the heavy volume: the meandering conversations, with all those surprising "(expletive deleted)"s and "(unintelligible)"s and "(inaudible)"s, several of them in crucial places; the "(Further conversation following unrelated to Watergate)"; the siege mentality; the seeming lack of concern for anything but limiting the damage; the mutual suspicions among the White House people, and the double-dealing; the President's uncertainty, need for guidance, even for being brought back to the subject, by his aides; the cold, cynical view of the men in the White House; the contempt for everyone—the public, the Congress, their colleagues, each other.

We had heard about the language, but that is not the heart of the matter. We had known that the White House was a place of suspicions, a place where the President taped his aides and the aides taped each other. We had long since had a picture of it as the court of the Borgias. We had known that it sacrificed whomever it was necessary to sacrifice. And we had had every sign that the President was not exactly straining to "get the story out"—not the true story, anyway. So the pain comes, as it has come before, in facing things we had known but, at least at times, chosen not to face.

Today, pursuant to a resolution passed by the Senate last December, was a National Day of Humiliation, Fasting, and Prayer.

MAY 1

The papers, as was to be expected, are crowded with stories about the transcripts. These are going to be long days. It is no time for slow readers, of whom I have the misfortune to be one. We learn that Dean assured the President that Gordon Strachan, Haldeman's aide, "is as tough as nails," and continued, "He can go in and stonewall, and say, 'I don't know anything about what you are talking about.' He has already done it twice, you know, in interviews." To which the President replied, "I guess he should, shouldn't he? I suppose we can't call that justice, can we?" That the President coached Dean on what should be in his report on the affair. "Make it very incomplete," said the President. And that the President used Henry Petersen to find out what was going on in the grand jury and then relayed the information to Haldeman and Ehrlichman, who were under investigation. Said the President to Petersen, "You have got to maintain the Presidency out of this."

Today is Law Day. The President has issued a proclamation saying, "Our freedoms survive because no man or woman is beneath the protections of the law. And the law retains its value and force because every person knows that no man or woman is above the requirements of the law."

Three years ago, there were Law Day anti-war demonstrations in Washington. There were mass arrests, most of them made without the required arrest forms. The Attorney General said that this was necessary because of the danger to the government (which some of the demonstrators had vowed to shut down). The courts dismissed the charges against almost all of the demonstrators.

Almost lost in the cascade of stories about the transcripts is one about an affidavit filed yesterday by Ehrlichman, for his trial in the Ellsberg break-in case, saying that the President had justified the break-in afterward to Henry Petersen as "in furtherance of national security and fully justified by the circumstances." Ehrlichman's affidavit says that the President had told him to tell Egil Krogh, one of the directors of the plumbers, "to do whatever he considered necessary to get to the bottom of the matter."

It seems noisier inside the Capitol today. There is the sense that something big has happened—a heightened atmosphere. The nervous system that is this city is once more jangled. Tonight, the Judiciary Committee will meet on the question of how to respond to the President's submission of the transcripts instead of the subpoenaed tapes.

There is the question now of what the committe will do. In the House members' dining room, a Republican member of the Judiciary Committee says that at yesterday's Republican caucus Minority Leader John Rhodes urged everybody to line up behind the President. At the caucus, the House Republican leaders said that the public would see the President's action as constituting compliance. Republicans are in a bad bind on this one.

The Chicago *Tribune,* of all papers, has printed the entire text of the transcripts. A copy of the *Tribune's* reprint is being passed around the House members' dining room, and the publishing feat is a subject of wonderment.

Railsback arrives for lunch weary and late. Judiciary Committee members are generally late for appointments today; they are being buttonholed for statements, television interviews. They are looking tired and distracted. Slicing a cheeseburger in half, Railsback says, "I think that the President helped himself with the television appearance and the release of the transcripts. He appears to be confronting the March 21st situation head-on. I think he's very wise, from a tactical standpoint, to do that. Also, there are parts of the transcripts that appear to exonerate him." Railsback has not yet read the transcripts; he had to go out last evening with representatives of the Chamber of Commerce from his district. "But I hear they're kind of bad," he says.

I ask him if he thinks that the President is in compliance with the committee's subpoena.

"No," he replies. "He is not really in compliance. But I think his offer could serve as a basis on which we might reach a future compromise. I think we're very close now. All that the committee wants are two things: they want Doar and Jenner to be able to listen to the tapes, and they want tapes instead of transcripts." He then says, "I wonder how many people will bother to read the transcripts."

I ask him if he thinks that the President's strategy of saying that the media would distort the transcripts will work.

"I don't think it will work with members of the Judiciary Committee, but I think it might work with members of the public," he says. "A lot of people do think that this is a Democratic plot and that the news media are trying to bring him down."

I ask him if these struggles over evidence are making his own position more difficult.

"Yes," he replies. "Any delays, regardless of what they are attributed to, hurt Republicans. They hurt the country, too, but they hurt Republicans. The closer this gets to elections, the more this hurts the Republican Party."

I ask him if it is hurting him in particular.

"Yes," he says. "It hurts me when I say that the President hasn't turned over enough. I said it yesterday, and I got six calls from people who are normally supporters of mine. Angry calls, saying why wasn't I supporting the President."

I ask Railsback if the President's withholding of the tapes themselves has made him suspicious.

"Yes," he says. "You can't help wondering. That's what it does—it makes you wonder. There are some who suggest that the President would be well advised to let a U-Haul come and take all the material."

An early edition of the Washington *Star-News* says St. Clair has said that he would move in court to have Jaworski's subpoena quashed. The headline is "Nixon Resisting New Tape Bids."

I go back to see James Mann, the South Carolina Democrat on the Judiciary Committee, to find out how he is reacting to the President's response. I ask Mann if he thinks that the President is in compliance with the committee.

He puts his foot on his desk. "Oh, he certainly is not," he replies. "I would have to ask you if there is anyone in the United States, or in the whole world, who could conclude that he has complied with what we asked for. If we accept it, we would be knuckling under to political pressure by not carrying out our full duty. The best thing now is to inform the White House that we consider it noncompliance—which would be futile—and then wait and see his reaction to our other request and have a whole record of noncompliance. His saying 'Now they can reach a decision' is a gross misrepresentation."

I ask him if he is concerned that there may be a party split this evening. The committee has been nearly unanimous in its actions thus far.

"Oh, yes," he replies. "What would worry me would be the Republicans' willingness to compromise their position on the subpoena because of politics. That would distress me. As for a party split, if it has to be, it has to be. There can be only one honest vote on the question of compliance and noncompliance."

Mann says that the substance of the transcripts is already having a negative effect on his colleagues. "They were not aware there was that much smoke," he says. The President's strategy "is really an assault on the system—a failure to respect the authority of the committee and the Senate to do their Constitutional duty," he continues. "To go to the people and release what material he wants them to have and then to represent that it's the entire case is the rawest kind of abuse of the system. And he took advantage of the public's thinking it is more of a political exercise than it is. As if the truth in the hands of James R. Mann weren't all that he needs." Mann is usually measured in what he says. I am surprised by the intensity of his reaction.

We go back to the subject of a possible party-line vote tonight.

"You know," Mann says, "it's so easy to play minority politics—for the Republicans to take an unreasonable position when the majority takes a reasonable position, and then say that the majority is 'partisan' and 'oppressive.' Taking advantage of the minority position and the President fixation—they're showing up so clearly, I'm sorry to say."

Mann refers, as people have been doing all day, to the "(expletive deleted)"s. They all seem curious to know what those parentheses are hiding. "The more that people know about him, it seems, the more trouble he's in," he says. "It's not that they think he's guilty of an impeachable offense, necessarily, but that he's not the man they thought he was."

The Judiciary Committee Republicans are meeting in Room H 219—the office of the House Minority Whip, Leslie Arends, of Illinois, just off the House floor—to decide on their strategy for tonight. The meeting was called for three o'clock. I was supposed to have an appointment with one of the committee Republicans, so I decide to watch the scene outside this room for a while. About a dozen reporters are here, some of whom are reading the large blue transcript books. One starts reading aloud from the conversation of the President, Haldeman, and Ehrlichman on April 17th. Dean has gone to the prosecutors, and the President and his aides are trying to figure out what to do.

> P. . . . What you want to do is get him out of the WH and yet Colson's recommendation is to get him out by firing him—
> E Colson would like to discredit him.
> P Well I know. But the question is what he could do to discredit us.
> E Well.
> P That's a problem.
> H Yeah. But I think at some point, like you do on anything else, you gotta face up to the fact that the guy is either a friend or a foe—or a neutral. If he's a neutral you don't have to worry about him; if he's a friend you rely on him, if he's a foe you fight him, and this guy—it seem[s] at this point—is a foe.

Haldeman and the President reconstruct the conversation of March 21st on whether to pay money to Hunt. They are worried about what was said in Dean's presence.

> P I didn't tell him to go get the money did I?
> H No.

Later, the President says,

> P But in that conversation I was—we were—I was—I said, "Well for (expletive removed), let's—"
> And Haldeman reminds him:

H You said, "Once you start down the path with blackmail it's constant escalation."

P Yep. That's my only conversation with regard to that.

A woman in the red jacket and navy skirt of a Capitol tour guide comes along, followed by a group of tourists. Standing outside the House chamber, she says, in a singsong voice, "This is the lawmaking branch of the government." The reporters try to suppress smiles. A reporter says that the consensus among members of Congress he has spoken with is that the March 21st conversation, which, according to the grand jury, was followed that evening by a payment of seventy-five thousand dollars to Hunt, is "it."

At three-forty, the meeting of the Judiciary Committee Republicans is still going on, but some Republicans come out, and the reporters surround them. The Republicans look tight-lipped. "See Hutch," they say, referring to Hutchinson. Cohen rolls his eyes toward the ceiling in a look of helplessness. Caldwell Butler, Republican of Virginia, is going into the meeting. "Would you characterize this as a strategy session?" asks a reporter. "It's a meeting with my counsel, and that's confidential," says Butler, and he smiles. McClory arrives, followed by more reporters. "It's an informational meeting," he says. "We're sharing information." Charles Sandman, Republican of New Jersey, struggling through the growing group of reporters, says, "I'm just trying to find the door."

Rhodes is spotted walking down the hall, and is immediately cornered by reporters. He says that a citation of the President for contempt would be "overwhelmingly defeated." He says yes, he would object to the sending of a letter to the President stating that he is in noncompliance. The committee got the information that is on the tapes, he says. What does he think of the transcripts, he is asked. "What I read is rather spicy," Rhodes replies. Does he think they confirm what the President said he had been doing? "Mainly," says Rhodes, although some parts "might have been a little surprising." Of March 21st, he says, "There were a lot of thoughts considered, but the action taken was not in accordance with the thoughts," and you don't, he says, "impeach for bad thoughts." Is he concerned that a payment was made to Hunt that night? "It's not clear that it was." What if it was? "Well," says the House Minority Leader, "we'll cross that bridge."

William Hungate, the wisecracking Judiciary Committee Democrat from Missouri, walks by the group of reporters still waiting outside the room where the committee Republicans are meeting. He says, "Are you (expletive deleted)s still hanging around?" A new term has entered our language.

One of the reporters who is standing outside the Republican meeting room has seen the separate volumes—like the ones shown on television

Monday evening—that were delivered to Rodino. One volume contained only one page.

At five o'clock, the Republicans are still meeting. They are obviously having trouble deciding on their strategy for this evening.

A House Democrat is encountered in one of the subterranean passages connecting the three House office buildings and the Capitol. "Have you read the damn thing?" he asks.

I ask him what impact he thinks it will have.

"It really hurts him," he says. "The first reaction in the country was 'God, he's come clean.' But the stuff won't go away. It sounds like the Mafia talking—a point that doesn't escape the public. It's loathsome."

There is a sense of excitement tonight in Room 2141, the House Judiciary Committee room. A long line of spectators is outside. There seem to be more photographers than ever inside, more people milling about, more noise. This is a meeting about what to do when one branch of the government has defied what another branch believes to be its authority. The fact that it is an evening session adds to the drama. Rodino, in a gray suit, looks, as usual, relaxed. Rodino is the star now. Or almost. Robert Redford is here. The word that Robert Redford is here spreads through the room. Some reporters want to know how to describe an amulet that Robert Redford is wearing. Washington, blase about its politicians, is struck by movie stars. Even the politicians are. Redford is spending time in Washington now as he prepares to play the role of Bob Woodward in a movie based on the book that Woodward and Bernstein have written about how they exposed the Watergate case.

Word is going around the room that there are now four versions of the March 21st tape: the White House transcript, the Special Prosecutor's transcript, the committee's transcript, and the tape itself. It is said that the committee's electronic equipment is more sensitive—able to pick up more words—than that of the White House. Which seems strange. "We care more," says a committee aide. Robert Redford is signing autographs.

Doar presents a chart showing the items that have been requested and those that have been turned over by the White House. The Republicans, led by Wiggins and David Dennis, of Indiana, attack the chart, pressing Doar to explain how he can say that something has not been turned over if he does not know whether it exists. The cloud of unreality which keeps fogging our view of the significant questions in these events has crept into this committee room tonight. They are arguing over whether it is proper to have a blank space represent the non-surrender of things whose non-existence has not been established. Mann asks Wiggins how the committee can be "clairvoyant in its knowledge of what is available at the White House," and continues, "I'm not concerned with partisanship; I'm not concerned with anything but the whole truth, and unless I get it I'm handicapped in my service to the American people in determining this issue." The committee is silent as Mann says this; what he thinks is important. He gets attention because he is quiet, he is courtly, and he is from South Carolina. But there is a certain giddiness to the atmosphere; people are keyed up, it seems—somewhat nervous in this most unusual situation. Jack Brooks, Democrat of Texas, is smoking a cigar, smiling, and making jokes about tapes. George Danielson, Democrat of California, confuses the words "tap" and "tape," and there is a ripple of laughter. Lawrence Hogan, the conservative Republican from Maryland, says of the tapes, "I have come to the inescapable conclusion that he must have forgotten they were being made." Laughter.

The room falls silent when Rodino reads his prepared statement: "We demonstrated time and again that we were not seeking any confrontation with the President of the United States. . . . Under the Constitution, is it not within the power of the President to conduct an inquiry into his own impeachment, to determine which evidence, and what version or portion of that evidence, is relevant and necessary to such an inquiry. These are matters which, under the Constitution, only the House has the sole power to determine." Rodino had wanted to put language along these lines in a letter that the Democrats are proposing that the committee send to the President, but Brooks, who has a number of objections to the deliberate style of Rodino and Doar, wanted a more abrupt communication, and on this point Rodino yielded to him.

Wiggins is emerging as the strongest man on the Republican side. A large man with a leathery California tan and wavy silver hair, he has the reputation of being an able lawyer. Whether that reputation is well-founded or not, the other committee members accept it and respect Wiggins and even seem to fear him. There are constant readings by members and the press as to which of the seventeen Republicans might vote for impeachment. As of now, according to some, William Cohen is considered likely to vote for it, and Hamilton Fish, Jr. (New York), and Tom Railsback might; Robert McClory, Lawrence Hogan, Henry P. Smith III (New York), Caldwell Butler and Charles W. Sandman are considered unpredictable.

At 11 P.M., Dennis reads a press release he issued yesterday. A compromise letter proposed by Cohen is rejected. And then the vote is taken, at last, on whether to send the Democrats' letter. It is suddenly clear that the vote is closer than was expected. John Conyers, Democrat of Michigan, and Jerome Waldie, Democrat of California, who support a contempt citation, are opposed. But Rodino does not want a House vote on contempt to precede the question of impeachment. And there is the practical problem of what to do about a President who is in contempt. Don Edwards, Democrat of California, said at lunch earlier this spring, "How can we enforce a subpoena? He has a bigger army than we do." So the committee is writing Nixon a letter. Then, as the Republicans' names are called, Cohen votes for the letter. He is the only Republican who does. The final vote is 20-18. Had Cohen voted the other way, there would have been a tie vote, and the committee would, in effect, have voted not to respond to the President.

The letter that will now go to the President says simply:

DEAR MR. PRESIDENT:

The Committee on the Judiciary has directed me to advise you that it finds that as of 10:00 A.M. April 30, you have failed to comply with the Committee's subpoena of April 11, 1974.

Sincerely,
PETER W. RODINO, JR., CHAIRMAN

MAY 2

The President spent last night at Camp David. Yesterday, Gerald Warren, the President's deputy press secretary, described the President as pleased by the public's response to the release of the transcripts. There are more exegeses of the transcripts in today's papers. We read the conversations, go back to what we knew about the events when they happened, to explanations given later. It brings on a slight dizziness— and also annoyance, because we have been lured into the contextual world of the tapes. All that is on the tapes is what is on the tapes. Will we become, as the President probably hopes, tired of them in time? One of the factors in this great struggle has been our brief attention span. Another question: When our national perturbation seems to subside, where does it go? Our perturbation over the war didn't really disappear. It eventually became impossible for our leaders not to end the war. They drew on the reservoir of silent tolerance until there was no more. The outcry over the firing of Archibald Cox came from some hidden wellspring of concern. Our outrage is an elusive thing, taking different forms; now you see it, now you don't.

Yesterday, the President invoked executive privilege once more in refusing to supply the tapes and documents subpoenaed by the Special Prosecutor for the trial of the President's seven former aides for the Watergate cover-up. The President said he had decided that disclosure of any more of his conversations "would be contrary to the public interest." The statement issued by the White House yesterday argued that "a President is not subject to compulsory process from a court," and it hinted that the White House was prepared to fight this issue all the way to the Supreme Court.

One friend of mine here has been saying for some time that it is not at all surprising that our current troubles were brought about by a group of largely clean-cut, wholesome-appearing types. Their appearance has become a cliché, but there is a serious point to it. "All the great usurpers," he once said, "spoke to something in their time." It was inevitable, he said, that those who played fastest and loosest with the American system would be terribly American in their style and use American symbols. "If there is a takeover in America," he said, "it will be done by people wearing conventional suits and using advertising techniques." I preferred not to think about what he said. But he is a sensible man, not given to overstatement. One of the great problems of living through this period and trying to understand it is that it is very difficult to judge just how dangerous it is, or might have been. But other people living through dangerous times probably had the same problem and preferred not to think about it, so from time to time one must. The path to tyranny, my friend said, can be undramatic. The actions can appear bland, incremental: a lie here, a call to a network executive there. A White House Office of Telecommunications issuing ukases. Businessmen being given to understand that it would be far more profitable to coöperate with those in power. All done by people with marvellously American styles—toughness with a smile—and bearing all the American symbols: flag, religion, family. It is important to remember now, amid all this debris, how frightened we used to be.

On tonight's news we see Gerald Ford saying that he is "convinced beyond any doubt" that the President is "innocent." The White House announced that the President rejects the committee's letter.

MAY 3

At lunch, someone stops by the table and suggests that certain pages in the transcripts be looked up. "Don't miss page 503," he says. "The President tells Ehrlichman to tell Magruder that he has his 'personal affection.' Right after that, the President says, 'That's the way the so-called clemency's got to be handled.' " Senators walked around this week trailed by aides carrying copies of the transcripts with paper clips on the pages on which the senators' names appeared. People are taking the same kind of pride in appearing in these transcripts that they did in appearing on the enemies list. But the amusement seems to have the same kind of nervous undertone.

Maryland's highest court, in a unanimous decision, has disbarred Spiro Agnew. Said the court, "It is difficult to feel compassion for an attorney who is so morally obtuse that he consciously cheats for his own pecuniary gain that government he has sworn to serve."

Sunday. Last night, in Spokane, at the opening of Expo '74, the President referred to Governor Daniel Evans, of Washington, as "Governor Evidence."

In an interview with reporters on Friday, Gerald Ford said that he was "a little disappointed" by the transcripts. He said that this was not the Nixon he had known for twenty-five years.

William Randolph Hearst, Jr., a long-time supporter of the President, has come out against the President. Hearst said that the transcripts "add up to as damning a document as it is possible to imagine short of an actual indictment." Someone rushed over to tell me about it at the tennis courts yesterday.

The White House has released a twenty-nine-page document that contains what it calls "important contradictions" between sworn statements made by Dean and the transcripts.

Ron Ziegler told the press accompanying the President on his Western trip that too much attention was being paid to the meeting of March 21st. "It's essential that the transcripts are read in their entirety for the American people to draw their conclusions," Ziegler said.

A Gallup poll published yesterday says that by more than two to one the people queried believe that the Judiciary Committee was right to reject the President's offer of edited transcripts instead of tapes. That's higher than the proportion of the Judiciary Committee who thought so.

It's a cold and rainy Sunday. Unfair. Snatch of conversation at a cocktail party:
"How are you?"
"Reading."

16

MONDAY. Time to try to get a sense of the reaction on Capitol Hill. I phoned Senator Robert Dole, Republican of Kansas, who is up for reëlection this year. I began by asking how he was. "Running hard, running scared," he replied. "I really haven't heard much. Last week, we were all going around saying, 'We haven't read it, we shouldn't comment.' Nobody thinks he's better off."

A Democratic senator: "My impression is it's hurting the President bad. I was interested in the poll [the recent Gallup poll on the committee's reaction to the transcripts] after his speech about the transcripts last week, which everyone thought was the best of his career. People will give you a chance. Then you slowly wear out your welcome. Then the burden shifts against you. He has no reservoir of good will. I haven't heard one person say the release of the transcripts was good for him. One pro-Nixon Southerner—at least, I assume he has been pro-Nixon—said, 'That does it for me.' I don't think anyone was surprised except by one thing: I don't think they knew what a small person he was. Senators, like everybody else, have built the Presidency up, and now they see this and don't know what to make of it. The tone and the language are having an impact—a greater impact, even, than what was actually said. The impression will last. So even if he stays in he won't be able to do anything."

MAY 7

A reporter stops me in a Senate hallway this morning. He thinks I would like to know what Hugh Scott just said. Hugh Scott, the Senate Minority Leader, just met with reporters and said that the transcripts reveal "a shabby, disgusting, immoral performance by all those involved." Scott did not say whether he found impeachable behavior in them, and did not say whether he thought the President was in compliance with the committee's subpoena.

I go to see Charles Wiggins. It is clear that this Republican, from Richard Nixon's original California congressional district, will be highly important in the House Judiciary Committee. A defense of the President by him would be powerful and effective. If he ended by voting to impeach the President, it could make the decisive difference among House Republicans. Wiggins is dressed, as usual, in California-sporty style: olive-green trousers, a green-and-white striped cord jacket, a green tie, white loafers that are either Guccis or a good facsimile. Wiggins also has the California style of apparent openness and easiness. What one is looking for is his cast of mind as he goes through this process. One clue: he says he will look to see "whether the totality warrants the kind of drastic surgery that involves the removal of a President."

I ask him what in his mind would constitute ground for impeachment.

"Something damn serious," he replies. "I suppose if I had to define a ground that would be appropriate to all cases, I would define it rather broadly, to prepare for all future contingencies. But the committee isn't called upon to find an answer that is chiselled in stone. In this case, the question is whether the President was deeply and personally involved in serious misconduct that would bar his continuing in office."

I ask him how he came to that conclusion.

"We're dealing with charges here, not hypothetical situations," he says. "The charges include everything from criminal misconduct to alleged inappropriate exercise of power. The latter would not serve the purpose of this case. That would not be in the national interest. It would be terribly divisive. You'd have millions of Americans lining up behind the President and millions opposed to him. There's a lesson to be learned from the Agnew situation. Agnew was going around the country making speeches, and he had a considerable following. Reflect for a moment on what might have happened if Congress had felt moved to remove Spiro Agnew for his insensitivity to the First Amendment. But Spiro Agnew was caught in criminality, and he has no friends now— except maybe Frank Sinatra. If we impeach on broad, vague grounds, we run the risk of tearing up the country. We have many serious allegations of criminal conduct. If the President is going to be impeached at all, it is going to have to be on these grounds, in order not to have a divided country."

I ask Wiggins if he feels, then, that the issue has come down to the Watergate break-in and cover-up.

"I think it will," he replies. "I don't think the other matters are out of the woods yet, but I think it will." Wiggins agrees that the milk issue is one that makes the politicians uneasy. "They would be nervous about expulsion on the ground of a government decision made around the time of a campaign contribution," he says. "If members of Congress in fact vote for impeachment for this, I think they should have to respond to a resolution of expulsion of members of Congress for a similar act. Where you have a hard bargain of action for money, I don't think there's a chance of proving it."

The cover of Wiggins' copy of the transcripts is tattered. He says that he has read up to page 1,247. He continues, "I get another impression— that the President didn't think he did anything wrong. It took a lot of explanations by his attorneys to explain obstruction of justice to the President. I have a gut feeling that generally you know you're doing something wrong. This guy didn't have a feeling of doing anything wrong. Maybe some technicians can point out that he's in technical culpability. From the tough stuff, it would be possible to contrive a technical violation by the President. But it would be only technical. And you weigh that against removal of the President, no matter what his popularity—that involves a lot of policy considerations, as opposed to technical ones. The question of whether a President is to be removed on the ground of some technical violation—that's what it gets down to, or will."

Says Wiggins, "The Republicans, given their bias in favor of the President and the Party, are inclined not to vote for impeachment unless the evidence demands it, and I don't think the evidence demands it."

At lunch, an aide to a Democratic senator says, "Releasing those transcripts made him more human, one of the boys," and continues, "Making him more human makes him more likely to be impeached." Many senators are appalled by the transcripts, he says, but "they are holding their fire."

I ask him about my impression that the President and St. Clair have succeeded in narrowing the definition of an impeachable offense to a crime.

"It's not that St. Clair and the President succeeded in narrowing it," he says. "That's the way it always was. They feel that things like the plumbers and the Huston plan are unclear. The politicians are worried about impeaching for infringing civil liberties and doing things where the illegality is not clear. They are afraid to do that. They don't want to set up a parliamentary system—congressional supremacy. The only other possibility is to follow the Ritter precedent: putting a series of acts together and, in this case, saying they amount to obstruction of justice."

I ask the aide if this would set the precedent that it is all right to do these things as long as one does not get caught.

"Yes," he replies. "That's the standard now, in public life and in private. Watergate isn't going to produce a law to make politicians more honest. Just as you can't say that putting one Mafia leader in jail will make the others behave. It won't. It will say, 'Be more careful.' There will be a sharper sense that people are watching. There will be more emphasis on integrity in politicians, a search for Mr. Cleans. These things go in fifty-year cycles, from Grant to Harding to Nixon. Don't worry about cynicism coming out of this. There is a loosening of the traditional hierarchies in the Congress. More new challengers are coming into House and Senate races."

I hadn't thought of it that way, but he's right. Signs of vitality and more questioning of the old order.

"One has a sense of a logjam breaking," he says.

This afternoon, I have an appointment with Peter Rodino. Concerned about the little time I have with him and the little time he has for anything, I sit on the edge of the chair next to his desk, eager to plunge into questions.

"Why don't you sit back?" he asks calmly.

If Peter Rodino can be relaxed, so can I. On Rodino's desk is a leather-bound book of Psalms and Proverbs, with his name embossed on it. I would have thought that Sam Ervin had retired that approach, but Rodino takes the book seriously. "Someone sent it to me," he says. "I just leaf through it. These things have lasted, you know." There is also a book of Robert Frost's poems on Rodino's desk, and a picture of Jesus.

I am hoping, in the limited time, to avoid the "awesome responsibility" and the "sense of sadness" on which Rodino has been quoted so often by now. I tell him that I have read his statements about how he felt upon finding himself in this role, and I do not want to take up his time with that. He smiles gratefully. I begin my questions by asking him if he feels that the White House may be succeeding in defining the issue—narrowing it to the Watergate break-in and cover-up, and saying that an impeachable offense has to be a criminal one.

"I think that's what they're attempting to do," he replies. "That's not what our staff is going to do. We have the authorization to conduct an inquiry where allegations have been made, and there are six broad areas. We make the allocations of resources and priorities. We're not being narrowed down because of the White House strategy. The inquiry is being made along the broad lines—which is the only way we can bring the scope of the issues before the committee and the Congress. Maybe it will come down to a criminal conclusion. I can't say that's necessarily the way it will turn out. I believe the members are going to ultimately ask themselves the question: Has the totality of the conduct of the President been such that the abuse of power has had a devastating effect on the government? Has it been so scandalous that it prejudices our government?" He is speaking with some intensity, his high-pitched voice strong. "Has the President faithfully executed the laws?" he goes on. "I'm not talking about piddling things. I'm talking about the Presidency as we understand it. I think that's what it will come down to—not just criminal conduct. And there could be a violation of a criminal statute, and in my judgment it doesn't necessarily mean that you impeach for that, because you're talking about removing the President of the United States from office. If there is a violation of the criminal code, the question is: Of what magnitude? How does it relate to his faithful execution of the laws? It's a question of the totality." Rodino is waving his arms, talking animatedly. "You have to consider so many individuals who held high office who are responsible to the President. Have they considered such acts? Is there that kind of involvement on the part of the President?"

I ask Rodino if he accepts the Madison concept, then—that the President can be held accountable for the acts of his subordinates. Almost every politician I have spoken with wants to steer clear of that argument.

Rodino says he could accept the Madison concept, but "one would have to recognize that those acts would have to be serious, and there has to be involvement with the President."

America is unpredictable in selecting its heroes, but it seems that Peter Rodino could become one. He already has a certain cachet, because now he is important. When the "awesome responsibility" landed on him, Rodino was generally viewed in Washington as a "lightweight." But he has earned the respect of the committee and of the press, and one can see his heroic possibilities: the simple man from Newark whose belief in God and country seems sincere. There was a time when Rodino's origins in Newark, a place of flourishing crime, caused uneasiness, but that uneasiness has largely evaporated. The general feeling is that if there were something there we'd have heard about it by now.

I ask Rodino how he will get across his view of the issues, as against the President's view, particularly now that the President's seems to be the prevailing view on Capitol Hill.

He replies, "I think that as we present the statements of detailed information, which will be supported by documents, these will have to be weighed by individual members. Then, in their own minds, they've got to define. While people talk about what 'you can't prove,' what we are doing is getting the relevant data that bear on the question, of whether or not the President was involved. We don't have to *prove* as such. We have to establish, as in a grand-jury proceeding, that these things did occur, and determine whether, put together, they in fact show impeachable offenses. Even with the edited transcripts, what do you consider that event to be? Is that a basis for impeachment? There are some parts that show the kind of conduct that would raise the question, I think, in the mind of the individual member: Is this in keeping with the faithful execution of the laws?"

John Doar comes into the office. His suit is, as usual, rumpled, but he has had a haircut. Rodino has another appointment, and has gone beyond the time allotted for our interview, but he is involved in what he is saying now, and wants to continue. He waves Doar away. I have a feeling that Rodino may almost be rehearsing a speech he will deliver on the House floor later this summer. Now *he* is on the edge of his chair.

"Does this contribute to the breakdown of our system of government?" he continues. "Does this bring the office into scandal and disrepute? I think these are the questions that will have to be asked."

I ask him if it is because he wanted the members to go through this entire process of thinking that he has avoided having the committee try to define an impeachable offense.

"Yes," he replies. "You can't expect, with different authorities saying different things—we've had only one impeachment of a President, and that was for a violation of a statute—that the committee could agree."

I say that I gather that he takes the broader view of what is an impeachable offense.

"I do have that broader view, I do," he says. "It's clear in my mind that the offense has to be serious. I'm aware of the fact that we're talking about the removal of the President of the United States."

With Charles Wiggins' dissection of the issues fresh in my mind, I ask Rodino if his problem, then, is going to be to put the picture together.

"That's it," he replies. "That's why you talk about the totality of it. If you separate it, and a member says, 'I'm not going to give any weight to that,' it's still there. We're still talking about the conduct of the President."

I suggest that it seems that the President has the advantage in defining.

Rodino smiles. "If the members of Congress recognize, as the people do, that the House has the sole power of inquiry, this is the question that *we* have to answer," he says. "We have to get it across to the people by doing a careful job, by being deliberate, by being thorough, by showing that we mean to come up with conclusions, whether we absolve the President or find him guilty. I think the people will see it in the way we handle ourselves. *We* have that responsibility to inquire. The President in this situation is a person who is being inquired into. I think, more and more, that the people are getting it. More and more, the people are beginning to respond. They do misunderstand in equating impeachment with the removal of the President, but I think they are learning. They have a sense of awe of the Presidency. We all have. I would have hoped that this would never come about. But if we are to prove that the system really works—that this is a government of laws, and not of men—then, by golly, we have to do it that way. The cynics say it's a lot of rhetoric. With me, you know, if the Constitution has any meaning—if this concept of democracy, which we've fought for, which we've fought several wars to protect, has any meaning—then we can have confidence in this process that the framers of the Constitution established. Terrible as it is, it's part of our Constitutional system. If we believe in it, we've got to go forward. There are no guidelines, no precedents. I knew when it happened. I knew that it was grave and would be awesome. I said I accepted it with a sense of sadness."

As I reach Tom Railsback's office, word comes that St. Clair has announced that the President will not give up either to the committee or to Jaworski the subpoenaed tapes relating to the Watergate break-in and cover-up. This is formal notice that no more tapes will be given to the committee, and also indicates that negotiations with the Special Prosecutor have broken down. In one stroke, the President is defying both the committee conducting an inquiry into his impeachment and the Special Prosecutor conducting an investigation of his Administration. Events are piling up fast again. Perhaps the President has no choice. Perhaps he has found that he is damned if he does and damned if he doesn't. Perhaps it's a preface to another retreat. We never know anymore. He may have decided that he is more damned if he does. Quotes from the transcripts are on the covers of *Time* and *Newsweek,* and no one seems to be saying they have helped him. I had wanted to see Railsback about last week's events. Now they have been overtaken by the events of the past five minutes. Calls are coming into Railsback's office for his comment on the latest development, and he is getting a statement ready. Callers are being told that a statement will be ready shortly. Railsback is wearing a pale-blue short-sleeved shirt and a bow tie. He asks an aide for two Diet Pepsis, and waves me into his office. He is obviously perturbed.

"You know what that's certain to do?" Railsback says. "It's certain to provoke a confrontation. It's going to contribute to the problems of the country. It's certainly going to hurt the Republican Party. It's really bad, I think. You know what I think? I think he's going to propel people here into voting for his impeachment, because the American people are going to be so outraged that he won't coöperate with the investigation."

Railsback takes a telephone call, and reads his statement, which will be broadcast over the radio: "I think the White House announcement is most unfortunate. It's certain to provoke a confrontation between the two branches of government, and the consequences will be bad for the American public and for the Republican Party as well."

Talking to me again, and perhaps to himself, Railsback says, "He's sounding the death knell for the Party. He's killing the Party. Have you seen the latest poll? Fifty-two percent would vote for the Democratic candidate for Congress, twenty-nine percent for the Republican. It's devastating. It's worse than '64."

I asked Railsback why, precisely, this latest Presidential move would hurt the Republican Party.

"The American people are going to take out their wrath on the Republican candidates for what they can't do to the President," he says.

And then he says, "It may be that eventually our difficult decision will be made for us. Who knows?"

At the President's direction, Roy Ash, director of the Office of Management and Budget has asked Cabinet officers to suggest "new thrusts" for the last "one thousand days" of the Nixon Administration.

A friend here says, "The great defeat for the President is coming in the field of public opinion. The erosion of confidence is enormously significant in terms of what he can do, what he can get away with. Public opinion is getting more and more negative. It's not just the Nixon-haters but the middle people, who began to surface a year ago. That's where the reaction to the transcripts comes in. Even a legal proceeding can never be totally insulated from the great tides of concern." There is a connection between atmosphere and fact. Atmosphere is substance. Everybody seems to have his anecdotal example of someone who had been for Nixon who has "had it," and says what "did it"—Agnew, taxes, tapes, too much. The shift of opinion has been marked, and the politicians sense it. Through their nerve fibres, it will affect the impeachment process. Powerful currents of public opinion go through those nerve fibres and are expressed in policy. When the public isn't interested, the politicians can be superbly arrogant—manipulated and manipulative, careless of the public interest. But let a real current start running, and their nerve endings respond. It is unrealistic to think that political men and women are not going to be influenced by the climate when they assess the phrase "high crimes and misdemeanors."

On our television screens tonight we see Father John McLaughlin, a Jesuit priest who works in the White House, saying that the President has given the nation "outstanding moral leadership."

I had almost forgotten about Father McLaughlin. In 1970, he ran for the Senate against John Pastore, the Democratic senator from Rhode Island. That was when a White House group—Harry Dent and Charles Colson and Murray Chotiner—worked hard to elect an "ideological majority" for the President in the Senate. Father McLaughlin lost, and went to work in the White House, and was rarely heard of. The last time he was very visible was during 1972, when he defended the President's policy on the war.

The Omaha *World Herald,* a conservative paper, has called on the President to resign.

Tonight, the President has gone on a cruise on the *Sequoia* with General Haig.

MAY 9

The Chicago *Tribune,* one of the strongest Republican and previously pro-Nixon papers, has called on the President to resign. It says that the transcripts show the President to be "immoral," with "a lack of concern for high principles," and to be "devious" and "vacillating." "He displays dismaying gaps in knowledge," it says. The *Tribune* says that the President made a strategic error in releasing the transcripts and his income-tax returns. "Both stripped the man to his essential character," it says, "and that character could not stand that kind of scrutiny."

It is a gray, chilly, rainy day. The presentation of evidence against the President begins today in the House Judiciary Committee. The networks had prepared to give extensive coverage to the presentation of evidence, but now it has been decided that that process will be closed, for both legal and strategic reasons. Some of the material comes from still secret grand-jury proceedings. And Doar wants a chance to lay out the scope of the case before the committee members without interruption by television and whatever distractions, and behavior of the members, it might cause. Some committee strategists were also worried that, because he must begin at the beginning—members of the press and much of the interested public are more familiar with the material than are members of the committee—Doar's presentation would come across as "dull," offering little that was "new." And that this, too, would affect the atmosphere. St. Clair will be present. The networks are televising the opening ceremonies, which take place before the presentation of evidence begins. Running as a leitmotiv through this broadcast are reports of the President's deteriorating situation. It is announced that John Anderson has said today that the loss of confidence in the President has assumed "truly tragic proportions," that the transcripts show the President to be "totally lacking in moral sensibility," and that the President should resign. John Rhodes is reported to have told reporters at a breakfast briefing today that the President should resign, and then to have issued a clarifying statement that what he meant was that the President should consider resignation as one of his options.

During the day, word comes that Ford has given a speech, in Charleston, Illinois, saying that there is "a crisis of confidence" in our government. The smoke signals that other Republicans have sent up this week are unmistakable. There is talk again of a delegation of Republicans going to the White House. But there is something that causes unease about the thought of a delegation going to the President and demanding (if that's the way they would put it) his resignation. On whose authority? We have Constitutional procedures for taking care of such problems. That is the point of having a Constitution. "While it may be easy to delete characterizations from the printed page, we cannot delete characterizations from people's minds," said Ford in his speech. Later, Ford said he was not "obliquely referring" to "the transcripts."

I phoned the moderate Republican House member I have spoken with from time to time, and he sounded more agitated than usual. "There are people who have said it's impossible to have a resignation, because that would set an intolerable precedent," he said. "Now there are people, including me, who still say that it is impossible to have a resignation but say that the present situation is even more impossible. The transcripts have been devastating. I thought we had a cool, calculating bandit there. Now it doesn't look as if there was even the competence I thought there was. The Republicans are very upset. It's not the thought now that he'll hurt us in the elections—it's on a moral basis, it's people saying, 'I wonder if I want to be in the same party as that guy.' It's a deep feeling. It's 'Can we stand it?' One of my colleagues took a poll and found forty-eight percent of the blue-collar workers in his district for impeachment, and sixty-seven percent of the Republicans. That describes the erosion of Republican support. It's a new kind of quiet outrage. It's not like the reaction to the Saturday-night massacre. But the talk is nondirectional: We think it's terrible, but what can we do? A lot of members talked with Rhodes before he made that statement. Who knows? By the end of next week, you may see something concrete. I think it will move very fast once it gets going. There is a very fast erosion of Republican support for the President. Pretty soon, you'll see no Republican support for him. You won't hear the little rats' feet going down the ropes, but it's pretty sure there will be nobody on the ship. The only ones left will be the retirees from Congress who want ambassadorships."

Ken Clawson issued a statement today that the President would not resign "even if Hell freezes over." Ron Ziegler discouraged reporters from using Clawson's statement, and issued one of his own. Ziegler said that the President was determined "to remain in office and fight the matter," and continued, "He feels he has a Constitutional obligation to do that." Ziegler also said that "probably the most disturbing aspect is the tendency of some to draw an erroneous picture of the morality, especially when they are those who have known him well for a long time and should be in a position to place this in better perspective." Clawson released a letter from Dean Burch to the Chicago *Tribune*. It said, "What emerges from the transcript is life as it is. It is life in government and politics, life in industry and business—and, yes, life in the editorial offices of every newspaper. It is how things actually are, warts and all." There have been rumors that the President is depressed. Gerald Warren described him as "positive and forceful and looking to the future." Some aides put some of their statements to reporters on a background basis, to guide the reporters in their thinking without having the statements attributed to them. One said, "The President is not going to be driven out of office by one-sided interpretations of morality."

On tonight's news we see, among other things, pictures of Bebe Rebozo on his way to appear before the Ervin committee. Rebozo, speaking to CBS correspondent Daniel Schorr about the President, says, "Public opinion sometimes can be distorted in such a fashion as to even make one wonder about himself."

MAY 10

More reporters than usual are at the White House today. The presence of each reinforces the feeling of the others that something is up. The President and Ford are meeting in the Executive Office Building. The rumor is going around again that the President might resign. Even some of the President's aides are wondering how he can stand the pressure. Word reaches the pressroom that Ford has left and will hold a press conference in Buffalo. A couple of reporters have received calls from stockbrokers wanting to know if the reporters think that the President will resign; the market rose yesterday, and the stockbrokers say that the thought that he might resign is what sent it up.

The White House will release a message to the Congress on housing today; the "governing" goes on. Now, even when the President tries to govern, or appears to, there is skepticism. (At the beginning of the year, when the President busied himself with programs and legislative proposals, Fred Zimmerman, of the *Wall Street Journal,* called his efforts "Operation Run-the-Country.") Shortly after 11 A.M., it is announced that there will be a "photo opportunity" in the Oval Office. We are led through a series of corridors and are suddenly in the President's office. There he is, at the end of this turbulent two weeks, sitting at a desk that is nearly bare. His face looks fatigued and puffed. His eyes seem sunken in his tired face. He is talking with James Lynn, the Secretary of Housing and Urban Development, who is sitting in a gold chair beside the desk. Nixon is sitting in a blue leather chair and making conversation about housing with Lynn while the photographers take their pictures, which will be on tonight's news and in the papers. The rug in the office is bright blue with gold stars around the border. It is a wonder that the President can go through this. His words seem forced. "What about your department?" he asks Lynn as the cameras whir and click, and he says, "Don't overlook the long term."

Milton Young, the conservative Republican senator from North Dakota, has said, "It would be a whole lot easier for members of Congress and myself . . . if he [the President] used the Twenty-fifth Amendment and stepped aside until this thing is cleared up." Republican Senators

Marlow Cook, of Kentucky, and Richard Schweicker, of Pennsylvania, have called for the President's resignation. Cook, Schweicker, and Young are all up for reëlection this year.

Rumors went around the Capitol today that the President was resigning. That Kissinger had been called back from the Middle East. That the President would hold a press conference. That the President had asked for television time to announce his resignation. There were rumors that plea-bargaining is taking place. The interesting thing is that the rumors were given more credence than before. It is a noisy and edgy Capitol today, and in the hothouse atmosphere the rumors burst into full bloom.

Tonight, the President went out on the *Sequoia* for a cruise with Mrs. Nixon and Julie and David Eisenhower.

MAY 11

Gerald Ford told reporters in Buffalo yesterday that the President had suggested to him that "maybe I was working too hard and should do less travelling."

Leon Jaworski, pressing his subpoena for more tapes of conversations relating to the Watergate break-in and cover-up, gave Judge Sirica a memorandum yesterday, which the Judge sealed. The Judge also said that hearings on the issue might have to be held in secret.

Dean Burch, Anne Armstrong, who is also a Presidential counsellor, and Mrs. Nixon's press secretary have made statements saying that the President will not resign. General Haig told the Associated Press, "I think the only thing that would tempt resignation on the part of the President would be if he thought that served the best interests of the American people. At this juncture, I don't see anything on the horizon which would meet that criterion."

Yesterday, the New York *Times* quoted Rogers Morton, the Secretary of the Interior, as having said in a speech, "We have seen a breakdown in our ethics of government which I deplore and which I am having a very difficult time living with." Today, the Washington *Post* quoted Rogers Morton as saying, "I'm not going to jump off the ship until there's evidence that the ship is sinking."

Billy Graham, in a telephone interview with an Associated Press reporter yesterday, said that we should pray for the Judiciary Committee and for the President. Dr. Graham said that the language in the transcripts is "not the language I've ever heard him use," and then he said, "The Lord is listening all the time. The Lord has got his tape recorder going from the time you're born until you die."

Tonight, the President is speaking in Stillwater, Oklahoma.

Julie and David Eisenhower held a press conference in the White House garden this afternoon. The President cannot hold a press conference now. There are too many questions.

"Absolutely not, no," Mr. Eisenhower replied to the question of whether the President would resign.

The President's daughter said, with some determination in her voice, that they had discussed the question of resignation last night on the *Sequoia*. "He had a very great quote—that he would take this 'Constitutionally down the wire,' " she said. "He said he would go to the Senate, and he said if there were one senator that believes in him that that's the way it would be."

Asked whom she blamed for the President's "predicament," Mrs. Eisenhower responded, "You begin with a break-in, third- or fourth-rate burglary."

Through his children, the President is sending a message to the politicians that he is not going to resign.

17

SUNDAY. The storm subsided even more suddenly than it blew up. The Republicans took the President at his word that he did not intend to resign. The idea of sending a delegation to advise him to do so seems to have evanesced in a combination of anticipation of rejection, unwillingness of key people to play messenger, and embarrassment. The Democrats contributed to the Republicans' discomfiture by speaking out against resignation, saying that the regular processes of impeachment and trial were preferable. Last Monday, Senator Mansfield, Senator Byrd, and Speaker Albert all issued statements. "Resignation is not the answer," said Mansfield. "This nation is going through a purgatory of sorts at present, but out of this turmoil will come a better U.S. . . . This is the time to keep cool." Said Byrd, "If the President were to resign due to such pressures as are now engulfing the country, and by so doing terminate the impeachment inquiry now under way in the House, a significant portion of our citizens would feel that the President had been driven from office by his political enemies. The question of guilt or innocence would never be fully resolved." Albert said it would be better for "the Constitutional process to run its course." In Oklahoma, Saturday night, the President said he'd "never give up." On the same day, Barry Goldwater said, "When the time comes to resign, he'll know it." Goldwater said he still thought that the President would resign if the House voted to impeach him.

Some people here believe that the Democrats were less interested in following the regular processes than in prolonging the Republicans' agony. But although a certain amount of cynicism is always in order here, there are a number of people—Democrats and Republicans— who, beyond party interests, are truly concerned about the manner in which this question is resolved. They were disturbed by the storm. They do not want it to appear—now or in the future—that Nixon was driven from office in an emotional whirlwind.

The Republicans may have been quieter this week than last, but they were no less distraught. I spoke with my moderate Republican House member again. "It looks as if the wagon started moving down the hill and got slowed down a little bit," he said. "These things always move in

fits and starts. Part of this week's reaction was to the President's statements. The light dawned that it was counterproductive to try to get a
group to go tell him to leave. At least, Republican members have gone
back to reading the transcripts, and saying, 'Come on, Judiciary, find
something and get it over with.' But I think that the effect of last week
is still critical, and may have been the turning point. It is going to sink
in. More and more people think he is guilty. I think the feeling among
the Republicans was that they were made to look like jackasses by the
Democrats. The Democrats are motivated by a desire to string it out,
and we are motivated by a desire to get it over with, and they were right
and we were wrong. That made us look like fools and slowed it down.
But nothing's gone away, nothing's reduced. His troubles are the same,
or even worse. They're just lying there. His White House people are up
here looking for support. Most of us tell them to go away. We didn't
stand up for him. I'm not sure that the White House got the message,
though. I don't think they understand anything at all."

The peer pressure within the Judiciary Committee against leaking
material held surprisingly well during the first days of the presentation
of evidence, until there were two leaks of material in the Committee's
version of the transcripts. One showed that on September 15th the
President vowed retribution against Edward Bennett Williams, counsel
to the Washington *Post* and the Democratic National Committee (the
President vowed to "fix the son-of-a-bitch") and against the *Post* ("The
Post is going to have damnable, damnable problems out of this one.
They have a television station . . . and they're going to have to get it
renewed"). Two months after the President was reëlected, challenges
to two stations owned by the Washington Post-Newsweek Company
in Florida were filed, one by a group headed by the chairman of the
Florida Finance Committee to Re-Elect the President, another by a
group that included two law partners of former Florida Democratic
Senator George Smathers, the man who introduced the President to
Bebe Rebozo, and who has turned up in this story from time to time.
Another leak showed that in the transcript of June 30th, two weeks after
the Watergate break-in, the President suggested in a conversation with
Haldeman and Mitchell that they "cut the loss fast." Mitchell's resignation as Director of the Committee for the Re-Election of the President
was proposed, the President suggesting to Mitchell that the resignation be put in "human terms," that it be "positive rather than negative."
"Otherwise," said the President, the resignation "will be tied right to
Watergate." And so the next day Mitchell resigned, in order, he said,
"to meet the one obligation which must come first"—to "devote more
time" to his wife and daughter. The White House complained about the
leaks, and the Committee staff arranged to lock up the transcripts every
evening.

The President, in an interview with James J. Kilpatrick, a conservative columnist, said that he would not resign "under any circumstances." The interview was published this week. Nixon said that those who proposed that he step aside under the Twenty-fifth Amendment were making a "fatuous suggestion." The President told Kilpatrick that, having learned from earlier crises, he has been able to survive his current one without "tingling nerves and a churning stomach." He would accept a House verdict of impeachment "with good grace," he said, and could conduct his job and undergo a Senate trial, because "I am a disciplined man."

This week, Dwight Chapin, once the President's appointments secretary, was sentenced to a prison term of from ten to thirty months for perjury before the Watergate grand jury investigating "dirty tricks."

On Thursday, the President went to Key Biscayne, and on Friday he went to Grand Cay, Robert Abplanalp's island retreat, with Abplanalp and Bebe Rebozo.

MAY 20

This morning, I talked again with William Cohen, "I think it was a mistake for the committee to begin the presentation with Watergate and the cover-up," he said. "It will take many more days, with many conclusions and ambiguities unresolved. The time pressure will be on us, and the impact of the other material will be diffused. The White House strategy of releasing the transcripts might be working. The purpose was to limit the scope of the inquiry to Watergate and the cover-up. After it played in the press long enough, people would become insensitive to it. Who cares about the eighteen-and-a-half-minute erasure now? The other issues will seem subordinate and insignificant. House members will say, 'You don't have it on Watergate, so you're trying to patch it up with these other things.' "

I asked him if he thought, then, that the White House would succeed in limiting the scope of the impeachment inquiry.

"I think it already has," he replied. "Members of the House are getting very, very anxious, getting distressed. They feel the forces that are pulling them toward a precipice. They have no control over this, and know that a number of them won't be back after November. The House won't act until the middle or end of July. Meanwhile, there is this pall hanging over the members. It's providing some very anxious moments. Other members say to us, 'Why can't you guys give us an answer sooner?' And we say, 'We can't, we don't have the evidence.' And when we ask for more evidence the White House says we're delaying. So we're squeezed by the members and the White House. The pressures to wind it up now come from members of the House. The later the vote, the more trouble they'll have, the less time to make amends. If I had to predict, I would say he's going to make it. There's not enough time. We haven't heard enough evidence yet. And there's going to be unbearable pressure exerted. There's St. Clair saying the Judiciary Committee has all the evidence to find the President innocent. It's Orwellian. We're caught in the catch phrases, the symbols, the emotion, the media, the Presidency, the life forces that drive people. It's not a judicial decision—it's a political one. I think you'll hear more and more about how impeachment will tear the country apart. It will if they keep saying it will. But we live by symbols and catch phrases, and we're stuck with them."

Today, Judge Sirica ordered the President to turn over the tapes of sixty-four conversations requested by the Special Prosecutor; the White House said that it would appeal; and Leon Jaworski, in a letter to the chairman of the Senate Judiciary Committee, said that in a secret hearing last week St. Clair argued that the Special Prosecutor, as an employee of the executive branch, cannot compel the President to produce documents. That seems to bring us back to where we were last fall. Jaworski says that it makes his position a "farce." The Senate Judiciary Committee has called a meeting for tomorrow. But what will or can it do? Other than sputter? It would seem to be too late now to try to establish a Special Prosecutor's office by legislation. This idea had wide acceptance just after Archibald Cox was fired, but as time wore on, and complications in writing such legislation arose, and other issues came along, and Leon Jaworski expressed concern that the President might use the opportunity of new legislation to get rid of him, the legislation was set aside. At the time, Senate leaders said that such legislation held in abeyance would be like a "sword of Damocles" over the President.

In an interview in this week's *Newsweek,* Barry Goldwater said that the President himself has to "seriously consider" the questions "Will his remaining in office be the death knell of the Republican Party? Is it best for the country that we maintain a viable two-party system?" And Goldwater continued, "I happen to believe very strongly in the two-party system. As of this moment, he is not about to resign. But if he begins to see that there is no way out, I think that rather than put the country through two or three months of televised horror, he would seriously consider stepping down." When Goldwater was asked if a delegation should go to the White House to urge the President to resign, he replied, "If I became convinced that this should be done, I would have no qualms about doing it. But I don't think the time is here yet. It could come at any time." If the House leadership thinks there will be "an overwhelming decision in favor of impeachment," he said, "then I think we might have to consider going to the White House before the vote."

The Senate Judiciary Committee met this afternoon and adopted a resolution saying that Jaworski is "acting within the scope of the authority conferred upon him." St. Clair has said that he will fight the issue of Jaworski's power all the way to the Supreme Court.

Jaworski has asked the Supreme Court to intervene on the question of his power to subpoena material from the President, skipping the Court of Appeals. A Supreme Court review now is critical, Jaworski argued, because the issue must be settled promptly—before the Court's term ends for the summer.

Judge Gesell, in a decision issued this morning, ruled that the Fourth Amendment guarantee against unwarranted breaking and entering cannot be suspended in the name of national security. It is one of the major events of this entire period—a legal landmark. The ruling was on the pretrial argument raised by Ehrlichman and Colson that they could defend themselves on the ground that the break-in at the office of Dr. Fielding was a legitimate national-security operation. The courts had never ruled on such a question. The President, in various statements, implied that they had, and that they had indicated "inherent power in the Presidency to protect the national security in cases like this." Today, Judge Gesell ruled that even for reasons of national security the President could not authorize a break-in without a search warrant. He also rejected specifically what he termed the "fall-back position" of Ehrlichman and Colson that—since neither defendant has claimed to have been given this authorization by the President—the President could properly delegate the authority to approve national-security break-ins. "Whatever accommodation is required between the guarantees of the Fourth Amendment and the conduct of foreign affairs," Judge Gesell wrote, "it cannot justify a casual, ill-defined assignment to White House aides and part-time employees granting them an uncontrolled discretion to select, enter, and search the homes and offices of innocent American citizens without a warrant." The Fourth Amendment "is not theoretical," he wrote. "It lies at the heart of our free society."

Gerald Ford let it be known at a press conference in Danbury, Connecticut, yesterday that he had told the President at last Thursday's meeting that his "stonewall attitude" could increase the possibility of "an emotional institutional confrontation." Much is being made of this by the reporters in Ford's entourage, apparently at the instigation of Ford or his aides. "Ford has now indicated that he won't defend the

President's defiance," says Phil Jones on CBS tonight. On the other hand, in a front-page story in this evening's Washington *Star-News,* Ford is quoted as saying, "We've had dirty tricks campaigns in years gone by. We've had all kinds of things comparable to I.T.T., to the milk thing. This is not an unusual situation. But there is an effort being made by some, in my judgment, to undo the 1972 election." The Vice-President added, "Most Democrats are not [involved]. . . . But you've got a few of the crazies who are undertaking an effort, I think, beyond responsibility."

In an interview today, Ron Ziegler said that a recommendation by the Judiciary Committee to impeach the President "will come as no surprise—[considering] the nature of the committee and the approach of the House Judiciary staff."

MAY 29

For the moment, the House Judiciary Committee has finished hearing the staff presentation on the Watergate break-in and cover-up, and on television tonight, once more, we see the members at the microphones.

Robert Kastenmeier, Democrat of Wisconsin: "A very compelling case was made."

Henry Smith, Republican of New York: "I haven't heard a compelling case."

Tomorrow, the committee will hold a business meeting, and next week the presentation of evidence by the staff will turn to the I.T.T. and milk cases. It will return to the cover-up later. The order in which the material is being presented has more to do with which areas are ready for presentation than with logic. The search for the "best evidence" has taken the committee inquiry down the evidentiary, legalistic trail, and seems to be reinforcing the idea that criminal culpability on the part of the President must be found. Even people who saw the question of impeachment as requiring a political judgment about the abuse of power have begun to think of it in terms of finding "proof" of criminal acts, in order to make the most persuasive case to the House and the Senate. And even members of the committee staff, in the process of looking for proof of a criminal act, have helped slip the definition of impeachment over into the area where the President wanted it. The question now is whether anyone will be able to pull it back.

MAY 30

On the radio this morning, it is announced that Gerald Ford has said that the President is justified in not giving more material to the House Judiciary Committee until it has digested the material it has and until it has called witnesses.

Today, the Judiciary Committee is to respond to the President's refusal to honor its last subpoena (dealing with conversations that might have been about the cover-up), and is to issue another one (this one dealing with possible conversations about both the cover-up and the plumbers). Rodino calls at the outset on Walter Flowers. That's interesting: Flowers, the conservative Alabama Democrat, will sponsor a letter to the President. Flowers says to the committee that the President's "open and continued defiance" of the committee is "a disturbing matter." He continues, "I say this committee is moving forward fairly, and I mean in every respect, including the issuance of subpoenas." He then says, "Under the Constitution, it is not within the power of the President to conduct an inquiry into his own impeachment." The committee letter, after some revising of language, warns the President that "committee members will be free to consider whether your refusals warrant the drawing of adverse inferences concerning the substance of the materials, and whether your refusals in and of themselves might constitute a ground for impeachment." The vote to send the letter is twenty-eight to ten—nine Republicans and Conyers opposed. Conyers had wanted to recommend that the President be held in contempt. It is a stronger letter than the one sent to the President after his release of the transcripts, and it has received more Republican support. The last time, Cohen was the only Republican who voted to send a letter. This time, he was joined by Smith, Fish, Sandman, Hogan, Butler, McClory, and Railsback.

During the lunch break, Hamilton Fish and his wife, Billy, who has been attending committee meetings, and I eat sandwiches in Fish's office, in the Longworth House Office Building. Fish—a tall man with wavy hair—is the fourth generation in his family to occupy a seat in Congress. He is, as it happens, the man who recommended that G. Gordon Liddy, whom he defeated in a primary, be given a government job. (Liddy went to work at the Treasury Department, before he went to the White House, and then served as counsel to the Finance Committee to Re-Elect the President.) Fish is considered one of the swing votes on the committee.

"I have been helped enormously by Mr. Jenner," he says. "In Republican caucuses, he has helped me in my thinking, which certainly has evolved. The scholarship and professionalism of Mr. Doar and Mr. Jenner made it easy for me to accept their memorandum about impeachable offenses. But the evidence is such a morass, and has been presented with objectivity—we'll have to get counsel to give us a theory of the case."

This morning, Fish voted to send the letter to the President, though he voted against the letter sent on May 1st. "Looking back, I don't think I'd vote that way again," he says. "I had no idea of the symbolic effect of the letter. I did think it was premature. We hadn't had a chance to look at the transcripts. We should have waited, as we did this time. Today was ten days after we received the President's refusal to honor the subpoena." Fish says that the fact that Doar and Jenner, at party caucuses, took members' suggestions for the letter, instead of having the letter presented to the committee at the last minute, also made a difference. "Another difference was that members were talking in terms of Constitutional grounds," he goes on. "The subject of the President never came up. Now there are only eight or nine members who have not bought the argument that we are proceeding according to our Constitutional authority, and that there is no counter-Constitutional authority. Some of them equate the principles of attorney-client privilege and confidentiality with the Constitutional principle of our authority. They haven't taken that leap, which is almost a religious leap of faith. It gets down to the matter of your acceptance of Mr. Jenner's position, which he gave this morning. [At the committee meeting this morning, Jenner advised the members that their "sole power" to conduct an impeachment inquiry could not be delegated to the courts, and a proposal by Railsback to submit to the courts the issue of the President's obligation to comply with the committee's subpoena was roundly defeated.] It's a novel theory that hasn't been used in a hundred years, and takes getting used to."

I ask Fish how he accounts for the differences of viewpoint among his colleagues on the question of whether there must be evidence of crime if the President is to be impeached, as opposed to a finding of general abuse of power.

He responds without hesitation, "It depends on your congressional district. Who it is that you are selling your conclusion to. People like Rangel [Charles B. Rangel, New York Democrat] and Drinan have no problems. We went through the same thing on the confirmation of Ford. Were we surrogates for our constituents? What did our districts think? What these political animals are concerned with is not so much the way it's going to end up as how they're going to justify it."

JUNE 1

Gerald Warren has refused to answer reporters' questions on whether the President would obey a "definitive" decision by the Supreme Court on the subpoenaed tapes.

Representative William L. Dickinson, Alabama Republican and one of the President's guests on the *Sequoia* a few nights ago (the President has been taking important Republicans and Southern Democrats cruising lately), says that the President vowed "there are some tapes that are so sensitive to national security that he wouldn't release them under any circumstances, even if it meant that he had to leave office."

Sunday. The second day of a drenching weekend. It has been raining since Tuesday. More than ever, we need to get outside, play tennis, try to shake our heads clear. Summer vacations are out. Some journalists can at least get the change of going to the Middle East and the Soviet Union with the President. Those of us who can't work up a justification for going will stay here and watch the processes unfold as the President appears nightly with one or another world leader.

At a dinner, a Cabinet officer says to me that recent events have not affected the management of his Department. When it is necessary, he says, he can still reach White House aides, and even, on occasion, the President, for a decision. Actually, now that Haldeman and Ehrlichman are gone, their *apparat* for trying to gain total control over the executive branch is in a state of disrepair, and Cabinet officers are freer than they might have dreamed possible in the past. (Some of the Haldeman-Ehrlichman *apparatchik* are still in the bureaucracies, though, and some officials, still unsure about how this will all turn out, are on guard.) "But you ask me how it is," the Cabinet officer says. "When your kids come home from school and say they were asked how their dad could work for a crook, that's when it's tough. That's when it's tough."

The bulletin cracked through Washington this morning: Colson has copped a plea. There had been earlier rumors of possible pleas prior to the trials, but in the rush of events we had forgotten about this. Colson has pleaded guilty to a charge of obstructing justice by scheming to defame and destroy Daniel Ellsberg and thus influence the outcome of Ellsberg's trial. The charge—a new one against Colson—is a felony, and could cost him a penalty of five years in jail or a fine of five thousand dollars, or both; his pleading guilty to it means that he will be prohibited from practicing law. In exchange for this plea, the charges against Colson for the break-in at Dr. Fielding's office and for the Watergate cover-up have been dropped. He has promised to coöperate in other investigations and trials of his former colleagues. Colson seemed to take some pains not to know things—to establish deniability—but still it is widely assumed that he has a lot to tell. Whether he has and whether he will tell it are in question as of now. (In the transcripts, Nixon said, "Colson would do anything.")

In court today, Colson said, "I now know what it is like to be a defendant in a celebrated criminal case," and he went on to say that he had "come to believe in the very depths of my being" that official threats to defendants' rights "must be stopped." Colson likening himself to Ellsberg. Tonight, we see Colson on television saying, "I have watched with a heavy heart the country I love being torn apart these past months by one of the most divisive and bitter controversies in our history."

Colson's problem now is that he is caught in his own trap. He may mean everything he says. He may feel contrition. His recent, publicized turn to religion may be sincere. He may be distressed at what is happening to his country, which he may truly love. When John Mitchell was exonerated in the Vesco trial, he said he loved his country, and so did Egil Krogh when he pleaded guilty. The people who surrounded Richard Nixon probably do and did love their country, and had their own peculiar sense of what that meant. It is still not clear that Colson understands why his country is being "torn apart." It is as if these people were utterly detached from what they did. And, having manipulated the symbols—country, flag, religion—they are inevitably suspected of continuing to do so. When Colson turned to religion, he was seen as engaging in the ultimate manipulation. That he then talked as enthusiastically about Jesus as he had once talked about Richard Nixon does not mean that he has not believed firmly in both. The religiosity of the men around Nixon was and is a striking thing, and it is something very hard to deal with. It is not polite to mock or suspect people's religious beliefs, and these men used that on us. They made their patriotism and their piety part of their politics. All of which gives fresh meaning to the point that we have a government of laws.

Gerald Ford has replied to those who say he "zigs and zags" in his defense of the President, "Zig and zag, that's what a good broken-field runner does."

JUNE 4

For the third time, the panel of experts approved by the White House and the Special Prosecutor's office last fall has reported that the eighteen-and-a-half-minute erasure was done manually, probably on a White House recorder. They repeated their earlier finding, in January, that the "hum" was the result of at least five and perhaps as many as nine separate erasures, none of them produced by the foot pedal, as suggested by Rose Mary Woods. They emphasized that the erasures "required hand operation of keyboard controls." This is presumably its final report.

Tonight, on the news, we see Jeb Stuart Magruder, thirty-nine, entering prison, and reporters asking him thoughtful questions about the morality and meaning of it all. This is getting to be a familiar scene. Watergate has given us a new generation of moralists.

The Associated Press reported today that at least sixteen members of the House Judiciary Committee—nine Democrats and seven Republicans—received contributions from the dairy coöperatives. Tomorrow, the committee is to take up the subject of the President's receipt of campaign contributions from the dairy industry.

Earlier this spring, it was also revealed—as the result of a report commissioned by the Associated Milk Producers, Inc.—that the milk producers had made contributions to the Presidential campaigns of Hubert Humphrey and Wilbur Mills, and that before Lyndon Johnson announced that he would not seek reëlection to the Presidency in 1968, the producers had paid over one hundred thousand dollars to print and distribute a book of Johnson's speeches. The report said that after the 1968 election the milk producers decided to "make peace" with the Republicans. We have read of the hundred thousand dollars in hundred-dollar bills delivered in a suitcase by a representative of the milk producers to Herbert Kalmbach in 1969.

In a "white paper" issued in January of this year, the White House acknowledged that President Nixon knew of the dairy industry's plans to contribute to his reëlection before he raised the price supports of milk in 1971. It said that Colson had "asserted in a memorandum to the President" that the milk producers had pledged two million dollars to his 1972 campaign. Last autumn, at his October 26th press conference, the President said that he had a rule that "I have refused to have any discussion of contributions. . . . I did not want to have any information from anybody with regard to campaign contributions." The White House White Paper said that the contributions by the milk industry were not discussed at the meetings between the President and industry representatives just before the price supports were raised, but of a meeting later that day with his advisers, it said, "The fundamental themes running through this March 23rd meeting were two: (1) the unique and very heavy pressures being placed upon the President by Democratic majority leadership in the Congress, and (2) the political advantages and disadvantages of making a decision regarding a vital political constituency." It also said, "Mr. Connally argued that the milk industry's case also had merit on strictly economic grounds."

JUNE 5

In California yesterday, the voters approved Proposition 9, the most rigorous campaign-reform measure adopted by any state, by a margin of more than two to one. In Seattle this week, the nation's governors, at one of their biannual meetings, adopted a resolution calling for reform of campaign financing, disclosure of conflicts of interest, and open meetings in state government. Both measures were backed by Common Cause. How long this reform wave will last and what changes it will leave in the landscape cannot be known now, but it is unquestionably having an impact. The more sophisticated reformers know that there is no perfect world and that there will be backsliding, but they recognize that this is their moment in history to move.

It was revealed today that last February, when the Watergate grand jury returned the indictments for the cover-up against the President's former associates, it named the President as an unindicted co-conspirator. The news stories say that it had wanted to indict the President but had been told by Leon Jaworski that there was a Constitutional question of whether a sitting President could be indicted. The rumor that the President had been indicted circulated last March but was not published. According to tonight's reports, the grand jury concluded that the President had set in motion a payment to Watergate defendant E. Howard Hunt. The story, broken by the Los Angeles *Times,* came out in the course of the negotiations between Jaworski and St. Clair over the subpoenaed tapes. Jaworski had informed St. Clair that he was prepared to argue in court that the President, as an unindicted co-conspirator, could not withhold evidence. It was during subsequent meetings *in camera* that St. Clair said he would still attempt to quash the subpoena, by arguing that Jaworski did not have the authority to subpoena the President. So these maneuvers were even more deadly than we thought.

St. Clair says on television tonight, "We've had many people charged by grand juries who were found innocent."

The field of psychophysics is built around the study of the increments in stimulus that lead to increments in perception. The unit of measurement is called the just-noticeable-difference, or J.N.D. According to this theory, if there is one candle in a room and one more is added, it makes a big difference; if one candle is added to a thousand candles in a room, it does not. Our J.N.D. factor may have just about run out.

Something else seems to be in the air. The President's extraordinary durability is making an impression. It appears to have self-fulfilling effects: he is an endurer; therefore he might endure; therefore what side does one want to have been on in this ultimate struggle over power? Nixon is still the President, and is still feared.

The news reports about the Judiciary Committee's presentation of evidence on domestic surveillance say that Administration-instigated wiretaps—and, presumably, some physical surveillance—turned up information such as that one person had been seen at a store that sold pornographic material, and that another had been seen dining with a woman when his wife was out of town.

We already know that taps on two of Kissinger's aides were maintained after they left the White House and were working as advisers to then Presidential candidate Muskie. The committee learned that information gathered from one interception enabled the White House to know about and make plans to counter an attack on the President's Vietnam policies in *Life* by Clark Clifford, Defense Secretary under Lyndon Johnson. At a press conference yesterday, Kissinger denied that he had initiated the taps, and said he had simply forwarded the names of those who had access to material that had been leaked, and he denied knowledge of the plumbers operation, despite the fact that one of its directors, David Young, had previously been on his staff.

At lunch, a White House aide says that it is important to make public the material on which the grand jury based its findings against the President, so as to "shoot it down." He says that even if a payment was made to Hunt, perhaps there is only a circumstantial case linking it to the President. He says that even if the President did say to pay Hunt temporarily, he knew that it couldn't be done forever. Should he be impeached for that the White House aide asks. He says that he does not see the "pro-impeachment" group as very strong; only the good-government people, the reform types—what he refers to as the "goo-goos"—are for it, he says. He tells me that John Rhodes, Richard Schweiker, and Hugh Scott all got strong "backfire" after they criticized the President or called on him to resign. The "hard-core" public support for the President is between twenty-five and thirty-five percent, he says, and for Republicans "that's a lot."

The aide feels that the President's case has been handled better legally than it has politically. Politically, there's a problem, he says. It is hard to get people to speak out for the President. They don't know what's going on. The Special Prosecutor does, the Judiciary Committee does, but others don't. And people don't want to go out on a limb. Members of Congress don't, Cabinet members don't, and even White House aides, himself included, have a problem. In effect, he says, the control of the news and events has passed from the White House. "Let's face it," the White House man says. "The press is with the Judiciary Committee. The media have deployed all those people to the Judiciary Committee, to the Special Prosecutor's office, so they have to come up with stories. They have made a big investment in Watergate."

I ask him how he feels that the release of the transcripts has worked out for the President.

He says he feels that either they should have been released in the first place, or the President, having "taken the heat" for not releasing the tapes, should have continued to refuse to release any version of them. The transcripts, he says, hurt him with "the spiritual types," and the intellectuals and opinion-molders—"ours and theirs." They hurt him, he says, with "the traditional Wasp Republicans but not with the average person, not with the working types." He says he doubts whether George Meany was really as offended as he professed to be. He says he sees the question of impeachment as a fluid one. If a vote had been taken after the Cox weekend, or not long after the transcripts were released, he says, the President would have been impeached, but he is not sure how things stand now.

A few days ago, a Washington lawyer, a Democrat, said that he no longer cares what happens. He said the fact that the President has flouted the processes does not mean that they will be flouted again. Nixon, he said, has created both a precedent and a cure. No future President, he said, would want to be accused of "acting like Nixon." The problem, said the lawyer, is that the vindication of the system has become an end in itself. The process, having been begun, has to be seen through. "So you have to go by principle instead of just what's practical," he said, and he added, "Too bad."

I put this to a wise man here this afternoon. He said that the lawyer was being too professional and technical. "You're dealing with two hundred million people who live by symbols and myths," said this man. "And the great national story has to have an ending." He said that the thing has to play itself out not just because of the process but because the whole thing—the whole national enterprise, national spirit, call it what you will—rests on caring people with an idea in their heads of what their society is or ought to be. "If that goes sour, we've had it," he said. "The American people is the ballgame on this. Their sense of equity and the dignity of the nation—the dignity of its rulers. How that comes out—that's the big thing."

Richard Kleindienst was given a suspended sentence of a month in jail and a one-hundred-dollar fine, and placed on one month's unsupervised probation today for the misdemeanor charge of not answering fully when he failed to tell the Senate Judiciary Committee in 1972 that he had been ordered by President Nixon to drop an appeal of a government anti-trust case against I.T.T. Kleindienst pleaded guilty to this charge on May 16th. ("I was not interfered with by anybody at the White House," Kleindienst had told the committee.) District Court Judge George L. Hart said that Kleindienst's was a "technical violation" of the law which "is not the type of violation that reflects a mind bent on deception" but "reflects a heart too loyal and considerate of the feelings of others."

JUNE 9

Sunday. Hot and humid. The beginning of a Washington summer. But this one will be like no other.

Senate Majority Leader Mike Mansfield says that the elections should not interfere with the conducting of a Senate trial, if necessary, in the fall.

The two editions of the transcripts are at the top of the New York *Times* paperback best-seller list.

The National Citizens Committee for Fairness to the Presidency held a luncheon for the President in Washington today. As the President watched, Rabbi Baruch Korff, head of the committee, read a resolution affirming the group's "faith in God and country, in Constitutional government, in the Presidency, and in our beloved President, who is one of the strongest links in the chain of the Presidency." The President told the crowd of fourteen hundred cheering supporters, "I shall do nothing to weaken this office."

JUNE 10

Walter Cronkite is at the Salzburg airport. The President has gone abroad, and the anchormen have gone with him, lending their importance to the trip. It is another of those airport scenes with which we have become familiar. This one is the first stop on the way to the Middle East. The President and Mrs. Nixon get off a plane. A band wearing tall hats with some sort of fronds dangling from them is playing. We also see a scene of the President on the White House lawn this morning—the Vice-President, the President's daughters and sons-in-law, members of the diplomatic corps, and a helicopter are in the background—just before he departs on what he calls his "journey for peace." They usually don't make journeys for war. This is total theatre, brought to us by the networks. The President's trip may have a serious purpose, but, if so, it's clouded by the lens of impeachment and rendered suspect by the hyperbolic P.R. Nothing the President does now can escape the cynicism engendered by his situation and his style. Someone said recently that he is doing to foreign policy what he did to the Presidency.

Shortly after the President departed, the White House released a letter to the chairman of the House Judiciary Committee rejecting the committee's May 30th subpoena for tapes and documents concerning Watergate and the plumbers. That subpoena fell due today. The President also left behind letters from St. Clair to Judge Gesell and Judge Sirica refusing to turn over materials. In his letter to the Judiciary Committee, the President said that this was not, as the committee had said in its letter to him, a case of "the President conducting an inquiry into his own impeachment." He said that he had given the committee "extensive and unprecedented coöperation." The question was, said the President, "where the line is to be drawn on an apparently endlessly escalating spiral of demands for confidential Presidential tapes and documents." He urged the committee to stop seeking "the chimera of additional evidence from additional tapes," and to call "live witnesses," subject to cross-examination. "The executive must remain the final arbiter of demands on its confidentiality," the President said. The President also said that the

impeachment inquiry "places a great strain on our constitutional system, and on the pattern of practice of self-restraint by the three branches
that has maintained the balances of the system for nearly two centuries."
It was essential, he said, to maintain the balance. He wrote, "Whenever
one branch attempts to press too hard in intruding on the constitutional
prerogatives of another, that balance is threatened."

JUNE 14

The President viewed the Pyramids today, and promised to give Egypt
the capacity for developing nuclear power.

On Wednesday, we saw pictures of what was said to be the biggest
reception Egypt had ever given a foreign leader. Egyptians in the large
crowd held up signs saying, "Man of Honor," and "Man of Peace." We
saw pictures of Nixon and Anwar el-Sadat, the President of Egypt, sitting and talking on a sofa, Nixon and Sadat toasting each other at a state
dinner, Nixon and Sadat riding in an open train to Alexandria, and the
Nixons and the Sadats watching a belly dancer. Tonight the President
arrived in Saudi Arabia, and we saw on our television screens a military
reception, and King Faisal and President Nixon kissing.

The big interest here is still in Henry Kissinger's emotional press
conference in Salzburg on Tuesday. Kissinger has, through friendly columnists, threatened to resign before, but this public threat, and what
came across on television as a near tantrum, has set this town fairly on
its ear. There seems, somehow, to be more fascination at this moment
with "Henry" than with the President. Perhaps because the President
is more remote, perhaps because he is less theatrical than Kissinger,
perhaps because we have become accustomed to Nixon and his crisis.
So there is endless speculation as to the meaning of Kissinger's statement on Tuesday that he would resign unless his name was cleared in
the wiretapping issue. ("I do not believe that it is possible to conduct the
foreign policy of the United States under these circumstances when the
character and credibility of the Secretary of State is at issue.")

The White House is, of course, making the most of the leaks of
information from the Judiciary Committee. At the White House yesterday, Vice-President Ford and Dean Burch attacked the committee
for the leaks. There have been leaks about Kissinger's role in the
wiretapping. And there have been leaks of a series of memoranda
from a staff lawyer for the Judiciary Committee (not a member of the
impeachment-inquiry staff) to one of the committee members showing discrepancies between the transcripts released by the White House
and transcripts of the same tapes made by the committee. One of the
memoranda shows that on March 22, 1973, the President said to John
Mitchell, "I don't give a—what happens. I want you to (unintelli-

gible) stonewall it, plead the Fifth Amendment (unintelligible) else, if it'll (unintelligible). That's the big point." The President is also shown to have told Mitchell, "Even up to this point, the whole theory has been containment, as you know, John." This material was not in the White House transcripts.

House Minority Leader John Rhodes, who has been coming to the President's defense lately, said a few days ago that if the President defied the Supreme Court he "probably could not survive" impeachment. Rhodes also told newsmen this week that after he had publicly suggested (following the release of the transcripts) that the President should consider resignation, "my mail switched from three-to-one anti-Nixon to eight-to-one pro-Nixon." Said Rhodes, "Any Republican who thinks he can win a congressional election without that hard-core support is more optimistic than I am." He also said that any member "will be in trouble at home" if he votes for impeachment and the Senate "knocks the case down flat."

Fred Buzhardt suffered a heart attack this week and is in the hospital.

The Presidential speechwriter Patrick Buchanan wrote a piece for the Op-Ed page of the New York *Times* (of all places) yesterday asserting that the grand jurors who voted to name the President an unindicted coconspirator were from "the most anti-Nixon city in the United States." He pointed out that George McGovern received seventy-eight percent of the votes in the District of Columbia, that seventeen of the twenty-three grand jurors were black, and that blacks across the nation had voted "upwards of 10 to 1 against the President."

JUNE 17

Monday. The second anniversary of the break-in at the Watergate. Herbert Kalmbach was sentenced today to a minimum of six months in prison for secret and illegal fund-raising.

China and France have conducted nuclear tests in the atmosphere. Ali Bhutto, the Prime Minister of Pakistan, says his country is developing its own nuclear capability. The President, still in the Middle East, has announced that the United States will also give the capacity to develop nuclear power to Israel. As the President left Saudi Arabia, King Faisal said, "Anybody who stands against you, Mr. President, in the United States of America, or outside the United States of America, or stands against us, your friends in this part of the world, obviously has one aim in mind, namely that of causing the splintering of the world." Tonight we see the President arriving at the Amman, Jordan, airport, where he is met by King Hussein. There is a fly-past of Royal Jordanian Air Force planes. In the background, a band is playing "The Washington Post" march.

JUNE 19

Down the hallway from Room 2141, reporters are standing behind ropes awaiting the emergence of committee members for a quorum call or their lunch break. The members are still hearing the evidence in closed session, and the reporters must do their best to find out what is going on. As members emerge, the reporters chase them, gathering what snippets they can. Representative Thomas M. Rees, Democrat of California and a member of the Banking and Currency Committee, which has rooms adjacent to the Judiciary Committee's, has likened the scene, in a newsletter to his constituents, to the running of the bulls at Pamplona. The reporters know by now which members will be helpful. Some members slip out through a side door, eluding the pack. Others head right for it, and for the television cameras just down the hall. And thus we get our few seconds each evening, on the television news programs, of what the members heard and how they interpret it. But the members must be watched for apparent tilts one way or the other, and reporters must write stories about what the committee is doing, so the reporters do the best they can.

In the committee's sixth week of hearing the evidence, the members are growing less accessible, more weary. One can see the strain in their faces. It is the strain of having heard so much material and, in the case of some, wondering what they will do with it; the strain of facing, and then having to explain, their vote; the strain of sitting in these long meetings while constituents continue to press for audiences and services, while mail has to be answered, while votes on other issues have to be cast, while campaigns for reëlection have to be run, and while— for those who take the trouble—the material that is put before them in great gobs has to be studied. Early on, Doar saw what he believed to be a pattern of misconduct and abuse of power. Jenner saw it, too. In seeing this pattern, Doar and Jenner were not unlike others who examined the material closely. And such was their reputation for integrity that others could feel that if they saw it, it was there—that their judgment was honestly arrived at. Most committee members felt this. Doar has been building the case before the committee, as one associate puts it, "brick by brick." His neutral presentation of one fact after another, together with his characteristically deliberate and undramatic manner, his delivery, in a monotone—intentionally monotonous—is calculated to have its cumulative impact on the committee members. It is also designed to convince them of his fairness, against the day when he may have to sum up the case for them.

Elliot Richardson has submitted to the committee an affidavit giving more detail than he had previously given publicly about White House attempts to limit the scope of Cox's inquiry: the White House, he said, objected to investigation of the financing of the President's homes, and of the Administration's use of electronic eavesdropping. Richardson also told the committee that the President, in a discussion about the investigation of then Vice-President Agnew, said, " 'Now that we have disposed of that matter, we can go ahead and get rid of Cox.' " The committee also heard how Haldeman's and Ehrlichman's papers were put with the President's papers, so that they could be covered by executive privilege.

The leaks, the long time that the committee seems to be taking, and the lack of public understanding of what it is doing have cast a pall over the committee's deliberations. It is one of those shifts in mood which have characterized this city's reaction to this issue for over a year now: at some given point it goes out over the nervous system and becomes the widely received truth that the President's fortunes are up or that they are down, that a particular investigation is going well or that it is going badly, that So-and-So is doing a good job or that he is "blowing it." At lunch today, one member says that the committee is "under a cloud." Moreover, the President's trip to the Middle East appears to have helped him, and from here in Washington, the polls notwithstanding, the public sentiment for impeachment does not seem to be very strong.

JUNE 21

Today, Charles Colson was given a sentence of from one to three years in prison, plus a five-thousand-dollar fine, for obstructing justice in the prosecution of Daniel Ellsberg. It was the stiffest sentence yet given to one of the Watergate defendants. Judge Gesell said, "The Court recognizes that men of ambition, affected by blind, impulsive loyalty, react to the atmosphere in which they work and which they helped create. But this does not change the individual responsibility of each public servant. Morality is a higher force than expediency."

Colson said after he was sentenced, "I can work for the Lord in prison or out of prison." He also issued a statement in the courtroom, saying that President Nixon "on numerous occasions urged me to disseminate damaging information about Daniel Ellsberg." Later, Ken Clawson issued a statement saying that Colson had been sentenced to prison for doing something that people on Capitol Hill do every day. Colson said in his statement in the courtroom, "During the time I served in the White House, I rarely questioned a Presidential order. Infrequently did I question the President's judgment. . . . I know that my popular image is that of an arrogant and self-assured man who revelled in the ruthless exercise of power. That is not an accurate characterization, and I think it is important that that be realized—not so much for my sake as for the sake of an understanding of how this kind of thing could have happened. Actually, I was often frightened by the enormity of the decisions I was asked to take part in. . . . I lost my perspective to a point where I instinctively reacted to any criticism or interference with what I was doing or what the President was doing as unfair and as something to be retaliated against. . . . I had one rule—to get done that which the President wanted done."

Today, the Judiciary Committee completed its six weeks of listening to the evidentiary material. In all, the committee covered seventy-two hundred pages of evidence, contained in thirty-six notebooks, listing six hundred and fifty findings of fact. The very voluminousness of the material seems to have left many committee members confused. Some are still searching for what has been termed "the murder weapon" or "the smoking gun"—the definitive piece of evidence that the President committed a crime. Now, too, some committee members have begun to see the pattern of behavior Doar has described—although Doar himself avoided using the term. One question now is how to define a pattern of misconduct as an impeachable offense. The staff has begun to try its hand at drafting articles of impeachment. Many subjects have been effectively dropped, as had been predicted from the outset. The I.T.T. issue has been converted by the staff from one of whether there was a *quid pro quo* between the Administration and I.T.T. to whether the President was aware that Kleindienst was giving misleading testimony—as part of a pattern of Presidential awareness of such conduct by his subordinates. Connections between contributions and agency actions eluded proof, and were not even energetically sought. It was understood that this would be a divisive subject. Moreover, the staff was not in a position—because of the pressure of time—to do much original investigating. It relied, therefore, on investigations conducted by other congressional committees, on the material that the President had given the Special Prosecutor, on the evidence forwarded to it from the grand jury, and on evidence from the F.B.I. about wiretapping. It has, however, held a number of interviews with former Nixon Administration and campaign officials.

Today is the first day of summer.

JUNE 24

Today, Monday, the Judiciary Committee met and subpoenaed tapes of forty-nine more conversations, bringing the total it has subpoenaed to one hundred and forty-seven. The conversations cover the subjects of the dairy industry, I.T.T., domestic surveillance, and the Internal Revenue Service.

These subpoenas of the President have become routine. McClory says something interesting: he asks if some of the material is being requested in accordance to what he refers to as the "take-care theory." This suggests that McClory has begun to think of the issue in terms of whether the President did, as the Constitution requires, "take care that the laws be faithfully executed." Even the Republicans who usually defend the President are not very feisty today. Only four Republicans— Hutchinson, Wiggins, Lott and Latta—vote against the subpoenas for the material relating to the I.T.T. and milk cases, and the other subpoenas are approved by voice vote.

At lunch in the Capitol Hill Club, a Republican gathering place a few blocks from the Capitol, Tom Railsback says, "A great deal is going to depend on the testimony of John Dean and Charles Colson before the committee. There are a lot of unresolved ambiguities. Impeaching the President of the United States is serious business, and you'd better have good evidence of his involvement, or it won't sell. I couldn't explain it to my district. I don't feel confident of doing it right now."

I ask Railsback if he accepts the theory that there may be a pattern of abuse.

He replies, "I don't accept the pattern theory. I think there has to be direct evidence of Presidential involvement in a serious offense— not a pattern of small events. But I don't rule out a series of smaller Watergate-cover-up events that, taken together, add up to obstruction of justice. That's a serious offense. But when members talk about patterns of misconduct and abuse of the system, a lot of them are viewing acts of subordinates as proved Presidential misconduct. I don't think we can do that. It's really arguable that the President was involved in these acts."

Later, Railsback says, "My constituents are against impeachment. I took a survey recently. A very small percentage favor impeachment. I asked, 'If you favor his resignation and he does not resign, should he be impeached?' and twenty-four or twenty-five percent were for that and sixty-seven percent were against. So what it means is I'd better know what I'm talking about if I vote for impeachment."

I ask Railsback what he thinks now about the domestic-surveillance issue.

He replies, "Again, the question is direct Presidential involvement. There are a lot of things I don't like, but you have to find direct Presidential involvement. The attempted manipulation of the F.B.I. and the C.I.A.—that bothers me, because that poses the greatest threat to our freedom in this country that I can imagine."

I ask what impact the presentation of evidence has had on him.

"It was a very clear account of the abuse of power, not necessarily by the President himself but by people who were in a position to wield great power," Railsback says. "What it means is that there should be more

oversight and more accountability. We have to provide for more accountability of the top non-Cabinet people in the White House, as we did for
the director of the Office of Management and Budget. We need to provide some mechanism for determining the validity of the assertion of
executive privilege. The presentation showed us overkill, overconcern,
pettiness, vindictiveness, greed."

On the CBS news tonight, Dan Rather reports that the President has
phlebitis.

JUNE 28

The committee broke into a partisan dispute this week over which witnesses—referred to as "live witnesses"—were to be called. Republicans
fought for St. Clair's list of six witnesses and for open hearings. Rodino
was concerned not so much about who was called as about the prospect
that the public's first extended view of the proceedings would be of a
string of witnesses defending the President. Dean Burch said that the
committee had "sort of the smell of a lynch mob."

The committee staff has interviewed Colson for two days and is very
nervous about calling him to testify before the committee. Apparently,
Colson is still causing confusion. Earlier this week, there appeared
press stories based on interviews with a private detective, Richard L.
Bast, who said that Colson had come to him just before he pleaded
guilty in court and had told him of his suspicions that the C.I.A. planned
the break-ins at the Watergate and at the office of Daniel Ellsberg's
psychiatrist, and that the C.I.A.'s apparent motive was to discredit the
President's advisers. Colson apparently told Bast much of what he had
earlier told Senator Howard Baker about the C.I.A. and the surreptitious
passing of White House documents to superiors at the Pentagon by a
yeoman assigned to the National Security Council. (Baker has from
time to time shown substantial interest in these matters.) According to a
story in the Washington *Post,* Colson "portrayed the President as a virtual captive in the Oval Office of suspected high-ranking conspirators in
the intelligence circles against whom he dared not act for fear of international and domestic political repercussions." Colson was reported to
have described the President as "out of his mind over the C.I.A. and
Pentagon roles."

On Thursday and Friday, St. Clair made his own presentation of
evidence before the committee. St. Clair argued that the President did
not know of the Watergate break-in in advance, was unaware of the
cover-up until March 21st, and did not approve any payment of money
for the silence of the Watergate defendants. St. Clair pointed out that
Dean told the Ervin committee that after he discussed Hunt's money
demands with the President the question had been "left hanging." St.

Clair's presentation was selective, the material offered being unabashedly intended to buttress the President's case. Hamilton Fish said afterward that St. Clair had offered no new evidence but had used available material in "making the President look good." Said Robert McClory, "I wouldn't call it persuasive." St. Clair told the committee members that he had not heard all the tapes. Said St. Clair, "That would not be the best use of my time."

On Friday, it was reported that Rodino had predicted to some reporters that all the committee Democrats would vote for impeachment. Ken Clawson said that Rodino should be "discharged." In the current atmosphere of raw nerves, each of these flurries seems monumental, and is reacted to accordingly. It is as if everything were of the same dimensions: a slip of the tongue by Rodino and a break-in; wiretaps and a partisan dispute over witnesses. There are reasons, having to do with the peculiar nature of Washington and the peculiar nature of the impeachment process, for this disproportionate attention. All that is visible to the eye now is the whitecaps—the leaks, the partisan fights. The deeper processes are going on unseen while we watch the day-by-day events. Moreover, what is seen is fed into what has become an overreactive nervous system. The mood of the moment sweeps through this city and is broadcast by word of mouth, in the newspapers, and on the nation's television screens.

This week, we saw the President arrive in Brussels, where he was greeted by guards wearing the Graustarkian uniforms that are said to have inspired the ones worn briefly by the White House police, and where he signed a new declaration on Atlantic relations. Then we saw him arrive in Moscow, and saw him and a beaming Brezhnev—Brezhnev wearing a medal and two stars and looking jovial, Nixon looking tired and seemingly forcing the joviality—toast each other. Nixon, raising his glass of vodka, said that past agreements "were possible because of a personal relationship that was established between the General Secretary and the President of the United States."

JUNE 29

Saturday afternoon. Hamilton Fish's eyes are red with fatigue. He has spent the day at the offices of the impeachment-inquiry staff, in the old Congressional Hotel, and in a few hours he will return to his district, in upstate New York, to do some campaigning. Some committee members have been taking the evidentiary notebooks home at night to study; some, like Fish, prefer to leave them in safekeeping at the staff offices; some have been going over to the staff offices at night to listen to tapes. It will not be long now before the committee members have to vote, and they must be able to explain their vote. It is particularly important for those who might vote for impeachment to be prepared to document their case.

Fish talked with Jenner today and will talk with him again on Monday. Fish is carrying legal pads on which he has made notes comparing arguments offered by the committee staff and by St. Clair. "All of a sudden, we are facing this terminal point," he says. "We need time to get our thoughts together. We have been thrown the evidence so fast—sometimes three notebooks a day. It was very cursory; some of the material was just referred to and passed over, leaving the questions of what it says and why it's there. And last week the House met every night until six or seven o'clock. One night, we met until eleven. Committee members can make life very easy for themselves if they accept that the Constitutional definition of impeachment is a criminal act. I don't think you can do that. They can make it very easy for themselves if they set up a very strict standard. But I don't think you can. If you accept our staff memo that the ground for impeachment is broader—and I do—it adds a burden for you. You have to find contempt of the Constitutional system, subversion of our institutions. I'm convinced that to the framers 'high crimes and misdemeanors' meant subversion of institutions and the Constitution. The other meaning of 'misdemeanors,' as you and I know the word, wasn't known then. 'Misdemeanors' meant 'misconduct,' in terms of crime against the people. If you take that approach, it seems to me proper to factor in considerations of what's best for the country. If you include the good of the country, which I do, then you also have to figure the good things he's done—foreign policy. Granted this is a capital-'P' Political process, would it be better for the nation not to go through with impeachment? You have to consider the state of the nation—to see if it might purify or might be the wrong thing to do."

I ask Fish what, having listened to the evidence, he thinks he has heard thus far.

"That is really what I'm trying to discover," he replies. "I'm trying to go through the evidence and see where things fit. It's hard to pull it all together. You may well ask as a preliminary question, 'Where is the Presidential involvement?' He has refused to comply with our subpoenas, and there is no question that the material subpoenaed is specific and highly relevant. The House is entitled to information in an impeachment. Especially since he produced some materials and not others, we're entitled to make adverse inferences. Still, we don't have much nexus between the President and specific events."

I ask if he thinks he has to find direct Presidential involvement.

Fish replies, "Republicans have a problem in going back to their districts and saying, 'I impeached him on grounds that he didn't take care that the laws are faithfully executed.' God, some of this stuff is subtle. When you look at the notebooks tab by tab, it doesn't necessarily show up. It's a matter of adverse inferences from his failure to produce evidence. The pattern is there. And you take each phase, and you find involvement by all these subordinates, and on the next dates you have meetings of these subordinates with the President, and in each case we don't get the tapes—that goes to his involvement. Then, separate that from the over-all pattern. If you didn't draw the adverse inferences, then you're left with obvious misfeasance on the part of subordinates, which they shielded from him, as your factual nexus. The legal nexus would be his responsibility to be diligent in the prosecution of these matters, insistent on certain conduct, not condoning other conduct. You get back to that pretty rarefied business of the responsibility to protect the institutions of government, their integrity. I'm just beginning to think that through.

"Of course, there is a pattern in the actions by the White House staff and CREEP after June 20th to control the investigation; the attempts by the President to influence Petersen; the Cox firing; the President's 'stonewalling' of the committee. The Fielding break-in bothers me very much. You have that in September, 1971, the Liddy plan in the winter of 1972. Domestic surveillance is something we'll have to go into a lot deeper."

Fish says, "It has become very uncomfortable to keep reading in the newspapers that the House will not impeach unless three or four committee Republicans vote for it. Every time someone draws up a list of three, four, or five possible votes for impeachment, I'm one of them. I'm on an open-minded search for the truth. I'm sorry more Republicans aren't that way. The week before last, I felt people firming up, people becoming unveiled defenders of the President. They had decided that the evidence didn't add up. Of course, the question is 'Didn't add up to what?' "

SUMMER

18

JULY 4

The President returned from his trip to Moscow last evening—on the eve of the Fourth of July—landing in Limestone, Maine. The arrival, exquisitely timed for 7:30 E.D.T., was broadcast on the television networks. Last night, President Nixon said, "It's always good to come home to America. That is particularly so when one comes home from a journey that has advanced the cause of peace in the world."

The United States and the Soviet Union failed to reach a comprehensive agreement on arms limitation. There are a number of indications that this failure resulted from the domestic troubles of the President, who is staking so much on the argument that he is indispensable to our foreign policy. It appears that, with Kissinger in the Middle East for much of the spring, and the President otherwise preoccupied, preparations for these talks were not accorded the necessary priority. Moreover, it appears that the President did not wish to risk giving further offense to conservatives, who opposed substantial arms-limitations agreements, and who also could decide the President's fate in a Senate trial.

Senate Republicans have retained an outside lawyer to help them prepare for a trial of the President in the Senate.

The inquiry staff of the House Judiciary Committee has completed a draft of articles of impeachment.

JULY 5

Dr. Walter Tkach, the President's personal physician, said in an interview today which appeared in the New York *Daily News* that the President had risked his life in making the trip to the Middle East: "He took a calculated risk. It could have killed him."

JULY 8

One of those really hot Washington days. Even in the early morning, one feels the moist heat, and knows that it will get worse as the day goes on. On days like this, it is almost too hot to move. Cars break down. Tennis is out of the question. Shortly after nine, the Popsicle man is doing a brisk business with the crowd that has been waiting—some of it for two days—in front of the Supreme Court for a chance to hear the argument today of the cases of United States of America v. Richard M. Nixon, President of the United States, et al., and Richard M. Nixon, President of the United States, et al. v. United States of America. When Leon Jaworski, the Special Prosecutor, arrived this morning, the crowd cheered, and someone in the crowd shouted "Go, U.S.A.!"

Inside this building, with its marble hallways, there is a special coolness—one would feel it whatever the temperature outside. It is as if this were a sort of temple, and people in it conduct themselves accordingly. They do not behave as if this were just another government building, or even another court. It is the supreme court. Inside this building, voices are hushed and steps are measured. We have come to think of this court as the guarantor of our safety, as the last refuge when other remedies fail. Sometimes, it has even performed as that. We do not think of it much as being composed of nine human beings, whose temperaments and degrees of intelligence vary—human beings appointed to lifetime terms by different Presidents for different reasons. One cannot help thinking today of what Nixon tried to do to this court. Of how he insulted it with his attempted appointments of Clement F. Haynsworth, Jr., and G. Harrold Carswell, both defeated in the Senate, and with the other highly undistinguished names that were floated—and perhaps even seriously considered. After the uproar, the two most recent vacancies were filled by Lewis Powell, the conservative and respected Virginia attorney, and William Rehnquist, the highly conservative Justice Department official. Referring to his Supreme Court nominations, Nixon used to talk about the need to "strengthen the peace forces as against the criminal forces." As it happens, he has filled four of the nine seats on the Court, almost a majority, and, as a result, on questions of civil rights and civil liberties the Court has, as he intended, become more conservative.

The issue of how to establish accountability for what has been done in the Nixon Administration has taken us to the Congress, to the White House, to the Justice Department, to the District Court, and now here. Once more, Nixon has drawn a line that must be put to institutional tests. To be argued here today is a melange of issues of great Constitutional import, and also, perhaps, of great consequence to the fate of the President—for we are here because Nixon clearly does not want to surrender some tapes that Judge Sirica has ordered him to turn over to the Special Prosecutor for the cover-up trial. Whether it is something about those particular tapes or it is that the President has simply decided that a line must be drawn somewhere, we can't know. The President has not said whether he would obey an order of the Supreme Court. Last fall, when it was thought that a similar issue might have to be brought to this court, he said he would obey a "definitive" decision. That pledge has not been repeated. The principal legal issue before the Court today is whether the President's right to invoke executive privilege is absolute, even in a criminal proceeding—an argument that was rejected by the District Court (and, in the tapes controversy last fall, was also rejected by the Court of Appeals).

The White House, in its brief to the Court, argued that only the President has the right to decide what information is privileged, and that the District Court cannot substitute its judgment. It argued that if the President is deemed to have abused this privilege, the only appropriate remedy is impeachment (in which proceeding the President is also invoking executive privilege). "The President is not subject to the criminal process," the brief says. The White House also argued that the court process was "being used as a discovery tool for the impeachment proceedings," because the material turned over to the District Court would go to the House Judiciary Committee. (This is not automatically the case. The President made the decision in March to give the House committee material he had given the Special Prosecutor, though perhaps as a practical matter he had no choice.) The White House brief also asserted that the dispute between the Special Prosecutor and the President is an intra-executive-branch dispute, in which the courts have no role, and, because of the impeachment inquiry, is a political matter, in which the courts should not intervene. The White House asked the Court, further, to review the grand jury's right to name the President as an unindicted co-conspirator.

The Special Prosecutor argued that because of the congressional arrangements with the Attorney General he has independent authority; that the courts do have the right to decide this issue; that "the public purpose underlying the executive privilege for governmental deliberations precludes its application to shield alleged criminality." The Special Prosecutor's brief asked, "Shall the evidence from the White House be confined to what a single person, highly interested in the outcome, is willing to make available?"

Beneath all these nice, and important, legal arguments is a very tough political and legal struggle, being fought by some very determined people. The President does not want to give up those tapes. Leon Jaworski is determined to call him to account. It was Jaworski who suggested to the grand jury that, since the question of whether a President could be indicted was unsettled (and could therefore be tested, and could upset the entire proceeding against the cover-up), Nixon be named an unindicted co-conspirator, and that the information on which the grand jury based its conclusion that the President should be indicted be sent to the House Judiciary Committee. The naming of the President as an unindicted co-conspirator then became another weapon that Jaworski could use to make evidence involving the President admissible in the cover-up trial, and to strengthen his argument that the President should not have the privilege of withholding evidence.

There were questions about Jaworski when this prosperous and well-connected Texan, a former president of the American Bar Association, succeeded Archibald Cox as Special Prosecutor. The main question was whether he would be as independent as Cox or would be deferential to the office of the President. But the Special Prosecutor's staff was still in place and had been gathering evidence, and it would have been difficult for any new Special Prosecutor to turn his back on it. And something seems to have happened to people who examined this case closely—some determination seems to have seized them. Beyond that, something else was working in the mind of Leon Jaworski: his experiences as one of the Nuremberg prosecutors. As he examined the evidence of what had taken place during the Nixon Administration, Jaworski came to believe—and he privately let some people here know that he believed—that there were some analogies between what had happened in Germany and what had happened here. He saw parallels in the way power is accrued, and the way the rights of individuals are undermined, and the way the public is apathetic until it is too late. The loss of freedom takes place incrementally and rather unostentatiously, he concluded; if it were attempted through a sudden great uprising, there would be great opposition, and it would fail. It begins, he came to believe, by small steps—by gradual erosion of the institutional safeguards. He felt that what Egil Krogh and Charles Colson said when they were sentenced indicated that it had begun to happen here—and how far it would have gone nobody knows. Both had talked of how the President's interest was seen as being paramount—of greater importance than individual rights. What struck Jaworski in his experience in Germany, and stayed with him—and what he thought about, and talked about privately, as he proceeded as Special Prosecutor—was the seemingly inconsequential way that it began there, and how it grew, and also how the German people kept their eyes closed until it was too late. They were not bad people, he felt, but they had become indifferent to what was moral and right—had preferred not to think about it.

The Supreme Court chamber holds only about three hundred people. Those of us who do not regularly cover the Court have to rotate seats, and are placed behind the row of massive marble columns at the left side of the courtroom. If we as much as rise slightly from our seats to peek around a column to see which Justice is speaking, one of the superintendents sternly motions to us to be seated. If one is not an expert at distinguishing the voice of Justice Byron White from that of Justice Potter Stewart, there is a problem. Haldeman is here, and so is Henry Petersen. Haldeman is seated next to Mrs. Leon Jaworski. Representatives Railsback, Cohen, and McClory are here. A few members of the public who waited and waited in line are also here.

The Justices, in their black robes, listen intently as the arguments proceed; several rock back and forth in their chairs. At the far right of the dais where they sit is the empty chair of Rehnquist, who has excused himself from this case because of his former association with the Administration. The tall marble columns on both sides of the room, the marble walls, the floor of red-and-black marble, the burgundy carpets, and the burgundy velour drapes along both side walls and behind the Justices add to the majesty of this chamber. People sit here reverentially, hushed, as if they were in fact in a temple.

"If there is any one principle of law that Marbury v. Madison decides," Jaworski says to the Justices, "it is that it is up to the Court to say what the law is." We are back to that, and this case could be just as important. Jaworski stands there—the familiar shock of wavy white hair above the round face with the bulbous nose, and the dark-rimmed glasses. He is asserting his right to sue for the tapes, saying that the office of the Special Prosecutor "to some degree could be described as a quasi-independent agency." Justice Stewart asks if Jaworski is arguing that "there is no right of executive privilege." Jaworski responds that he is not, and says, "It has been traditionally recognized, and appropriately so, in a number of cases, as we see it. We do not think it is an appropriate one in this case. But, we certainly do not feel that it has any Constitutional base." Powell, in his soft Virginia accent, asks, "Is it your view that there are no inferences to be derived from the doctrine of separation of powers?" Jaworski says that "the privilege" as recognized judicially may have been tied to a separation-of-powers doctrine but that "the separation-of-powers doctrine in the exercise of and calling for executive privilege has not been applied in a number of instances." Jaworski goes on to say, "What it really narrows down to is a somewhat simple but very important issue in the administration of criminal justice, and that is whether the President, in a pending prosecution, can withhold material evidence from the court, merely on his assertion that the evidence involves confidential communications." (The more narrowly the point is drawn, the easier it might be for the Court to decide in his favor.) Jaworski adds that, "painful as it is"—and he lowers his voice slightly as he says that—the grand jury's finding that the President was to be named as an unindicted co-conspirator is "sufficient to show *prima facie* that the President was involved in the proceedings in the course and in the continuation of the particular conspiracy that was charged." In order to get around the sticky problem of whether the Court must approve the grand jury's finding of the President as an unindicted co-conspirator in order to find that the President must surrender the tapes, Justice Stewart takes Jaworski through a series of questions designed to separate the two issues. Even if that finding had not been made, Justice Stewart suggests, "you would still be here." "That is right," Jaworski says.

A Supreme Court oral argument is not, as many often expect, like a declamatory contest but is conducted more in the low-key style of reasonable men talking over interesting questions. The Justices have usually read the briefs, and they want to pursue with counsel the questions that trouble or interest them. There is an art to appellate arguing—it requires skills different from the pyrotechnics of convincing a jury—and this is the Wimbledon of appellate arguing. Counsel must be prepared to drop his line of argument, answer the Justices, perceive what is troubling them, and refashion the argument to deal with what is in the Justices' minds. Today, the Justices have clearly read the briefs and have undoubtedly discussed the issues with their clerks, and they are particularly active in asking questions. Jaworski is not conspicuously good at dealing with this form of courtroom argument, and St. Clair is only slightly better. They have not trained for it. But this case will be decided on the issues, not on the style of the argument. Sometimes the Justices help the counsel out of a difficult spot; sometimes they make a point by way of asking a question. Both Jaworski and St. Clair are in business suits. (I remember seeing Archibald Cox some years ago, as Solicitor General, arguing here in a swallow-tailed coat. Government attorneys usually wear swallow-tailed coats when they argue here, but Jaworski has chosen to wear a suit today as an illustration of his point that he is not a member of the executive branch.)

St. Clair, slightly stout and in a blue suit, talks about the "co-pendency" of the impeachment inquiry and about the value of the tapes to that inquiry.

Justice Thurgood Marshall observes, "I don't know what is in the tapes. I assume you do."

"No, I don't," St. Clair responds.

"You don't know, either?" says a puzzled Justice Marshall. "Well, how do you know that they are subject to executive privilege?"

St. Clair, speaking more forcefully than Jaworski, says that they are subject to executive privilege because "there is a preliminary showing that they are conversations between the President and his close aides." St. Clair takes off and puts on his glasses as he speaks, and refers to Jaworski as "my brother." (All lawyers are "brothers" at the bar.) St. Clair argues that there are only three branches of government, and that the President is "the chief law-enforcement officer," adding, "He shall take care to see that the laws are enforced. The executive power is vested in him, in one man."

Justice Stewart, who usually votes with the conservative bloc, says, "Your argument is a very good one as a matter of political science, and it would be a very fine one as a matter of Constitutional and probably

statutory law—except hasn't your client dealt himself out of that argument by what has been done in the creation of the Special Prosecutor?"

All this makes one wonder whether a President in trouble would ever
again establish a Special Prosecutor. St. Clair argues that the President
is the prosecutor, and that only he can decide what material is needed.
"If anything, a decision in this case against the President would tend to
diminish the democratic process," St. Clair argues. He continues, "This
President ought not to have any less powers than any other President
ought to have," and he says, "One of the necessary results as I view them
from my brother's argument is that because of the circumstances of this
case, Richard Nixon is, let's say, an eighty-five-percent President, not a
one-hundred-percent President. And that can't be, Constitutionally. The
framers of the Constitution had in mind a strong Presidency."

St. Clair is doing his best, using his wits, but he has a difficult argument to make. He served as a staff assistant to Joseph N. Welch, the
special Army counsel at the McCarthy hearings in 1954. A member of a
highly regarded Boston law firm, he went to work for Nixon in January,
and now he is here. Gray-haired and gap-toothed, St. Clair is more
portly than he appears on television. One often wonders what he really
thinks. Other lawyers tell me they would insist upon seeing (or hearing) their client's best evidence, even if the client were the President.
How has he felt in serving not just as the President's lawyer but also
as his public-relations man? How does he really feel about making the
circular argument he is making here—that the Special Prosecutor has
not shown that the tapes are relevant to the case, and that the Prosecutor
cannot show that the evidence he seeks is relevant, because he doesn't
know what is in the tapes?

Justice Powell, whose conservative philosophy embraces a feeling
for the preservation of institutions, is the focus of much attention today.
Powell has a good mind, and will be influential with the Court in this
case. And so it is noticed in this courtroom when Powell asks, "What
public interest is there in preserving secrecy with respect to a criminal
conspiracy?"

St. Clair says, "The answer, sir, is that a criminal conspiracy is criminal only after it's proven to be criminal."

It is also noticed when Chief Justice Warren Burger, Nixon's appointee, asks if Judge Sirica couldn't screen the tapes, to withhold parts that
are irrelevant or involve sensitive material.

Philip Lacovara, a thirty-year-old attorney in the Special Prosecutor's
office, mustachioed and wearing steel-rimmed glasses, makes the rebut-
tal argument for the Special Prosecutor's side. Lacovara, who has served
in the Solicitor General's office, knows how to deal with this court. He
takes the Justices' spoken concerns, and points that St. Clair may have
scored, and weaves them into a flowing argument for his side of the
case. Responding to Justice Powell's concern that this case might set a

precedent for other grand juries to name a President as an unindicted co-conspirator, and so might give "a politically motivated prosecutor . . . a rather far-reaching power," Lacovara concedes that this could be a problem but argues that "grand juries usually are not malicious" and "even prosecutors cannot be assumed to be malicious." He goes on, "We have a resilient society, where people can be trusted to sort out truth from falsehoods. . . . And I think the inherent dignity of the Presidential office on any incumbent provides him with a notable check against being defeated, or, as my colleague says, impeached by the action of a grand jury." He says, "This is perhaps the most notorious event—notorious case—in recent times." He says, "The President has not been displaced from office—he still is President, he still functions in accordance with his Constitutional powers." A subpoena is "a traditional, ordinary, prosaic remedy," he says, for "a trial that was brought to a head without regard to the impeachment inquiry." And he argues that the fact that there might be political consequences should not prevent a court ruling—that that argument would have prevented the court from deciding Marbury v. Madison. He cites the late Justice Felix Frankfurter, and he even manages to cite Rehnquist. He cites momentous decisions by the Supreme Court over the years, and says that in those cases "the Court understood its duty to interpret the Constitution." He continues, "That's all we ask for today. And we submit that this Court should fully, explicitly, and decisively"—he pauses, and then adds—"and definitively" uphold Judge Sirica's order that the tapes be produced.

Courtroom 6 of the United States District Court House, on Constituion Avenue, a short distance from Capitol Hill. The second courtroom of the day—the décor plainer and the proceedings more routine. But this afternoon John Ehrlichman is on the stand. Once, he was in virtual charge of the government. Now he is on trial here for his role in the break-in at Dr. Fielding's office. Ehrlichman, forty-nine, is wearing gold-rimmed aviator-style glasses, which seem new, and he is tanned and looks a bit heavier than when he was in power. But he has the same sure, confident style as before. He juts his chin forward and nods as he says, "Yes, sir," or corrects William Merrill, the Associate Special Prosecutor, who is trying this case, or even chastises Merrill. ("You have generalized from the specific; and I've watched you do it.")

Merrill, a fifty-one-year-old attorney from Detroit, is low-key, undramatic, and unruffled. He has wavy graying hair and wears dark-rimmed glasses; a Midwestern accent is detectable in his quiet voice. He reads from papers atop a briefcase atop a table, sometimes pausing at length between questions. Each man, in his own way—Merrill's unassuming, Ehrlichman's confident—is performing for the jury, the six men and six women who are the regular jurors, and who sit, with their six alternates, in the box on the left. Nine of the regular jurors are black.

Ehrlichman's chief attorney is William Frates, a middle-aged man with wavy hair and a Southern accent—Bebe Rebozo's attorney. (Ehrlichman has dropped John J. Wilson, who continues to serve as Haldeman's attorney.) Ehrlichman has also retained two black attorneys for this trial.

The arrangement in this courtroom is like a scene from *Separate Tables*. Ehrlichman's table is in the front. Behind it is a table where two other defendants, Bernard Barker and Eugenio Martinez, are seated with their attorneys. Martinez is slight, with curly gray hair and olive skin, and is nattily dressed. It has recently been reported that in connection with his various C.I.A. activities Martinez participated in some three hundred break-ins. Bernard Barker has a seedier look; he is stumpy and wears thick, tinted glasses. These historic figures—veterans of the break-ins at the Watergate and at Dr. Fielding's office—are suddenly very human-looking, not very interesting, and rather sad. Last week, Howard Hunt testified here that when he hired them for the Ellsberg break-in he told them it was an operation against a "traitor" to the country.

At a third table, off to the right, is Gordon Liddy. Liddy has a prison pallor, dark hair, and a dark mustache. His eyes dart about a lot, and he takes many notes. One wonders about the silent Liddy: what he knows, what he did, why he is keeping quiet. Judge Gesell's pinkish face is slightly rounder than it appears in photographs, and his glasses sometimes slip down his button nose. Ehrlichman is charged with, among other things, lying to the grand jury when he said he did not know that before the break-in the C.I.A. had been asked by the White House plumbers to prepare a psychological profile of Ellsberg. (The profile said that Ellsberg had acted out of patriotic motives in leaking the Pentagon Papers, so the C.I.A. was asked to prepare another psychological profile. The second profile said that the leaking of the Pentagon Papers was an "act of aggression" against his father, against Lyndon Johnson—whom he identified with his father—and against his analyst.) Ehrlichman is asked about the memorandum in which Egil Krogh and David Young, the directors of the plumbers, proposed "a covert operation . . . to examine all the medical files still held by Ellsberg's psychoanalyst"—the memorandum that Ehrlichman initialled, adding the notation "If done under your assurance that it is not traceable." This memo is one of several "overt acts" cited in the indictment.

Today, Ehrlichman says that he did not explore the "philosophical or deeper meaning" of the word "examine." Ehrlichman also says, "I was simply reasserting our understanding that these people would not be identified as White House people."

Ehrlichman says that when Krogh told him of the break-in, Krogh said that Hunt and Liddy or people obtained by them had gone into Dr. Fielding's office to get Ellsberg's psychiatric records, that they hadn't found them, that they had attempted to mask what they had done by tearing up the place to make it look as if a burglar had been after drugs. (Krogh has said that he and Ehrlichman were upset when they saw pictures of the damage that had been done to Dr. Fielding's office; it has never been clear whether their perturbation was over the break-in or over the damage.) Ehrlichman says that he told Krogh, "It was incredibly bad judgment."

Liddy grimaces.

And then Merrill asks Ehrlichman a series of questions in rapid succession:

"Did you ever report this to the Beverly Hills Police Department?"

"No."

"Did you ask Mr. Krogh to report it to the Beverly Hills Police Department?"

"No, I certainly didn't."

"Did you instruct Mr. Krogh to write a memorandum about it and how it had all happened?"

"No, I didn't."

"Did you write a memorandum about it?"

"No."

"Did you advise the Department of Justice about it?"

"Did I? No, I did not."

Merrill asks Ehrlichman if after that Labor Day weekend in 1971, when the break-in occurred, Ehrlichman informed the President of what happened.

"I discussed it with the President."

"When?"

"In March of 1973."

It is steaming hot outside this afternoon; the temperature is in the nineties, and we are having our first air-pollution alert of the summer.

The Dow-Jones average declined twenty-one points today—to its lowest point in three and a half years.

Charles Colson went to jail today. Asked what reading material he was taking, he replied, "I have a couple of editions of the Bible with me. That's all."

JULY 9

The partisan lines within the Judiciary Committee are said to be "hardening." The talk is that the "drift" is against the committee, against impeachment by the House, and perhaps even against a committee vote to impeach. The Southern Democrats—particularly Flowers—are said to be uncertain about how they will vote. Barbara Jordan, Democrat of Texas, is said to be uncertain. There are other things—

whitecaps, perhaps—strengthening the sense that the current is against definitive action by the committee. What Democratic leaders fear most is a partisan vote for impeachment. There is even some thought among Democrats—not well formed yet, but there—of having the President censured rather than impeached. Around Washington, one is aware of a growing doubt—even among those who have favored impeachment— whether it is worth it all anymore. There is a growing fatigue with the whole thing. There is an increasing desire to turn it off—if the people who wish to could only figure out how. The extent to which the diminished interest in seeing it through is fed by fears of failure is not clear, because people do not express those fears very much. But they are there. Many people feel that it would be worse to lose this fight than not to go through with it. To lose this fight might be to condone the Administration's actions, and to vindicate Nixon. (An aide has said that Nixon would be "magnanimous" if he was vindicated. The transcripts leave another impression.) Some of the fears may result from the realization that decisions of great moment are almost upon us. Decisions are going to be made this summer which will determine what kind of country this will be far into the future.

It is not surprising that many of the Judiciary Committee members are, or appear, indecisive. The decision they face is a formidable one. Moreover, it is in the nature of the political mind—most such minds, at least—to put off the big decisions. The political mind is opportunistic, rides the wave of the moment, avoids the difficult decisions until they must be made. With luck, they may not have to be. The Democrats fear a partisan proceeding. The fears of the Republicans are more complex. The fear of that supposed twenty-five percent of the Party who are die-hard Nixon supporters doesn't quite explain it. I talked today with an important Republican who is in touch with members of various segments of the Party. He predicted that impeachment would fail in the House.

I asked what had become of the Republicans' desire to have Nixon out of office.

He said that there was a big difference between wishing the President out of office and voting to impeach him—"a one-hundred-and-eighty-degree difference." A Republican member of Congress who voted to impeach, he explained, would have to spend a great deal of time during his reëlection campaign explaining the vote. If he voted against impeachment, the Republican candidate could say that the evidence was not sufficient, and then he could get on with talking about other issues. This man said that the estimate that twenty-five percent of the Republican voters are unyielding in their support of Nixon is probably too high. He added that Republican politicians like to inflate this figure and exaggerate the amount of mail they receive, so that people will be impressed by the difficult spot they are in. The amount of mail that the politicians are receiving on this issue is not all that high, he said. However, he said, it would not take very many Nixon supporters to give a Republican who had voted for impeachment a hard time. All that would be needed would be two or three people at each political meeting raising questions, making the candidate defend his vote. Politicians know that, he said.

Furthermore, this man explained, Republican leaders across the country—such as the county chairmen—are by no means united on the question of whether it would be preferable for Nixon to leave office. Some do not want Ford as the incumbent in 1976, because they are for Rockefeller, or Reagan, or want to stay loose. Rockefeller has been travelling about the country cultivating local Republican leaders. For Republican leaders, the 1976 nomination is the highest stake. Therefore, he went on, there are many Republican leaders who, in pursuit of the longer-range goal of the 1976 nomination, would not mind—as the specifically affected members of Congress would—Republican congressional losses in November. In fact, he said, there are those Republicans who would not mind at all if in the next two years there was an overwhelmingly Democratic Congress, on which to place much of the blame for whatever goes wrong.

There is another factor in the county chairmen's minds, this man said. Many perquisites can flow from the party in power, and the person who is in power can determine the course of that flow. Given the right flow, the county chairman can be the one to parcel out such attractive and lucrative federal largesse as the designation of who will do the Federal Housing Administration or Veterans Administration home-loan closings in that area. These perquisites are of more value to the county chairman than such things as federal judgeships, this man explained. Right now, with CREEP demolished and the President clinging for dear life to what remains of his Party support, the county chairmen are doing rather nicely in obtaining such benefits through the Republican National Committee. A new President might—as most Presidents have done in the past—establish his own structure for consolidating power within the Party, with federal largesse as an instrument.

This man, who knows Nixon, said that the President would never resign. He said that he had never met anyone in politics who was as tough as Nixon. He suggested that this might be because Nixon had such a difficult early life—a harder life, this man said, than any other President he could think of. The difficulties of Nixon's early life—the poverty, the tuberculosis-stricken brothers, the father's business failures—had, he said, made the President incredibly disciplined, tough. Trouble can affect people in different ways, and the way it seems to have affected Nixon is to have given him a very hard shell. Said this man, "He is not bothered by things that would get to other men. There is no group he would listen to. No group. No one. Not his wife. Not Bebe. No one. He doesn't read the messages sent to him in the press. God, he's tough!"

It seems possible as of now that the White House is getting through to the people—that its repeated attacks on the Judiciary Committee, its assertions that its problems have been brought about by the "media" are sinking in. This period makes one think about where public relations ends and propaganda begins.

The committee's version of the transcripts of eight conversations which have already been released by the White House shows the President saying on March 13th, in response to his own question as to whether it was too late to "go the hang-out road," "Yes, it is." The White House version did not have any answer. The committee version shows the President saying, "The hang-out road's going to have to be rejected. I, some, I understand it was rejected." The White House version of this was "The hang-out road (inaudible)." On March 21st, according to the committee version, the President says about Hunt's demand for money, "We should buy the time." The White House version had the President saying, "We can buy the time." The committee transcript has the President referring to the possibility that Hunt may "squeal." The White House transcript doesn't. The committee transcript also shows that on March 22nd (the meeting in which the President and his aides discussed the nature of the "hang-out"—whether it would be, as Haldeman and Dean described it, a "limited hang-out" or, as Ehrlichman suggested, a "modified limited hang-out"), when the President instructed Mitchell to "stonewall," he went on to say, "On the other hand . . . I would prefer, as I said to you, that you do it the other way. And I would particularly prefer to do it that other way if it's going to come out that way anyway." But then the President also said, "But that's, uh, you know, up to this point, the whole theory has been containment, as you know, John." In the White House transcript, the President, discussing the appearance of some of his aides before the Watergate grand jury, said, "But you can say I don't remember." In the Judiciary Committee version, the President says, "Just be damned sure you say I don't remember."

Yesterday, Ron Ziegler accused the committee of having embarked upon a "hypoed public-relations campaign."

The amount of material with which we are being bombarded now is simply getting out of hand. The Judiciary Committee has released the first eight of eighteen beige-bound volumes of evidence, and today three fat green-covered volumes constituting the final report of the Ervin committee arrive. The Judiciary Committee volumes, entitled "Statement of Information," lay out the case the way Doar did before the committee: statement of fact and supporting evidence following statement of fact and supporting evidence. The first eight volumes cover the Watergate break-in and cover-up. The Ervin-committee report is for release on Sunday.

The Judiciary Committee's presentation begins with memos from Gordon Strachan, Haldeman's deputy, about the fact that "Operation Sandwedge," a plan to form a covert intelligence unit through a private security organization to be established by John Caulfield [and to include Rose Mary Woods' brother, Joseph, a former Sheriff of Cook County, Illinois, and a former F.B.I. agent], had fallen through, and mentioning that "The Attorney General discussed with John Dean the need to develop a political intelligence capability," and that Gordon Liddy, who had been working in the White House, would become general counsel to the Finance Committee to Re-Elect the President, and would "handle political intelligence as well as legal matters. Liddy will also work with Dean on the 'political enemies' project." In his Dictabelt recording about the meeting on March 21st, the President said, "The, uh, very great danger [is] that somebody like H-Hunt is going to blow." The President also told the Dictabelt: "I learned for the first time that, uh, Ehrlichman apparently had sent Hunt and his crew out to check into Ellsberg, uh, to see something about his, uh, check something about his, uh, uh, psychiatric problem with his doctor, or something like that. That seemed to me to be a very curious junket for, uh, Ehrlichman to be involved in." The President has said that he was told about this for the first time on March 17th, and the transcripts show him discussing the Ellsberg break-in with Dean on that date. This Dictabelt was volunteered to the court by the President when the White House said that the Dictabelt of another meeting with Dean was missing.

On a CBS News Special Report last night about the newly released committee evidence, Ron Ziegler said that "to release all the material dribble by dribble . . . in my view manipulates public opinion." Said Ziegler, "One reason why I can spot a public-relations campaign is I know one when I see one."

John Ehrlichman was found guilty today of conspiracy and perjury in connection with the break-in at Dr. Fielding's office. Barker, Martinez, and Liddy were also found guilty of conspiracy.

I wondered what impact the release of all the material was having on House members. The moderate Republican told me, "None. Zero. Nobody really understands it. Nobody but the committee has taken the time to listen or read. Around here, it's the same old refrain: they want to wait until the committee makes its recommendations. When I read in the papers about the comparative transcripts, I nearly jumped out of my skin, but I came down here and found people yawning. There is a feeling that the moment of truth is not here yet. We have given our proxies to the Judiciary Committee. The whole issue still seems kind of remote. It's strange and it's scandalous; it's sort of as if we had parked our morals on some obscure shelf."

JULY 14

Sunday. On Friday, when the Ervin committee met with the press for the last time to distribute its report, Sam Ervin, referring to the fact that in the light of the House Judiciary Committee's consideration of impeachment the report refrained from drawing ultimate conclusions about whether the President had carried out his Constitutional responsibilities in an acceptable manner, said, "There are two ways to indicate a horse. One is to draw a picture that is a great likeness. And the other is to draw a picture that is a great likeness and write under it 'This is a horse.' We just drew the picture."

The report raised again a question that we had almost forgotten, and one that the House Judiciary Committee, for its own reasons, is treating only peripherally—the question of whether in 1972 we had a genuine election. Ervin, in a section of the report setting forth his own separate views, wrote that the first objective of the "various illegal and unethical activities" studied by the committee was "to destroy insofar as the Presidential election of 1972 was concerned the integrity of the process by which the President of the United States is nominated and elected." The report covered the extensive intelligence-gathering by the Administration, beginning soon after Nixon's inauguration in 1969 (the committee has also found that John Caulfield and Anthony Ulasewicz, the private White House detectives, carried out some seventy investigations); it said that the Watergate break-in had to be seen in the context of other White House activities, including the Huston plan and the plumbers; it spoke of the "misuse of large amounts of money, especially difficult-to-trace cash that was held in secret places in the White House and elsewhere"; it talked of the use of the I.R.S., the F.B.I., and the C.I.A. for political purposes (it said that the I.R.S. was "a preferred target of the White House staff in its attempts to politicize independent agencies"); it mentioned the "Responsiveness Program," in which there was an attempt to shape the activities of departments and agencies in ways that would help the President's reëlection; it dealt with milk and with the sale of ambassadorships; it alleged that some money that Rebozo had sworn was turned over to the Nixon campaign committee was actually diverted to pay for improvements on the Nixon properties (including a swimming pool and a new roof extension) and to buy a pair of platinum-and-diamond earrings (costing $5,650) for Mrs. Nixon.

Among the proposals that the Ervin committee made was one for the establishment of a permanent "public attorney," to be appointed by the judiciary and confirmed by the Senate. The committee also recommended curbs on intelligence-gathering activities in the White House, prohibition of the examination of tax returns of others by anyone in the executive office, prohibition of wiretapping without court orders, and a number of new regulations covering campaign activities.

And so this committee, which in its fumbling way fixed in the public mind an indelible picture of abuse of power, has gone out of business, and left the country an agenda worth thinking about. The question is whether the people and the politicians will want to think about it.

After meeting with the President at San Clemente yesterday, Vice-President Ford said that there is a "possibility" that the Judiciary Committee may vote to impeach the President but that he does not consider the committee to be reflective of the House, and that he felt "strongly" that the House would reject impeachment, because "the preponderance of the evidence favors the President."

JULY 18

Commenting on Charles Colson's elusive testimony before the Judiciary Committee this week, Caldwell Butler, the Republican from Virginia, said, "He seems to be trying to be candid, but he hasn't had much experience in that area." Kalmbach's testimony this week about how the dairy representatives had had to reaffirm their two-million-dollar commitment—in a midnight meeting with Kalmbach and Murray Chotiner at the Madison Hotel here—before the price-support increase was announced was said by several committee members to have been very damaging. Although the committee is not expected to include the milk episode in its list of charges, Kalmbach's testimony seems to have contributed to a darkening picture in many members' minds of the way business was conducted in the White House. Trent Lott, the Mississippi Republican, who is a strong supporter of the President, remarked that Kalmbach's testimony gave "more of an impression . . . that there was some sort of understanding." Lott added, "I'd just as soon he hadn't said some of the things he said." Kalmbach told the committee of arrangements with three people for contributions in exchange for ambassadorships. Of that testimony, Lawrence Hogan, the Republican from Maryland, said, "This is the most damaging stuff I've heard yet."

Many of the witnesses, it may be remembered, were called at the behest of St. Clair, and the Democrats feared a display of them on television. (Rodino achieved the trade-off of closed hearings in exchange for calling all the witnesses on St. Clair's list. One of these—Haldeman—refused to testify.) But if those witnesses were supposed to somehow demolish the case against the President, they have apparently failed to do so. One Democratic member thinks that perhaps the witnesses who might have helped the Administration fell flat because they had nothing new to say. As for Dean, whose questioning by St. Clair yielded little, the member said, "Dean knew exactly what he was going to say. He has been saying it for a long time." Dean remained cool and poised, and impressed the members with what appeared to be a good memory. Robert McClory said, "He has done very well in the face of very skillful cross-examination. He was a damaging witness as far as the President was concerned."

In this, the last week before the committee begins consideration of the articles of impeachment, the tension and the frayed nerves have been even more apparent—and so have the theatrics. One can hear the tension in the voices of the committee members, and even of the usually polite members of their now overworked staffs. The committee has been meeting evenings. Last night, a committee member I had called returned my call at ten-forty-five—he had just returned home after the committee recessed—and said, "I haven't signed any mail. I haven't done a damn thing. We get only a half hour for dinner now. Everybody is kind of on edge now." On Tuesday, Charles Wiggins told reporters that he expected all the committee Republicans to vote against impeachment. Some Republicans (and committee staff members as well) interpreted this as a form of pressure and went into a state of high dudgeon. Railsback told reporters that he and "at least" three other Republicans—Cohen, Fish, and Butler—would remain undecided until they heard St. Clair's and the committee lawyers' final arguments. Cohen asserted that Wiggins was not speaking for him. McClory told reporters that he wanted to be on the undecided list, too. (Some skeptics thought that this was because the Republican "undecideds" are now the center of attention—might even be on the cover of next week's *Time.*) McClory told reporters he was troubled by the fact that "so many of those who were in the White House are now in jail or have completed their terms or are awaiting sentence." Said McClory, "There was obviously wrongdoing taking place right under the President's nose, and I'm very concerned. Is that any way to run a White House?"

While Albert Jenner conducted the questioning of Kalmbach, John Doar remained in the inquiry-staff offices writing his summary of the case and continuing to prepare articles of impeachment. Doar wants to show the committee the patterns now—to get across such things as the Administration's pattern of establishing deniability. What one staff aide calls "the consciousness-raising sessions"—briefings of committee members by staff members—are taking place in the mornings and at night. Doar has had sessions with Flowers, Mann, Ray Thornton (Arkansas Democrat), and Barbara Jordan. Mann and Flowers are said to be especially uncertain. Doar has shown Mann the articles—referred to as the R (for Rodino) articles—that will be placed before the committee; the other members of the committee have not seen them. Rodino has had talks with Thornton and Flowers. Some Democratic members, including Elizabeth Holtzman, Jack Brooks, and Don Edwards, have prepared articles. Paul Sarbanes (Maryland Democrat) has prepared a sort of outline of the case, covering a spectrum of misbehavior, including the number of times the President has lied to the public about the events that the committee has been looking into. Ad-hoc strategy meetings of Rodino and other Democrats take place just before committee meetings, or on the House floor during votes.

Some of the Republican "undecideds" have been talking among themselves. Cohen and Butler, who sit next to each other in committee meetings, have been talking over the case during the hearings. Cohen and Railsback have gone out to dinner twice this week, and once Charles Sandman joined them. Last Sunday, Cohen and Fish met at Cohen's house with Richard Cates, the inquiry-staff expert on the cover-up, and three members of the minority staff. Some members noticed a different, tougher tone in Hogan's questioning of Kalmbach last night.

On Tuesday, Republicans asked Jenner to draw up a summary replying to Doar's and making the arguments against impeachment. Jenner refused, saying that his role was to provide "a professional opinion to a client, which is the entire committee." He told reporters that what he was doing was part of a Constitutional process, involving the highest privilege in the Constitution—impeachment—and that what was called for was the judgment of a lawyer with a professional responsibility to the committee and to the people.

St. Clair presented his final argument against impeachment to the committee today, saying that no case had been made against the President on any of the charges. And he offered an excerpt from a transcript of a conversation of March 22nd—the tape of which was subpoenaed by the committee and refused by the President. The excerpt quoted the President as saying, "I don't mean to be blackmailed by Hunt—that goes too far." St. Clair told reporters that elsewhere in the meeting the President "indicated it would be right to pay money to Hunt for humanitarian purposes." Which doesn't seem to help the President's case.

The volumes of the committee's evidence have continued to pour forth this week. They tell of White House pressures on the I.R.S. to audit a list of McGovern supporters, to place Caulfield and Liddy in sensitive I.R.S. positions, to create tax problems for Lawrence O'Brien when he was chairman of the Democratic National Committee—all of them pressures that, according to affidavits supplied by two former I.R.S. commissioners, were resisted. The committee says that the President met with Haldeman and Dean on September 15, 1972, to discuss "taking steps to overcome the unwillingness of the I.R.S. to follow up on complaints," and Dean has said that he discussed the O'Brien case with the President. The committee evidence also shows that Ehrlichman complained to I.R.S. Commissioner Johnnie M. Walters, when Walters reported that he considered the O'Brien case closed, "I'm god-dam tired of your foot-dragging tactics." (The Ervin committee had quoted Ehrlichman as saying in executive session, "I wanted them to turn up something and send [O'Brien] to jail before the election, and unfortunately it didn't materialize.") And that Haldeman invoked the President's name in asking another White House aide to obtain informa-tion from the I.R.S. about the tax problems of George Wallace's brother Gerald, which was then leaked to Jack Anderson, the columnist. And that Mitchell, while he was Attorney General, apparently passed on ambassadorships. ("Concerning ambassadorships," Gordon Strachan wrote to Haldeman on December 2, 1971, in one of several memoranda about how the 1972 campaign would be organized, "Kalmbach will get a case by case determination from the Attorney General." In another memo, Strachan wrote that two donations "should be returned, since the European commitments cannot now be met.")

The committee evidence also contains memoranda indicating that Kissinger was concerned about news leaks in 1969 and asked Hoover if he could make an effort to find where they had come from, and that this was followed by a visit to the F.B.I. by Haig, then Kissinger's deputy, who proposed names of people to be tapped, and that shortly thereafter Kissinger went to the F.B.I. offices to read the logs of the taps. It shows that subsequently the President, Kissinger, Haldeman, and Ehrlichman received reports on the taps. It shows that Haldeman later requested the reinstitution of a tap of a member of the National Security Council. It states that none of the members of the National Security Council who were tapped were found to have been the source of the leaks that perturbed their superiors, nor were the other tapped White House staff members found to have leaked classified information. It shows that the President ordered the tapping of a television commentator. (Mitchell also requested physical surveillance of the commentator but was dis-suaded by the F.B.I.).

Not all of the taps were carried out through the F.B.I.: John Ehrlichman directed Caulfield to have a tap placed on the phone of columnist Joseph Kraft, and we have already learned that the Secret Service tapped the President's brother, Donald. The committee evi-dence indicates that the F.B.I. tapping program was terminated in 1971 at the insistence of Hoover. (One reason suggested for this particular timing was that Hoover was about to testify before Congress and cus-tomarily preferred to give a low figure for the number of taps that were being maintained.) The evidence also shows that about January, 1970, Ehrlichman, apparently referring to the use of information that the committee said was "contained in one of the summaries of the 1969-71 wiretaps to be used in connection with political action in opposition to persons critical of the Administration's Vietnam policy," wrote in a memo to Haldeman, "H. This is the kind of early warning we need more of. Your game planners are now in an excellent position to map anticipatory action."

The President is in San Clemente.

JULY 19

John Doar summarized the case against the President before the Judiciary Committee today. He said, "Reasonable men acting reasonably would find the President guilty." Speaking with unaccustomed passion, Doar talked of the President's "enormous crimes," and said that he could not remain indifferent if President Nixon or any other President committed "the terrible deed of subverting the Constitution." Jenner supported Doar's argument, and told the committee members that they had an obligation to live up to the ideals of the nation's founders and to determine "whether that country and that Constitution are to be preserved." In addition to the written summary of the case, Doar submitted several sets of articles of impeachment, of which one set, the work of Doar and the staff, contained four articles—the R articles. They would impeach the President for the cover-up; for "a pattern of massive and persistent abuse of power for political purposes involving unlawful and un-Constitutional invasion of the rights and privacy of individual citizens of the United States," including the break-in at Dr. Fielding's office, unlawful surveillance and wiretapping, and attempted use the I.R.S. for political purposes; for failure to comply with the committee's subpoenas; and for the "fraud" of backdating the deed of his Vice-Presidential papers for the purposes of taking tax deductions.

The article on taxes is a surprise, but Rodino and his staff feel that the tax issue is an "attractive" one, and also one that, since the Special Prosecutor is now looking into the matter of the President's taxes and finances, should be kept alive until the case reaches the Senate. The tax article says that other investigations—by the I.R.S. and the Joint Committee on Internal Revenue Taxation—were thwarted "solely by reason of the fact that Richard M. Nixon was President of the United States and that impeachment proceedings against him had been instituted."

A second set of articles, also drafted by the staff, makes similar charges against the President, each article charging that the actions were in violation of the President's oath of office and his "duty to take care that the laws be faithfully executed." The staff has still other drafts, which it has not submitted. And articles drafted by members have been submitted. The idea now is to put articles before the members, for them to talk about and think about over the next few days, and see what sort of consensus might arise. The committee will meet again tomorrow—Saturday.

On television tonight, Ron Ziegler, at San Clemente, is clearly much upset. He looks stung. He calls Doar a "partisan ideologue," who has been proceeding in a "partisan, duplicitous, false way." Ziegler says that there is no justification for the fact that the articles were drawn up before all the evidence was presented, and that Doar has proceeded as if he were operating "a kangaroo court."

19

Monday morning. A bright, clear day—not too warm. This is the week that will have been. By the end of the week, according to the House Judiciary Committee's predictions, it will have voted on articles of impeachment. Over the weekend, members of the committee have been considering the articles offered by the staff last Friday, and studying the three-hundred-and-six-page summary of the case presented that same day by Doar, when he recommended that the President be impeached. Since Jenner, on the ground of his own belief, had refused a request by the committee Republicans to present the case against impeachment, Jenner's deputy, Sam Garrison, a thirty-two-year-old Virginia attorney and former member of Vice-President Agnew's staff, has prepared an anti-impeachment argument and will present it to the committee this morning. The President has now been in San Clemente for ten days, on a "working vacation." According to his aides, he has been taking long walks on the beach, swimming, and working on the economy. His aides, meanwhile, have been continuing their attacks on the committee. Following up the "kangaroo-court" accusation by Ron Ziegler, Dean Burch called the committee's proceedings "a black spot on jurisprudence." He added that the President himself thought the committee had acted unfairly. Within the next few days, the Supreme Court is expected to rule on the question of whether the President must surrender the tapes subpoenaed by Special Prosecutor Leon Jaworski. During the noon recess today, the committee Democrats will caucus to plan the debate on the articles. Nobody seems to have a clear idea of just what form the debate will take. This process is still being invented.

This morning, on the steps of the Capitol, Neil Salonen, president of the National Prayer and Fast Committee, is holding a press conference. He is wearing a red button that says "NATIONAL PRAYER AND FAST," and an American-flag pin is in his lapel. A few dozen people are with him, and he says that six hundred are expected. The committee was founded in late 1973 by the Reverend Sun Myung Moon, the evangelist from Korea whose followers have been turning up for the President at crucial moments since then. At twelve-fifteen, Mr. Salonen says, Rabbi Baruch Korff will arrive and express solidarity with this group. The

White House has worked closely with Rabbi Korff, helping him to organize his National Citizens Committee for Fairness to the Presidency. Most of the people standing on the Capitol steps with Mr. Salonen are young, wearing heavy suits with flags in their lapels. Most of them stand very quietly, looking intent. This group has an ascetic look—a look of religiosity and apartness. They look neither like the anti-war demonstrators nor like the clean-cut young Nixonians who turned up at the 1972 Republican Convention shouting "Four more years!" Members of the Prayer and Fast Committee will maintain a three-day prayer vigil this week for individual members of Congress, hoping, Mr. Salonen says, that "God's will will be revealed" to them. Under questioning, one of several public-relations representatives of the Prayer and Fast Committee says, "Many people feel that it is God's will that the President should not be impeached."

The striking thing is how little demonstrating over this issue—this issue that was to inflame public passions—there has been. Aside from the people on the Capitol steps, hardly anyone is here, and Rabbi Korff and Reverend Moon do not, to put it politely, seem to represent great masses of Americans. And no one is marching on the Capitol *for* impeachment. There seems to be some unspoken understanding that marching is not in order. And many Americans seem not to care, or to figure that the politicians will or will not handle it. Many are on vacation, or are home worrying about inflation. And so the country is not, as so many predicted, being, "torn apart" by the question of impeachment.

Shortly after noon, the members of the House Judiciary Committee come out of Room 2141 of the Rayburn Building, and, as usual, the reporters pursue them. The members and reporters are tired; the reporters have had to do all that reading of the committee's material. Some members of Rabbi Korff's organization have been assigned to individual committee members. A black woman pursues Barbara Jordan, the black Democratic representative from Texas, down the hall. The woman says to Barbara Jordan, "I'm for the President." Miss Jordan, her face grim, fatigued, continues her determined stride, shoulders forward, down the corridor, and turns her head to snap at the pursuing woman, "A lot of people are."

In a crowded elevator in the Rayburn Building, a woman wearing a button that says "GET OFF THE PRESIDENT'S BACK" and carrying a small American flag says to Tom Railsback, "Do you think it's fair to convict the President on circumstantial evidence?" Reporters are questioning Railsback as the elevator descends to the subway level of the building. The elevator is filled with elbows and notebooks and purses and the flag. The lady with the button and the flag says to Railsback, "Please be fair and have a clear conscience when you vote." She is pleasant, and smiles when she says these things.

Over lunch, Railsback tells me, "I've discovered that some of the key undecided people seem to be focussing on the same areas. Walter Flowers is concerned about the use of agencies and about the cover-up, and those are what I've been interested in." Railsback says that he began talking with Flowers a couple of weeks ago. "I visited with Caldwell Butler, and I visited with Ham Fish. I had a briefing from Dick Cates [Richard Cates, the inquiry-staff expert on the cover-up]. I've been going through the staff summary, which I think has been very well done. Some of us had a little discussion meeting; it wasn't very planned." Last week, Butler and Railsback had lunch, and Railsback and Cohen had lunch, and Fish and Butler and Cohen had lunch and Railsback joined them later. (Railsback had been getting a briefing from an inquiry-staff member on the President's involvement with Henry Petersen when Petersen was in charge of the Watergate investigation.)

It is now considered possible that these Republicans will vote for impeachment; these meals may turn out to have been of great importance. One evening last week, Railsback, Butler, and committee members George Danielson (Democrat of California) and Charles Sandman (Republican of New Jersey) went out for dinner. Sometimes the members talked about their impressions of the witnesses. Railsback says that they felt sorry for Herbert Kalmbach—felt that he had been badly used by the Nixon Administration. When Butler, Cohen, Railsback, and Fish got together, they talked about what the evidence seemed to point to. This past weekend, Railsback took Raoul Berger's book *Impeachment: The Constitutional Problems* home with him. But in general, he says, broad Constitutional questions were not discussed among the members. "I had one discussion with McClory," he says. "He is very incensed over the noncompliance with the committee's subpoenas, and I am, too. It seems to me that if the Congress doesn't get the material we think we need and then votes to exonerate, we'll be regarded as a paper tiger. Let's face it. This whole thing deals with Presidential power and the excess of power. I think that the most serious charges against the President are the cover-up and the attempted misuse of the agencies. The misuse of the I.R.S. on a massive scale for political purposes poses a threat to individual rights and freedom. Over this weekend, as I thought very carefully about the staff presentation, I realized that there's a much better case on the Watergate cover-up than I'd thought there was. This was the first chance I'd had to put things in context. Whether the cover-up is of a magnitude to impeach him for is what I've got to decide. I want to read St. Clair's brief again and go through the staff brief again and see what I have."

Today, Railsback is wearing a navy-blue suit with two rows of white stitching around the lapels. Since he is a gregarious and political man, and seems to be leaning toward impeachment now, I ask him what he has been doing about staying in touch with House Republicans who do not serve on the Judiciary Committee.

"Some of the Republican members have been talking about getting together pretty quick," he says. He has talked with a number of them, including several conservatives—John Rhodes, the House Minority Leader, among them. "They are conservatives and friends," he says. "I advised them to wait until they hear all the evidence. I told them to keep their options open."

I ask him whether the committee's sentiment has undergone changes.

"I guess there were changes," Railsback replies. "After the staff presentation left Watergate, we went into these other things, where I didn't think they had a very good case—milk, I.T.T. And then we got back to Watergate and agency abuses. And then we got the staff summary of the case. It's one thing to have four great big volumes of evidence that tell you the facts about Watergate. It's another thing to have an advocate's brief that boils down the relevant facts and gives you legal theories. You get a much better picture of the case."

"And so it came together?" I ask.

"It's coming together," he replies. "Impeachment to a certain extent is going to depend on the articles that are drafted. They can't be too broad or too general." He says that the staff articles must be amended.

Railsback says that he hasn't told anyone his position yet.

I ask him if he has decided on it.

He replies, "I have suspicions. I do worry about the system. Is it working? Do the people think it's working? I'll tell you something else I worry about. I worry about what happens to Pat Nixon and Julie Eisenhower. I worry about that. What effect does this have on them? I don't seem to have that same feeling about the President himself, for one reason: he has not been contrite. He has not been remorseful; he has not been repentant. He has never admitted that he has made a mistake."

I ask if he worries about the consequences for the future as he considers whether the President should be impeached.

"Yes," Railsback replies. "I put myself in the position of being on the receiving end. Suppose we have a Democratic President who wants to harass Republican congressmen and senators and their supporters. Suppose we have a Democratic President who wants to have my tax returns audited. I wouldn't like it. I find it very offensive. I don't care if it's been done before. I don't think it's been done on this massive a scale."

Of the several conversations I've had with Railsback, this is the first one in which he has alluded to the Internal Revenue Service; clearly he has come to think of this—and rather recently—as an important issue. He also refers to the conversation among the President, Haldeman, and Dean on September 15, 1972, when the President told Dean that after the election they would use the agencies, including the F.B.I. and the

Justice Department, against their opponents. And Dean replied, "What an exciting prospect." "The Watergate cover-up is an understandable, human thing—trying to protect your own," Railsback continues. "Compare that to using agencies to harass political opponents and private citizens."

Walking back to his office with him, I ask Railsback what his thinking is on the activities of the plumbers—specifically, the break-in at the office of Daniel Ellsberg's psychiatrist.

"The President told Petersen to stay out of it," he replies. "That's his direct connection with that. He set up the unit that did it. He found out about it afterward. He didn't tell anyone about it. The government didn't offer to pay Fielding. The only way we found out about it was through Kleindienst's insistence that the Justice Department had to inform the trial judge of the break-in."

And then Railsback goes back to talking about the use of agencies. "I don't like the big federal government playing around with people's lives—newsmen, political contributors. That's not the purpose of government." A conservative thought. It is clear how this is coming together in Railsback's mind, and where he is going.

During the walk to his office, I ask Railsback to describe the pressures he has been receiving from his district.

He replies, "People say, 'I'm not going to vote for you.'" He smiles. "Some say, 'What's happened to Tom? He's said he'll impeach the President.' My defenders say, 'No, he hasn't.' What'll they say if I vote to impeach him?" And he smiles again.

JULY 23

Last night, in San Clemente, St. Clair held a televised press conference, at which he said that the Judiciary Committee staff had "assumed the role of prosecutor." Under insistent questioning, he refused to say whether the President would comply with a Supreme Court ruling on the tapes.

How, I have been wondering, will the Democrats be able to persuade contemporary Americans, and history, that this was not a partisan proceeding, which reached a partisan conclusion? I put the question this morning to Paul Sarbanes, a Democratic member of the committee from Baltimore, who is in his second term in the Congress. In the 1970 Democratic primary in Maryland, Sarbanes successfully challenged a longtime incumbent, who was then also chairman of the House Public Works Committee. A graduate of Princeton (where he was a friend of Ralph Nader) and of the Harvard Law School, and also a former Rhodes Scholar, Sarbanes has one of the best minds on the committee. He has said little during the proceedings thus far—in itself a mark of wisdom—and when he has spoken up it has usually been to clarify a point.

Sarbanes answers my question about partisanship as we walk from the Rayburn Building to the Capitol, where the House Democrats are caucusing on the controversial issue of reorganizing the jurisdictions of House committees. (Proposals to reorganize the committees, which have not been reorganized since 1946, are in trouble because nobody wants to give up power.) "It can be partisan from either direction," he says. "You'll have to look at all the evidence and conclude what was the right decision. Maybe it's the person who looks at the evidence and votes the other way who is partisan. Why isn't it looked at in that light? That point hasn't been made. You have to engage in the ultimate evaluation. You have to look at the process and procedures the committee followed. The fact that Doar and Jenner, after they had been through the whole thing, said they felt there was sufficient evidence to impeach does not mean it was partisan. Probably, at some point, members said to themselves, 'What's going on here?' " And then Sarbanes—choosing a forceful and homey image—says, "It's like you go to your vegetable store and go over to the tomatoes and the first one is rotten and the next one is rotten and you go over to the other side of the bin and it's rotten, and then you try some other vegetables and they're the same way. After you've been through this for a while and it keeps happening, you say, 'What kind of a store is this?' You have the same thing here. At some point, after you look at this stuff, you say, 'What's going on here?' You have an abuse here, and there, and there, and then you have the question of how power is being exercised, by whom, on whose behalf, and by what standards. How were these Constitutional powers that were granted to the President being exercised? There is a difference between reading stories about all this and going through the presentation that Doar and Jenner put together. If there was a conflict in the information, they told us there was a conflict. You have a record before you that is firm as you press against it. You have a kind of substratum you're resting on."

A group of committee Democrats—including Rodino; Don Edwards, of California; John Conyers, of Michigan; and Sarbanes—is reported to be redrafting the articles prepared by the staff. The committee's debate on the articles is to begin tomorrow, but as of now no one knows when. It was originally to have begun in the morning, but there have been later reports that it will not begin until tomorrow evening. One reason, it is thought, is that the articles the committee will debate are not ready. Another may be that the committee leaders are attracted to the idea of beginning the debate in prime time.

At eight o'clock this morning, four committee Republicans (Railsback, Butler, Cohen, and Fish) met with the committee's three Southern Democrats (Mann, Thornton, and Flowers) in Railsback's office. At the moment, the meeting is still something of a secret. The group explored tentatively whether there was any solution to what they had seen which would be less severe than the impeachment of the President—such as censure—and decided that there was not. That point, the participants seemed to realize, had been passed. They also toyed briefly with the idea of delay, and realized that it was too late for that, too. They then agreed with little difficulty that they would support articles of impeachment on the cover-up and on abuse of power, if the articles were properly drafted. They would, they agreed, proceed within the framework of the staff articles, but they wanted the articles to encompass only charges that could be traced to Presidential action—a distinction that may be unreal, and a criterion that may be difficult to meet. The issue of the President's noncompliance with the committee's subpoenas would be, the group agreed, folded into the article on abuse of power. Mann had already prepared a new draft of the article on the abuse of power. The group will meet again this afternoon or tomorrow.

This group knows that it holds the critical votes on the committee. The votes of the Southern Democrats and of as many Republicans as possible have come to be considered crucial, in order to make a convincing case to the House—and the nation—that the articles of impeachment bridged partisan and philosophical differences. Working together, the members of this group could both provide each other with protective coloration ("Misery loves company," said one of the participants) and wield considerable power over Rodino and the other Democrats on the committee. Some members of the group say—and perhaps even believe—that what they finally do will depend on how the articles are drafted. But it is clear that they have passed the point of no return.

On the floor above the Judiciary Committee's meeting room—in Room 2237, where Rodino used to conduct his briefings for the press after the closed committee sessions—cameras are being set up for a press conference by Lawrence Hogan, the Maryland Republican member of the Judiciary Committee. There are eight television cameras and innumerable microphones. Reporters are fairly cynical about this event. They assume that Hogan has decided to vote for impeachment and is dramatizing the decision—announcing it before the debate opens tomorrow—because he is running for governor of Maryland. Hogan is not particularly well liked, so his move is seen as one of opportunism rather than as one of courage. Still, it is a major event, and the room is crowded.

Hogan, a conservative, is a sandy-haired man of medium build who was once an F.B.I. agent and then a public-relations man; he scowls a lot and has a reputation as a "law-and-order" man. As he enters the room with his wife, aides are passing out a mimeographed statement headed, like a report for school, "Why I Will Vote for Impeachment, by Congressman Lawrence J. Hogan." Hogan reads the statement, the television lights causing him to squint slightly. He slows up his reading when he reaches the point, on page 5, that says, "After having read and reread, sifted and tested the mass of information which came before us, I have come to the conclusion that Richard M. Nixon has, beyond a reasonable doubt, committed impeachable offenses which, in my judgment, are of sufficient magnitude that he should be removed from office." He continues, "The evidence convinces me that my President has lied repeatedly, deceiving public officials and the American people." Interesting that he begins his reasons with that one. He reads it with some feeling. "He has withheld information necessary for our system of justice to work," Hogan goes on. "Instead of coöperating with prosecutors and investigators, as he said publicly, he concealed and covered up evidence, and coached witnesses so that their testimony would show things that really were not true. He tried to use the C.I.A. to impede the investigation of Watergate by the F.B.I. He approved the payment of what he knew to be blackmail to buy the silence of an important Watergate witness. . . . I know that some of my financial contributors (who have staunchly supported Richard Nixon and me) will no longer support me. I know that some of my longtime campaign workers will no longer campaign for me." And then he quotes John F. Kennedy, saying that "sometimes party loyalty demands too much." To base the vote on politics, says Hogan, not only would violate his conscience "but would also be a breach of my own oath of office to uphold the Constitution of the United States."

When he is finished, he invites questions, and a reporter asks if he would be making the announcement "at this time" if he were not running for governor.

Hogan replies slowly, "I don't really know the answer to that. Perhaps not. But this is a no-win situation for any candidate this year."

After Hogan's press conference, Charles Wiggins, who had made some bets in favor of his prediction that all the Republicans on the committee would oppose impeachment, said to reporters, "I'm going to take a cold shower."

Representative Barber Conable, Republican of New York and an important member of the House, notices a knot of reporters in an elevator in the Capitol and says, "Join my bandwagon—of the undecideds." Conable is on to something. This is taking on the atmosphere of a political convention: rumors and announcements and back-room negotiations and talk of "erosion" in the President's position; media covering the media that are covering the event. Hogan's announcement, whatever its motivation, is the subject of a lot of conversation on the House floor this afternoon. A conservative has looked at the evidence and decided that this is how he will vote; the possibility that Hogan also considers this the politic position does not diminish its importance in the eyes of the politicians in the House.

In the subway between the Capitol and the Rayburn Building, Walter Flowers puts his hand on his stomach and says, "I'll tell you, for the first time since I was trying lawsuits ten years ago, I've got an ulcer."

It is a cool evening, and there is a light rain. On the Capitol steps, ten people are maintaining the prayer vigil for members of Congress.

JULY 24

Today, I have a seat in the Supreme Court chamber. At eleven o'clock, the Court is to issue a ruling, and the assumption is that it will be on the tapes. At ten-forty-seven, Leon Jaworski comes in. With him are Special Prosecutor's office staff members James Neal, who will try the case of the cover-up, and Philip Lacovara and Jill Wine Volner. By ten minutes to eleven, the large chamber is full. At two minutes after eleven, there are sudden sounds—the buzz of a buzzer and the bang of a gavel and a voice commanding "All rise." As the Justices file in, the voice, binding us to a distant past, says "Oyez, oyez, oyez," and ends with "God save the United States and this Honorable Court." Another bang. The Justices take their seats, and we take ours, and there is a dead stillness. Then Chief Justice Warren Burger gives a simple, brief history of the case. As he talks, quietly and unemotionally, some of the other Justices watch him, and others stare out into the chamber. They know what they have done. And then, as Burger continues to speak, one begins to sense what they have done. He affirms the Special Prosecutor's authority "to represent the United States as a sovereign." The Chief Justice says that "the District Court acted within its powers" in authorizing the Special Prosecutor's subpoena of the evidence. Then, quoting from Marbury v. Madison, 1803, he says, "It is emphatically the province and duty of the Judicial Department to say what the law is." He cites grounds for a President's claiming executive privilege, including "the need to protect the confidentiality of the communications of a President with his aides and advisers," and says that protection of the confidentiality of Presidential communications "is Constitutionally based." He cites cases upholding that claim, and then says, of those cases compared with the present one, "However, there are important differences." They "were not criminal cases." And here, he says, there is a "generalized, undifferentiated claim of executive privilege."

As we sit here in this cool chamber, we hear Chief Justice Burger— Nixon's appointee as Chief Justice—peel away the President's arguments one by one. A presumption of Presidential privilege, he says, "does not mean that all material in the possession of a President is immune in all circumstances from judicial process." He says, "No case of this Court has extended this high degree of deference to a President's generalized claim of the need of confidentiality." The claim, he says, must be weighed against the claims of "criminal justice." "We cannot conclude," he says, "that advisers will be moved to temper the candor of their remarks." At eleven-twenty, Chief Justice Burger says, "Accordingly, the judgment under review is affirmed." Bang. We stand. They are gone. The President has been ordered by a unanimous decision of the Supreme Court to give up the tapes.

In the Capitol, inevitably, the politicians are making statements in reaction to the Supreme Court's ruling. Henry Smith of New York, Republican member of the Judiciary Committee: "A whole new ballgame." Even if one isn't interested in their statements, one cannot escape them. Someone says McClory is in the television-radio gallery now. It is shortly before noon, and the group of seven "swing" members of the committee—the four Republicans and three Southern Democrats—are meeting in Railsback's office. The group has been discovered, and several reporters are waiting outside. Word comes that McClory says that the Court decision means that the committee ought to delay its proceedings. In Railsback's office, a secretary is saying to two constituents—very nicely—"I'm sure he'd like to talk to you. Time is the main problem." The group of seven is now going over the third version of its draft of Article I. It is talking about dropping the offering of clemency as one of the charges against the President, because there are several Presidential remarks in the transcripts which say there should not be clemency, and the group wants only clear-cut cases. It is talking about separating the charges of "destruction" of evidence from "concealment" of evidence, because some things were destroyed but not concealed and some were concealed but not destroyed. The group is not finished and will meet again this afternoon.

McClory's office is calling the offices of other committee Republicans, to test the sentiment for delaying the committee's proceedings.

It is after six and the compromise articles—based on negotiations between the "swing group" and the Democratic drafters—are still not ready, so some articles will be placed before the committee for the purpose of having articles there when the debate begins tonight, and the work on the compromise will continue. Says one tense Democrat, "This last-minute drafting is a very unpleasant way to do business."

From San Clemente, throughout the day, have come announcements that there would be a statement on the Supreme Court decision, and then announcements that the statement has been postponed. Finally, at seven o'clock, James St. Clair is on television, reading a statement by the President: "While I am, of course, disappointed in the result, I respect and accept the Court's decision, and I have instructed Mr. St.

Clair to take whatever measures are necessary to comply with that decision in all respects. For the future, it will be essential that the special circumstances of this case not be permitted to cloud the rights of Presidents to maintain the basic confidentiality without which this Office cannot function. I was gratified, therefore, to note that the Court reaffirmed both the validity and the importance of the principle of executive privilege, the principle I have sought to maintain." Says St. Clair, "As we all know, the President has always been a firm believer in the rule of law," and he adds that "the time-consuming process" of preparing the material to be submitted to the Court "will begin forthwith."

There aren't many people in the corridors of the Rayburn Building this evening as the formal impeachment proceedings are about to begin. Police are stopping people at the doors, and the security is tight. Members of the press have been given special green passes. There isn't a very long line of spectators outside, either. Inside the building, Charles Wiggins walks toward the committee room, holding his wife's hand. Walter Flowers is being interviewed for television. An American flag is in the lapel of his blue-gray jacket, and he is wearing red-white-and-blue saddle shoes. As the members take their place on the two-tiered dais in Room 2141, there is an exceptionally heavy crush of reporters and photographers surrounding them. It is seven-thirty—time for the meeting to begin. But, as is customary, it will begin late. This scene can't look very stately on television. A number of members are wearing blue shirts tonight, for the television cameras. John Doar is wearing a light-gray suit. Tall, and lanky, he moves slowly. Doar always manages to look calm. But the fatigue shows. His ordinarily expressionless face seems to grow more ashen, and to age, with each passing week. Albert Jenner is in a navy-blue suit. As usual, he is ruddy and smiling. Peter Rodino is in a gray suit with a blue shirt; the rosette of the Knights of Malta is in his lapel. Father Robert Drinan, the tall and generally stern-looking Democrat of Massachusetts, who sponsored an impeachment resolution as early as the summer of 1973, looks healthier and more relaxed than he has in weeks. James Mann looks tired.

Finally, the debate on President Nixon's impeachment begins. At seven-forty-five, Rodino bangs the gavel—for the benefit of the photographers, he bangs it three times—and calls the committee to order. In his introductory remarks, Rodino says, "Make no mistake about it. This is a turning point, whatever we decide." He seems to mean it. For months, when Rodino has talked to his colleagues and the press about the impeachment process, he has used language that placed it in its historical context and accorded it its full Constitutional seriousness, and tonight, as it enters its climactic stage, he talks of it this way to the nation. In the opening moments, he says, "Each generation of citizens and their officials have been faithful custodians of the Constitution and of the rule of law. For almost two hundred years, every generation of Americans has taken care to preserve our system. This committee must now decide a question of the highest Constitutional importance. For more than two years, there have been serious allegations, by people of good faith and sound intelligence, that the President, Richard M. Nixon, has committed grave and systematic violations of the Constitution." The framers of the Constitution, "in their determination that government be accountable and lawful, wrote into the Constitution a special oath that the President, and only the President, must take at his inauguration," he says. "In that oath, the President swears that he will 'take care that the laws be faithfully executed.' " And he quotes Edmund Burke during the impeachment trial of Warren Hastings, in 1788: " 'It is by this tribunal that statesmen who abuse their power are accused by statesmen and tried by statesmen, not upon the niceties of a narrow jurisprudence, but upon the enlarged and solid principles of state morality.' " Our Constitution is being put to the test, he says, and he adds, "Such tests, historically, have come to the awareness of most peoples too late." Then he says, "Let us go forward. Let us leave the Constitution as unimpaired for our children as our predecessors left it to us."

Rodino calls on Edward Hutchinson, of Michigan, the senior Republican on the committee. In the course of his introductory remarks, Hutchinson says, "Perhaps ours is more of a political than a judicial function after all."

At eight minutes after eight, Harold Donohue, Massachusetts Democrat, who is ordinarily silent unless he is carrying out chores for Rodino, speaks in his deep voice, with a Massachusetts accent. At seventy-three, he is retiring after this Congress, and will introduce the articles of impeachment. This will have been the most important thing he has ever done here. Harold Donohue—the white-faced congressman from Worcester, Massachusetts, who worked as a streetcar conductor while putting himself through law school—says, "I move that the committee report to the House a resolution together with articles of impeachment, impeaching Richard M. Nixon, President of the United States." His head bobbing up and down, he says, "No individual is above the law." He says that "Richard M. Nixon engaged in certain activities designed to obstruct justice, to unlawfully invade the Constitutional rights of private citizens." He goes down the list of charges against the President of the United States: defiance of "the duly authorized and properly served subpoenas of a committee of the Congress," "misuse [of] executive agencies for personal and political benefit," failure "to fulfill his Constitutional obligations to insure the faithful execution of our laws." And then, having completed his recital of the charges against the President,

Donohue says that the committee must decide whether "the President has seriously, gravely, purposefully, and persistently abused and misused the power entrusted in him by the people of these United States."

Each member has been allotted fifteen minutes to make an opening statement. There has been some concern as to how interesting this can be. Some members don't want to give their positions away until they cast their votes, so the question is: What can they say? And how likely are people to stay glued to their television sets while thirty-eight House members make fifteen-minute speeches? This could be a disaster.

As some members speak, others listen, and some revise their own remarks. They have had little time to prepare their statements. Those with less seniority will have to continue revising as some of their points, and better lines, are used.

While Henry Smith, New York Republican, is speaking—saying, he is not convinced that the President is personally responsible for any of the activities he is being charged with—copies of the Donohue resolution, including two articles of impeachment, are distributed. (Some reporters tear out of the room to file stories on them.) These articles represent the latest version of the compromise between the "swing group" and the Democratic drafters. The first article proposes to impeach the President for his role in the cover-up. The tone of the staff-prepared article has been tempered. Unlike the staff article, this one does not attempt to tie the break-in at the Democratic National Committee to the President, through his staff. The new version seems cleaner and stronger. The strategy of surfacing the articles before the debate began has worked, and so, surprisingly, has the process of redrafting, carried out by several groups. Such honing and shaping and redrafting—and last-minute compromising—took place at Philadelphia in 1787, too. Article II, which will undergo even more revision, lists various ways in which the President "has abused the powers vested in him as President by one or more of the following, either directly or through his subordinates or agents." Included in the list are wiretapping and the Fielding break-in.

As Robert Kastenmeier, Democrat of Wisconsin, finishes his speech, in which he says, "President Nixon must be impeached and removed from office," Rodino suddenly bangs the gavel and calls a recess. Apparently, there is a bomb threat.

While committee members, press, and public mill around in the soft air outside the Rayburn Building and relax in an impromptu picnic-like atmosphere, security officers sweep Room 2141 with bomb-detectors and a team of German shepherds. No bomb is found, and the proceedings resume.

Charles Sandman comes on strong—stronger than I have ever before seen him. "To say that this is the most unusual proceeding that I have ever been a part of would be a tremendous understatement," he says. He says that there have been leaks "every hour on the half hour." The audience is amused by his sarcasm. The dignity that preceded the bomb threat has not been retrieved. Sandman seems a figure out of the movies. He is a heavy-set man, with a broad face and slicked-back black hair; his eyes peer over black-framed half-glasses, and he speaks in a powerful voice with an exaggerated New Jersey accent. Sandman says, referring to Nixon, "Is there direct evidence that said he had anything to do with it? Of course there is not." He attacks the media, and also gets into some of the substance of the issues before the committee. When he first heard the tape of the first of two March 21st meetings, he says, it "worried me to death." He continues, "When I went to bed that night, I made up my mind, The President's goose is cooked." But then the next day, Sandman says, he heard the tape of the second meeting on the twenty-first, "and that completely did away with what was happening in the first tape."

Don Edwards, dark-blond and somewhat elegant, talks of the value of "this relearning process," of relearning "the value and the beauty of our Constitution," which he describes as "the compact we have with each other that enables us to live together in peace" and as "the cement that holds us together as a decent and humane society." Edwards has been of major help to Rodino in formulating strategy. A former F.B.I. agent who became a successful businessman and who a few years ago was chairman of Americans for Democratic Action, he says that he supported Nixon in 1950. That's a surprise. But now he says, "I do believe that the President has consciously and intentionally engaged in serious misdeeds, that he has corrupted and subverted our political and governmental processes to the extent that he should be impeached."

When Railsback begins his statement, shortly after 10 P.M., he appears a bit pale, tense. He has no prepared speech; he just talks—the way he always talks. "Let me begin by saying that you, Mr. Chairman, I think . . . I think that you have handled yourself very well." His voice is high and boyish. He makes a little joke about being on the Judiciary Committee and another little joke about playing golf with Wiggins, and these jokes don't fit the tone of the proceedings. But Railsback, characteristically, is touching his bases, because he knows what he is going to do. The President, he says, "has been in my district twice campaigning for me," "has only treated me kindly," and "has done many wonderful things." And then he says he has "two serious areas of concern" that "I want to share with my colleagues and I want to share with my constituents." He talks about abuse of power, and says, "I cannot think of an area where a conservative or a moderate or a liberal should be more concerned." And then he starts talking fast, crowding as much as he can into this major chance to explain himself on national television. And out it comes: about John Dean and the President talking about the I.R.S.; about the cover-up; about getting hold of the C.I.A. and using it to keep the F.B.I. away—"and the President knew about this." He talks of Pat Gray's warning the President that "some of your top staff are mortally wounding you." (Gray, the former acting F.B.I. director, told the Ervin committee that the President responded by simply saying, "Pat, you just continue to conduct your aggressive and thorough investigation.") He talks of the attempt to get Dean to write an absolving report. He reads from the transcripts. His voice becomes higher. He is not talking Constitutional principles; he is tossing out facts as fast as he can—facts that he has decided trouble him and that he wants to convince others should trouble them. Rodino watches him carefully.

Railsback talks about the President's getting information from Henry Petersen, and—chopping the air with his arms—demands, "What did he do with the information that Henry Petersen gave to him?" He is running over his allotted time, and Rodino, who, with apparent reluctance, has been fingering the gavel for a few moments, waves it in the air as if he can't bring himself to bang it. Railsback is still going: "The President on April 17th met with Haldeman, who had been implicated again by information that was given to Henry Petersen, and Henry Petersen had revealed it to the President and the President advised at that point Haldeman that he better get together with John and map out some kind of a strategy on the money." Rodino taps the gavel lightly. The next speaker, William Hungate, Democrat of Missouri, yields Railsback two of his allotted minutes. The Democrats want to give Railsback a chance to make his case; they know that he is important—to the Congress and to the audience that is watching.

Railsback goes on: "I just—I just can't help but wonder, you know, when you put all of this together in that kind of perspective, I am concerned and I am seriously concerned. Let me say just one thing in the remaining minute. Some of my friends in Illinois . . . say that the country cannot afford, that we cannot afford, to impeach a President. Let me say to them, I have spoken to . . . many, many young people, and if the young people in this country think that we are going to not handle this thing fairly, if we are not going to really try to get to the truth, you are going to see the most frustrated people, the most turned-off people, the most disillusioned people . . ."

We will never know Railsback's mind—what combination of concern about what he had seen and of his belief that the future does not lie with Richard Nixon and of his ideas about the way government is supposed to work has brought him to this point tonight. Perhaps Railsback will never know, either.

JULY 25

Rodino and Doar were up very late last night, going over the draft of the compromise articles. They are worrying about the history that the articles will establish, concerned over the insistence of the "swing group" that there be nothing in the articles which cannot be proved to have been approved or condoned by the President. It is an unrealistic requirement. The insistence by the "swing group" that a distinction be found between the acts of the President and the acts of his subordinates raises one of the major issues in this whole chain of events—whether the President is culpable for the carrying out of acts by his subordinates on his behalf in such a manner as to establish deniability for him, and even for his top aides. Walter Flowers has indicated to Rodino that he is still uncertain about how he will vote. Liberal Democrats are expressing displeasure at the concessions being made to the "swing group." So Rodino is still negotiating, and at some point today, while the members continue to make their opening statements, he will turn the gavel over to Donohue and slip out of the room to continue the negotiating and drafting. Though this last-minute uncertainty seems real, so does the certainty about the outcome. Yet that final wording is crucial, not just to the number of votes there will be in favor of the articles but also to history, and at the moment these two goals are in some slight conflict. At this morning's caucus of the committee Democrats, Rodino will urge them to be more specific in their opening remarks—to use that time to lay out the case. He is concerned that they did not do so last evening.

Today, Charles Wiggins is conservatively dressed; it is the first time that I have seen him so. He is wearing a navy-blue suit and a blue-and-white striped shirt. He is the first to speak this morning, when the committee convenes at ten minutes past ten. He talks quietly, in the flat, non-accented California style. Someone says that he sounds like Jack Benny—an improbable likeness but an accurate one. Wiggins commends Rodino for having "set the right tone for these proceedings." And then he argues that much of what the committee is considering is "material" but is not "evidence." He says he guesses that "you can put all of the admissible evidence in half of one book." The President can be impeached, he argues, only "for demonstrated and proved high crimes and misdemeanors." Wiggins will address himself, he says, to two charges that seem to bother people—that the President misused the C.I.A. and the I.R.S. He will try, for the benefit of the audience, if not of the committee, to break down the charges against the President. Railsback, sitting beside Wiggins, watches and listens carefully.

By June 23, 1972, Wiggins says, the President had reason to think that an investigation of the break-in might lead to C.I.A. activities: James McCord was a former C.I.A. agent; Bernard Barker was "an active C.I.A. agent until recently before this incident and perhaps [was] still on retainer with the C.I.A.;" Eugenio Martinez was "an active C.I.A. agent." "The name of Hunt had surfaced," says Wiggins, and "Hunt characterized himself . . . as a spy." Hunt, Wiggins says, had been an employee of Mullen & Company, a public-relations firm and "a C.I.A. front." The fact, Wiggins argues, that Nixon knew about the "Mexican checks in the context of a former C.I.A. agent"—the checks for Nixon's reëlection that were "laundered" in Mexico and turned into the hundred-dollar bills found on some of those caught on June 17, 1972, in the Democratic headquarters—means that the President was legitimately worried that the F.B.I. investigation might compromise the C.I.A. He says that only the President and Haldeman were present at the June 23rd meeting, after which the F.B.I. was instructed to keep its investigation of the Watergate break-in away from C.I.A. activities. (The committee has subpoenaed but has not received a tape of that meeting.) That action, argues Wiggins, was "wholly responsible and wholly reasonable."

As Joshua Eilberg, Democrat of Pennsylvannia, speaks, Cohen, in the front row, and Railsback, behind him, are conferring. Doar has slipped out of the room.

Then Fish, in the back row, reads his statement, in a soft voice. He talks about the larger questions. Mrs. Fish, a tall woman in yellow slacks and a yellow shirt and sunglasses, is watching from the audience. Fish says that for him the tests of an impeachable offense are that it must be "extremely serious," and that it must be "an offense against the political process or the Constitutional system of our country," and "one that is recognized as such by the broad majority of the citizens of this country." And then he speaks of the President's oath of office. The issue, interestingly, is really coming back to that—to those few words that are uttered on the Capitol steps on a usually cold day in January, those words to which we usually listen with so little attention. Fish says that when the President takes that oath, "he vows not only to perform the duties of the President but to perform those duties *faithfully*," and he goes on, "I would suggest that a President is required to keep faith with the public trust that is placed in his position. . . . A President is required to safeguard the Constitution to the *best* of his abilities. . . . It is his responsibility to exercise his powers to insure the liberties and Constitutional rights of the people." The President is charged with the *"faithful* execution of the laws," says Fish, and this means not just that he is responsible for obeying the law but that "he is responsible both for carrying out the enactments of Congress and for supervising the thorough and impartial administration of justice." Says Fish, "Here the issue is the Constitution, and in assessing the fitness of the President to remain in office the Congress becomes the conscience and protector of the state. What is best for America . . . is that our people know that the rule of law applies equally to those who govern as well as to the governed."

Since what has come to be called the "smoking gun" or the "murder weapon"—which would have made the decision so much easier for many of the committee members—has not been found, the question of

whether the President should be impeached remains one of mental context, of philosophy, of views of the meaning of the Constitution. Which
is just as well. The probabilities are against another cover-up like the
one carried out under the Nixon Administration. The problem of abuse
of power is more likely to recur. And it is just as well that the politicians
have had to decide these issues. At some point, many of them have faced
the fact that this is a question of the Constitution, and now we hear it in
their speeches. There are, of course, political ingredients in their decisions. And that is not so bad, either. The framers of the Constitution
deliberately put this process in the hands of politicians, beginning with
members of the House of Representatives, who have to receive the affirmation of the people most often. In Federalist Paper No. 65, Alexander
Hamilton asked, "What is the true spirit of the institution [of impeach-
ment] itself? Is it not designed as a method of National Inquest into
the conduct of public men? If this be the design of it, who can so properly be the inquisitors for the nation as the representatives of the nation
themselves?" The framers gave it to people who must work out political
equations, and the working out of political equations is what keeps our
country going. The politicians are our mediators. Sometimes we don't
like their decisions, but someone has to mediate.

Jerome Waldie, Democrat of California, talks about the evidence. He
says, "Common sense tells you that a President of the United States
does not condone the payment of over four hundred thousand dollars
to seven people occupying a D.C. jail because they have committed a
burglary unless he wants something from them."

While Wiley Mayne, Iowa Republican, is speaking, John Doar, back in
the room, is writing on a yellow tablet—presumably still drafting. Now
an aide brings Doar an envelope. Jenner sends a note to Mann. While the
speeches are being made for the television audience, the words are being
chosen for the tablets that will be handed down to the future.

Shortly before noon, Walter Flowers begins to speak. Flowers is
ready to vote for impeachment, and he has these few minutes to explain
himself to his constituents, who do not yet know what he will do. His
constituents are mostly white, conservative, and supporters of the
President—any President—and, as he implied in a conversation I had
with him in April, they equated a vote against Nixon in 1972 with being
pro-black. Today, Flowers is wearing a navy-blue jacket and a blue shirt
with a white collar. He has an American flag in his lapel. He begins
by saying that there are "things I would like to get off my chest." He
says that the committee has been fair, except for "the unfortunate and
grossly overemphasized leaks." And he wants to say some things to the
press "before I slip back into anonymity." He asks the press to "look
inward" and "decide for yourselves if you have treated fairly with the
President," and he also suggests that "the perspective of Middle America
does not receive equal time." Then he gets to "the problem at hand,"

which he describes as "a terrible problem," to which there is "no good solution." He says, "I wake up nights—at least on those nights I have been able to go to sleep lately—wondering if this could not be some sordid dream: to impeach the President of the United States, the Chief Executive of our country, our Commander-in-Chief." He goes on, "The people that I represent—just as I do, and most Americans, I think—really *want* to support the President." This is the other side of the political equation: here is a politician speaking to the fears and concerns of his constituents, understanding his people, and leading them. It is an intrinsic part of political communication that as a politician embraces Proposition A he tries to propitiate the proponents of Proposition B. And that is what some of these people, with divided constituencies, or even constituencies that might be largely opposed to the decision they have made, are doing in these speeches. "What if we failed to impeach?" Flowers asks. "Do we ingrain forever in the very fabric of our Constitution a standard of conduct in our highest office that in the least is deplorable and at worst is impeachable?"

Speaking again within the frame of reference of his constituents, he says, "Some of the things that bothered me most are troubling to all people who fear that big government can encroach on the freedom of people." Like his friend Railsback, Flowers is pointing to things that might offend the conservative mind. He says, "The institutions of this country have been set up by the people to serve them, to carry out those functions that are necessary to a peaceful and a free society. They are not created to serve the interests of one man or one group of men or the political gain of anyone." He speaks of the F.B.I., the Justice Department, the C.I.A., and the I.R.S. He points to evidence that in 1970 the White House leaked information about the tax problems of George Wallace's brother Gerald "in an apparent attempt to affect the Governor's campaign that year." (We also know that the White House funnelled money to Wallace's gubernatorial opponent in 1970.) He points to "evidence that the F.B.I.—the nation's police—were used to spy on those who disagreed with the Administration."

Then Flowers, the conservative Southern Democrat, the youthful-looking, heretofore anonymous congressman with the curly hair and the intelligent, country face, says, "The power of the Presidency is a public trust, just like our office. And the people must be able to believe and rely on their President. . . . If the trust of the people in the word of the man to whom they had given their highest honor or any public trust is betrayed, if the people cannot know that their President is candid and truthful with them, then I say the very basis of our government is under-mined." Rodino, back in the room now, watches him carefully, and so do Jack Brooks, Democrat of Texas, and several Republicans, and Doar and Jenner. Flowers knows how to weave the patriotic traditions that he grew up with—and that his constituents still hold dear—

together with the Constitution. His speech is a political work of art. "I have said many times that we can make great progress and improve our society and still not have anything that will live or last unless we concern ourselves with our underlying values," he says, and he goes on, "We have in the tradition of this nation a well-tested framework of values: liberty, justice, worth and integrity of the individual, individual responsibility. Our problem is not now to find better values, but I say our problem is to be faithful to those that we profess—and to make them live in modern times." And he cites the preamble to the Constitution: " 'We, the people of the United States,' and surely there is no more inspiring phrase than this—'We, the people of the United States,' not we the public officials of the United States, not we the certified experts, or we the educators, or we the educated, or we the grownups over twenty-one or twenty-five, not we the privileged classes, or whatever, but just simply 'We, the people . . .' We acting in our communities across the nation can pull our fragmented society together."

This is no ordinary set of speeches. It is the most extraordinary political debate I have ever heard—perhaps the most extraordinary since the Constitutional Convention. And perhaps the most important political debate since that one. These people are drawing on history, attaching themselves to it, and becoming part of it.

As the committee breaks for lunch, John Seiberling, Democrat of Ohio, and George Danielson, Democrat of California, who have been scribbling during the debate, tell reporters that they are going to get more specific facts into their statements, so as to rebut Wiggins. Danielson says, "I've written an evidentiary addendum to my compendium of generalities." Hamilton Fish goes to the Capitol Hill Club, where he relaxes over lunch with his wife and son. William Cohen, tense, goes to his office to work over his remarks, to be delivered this afternoon. Walter Flowers and his wife—blond, in a sleeveless white blouse and with a small gold cross around her neck—are lunching with another couple in the members' dining room. In the inquiry staff's offices in the old Congressional Hotel, an annex across the street from the House office buildings, John Doar and James Mann are still drafting the articles of impeachment.

During the lunch break, I drop in on the moderate House Republican—not a member of the Judiciary Committee—with whom I have been talking from time to time since last fall. "The dam has sort of burst around here," he says. "As near as I can figure, the Republicans around here have just started talking about this matter seriously. Now, whenever there are two or four or twenty of them together, they talk about it in a thoughtful way. Although a lot of them are usually listed as against impeachment or as holding unknown views on it, the thrust is against the President. From what I see in the committee, I think the vote could be at least two to one against the President in the House. Three hundred votes for impeachment seems like a lot, but it's not impossible. [With all the members voting, a majority of two hundred and eighteen would be required to impeach.] It all just hit this week. It was like after the transcripts were released. At first, it fell with a dull plop. Then came the reaction. It was the same with the committee's evidence. Especially for the conservatives: the idea of going to the I.R.S. with a list of three hundred names of McGovern supporters and others and saying 'Fry these people'—man, that's hard to swallow." (There is some puzzle in the fact that House members are suddenly expressing so much concern about this list, which has been known about for some time; perhaps the answer is that the House members chose not to face it until they had to.)

The moderate Republican continues, "In the last couple of days, we've begun to get the committee's comments, and we're learning the details of the cover-up. A lot of guys who were standing firm against impeachment are now leaning toward it. That's my position now. I'd have to hear some super-duper evidence to change. What got to me was the misuse of government agencies—principally the I.R.S. but also the C.I.A. and the F.B.I.—and the cover-up. I listened to Railsback last night. I've talked with Railsback a number of times, and also with Butler, Froehlich, Cohen, and Fish. I've talked with Wiggins and Dennis, too. [Harold Froehlich, of Wisconsin, and David Dennis, of Indiana, are Judiciary Committee Republicans.] Hogan is damned important. Everybody's underestimated that. Hogan made it respectable for non-liberals to be for impeachment. Call it politics, call it what you want, it was damned important. This was a supporter of the President who had heard all the evidence and came out for impeachment. It's been about a forty-eight-hour phenomenon. The game's over."

After lunch, Hogan begins his fifteen-minute statement. We heard him at his press conference, so the attention wanders. But suddenly one realizes that Hogan is speaking with even more passion than he did two days ago, and saying some striking things. He says, "I was accused of making a political decision," and he goes on, "If I had decided to vote against impeachment, I venture to say that I would also have been criticized for making a political decision. One of the unfortunate things about being in politics is that everything you do is given evil or political motives. That I personally resent." As he says this, his voice quavers, and the room goes silent. Speaking of Nixon, Hogan says, "It is impossible for me to condone or ignore the long train of abuses to which he has subjected the Presidency and the people of this country." Addressing himself to Sandman and the others who say there is no evidence of direct Presidential involvement, Hogan says, "What they are looking for is an arrow to the heart. . . . We do not find in the evidence an arrow to the heart. We find a virus that creeps up on you slowly and gradually until its obviousness is so overwhelming to you. It is like looking at a mosaic and going down and focussing in on one single tile in the mosaic and saying, 'I see nothing wrong in that one little piece of this mosaic' "

Then it's time for James Mann to speak. Mann, the tall, courtly, soft-spoken South Carolina conservative with wavy gray hair, is perfectly cast for the part of definer. He looks like a lineal descendant of what we want to think the framers looked like. Mann gazes right into the camera and gives a little talk about the committee ("You know, it is impor-tant that the American public have respect for these proceedings") and about government. Several of the things he says echo the concerns he expressed in a conversation I had with him earlier this year. He talked then about the power of "the electronic throne" at the White House, and about the question in his mind as to whether the people really want self-government. Today, he is raising these questions before the people, on television. He is saying, "In this era of power that our governmental system has brought us to in the world, where our involvement in foreign trade and foreign affairs puts the President out in front as the symbol of our national pride and as the bearer of our flag, and here we have in the House of Representatives four hundred and thirty-five voices speak-ing on behalf of different constituencies, with no public-relations man employed by the House of Representatives, and I wonder if the people still do want their elected representatives to fulfill their oath to 'preserve, protect, and defend the Constitution of the United States.' Do you want us to exercise the duty and responsibility of the power of impeachment? . . . Are we so morally bankrupt that we would accept a past course of wrongdoing or that we would decide that the system that we have is incapable of sustaining a system of law because we aren't perfect?"

This is Mann's moment to try to reach the public, and he is bringing all his powers to bear on it. The room is hushed; there is admiration for his performance. But, beyond that, he has caught up many in the room in what he is saying, his words cutting through whatever cynicism there is here, some of it affected—the sense that this is a show. He says, with some emotion now, "Our country has grown strong because men have died for the system. . . . We have built our country on the Constitution. . . . That system has been defended on battlefields, and statesmen have ended their careers on behalf of the system." And then Mann talks about how much he would have liked to have more evidence. He speaks slowly, his voice getting softer and softer, and Rodino is watching atten-tively, and other people in the room are straining to hear every word. Mann's face seems paler than usual; there are long pauses between phrases. He says he expects others to disagree with what he will do but asks them to "recognize my role and their responsibility to know the facts as I know them." Then, marching right up to one of the questions that the committee members have had the most difficulty with, he says,

"We're faced in the future with a very, very serious problem": can we permit "a President to escape accountability because he may choose to deal behind closed doors or to deal between two close, longtime, alter-ego, trusted subordinates?" He says, "We must examine our options to preserve our freedom," and then he speaks again of the evidence, saying that he would still like to have more of it. "I am starving for it," says Mann impassionedly, and then, quietly and abruptly, he concludes, "But I will do the best I can with what I've got."

As Caldwell Butler begins to speak, I glance back at Mann. There are tears in his eyes. Butler speaks quickly and without emotion. Butler, Republican from Virginia, talking of Nixon, points out that there are many who believe that he himself would not be in the Congress "if it were not for our joint effort in 1972," and says, "I am not unmindful of the loyalty I owe him." Therefore, he says, this proceeding is very "distasteful." The proponents of Proposition B having been propitiated, he turns to Proposition A. He points out that "for years we Republicans have campaigned against corruption and misconduct in the administra-tion of the government of the United States by the other party," and he goes on, "But Watergate is *our* shame. . . . These things have happened in our house, and it is our responsibility to do what we can to clear it up." Butler—black hair, egg-shaped face with receding chin, black-rimmed glasses—reads on quickly: "There are frightening implications for the future of our country if we do not impeach the President of the United States. Because we will by this impeachment proceeding be establish-ing a standard of conduct for the President of the United States which will for all time be a matter of public record. If we fail to impeach, we will have condoned and left unpunished a course of conduct totally inconsistent with the reasonable expectations of the American people; we will have condoned and left unpunished a Presidential course of conduct designed to interfere with and obstruct the very process which he is sworn to uphold; and we will have condoned and left unpunished an abuse of power totally without justification."

Butler continues, "The people of the United States are entitled to assume that their President is telling the truth." Then he recounts some instances in which Nixon was not. The emphasis in these proceedings on Nixon's lying is interesting and somewhat surprising. Politicians know that politicians, including Presidents, lie. Perhaps this, too, bears witness to the wisdom of the framers in putting the impeachment pro-cess in the hands of politicians—a point that William Hungate has made to reporters a number of times. Politicians know when some line has been crossed. Butler goes on to observe that "throughout the extensive transcripts made available to us of intimate Presidential conversation and discussion there is no real evidence of regret for what occurred, or remorse, or resolution to change, and precious little reference to, or concern for, Constitutional responsibility or reflection upon the basic

obligations of the office of the Presidency." Then, with startling direct-
ness, he says, "In short, power appears to have corrupted. It is a sad
chapter in American history. But I cannot condone what I have heard; I
cannot excuse it, and I cannot and will not stand still for it. The misuse
of power is the very essence of tyranny."

A few minutes before three o'clock. Rodino slips out; Doar has
already left. Paul Sarbanes, following up on Rodino's request, deals
in particulars in his speech—in this instance, the President's use of
information about the grand-jury proceedings which he received from
Henry Petersen. Sarbanes also holds up a copy of the Constitution, in
a green cover, and works into his speech some talk about that document, and about the requirements of a free society. Addressing himself
to one of the key issues, now and for the future, he refers to the Madison
superintendency theory—that, as Madison put it, a President is subject
to impeachment if he "suffers them [subordinates] to perpetrate with
impunity high crimes or misdemeanors against the United States, or
neglects to superintend their conduct, so as to check their excesses."
Says Sarbanes, "You must ask yourself whether a Chief Executive of
this land who surrounds himself at the highest levels with men who flagrantly abuse our Constitutional processes should be called to account
for their actions. What concept of government is it if the person at the
head is to walk away claiming that he knows nothing, sees nothing,
hears nothing, while those closest to him, those that have been referred
to as the alter egos, proceed about their destructive business?"

William Cohen speaks earnestly and rather quickly. Thirty-three, a
freshman congressman, he understood early what the issues were, and
though he kept an open mind until he was sure that the evidence was
sufficient, he did not play games; it was widely understood that he was
the Republican most likely to vote for impeachment. Cohen has evidently enjoyed his share of the limelight, which has been considerable,
and he and his attractive wife, Diane, have been quickly gathered into
Washington's social life. But he also risked—and for a time was subjected to—near-isolation within the Republican Party. In May, when
the President submitted the transcripts, Cohen's vote—the only one by
a Republican—kept the committee from failing to send a letter to the
President finding him not in compliance with its subpoena. Cohen did
not shrink from dramatizing his position to reporters, but he also stayed
up night after night reading the books of evidence and preparing for close
questioning of the witnesses—questioning that impressed and influenced some of his colleagues. And so one must ask: With whom were
our liberties safer—with William Cohen, thirty-three, or with those politicians who preferred not to face the problem and kept looking for exits?
Today, Cohen cuts right through the argument, raised by some of the
opponents of impeachment, that all that the committee has is "circumstantial evidence." The man from Maine offers an example that reflects

his origins: "If you went to sleep at night and the ground was bare out-side, and you woke up with fresh snow on the ground, then certainly you would conclude as a reasonable person that snow had fallen [even] if you had not seen it."

Cohen is tense and tired. He has been revising and revising his speech, in the intervals between these meetings and the informal meet-ings to work out the articles. Still he, too, manages to get to fundamental issues, and to define. "It also has been said to me," he says, "that even if Mr. Nixon did commit these offenses, every other President—we have heard this argument today—every other President has engaged in some of the same conduct, at least to some degree. The answer is that democ-racy . . . may be eroded away by degree. Its survival will be determined by the degree to which we will tolerate those silent and subtle subver-sions that absorb it slowly into the rule of a few in the name of what is right. Our laws and our Constitution are—and they must be—more than a sanctimonious recital of what we should prefer but will not insist upon. . . . It has been said that impeachment proceedings will tear this country apart. To say that it will tear the country apart to abide by the Constitution is a proposition that I cannot accept."

Short, rotund Harold Froehlich, Republican of Wisconsin, with dark-blond hair and black-rimmed glasses, first makes jabs at the "million-dollar" impeachment-inquiry staff, and, as Wiley Mayne did, at Lyndon Johnson's accumulation of wealth while he was in public office, and then gets to "the evidence that troubles me." Recalling the testimony of Alexander Butterfield, the former White House aide, that Nixon was, as Froehlich puts it, "a man concerned with the salad at the banquet table," he wonders how Nixon could have known so little about more important matters. The testimony of Butterfield (it had been Doar's idea to call him) about the President's attention to detail and his close rela-tionship to Haldeman has been referred to by others in their statements. It has clearly made a strong impression on the members.

The committee members have a sense of the moment. They have worked hard, and they are serious. Watching this makes one think about Rodino. He has set the tone—one of decorum and dignity. It takes inner reserves of strength to approach this thing as he has approached it: to be patient, to know when to wait, to maintain balance. Rodino has drawn on qualities that are within a man—qualities that cannot be cultivated or imparted. One notices his taste in people: Doar; Francis O'Brien, Rodino's twenty-seven-year-old administrative assistant. O'Brien spent long evenings talking over strategy with Rodino and Doar, and was the link between them and the outside world, particularly the press. O'Brien was that "sources close to the inquiry" who kept turning up in news stories. Somehow he got through it all with good humor, unpretentious-ness, and a surprising amount of candor. And Rodino's effect on the committee is noticeable: the members praise him and, for the most part, follow his lead in trying to maintain dignity in these proceedings. The members trust him, and something happens in a group when its members trust the man in the chair, when they do not think he will double-cross them. In this most dramatic of situations, Rodino himself has avoided showboating (as Sam Ervin did not, and even Archibald Cox did not). In this potentially most partisan of situations, Rodino has been fair.

This proceeding is also demonstrating that there are several members of the Congress who are not the hacks, the cartoon figures, that they are often taken to be. The misunderstanding—the belief that the Congress is a collective cartoon—comes not just because its members receive stereotypical treatment in the press but also because there is little opportunity for most of the talented members to show, or use, their capacities. History and process lift people, and they have lifted this group—and given the public a chance to see it. Paul Sarbanes would not have looked at all bad at the Constitutional Convention; he might have been one of the great ones. But there are institutional and atmospheric and generational attributes of the Congress that make it almost impossible for the gifted members of the House, in particular, to find their role, to be what they can be, to have an impact. When a member does break through, it is the exception.

During the dinner recess tonight, most of the members of the "swing group" met, and Hogan and Froehlich joined them. The committee's meeting tonight is postponed until eight-fifteen, because at seven-thirty President Nixon is giving a speech on the economy, which is being carried on the television networks.

Charles Rangel, the black Democrat from Harlem, in his speech this evening, asks, "Why is my President talking about paying one hundred twenty thousand dollars to any common burglar?"

The star tonight, as was expected, is Barbara Jordan. Her brains, eloquence, and tough-mindedness have made her a sort of pet of the committee and the press, and tonight she does not disappoint them. Picking up Flowers on his citation of the preamble to the Constitution, "We, the people," Miss Jordan, the large black woman from Texas, says, "When that document was completed, on the seventeenth of September in 1787, I was not included in that 'We, the people.' I felt somehow for many years that George Washington and Alexander Hamilton just left me out by mistake. But through the process of amendment, interpretation, and court decision I have finally been included in 'We, the people.' " And then she says, "Today I am an inquisitor, and I believe it would not be fictional and would not overstate the solemnness that I feel right now to say"—and, in her strong, clear voice, speaking slowly and clipping the words for emphasis, she goes on— "my faith in the Constitution is whole, it is complete, it is total, and I am not going to sit here and be an idle spectator to the diminution, the subversion, the destruction of the Constitution." As she says this, one senses that she believes it in her bones.

And then Barbara Jordan, whom the framers of the Constitution left out, speaks some words that future students of the meaning of the Constitution may well be quoting. Impeachment, she says, "is designed to bridle the executive if he engages in excesses. It is designed as a method of national inquest into the conduct of public men." She says, "The framers confined in the Congress the power if need be to remove the President in order to strike a delicate balance between a President swollen with power and grown tyrannical, and preservation of the independence of the executive." She reads the statements of the framers as to the meaning of impeachment, and juxtaposes against these the actions of Nixon. "If the impeachment provision in the Constitution of the United States will not reach the offenses charged here," she says, "then perhaps that eighteenth-century Constitution should be abandoned to a twentieth-century paper shredder."

Rodino, who has been presiding with great calm, shows emotion as he makes some closing remarks. He pays tribute to John Doar: "A great American who has contributed a great deal." And Albert Jenner: "A man who has stated before this body that he loves the Constitution above any party." His colleagues: "You have left no stain upon your effort." Echoing his statement of February 6th on the House floor, when he sought official House sanction for this inquiry—a statement of which he is proud—he talks again about the necessity of proceeding "with care, and with fairness, and with decency, and with honor, so that all Americans and those who come after us will be able to say there was only one way and that was the way we did it." The room is utterly still. To his colleagues he says, "I am proud to be a part of you, to be among you, to be of you." Almost all of them are looking at him: he has come through; they have come through; he has given them dignity. And then Rodino says, "I revere the Presidency. . . . I have searched within my heart. . . . I find that the President of the United States, in accordance with the tests that I feel we must confront, I find that the President must be found wanting. And so tomorrow I shall urge, along with others, the adoption of articles of impeachment."

JULY 26

The redrafting of the articles is still going on this morning. John Doar was up most of the night working on a final draft of Article I, and now he and Rodino are meeting with Edwards, Mann, and Sarbanes. Some of the press is being told that they are working just on "words," but the words they choose could be crucial to history. There are still uncertainties within the certainty.

A Gallup poll published in this morning's paper puts the President's popularity at twenty-four percent.

Railsback and a few members of the press here have suffered from a stomach disorder in the past twenty-four hours; perhaps a virus has made its way among those in this room. These exhausted people, threading their way through important Constitutional deliberations, get sick, too.

As the committee finally convenes, shortly before twelve, McClory moves that the deliberations be delayed to see if the President will supply the committee with the tapes that the Supreme Court has ordered him to turn over to the Special Prosecutor. But even Sandman is opposed. "You have the votes," he tells the majority. "Move the resolution, and let's go home." He seems to be speaking for most of them. John Seiberling, who sometimes talks too much, and often bores the members, reaches them today when he says that "some concession must be made to the shortness of human life." As this is going on, Sarbanes is crouched behind the counsel's table, next to Doar, who is showing him a marked-up copy of Article I—numerous circles and arrows are drawn in ink on the typed sheet. McClory's motion is defeated, twenty-seven to eleven. Mann, who made a point yesterday of wanting more information, votes with McClory, covering this base.

And after all this time, and even with the doubt now removed about the outcome, one is still not prepared for how it sounds as Garner Cline, associate general counsel of the committee who is serving as clerk during this debate, from his place at the counsel table, reads, in his clear, flat voice, the proposed articles of impeachment of the President. There have been many chilling moments in this past year, and here is another one as the clerk reads:

> RESOLVED, that Richard M. Nixon, President of the United States, is impeached for high crimes and misdemeanors and that the following articles of impeachment be exhibited to the Senate:

> Articles of impeachment exhibited by the House of Representatives of the United States of America. In the name of itself and of all of the people of the United States of America, against Richard M. Nixon, President of the United States of America, in maintenance and support of its impeachment against him for high crimes and misdemeanors.

Then the clerk reads a substitute article offered by Sarbanes, to replace the version submitted Wednesday evening:

> In his conduct of the office of President of the United States, Richard M. Nixon, in violation of his Constitutional oath faithfully to execute the office of President of the United States and, to the best of his ability,

preserve, protect, and defend the Constitution of the United States, and in violation of his Constitutional duty to take care that the laws be faithfully executed has prevented, obstructed, and impeded the administration of justice, in that . . .

And the listing begins where this all ostensibly began:

On June 17, 1972, and prior thereto, agents of the Committee for the Re-Election of the President committed illegal entry of the headquarters of the Democratic National Committee in Washington, District of Columbia, for the purpose of securing political intelligence.

The article continues:

Subsequent thereto, Richard M. Nixon, using the powers of his high office, made it his policy, and in furtherance of such policy did act directly and personally and through his close subordinates and agents, to delay, impede, and obstruct the investigation of such illegal entry; to cover up, conceal, and protect those responsible; and to conceal the existence and scope of other unlawful covert activities.

And then it lists "the means used to implement this policy," and the clerk reads the charges against the President:

Making false or misleading statements to lawfully authorized investigative officers and employees of the United States; withholding relevant and material evidence or information . . . ; approving, condoning, acquiescing in, and counselling witnesses with respect to the giving of false or misleading statements to lawfully authorized investigative officers . . . and in . . . duly instituted judicial and congressional proceedings; interfering or endeavoring to interfere with the conduct of investigations . . . ; approving, condoning, and acquiescing in the surreptitious payment of substantial sums of money for the purpose of obtaining the silence or influencing the testimony of witnesses . . . ; endeavoring to misuse the Central Intelligence Agency . . . ; disseminating information received from officers of the Department of Justice of the United States to subjects of investigations . . . ; making false or misleading public statements for the purpose of deceiving the people of the United States into believing that a thorough and complete investigation had been conducted . . . ; endeavoring to cause prospective defendants, and individuals duly tried and convicted, to expect favored treatment and consideration in return for their silence or false testimony, or rewarding individuals for their silence or false testimony.

The clerk then reads—and one sits stock still, hardly breathing, never having heard anything like this before:

Richard M. Nixon has acted in a manner contrary to his trust as President and subversive of Constitutional government, to the great prejudice of the cause of law and justice and to the manifest injury of the people of the United States.

And he concludes:

Wherefore, Richard M. Nixon, by such conduct, warrants impeachment and trial, and removal from office.

Sarbanes explains, in accordance with his briefing by Doar moments ago, the differences between this version and the one submitted Wednesday evening. Some of the changes are indeed just "words," such as corrections of titles. Some of them are for the purposes of precision. And some are substantive: the cover-up is now called the President's "policy," rather than his "continuing policy"; it has been added that he sought to "protect" those responsible.

Railsback, following a procedure customarily used on the House floor to establish "legislative history," asks Sarbanes a series of questions designed to show that the allegations in the article are intended to be limited to "matters that include the President himself either in respect to knowledge that he had or participation that he entered into, rather than to in any way try to impute criminal responsibility to him for acts of misconduct on the part of his subordinates that he had no knowledge of." Sarbanes responds that the acts of the President's subordinates would have to be in furtherance of the President's policy, and, under further questioning by Railsback, assures him that the language of the article "would not reach to the limits of the Madison superintendency theory." So that is how, for the moment, they are getting around the problem of holding a President accountable for the acts of his subordinates: for the purpose of dealing with the cover-up, they are saying that the problem does not exist.

But then Wiggins, dressed today in dark-brown suit and a white shirt, closes in, asking Sarbanes, as "the author of the proposed article" (Wiggins knows better, presumably), just when the "policy," which is the heart of the article, was declared. Sarbanes has a problem—or appears to have one. He talks about the fact that the "evidence" shows that this was the policy. Wiggins is being literal, and trying to trap the drafters in their own escape hatch—the assertion that the acts were carried out pursuant to a Presidential policy. There is a great deal of evidence—like William Cohen's snow—that there was such a policy, but Wiggins is asserting that if there is no declaration of the policy by the President at a specific time and place it did not exist. Then Sandman, moving in like a heavy tank, hits Sarbanes with a second line of questioning. "Is it your understanding of the law," he asks, "that the articles of impeachment must be specific, in order to meet the due-process clause of the Constitution? Do you not believe that under the due-process clause of the Constitution every individual, including the President, is entitled to due notice of what he is charged with? Do you or do you not believe, and you can say 'yes' or 'no,' that the President is entitled to know in the articles of impeachment specifically, specifically on what day he did that thing [for] which you say he should be removed from office?" Sarbanes has been trying to respond by referring to the fact that extensive material has been gathered by the committee, and that the President's counsel was present at the proceedings. But he is blinking now, and seems taken aback. Rodino has left the chair and is over on the left, talking with Flowers. And then, at one-twenty-seven, Rodino, Flowers, Doar, and Richard Cates, the staff expert on the cover-up, leave the room. Danielson, trying to help Sarbanes out, says that a bill of impeachment is not the same as an indictment but that the proposed article does meet the test of an indictment, and sets forth the charges "with great particularity." At one-twenty-eight, Donohue, now presiding, announces a recess until three o'clock. I ask a committee aide what Rodino and the others are doing with Flowers. "Explaining," he replies.

At lunch, Railsback says he thinks that Sandman and Wiggins have done their damage. "I think they muddied up the streams real good this morning," he says. "People want to see the President treated fairly. It made a bad impression on television. Our staff should have been prepared with specific backup stuff. Now the staff is going back to draw up itemized information." So they really were not prepared for this debate, had not thought through how to handle it, had not anticipated tactics. A substantial oversight, and, for the moment, a costly one. But the staff has been overworked for some time now, and the attention of late has been on the re-drafting of the articles. Moreover, a recitation of facts can devolve into arguments over the validity and significance of each fact, and narrow the focus once more. The issues are fed by the facts but are also above and beyond them. The majority has made the mental shift from the specific facts to the larger picture of misconduct; they and Wiggins/Sandman are talking different languages.

Still, Railsback is not really very worried. "I think it's almost all over but the shouting," he says, "We'll work out the specifics." He agrees that the majority would just as soon avoid argument now over each of the facts. But this seems to be another case in which the majority will have to accede to the minority—will have to let the minority set the agenda. Every precaution must be taken to assure that the proceeding is fair.

Railsback wanted to get away from the Capitol for a bit, so we are eating at a seafood restaurant a few minutes away by taxi, overlooking the Anacostia River. Railsback is still not feeling well. The view of the

river, the quiet of the restaurant make the Capitol seem remote. Railsback describes how the seven members of the "swing group" got
together. Two weeks ago, he talked things over with Flowers. Flowers
and Railsback are social friends; Sandman used to keep a boat in
Washington, and they used to go out on Sandman's boat. Two weeks
ago, Railsback and Flowers had dinner together. "I said, 'Walter, where
do you think there are problems?' " Railsback tells me. "He said he
thought there were problems in the abuse of power and in the cover-up.
I think the staff had a theory, based on the testimony of Butterfield and
other things, that because Haldeman and Ehrlichman were so close to
the President their knowledge was his knowledge, and this was one of
the theories of the case. But if you're going to impeach the guy it should
be for what he did. There are some very simple things that occurred:
Nixon asking Dean to write the report, when Dean had been involved;
then asking Ehrlichman to write the report, when he'd been implicated
himself. Then you get into the Henry Petersen period, in April, because
Dean and Magruder and LaRue started to blow the whistle in April.
These are irrefutable facts."

Railsback's concerns with what the Administration did seem broader
now, and stronger, than when we talked on Monday. Perhaps this is a
result of his having crossed some mental line; the same thing seems to
have happened to Hogan. Once the mind unlocks and becomes recep-
tive to an idea, it is more likely to entertain and accept ramifications,
elaborations, of the idea. So now Railsback is seeing the broader can-
vas. He is concerned about the electronic surveillance. He expresses
more concern than he did Monday about the Fielding break-in, and now
thinks he will speak to that issue when the articles of impeachment are
debated on the House floor. He is even considering the possibility of
being a manager in the Senate trial. "But," he says, referring to Nixon,
"the guy's been good to me."

As Railsback finishes a chocolate marshmallow sundae, he remarks
on the fact that Gerald Warren has announced from San Clemente
that the President is not watching the committee's proceedings. "The
President doesn't want to watch us," he says. "That's one of the problems. We were never able to communicate enough."

The afternoon and evening sessions take on the character of a somewhat haphazard opera, with various members finding their roles, with
three choruses—each with its own theme—and with several principals
returning time and again to resume their particular recitatives. Sandman,
with his raspy voice, is assuming a starring role, the role of the heavy,
and he seems to enjoy it. The proceedings are at once a serious debate
and a disorganized opera. The committee members know each other
well by now, and know how this is going to turn out, so they are making
their points for the television audience, including their own constituen-

cies, and also for the record. They know Sandman and rather like him, and see that he is enjoying his newfound role, putting on something of an act. "Isn't it amazing?" becomes Sandman's theme, and he makes "amazing" into a very long word. "Isn't it amazing," he asks no one in particular, "that they [the proponents of impeachment] are willing to do anything such as resistance to making the thing specific? Isn't it amazing that they have so much but they are willing to say so little? Isn't it amazing? They are willing to do anything except make these articles specific."

The chorus composed of the opponents of impeachment keeps playing on this theme—that the articles are not specific. "Specificity" becomes a pronunciational hurdle that members trip over or, with some satisfaction, clear. Delbert Latta (a senior Republican from Ohio, whom Republican leaders chose to fill a committee vacancy for the course of the inquiry) says, "A common jaywalker charged with jaywalking anyplace in the United States is entitled to know when and where the alleged offense is supposed to have occurred. Is the President of the United States entitled to less?"

Democrats who support impeachment form the second chorus. They pick up, one after another, the account of the cover-up, and it takes on the attributes of a bedtime story. "Well," says Don Edwards as he tells his part of the tale, "here is the key to it. Immediately—the next day, actually—the White House knew that Hunt was involved." Edwards makes little gestures, acting out the story, when he tells of Hunt's obtaining the wig and the voice changer from the C.I.A. Jerome Waldie becomes the chief storyteller. Waldie—who does not disguise the fact that he dislikes Richard Nixon intensely, who introduced a resolution of impeachment after the weekend last fall when Special Prosecutor Archibald Cox was fired, who has lost a primary race for governor of California and is concluding his political career with this impeachment, and who has a very acute mind—tells the Richard Nixon story, referring to a black-bound notebook as he does so. His voice is heavy with sarcasm as he relates now familiar events. A mistake, it seems: we have passed the point where this story was viewed as comic—a giant Brueghel filled with grotesques. Yet there is much to the story that is patently ridiculous, and one of the problems all along has been whether to be enraged, to feel insulted, or to laugh. In the course of his recitative, Waldie refers, for example, to the practice of "picking up money with gloves on because you don't want fingerprints when you are going to deliver it for a compassionate purpose." (Fred LaRue, formerly an assistant to Mitchell at the Re-Election Committee, testified to the Judiciary Committee that once when he received money from Gordon Strachan for the Watergate defendants, and counted it, he wore gloves.) But the dignity in which this proceeding has been wrapped begins to slip away.

Hungate also uses humor; it is his language. Hungate, the white-haired representative from Missouri, likes to associate himself with some of his state's illustrious contributions to America—Harry Truman and Mark Twain. In fact, he represents Hannibal, Missouri, where Mark Twain grew up. "There is lots of evidence," Hungate says tonight. "We sit through these hearings day after day. I tell you, if a guy brought an elephant through that door and one of us said, 'That is an elephant,' some of the doubters would say, 'You know, that is an inference. That could be a mouse with a glandular condition.' "

The third chorus is that of the members of the "swing group," who are anxious to establish that this is a fair proceeding. James Mann, referring to the thirty-six books of evidence that the committee has released, says he is "astonished" that "there are those here who would assert that we should list in this article all of the evidence that applies to this charge," and explains, "It is very clear, of course, that if we were to attempt to do that we would have a document equalling several of these books." The other members listen to Mann when he speaks, watch him carefully, know that he is very important. He talks of the "loose statements" that "the President is going to go to trial without knowing what the charge is," and says, "The President, if he goes to trial, is going to trial not only knowing what the charge is but knowing every iota, every word, every 'i' and every 't,' every bit of evidence that has been made available to this committee. . . . I do not find that this proceeding, which admittedly has sparse precedent, is in any way violating anyone's Constitutional rights. . . . I conclude [that] this is not a substantive objection; it is a procedural matter—is a matter that I must suggest that I somewhat predicted as I realized that the arguments made here in front of these cameras would not be made for the benefit of me as a member of this committee. I do not think Mr. Sandman would be so strident, or even so partisan, if these proceedings were not being conducted to influence the opinions of the American people." (Mann can make this unusual personal reference to another member because he is respected—and also because he and Sandman are friends.) Slowly and quietly, Mann says, "Let us be reasonable."

Butler puts his finger on it. Speaking of the amount of information available to the committee members, he says, "We really have so much that we do not have any." They are drowning in evidence, thrashing about in it; they have so much evidence that they don't know what to do with it. There is a tactical point here, too: members of the majority do not want to limit the evidence now—to narrow the case. Further evidence may turn up. And, more important, this case is not about specific incidents but, as Sarbanes says, about a course of conduct—as Hogan said, a mosaic. Prior impeachments are no guide, because there has never been a case like this. Most of the charges against Andrew Johnson centered on one act—the firing of the Secretary of War. The problem with this case is that Nixon did so much. There are so many facts that

Charles Wiggins has somehow managed to turn the situation inside out and say that there aren't any facts. "Wouldn't it be a damning indictment, Mr. Chairman," asks Wiggins, "if after all this time and all this money we were unable to state with specificity what this case is all about? I think it would."

This monumental proceeding in this small room is taking on more and more aspects of a debate on the House floor, or of a political convention. Around the two-tiered dais, there are little caucuses. Several of the junior members consult with Rodino, presumably to receive his instructions or seek his advice. After Harold Froehlich poses some questions to counsel, which suggest that Froehlich—who, although he has remained mysterious, is now thought very likely to vote for impeachment—is troubled and may be backsliding, Railsback leans forward from his back-row seat to talk to him in the front row. (Froehlich, a freshman, faces reëlection difficulties. He won in 1972 by only 50.5 percent.) As the committee breaks for dinner, Railsback arranges for the "swing group"—with Froehlich and Hogan added—to go to the Capitol Hill Club for dinner.

After the dinner recess, Rodino calls first on Barbara Jordan. Earlier in the day, he more than once beckoned her over to talk with him. Miss Jordan has a particular ability to reduce a problem to its essence, and seems unafraid to take on the most skillful debaters. Now she says, "It apparently is very difficult for the committee to translate its views of the Constitution into the realities of the impeachment provisions. It is understandable that this committee would have procedural difficulties, because this is an unfamiliar and strange procedure." As she continues, her voice resounds and she speaks with great certainty. "But some of the arguments which were offered earlier today by some members of this committee in my judgment are phantom arguments, bottomless arguments." Those words—"phantom," "bottomless"—ring out.

Later on, Sandman moves to strike the first item in Article I ("making false or misleading statements to lawfully authorized investigative officers and employees of the United States"), and, finally, after eleven-thirty, the committee votes on his motion. It is a sort of rehearsal for the vote on the article, yet there may be changes in the votes of some members. Smith votes not to strike the item, and Froehlich votes to do so. Sandman's motion is rejected, twenty-seven to eleven.

JULY 27

The morning papers say that the White House will begin to turn the subpoenaed tapes over to the District Court on Tuesday. In court yesterday, St. Clair said that the turning over of the tapes might take time, partly because the President wants to listen to those he has not heard. "The President feels quite strongly that he should know what he is turning over," said St. Clair. Judge Sirica told Jaworski and St. Clair that he wanted the cover-up trial to begin on September 9th, as scheduled. Jaworski revealed in court yesterday that in early May he and St. Clair had considered an out-of-court agreement under which the President would surrender tapes of the eighteen conversations that Jaworski considered most crucial, plus the tapes of certain conversations included in the White House transcripts, and Jaworski would drop his pursuit of the remaining tapes. But the President, according to Jaworski, rejected the compromise after listening to some of the tapes.

The Judiciary Committee staff again stayed up most of the night, this time preparing the documentation for each item in Article I. Harold Froehlich must be assuaged, in the hope of winning his vote to impeach. Moreover, Flowers has become rather attracted to the idea of offering a motion to strike each section of Article I, and so giving the proponents of impeachment an opportunity to spell out, for the television audience, the documenting evidence. Some members of the "swing group"— Railsback, Mann, Butler, Flowers, and Cohen—met this morning in Railsback's office to discuss Article II, which is in fact the more important article. Hogan, the former F.B.I. agent, does not want it to contain language suggesting that the F.B.I. acted improperly. McClory, for his part, in a move that surprised many, has proposed a broad article that would impeach the President for failing to "take care" that the laws were faithfully executed; some of the "swing" members think that McClory's proposed article is too broad. But the group is considering ways to draft Article II so as to win McClory's vote.

The more one thinks about it, the more sensible the consensus process followed by the Judiciary Committee appears. There are all kinds of charges that got left behind along the way—charges having to do with money, with interference in the affairs of the other party, with the dismantling of the Office of Economic Opportunity (never taken seriously as a subject for impeachment), with the Vietnam war, with milk. The committee moved toward issues that subsume other issues, issues behind which there is the greatest consensus, issues that rise far above the claim that there were precedents for these things. Similarly, though it was not essential to let the President's counsel participate and suggest witnesses to be called—and even Rodino sometimes regretted the committee's leniency—those concessions are now proving helpful. The committee is ending up with a solid bipartisan group—including conservative Southern Democrats—in favor of impeachment, and this fact has already had a powerful impact on the House, and will have a similarly strong impact on the Senate and on the country at large. It will be realized that this widely disparate group studied the evidence at length—and now its seemingly deliberate pace is seen as helpful, too—and took a stand for impeachment.

Today, shortly after the committee reconvenes, Railsback offers an amendment to Article I to change that controversial word "policy"— the "policy" of cover-up that the proposed Article I says the President adopted and carried out "directly and personally and through his close subordinates and agents"—to "course of conduct or plan," and it is quickly agreed upon by voice vote. The Democrats heap praise on Railsback for his draftsmanship: "a very constructive suggestion" (Sarbanes); "superior" (Thornton); "more definitive language" (Mann). Flowers moves to strike section two of the article, which charges the President with "withholding relevant and material evidence or information," and Cohen recites instances in which he did so, Cohen beginning each example with the word "specifically." Unhappily hoist on his own stratagem, Sandman complains, "Please, let us not bore the American public with a rehashing of what we have heard."

As the committee is about to resume its afternoon session following a break, Caldwell Butler, smiling and fingering some papers, tells reporters, "I've got my script." One reason for the break was to get more material ready. Another was to get the choreography straight for the rest of the day. More people spoke than were supposed to on Flowers' motions this morning—they became rather enthusiastic about laying the case before the public, about appearing on television—so the discussion took longer than had been planned. During the afternoon recess, Flowers has checked with other Southern members of the House, and they have said that they like the idea of getting "the facts" before the public, so the process will continue. The staff, accordingly, is continuing to work up specifications for Article I, while Article II is still being drafted by Doar, Mann, and Rodino. At the moment, Flowers' great importance to the committee is that—like Railsback, on the other side of the aisle—he has been keeping in touch with colleagues in the House who might follow his lead. Mann's major importance now seems to lie within the committee, as a negotiator and framer of the article. But both Mann and Flowers will be very important on the House floor, as what they have said in the past two days has been. The committee wants to finish its work on Article I by tonight. For some of the people in this room, the big question is whether this will be over by dinnertime or in time for press deadlines.

There are few people waiting outside the Capitol on this Saturday afternoon. It has the deserted look of the Capitol on almost any Saturday. The lush green summer lawns and trees stand out against the backdrop of the white marble buildings. Saturday. Archibald Cox was fired on a Saturday evening. Inside the committee room, there is a growing sense of what is going to happen this evening. Flowers moves to strike

subsection three ("approving, condoning, acquiescing in, and counselling witnesses with respect to the giving of false or misleading
statements"), and Butler reads his script. Butler, too, makes frequent
use of the word "specifically," and, like the others, he reads from the
transcripts. Those transcripts keep coming back to haunt the President.
Something of a contest has developed in the reading of the transcripts
here, and Butler's performance ranks high; when, in a deep voice, he
reads conversations in which the President of the United States is saying "Yeah" and his counsel John Dean is saying "Uh huh," he wins the
bipartisan admiration of the galleries.

Sandman keeps up his role to some degree ("What a difference
twenty-four hours makes. . . . Now today every other word they breathe
is 'specify.' Isn't that unusual? So unusual. Everything is so specific.
But they have not changed one word in the articles"), but his heart
doesn't seem to be in it. One senses that many members want to recoup
from the disarray of last night—that they may have got bad reviews
from colleagues or constituents. In the room, Sandman looks smaller,
and comes across as less heated, than he does on television. It is all proceeding perfunctorily now, moving toward the inevitable conclusion.
The committee members are almost casually approaching a historic
moment—a moment of extraordinary drama. Article I, though not as
important as Article II, is important in terms of what it says about the
accountability of the President to the processes of law. Moreover, it was
the one on which it was easier for the members to cross the line, and so
it comes first.

At six-fifteen, the committee members are handed large manila enve-
lopes. In them is the written back-up material for the charges in Article I.
Then the vote nears on Flowers' last motion to strike, and the room gets
quieter. There is a growing sense of what is coming. Hungate gives a
sort of peroration, apologizing to those who may have found his occasional attempts at humor offensive. "I felt it better to have a sense of
humor than no sense at all," he says. Then he refers to the national cem-
etery at Omaha Beach, where Americans who died in the Second World
War are buried, and he quotes from the inscription on the stone there:
"They endured all and suffered all, that mankind might know freedom
and inherit justice." He says, "I hope our deliberations here will pro-
mote that cause," and one senses that he means it.

Just before the vote on the question of impeachment, Flowers, reading from notes, takes one last opportunity to explain what he is about to
do. He says, "There are many people in my district who will disagree
with my vote here. Some will say that it hurts them deeply for me to vote
for impeachment. I can assure them that I probably have enough pain
for them and me." And then, looking beyond what is happening in this
room, at once raising a basic issue and touching a base, Flowers says
to his colleagues, "I suggest to my friends here that they do not have to

wait one hundred and seven years to vote on the next impeachment to prove responsibility. . . . We will and should be judged by our willingness to share in the many hard choices that must be made for our nation, such as allocation of scarce resources, such as management of the forces of inflation and recession, such as balancing priorities and controlling the spending of the taxpayers' money. In the weeks and months ahead, I want my friends to know that I will be around"—and some of his colleagues nod assent, as if affirming that Flowers will survive politically what he is about to do—"to remind them when some of these hard choices are up."

At seven o'clock, the roll is called on whether or not the House Judiciary Committee will recommend to the House that the President be impeached. Technically, the vote is on whether the Sarbanes substitute article should be adopted, but it is in effect the definitive vote. And, no matter how seemingly inevitable this vote has been for some time now, no matter how well we know the outcome, there has been no way of preparing ourselves for this moment. More than any of the several other moments when the emotional reverberations outran the intellectual anticipation, this one has stolen up on us, taken over, leaves us sitting here feeling stunned, drained, almost disbelieving as the clerk calls the roll and the members cast their votes. The room is utterly still except for the call of the roll and the sound of cameras clicking. The moment has taken over the members; they know what they are doing, and they are physically, mentally, and emotionally spent. They have been through a long period of strain. No other group in the Congress has ever had to go through anything like this. One can barely hear the members as they respond to the clerk.

First the Democrats. Even those for whom this is not a difficult vote are somber as they respond "Aye"—perhaps in part because they know that they should be. Mann, for whom this has not been easy, stares into space as he says "Aye." His voice is all but inaudible. Again there appear to be tears in his eyes. Father Drinan, his long, thin face looking stern and sober, ever more like an El Greco painting, quietly says "Aye." Barbara Jordan, usually of full voice, also responds quietly. Ray Thornton looks at the ceiling, closes his eyes, and says, softly, "Aye." They are impeaching Richard Nixon. They are setting loose an unimaginable course of events, and they know it.

The first vote cast with a loud certitude is Hutchinson's "No." Hutchinson smiles—the only one who does.

"Mr. McClory."

"No."

"Mr. Smith."

"No."

"Mr. Sandman."

"No."

Railsback, next, is sitting with a red Coca-Cola can in front of him. He is drinking Coca-Cola to soothe his stomach. One can hear the cameras clicking furiously at this moment. Railsback's brow is furrowed. He purses his lips and looks up and off to his right, perhaps at the clock, perhaps at space, and says, softly, "Aye."

Wiggins says a quiet "No."

Hogan stares straight ahead and says "Aye."

Butler, not one for drama, says a quick "Aye."

Cohen says a quiet but certain "Aye."

Froehlich votes "Aye."

Rodino, who casts his vote last, undramatically says "Aye." The clerk announces, "Twenty-seven members have voted aye, eleven members have voted no." All twenty-one Democrats—including the three Southerners—and six Republicans have voted to impeach the President for the cover-up.

The vote on the article as amended is a ceremonial vote now, but it must be taken, and again it is taken solemnly. This time, Rodino's voice cracks as he speaks the final "Aye." The room is utterly silent, and then, at a few minutes after seven, Rodino announces, "Article I . . . is adopted and will be reported to the House."

Hamilton Fish comes out of the committee room holding his wife's hand. Some members are being interviewed on television. Barbara Jordan, preparing to be interviewed, is having difficulty composing herself. Some members—Rodino included—went into the anteroom behind the committee room and wept. There is a small group of observers, dressed in casual summer clothes, standing quietly outside the Rayburn Building. When Barbara Jordan comes out of the Rayburn Building, several in the group applaud. She smiles and waves vaguely. Reporters have gone back to the pressrooms to file their stories. It is good to have something that must be done.

The Capitol grounds are very quiet tonight. Across the way is the Supreme Court Building. Could it really have been only three days ago that the Court ruled against the President? The committee members have taken the first step—the hardest step, making it easier for those who will follow. They didn't walk away from it; they became the definers. But there doesn't seem to be much of a sense of triumph on anyone's part tonight. Perhaps this will be written of in the future as a moment of triumph—"the system worked"—but that is not how it feels now. There is a feeling of sadness, and exhaustion, at what everyone has been through. A feeling, too, of foreboding about those unimaginable next steps. It is a drained feeling. When history records events, it tends to leave out this kind of human emotion.

20

SUNDAY. It has been announced that the President was walking on the beach at San Clemente while the committee voted to recommend his impeachment. After consulting with the President, Ron Ziegler issued the following statement last night: "The President remains confident that the full House will recognize that there simply is not the evidence to support this or any other article of impeachment and will not vote to impeach. He is confident because he knows he has committed no impeachable offense."

On *Face the Nation* today, Caldwell Butler said of being a congressman that "the job really isn't that good that you want to compromise yourself to what you think is right."

Monday. There were several meetings on Capitol Hill yesterday to work out the substance of and strategy for the debate on Article II. This is the crucial article—the one that will define limits on Presidential power, reassert guarantees in the Bill of Rights, and reaffirm our liberties. On Saturday, the "swing group" decided to adopt McClory's construction of the issue: to attach the charges to the President's failure to "take care that the laws be faithfully executed." In the midst of these busy meetings, they were settling an important Constitutional question of the President's responsibility. One reason for moving to McClory's framework was that the "swing group" was having trouble meeting its own requirement—that each event must be directly traceable to the President. Another reason was to win McClory's vote. After some backing and filling, it was also decided to split off the question of the President's failure to comply with the committee's subpoenas, and to deal with that in a separate article.

In the midst of these busy meetings, the members were deciding the difficult Constitutional question of the President's failure to coöperate in his own impeachment—what that does to the impeachment process itself. Mann, deeply involved in all these negotiations, preferred to see the issue of noncompliance as part of Article II, coming under the heading of abuse of power. He felt that it was in fact an abuse of power, and he was uncomfortable with the idea of impeaching a President on a "procedural" issue alone. However, there were, once again, practical considerations for making the issue of noncompliance a separate article. This was the way McClory wanted it, and Mann was concerned that some of the Republicans who otherwise supported Article II might oppose it if the charge of noncoöperation with the committee were in it. Moreover, Doar believed that noncoöperation with the committee was in itself a serious issue, and in the meetings on Sunday he came down in favor of dealing with it separately, as Article III. But Doar also had concern over the Fifth Amendment implications of Article III, and said that this might cause problems on the floor of the House and the Senate. And Mann, despite his misgivings, was prepared to vote for a separate article on noncoöperation with the impeachment investigation. He is, it seems clear, considering the possibility that he might be one of the managers of the Senate trial, and feels that the appropriate Constitutional history can be made there—that such a charge should be levelled only in the context of other serious and impeachable misconduct. (That Mann, who looks typecast for such a role in the Senate—and, as a conservative Southerner, is politically well suited for it—is considering such a possibility is another indication of how those who now favor impeachment have become believers. It may also indicate that some of them are warming to the possibilities of their historic roles.) Early yesterday morning, Rodino, Mann, and McClory met and agreed upon the outlines of Article II.

Senate Majority Leader Mike Mansfield and Senate Minority Leader Hugh Scott are meeting this morning to work out procedures for a Senate trial. Over the weekend, there was a babel of predictions about the President's fate. House Majority Leader Thomas O'Neill predicted impeachment by a margin of about seventy votes. John Rhodes, the House Minority Leader, said that the "only viable possibility" for avoiding impeachment was for the President to "go on television and exhaustively explore and refute the evidence." It appears to be too late for that—as Rhodes may realize. He said that the vote by six committee Republicans in favor of impeachment "is going to have some effect" in reducing House Republican support for the President. Senate Majority Whip Robert Byrd said that if the President refused to produce tapes or other required evidence for a Senate trial, it would "sound the death knell for the President so far as some senators are concerned, my vote being one." Alexander Haig said that "the case for impeachment is not there," and that the committee's charges were "a grab bag of generalities." Haig said that it had long been felt in the White House that the committee was a lost cause, and "there were discussions that perhaps we could hold three or four Republicans." Ron Ziegler said that the President has "a tremendous capacity of discipline," has "no feeling of despair," and has not allowed "anger to overtake him." Ziegler added, "Certainly there is anguish . . . certainly there is disappointment." The President is a man "with feeling and compassion," said Ziegler, and this period has been "very tough."

The President returned to Washington from San Clemente last night.

This morning, the committee is again late in getting started. Article II is still being refined, and the members are holding strategy huddles. Railsback is talking with Flowers in the committee room, and the photographers rush to record the scene. They must have a million photographs of these people by now. Railsback looks tanned and rested; he played golf yesterday with Wiggins. Railsback says that his district's reaction to his vote has been "sixty-forty favorable." Cohen has a hemorrhaged ear, from flying back in a small plane from Maine— where on Sunday he made a televised speech explaining his vote to impeach. Doar looks exhausted. The new version of Article II will be offered by Hungate. The Southern Democrats will not themselves sponsor these articles; other senior Democrats are too identifiably pro-impeachment; and Sarbanes, a junior member, has already done his job. So this one falls to Hungate, a border-state representative. At eleven-nineteen, a new draft of Article II is passed out to the members, and they are told to throw away the former version. Those Xerox machines must be indestructible.

At eleven-thirty, word circulates through the room that John Connally has been indicted for accepting ten thousand dollars, when he was Secretary of the Treasury, in exchange for urging that price supports on milk be raised, and for lying about the money to the grand jury. Jake Jacobsen, a lawyer for Associated Milk Producers and, like Connally, a Texan and former associate of Lyndon Johnson, was also indicted, for making the payment. Trent Lott, the thirty-two-year-old conservative Republican from Mississippi—whose district in 1972 gave Nixon the highest vote of any district in the country—says to reporters, "Secretly, maybe all of us are hoping for resignation, and maybe I care enough for my colleagues to think that's the best course."

The new version of Article II states that the President, "in violation of his Constitutional oath faithfully to execute the office of President of the United States and, to the best of his ability, preserve, protect, and defend the Constitution of the United States, and in disregard of his Constitutional duty to take care that the laws be faithfully executed has repeatedly engaged in conduct violating the Constitutional rights of citizens, impairing the due and proper administration of justice and the conduct of lawful inquiries, or contravening the laws governing agencies

of the executive branch and the purposes of these agencies." The first
charge is that the President "has, acting personally and through his subordinates and agents, endeavored to obtain from the Internal Revenue
Service, in violation of the Constitutional rights of citizens, confidential
information contained in income-tax returns for purposes not authorized by law, and to cause, in violation of the Constitutional rights of
citizens, income-tax audits or other income-tax investigations to be
initiated or conducted in a discriminatory manner." The I.R.S. issue,
the members have recently discovered, is politically very potent, so it
has been incorporated in a separate subsection, which is put first. The
President is held accountable for the various instances of misuse, or
even of attempted misuse of the I.R.S. by the inclusion of the phrase
"acting personally and through his subordinates and agents."

The article does not assert that the misuse of the I.R.S. actually took
place, but charges that the President, via his aides, "endeavored" to misuse it. It remains somewhat unclear to what extent the Nixon White
House was able to use the I.R.S. for political purposes, as opposed to
trying to use it and talking about using it. While it has been said that
those on the enemies list and the list of McGovern supporters were not
singled out to be audited (the study of this by the Joint Committee on
Internal Revenue Taxation is continuing), many of us know of several
people on the lists who were—perhaps only at random. We do know
that information about George Wallace's brother was obtained and
used; and, according to committee evidence, that information on others,
including Lawrence O'Brien, was obtained; that the President on several occasions expressed interest in overcoming the resistance of I.R.S.
officials. We now know (through a piece of tape that was accidentally
recorded by the Secret Service, which was recording tapes to be turned
over to the committee) that on September 15th, before Dean entered the
Oval Office, Haldeman informed the President that Dean was "moving
ruthlessly on the investigation of McGovern people, Kennedy stuff,"
and also that "Chuck has gone through, you know, has worked on the
list and Dean's working the, the thing through I.R.S." There have also
been testimony and affidavits to the effect that in their meeting that
day, Dean, Haldeman, and the President discussed the reluctance of the
I.R.S. to coöperate, and that Dean reported on the I.R.S. investigation
of O'Brien. The White House has refused to surrender this portion of
the tape. But it is not clear to what degree the committee members are
moved by the seriousness of the interference with the I.R.S., its potential seriousness, or its political potency as an issue.

The second charge covers the wiretapping, which was dealt with only
indirectly in the original version of Article II, submitted to the committee last Wednesday. To skirt the issue of whether the wiretaps should
be termed illegal, the earlier draft charged only that the President had
directed that the F.B.I. not maintain proper records of them. On the

wiretapping issue, there were deep divisions between the Democratic drafters and the "swing group," and even within the "swing group." Some of the members thought that all the tapping was illegal; some thought that at least part of it had justifiable national-security purposes; some thought that in order for the tapping—even if illegal—to be deemed impeachable there had to be a showing that it was done for the President's personal political gain. This version of Article II charges him with misusing the F.B.I., the Secret Service, "and other executive personnel in violation or disregard of the Constitutional rights of citizens by directing or authorizing" them "to conduct or continue electronic surveillance or other investigations for purposes unrelated to national security, the enforcement of laws, or any other lawful function of his office"; thus it gets around the misgivings of those members who felt that some of the wiretaps may have had a national-security basis at least at the outset. This subsection on wiretapping also charges that the President "did direct, authorize, or permit the use of information" gained from the wiretaps "for purposes unrelated to national security." Therefore, the charge that this wiretapping was for his personal political benefit is included, indirectly, but such words as "personal political benefit" are left out.

The third charge is that the President, "acting personally and through his subordinates and agents, in violation or disregard of the Constitutional rights of citizens, authorized and permitted to be maintained a secret investigative unit within the office of the President [the plumbers], financed in part with money derived from campaign contributions [milk money], which unlawfully utilized the resources of the Central Intelligence Agency, engaged in covert and unlawful activities, and attempted to prejudice the Constitutional right of an accused to a fair trial." This deals with the issue of attempts to smear Daniel Ellsberg—surfaced in Colson's recent guilty plea—without giving it more emphasis than the committee members wish. (Members of Congress were not eager to frame the issue as one of defending Ellsberg against the President.) It also encompasses the break-in at Dr. Fielding's office without necessarily linking it directly to the President. The use of the milk money to finance the Fielding break-in is included because several committee members find the concept of using campaign funds to finance secret intelligence operations conducted from the White House exceedingly disturbing. Last fall, when we first learned of the circuitous way in which Colson, at Ehrlichman's request, had raised five thousand dollars to finance the travels of the plumbers to the West Coast, it seemed like any number of bizarre and slightly disconcerting news stories we were reading. Now it is part of an impeachable offense.

The fourth charge included in Article II is that the President "failed to take care that the laws were faithfully executed by failing to act when he knew or had reason to know that his close subordinates endeav-ored to impede and frustrate lawful inquiries" into the break-in of the Democratic National Committee "and concerning other matters." This, in effect, encompasses Article I, but in a different form, with a lower burden of proof. This subsection holds the President account-able—under the "abuse of power" concept—for the cover-up on the basis of misconduct of his close subordinates, and "failing to act when he knew or had reason to know" of it; as opposed to—in Article I—saying that the President was himself engaged in the obstruction of justice.

And the fifth charge: "In disregard of the rule of law, he knowingly misused the executive power by interfering with" various government agencies, including the F.B.I., the Criminal Division of the Justice Department, the Special Prosecutor's office (presumably, this includes the firing of Archibald Cox, and though the destruction of evidence—the responsibility for this not having yet been proved—is not specifically included, it was on the drafters' minds), and the C.I.A., "in violation of his duty to 'take care that the laws be faithfully executed.' " So now those words, conveying one of the Constitutional obligations of the President, are to have meaning. The Congress, which had paid little attention to whether the laws were being faithfully executed, will now give those words force. But will the Congress continue to pay attention after this is over?

The criterion of charging the President only with actions that could be traceable to him proved impossible, and in this draft the issue has been fudged. Language was adapted to pick up votes. These were legislators legislating; accommodations were made to satisfy various members, and even staff members. There has sometimes seemed to be more emphasis on the fact that agencies were misused than concern for the citizens whose Constitutional rights were thereby violated—a result of political judgments that misuse of the agencies was a stronger political issue. This article still holds the President accountable, at least indirectly, for the actions of his subordinates, leaving the question of the Madison superintendency concept unresolved. Perhaps this is the way it will always be: those actions will always be traced, however indirectly, to the President. Acting through subordinates is the only way a President can act. In order to deal with the deniability problem, the staff had stressed Haldeman's close association with the President, so as to get across the idea that Haldeman and those he directed were doing the acts at issue here on the President's behalf, and that the President failed to superin-tend his highest aides. There is, of course, the possibility that a similar White House group—should this country ever be faced with one—acting for a future President would be more skillful at establishing deniability. But it seems that the critical thing that is happening here is that the committee is establishing that there is certain executive behavior, including infringements of the Bill of Rights, that will not be tolerated. This article reaffirms the First, Fourth, and Sixth Amendments of the Bill of Rights. Our language in talking about these articles has been turned inside out: it is said that this version of Article II, encompassing McClory's "take-care" framework, is "looser" than previous versions; it in fact encompasses a stricter code of Presidential behavior.

The debate on Article II begins. It is as serious, defining, and crucial as any that has taken place since the Constitutional Convention. Striking at the heart of it, Charles Wiggins, who has become the most effective opponent of impeachment on the committee, argues that Article II "fails to state an impeachable offense under the Constitution." He says, "The question is whether an abuse of power falls within the meaning of the phrase 'high crimes and misdemeanors.' " And Wiggins asks, "Just what is abusive conduct? I suggest that it is an empty phrase, having meaning only in terms of what we pour into it. It must reflect our subjective views of impropriety, as distinguished from the objective views enunciated by society in its laws." Article II, he says, "would embed in our Constitutional history for the first time, for the very first time, the principle that a President may be impeached because of the view of Congress that he has abused those powers, although he may have acted in violation of no law."

Wiggins is exactly right, and has stated what the fundamental argument is about: he is asking whether, in the absence of codified limits, the Congress can safely decide that the President has overstepped limits. Taking it a degree further, he says, "By declaring punishable conduct which was not illegal when done, this Congress is raising the issue of a bill of attainder, contrary to the express terms of the Constitution. The argument of ex-post-facto legislation is now before us. . . . We are taking a step toward a parliamentary system of government in this country rather than the Constitutional system which we now have. We are, in effect, saying, Mr. Chairman, that a President may be impeached in the future if a Congress expresses no confidence in his conduct, not because he has violated the law but, rather, because that Congress declares his conduct to be abusive in terms of their subjective notions of propriety. In terms of the future, Mr. Chairman, what standard are we setting for the Presidents in the future? How will any future President know precisely what Congress may declare to be an abuse, especially when they have failed to legislate against the very acts which they may condemn?"

George Danielson, Democrat of California, responds. Danielson, pink-faced, with white-blond hair stretched straight across his partly bald head, is usually pleasantly low-keyed. But there is passion in his voice as he responds to Wiggins. "This is possibly, probably—I can make that stronger—it is certainly the most important article that this committee may pass out," he says. "The offense charged in this article is truly a high crime and misdemeanor within the purest meaning of those words as established in Anglo-American jurisprudence over a period of now some six hundred years. The offenses charged against the President in this article are uniquely Presidential offenses. No one else can commit them. You or I, the most lowly citizen, can obstruct justice. You or I, the most lowly citizen, can violate any of the statutes in our criminal code. But only the President can violate the oath of office of the President. Only the President can abuse the powers of the office of the President."

This debate conducted by these two men from California—one a Democrat, the other a Republican—will be consulted for decades to come. Danielson concludes by saying, "And it is our function, acting under the impeachment clause, to preserve and protect the Presidency as we preserve and protect every other part of our marvellous structure of government. . . . The offenses charged in this proposed article, I respectfully submit, Mr. Chairman, are offenses which go directly to that solemn breach of a solemn oath of office. Can anyone argue that if the President breaches his oath of office, he should not be removed?"

William Hungate describes his latest version of the substitute Article II as "a distillation of the thought of many members from many areas, and of differing political philosophies." The truth—and a nice way to think about it. Wiggins has raised an important point—whether there is or should be some explicit understanding of the limits, whether it is fair to impeach a President when no notice has been given of what would be grounds for impeachment. It is, by itself, a question with a certain plausibility. If the criminal code is not the guide, what is? By what fair test can it be decided that a President has "abused power"? Hungate responds to these questions. He says that the article refers to "repetitive conduct." He goes on, "I would think that if [there had been] only one instance of improper conduct—and it perhaps could be quite serious—I do not know that we would be here today. I think this sort of impeachment trial was deliberately set up historically so that those who are in political life, and political figures, try the President, a political figure— those who can understand some of the pressures and nuances involved in serving in a public office. And, for my part, I think there is more tolerance in such a political body than one would find in just a body without the experience . . . of the pressures and difficulties in public life. I say again if only one violation had occurred, I would doubt that we should be here. Men are human. Humans are frail. But I think we discuss and consider here and see here a consistent disregard of the law." So, as Hungate defines it, it is a matter of degree. Not everything can be codified. In the end, it is a political question, which the framers put in the hands of political people—people who are not without their own transgressions, who sometimes seem too tolerant of the transgressions of other politicians—trusting them to know when a line had been crossed. This responsibility was not without its dangers (as Alexander Hamilton pointed out), but there seemed to be no better solution.

Yet, asks Edward Hutchinson, does the "supposed repetition" make the charge more justifiable? Would each offense be impeachable if it stood alone? The Republicans are well prepared today, too, and we are hearing a serious and important argument.

Robert McClory, defending Article II, says that his support of the article is founded on the "take-care" clause. And, as he defines it, "there is a clear violation of the President's responsibility when he permits multiple acts of wrongdoing by large numbers of those who surround him in possession of greatest responsibility and influence in the White House." The purpose of impeachment, he says, is "to set a Constitutional standard for persons occupying the office of the President." He goes on, "I view the duty of the House of Representatives as something other than serving as a district courthouse," and, "We must phrase our charges in Constitutional terms so that the Presidents to come may know what is meant by our action. If we are to establish our proceedings as a guide for future Presidents, we should speak in terms of the Constitution and specifically in terms of the President's oath and his obligation under the Constitution. It will be of limited value to admonish a future President not to obstruct justice or engage in a cover-up. However, it will aid future Presidents to know this Congress and this House Judiciary Committee will hold them to an oath of office and an obligation to 'take care' to see that the laws are 'faithfully executed.' " It is hard to imagine that the words of Robert McClory, from Lake Bluff, Illinois, this man with the nasal voice and wide eyes who has so often seemed confused, will be as carefully attended to in the future as those of James Madison have been. But they may well be, because today McClory is making Constitutional history.

Wiggins then strikes at another crucial point—that of whether it must be shown that the President had knowledge of or condoned all the actions for which he might be impeached—by offering an amendment saying that in the matters included in Article II the President acted "through his subordinates and agents acting with his knowledge or pursuant to his instructions." Doar watches, looking worried, and shakes his head, signalling no, as Hungate, apparently unaware of what Wiggins is doing—establishing a criterion of proof that perhaps cannot be met and, according to this article, is not necessary—says that Wiggins' amendment encompasses the intention of the article and is "superfluous." Doar quietly sends an aide to the dais to talk with another aide, who is sitting behind Hungate, and while other members are speaking, the seated aide talks with Hungate. Later, Hungate says that he cannot agree with the language of the amendment. McClory, speaking against

Wiggins' amendment, makes another definitive statement when he says that "the Constitution does not say that the President shall execute the laws but that he shall 'take care that the laws be faithfully executed.'"

During the noon recess, Railsback circulates on the floor of the House, moving among several groups of Republicans. Railsback is doing the talking. He is at work. He is explaining his position. He is hastening the end of the Nixon Presidency. Then he goes to the House members' dining room and seats himself at a large round table toward the back of the room, at which Republicans regularly gather for lunch, and talks some more.

Before the committee reconvenes, I drop in to see Walter Flowers in his office. Flowers says that he is exhausted, "physically, mentally, emotionally." He says that, in addition to an ulcer, he had a partly collapsed lung during the proceedings.

I ask how the decision to vote for impeachment had formed in his mind.

"It was a late-blooming thing," Flowers replies. "It was kind of like all the seed was in and the plowing and fertilizing germinated in the last two weeks. The more I thought about it, and tried to think about doing something else, I realized I couldn't. Then the undecided people got together and we started talking among ourselves. Most of us probably started out looking for a way to support the President."

I question him on that, asking if this was really so.

"My whole background and upbringing would make me that way," Flowers replies. "Who I am and where I come from." He goes on, "But when you got all of the evidence before all of us so-called 'persuadables' and we all came down on the same side, it really struck us."

I ask him what did it.

"I can't put my finger on it," Flowers replies. "I can't do it. It was the whole thing. I tried to look at it from the side of what happens if we fail to impeach. It's worse. It's worse. I do not accept the fact that the President can mislead and misrepresent to the public. I do not accept the fact that the President can misuse sensitive agencies. I do not accept the fact that he can obstruct investigations. The Petersen thing zapped me more than anything else. The live witnesses affected me. And when it all got put together the pieces fitted. Kalmbach was a particularly persuasive witness. There was something massively wrong that this thoroughly decent man, a picture of what a lawyer ought to be, got into this whole seamy thing." (Railsback had mentioned Kalmbach, too. These lawyers seem to have found him sympathetic, somehow even to have identified with him—considered him one of them, and had been greatly disturbed by his having been drawn into the corruption.) Says Flowers, "There was a lack of sensitivity to the barest requirements of human behavior. You've got to assume that the standard of conduct is set by the man in charge. The President never tried to stop all this. He was kind of like a pumping station on a pipeline. He kept applying the pressure."

I ask Flowers what feedback he has been getting from his Southern colleagues in the House since he voted for impeachment.

He says that the fact that Butler, the conservative Virginia Republican, and the three Southern Democrats on the committee all voted to impeach has impressed several of his Southern colleagues. He says, "I happen to think that the system is more important than the man, and I think that the moderates and Southerners will see this as they look at it some more." He adds, "There are some people in the South who think that McGovern is going to be President if Nixon is impeached. Did you know that?"

An elevator operator in the Cannon Building, where Flowers' office is, says as Flowers and I get out of the elevator, "Have a good day." Flowers laughs, and says, "That sounds kind of funny—somebody telling me to have a good day."

In the afternoon session, Wiggins' amendment that would specify that all the actions covered in Article II had been taken with the President's "knowledge or pursuant to his instructions" is defeated. He offers another one, to delete the words "and concerning other matters" from the section charging the President with failing to act when he had reason to know that his aides were impeding the inquiries into the Watergate break-in "and concerning other matters." Wiggins has struck again. He says that the language is "vague" and "uncertain." Flowers agrees, and says he will support the amendment, and so does Railsback. They are propitiating. But the point of the language was to include other matters, and the pattern of blocking investigations is one of the major elements of the case. Doar sends another message, via an aide, to Hungate, and Butler leaves his seat on the dais to speak with Doar. McClory opposes the amendment, saying that the break-in at the Democrats' headquarters "is only a small part of the misdeeds, the misconduct which is attributable to these aides and assistants of the President." Rodino signals to Doar to come and speak with him, and Barbara Jordan joins them at Rodino's seat. They are regrouping on this one.

Cohen, who has often perceived an opposition stratagem and quickly moved to meet it, asks Hungate if he would be prepared to accept a list of specific instances, and Hungate says he would. Cohen drafts such an amendment as others stall for time to get it honed and reproduced; Butler offers it; and it is quickly accepted by the committee. Wiggins, the good advocate, succeeds by his questions in sharpening the articles, and the arguments for them. That particular subsection of the abuse-of-power article, charging the President with failing to act when his subordinates thwarted the administration of justice, is one of the most important subsections in terms of establishing Presidential accountability. It now covers condoning a pattern of blocking investigations of the break-in at the Watergate and of the cover-up, and also of frustrating lawful inquiries during the confirmation hearings of Richard Kleindienst as Attorney General; of the wiretapping (including the removal of information about wiretaps from the offices of the F.B.I.); of the Fielding break-in; and of the campaign-financing practices of the Committee to Re-Elect the President. (The last is the only reference to the broad subject of money in either Article I or Article II.)

Then the Judiciary Committee members debate wiretapping and the plumbers. There was a time when it seemed that the politicians in Congress, intimidated by the national-security rationale for the plumbers, and persuaded that the public was apathetic toward such an "abstract" issue as the Fourth Amendment, would not come to grips with the issue of the plumbers or wiretapping. Now Hamilton Fish, the patrician representative from upstate New York, is arguing that the plumbers' operation was not justified and is impeachable. "It was a public-relations effort they had in mind," he says. "National security . . . was not the issue."

During the dinner break, James Mann, relaxing over a drink in his office, talks to me about the difficulty of establishing and codifying Presidential involvement in offenses that are deemed impeachable. He says, "Although each of us in the so-called 'swing group' was convinced that there was enough Presidential involvement to satisfy his conscience, we weren't able to separate all the facts and concerns that bore on but did not directly relate to Presidential involvement. A lot of the Presidential involvement was suggested by things that were not Presidential involvement. How do you set down in writing, then, all the specific acts? How do you set down a negative—that someone failed to do something? It's going to be a difficult case to state. It's above and beyond the facts. It permeates your whole being, once you get the feel of it. You climb up on this pile of garbage and you say, 'Where's the garbage?' You're standing on it."

I ask Mann when the picture came together in his mind.

"It came together in my mind very, very recently," he says. "Two or three weeks ago, I was not at all clear. You know, you're looking for a way out. You're rationalizing that the clear and present danger is gone and you've accomplished a great deal by causing people to think about their responsibility. [I recall that Mann talked this way when we spoke in April. He said then that perhaps the danger had been sufficiently recognized and therefore was past.] So everyone's alerted to the danger, and if you were to go ahead with the process and not be successful you might do more harm than good. Stopping would have been preserving the gains—having stopped the abuse of power and pointed out the inadequacies to the public and the Congress. And you would have accomplished a great deal and maintained respect for the system."

I ask whether the process could have been stopped without an appearance of condoning the abuses.

Mann replies that it could have been stopped on the basis that there was insufficient evidence. He says that he was prepared to vote against impeachment, and sign a harsh report saying that the clear and present danger was removed and that there was not sufficient evidence to impeach. "I was genuinely undecided," he says. "Roughly two weeks ago, the week before last—as that week went by, I started my decision-making process. We finished hearing the witnesses on Wednesday. By training, I wait until the end to make up my mind."

It appears that Mann, like Flowers and Railsback, decided—with some reluctance—that there was something he could not walk away from. It appears not to have happened at any particular moment but to have occurred more as a realization that developed. Perhaps asking these people when they made up their minds is putting an unanswerable question to them. In many of our most important "decisions," the awareness of having made a decision occurs some time after it has happened; the process is deeper, more subtle, less commanded by reason or logic than we would like to think. Falling in love. Turning against the Vietnam war. Changing jobs. Do we know exactly when these decisions were made, or exactly why? When and why did people decide that something was terribly wrong with the Nixon governance? When the hundred-dollar bills found on the burglars at the Watergate were traced to the Finance Committee to Re-Elect the President? When John Dean testified before the Ervin committee? When the President made his third evasive statement about these matters? If these people are to be taken at their word, there was a time when some of them did think they could walk away from it—and then decided that they could not. Perhaps they never really could have. We, and perhaps they, will never know. I ask Mann if he can describe at least what it was that he felt he could not walk away from. He thinks for a few moments, then says carefully, "The obvious failure to give proper recognition—I'm putting it as mildly as I can—to the rule of law. That just has to be the core of the whole philosophy of this. The evidence that was available to us just broke through the specifics."

Mann can describe the steps that led him to be the chief draftsman of the articles of impeachment. "One day, Bill Cohen, Walter Flowers, and I were standing there talking," he says. "I had been talking about it with Walter and hearing through him from Railsback, because he and Railsback are better friends. Walter had expressed to me some doubt that Railsback would be for impeachment. Cohen asked if we would be interested in talking. Frankly, I had no intention of letting it go with-

out our getting together. Within a day or two, I got a call from Flowers."
That call led to the meeting last Tuesday morning in Railsback's office.
Mann had spoken with Butler, and several members of the group knew
that Fish might be leaning toward impeachment, so the seven swing
members began meeting.

"We met," says Mann, "and it was very comfortable." He confirms,
as the others have, that "it became quickly apparent at that meeting that
we were agreed on two propositions—one was obstruction of justice
and the other was abuse of power." He goes on, "It fell to my lot to
work on some articles. It wasn't over seventy-two hours before that
that I had it locked in my mind—but it was a contingent locking—
that we would be able to put together a series of articles that could
be supported. Something had happened to me, and I said to myself I
couldn't let this thing pass. It didn't come to me until a few days after
the witnesses had testified. It was a conclusion that came on slowly, a
conclusion that there was no way out, despite all your rationalizations.
The Democrats realized that they had to work with us and accept the
lowest common denominator. I called it that, and Jerry Waldie called it
that. That became clear in a caucus or two." Mann feels that they also
have a "semi-commitment" that articles on Cambodia and taxes will
not be passed—"so that there will be no dilution of the principles that
we are willing to support." He adds, "I'm of the opinion that we are in
a position to enforce that commitment. We'll use whatever force we
must use to see that those articles don't pass. Of course, I'm not asking
people to vote against their consciences."

And so Mann proceeded to consult with staff members, do some
drafting of his own, check language with Doar, shuttle between the
"swing group" and the Democratic drafters, work out political equations. And so the articles of impeachment were drafted.

In prime time, the committee completes its debate on abuse of power.
Wiggins argues, "Richard Nixon believed the Pentagon Papers issue
was a national-security issue, and his actions after learning in March
of 1973 were wholly consistent with that belief on his part. Now, if a
majority of the committee really believes that a President of the United
States should be impeached because of his honest and good-faith belief
that the security of this nation is in jeopardy, and that decisive and bold
action is required on his part, then so be it. . . . History is going to judge
you ill if you make that judgment."

Paul Sarbanes, referring to the Fielding break-in, replies, "I ask every
doctor and lawyer and every insurance agent and accountant in the
country, what kind of a land would you be living in if a group of hired
hands have the power to come into your office in the dead of night in
order to get one of your files?"

And, in prime time, Brooks moves to strike the subsection about the

I.R.S., thereby gaining another opportunity to spread the issue before the nation. They know they have hit home with this issue.

Says Sandman, "It is obvious that this is a game. . . . I'm mindful of the fact that they tell me we have about a twenty-percent audience, which is about forty-four million people."

Fish, speaking to the philosophy of Article II, says, "To faithfully execute the laws of our country does involve policing your lieutenants and does involve an obligation to stop them when you see the course they are following." Fish has said little during the debate, but now he says, in a few words, a great deal. For a long time, people struggled to find the imagery to describe this set of events, or even to describe the difficulty of describing it. Then the images began to emerge. Hogan spoke of tiles in a mosaic, Mann of a pile of garbage, Sarbanes of the vegetable store. Now Fish says, "For those who are looking for the smoking pistol, I am just afraid they are not going to find it, because the room is too full of smoke."

As the vote on this article approaches, there is not the same tension in the room that there was on Saturday. The first vote to impeach was the more difficult one. Having cast such a vote once, it will not be so difficult to do it again. In their closing statements, however, the members on both sides show that they recognize the special significance of Article II.

Sandman: "What we do we had better do right, because the effect of it is going to make a precedent for a thousand years."

Mann, quoting Thomas Paine: "Those who expect to reap the blessings of freedom must, like men, undergo the fatigue of supporting it." And then Mann says, "If there be no accountability, another President will feel free to do as he chooses. But the next time there may be no watchman in the night."

At eleven-seventeen, the committee votes on the Hungate substitute—in effect, a vote to impeach the President of the United States for abuse of power, for failure to "take care that the laws be faithfully executed." It is not as emotional or dramatic a moment as the one on Saturday, but it is more important. Flowers tilts his head back slightly as he says "Aye." Mann again stares off into space as he votes. Some of the Republicans are defiant as they say "No." This time, McClory votes "Aye." His is the only vote that has changed since Saturday. Railsback looks off somewhat balefully as he votes. Hogan's head is down. And Rodino nods his head slightly as he says "Aye." The vote is twenty-eight to ten to impeach the President for abuse of power.

JULY 30

Tuesday. Yesterday, the White House announced that the President would not resign if he was impeached. The President was said to have been spending time on the talks between the Greeks and the Turks about the recent fighting in Cyprus, and also to have met with his lawyers James St. Clair and Fred Buzhardt to review the tapes that the Supreme Court ordered him to turn over to the Special Prosecutor.

Edward Hutchinson has predicted that the President will be impeached. The Senate yesterday, in its first formal step in the process, referred the question of revising the decades-old rules for a Senate trial to the Rules and Administration Committee. It is still not clear whether the trial will be held before the election, or even before the beginning of the next Congress. Mansfield, Byrd, and aides to other Democratic senators, such as Edward M. Kennedy, Philip Hart, and Birch Bayh, have already been working on revisions of the rules, and, characteristically, there is some rivalry over whose rules will be adopted.

The Washington *Post* reports that a survey it has made indicates that fewer than half of the Southern Democrats in the House may support the President on impeachment, and that Midwest Republican leaders "indicated there may no longer be any clear advantage for Republican congressmen from that region in voting with the President." The *Post* quotes Representative Richardson Preyer, an influential Democrat from North Carolina, publicly "uncommitted," as saying that the Judiciary Committee and its staff "have done a very careful job of fitting the pieces together," and adding, "When people like Mann and Flowers come out for impeachment it will make it easier for other members from my area who might be inclined to support impeachment. Everyone knows they aren't secret liberals." Representative Gillis Long, Democrat of Louisiana, also "uncommitted," predicted that there would be votes against the President by representatives from his state, from Georgia, and possibly even from Mississippi. Long said that the Judiciary Committee's conduct had been "exemplary" and "tends to shore up the confidence of people that the matter's being handled fairly." There are stories about the "erosion" of the President's support among conservatives in the House. John Ashbrook, conservative Republican representative from Ohio, said, according to the *Post*, that he was now prepared to vote for impeachment and it would take "a miracle of evidence to change my mind." Howard Phillips, once President Nixon's chosen instrument, as director of the Office of Economic Opportunity, for the dismantling of the agency, announced the formation of a group called Conservatives for the Removal of the President. Other conservative Republican representatives who had said they were opposed to impeachment are now placing themselves in the "undecided" category.

Article III, to impeach the President for his failure to comply with the committee's subpoenas, was adopted today after a debate that was at once solemn and confused, of great historical significance and fed by momentary political considerations. But so were the debates at Philadelphia. The question here, simply put, was whether, if a President refuses to coöperate with an inquiry into his impeachment, he should be impeached. There were two very strong, and opposite, arguments to consider. If a President could with impunity refuse to submit evidence to an impeachment inquiry, he could destroy the power of impeachment. On the other hand, to impeach a President on this ground might establish a precedent for an irresponsible Congress to launch an impeachment inquiry that was without serious grounds, and then impeach a President simply for refusing to turn over whatever evidence it demanded. It might establish that there were no justifiable claims of executive privilege or national security. And, as some members pointed out, the issue raised the problem of self-incrimination. Ultimately, it appears that great power requires great constraints, and that this outweighs the consideration that a responsible President could be harassed by an irresponsible Congress. Better to have him turn over material he would prefer to withhold than to nullify the impeachment process.

While some members, such as Cohen and Mann, felt that the principle of Presidential coöperation was important, they wanted it to be considered in context, not codified as a separate impeachable offense. Mann, who a few days ago had, mainly for political reasons, supported a separate article on noncoöperation, changed his mind, and decided to vote against Article III. It seems, also, that for most of the members of the "swing group" voting for two articles of impeachment was enough. Railsback, during the debate on Article III, called it "political overkill," and even warned that if it was adopted the "fragile coalition" on the committee would be threatened. (Cohen made a point of dissociating himself from this threat.) Doar, who had espoused treating the President's defiance of the committee as a separate impeachable offense, was still troubled by the Fifth Amendment implications and the possibility that the article might be rejected by the House or the Senate. Rejection of Article III might be viewed as approval of Presidential noncoöperation. Rodino stayed up late last night worrying about the question, and finally decided to proceed with the article. An amendment by Ray Thornton, of Arkansas, adopted by the committee, limited the article to covering situations in which there is "demonstrated by other evidence to be substantial grounds for impeachment of the President."

On the final vote on Article III, Hogan and McClory vote with nineteen Democrats in favor, and Flowers, Mann, Fish, Cohen, Railsback, Butler, and Froehlich join the ten remaining Republicans in opposition. (Lawrence Hogan has thus become the one Republican to support all three articles.)

Conyers' motion to impeach the President for the secret bombing of Cambodia and the falsifying of information about it is, as had been expected, rejected—by a vote of twenty-six to twelve. From the outset, there was little disposition within the committee to inject the bitter question of the war into the impeachment.

In the debate, Caldwell Butler draws from Elizabeth Holtzman, Democrat of New York, the fact that several congressional leaders knew about the bombing, and, concludes Butler, "That's a responsibility the Congress must share with the President. We can't impeach ourselves." Cohen points out that after the Congress learned of the bombing it did not act immediately to stop it but ultimately voted to cut off the bombing as of August 15, 1973—in effect, as several members saw it, ratifying the President's action. Sandman, coming at it on another level—a level that Rodino and others had hoped to avoid—says, "Do you want to be remembered as that part of that Congress that tried to impeach a President of the United States because he did something which ended a war that his two predecessors could not do?"

And, as the Republicans angrily point out, the Democrats choose prime time this evening for the debate on a proposed article to impeach the President for receiving "emoluments"—the government spending on his homes at Key Biscayne and San Clemente—in violation of Article II, Section I of the Constitution, and for "willfully" attempting to avoid full payment of his income taxes. Both sides knew that this was an article that would not pass but that the issue of the President's taxes and homes was one that particularly annoyed the public. This article, too, is defeated by a vote of twenty-six to twelve.

It is odd how quickly the perception of reality has changed again. There was a time when it was said that the Judiciary Committee, being "stacked" liberal, would, of course, vote for impeachment but that it did not follow that the House would do so; it was not just the opponents of impeachment who discounted in advance a possible recommendation by the committee that the President be impeached. Now the general perception is that a vote to impeach is a foregone conclusion in the House and that the President's fortunes are slipping rapidly in the Senate. There were some who always thought that it would be this way once the House committee had voted. The manner in which the committee conducted its proceedings and the size of the votes to impeach—the fact that three Southern Democrats and six, and then seven, Republicans supported two articles of impeachment—have become the decisive factors. There was a time when some said that the committee's deliberations were just the preliminaries—and in one sense they are. It will be a long summer—and perhaps autumn and winter—as the House and the Senate go on with this process. But it also seems now that the Judiciary Committee's action was the defining one.

At eleven o'clock tonight, July 30, 1974, Chairman Peter Rodino says, "This concludes the work of the committee." The moment is less dramatic than might have been expected. Since Saturday, people have become more accustomed to the idea of what the committee has done. It is hard to remember that this is the first time since 1868 that the impeachment of any President has been recommended by a congressional committee. It is still hard to realize what this means—that Richard Nixon may be the first President in American history to be removed from office.

21

WEDNESDAY. The lead story in today's Washington *Post* is that if the President is convicted by the Senate he will lose the perquisites he would have upon leaving the office under other circumstances, including resignation: a pension of sixty thousand dollars a year; a stipend of ninety-six thousand dollars a year for staff salaries and allowances; free office space for himself and his staff; and a widow's pension of twenty thousand dollars a year for his wife. The story also points out that if he is convicted by the Senate he may be disbarred. It is a strange non-news story, given odd prominence. Is someone trying to send him a message? The story was written by Spencer Rich, the *Post's* Senate correspondent. Will this story be put in the President's daily news summary?

One can almost hear the sound of the walls crumbling. The New York *Times* reports that John Rhodes, "hoping to head off what could become a stampede for impeachment," has scheduled informal meetings for Republicans to debate the issue. The *Times* quotes a "Northern Republican" as saying that there might be nearly a two-to-one margin for impeachment in the House. "It looks like a runaway," he is quoted as saying. Republican House members have been discussing the possibility of having the President ask the House to forgo a debate on the impeachment articles and to cast a "pro-forma" vote, so that there could be an immediate trial in the Senate. The White House is also showing interest in such a plan. The House members say that this is in the President's interest, but it appears also to serve their own.

Yesterday, the President turned over twenty of the subpoenaed tapes to Judge Sirica. Others are still to be produced. Yesterday, it was announced that the President was spending time in the Lincoln sitting room—where we used to be told that he sat in lonely isolation with a yellow legal pad drafting speeches—listening to subpoenaed tapes.

The Senate aide who is in the traffic patterns on Capitol Hill says, "It's all over. It's only a matter now of how the eggs are cooked."

Jack Anderson, the columnist, reports today that the Special Prosecutor's office, picking up where the Ervin committee left off, is continuing an investigation into the financial affairs of Bebe Rebozo.

AUGUST I

Thursday. John Ehrlichman, after he was sentenced yesterday by Judge Gesell to a period of from twenty months to five years in prison for conspiracy and perjury in connection with the break-in at Daniel Ellsberg's psychiatrist's office, said that he would appeal and that he was "confident ... that I will ultimately be exonerated and vindicated." Ehrlichman is the highest former aide to the President—and the fourteenth of his former aides or associates—to be convicted, or to plead guilty. (Seven more have been indicted and still face trial.) Speaking to reporters on the steps of the District Courthouse, Ehrlichman described what he thought were "the fundamental issues and principles" involved. He said, "People who are in government are constantly required to balance the rights of an individual against the larger rights of the nation as a whole. . . . The obvious example is the farmer who is asked to give up his farm in order to build an airbase in wartime." These "balancing judgments are involved day to day in various aspects of government life," said Ehrlichman. "There was a balance of that kind involved in this case."

Charles Wiggins and Senator John Tower, Republican of Texas, have said that they now believe that impeachment is almost inevitable. John Brademas, the chief deputy House Democratic Whip, predicts that there will be three hundred votes for impeachment. Plans are being made for informal sessions of House members to hear the arguments on both sides preceding the formal debate. And now they have to invent a way of conducting a floor debate on the articles of impeachment. The debate is scheduled to begin August 19th and to last about two weeks; the committee staff needs time to write the committee report. Sarbanes, Edwards, McClory, and Railsback have been meeting with Rodino to plan strategy for the floor debate; new alliances have been forged. The Judiciary Committee got such good reviews that it seems more likely than before that the proceedings on the House floor, and in the Senate as well, will be televised. Other members of Congress want their time under the lights. Even some members of the House Rules Committee, which will formally set the debate rules, want its proceedings televised.

A Republican Senate aide says that the impact that the House Judiciary Committee's televised proceedings had on the Senate was "overwhelming." The Senate has always had a rather patronizing view of the House, and senators were struck—as, apparently, much of the country was—by the quality of the House members' performance. The aide—who gets around the Senate—says that he has thought for some time that the President had no more than twenty-eight votes in the Senate. (If every senator were present and voting, he would need thirty-four to spare him conviction.)

White House lawyers told Judge Sirica yesterday that more than five minutes of a subpoenaed conversation was missing. The conversation involved the President, Haldeman, and Ehrlichman on April 17, 1973, in the Oval Office. It was on that day that the President announced to the public that there had been "major developments"—our first real clue that the case was indeed breaking.

Today, a White House aide told one of my colleagues that he thought there were fifty certain votes for the President's conviction in the Senate and only twenty certain votes against it. Said the aide, "It isn't down the chute yet in the Senate, but it's damn close." A Senate Republican leader estimates that at the most, counting all the "maybes," there are thirty-six votes for the President. He refers to what is happening now as "a growing political snowball," and says that the end will come when Republicans realize that the President might scrape by in the Senate and they would be stuck with him in office for two more years. At the White House, Gerald Warren announced today, "The President will not resign." But the heated atmosphere and cancellations of meetings at the White House suggest that something is up. We have tried to train ourselves not to get caught up in these heated moments, not to think that the President would resign. He has ridden out heated moments before. But the other possibility has also been there: that events would finally come together in some combination of impeachment and resignation.

AUGUST 2

Friday. "Frankly," says John Anderson, the Illinois Republican and chairman of the House Republican Conference, as we talk in his office this morning, "it is a *fait accompli* in the minds of the members." Anderson has just come from a lengthy meeting of the Wednesday Club, a group of about twenty-five moderate House Republicans, at which they heard Wiggins discuss the issues in the articles voted by the Judiciary Committee. Several more meetings of Republicans are scheduled for next week, so that members can hear from proponents of both sides. Butler, Cohen, and Lott are to speak at a meeting of the House Republican freshmen—a fairly conservative group, who have already met on the matter and are in some anguish, because their positions with the electorate are less secure than those of more senior members. Even though the House members now know that the President will be impeached, "we feel we have to go over and over the details and the law," says Anderson. "We have to be able to debate. We have to be able to explain to our constituents. We've got to be able to convince people that this process was fair." The Republicans are particularly busy having meetings, he says, "because we feel it's more poignantly a Republican problem."

I ask him when it became a *fait accompli.*

Anderson lists a number of events. "This thing has been one of peaks and valleys," he says. "Lately, there were the Ehrlichman conviction and the 'kangaroo-court' line by Ziegler. There was the committee's release showing the discrepancies in the two sets of transcripts. Then the Supreme Court decision. There had been a noticeable buildup of tension in the cloakrooms for two or three days before that. Granted that the Court ruling did not cover the question of Congress's prerogatives, it demolished Nixon's argument of executive privilege. Then the Judiciary Committee proceedings gave the Congress a much-needed lift. They restored to the Congress a sense of dignity, and imbued it with the courage to do what it has to do. Those televised proceedings were hung on very carefully by members of Congress. Members of Congress don't often listen to each other. Nothing is more boring. But this was different. Then members began to gather in little knots in the cloakroom and on the floor and say, 'He's had it.' "

I ask what has become of the Republicans' concern for that presumed twenty-five percent of die-hard Nixon supporters.

"As time went on, the twenty-five-percent figure became displaced by a great many polls that have been taken in a number of districts," Anderson replies. "Members began to do a little more careful analysis and realized that the shouters were being overcounted. When you counted Democratic voters who might vote for some Republican, and Republicans who were for impeachment, and the growing block of independents, you came up with a majority. A lot of different members polled, and compared the results. Those polls were floating around here. I don't want to suggest that it's just the polls. It's also the evidence. Some of us have been lugging the evidence books around. Many weeks ago, I formed the theory that you could make a case for impeachment on obstruction of justice. That's what led me to call for the President's resignation. And that issue had been built up in the media. But something that caught fire—that came up quickly— was the theory of abuse of power. It was just amazing to me how the members grasped at it as an impeachable offense. They clearly thought that the part about the I.R.S. was salable back home. The I.R.S. as 'the jackboot of the federal government.' The idea of the abuse of power just emerged. The media hadn't built it up. Now the members are reinforcing each other. There is a relief in finally deciding. They got tired of this thing hanging over their heads. You can't neatly categorize the factors—you can't say that it's twenty-percent evidence and twenty-percent politics and sixty-percent courage, or whatever the proportions. The climate just built up."

The only question remaining in the House is the size of the vote by which the President will be impeached. One member whom many members of the House and of the press are looking to is Barber Conable. Fifty-one, he is a Republican from upstate New York; the chairman of the House Republican Policy Committee; and a member of the Ways and Means Committee. And, as one who is already important, he is generally considered to be a possible top House Republican leader. Just as at one point Railsback was the center of attention, it is commonly said now that what Conable does will determine the size of the impeachment vote in the House.

Conable arrives late for our lunch appointment today. "I'm in the unfortunate position of being identified as a key man," he says. "When I say I'm undecided, people say, 'Isn't that cute. He is going to vote against the President.' People throw the searchlight on the 'undecideds' and say, 'They'll vote against the President.' The President isn't very likable, so it is assumed that the 'undecideds' are against him. I'm taking home six books of Judiciary Committee evidence on abuse of power this weekend, and meanwhile I have to meet with my political advisers on the political race of my life. People have identified me as a key man who will vote for impeachment, and call me a key man in order to maximize my influence. The problem is that it will take me so long to get my thoughts together that I might not be key by then. I'll be more 'sicklied o'er with the pale cast of thought,' and that's not a bad posture at this point."

As Conable and I talk, a House Republican stops at the table and says he wants to talk with Conable about something later. Conable says it's about the idea—put forward by some Republicans, and briefly floated by White House aide Patrick Buchanan yesterday—of having a censure vote rather than impeachment. He goes on to say, "People are still hoping that something will come along to dilute that cup of hemlock."

Today, Gerald Warren, reading from notes that are presumed to have been approved by the President, described Mr. Nixon as "an underdog" in the impeachment battle. Calling it a "political struggle," Warren said, "We face an uphill struggle, but in a political struggle you have a chance to win."

Today, John Dean was sentenced by Judge Sirica to a term of from one to four years for his role in the conspiracy to cover up the Watergate break-in.

Also today, Judge Sirica ordered White House lawyers to speed the delivery to the court of the remaining subpoenaed tapes, and set a deadline of next Wednesday.

Sunday. The lead in today's New York *Times* is another story about the fact that the President will lose his sixty-thousand-dollar pension and ninety-six thousand dollars for staff and other expenses if he is impeached and convicted. This one, by the *Times* political correspondent R. W. Apple, says that "several" of the President's "longtime financial backers" have, according to White House aides, "sent word to Mr. Nixon that he should weigh his financial future carefully before reaching a final decision." Apple also writes that "some Republicans on Capitol Hill, still convinced that resignation is preferable to the trauma of impeachment, have discussed the idea of using his finances as a lever to persuade the President to quit." The "trauma" seems to be that of the politicians. The striking thing is that, except for the buzzing on Capitol Hill and among the press about how high the impeachment vote in the House might be, it is so calm here—and, apparently, in the rest of the country, too. A Harris poll published today says that sixty-six percent of those polled think the House should vote to impeach—up from fifty-three percent since the House Judiciary Committee voted the articles of impeachment.

Gerald Ford is quoted in today's Washington *Post* as saying that he thinks "the odds are such" that the President may be impeached. "I think the situation has eroded," said Ford. The Vice-President also said, "I believe the President is innocent. I don't want any impression created that I've changed my mind about the President's innocence." There have been messages to Ford, in various news stories and columns, from allies and from various journalists who give freely of their advice: to stay home, keep quiet, and get ready. Ford has been out of Washington for most of the past few months. He is in Mississippi and Louisiana this weekend, and on Thursday he is to leave for California and other Western points, and will be out of Washington during most of the two-week House debate on impeachment. Many observers think that his absence during this period is not accidental.

The President is meeting at Camp David with some aides this weekend, and is said to be mapping strategy for the forthcoming impeachment fight. James St. Clair and two speechwriters are there. But what strategies can be left?

Monday. The New York *Times* reports that Senate Minority Whip Robert Griffin has written to the President that he would vote to convict if the President defied a Senate subpoena of tapes. Word comes that John Rhodes has cancelled a scheduled statement for today on his position on impeachment, because he has a cold. Since I have one, too,

I am inclined to believe this, but some of my colleagues are skeptical. Then word comes that Griffin has called on the President to resign, saying that "the national interest and his own interest would best be served by resigning," and that "I believe he will see it that way, too." Carl Albert has said that the process of impeachment should be carried through. On the radio this afternoon, George Meany's voice is saying that he is not interested in seeing the President punished. Says Meany, "All I want is the President just to go away."

Despite all the signs that something was about to break, there was no being prepared for the five o'clock news today. It is reported that the President has announced that he will release transcripts of three tapes and that these tapes "may further damage my case." According to the news, these tapes—of three conversations with Haldeman on June 23, 1972, six days after the Watergate break-in and three days after the Nixon-Haldeman conversation of which eighteen and a half minutes was erased—show that the President knew that the F.B.I. was tracing the break-in to the Finance Committee to Re-Elect the President, and that he was concerned about the political consequences and directed the C.I.A. to try to stop the F.B.I. investigation. Since May, 1973, the President had been saying that he was concerned that the F.B.I. investigation might expose sensitive "national-security" C.I.A. operations. Today, in a statement, he has acknowledged that he "also discussed the political aspects of the situation." The President said today that when he had said, on releasing the earlier transcripts, that they told the whole story of Watergate, he had not been aware of the "implications" of the conversations he is releasing today. On an unusually contrite note, he now says that he listened to these tapes in May, after they had been subpoenaed by the Special Prosecutor, but concealed the conversations from his attorneys, other members of his staff, and the House Judiciary Committee, which therefore based its inquiry on "incomplete and in some respects erroneous" information. He also says that it is "clear that portions of the tapes of these June 23 conversations are at variance with certain of my previous statements." The President said that a House vote to impeach was a "foregone conclusion," and that he would turn over to the Senate any tapes that Judge Sirica might rule should go to the Special Prosecutor. He asked that the case be viewed "in perspective," and said that he did not believe that the evidence warranted the "extreme step" of impeachment and removal of the President.

Why is he putting these transcripts out now? It seems clear that others who heard these tapes must have told him that he was cornered. Perhaps it is another exercise in damage limitation—like the earlier transcripts. The tapes will become public eventually, so put them out yourself, cut the losses. Perhaps this new information can become enveloped and lost in the House action, precluding new discoveries during the Senate trial.

On the six o'clock radio news, Wiggins, who was informed about these new transcripts at the White House three days ago, is saying, "The President of the United States should resign." It's coming fast now. On the NBC and CBS evening television news programs, the Republican statements unroll, all of them bad for the President. The Judiciary Committee Republicans were shown the transcripts this afternoon by St. Clair and Buzhardt. Tonight, Charles Sandman says, "It certainly changes my vote. This is devastating." And Delbert Latta says he is reconsidering his position against impeachment. Barber Conable, who was agonizing just three days ago, says, "It's tough to put your loyalty in someone who abuses it. I think the issue becomes one of how to transfer the government in an orderly fashion." Robert Dole, the Republican Senator from Kansas, who is up for reëlection, says, "Jerry Ford by Labor Day would ease our load." The NBC news shows Wiley Mayne in Iowa, over the weekend, explaining that he voted against impeachment because he thought the case was weak. This afternoon Wiley Mayne is saying he will vote for impeachment.

Now, on CBS television, Wiggins is shown reading his statement. "I believe that this is not the time for the President to meet with his attorneys to plan for his defense in the Senate," Wiggins says. The tone is one of cold rage. But then the voice quavers as he says that it is time "to discuss the orderly transition of power from Richard Nixon to Gerald Ford." It is as if he were pronouncing a death sentence—which, in a way, he is. "The magnificent career of public service of Richard Nixon," Wiggins says, struggling to contain his emotions, pausing, clearing his throat as he tries to regain his composure, "must be terminated involuntarily." It seems to be the anger and distress of a man who has been used and betrayed, who has been through too much, can take no more. Wiggins says that if the President does not resign he will now vote for Article I in the House.

Gerald Ford has issued a statement saying that he has "come to the conclusion that the public interest is no longer served by repetition of my previously expressed belief that on the basis of all the evidence known to me and to the American people the President is not guilty of an impeachable offense." Therefore, said the Vice-President, he would "respectfully decline" to discuss the matter further. He is saying, in effect, the same thing that the others are saying, but saying it backward, as circumstances dictate.

Now the news is bombarding us again, and one has no choice but to receive it, to stay by the radio and the phone. Events are hurtling forward, and all one can do is try to keep up. There is little time to think. Momentous decisions are being made. We shall have to live with the consequences. If in fact the transition is coming, are we really prepared for it? We have been talking about it, thinking about it, for so long, sensing—except for that one period of doubt before the House Judiciary Committee acted—that it would take place. But as it begins to appear possible it seems that we can't separate ourselves from Nixon's disgrace. It seems that we have all gone through this with him, and have all been brought low. As long as he is President, a blow to his dignity is in some inescapable way a blow to ours.

Late this evening, a colleague brings me a copy of the transcripts of the June 23rd meetings. It is hard to believe that one can still be astonished, but the transcripts themselves give a far more devastating picture than the news stories suggested. For those who believed that the President was aware of, and even directed, the cover-up, it must still be a shock to *read his conversation* about it.

Here—on these photocopied, stapled-together, double-spaced pages—it is:

H Now on the investigation, you know the Democratic break-in thing, we're back in the problem area because the FBI is not under control, because Gray doesn't exactly know how to control it and they have—their investigation is now leading into some productive areas—because they've been able to trace the money—not through the money itself—but through the bank sources—the banker. And, and it goes in some directions we don't want it to go. Ah, also there have been some things—like an informant came in off the street to the FBI in Miami who was a photographer or has a friend who is a photographer who developed some films through this guy Barker and the films had pictures of Democratic National Committee letterhead documents and things. So it's things like that that are filtering in. Mitchell came up with yesterday, and John Dean analyzed very carefully last night and concludes, concurs now with Mitchell's recommendation that the only way to solve this, and we're set up beautifully to do it, ah, in that and that—the only network that paid any attention to it last night was NBC—they did a massive story on the Cuban thing.

P That's right.

H That the way to handle this now is for us to have Walters call Pat Gray and just say, "Stay to hell out of this—this is ah, business here we don't want you to go any further on it." That's not an unusual development, and ah, that would take care of it.

Then Haldeman, referring to the F.B.I., asks, "And you seem to think the thing to do is get them to stop?"
And Nixon replies, "Right, fine."
Haldeman tells the President that after the F.B.I.'s "interrogation of

Colson yesterday, they concluded it was not the White House, but are now convinced it is a C.I.A. thing, so the C.I.A. turnoff would—"

Says Nixon, "Well, not sure of their analysis, I'm not going to get that involved. I'm (unintelligible)." And he tells Haldeman, "You call them in."

Replies Haldeman: "Good deal."

There is an inexplicable difference between the experiences of suspecting a lie and being whacked in the face with the evidence of one. Many Americans had become accustomed to thinking of the President as a liar, and had alternately suspended belief in, scoffed at, or become enraged at his statements. But I wonder whether the enormity of his lying has sunk in yet—whether we have, or can, come to terms with the thought that so much of what he said to us was just noise, words, and that we can no longer begin by accepting any of it as the truth. This is a total reversal of the way we were brought up to think about Presidents, a departure from deeply ingrained habits. One's mind resists the thought of our President as a faithless man, capable of looking at us in utter sincerity from the other side of the television camera and telling us multiple, explicit, barefaced lies. One is torn between the idea that people must be able to have some confidence in their leaders and the idea that in this day of image manipulation a certain skepticism may serve them well. I do not think there is much comfort to be taken from the fact that eventually Nixon's lies—like Johnson's—caught up with him. It took a long time, and a great deal of damage was done meanwhile.

These transcripts tonight are stunning on a number of grounds. There are bits of conversation about the number of misdeeds that the President and his aides were intent on concealing. The President rehearses the reasons the C.I.A. must be told to try to call the F.B.I. off the investigation:

> P Of course, this Hunt, that will uncover a lot of things. You open that scab there's a hell of a lot of things and we just feel that it would be very detrimental to have this thing go any further. This involves these Cubans, Hunt, and a lot of hanky-panky that we have nothing to do with ourselves. Well what the hell, did Mitchell know about this?

What hanky-panky? While this transcript makes it clear that the President was trying to block the investigation, one cannot help suspecting that an investigation might have turned up some things—related to the break-in or not—that were real enough. Says the President in this conversation, "We protected Helms [Richard Helms, former C.I.A. director and now ambassador to Iran] from one hell of a lot of things." We know that Hunt and the Cubans had been involved in other matters. We know that the public relations agency Hunt worked for after he left the C.I.A. had C.I.A. connections. The C.I.A., too, needs untraceable money.

There are exchanges that indicate that these people knew things well in advance of when they said they knew about them. Haldeman explains to the President how the money found on those caught in the Watergate break-in is traceable, via a Mexican bank, to the Finance Committee to Re-Elect the President. The President, who presumably had no idea of such matters, asks whether it was Liddy who knew how the financing of the operation would be arranged. Observes the President, "He must be a little nuts!" Haldeman concurs, but also explains that Liddy "was under pressure, apparently, to get more information, and as he got more pressure, he pushed the people harder to move harder—" The President asks, "Pressure from Mitchell?" To which Haldeman replies, "Apparently."

There is also the sheer incoherence and triviality of these conversations. One does not expect, as someone said, iambic pentameter in the Oval Office. It is understandable that busy people might cover a wide range of subjects when they meet. But these conversations meander mindlessly around a cluttered field that includes the cover-up; Mrs. Nixon's concern, brought up by the President, that helicopters might disarrange her and her daughters' hairdos at the Republican Convention at Miami Beach; the fact, mentioned by Haldeman, that the British have floated the pound (the President asks "That's devaluation?" and he goes on to say "It's too complicated for me to get into"); the fact, also mentioned by Haldeman, that Arthur Burns, the chairman of the Federal Reserve Board, is concerned about the lira—to which the President replies, "Well, I don't give a (expletive deleted) about the lira"; the Congress's action on a pending proposal to increase Social Security benefits; the fact, mentioned by the President, that when his daughter Tricia presented some Chinese artifacts to an art gallery in Boston, two people, one of them from the press, refused to shake her hand in a receiving line. Says the President, "The worse thing (unintelligible) is to go to anything that has to do with the Arts. . . . The Arts you know—they're Jews, they're left wing—in other words, stay away." He talks of the importance of reaching "Middle America," and of some of the things the President's daughters might do toward that end ("ride a bus for two hours"), and of his interest in calling "key contributors." He speaks of *Six Crises,* saying that he was "thumbing through" it the night before, and he repeatedly instructs Haldeman to reread it and says he wants Colson to read it, "and anybody else." (Colson told the Judiciary Committee in July that "all of us who were in daily contact with the President from time to time received instructions to read certain portions of *Six Crises.* I think I read it fourteen times.") "Actually," says the President, "the book reads awfully well."

In these transcripts, we find, not for the first time, Haldeman suggesting the President's course of action. I have been told several times by people who worked with them that in order to understand the Nixon Administration I must understand the relationship between Nixon and Haldeman, and must understand Haldeman. And that an understanding of these two men would also help me to understand the existence of the tapes. It has been explained to me that Haldeman played to Nixon's weaknesses—his uncertainty, his lack of self-definition, his constant need to master his profound indecisiveness. Haldeman once told Allen Drury that he acted as a screen for the President, "because there is a real danger of some advocate of an idea rushing in to the President . . . and actually managing to convince [him] in a burst of emotion or argument." So Haldeman's judgment—such as it was—very frequently became Nixon's. And it has even been suggested that I must consider the fact that Haldeman is a Christian Scientist (as is Ehrlichman): that this explains his broader rejection of what other people regard as realities, and his minimizing of the importance of deeds as opposed to thoughts. And explains what can be seen as a preoccupation with Nixon's immortality. Tapes. (Of the President's top aides, only Haldeman knew about the tapes.) Dictabelts. Memoranda. We used to read how Haldeman and Ehrlichman made home movies of Nixon and, for relaxation, went to each other's house and watched them. To Nixon, the tapes might have been, among other things, a means of establishing his authenticity as President. In the Nixon White House, the Nixon Presidency became a kind of religion in itself—one that we were all asked to believe in.

Again the question: Why weren't the tapes destroyed? After Butterfield disclosed their existence to the Ervin committee, in July, 1973, Nixon consulted some of his aides about whether to destroy them. Once more, his indecisiveness was his undoing. Having asked others, he placed others in the position of either advising against the destruction of the tapes or countenancing the obstruction of justice. And there were people in the White House who—whether for reasons of conscience or because they had seen the damage to their former colleagues, or both— were not about to do the latter. Moreover, there is every indication that the President did not—still does not—believe he did anything wrong. He wrote to the Ervin committee, "As in any verbatim recording of informal conversations, they contain comments that persons with different perspectives and motivations would inevitably interpret in different ways." So he took his chances and did not destroy the tapes.

22

The Washington *Post* reports this morning that over the weekend, at Camp David, the President seriously considered resigning. Yesterday evening, he and Mrs. Nixon and their two daughters cruised on the *Sequoia*. Bebe Rebozo, who had been a guest of the Nixons since last Thursday, returned yesterday to Key Biscayne.

The noon news. Some Republicans are suggesting that the impeachment debate in the House be shortened, and be held earlier than had been planned. Robert McClory suggests one day of debate, to be held next week rather than two weeks from now. Rhodes has said that "this disclosure makes a quick House vote on impeachment an imperative in the best interests of our country." Then one hears the voice of David Dennis saying that now he will vote for Article I. "I was shocked and I was sorry, but I was not all that surprised," says David Dennis slowly. "I've practiced law a long time. I've had clients lie to me." In the first half hour of trading on Wall Street this morning, prices shot up by twenty-five points on the Dow-Jones industrial average. The President has met with his Cabinet this morning. Reporters are standing by.

The 1 p.m. news. The Cabinet has emerged from its meeting with the President, and William Simon, the Treasury Secretary, has said that the President won't resign and sincerely does not believe he has committed an impeachable offense. The President is saying he won't resign. He won't say he will until he does. But all logic is now with his doing it soon, before he is impeached. If he wants to do it before the Senate convicts him, he may as well do it before he is impeached by the House. This is a rather banal ending. A piece of tape. The President caught in his own words. One has to think again about what this story would have been like tapeless. We can never be sure.

A telephone call to the Senate Democratic aide who is in the traffic patterns. "No one knows what the hell is going on," he says. "We're taking him at his word that he wants a trial. I think resignation now would not be satisfactory from his standpoint. He would be criminally prosecuted. His culpability should be determined in a public forum—

House impeachment. Then prosecution could be avoided on the ground that it would be kicking a corpse. I don't think resignation would be enough. There has to be some recitation of the charges, as there had to be in court against Agnew. For Congress to give him immunity if he resigns is the worst of all options. It would be the cowardly way for Congress to act. The question is at what point the mood in the country would be that he has had enough. That isn't the mood yet. The idea that he can just quit is not enough. That does not hold him accountable. I don't think the system is strengthened by taking that route. So there is a growing division of opinion on this—between those who want to let the processes work and those who want him out and who say the record is already clear. I don't want history to say he was scared out of office. I want him to be judged by the people's representatives."

There seems to be another problem. No one seems to be willing to take responsibility for giving the President immunity. Griffin said today that he doubted that Congress had the power to grant immunity. Someone else says it's up to the Special Prosecutor. But it seems unlikely that either a new President or the Special Prosecutor would want to take this action on his own. So there is the problem of how to extricate the President from this situation, even if that is thought desirable. The politicians are worried about getting wrapped in his disgrace if they let him off. The leniency accorded Agnew was very upsetting to much of the public, and now it is coming back to haunt Nixon.

In January, when the President was quoted as saying he would "fight like hell," he also said that "there is a time to fly."

John Rhodes, apparently recovered from his illness, has made a statement calling the latest revelation "a cataclysmic affair which did cause me to change my position on Article I." He says he will support it. Does that mean he was going to vote against it? The Republicans seem to be falling on this latest scrap of tape, grasping it, as if it were their lifeline to safety. For the hesitants, it makes a vote for Article I respectable, and there will now be safety in numbers. It might even hasten the President's departure—an outcome that many have harbored in their breasts since last fall, and that they now fervently wish. Article I, dealing with the cover-up, is the easiest article to embrace. And, in fact, it leads us back to the White House definition of an impeachable offense—a crime. Will the lessons of all this be: Don't cover up a crime, and, if you do, don't tape yourself while you do it? What about Article II, having to do with abuse of power—the far more serious charge? And what about the question raised in Article III: whether a President must coöperate with the Congress in an impeachment inquiry? These articles were to be the tablets handed down to the future. The sudden outrage of some

Republicans has a hollow ring. Where are they on the question of abuse of power? Where are they—where have they been—on the question of our liberties? These politicians are responding to the moment. Many of the Republicans tell themselves that the last tapes are a kind of confession. They came to see the President as an unclean thing, and they want to get him out. They are thinking of these things, not the processes.

Many of these people are what a friend calls King's-party men. King's-party men rally around the Crown until it becomes clear that the King must be beheaded. King's-party men impute great authority to the Crown, but they also impute to themselves the authority to make that kind of decision. And then they move on, in the tradition of "The King is dead. Long live the King." What James Buckley referred to in March as "the regime" is preserved. The question of laying out the boundaries within which the King may act is now secondary to the question of succession.

We still don't know if this country can carry out the process of impeachment and conviction of an incumbent President. Perhaps, if there are future impeachments, it will always end something like this. Perhaps it will be seen that the House Judiciary Committee examined the evidence and came to conclusions not only about the obstruction of justice but also about abuse of power and—with some misgivings—about the authority of the Congress in an impeachment proceeding. It is clear that the House would approve Articles I and II and impeach the President; and it now seems probable that the Senate would convict. But we may be left with probabilities rather than certainties. Perhaps the lesson will go down that the abuse of power is a dangerous business—something that Presidents had better not engage in, and something about which we will be more alert. One can't be sure now. We may be more sensitized to it at the moment, but precious few steps have been taken to institutionalize safeguards. Will the Congress remain alerted—to the extent that it is alerted at all—or will it go back to sleep? The public and the Congress—in that order—did finally become alarmed, and reacted, but it took a great deal to get them to do so. I remember James Mann's point, when I first spoke with him, in April, about the need for the Congress to maintain constant oversight. Will he be listened to now? Or will the Congress—and will we—revert to the habitual limited attention span? Will there be the assumption that with the exit of Richard Nixon the danger is past? Will there be, as seems all too likely, a great national desire not to think about these things anymore?

Several people have said in the past two days that one thing that troubles them—in the light of the President's possible resignation—is John Ehrlichman's statement last week suggesting that he still does not think he and the President did anything wrong. These people want a definitive statement from the legislative branch that they did.

The afternoon news. Now all ten Republicans on the Judiciary Committee who voted against all the articles have announced that they will vote for Article I. John Tower, chairman of the Senate Republican Policy Committee, emerged from a meeting of the Republican senators this morning and said that a majority of the senators now favor the President's resignation. Tower said that the President "does not perhaps comprehend the great hazard he faces in coming to trial in the Senate," and that after a few days, in which things should cool off, the senators will try to get a message to him. Carl Albert has emerged from a meeting of House Democratic leaders to say that the House debate on impeachment will be reduced from two weeks to one but that the debate will still not begin until August 19th. There remain the mechanical problems of producing the Judiciary Committee's report (to be further amended, in light of the new evidence) and of going through procedural steps before legislation can be debated on the House floor. Said Albert, "This is one of the most important things we've ever done in this House, and we are not going to have any summary operation." John Anderson has made a statement saying that if the President wants a Senate trial he should have one, and should not be "dragooned" into resigning.

On tonight's news, we see Secretary of State Kissinger on the White House lawn after the Cabinet meeting, looking grim. Clearing his throat, as he does when he is very tense, Kissinger says to the reporters, "When questions of peace or war are considered, no foreign government should have any doubts about the way in which foreign policy will be conducted." Kissinger is sending his message—whatever its precise meaning—to the world through these reporters on the White House lawn. For some time—it seems since last fall, at least—Kissinger has spoken privately with friends, and publicly in somewhat more veiled terms, of his fears that Mr. Nixon's troubles might undermine Kissinger's foreign-policy efforts, might tempt the Russians in the Middle East or elsewhere.

Tom Brokaw reports on NBC tonight that the President spent thirty-five minutes today with Rabbi Korff.

Senator Barry Goldwater is reported on tonight's news to have made an emotional speech in the Republicans' meeting this morning, and to have said, "You can only be lied to so often."

Tonight, we see Tower saying that the senators' view is that "it would be best for the country" not to have a trial, that a Senate trial would be "a wrenching experience." "That's their rationale," said Tower. Robert Byrd is quoted as saying that if the vote were taken in the Senate today the President would be convicted.

And then we see still more of the ten Judiciary Committee Republicans—who had wished to see no evil and hear no evil—announcing their turnabouts. The speed with which these turnabouts are occurring gives one the sense that at least some of the Judiciary Committee Republicans who opposed impeachment may have been living with more doubts than they displayed. Hutchinson: "I have been deceived." Sandman: "I'm prepared to vote to impeach." Latta: "If I were in his shoes, which I'm not, I would resign." This is something out of fiction, or out of the movies. In actuality, members of Congress don't vote one way on a big issue and then file back before us on television only a little more than a week later and tell us they've changed their minds. But here they are—one by one. Trent Lott, whose Mississippi district voted eighty-seven percent for Nixon: "I feel let down. . . . The fact that there have been so many bombshells . . . You reach a point of no return."

The President's Senate "friends" are reported tonight to have sent a warning to the White House that the longer he waits, the harder it may be for him to get even a "gentlemen's agreement," much less legislation, granting him immunity from further prosecution once he leaves office. (Tonight's Washington *Star-News* reports that Griffin knew there would be a new disclosure when he made his statement yesterday that the President should resign. Haig had telephoned him on Sunday.)

Today, the Senate Foreign Relations Committee voted unanimously to clear Kissinger of allegations that he misled the committee during his confirmation hearings in September, 1973, about his role in the wiretapping of seventeen government officials and newsmen. He told the committee two weeks ago that he had simply "furnished the names of individuals with access to sensitive leaked information." The Judiciary Committee had received information that Kissinger "initiated" the taps, despite his denial during his confirmation hearings that he had done so. (Even before the Foreign Relations Committee held its recent hearings on the subject—at Kissinger's request, during his press conference in Salzburg—a majority of the Senate had signed a resolution attesting to Kissinger's "integrity and veracity.") The State Department announced this afternoon that the Secretary was "gratified" and "no longer sees any reason for resignation."

James St. Clair has let it be known, without confirming it directly, that he was instrumental in having the June 23rd tape made public. (But this tape was to go to the court, and would have been made public in due course.) St. Clair seems to be taking pains to look after his reputation.

It has been noted today that in *Six Crises,* in the chapter on Alger Hiss—which the President instructed his aides to read when the plumbers' unit was established—Nixon wrote that Hiss's fatal mistake was in not telling his lawyer everything. Last May, John Ehrlichman told the House subcommittee studying the role of the C.I.A. that the President wondered whether C.I.A. officials were covering up for subordinates, and he said, "The President said substantially: A man makes a grave mistake in covering up for subordinates. That was President Truman's error in the Hiss case when he instructed the F.B.I. not to coöperate."

After William Simon said today that the President did not intend to resign, the stock market went back down.

Senate Republicans met again this afternoon. There are reports tonight that Goldwater is seeking an appointment with the President.

On an NBC Special late tonight, Robert Dole is interviewed by Douglas Kiker. Dole says that at this morning's meeting of Senate Republicans "there was very little support" for the President. "I just have a gut feeling" that something is in the air, Dole says, and he says that this afternoon he conveyed his view to Haig that the President's situation in the Senate "had deteriorated greatly." The President's resignation, says Dole, "would be good for the Party, but it would also be good for the country." Dole says that he's heard the President say he wouldn't do a lot of things that he then did, and Dole, looking into the camera, as if speaking to the President, his eyes hard, says, ostensibly to Kiker, that, yes, the votes are there in the Senate today to convict the President.

AUGUST 7

The Washington *Post* Senate correspondent, Spencer Rich, reports that Senators Griffin and Tower favor "absolution from any criminal prosecution if Nixon resigns." Griffin also said he was considering drafting immunity legislation. Said Griffin, according to the *Post,* "The offenses—I mean the alleged offenses—with which he is charged may not be so serious that people want to see a former President go to jail."

A Democratic senator says on the telephone this morning that he thinks recent events will give the Republicans twenty seats in the House which they might have lost in November. "They're off the hook now," he says. But he also describes himself as relieved. In December, he said to me, "Why should we give Jerry Ford six years in the Presidency?" Today, he says, "The fear that was welling up within me over what I thought was the impotence of the institutions was such that I wondered whether they would last. Suddenly, I realized that your position on the issues wasn't very important—that you had to have a framework of institutions within which to fight for your position on the issues, and that without the system nothing else matters."

There *is* a sense of relief. It is important to remember the fears—how deep they were, and on how many levels they worked. The stakes *were* enormous. The actions of each of the other branches—the Congress and the courts—were not as neat or inevitable as history may show. Those branches consisted of human beings who were groping. The framers of the Constitution understood that that's how it would work. James Madison wrote in Federalist Paper No. 51, "The great security against a gradual concentration of the several powers in the same department consists in giving to those who administer each department the necessary Constitutional means and personal motives to resist encroachments of the others. The provision for defense must in this, as in all other cases, be made commensurate to the danger of attack. Ambition must be made to counteract ambition. The interest of the man must be connected with the Constitutional rights of the place. It may be a reflection on human nature that such devices should be necessary to control the abuses of government. But what is government itself but the greatest of all reflections on human nature." They were not beguiled by illusions about human nature, nor should we be. There is not much cause for serenity in how this is turning out.

The events of the past several months were without precedent in our national life. At the heart of it all was the question of whether our Constitutional form of government would continue. This was a new question. President Nixon's resignation might appear to be the decisive event, but it is not. Perhaps, in the future, it will be clear that what was decisive was the action taken by the thirty-eight members of the Judiciary Committee of the House of Representatives. It was these men and women who, by what they did, compelled the President to give up his office, established what Presidential conduct was intolerable, and handed down the tablets for the future. Thus far, the committee has carried out the only process by which the President was called to account for the conduct of his Administration. It was a process that was not an easy one for political beings to face, and was one that many politicians—to the end, and with apparent success—sought to avoid. In the course of reaching their conclusions, the elected representatives on the Judiciary Committee conducted the most fateful deliberations about the meaning of the Constitution since the document was drafted at the Philadelphia convention in 1787.

The President's leaving office would be all that prevented an overwhelming vote of impeachment in the House, which would have been only the second impeachment of a President in American history, and what appeared to be an inevitable conviction in the Senate, which would have been the first. It is already coming into fashion to say that "the institutions" have performed, that "the system" has worked, but this is not really so clear. The ending of the Nixon Administration which, it now seems, could come at any moment, was not as certain, or the series of events that preceded it as impersonal, as history may make them seem. The "institutions" and the "system" are not self-implementing. They can work only if there are enough people who are sufficiently concerned and wise—as well as in a position—to make them work. There were such people—in the Congress, in the Special Prosecutor's office, in the courts, and in the citizenry. But while we learned that the forces that can make our system of government work are powerful, so are the countervailing forces. There were several times during the past year when there was reason to question which would prevail.

This story has a number of "what if"s, and we shall never be able to go back through it and find the answers to all of them. There is the big "what if" about the tapes, of course, but there are also others. What if Archibald Cox had been a different sort of man? What if there had been no Special Prosecutor? (And what is the likelihood that a future President with something to hide will appoint one?) What if the chairman of the House Judiciary Committee had been someone other than Peter Rodino—had been a fool or a demagogue, or even a man of less good judgment? Or what if the chairman had retained a counsel with poor judgment?

Our safety lay in those who saw what the issue was, and who, when it wasn't easy to do so, pressed on. Now we know what real danger is. Perhaps we actually needed some people to come to power who would test the limits. Fortunately, they were incompetent. But we cannot rest easy—because of that very incompetence, and those obsessive tapes. And, even with the incompetence, a great many things happened. They weren't incompetent at raising untold millions of dollars from people who did business with the government. They weren't incompetent at making newspaper publishers and broadcasters uneasy—at the very least—and we, and perhaps the publishers and broadcasters themselves, will never know how many of their decisions were affected. They weren't incompetent at getting laws passed and taking actions that had the effect of reducing our rights. They weren't incompetent at causing people to think again before marching, signing, or speaking out. We shall never know if it was the end or the beginning of something. I keep remembering what Leon Jaworski has said—how Jaworski, the former Nuremberg prosecutor, has told people he thought there was an analogy between the way it began in Germany and what was happening here. Nixon may have been, as a friend of mine has suggested, our greatest reformer. He showed us the possible consequences of our acquiescence, inattention, cynicism.

At three o'clock, a friend calls from Capitol Hill. I had kept the radio off for a few hours in order to get some work done, and it was as if I had spent a week on Mars. My friend says that the atmosphere on Capitol Hill is "electric." Today's Phoenix *Gazette* quoted a "highly reliable" source—assumed to be Goldwater—as saying that the President would resign this afternoon. The Providence *Journal-Bulletin* has also said that the President would resign, and the speculation is that the source of that story was Rabbi Korff, whose National Citizens Committee for Fairness to the Presidency was founded in Providence. There goes the rest of the day. It was Goldwater, despite his denials, who predicted Agnew's resignation. Could that really have been only eleven months ago?

There are rumors on Capitol Hill that the television networks are preparing to broadcast a Presidential statement. Some aides on Capitol Hill have done research and found that a President can be impeached and convicted even if he is not in office. Senator Mansfield has said that the processes of impeachment and a Senate trial should go forward if the President resigns. Senate Republicans met in caucus this morning and decided that a delegation—Scott and Goldwater—representing the moderate and conservative wings of the Party should go to the White House. A "delegation" to the White House. I always thought that that was something out of mythology.

CBS radio says that "high-ranking Republicans" in the House and Senate—who would not permit their names to be used—were telling fellow-Republicans to expect a resignation soon.

At 3:35 P.M., the radio says that the White House press office has said that the President's position has remained unchanged since this morning—that he is going to stay on, will not resign, is determined to go through the processes in the House and Senate.

As the four-o'clock radio news comes on, a senator returns my call. With one ear I hear the news ("Senator Goldwater has just come from a meeting with . . ."), and with the other I hear the senator, a Democrat, who is trying out a statement he has prepared ("This is a sad day in the history of our country . . .").

Now the radio says that Scott and Rhodes met with the President. Half an hour ago, the radio said it was Scott and Goldwater who met with the President. Ford cancelled a breakfast meeting on Capitol Hill in order to meet with Haig. Then Ford went to Capitol Hill to meet with Rhodes and Representative Albert Quie, Republican of Minnesota. Afterward, it was announced that this was a regular prayer meeting.

CBS radio, 5:45 P.M. Goldwater, Scott, and Rhodes have come out of the White House. All three of them met with the President. They are outside the West Wing of the White House, surrounded by reporters. It is the kind of moment in which one expects solemn evasions rather than candor, yet one listens intently. If they did not want to see the press, send a message through it, they could have slipped out through a side door. Goldwater's voice says, "Whatever decision he makes, it will be in the best interest of our country. There have been no decisions made.

We made no suggestions. We were merely there to offer what we see as the condition on both floors." Hugh Scott's voice is saying, "The President stressed that his decisions are made and will be made entirely in the national interest." Scott says that they told the President that the situation was "gloomy on Capitol Hill," that it was "a very distressing situation." Scott also says, "We gave him further evaluations," which Scott will not now discuss.

I turn on the television set, and the same scene is on NBC, live. Goldwater says the President "invited us." Of course. That's the proper thing to say. Goldwater looks solemn. Scott, holding a pipe in his right hand, looks confused. Goldwater is asked about immunity for the President. "That subject was not touched on," he replies. "The discussion was quite general in tone. We were four old friends talking over a very painful situation." Rhodes, smaller than the others, is in a gray suit. He looks calm, impassive, his narrow eyes expressionless. This is an extraordinary scene. Who are these people, and for whom do they speak? Are these our leaders? Might this visit be exactly what the President wants, enabling him to say he was pressured into leaving office? Gerald Warren is glimpsed off to the side. This little press conference has White House approval. The three Republicans say that the subjects of resignation and immunity did not come up. It sounds plausible. The three men may have been delivering bad news, but they were still speaking to the Presidency; besides, some things don't have to be said.

Scott is saying, "The President is in entire control of himself. He was serene and he was most amiable."

Rhodes is asked whether, if the President resigns, the House and the Senate might go ahead and vote on the articles of impeachment. Replies Rhodes, "No useful purpose would be served by that."

The Dow-Jones went up 23.78 points today.

Rabbi Korff was at the White House again today, and tonight on television we see Mrs. Korff picking him up in a red Mercedes. The Rabbi has issued a statement saying that the President may resign unless there is a flood of support from Americans of all persuasions.

It is reported that just before nightfall Kissinger was seen going into the White House.

Charles Wiggins is interviewed on CBS by Bruce Morton. Wiggins still looks troubled. He says that when he learned on Friday at the White House what was in the June 23rd tapes he told White House aides that the reaction would be greater than the reaction over the firing of the Special Prosecutor. He says that he returned from the White House to his office "in a state of some agitation." He says he had been working all day on organizing the House debate against the articles of impeachment. And then, he says, "I remember coming in here and tearing up my notes."

Much attention is now being given to who has the power to do what in order to spare the President future criminal prosecution. There seem to be four possibilities: the Congress might try to do it, but there are legal doubts about whether it is empowered to; the Special Prosecutor could do it; some say that Nixon could pardon himself; Ford, as President, could pardon Nixon. None of these possibilities could spare the ex-President from being summoned to appear as a witness in trials (though what would he say?), from being prosecuted in state and local jurisdictions, from civil suits, or from being disbarred. Today, Attorney General Saxbe said that the question of granting immunity was in Jaworski's hands. Jaworski's office wouldn't comment, but I am told that Jaworski has for some time been consulting people on what to do about this question. On television tonight, we see a replay of the moment in Ford's Vice-Presidential confirmation hearings in the Senate when he was asked whether a new President could pardon an outgoing one, and Ford replied, "I don't think the public would stand for it."

Today, Jake Jacobsen pleaded guilty to giving John Connally ten thousand dollars in exchange for a rise in milk-price supports, and it was announced that Jacobsen will testify against Connally in court.

Today, James St. Clair told Judge Sirica that nine of the sixty-four conversations that the Special Prosecutor had subpoenaed and the Supreme Court had ordered turned over by the President had not been recorded or could not be found.

Almost unnoticed, an odd situation has developed. Sometime in the past seventy-two hours, the capacity of our Chief Executive for acting with the support and confidence of our national leaders and the people—a capacity that had been waning—has totally vanished. It is as though he were already gone, with no successor yet in place. One thinks of Woodrow Wilson when he was incapacitated and, unbeknownst to the nation, his wife governed. Another thought—a lurid one—has struck some observers. Though incapable of acting with national support, the President—a man under crushing strain—may be capable of some act of desperation. But this possibility, if it ever existed, probably exists no longer. There are all kinds of constraints on what the President can do at this point. I remember last fall a friend's saying that somewhere along the line the President's situation might have so deteriorated that if he did anything rash the "Tilt" sign would light up. That seems to be the situation now.

Last fall, they had to invent a way of approving a Vice-President selected under the Twenty-fifth Amendment. This winter, spring, and summer, they had to invent a way of conducting an impeachment of a President. And now they have to invent a way of arranging for the resignation of a President and the transfer of power.

AUGUST 8

This morning, I phoned someone who knows the President fairly well. Last November, when the calls for the President's resignation were widespread, this person said that the President would resist and fudge and fight to the end. Now the President's friend said that Rose Mary Woods was calling various people who had been friends of the President and talking over his situation. This person had offered Miss Woods the opinion that the President had no choice but to resign, and immediately—that the longer he remained, the more he jeopardized himself and the country. With the outcome of a Senate trial clear, there would be no point in his going through it. Moreover, a trial could last for months, and meanwhile the economy would be getting in deeper trouble. If the President made a proper withdrawal, this person suggested to Miss Woods, he might receive more consideration of leniency.

"He is living on his viscera," this person said to me this morning. "The President has blocked out reality. He externalizes the situation, as if it weren't he who was involved. It's a horrible end. He defied the best advice all along—at the beginning, to make a clean breast of things, and then at various stages later. He believed to the end that the Court might be closely divided or not rule against him. He could have saved himself a number of times. That's why there's a feeling that he is irrational, responding to some inner belief that he was right when he was actually wrong. Lawyers have seen the same thing over and over in clients. Lawyers have to say to a client, 'The facts are not this, they are that.' Why didn't he destroy the tapes? That may again have been his inability to grasp reality, his belief that he would never get caught up in this. The only explanations lie very deep in the man. Your reaction to trouble always comes from within you. It may still be his disposition not to give up. But the reality has just got to penetrate."

This person pointed out that Brezhnev had staked a great deal on détente, and that Sadat was in some difficulty. The more often people mention the maintenance of foreign policy as a consideration, the stronger one's impression is that Kissinger has been calling around. In fact, last fall a friend of Kissinger's said that he was cementing his relationships on Capitol Hill and getting ready for "the inevitable." Yesterday, in the New York *Times,* James Reston wrote, "The need for a rapid transition is obvious. The Chinese in particular have been asking for reassurances of continuity in American foreign policy ever since the impeachment of Mr. Nixon seemed certain, and Mr. Kissinger twice this week, once at the Chinese mission here, and again in public, has been trying to assure them and other nations that the foreign policy of the United States has been settled on a steady course, with bipartisan support." There are also stories and speculation about the President's emotional state—actually, a subject of interest for years about this unusually self-absorbed man. But few people have seen the President for any length of time in the past week, and it is a very tricky business to diagnose someone's emotional state. Someone describes the President as "distraught," and that figures. It is said that he is "out of touch." If so, that would be understandable, too.

Nixon still the center of the piece. This man who took us through his crises, talked of winning, fighting, never quitting, made personal the most important political processes in this country. On the one hand, we had a system that was supposed to rest on accountability, due process, the rule of law, and limited power; on the other, we had a man driven by his own character. So one must think about Nixon. Volumes will be written about his psychopathology. But there was so much that was right out there in plain view for years. The fabricated man, the man who invented himself, shaping his image with almost every move, tirelessly touching up his self-portrait. (I'm tough. . . . I never take the easy way. . . . I'm calm, a Quaker, with peace at the center, etc.) The limitless faith in manipulation, in his capacity for conning the public, and even his own associates; the extraordinary capacity for piling lie upon lie. The almost perfect pitch with respect to the hypocrisies that conventional people live by—the fears they don't admit, the hatred they want to express but can't, the images they would like to have of themselves—and a sense of how to exploit all that. The overreaching, the absence of any sense of limits, of the unwritten rules. The deep well of vindictiveness, even when he was expressing just the opposite. (The press has a perfect right to report it that way. . . . I shall be very lenient about amnesty. . . . People have a perfect right to disagree with me.) The faith in power and the tough exercise of power: punitiveness toward opponents; using the levers of control against those, within government and outside it, who disagreed too loudly. The "loner" quality, the man without many deep human connections, the man who used and discarded people wantonly, who perceived himself—and became—the solitary figure fighting against overwhelming odds. He is ending his Presidency as he began it: the lonely man in the Lincoln sitting room.

There is another "what if." What if Richard Nixon had been a more plausible figure? It may be that a more plausible figure would not have got into this mess, but we can't be sure. As it was, a great deal of plausibility was imputed to Nixon for a very long time. He was twice elected President of the United States.

A bulletin on the radio shortly before 11 A.M.: Gerald Warren has announced that in about two minutes the President and the Vice-President will meet in the Oval Office. Warren is said to have made the announcement in "a grave manner."

The radio, a few minutes later: Helen Thomas, the U.P.I. White House correspondent, has written that the President has decided to resign.

One cannot reach the White House by telephone. The switchboard is overloaded. The last time, to my knowledge, that the White House switchboard was overloaded was on that Saturday night when Special Prosecutor Cox was fired.

This morning's New York *Times* says that Goldwater told the President that he could count on no more than fifteen votes against his conviction in the Senate. It also says that Goldwater said he would be willing to serve as the next Vice-President.

Scott is quoted in the *Times* as saying that the President had his feet on the desk when the Republicans spoke with him yesterday, and that he, Scott, had told him that the situation in the Senate was "gloomy." According to Scott, the President inquired, "Damn gloomy?" And Scott replied, "Yes, sir."

The *Times* also reports that Haig was leading a "movement" within the President's staff to convince Mr. Nixon that he should resign.

The Washington *Post* reports that Ford's contingency plans for assuming the Presidency, according to one of Ford's "associates," began Monday night.

So Ford, handpicked by Nixon and confirmed by a Congress anxious to have a successor in place, is about to become President. Ford was chosen, it seemed at the time, because he was loyal, uncontroversial, a regular Republican, and perhaps precisely because he did not seem especially well qualified to be President. But then the parties themselves do not exactly set out to nominate the best-qualified people. And things could be worse now. Agnew could be the Vice-President. And though the processes by which a new Vice-President was chosen under the Twenty-fifth Amendment are troubling, one must consider how much more complicated this situation would be if there had been no provision for selecting a new Vice-President, and, with the Democrats in control of the Congress, Nixon's leaving office would have involved the accession of the Speaker of the House and a change of parties in power. Now people are speculating on who the *next* Vice-President will be. Melvin Laird, who was instrumental in the selection of Ford, is pushing Nelson Rockefeller.

Ford has his limitations, and is more conservative than most people seem to think, but his relaxed and apparently open style has made him

popular. Ford is also a creature of the traditional political and congressional processes. Will the public grasp at this opportunity to assume that
most of our problems are over? The particular grotesqueries of Watergate
may be gone, but many issues involving how decisions that affect our
lives get made, how power is allocated and superintended remain. There
is still a lot of work to be done. It is still not settled whether government
can be bought. It is still not clear whether government agencies can be
used to harass us. Or whether Presidents can be called to account.

John Rhodes has reported that the President will resign. Says Rhodes,
"I feel relief, sorrow, gratitude, but also optimism."

Shortly before 12:30 P.M., we suddenly hear Ron Ziegler's voice on
the radio. Ziegler sounds shaken and out of breath, barely able to speak,
as he announces, "Tonight, at nine o'clock Eastern Daylight Time, the
President of the United States will address the nation on radio and television from his Oval Office."

Now we await this last speech. How many times Nixon has pulled us
to the television set, starting with Checkers. With that speech in 1952, as
the then Vice-Presidential candidate attempted to explain the existence
of a fund for his senatorial expenses maintained by some backers, a dog
and a cloth coat entered American political history. I remember watching the broadcast as a child. I didn't know what to make of it. (Perhaps
today's children, who have seen so much, would not have had that difficulty.) One prays that he will leave us in dignity tonight.

It has been a gray morning, and now it is beginning to rain. For most
of this week, it has been sunny but not too warm. Dan Rather and Tom
Brokaw are broadcasting from Lafayette Park, across the street from the
White House.

The Dow-Jones average has been falling today. The stock market
never did make sense.

Reports are coming from Capitol Hill about proposals by both senators and House members that the President be given immunity. Senator
Edward Brooke, Republican of Massachusetts, has hedged his proposal
for a sense-of-the-Senate resolution that the President be given immunity by adding the condition that he "confess" his wrongdoing. Unlikely.
A number of the statements about immunity are couched as warnings
to the President against making a divisive speech tonight (they are still
afraid of him), and several call for contrition. Democratic leaders are
opposing legislation to grant immunity. Carl Albert says that this "is a
matter for the courts, the executive branch of the government, and not
for the legislative branch." Apart from the Constitutional niceties recited
by the politicians, there is fear of public outrage if the Congress grants

the President immunity now. One Senate aide tells me that the calls and telegrams coming into his senator's office against granting the President immunity are as numerous and as intense as was the reaction against the firing of Special Prosecutor Cox. The Senate aide in the traffic patterns says, "Why have two standards of justice—one for the President and Vice-President, and one for the rest of us? Dual standards are wrong. There is something beyond the present. This whole thing was about the rule of law. Where was the compassion when they voted to restore the death penalty? What about the kids living in Sweden and Canada because they opposed the war? Compassion is marvellous, but why be so selective?" Some of the politicians are sensitive not only to the public reaction against special legal treatment for our highest officials but also to the fact that Nixon will be leaving with a comfortable pension, a staff, and arrangements for an office.

Those few on Capitol Hill who are still interested in seeing the processes of impeachment carried through are being overtaken by events. The House Democratic leaders have come out against going ahead with impeachment. The House Judiciary Committee's report, still being prepared, becomes all the more important. It may turn out to be the only definitive document.

There is already some talk about what "the historians will say"—the historians, those unknown people who in the future will have the franchise to interpret what is going on now. We tend to assume that out of their years of accumulation of fact they will sift the truth—a truer truth than any we can hope to grasp. They will have many more facts, and they will have what is called "perspective" (which means they will not be trapped in the biases of our day and can freely write in the biases of *their* day—can find what they are looking for). But I wonder if they will really understand what it was like. Will they know how it felt to go through what we have gone through? Will they know how it felt to be stunned—again and again—as we learned what had been done by people in power? Will they know how it felt to be shocked, ashamed, amused by the revelations—will they understand the difficulty of sorting out the madcap from the macabre? (What *was* one really to think about someone in the pay of the White House putting on a wig and travelling across the country to visit a sick, disgraced lobbyist?) Can they conceivably understand how it felt as we watched, on our television screen, our President say, "I am not a crook"? Will they be able to understand why, almost two years ago, some very sensible people wondered whether it was the last election? Will they understand how it felt—as it did last fall at the time the President fired Special Prosecutor Cox, and on several later occasions—when it seemed that there were no checks on power? Will they understand how degrading it was to watch a President being run to ground? Will they know how it was to feel in the thrall of this strange man, who seemed to answer only to himself? Knowing the conclusion, as they will, will they understand how difficult, frightening, and fumbling the struggle really was?

This afternoon, the House of Representatives passed a bill to provide for the public financing of Presidential—but not congressional—campaigns.

The Nixons will go to San Clemente tomorrow. They have promised to give that house to the nation. But no papers have been signed, so it remains only a pledge. The President can still change his mind.

A Republican says that the politicians who are talking about immunity for the President are thinking personally, not institutionally. They are seeing Nixon as a former colleague. They are seeing the loss of power as "punishment enough." That is a very "Washington" way of looking at it. It is a hard question. But one must think of the damage that was done this country. And so much of that—which brings us back to where we began on the question of impeachment—is not covered in the criminal statutes.

The real transfer of power is going on out of sight. Tomorrow, it will be marked by another ceremony, signifying still another beginning. Soon we shall have both a President and Vice-President who were not elected.

There are reports tonight that the President made the decision to resign Monday evening on the *Sequoia* but that his family, who were along, begged him to reconsider, and that at dinner last evening he once again told his family that he would resign. Then the speechwriters were called in.

The stories are continuing to come out—some in print, some in conversation—about what went on in the White House and on Capitol Hill in the past few days. On the day that the Supreme Court ruled on the tapes, the President phoned Buzhardt from San Clemente and asked him to listen to the June 23rd tape. Even before then—for some time, in fact—some of the President's aides had seen that it was over, that the House would impeach and that very probably the Senate would convict. And they had reached a point where, whatever the prospects, they, like the Republicans in the Congress, wanted to get it over with. The President's aides were exhausted, battle-weary, shell-shocked, and, as one of them put it, nearly fit for psychoneurotic discharge. They had lived with this thing for more than a year. Some felt that such was the distraction at the White House that it had cost the nation a year in dealing with its problems, its allies, its adversaries. It was, says one, more an unconscious perception that grew, and worked on these exhausted people. So the last tape was only the precipitating event; there were people in the White House who seemed to grasp it as eagerly as did the Republicans on Capitol Hill, and who did what they could to persuade the President that he must give up his office.

At lunch in the White House Executive Dining Room on the day of the Supreme Court decision, Dean Burch, Buzhardt, William Timmons, who is in charge of congressional liaison, and Leonard Garment discussed whether the President should resign. All of them thought so, but Garment had some reservations; he considered that there was something to be said for seeing the processes through. Only Buzhardt had heard the June 23rd tape, and the others took notice when Buzhardt, the last to speak, said quietly, "He should resign." In California, Haig was trying to get through to the President about the degree of the trouble he was in.

Then there followed the showing of the transcript of the June 23rd tape to Wiggins by St. Clair and Haig, and telling Griffin and Rhodes about new evidence. During the last week, there was, in fact, a movement within the White House to get the President out. The President's declaration at the last Cabinet meeting that he would not resign, the importunings of his family that he not resign, even the call by Rabbi Korff for the country to rally round the President worried those who thought he must go. Bryce Harlow, the former White House counsellor and now a lobbyist for Procter & Gamble, went to work. Harlow made calls to the Hill. We have learned of some of the calls these various people were making to the Hill, but there were many—many of them redundant. Key Republicans—Goldwater, Tower—were got in touch with, and it was seen to it that Mississippi Democratic Senator John Stennis—"Judge Stennis," who was to listen to the tapes last fall, and who is one of the most influential men on Capitol Hill—conveyed word to the President about the depth of his trouble. Therefore the statements by key Republicans. Therefore the delegation to the White House. Therefore the aborting of the processes. Inevitably, the anxious conversations and meetings will come out in multiple versions, told from the perspective, and to the advantage, of the various participants—this will be the *Rashomon* to end *Rashomons*—but the show was over before they began.

The speech. During the day, researchers have found that it was six years ago tonight that Nixon made his acceptance speech at the Miami Beach convention. It is hard to believe that this is the last speech Richard Nixon will make as President. Yet there he is, sitting in that familiar scene, at the familiar desk, one flag in his lapel, one by his side, holding white sheets of paper. Just as when he talked about the economy, or the war. Johnson stunned us when he looked up from his white paper and said that he would not run for reëlection. Nixon's speech will not stun us. It is just there. He looks bad—the face more creased and drawn. He is wearing a dark suit, a dark tie, and a white shirt. He begins by telling us that this is the thirty-seventh time he has spoken to us from that office, and we recall that he is our thirty-seventh President.

He gets down to it quickly. He says that he will not continue "to make every possible effort to complete the term of office to which you elected me," because it has "become evident to me that I no longer have a strong enough political base in the Congress to justify continuing that effort." A euphemism, but so be it. Yet this makes it sound as if the President were resigning for the very reason that he insisted so often he would not resign for; he is talking as if we had a parliamentary system. Perhaps, *in extremis,* we do. He says he has concluded that "because of the Watergate matter I might not have the support of the Congress that I would consider necessary to back the very difficult decisions" he has to make. "I have never been a quitter," he says. "To leave office before my term is completed is abhorrent to every instinct in my body," he says, and one believes him. Yet, he says, to continue his fight "would almost totally absorb the time and attention of both the President and the Congress in a period when our entire focus should be on the great issues of peace abroad and prosperity without inflation at home." And then he says the flat, straight sentence—a sentence one thought one would never hear but now hears numbly: "Therefore I shall resign the Presidency effective at noon tomorrow." He says some graceful things about giving the next President our support. He talks about putting "the bitterness and the divisions of the recent past behind us," and says, "I regret deeply any injuries that may have been done in the course of the events that led to this decision. I would say only that if some of my judgments were wrong—and some were wrong—they were made in what I believed at the time to be the best interest of the nation." He looks straight into the camera, projecting a look of sincerity. He probably believes this. We have had no indication that he believes anything else. He says, "I leave with no bitterness toward those who have opposed me." Doubtful. Then he speaks with deep pride of his foreign-policy achievements, which he used to say so often would bring us "a generation of peace." He does not seem to understand that so much of what went wrong was done in the name of that foreign policy. From time to time, he manages a wan smile. He says that he will continue to work for his "great causes," and tells us that because of him "the world is a safer place." Shortly after that, he says, "May God's grace be with you in all the days ahead," the camera pans to the Presidential seal, and it is over.

AUGUST 9

Leon Jaworski issued a statement last night, saying, "There has been no agreement or understanding of any sort between the President or his representatives and the Special Prosecutor relating in any way to the President's resignation." It seems uncharacteristic that Nixon would leave office without having made arrangements about his legal future. Perhaps it is simply understood that if the President goes—without tearing us apart in the process—he will be given immunity. There was that comment by the President's Senate "friends" earlier in the week about a possible "gentlemen's agreement." It may be that the only way immunity might be possible would be if it is *not* talked about. Nixon has a subtle enough mind to understand that. Again, perhaps the only hope lay in getting out and taking his chances. On the other hand, it seems uncharacteristic that he would take such a big chance.

On television last night, we were told about Ford's life and his children. The building of the next totem has begun.

Late last night, Nixon was up making phone calls. In one post-midnight call to an aide, who told me about it, the President expressed some anxiety that he would be pursued and prosecuted in the courts. And then Nixon joked, "Some of the best political writing in this century has been done in jail."

On television this morning, we hear "Hail to the Chief" played for Nixon for the last time. Perhaps it is only in the imagination that it sounds slightly like an echo of itself. Staff members and their wives are seated in chairs in the East Room. The East Room: site of press conferences, religious services, and the naming of Gerald Ford as the next Vice-President. Today, the applause for the President goes on and on. James St. Clair and Raymond Price, a speechwriter who worked on last night's speech, are in a front row, applauding. Henry Kissinger and his new wife and William Simon and Alexander Haig are also in a front row, applauding. They all look grim. One wonders—watching them applaud—how much each of them had to do with bringing this moment about. The President and Mrs. Nixon—in a pink dress—and their daughters and the daughters' husbands stand on a platform in the front of the East Room. A gold curtain is behind them. Nixon looks better than he did last night. Mrs. Nixon is composed, as always. James Schlesinger, the Secretary of Defense, puffing on his pipe, applauds. Fred Buzhardt applauds. That's all he can do for Nixon now. Rabbi Korff, in a front-row aisle seat, applauds lustily.

Nixon, almost as if he couldn't help himself, begins with a jab at the press, suggesting that the press will be skeptical that this is a "spontaneous" event, and the skepticism "will be so reported in the press, and we don't mind, because they've got to call it as they see it." The President says that he is saying not goodbye but *"au revoir*—we'll see you again." He expressed his gratitude to the unseen staff people—the upstairs people—who keep the White House going. The President seems more human today. Again he is wearing a navy suit and a white shirt, and again a tiny American-flag pin is in his lapel. (What happens to the American-flag pins now?) He is trying to buck up his staff. Then he says some strange things. "Sure we have done some things wrong in this Administration," he says, "and the top man always takes the responsibility, and I've never ducked it." But, he says, "no man or no woman came into this Administration and left it with more of this world's goods than when he came in." Remarkable in several respects that he is standing there and saying that now. He talks of the importance of America's leadership in the world, and gets back to the point that no one in his Administration was "feathering his nest," and that government service is important but so are other careers. ("This country needs good farmers, good businessmen, good plumbers, good carpenters.") Then he talks of his father. Despite the hardships and the business failures, his father was "a great man," he says. "Nobody will ever write a book probably about my mother," he says. (Is he thinking of the book about Rose Kennedy?) Then, his eyes brimming with tears, he says, "My mother was a saint." (My mind flashes back to Egil Krogh telling me, four years ago, about that morning in May, 1970, when there were demonstrations here against the invasion of Cambodia, and the President, at dawn, went to the Lincoln Memorial and talked to the demonstrators about football, and then went to Capitol Hill, where he encountered, in the near-empty corridors, a cleaning woman. Krogh told me that the cleaning woman was carrying a Bible and asked the President to sign it, and as he did so the President told the cleaning woman that his mother had been a saint. "You be a saint," said the President to the cleaning woman.)

Now, choking back sobs, the President tells of his mother's having two sons die of tuberculosis and taking care of four boys not her own so that she could afford to take care of his older brother. One thinks of how often, through all the campaigns, he told us of his hard childhood, how deeply this is still in him. And there are some other touches that are pure Nixon. "I'm not educated, but I do read books," he says, and then he says that he was reading last night, which is hard to believe. In his speech last night, he quoted from Theodore Roosevelt about the importance of being in the arena, of being a man who "if he fails, at least fails while daring greatly." This morning, he reads from Theodore Roosevelt's diary upon the death of Roosevelt's first wife: "And when my heart's dearest died, the light went from my life forever." One thinks of the times Nixon has been Disraeli, Woodrow Wilson, Lincoln, Patton. The Theodore Roosevelt phase seems to be new. (So are the glasses, which he puts on while reading from Roosevelt's book.) This is a very painful sight. Nixon has this emotional side, too, and we have been through so much with him that one cannot help feeling his pain now. Distraught, destroyed, confused, broken, telling himself, because he has to, that this last defeat is "only a beginning." He says some true things about the tests and the strengthening that can come from the deepest disappointments and sadness. He puts it, characteristically, in terms of "the deepest valley" and "the highest mountain." And then one watches, transfixed, as he advises his staff, "Never get discouraged. Never be petty. Always remember others may hate you but those who hate you don't win unless you hate them. And then you destroy yourself." This speech will be much studied. But it shows almost nothing that we did not know about him before. And so the grief that one feels at the moment is for him, this man whose character was his fate, and for us, that we went through so much with and because of him. He did make his ordeal ours.

On the South Lawn of the White House, a red carpet has been rolled out to the waiting helicopter. The helicopter is olive-colored; a flag is painted on its side. President and Mrs. Nixon, together with Vice-President and Mrs. Ford and the Nixon children, walk toward the helicopter. Tricia and Edward Cox are going with the Nixons to California; Julie and David Eisenhower will stay behind to pack. Ron Ziegler is going with the Nixons to California. As the President boards the helicopter, he stands in the doorway, faces the crowd, and shoots his arms in the air, the fingers of both hands shaping the characteristic "V"s. The helicopter lifts off into the gray sky, circles over the Jefferson Memorial, disappears momentarily behind the Washington Monument, and is gone. Nixon seems to have just floated away. Moments later, he will land at Andrews Air Force Base. At twelve o'clock noon, when the President's plane—the "Spirit of '76"—is midway across the country, Nixon's resignation as President will take effect.

AFTERWORD

*"A man is not finished when he is defeated.
He is finished when he quits."*

Since Richard Nixon left office, we've learned a number of things about him that shed light on how he got into such terrible trouble, how he handled the biggest crisis of his crisis-ridden life—and more of what was going on inside the White House while we were watching, agape, from the outside. Moreover, looking back at the events of 1973–1974 offers new insights as to what Watergate was really about.

The story of what happened to Richard Nixon after he became the first president to have been driven from office is as interesting and compelling as most of the rest of his life. Nixon never managed to be boring. Little has been known about what he proceeded to do after he landed at his "Western White House," in San Clemente on August 9, 1974. He was now essentially out of sight. The nation might have thought that Richard Nixon, having met with the ultimate political humiliation, had finally gone away and disappeared from public life. But—as he'd said so many times before—he wasn't "a quitter." It wasn't in his nature to give up.

And so this remarkably resilient man wasn't about to quit now. Determined and methodical as usual, Nixon soon had a plan. With the help of aides who had gone with him to California, at government expense, he drew up a secret plan for his restitution, to regain respectability. It was given the code name Wizard. This plan took place out of sight because with the exception of those few aides, Nixon was more on his own than since he'd begun his long and tumultuous political career. He'd struggled virtually all his life, had pulled himself out of deep troughs before, and he wasn't about to stop now, not when all that he had fought for lay in ruins. This was the deepest trough of all, the most difficult situation to surmount. And now he was fighting a new kind of battle—not for something as tangible and requiring fairly conventional means (even for him) as political office, but to rehabilitate his reputation. How, exactly, does one in this unprecedented situation go about that? Most people wouldn't have dared to try. What would have crushed most people was to Nixon yet another challenge to be met and overcome. He was as driven about this one as he had been about all those that had gone before.

Nixon's defenders have argued that it's unfair to look at the man's record as president only through the prism of Watergate. That's a valid point, and this section will also attempt to put his presidency in that larger perspective.

What follows is a more rounded picture of Nixon's presidency than could be assessed in the midst of Watergate, as well as a new view of what that crisis was about—the crisis that cost him his lifelong-desired place at the pinnacle of political power and the desperately sought affirmation that this country bestowed by electing him to that position. Richard Nixon may have been more disgraced than any other president in history, his career up in smoke, but he wasn't done yet.

Down and Out in San Clemente

When friends and acquaintances picked up Nixon's phone calls from San Clemente shortly after he arrived there, they heard a deeply depressed man, sometimes in tears about having been brought so low, convinced that "they" would never relent: "They won't be satisfied until they have me in jail," Nixon said. He also fell ill from a serious recurrence of phlebitis, contracted during his Middle East trip in June, shortly before he left the presidency. A later recurrence almost killed him.

Yet for all his self-pity and sense of persecution by his "enemies," Nixon had a striking degree of self-knowledge. In a startling conversation with an aide in the early weeks of his exile, Nixon reflected on what had brought about his downfall. He said to the aide, "What starts the process are the laughs and snubs and slights that you get when you are a kid. But if you are reasonably intelligent and if your anger is deep enough and strong enough, you learn that you can change those attitudes by excellence, personal gut performance, while those who have everything are sitting on their fat butts." He had appointed tough guys as his aides, he said, because he wanted people around him who were, like him, fighters. He went out for high school and college football, and the fact that he had no real athletic ability "was the very reason I tried and tried and tried. To get discipline for myself and to show others that here was a guy who could dish it out and take it. Mostly, I took it."

If he was poorer and physically weaker than others his age, he triumphed by working harder than they did, and: "You get out of the alley and on your way." But then came the danger—and the trouble: "In your own mind you have nothing to lose, so you take plenty of chances. It's a piece of cake until you get to the top. You find that you can't stop playing the game because it is part of you . . . So you are lean and mean and resourceful and you continue to walk on the edge of the precipices because over the years you have become fascinated by how close to the edge you can walk without losing your balance."

"This time it was different," the aide responded.

"Yes," Nixon replied quietly, "This time we had something to lose."

His political career had been marked by unlikely comebacks. Only three others had lost a presidential race and then gone on to win one, and none of them in modern politics—Jefferson, Jackson, and Cleveland. When, two years after losing the presidential election to Kennedy, Nixon lost the California gubernatorial election, it was generally assumed that he was finished, as there were no more high political offices he could run for and win. Conceding the California race, he famously told the press corps, "You won't have Dick Nixon to kick around anymore."

His memoir, oddly named *Six Crises* (1962), approached his autobiography from an unusual perspective: each chapter described a time when, as he saw it, he'd been confronted with a challenge so great that it was a crisis, and he'd prevailed. Nixon talked about the book frequently, urging people to read it. (When Nixon met Mao on his breakthrough trip to China, in 1972, the wily Chinese leader flattered and preempted him by telling him he'd read *Six Crises*—before Nixon had a chance to tout it. Each had read up on the other, and Nixon for his part recited some of the Great Leader's philosophical thoughts.) Nixon even instructed his staff to make sure that the "plumbers"—the ragtag group, most of them veterans of the failed Bay of Pigs operation against the Cuban communist leader Fidel Castro, who conducted the famous Watergate break-in and other underhanded and illegal acts against the president's "enemies"—read the chapter about his confrontation with Alger Hiss. As soon as Nixon was elected to the House of Representatives, in 1946, at the height of the Red Scare, he sought and won a seat on the communist-hunting Un-American Activities Committee as a forum for getting attention—and his pursuit of Hiss, a suspected spy for the Soviet Union, brought Nixon to national attention and propelled him into the Senate. Hiss, then a respected member of the Eastern establishment (which Nixon so hated), ultimately went to jail for perjury, though later evidence arose that appeared to confirm Nixon's charges. A mere two years and some devious pre-convention maneuvers later, Nixon was on the Republican ticket as the party's vice presidential candidate. But then, facing charges of corruption through a slush fund collected by his friends and supporters, he fought to stay on the ticket by giving the "Checkers speech"—another chapter in *Six Crises*.

The Rootless Man

Nixon had bought the house in San Clemente—a large Spanish-style building overlooking the Pacific Ocean—during his presidency with the help of his friends Bebe Rebozo and Robert Abplanalp. But he was essentially a rootless man—unlike other presidents he had had no place with which he was identified, no real hometown. Just as he invented himself, Nixon invented "homes." The larger spread at San Clemente made more sense for him at this point than his other house, at Key Biscayne, and to the extent he belonged anywhere, it was California, where he had grown up and begun his political career.

From early in his presidency, Nixon spent an uncommon amount of time fleeing the White House and Washington. He went to Camp David often with Rebozo, his closest and only real friend. But it wasn't a friendship of

420

equals: Nixon valued Rebozo's company for the latter's ability to remain silent for long stretches of time. The two men also engaged in heavy drinking together.

During his White House years, there had been indications that the President liked his liquor, but the full extent of his fondness of the drink, or its effects, was unknown to the general public throughout his presidency; it began to become apparent later to some people when they read the transcripts closely. And even though the transcripts suggested that he had been drinking, it wasn't until later that people learned how serious his drinking problem was. When he drank a lot, Nixon slurred his words to such an extent that it was difficult for his aides and others to understand him, and he sometimes seemed out of control. He would call aides and others at all hours of the night, issuing outlandish instructions—for example, to fire an entire floor of the State Department—and then slamming down the phone—often as not only to pick it up again to emphasize the order. ("This order is not appealable." Slam.) It was left to the judgment of aides—whose judgment was clearly questionable—to decide which of the middle-of-the-night orders by the president of the United States to carry out and which to ignore.

Adding to the problems caused by his drinking, Nixon began to take Dilantin—a medication supplied to him by the financier Jack Dreyfus—to deal with his deep depression. Dilantin was an anti-convulsive drug that had never been approved for depression, and its effect was to exacerbate the characteristics of drunkenness: mental confusion, slurring one's words, irritability. A man in this state was making fateful decisions.

I learned later that Rebozo and Nixon were drinking heavily together at Camp David on the eve of the invasion of Cambodia. During the run-up to the invasion, Nixon made so many calls to his national security adviser that after midnight one night, Kissinger ordered a member of his staff back to the White House, saying "Our peerless leader has flipped out." Kissinger sometimes referred to the President as "our drunken friend," and had aides listen in to hear what he was hearing. Nixon had taken to watching *Patton* over and over, and he ordered his staff to view it before the invasion of Cambodia. The recollections of various Nixon associates of that period makes it quite evident that the orders to invade a neutral country without authorization from Congress—an invasion that set off riots on campuses across the country and led to the killing of four students at Kent State by National Guard officers— was heavily affected by Nixon's anxiety and inebriation.

A Pursuit of Money
In the national uproar that ensued when Gerald Ford pardoned Nixon on September 8, 1974, a month after Nixon announced his resignation, inevitably there was widespread suspicion that there had been a deal: that in exchange for Nixon selecting Ford to succeed him, Ford would repay Nixon by protecting him from criminal prosecution. Ford even felt compelled to

appear before a congressional committee to deny that there had been such a deal, and there was never any evidence of one. Though I felt at the time that Ford had done the right thing—that the country had been through enough upheaval and it was time to move on—some whose opinion I respect thought that the legal case should have proceeded, to make it clear that no one was above the law. According to this view, Nixon shouldn't have gone to jail— removal from office would have been punishment enough—but the legal process should have been seen to its conclusion. Nixon was actually troubled about the pardon and hesitated for a while about accepting it for fear it would be seen as an admission of guilt. Yet he reconciled himself to accepting the bad publicity in exchange for avoiding years of expensive trials and perhaps even jail time.

Nixon's most urgent order of business was to make money, though money wasn't a new preoccupation. Rather than risk impeachment on the matter, Nixon agreed to pay $465,000 in back taxes (the IRS had said he owed at least $11,000 more); among deductions the IRS disallowed were for claimed business use of his vacation homes, for a masked ball given by Tricia Nixon, $22.00 for the cleaning of Mrs. Nixon's bathroom rug, and $1.24 for interest on a department store bill. He paid no state or local income taxes for any of his residences.

Even as Nixon was giving his farewell speech to his staff, a longtime military aide was packing up crates full of presidential documents from the West Wing to ship them to San Clemente. The purpose was to use them as material for another book, from which he'd presumably earn substantial income. Nixon's plan was to get everything useful out of the White House before the incoming Ford people noticed. And taking his Presidential papers to California would also prevent them from becoming public and causing him embarrassment. Nixon first tried to get hold of the papers semi-legitimately by persuading the General Services Administration to give him control over them for five years—at the end of which he could destroy them. (His failure to destroy the tapes had been a lesson.) But Congress stepped in to stop this egregious arrangement and passed a law stipulating that the presidential papers would go to the National Archives. Desperate to keep his reputation from sinking further, Nixon made a deal with the National Archives that documents and transcripts concerning Watergate and Vietnam wouldn't be made public for some time. But despite the signed agreement to turn over his papers and transcripts to the Archives, Nixon proceeded to purloin them from the White House.

The Nixon military aide managed to collect the equivalent of three railroad boxcars of documents and began transferring them to California. (Other documents were shredded using a special chemical.) But the plot was foiled when in an off-hour a Ford aide noticed strange trucks in the White House driveway and inquired what was in them. A revelation in the *Washington Post* just before Nixon left office interrupted another bit of kleptocracy—to ship to San Clemente millions of dollars in gifts from foreign leaders, including elaborate jewelry for members of his family. Under the law, any gift worth over $50 was to be turned over to the federal government. As a result of the disclosure the Nixons had to surrender the gems.

Nixon's book was a great success. He received a handsome advance of $2.5 million for his memoirs, which he wrote with the help of some aides who had gone with him into exile. The resulting book, *RN: The Memoirs of Richard Nixon*, sold an astonishing 330,000 copies in just the first six months. (Nixon had sought to emulate his idol Theodore Roosevelt—or TR—by having his own initials, RN, be the title of the book, but the publishers talked him into merely putting them at the front of the title.)

While Nixon was working on the book he decided on another money-making venture: to grant a series of televised interviews. While American broadcasters vied for the opportunity, Nixon decided on the English talk show host David Frost. Nixon assumed that Frost wouldn't ask him the kinds of troublesome questions that American journalists were likely to. Frost also offered Nixon a sweet deal: in a highly unusual arrangement, Frost agreed that Nixon would be paid a fee of six hundred thousand dollars, *plus* 20 percent of the profits from sales of the interview to television stations.

Thus, according to this agreement, Nixon had a financial incentive to say something that would guarantee headlines—and lots of sales. It was a fix. The supposed gladiators were in business together—a fact unknown by the viewers. But the deal almost didn't pay off. Part of the arrangement between Nixon and Frost was that only one of the four sessions would be about Watergate. For the first three Nixon rambled through his foreign policy successes (as he defined them, including Cambodia); the interviews were considered soporific. So everything rested on the final Watergate segment. For a while Nixon remained unrevealing; both Frost's and Nixon's aides were becoming desperately worried that the whole thing would be a flop. But suddenly, through Frost's misreading of a sign the Nixon side held up—he thought it said that they wanted a pause in the interview—there was an unplanned break. In the dressing room, Nixon's aides told him that he had to be more forthcoming, and at the end of the break a Nixon aide told Frost that Nixon knew that he had to say more, "He's got more to volunteer." The deal was on. And so Nixon returned and uttered his more famous lines, "I let down my country." And, "I gave them a sword." He insisted that his mistakes "were mistakes of the heart rather than of the head." These were unusual things for an ex-president to say, but they weren't stunning revelations. It was highly improbable that Nixon, a lawyer and skilled debater, would start confessing now to the commission of crimes. Most open-minded observers concluded that the interviews had resulted essentially in a draw.

Unfortunately, the popular play and movie *Frost/Nixon* distorted the transcript of the Watergate interview. Both the play and the movie have Nixon confess to Frost that he he'd been involved in a cover-up—with Nixon's face distorted in agony, this was the climactic moment of the drama. Such a confession to criminal behavior would have been dramatic indeed, had Nixon actually said it. But the line in the script for the play and the movie omitted the first several words in the sentence that Nixon had actually said—which can be heard on recordings of the interviews—and an ellipsis was substituted, so that the script read, ". . . I was involved in a cover-up as you call it." The audience of course could know nothing of the ellipsis, and so it was deceived into believing that Nixon had made a damning disclosure when no such thing has occurred. It made for high drama, but it wasn't true. The actual line uttered by Nixon, when Frost pressed him to confess that he had more than made "mistakes," that crime may have been involved, was, "You're wanting me to say that I participated in an illegal cover-up. No." On the doctored line rested the plot's conceit that the canny Frost had bested the shrewd, evasive Nixon. The play had been set up as a David/Goliath confrontation: thus the sequence of the names in the title *Frost/Nixon*.

Despite Nixon's efforts to make the subject of Watergate go away, it kept lapping up on the shores of San Clemente. By the end of 1974 and into the following year, a substantial number of his aides were sentenced to prison terms. Among the former top aides to go to jail were his former Attorney General and chairman of his reelection committee John Mitchell; his top assistants Bob Haldeman and John Ehrlichman; and also Charles Colson and John Dean—virtually the entire higher level of the Nixon White House. Some smaller White House fry, as well as the plumbers and their leaders, were also sentenced to prison.

The Sagehood Plot
Nixon's preoccupation, even obsession, after being forced from office was to redeem his reputation, to become a respected figure, to raise himself up from his disgraced state, according to the Wizard plan. He wanted to become someone people listened to—a senior statesman, a sage. And the best way to be considered a sage, Nixon understood, was to establish one's credentials as an expert in foreign policy, a man known to world leaders. Domestic policy didn't cut it the same way: lectures and articles on education or the environment didn't attract the Brahmins and the business leaders Nixon wanted to attract, didn't occupy nearly as much space on the stage. No splashy trips. Nixon hadn't been much interested in domestic policy. Various descriptions have been offered of Nixon's domestic philosophy, but essentially there wasn't one: he was a pragmatist—he moved left and right as the situation suited him. His approval of relatively moderate bills on domestic policies—certainly by the later standards of the Republican Party—were for the most part responses to initiatives by leading Democratic senators.

This was particularly true of the environmental policies he signed onto: the environmental movement took hold during his presidency, and Nixon wasn't going to get isolated on the matter. And so the role of the federal government in regulating the environment grew considerably under Nixon—though in conversations with aides he referred to environmentalism as "crap for clowns." Ehrlichman later wrote of his own frustration with the difficulty of getting the president's attention to domestic issues and his efforts to keep Nixon from veering further to the right, as other aides urged.

The radical family assistance plan Nixon proposed—to replace welfare payments with cash assistance—was foisted on him by then-urban affairs adviser Daniel Patrick Moynihan, who convinced Nixon that he could be Disraeli, a conservative who backed proposals that liberals could support. For a brief while, the grand notion of the family assistance plan, plus emulating a great statesman, appealed to Nixon. The plan would also enable him to reduce significantly the size and the power of the welfare bureaucracy—in general Nixon loathed the bureaucracies, viewing them with suspicion as definitely not on his side. Though Nixon announced his proposal with great fanfare on television, he quickly lost interest in it. In congress both liberals and conservatives disliked the plan, but for different reasons: many liberals felt that the payments were too low—and conservatives wanted nothing to do with cash payments for the poor. And so the program died on Capitol Hill. This was fine with Nixon, who in fact had told Haldeman that his goal was to convince liberals that he wanted to propose something progressive that conservatives would kill.

In the case of race, the most thorny domestic issue, Nixon's policies were a mixed picture. He campaigned in 1968 on the "Southern strategy": to appeal to both Southerners and blue collar workers in the North perturbed by efforts toward racial integration. In other efforts to have it both ways, Nixon sought to please liberals by ordering the Justice Department to enforce court orders on integration—and conservatives by making it clear that he would go no further than that. He openly opposed the busing of children in order to achieve racial integration of schools, a problem of particular sensitivity in the urban North. Nixon ordered the firing of Leon Panetta, then a Republican, from his job as head of the civil rights division of the Department of Health, Education and Welfare because Panetta openly complained that the administration was moving too slowly toward school integration. Nixon wanted to get George Romney, his Secretary of Housing and Urban Affairs, who pressed for housing integration in suburbs, out of his cabinet, but, characteristically, he couldn't bring himself to fire him, and turned the matter over to John Mitchell, but Romney resisted Mitchell's suggestions that he go.

Nixon displayed a marked indecisiveness at times, especially when it came to personnel, and his hesitation to fire Romney was fed by the storm that had broken out not long before over the fact that he *had* fired Interior Secretary Walter Hickel, who was popular among environmentalists and younger people. Hickel had been an anti-environmentalist when Nixon selected him, but he changed as he got closer to the subject. He had also infuriated Nixon by openly criticizing the administration's policies in Vietnam, saying that the president should show more sensitivity to the concerns of student protestors. Nixon had turned to Mitchell to do his dirty work and get rid of Hickel, but Hickel refused, and Nixon had to carry out the unpleasant mission himself.

He may not have had very firm principles about domestic policy, but Nixon wasn't benighted, either. The result, however he got there, was—with the exception of race—a relatively progressive record on domestic issues. He accepted the idea that the federal government could be put to use to help the citizens. He was the last Republican president to do so.

Mr. Foreign Policy

Nixon was far more interested in foreign policy, where a president could make decisions with less interference from the congress—until the latter stages of the Vietnam War, that is—and where he could have the greater impact, for good or for ill. As President, Nixon eagerly embraced the role of international statesman. After losing the presidential and California gubernatorial elections he had traveled abroad and met foreign leaders—not all of whom were enthusiastic to meet a man who had lost two successive elections. But Nixon wasn't easily embarrassed. Then, one of the first things Nixon did upon becoming President was to take a trip to Europe in February, meeting with heads of state. He was partial to Charles de Gaulle, who had taken the time to meet with him during his wanderings, and who implanted in him the idea of *détente*, a lessening of tensions with the Soviet Union. While biding his time before he ran for president again, Nixon wrote about this and also about the need to open up dealings with China. His openings to the Soviet Union and China were historic achievements. His policy on the Vietnam War remained controversial beyond his lifetime and is likely to remain so: the heart of the issue was whether he and Henry Kissinger carried on the war for an additional five years for a peace agreement very close to one they could have had that much earlier. He also engaged in serious arms control efforts as he pursued *détente* with the Soviet Union. Nixon's record looked better the longer he was out of office and occasionally produced waves of nostalgia.

And now the former president would burnish his credentials by a number of foreign trips; he also wrote and spoke, his speeches mainly about foreign leaders he had known. In early 1976, he returned to China, the place of his greatest triumph, where he issued foreign policy pronouncements as if he were still president, or thought he was. His trips, and apparent confusion about his role, weren't necessarily appreciated by Republicans who were engaged in their own attempts to lead the nation, or the numerous party members who wanted Nixon to just go away.

The China trip, coming as it did during the 1976 contest for the Republican nomination, displeased Ford, who was seeking a real election to the office Nixon had put him in, and was facing a strong nomination challenge from Ronald Reagan. (Ford was constrained to jam in a trip to China of his own during the primaries.) Soon after his heady China trip, Nixon planned a six-week worldwide tour, but a number of heads of state sent word that they had no time to see him, and his two former Secretaries of State, Kissinger and William Rogers, told him that such a trip was ill-advised. Nixon failed to grasp that it was too soon since he had been forced to leave office to start playing world leader again, though he agreed to postpone that trip. He did appear at the Oxford Union, where he was greeted with jeers but at the end of his appearance received a standing ovation. Upon his return, Nixon told a reporter his guiding philosophy: "A man is not finished when he is defeated," Nixon said. "He is finished when he quits."

Nixon became increasingly audacious in his climb back toward respectability as the years went on. He sought to make himself the indispensable advisor to presidents on foreign policy dealings—sometimes by devious methods—and he often succeeded. Though Jimmy Carter loathed Nixon, in 1979 the former president got himself invited to the first state dinner for Chinese leaders—at the insistence of the Chinese—despite the fact that Carter wasn't at all eager to have him there. After Nixon took yet another trip to China later in 1979, he was voted one of Gallup's ten most admired men in the world.

Nixon was playing fantasy president, which meant attending all of the most important funerals, since that's what presidents and ex-presidents do. But the circumstances of Nixon's ex-ness made for a most unusual situation and discomfited former presidents who hadn't been thrown out of office. In 1981 he attended the funeral of the Shah of Iran and later that year managed to get himself included—along with former presidents Ford and Carter—in the official delegation to the funeral of Anwar Sadat, making for a rather tense threesome. At the end of the Cairo ceremonies, having told no one but Reagan's national security adviser Al Haig (who had urged Reagan to include Nixon in the funeral entourage), Nixon slipped away from the delegation and took an extensive tour through the Middle East, despite a recurrence of his painful phlebitis. When Nixon returned from the trip, he sent a supposedly private report on his findings to the president—and released it to the press. This was a to be a technique he would use often to get attention to himself as the elder statesman: he would send some very important figure a "secret" document stating his views on this and that and simultaneously make it available to reporters.

And then in perhaps Nixon's most brazen act of his effort to climb back to respectability he blackmailed Bill Clinton into consulting him on Russia. He got word to Clinton that if he weren't paid proper respect as a foreign policy guru he would write an op-ed in a major newspaper attacking the President's handling of foreign policy. Following Nixon's subterranean threat and some lobbying by Nixon allies, Clinton telephoned him, appearing to seek his counsel, and then, still under pressure from the Nixon camp, on the eve of a two-man summit with Boris Yeltsin, Clinton reluctantly invited Nixon to the White House supposedly to give him advice. The meeting was held at night so that no press would be around to ask questions and take pictures of Clinton and Nixon together.

Nixon was a smart man—intelligence and judgment being different qualities—he impressed with his talks. His sonorous voice and certitude projected confidence, and he appeared a font of knowledge. To add to the dazzle he made a point of speaking without notes or a podium. Nixon the foreign policy expert wasn't the Nixon of Watergate memory—wriggling, perspiring, defensive, toying with the truth. But his name-dropping speeches could take him only so far, and he was limited by having San Clemente as his base of operations and, understandably, he was becoming bored with its relative isolation.

"The Fast Track"

And so, in 1980, despite his many vows to leave it to the federal government, Nixon sold the house in San Clemente, and he and Pat moved to New York, locale of many of the poobahs—publishers, bankers, captains of industry, and foreign policy eminences—whom he needed to cultivate in order to implement Wizard. New York was where, as Nixon put it, he could be "on the fast track." (He had repaired to New York before, after losing the California governorship, and it had helped him get on his feet then.) The Nixons moved into a townhouse on the Upper East Side of Manhattan (having been blackballed by various co-op boards). In time, movers and shakers flocked to Nixon's townhouse, having eagerly accepted one of the most coveted dinner invitations in New York.

Nixon's dinners, most of them stag, were ritualized affairs. At 7 p.m. sharp, he greeted his guests in the foyer; this was followed by light conversation, along with drinks and hors d'oeuvres in the upstairs library. (Nixon mixed the drinks himself, specializing in dry martinis.) Nixon's new home was fixed up in Chinese décor. At dinner, where delicious Chinese food was served by Chinese waiters the conversation was focused on a topic Nixon selected. Following dinner the group repaired to the living room for more light conversation, with the host, though still awkward, often telling stories. Then, precisely at 10:30, Nixon would look up at the clock and remark, "Well, I promised to get [so and so, naming a prominent guest] to a house of prostitution by 11:00, so I guess we'd better call it a night." Everyone knew it was time to leave. Afterward they talked about the dinner all over town.

In time, Nixon became a New York celebrity—dining in fine restaurants with other famous people, local powers, and visiting dignitaries; his attendance at football games was pictured in the papers, as were sightings of him around town. He wrote articles for *Foreign Affairs*, the *New York Times*, and the news weeklies. He was having, for him, a wonderful time. Newspaper stories began to appear hailing Richard Nixon's latest comeback—reminiscent of all the times in his career when he was down and seemingly out and pundits would call on him and return to announce a "new Nixon."

But in just three years, disturbed by the seamier side of New York and worried about its effects on his grandchildren, on whom he doted, Nixon moved again, this time to the quieter, suburban Saddle River, New Jersey. And he still wasn't done: now there was a new generation to cultivate. So he held a series of cocktails and dinners at his new home for journalists who hadn't yet come of age during Watergate and presumably had no preconceptions. Nixon set out to impress them with his worldly knowledge, and most came away awed. In 1984 and 1988 he went to the belly of the beast, and addressed conventions of newspaper editors and publishers in Washington, D.C. Each time, he was asked to opine on the upcoming presidential election, and though he sometimes got it wrong (his predictions were evidently questionable at the time) he received standing ovations from people who had driven him from office.

A bona fide ex-president would in the normal course have his own library, and Nixon was determined to have one as well, despite his unusual circumstances. A library would guarantee immortality and present a proper picture of his presidency—as he saw it. Since the government wasn't going to pay for a library for him, he and his wealthy backers had to raise the money. The library would be located in Yorba Linda, where Nixon was born and spent his early years. (His modest birthplace was to stand in its original place, on the grounds of the library.) Because his presidential papers belonged to the federal government in Washington, the library would be essentially a museum. Under the control of his family and allies, the Nixon Library downplayed Watergate by darkening the room that housed its display—his daughter Julie explained to Larry King that the purpose was "so that you want to move on." The record was adjusted. The text of the transcript of the crucial "smoking gun," the August 23, 1972, conversation in which Nixon told Haldeman to instruct the CIA to call the FBI off its investigation, the one that sealed Nixon's fate, was doctored. The library declared the entire Watergate episode a "coup" perpetrated by Nixon's "enemies."

Nixon's faux library was given a grand opening in July, 1990, a ceremony solemnly attended by President George H.W. Bush and former Republican presidents Ford and Reagan. Later, in early 1994, after a great deal of controversy, congress passed a law that provided federal funds for Nixon's Library, and in time, transcripts of the tapes were transferred there from the Archives. But though the library was now technically under the control of the Federal Government, Nixon's family and allies kept a strong hand in its management through the Richard Nixon Foundation, which was officially given a voice in its operation. Inevitably this collision of interests caused difficulties: the first director, Tim Naftali, a respected historian of the Cold War and a former employee of the National Archives, collided with the Foundation over his inviting speakers who had been critical of Nixon. And then, a protracted and bitter row occurred when Naftali, with great effort, mounted a more honest—and far tougher—Watergate exhibit. The Nixon Foundation made hundreds of suggestions for changes to the new exhibit, including the omission of certain episodes, but all of them were ignored. In 2011, Naftali was forced out. While a long search for a new director was supposedly taking place, Nixon's allies unveiled a new exhibit called "Patriot, President, Peacemaker," which covered Nixon's entire life but left out Watergate altogether. The Nixon backers explained that Watergate was already covered in the permanent exhibit—which of course covered the rest of Nixon's life as well.

Patricia Nixon died in June 1993 and the nation saw a distraught Richard Nixon sobbing at her funeral. Recent discoveries suggest that they were closer than it appeared in public—their attachment apparently having grown stronger during Nixon's exile. (Pat was delighted to be out of politics.) Nixon himself died of a stroke the following April 29, less than a year after his wife's death. A grand array—President Clinton and his wife, along with three ex-presidents and their wives, and Henry Kissinger, Bob Dole and numerous other grandees—gathered in Yorba Linda for Nixon's funeral. Over a hundred members of congress were in attendance, as were a couple of hundred members of the diplomatic corps. Kissinger's and Dole's voices cracked as they delivered their eulogies (though Dole used to wisecrack about Nixon). The funeral was carried on national television.

Nixon would have been pleased.

Who Was This Man?

So, what are we to make of this man, and what is the meaning of his extraordinary presidency, unique in all of American history?

The tragedy of Richard Nixon is that he was a very smart man who had reached the pinnacle of political life in America only to lose it as a result of his own inner torment. No matter how high he went, or his historic international achievements (for which he became as noted in the foreign policy circles that meant so much to him as for his blatant disregard for the constitution), or the bankers and publishers he managed to impress, he never lost his resentments, his anger at those he thought had had it better than he did and he was sure lorded it over him, and his desire for revenge. Nor did he shake his awkwardness.

A former Republican congressman recounted having been summoned, along with some other back-benchers (led by the insurgent Newt Gingrich) to a meeting with Nixon at the Madison Hotel in Washington in1984. Nixon had been observing the group, and he wanted to meet some of its members—but only the new ones, no one with a direct memory of Watergate. Altogether about a dozen young congressmen met with Nixon in a large suite: the former congressman recalled meeting a very awkward man who didn't know quite what to do after he greeted his visitors in the foyer of his hotel suite. It took an aide to suggest that they should move to the living room and talk. Nixon didn't know how to begin the conversation—but after an uncomfortable pause a congressman asked him to talk about foreign policy. Whereupon Nixon brightened and performed his lengthy disquisition about what was going on in the world and leaders he had known, enthralling his audience. He even made a couple of prescient comments about the forthcoming presidential election.

He couldn't remove himself from politics. Nixon wasn't invited to the Republican conventions, but he made it his business to know what was going on, calling candidates and operatives, offering advice; he learned the names of who was running each campaign and what were the poll numbers in almost every district. Nationwide, people were astonished to hear his voice on the phone, and it apparently never occurred to him that his advice wasn't necessarily desired. After Reagan was reelected, Nixon was so disconnected from reality that he made a run at getting a high-level position in the administration. He felt that he had earned it.

Sometimes it seems that Nixon never had a chance. He was trapped in a character that wouldn't permit him to be content—he felt over and over that he had to prove himself, he was at war in his imagination. In Richard Nixon's tormented mind a large array of "enemies" was out to get him—so he had to retaliate, "get the goods" on them, or even, as he put it, "destroy" them. He would never be accepted, he believed, because of his modest roots. Even after he won scholarships, his parents couldn't afford the other costs of sending him to an elite college or law school. Certain that Ivy League graduates would always look down on him, he had to show 'em. There could never be enough success. He was a lonely man—there was no one to challenge his assumptions, to set him straight in his confusion of political opponents with enemies. He didn't recognize boundaries. He never learned to observe limits—anything went—and one thing led to another until he was in too deep to extricate himself.

For a man whose exposure to the world was extensive, his prejudices blinded him and led to some of his darkest moments. Count the Jews in the Department of Labor, he instructed an aide, and he had hired the kinds of people who would carry out such instructions. He simply couldn't stop himself until he arranged his own doom. One can almost empathize with a man who was a prisoner of his own resentments, suspicions, hatreds. It's tempting to indulge in amateur psychology in Nixon's case, in part because his interior became so public—but that's tricky business. Books have been written containing amateur analyses of the man, but most rely on a shaky determinism. The violent father and the mother who has been variously described as warm and cold, loving and distant, whose approval was, by most accounts, hard to win. Nixon's childhood was marked by her long absences while she took care of two tubercular sons, both of whom died of the disease. With the poverty thrown in, Nixon's is almost a Dickensian story. Nixon lacked the sort of support that might have saved him from himself: he had no stabilizing mentors, no lifelines to a more normal existence, no one to give him satisfaction with his talents and achievements. Yet people who have had difficult childhoods don't necessarily end up nearly destroying constitutional government.

What, In the End, Was Watergate?

Though Nixon was named an unindicted co-conspirator by the Watergate grand jury for having obstructed justice, it's a major mistake to think of his role in the whole of Watergate narrowly, merely in terms of criminality—the menace and the danger were far greater. The more I looked back some years later on the kaleidoscopic events of Watergate, the clearer became a pattern of activities that amounted to an attempt to subvert the democratic process. The President of the United States intervened in and attempted to undermine the nomination of a presidential candidate by the opposition party; the extent to which he caused the outcome doesn't matter. Nixon used the powers and prestige of the White House to obtain money to pay for his own personal goon squad. Their activities were more than objects of curiosity, and whatever mirth (albeit nervous) they stirred at the time evanesces when they're seen as part of the larger purpose of undermining the workings of the opposition party. That way lay fascism. And Watergate was the second greatest test of the Constitutional system in our nation's history: was the President accountable to the Congress and the courts?

Thus, Nixon's nearly lifelong pattern of confusing opponents for "enemies" was carried right into the White House, where there was little hesitation to use the instruments of power at the top of the government to spy on, harrass, "destroy" them. (George Shultz, then Treasury Secretary, did refuse to implement the use of the IRS to audit those on the enemies list, thus earning Nixon's sobriquet "candy-ass.")

Fortunately, the plumbers were stumblebums, more fit for Marx Brothers movies than sinister plots on the part of the President of the United States and his aides. They bungled every assignment they were given. But the comic aspect of their cloddish performances collides in the mind with their role as an off-the-books operation to carry out the President's personal vendettas—in the process tearing up Constitutional and other long accepted restraints.

I discovered later that the plumbers' history-making break-in of the Democratic party's headquarters in the Watergate complex on June 17, 1972 was actually their fourth attempt to get into the DNC's offices—and in fact their second successful entry. By now conducting break-ins was rather routine for these misguided zealots—nothing special. (Though there were various theories, it has never been settled exactly what the burglars were looking for, or why they put taps on a couple of phones, including that of party chairman Lawrence O'Brien—but in the end those aren't important matters. The point is that this was considered an okay thing to do to the opposition party.)

The plumbers' first attempt to get into the DNC headquarters was through an elaborate ruse in which they staged a dinner within the Watergate building, which, they figured, would provide them a way to get into the DNC offices later. But the burglars ended up spending the night locked in a closet. On the second attempt they got as far as the DNC office, but they'd failed to bring the right equipment to break the lock on the door. So one of the burglars had to return to Miami to obtain the proper tools for their mission. The burglars did succeed in getting into the DNC offices on the third try, on Memorial Day weekend of 1972—but they made a hash of the job. (The bug on O'Brien's phone didn't work, and the documents they photographed were barely readable.) A highly dissatisfied John Mitchell ordered the burglars to go back to the DNC's Watergate offices and get it right. But they got a bit careless with tape.

It was clear from a conversation Nixon had with Haldeman in the White House three days later, after he returned from a vacation in Key Biscayne, that he was worried that the capture of the burglars would lead to Colson and the number of things the plumbers—whom Nixon kept referring to as "the Cubans"—had done. In particular, he feared that the arrest would uncover the break-in of the office of Daniel Ellsberg's psychiatrist, Dr. Lewis Fielding, in Los Angeles, on September 19, 1971, nearly a year before. This raid was a flagrant violation of the Fourth Amendment. It's also clear that the cover-up had more to do with the raid on Fielding's office than it did with the Watergate break-in. Ehrlichman said later that Nixon had known about the raid on the psychiatrist's office beforehand. The purpose of this break-in was to get hold of Ellsberg's file in order to see if there was anything in his talks with his psychiatrist that they could smear him with (imagine!). Such material might also be useful in swaying the jury in Ellsberg's trial.

Haldeman, a little blind to the details, said to Nixon, "They've been doing other things very well, apparently." He and Nixon discussed the relationship of the various Cubans and their leaders to the White House; Haldeman suggested their line of defense for having broken into the Watergate: "We went in there to get this because we're scared to death that this crazy man [McGovern] is going to become President and sell the US out to the communists." In this and a meeting the next day, it became clear that Nixon and his aides were especially concerned about the arrest of Howard Hunt: "He's done a lot of things," the President said. The swashbuckling Hunt, who directed most of the plumbers' operations, was the hyper-belligerent Colson's man. And they became apprehensive, fatally so, about what the FBI might learn. The President asked his aides, "Can you get a little better protection for the White House on that?"

It was from this conversation between Nixon and Haldeman that the famous 18 ½ minute erasure was made. Though the "18 ½ minute gap" remained a mystery during Watergate and for a long time after—White House aides had tried to place the blame on Nixon's secretary Rose Mary Woods—

the evidence is compelling that Nixon had sat at Camp David working the keys to delete a large portion of this dangerous conversation. But what remained was incriminating enough—the cover-up was being planned right then and there. The disclosure of these conversations three days after the discovered break-in put the lie to the countless statements Nixon made to the public as to when he learned of any White House role in the break-in, or any attempt to cover it up.

The plumbers botched the job of the breaking into Dr. Fielding's office, too. Though their two leaders, Howard Hunt and G. Gordon Liddy, cased Dr. Fielding's office beforehand, when the plumbers, using CIA-supplied wigs and other disguises, including voice-altering devices, broke in they found no files at all, not to mention one on Ellsberg. Even so, the break-in still managed to defeat its purpose. In the course of Ellsberg's trial on federal charges, the Justice Department, over Nixon's strenuous objections, disclosed the raid on Dr. Fielding's office. After that disclosure, the district judge presiding over the case ruled that the administration's efforts to interfere in the trial "offend a sense of justice," and he dismissed the case. The raid on Ellsberg's psychiatrist's file was the single most damning—and alarming—act of the entire Watergate period.

The craziest idea of all: to firebomb the Brookings Institution in order to find material about Vietnam that Nixon was convinced was squirreled away there. The stratagem, cooked up by Colson, whom even his White House colleagues considered unrestrained, resulted from insistence by the president: "Goddamn it, get in and get those files. Blow the safe and get them." It's been speculated that the material Nixon was after was, variously, two unreleased chapters of the Pentagon Papers, information about the bombing halt just before the 1968 election, or perhaps a document that would disclose Nixon's role in interfering with the peace talks—the collapse of which may have decided the election. (When an election is that close, any number of things can have caused the outcome.) Colson's scheme was that the White House's private goon squad start a fire in the building on Massachusetts Avenue and in the confusion when a fire truck that they themselves mocked up was arriving, the plumbers would blow open a safe in the office of Leslie Gelb or Morton Halperin, two former Pentagon employees who had worked on the Pengagon Papers, and seize the contents. But as it happened, neither Gelb nor Halperin had any such papers—they didn't even have a safe. Some presidential aides realized the recklessness of the Brookings plan and called it off.

Was the Ending Inevitable?

In retrospect, the denouement appeared inevitable—but it certainly didn't feel like that at the time. Not until quite close to the very end, once the "smoking gun" was discovered and Republican leaders, in an act more of self-preservation than courage, went to the White House and told Nixon he had to go. If Nixon didn't accommodate them, they would have had to stage a trial in the Senate and cast some—even at that point— difficult votes. Nixon, it must be remembered, still had a base. It was a foregone conclusion that the House would adopt the Judiciary Committee's Articles of Impeachment: they had been arrived at through a process that—as envisioned by chairman Peter Rodino, his young strategist Francis O'Brien, and the calm, methodical, un-partisan counsel, John Doar—ended in three articles that were adopted by bipartisan votes and that the country overwhelmingly deemed fair. But even then Nixon's departure wasn't a sure thing. With his presidency hanging in the balance, Nixon alarmed to the end—there simply was no telling what this desperate, out-of-control (and, we now know, heavily drinking) man would do. It's to be recalled that the Secretary of Defense, James Schlesinger, felt constrained to tell Pentagon military officials not to take any orders from the White House that hadn't gone through him.

It wasn't Nixon's intent, of course, but the Watergate period ushered in an era of government reforms. Nixon had greatly expanded the president's powers, and his downfall caused the congress to try to curb them or to take many of them back, as well as to reform some of its own procedures. In the 1974 midterm landslide for the Democrats, a reaction to Watergate, the Democrats picked up forty-nine House seats—the "Watergate Babies"— and gained five seats in the Senate. A flood of reform legislation ensued; among these were: campaign finance reform; the Freedom of Information Act, which gave citizens greater access to government records; more congressional committee deliberations were opened to the public; ethics rules for members the adminstration and congress, including a requirement to file financial disclosures; a Congressional Budget Office to prevent a president from refusing to spend funds authorized by congress (as Nixon had in his "impoundments"); authorization for special prosecutors to investigate alleged crimes in the Executive Branch; the War Powers Act, intended to limit the president's power to wage war without the approval of congress (though this didn't actually work as intended).

Some of these reforms had a more lasting impact than others; campaign finance reform remained the subject of an unending struggle, and the law's impact was severely diminished by the Supreme Court under Chief Justice John Roberts once Samuel Alito replaced Sandra Day O'Connor, in 2006; some decisions upholding the campaign finance law were overturned two years later, and the Citizens United case reversed a century of limits on contributions by corporations. Justices who didn't understand politics or had a conservative agenda gradually opened up our political system to great floods of private money aimed at fixing nominations and turning elections at several levels—and also at affecting federal and state policies. There weren't great grounds for optimism about returning to the post-Watergate campaign finance reforms, in fact or in spirit.

Government will always create opportunities for corruption. And not everything that is politically influenced is corrupt—and there's more public alertness. The orgy of excitement over faux scandals in the fall of 2013 brought home the truth that scandals are a lot of collective fun for the press—certainly more so than the details of the federal budget. The difference lies in whether there's systematized corruption sanctioned at the highest levels—as occurred during Watergate.

The temptation—born partly out of nostalgia, partly out of dimming memories, and partly out of partisan revenge—has existed since Nixon to analogize real or suspected egregious actions on the part of a president or his top people to Nixon or Watergate, but nothing has come close to the pattern of illegal and abusive activities at the top of the government that went on then, directed or sanctioned by the President himself—or for which he was accountable.

Watergate wasn't this event or that one, but a pattern of behavior, a mentality that sanctioned activities that were without precedent or successor. Nixon told David Frost, "If the president does it it isn't illegal," and he was surrounded by toadies that largely went along with this stunning view. It's not clear that Nixon actually believed this throughout his presidency: he was deeply worried about being found out. Though the Watergate period was alarming, honesty requires an admission that it was also a high—that for all its deeply worrisome nature, it was an exciting time, a wild ride through history, including several moments of hilarity. But it was essentially nervous laughter, giving cover to the fact that most of us were frightened, at least some of the time, many for most of it. Power was in the hands of people who gave the clear impression that they would do anything to maintain it.

In real time, we watched with fascination as the story played out in ensuing years—as some of his aides who'd gone to jail came out devoted, proselytizing Christians. Was all to be forgiven? It was a hard sell, but not for lack of trying. Nixon's devotees continued to play down or redefine Watergate as a sideshow, a coup against him by his enemies. Former participants produced stacks of books, many justifying their role at the expense of others; and thereby we were treated to an extended viewing of the nest of vipers that was the Nixon White House. The Nixon family and historians continued to battle over what Watergate was. Little that Nixon touched or affected escaped the long struggle over the definition of the man and his presidency.

Richard Nixon would probably be surprised and also bemused that over time he became a cult figure. It's unarguable that Nixon was one of the most fascinating political characters in all of American history. His awkwardness and characteristic colloquialisms made him an entertaining figure. But this was a man whose long-nursed angers caused him to destroy the presidency he had sought for so long. This was a man whose drinking and consumption of unprescribed medication caused him to be out of control at critical times, and it's doubtful that we will ever know all of them or just when they were. Was this the case when he ordered two worldwide nuclear alerts for no apparent reason from the White House residence, where he had taken refuge during deep depressions? His aides considered it the highest duty to protect him, rather than the country from him. This was a man with no real friends, no one to remind him of the boundaries. He tested the constitutional system, and it held firm through a fortuitous collection of personalities who rose to the occasion. A misfit almost all his life, he convinced some of the press time and again that he had changed, and the establishment that he was a wise man. Do we have a screen adequate to prevent such a person from again gaining power?

That is not clear.

ACKNOWLEDGMENTS

This book bears witness to the fact that a lot of very busy people took a lot of time to talk to me about what was going through their minds during the upheaval that was Watergate. I cannot list them all. Some, of course, are no longer alive. I think of the quiet, shy, usually barely articulate Peter Rodino, who was transformed into the wise, dignified, eloquent leader of the House Judiciary Committee in its Inquiry Into the Impeachment of Richard Nixon. Rodino was among the number of apparently unremarkable people who rose to the occasion and acted remarkably. They were deadly serious as they went about their job of deciding whether Nixon was to be impeached and on what grounds. Or even what impeachment was or what it should be: what were the grounds for voting to in effect indict a president, or in the Senate to convict him. They understood the gravamen of the situation, sifted the evidence, considered what the country could bear in this first, and only, serious impeachment process in our history. And they made no bones about that this was also a highly political decision, as well as a momentous, historical one. I can tell it here that the figure I referred to as "the man in the traffic patterns" on Capitol Hill, who had an unerring sense of where things were moving, was Charlie Ferris, a Boston pol type, who was Staff Director of the Democratic Policy Committee and a close adviser to Majority Leader Mike Mansfield .

Two people above all made this book possible, and were major influences on how I went about it. William Shawn, then the editor of the *New Yorker*, was as remarkable as legend has it. Other writers would agree that his quiet encouragement, severe but gently applied high standards, and love for writers, lifted us all and made us better at what we did. When at last he had to retire, the *New York Times* editorialized: "For several generations of [writers], being asked to write for William Shawn was like being asked to dance with Fred Astaire." Exactly.

The other major influence, John Gardner, was a mentor throughout this project and for much of my life: pillar, adviser, inspirer, friend. I was honored by the support of these two exceptional men.

I first met Francis O'Brien, Rodino's Administrative Assistant in early January of 1974, when the time had come to familiarize myself with the House Judiciary Committee and understand how it would set about its extraordinary task. We became lasting friends and he's no less wise, interesting, and funny now than he was then. If Francis didn't invent loyalty he put his own unrivalled stamp on it. Others, then and now, gave me the moral and other support to see this project through. Among them are Molly Ball, Dan and Nancy Balz, Stephen Breyer, Barbara and John Cochran, David Cohen, Ezra Klein and Annie Lowrey, Molly Raiser, Deborah Tannen, and Catherine Wyler. And of course my dear Daniel and Alexander Webster—as well as the Villegas family, in particular the incomparable Tessie, without whom I cannot imagine getting much of anything done for more than a decade.

This book is also dedicated to the beloved Haynes Johnson.

Index